Writing Successfully

Revised Sixth Edition

With 2020 MLA, APA, CSE, AND CHICAGO DOCUMENTATION STYLES

Richard Hanson

*Jefferson Community
and Technical College*

Cover © Martin Rollins

www.kendallhunt.com

Send all inquiries to:

4050 Westmark Drive

Dubuque, IA 52004-1840

This book was previously published by Allyn & Bacon (1996)

Published in the United States of America

Table of Contents

THE RHETORICAL PROCESS

I

II

III

THE RESEARCH PROCESS

IV

DEVELOPING ESSAYS IN
OFTEN ENCOUNTERED GENRES

VII

STYLE MANUAL AND HANDBOOK

X

XI

Permissions Acknowledgments

Preface to Instructors

Writing Successfully was written to achieve three primary goals:

- That it be concise, but complete – giving students and teachers more time for writing, revising, and peer reviewing.

- That it be accessible and readable by students – giving a variety of suggestions and choices for them.

- That it demonstrate the recursiveness of the writing process.

Through years of teaching and six editions of *Writing Successfully*, I have often noticed that those students who write well from the beginning of introductory composition classes need short, succinct rhetorics to reinforce what they already know about their writing processes, and they improve the most (at the freshman level) with less reading about writing and more practice writing and revising. However, I have found that even those more experienced student writers each have a few holes in their knowledge, usually concerning specific, discreet revision or editing skills. *Writing Successfully* has short, but thorough, sections concerning research, revision, and editing processes. I tell students that freshman writing courses are often the last writing courses students will take, and that they need competence in ALL research, revision, and editing skills to succeed in college and the world. So to find out what they know and what they need to learn, I have students read all the process chapters while they do the editing for their first essay, and take students slowly through the multiple writing processes for predrafting, revision, and editing so they can learn and use the many discreet skills they may have missed in high school, skills for the most experienced of them like college level research, or editing skills like using action verbs and the active voice, or eliminating wordiness and repetition.

At the same time, those students who need some remedial instruction in areas of the composing or editing processes continue to have problems. Teachers most often accomplish remedial instruction through student/ teacher conferences and, for some professors, textbook assignments geared toward individual student's needs. One reason these students do not become better writers is that they are daunted and intimidated by longer handbooks. *Writing Successfully* mediates between these two concerns with its short, concise descriptions and its comprehensiveness. As a writer and composition professor, I have struggled for thirty-five years with this text and its revisions to balance the opposed poles of being prescriptive (which allows for brevity and which students seem to want, "just give me the rules") and being descriptive (which takes more pages, yet not only better demonstrates the writing process, but also constitutes a better teaching *and* writing tool; don't we always ask students to "show, don't tell"?). This text reaches a balance between these two pedagogies. The text does a considerable amount of "showing" with student texts that have comments in the margin discussing the students' choices.

Too many students cannot even navigate their way around rhetorics and handbooks; the simplicity of the structure of *Writing Successfully* serves them well. Writing well, as we all know, involves a process, a series of discreet steps involving predrafting, drafting, revision and editing. *Writing Successfully* has a unique organization of chapters, with a similarly organized *revision and peer review checklist* on its front and back inner covers. Students are invited to break the process into discreet steps with their first essays. Much thought has gone into the ordering of this process (and the organization of *Writing Successfully*), so that students learning to write better do all of the processes that professional writers do, in the most advantageous order. As students re-do the steps of the process with succeeding essays, they are invited to combine steps.

Writing Successfully's innovative invention and revision heuristics have been tested in the classroom, and they produce excellent context and content results for average and poorly prepared students, and above-excellent results for more experienced student writers. Editing strategies contain easily learned problem/solution techniques.

Dr. Richard Hanson

Jefferson Community and Technical College

Louisville, KY

Innovative Features of *Writing Successfully* (6th ed.)

The Rhetorical Process

Chapters 2-5 move students through developing context, then content, followed by revision strategies for context and content. There are **four innovative features** in these first chapters:

- In Nancy Sommer's seminal essay, "Revision Strategies of Student Writers and Experienced Adult Writers," she demonstrates that student writers rarely perform global revision as more experienced writers do to discover – or rediscover – their subject, audience, and purpose. Many studies corroborate Dr. Sommer's findings, and pedagogical theory for forty years has stressed invention theories (see the works of James Berlin, Ann Berthoff, Peter Elbow, Linda Flower, and Karen LeFevre, to name the authors of seminal studies and overviews). As with most rhetorics, *Writing Successfully* begins with a discussion of focusing and gaining knowledge of a subject, analyzing audience and writing situation, and developing a thesis and tone (with appropriate predrafting heuristics and two student examples). Few are as concise, but complete, as Chapter 2 of *Writing Successfully*. **A writing exercise at the end of chapter 2, to which students and teachers can return with each succeeding essay, asks students to envision and re-envision their contexts by creating context cards that specifically describe their focused subjects, their audience and writing situation, their thesis, and the appropriate tone they will use.** Students can use the cards to focus their revisions, and peer reviewers and teachers can use them to understand a writer's intention specifically, and thus can better evaluate drafts. There are multiple student examples in which the student writers perform this task.

- As the next chapters take writers through developing content, writing a draft, and revision for content, **Chapters 3-4 stress again and again at appropriate junctures that no writing will be successful until the writing context (a FOCUSED subject, a PRECISE thesis, a SPECIFIC audience) has been finalized.** Writers cannot know what to include or exclude in terms of content, nor can they decide on an appropriate tone for their essays, until finalizing context decisions. Too many students write mediocre and average essays because they are not reminded throughout the predrafting AND initial revision steps that a precise finalized context is essential for success.

- The revision for content divides into three stages. The two innovations above finalize the first stage: specific context decisions. The second revision stage (discussed in ch 4) asks students to make global revisions until the main ideas support the finalized thesis and that the essay flows well (containing a workable organizational strategy). The third stage (discussed in ch 5) has two distinct innovative strategies. How many students, after they have revised a draft for content, think there is something missing but they can't identify it? Since their work generally discusses the thesis, they turn it in. Then, writing professors return the essays with notes about a lack of specific evidence for the thesis. **Chapter 5 asks students, after they have successfully completed revision stages one and two for context and overall content and organization, to look at each individual paragraph with a microscope and decide whether each paragraph contains ALL the specific evidence and illustration to prove its sub-point, and to add and subtract evidence until each paragraph does this. After revising each paragraph, they are invited to revise their introductions and conclusions.** How can students introduce something before it is finished; how can they end something that isn't finished yet? This attention to detail creates essays with much more in-depth content.

- Finally, in this same chapter 5, **in the section on paragraph completeness, Precise Word Use has been put in its proper place in the revision order. Professional writers, when they are revising their texts for thoroughness, always find that some or most of the additions for completeness occur at the word level. In earlier drafts they have used vague words, and sometimes just replacing a vague word or phrase with the specific one that is at the heart of the paragraph is enough to make the paragraph complete.** With the text's placement of the discussion of Precise Word Use within the context of paragraph revision, as opposed to yet another discreet step usually placed in a section of a handbook on diction (along with denotation and connotation), students save time, and actually do a necessary step that has historically been skipped by most freshmen writers.

The Research Process

The research chapters offer these **innovative features**:

- Most students come to college with the skill of highlighting important ideas in a text as they read it; however, **few students have learned these essential college and workplace skills: Chapter 6 teaches students to become active readers, with specific suggestions that include writing summaries for specific purposes, audiences, and writing situations, evaluating texts and their author's stances as they read, and responding to texts as they read.**

- One of the most used forms of discourse in both college and the workplace is the literature review. **Chapter 6 concludes with an assignment (including a student example) asking for a summary/evaluation/ response to an essay (a literature review).** Professors can also use this section to show students how to do in-depth annotated bibliographies which are discussed in chapters 7-8.

- **Students learn the valuable skill of synthesis of sources in chapters 7-8**, with heuristics for, and examples of, methods to integrate sources into a researched essay.

- Many professors ask students to conduct interviews, detailed observations, or even conduct informal surveys (the tried and true social sciences component of the Writing Across the Curriculum pedagogy). **Chapter 9 includes concise but thorough explanations of how to perform primary research, with six student essays that incorporate observation, interview, surveys, case studies, experiments, and the scientific proposal.**

Looking at the Genres College Students Encounter Today

In the last decade, schools and rhetorics have moved more toward discussing student essays in terms of the genres they will be writing in (analysis, persuasion, narrative, evaluation). We've come a long way from the "rhetorical models" approach that I was taught, and began my teaching career with in the 1980s as it faded out. However, we are again speaking of writing in terms of the writing situation: what are the expectations for the kinds of content used in a particular student essay?

- The textbook begins with a brief Chapter 1 that discusses the kinds of essays students will be asked to write in all of the major college disciplines and the work world, as well as contrasting these genres with ones they already know how to write from high school and any differences between high school and college.

- Chapter 10 is a lengthy chapter that covers Analysis, Evaluation, and Narratives, further breaking these broad categories down into causal and process analysis, rhetorical analysis, textual analysis, literary analysis, evaluation, personal narratives/memoirs, literacy narratives, and essay exams. There are student examples for each of these rhetorical categories.

- Chapter 11, Developing Persuasive Essays, in forty-two pages stresses in-depth predrafting and research to analyze opposing arguments, their evidence, and both students' own and their opposing arguments' warrants. Students are invited to analyze a subject in detail and only after careful, objective analysis arrive at their thesis for a persuasive writing assignment. Warrants are also fully explained, so students understand that many times positions they and others believe are not always grounded in objective fact, but come from philosophical beliefs (warrants) that underlie a persuasive claim. Both Aristotelian (appeals to logic, authority, and emotion) and Toulminian (finding a common ground) concepts are offered as methods to develop content. To reinforce the necessity of answering opposing arguments, the second half of the chapter illustrates four organizational strategies designed around the placement of opposing arguments: 1) introducing opposing arguments first, 2) answering opposing arguments throughout the essay, 3) placing opposing arguments at the end, and 4) answering opposing arguments in a problem/solution essay. Four exemplary student essays demonstrate persuasive writing.

- Finally, with the new emphasis on genres, a brief Writing for Business (ch 12) has been included in this section on genres.

Style Manual and Handbook

Students who most need a style manual and handbook do not use it because it is too lengthy and hard to navigate. Pulling one of the standard "complete" handbooks from the shelf, I counted the pages on sentence style, word use, punctuation, grammar, and usage: 315 pages. I pulled a second rhetoric advertised on the cover as a "Brief Handbook": 215 pages. I pulled two more from the shelf and they had just 35-50 pages with major proofreading errors (not nearly enough detail for students with editing problems). *Writing Successfully* is brief, BUT THOROUGH (106 pages for editing strategies), containing enough information and examples for students struggling with either an immature style or with surface problems. There is also a careful grouping of subjects so that with a first essay students can go through 17 discreet editing processes found in chapters 13-22. If they conscientiously study each process, they will, first, learn that they are competent in many of them, and second, they will know which ones to study and practice. In practice, I have seen that students who follow this method will reduce the number of discreet editing processes (through combination) from 17 to 7 or 8 with the second essay, and by the end of a course can reduce the number of processes they need to produce stylistically mature and practically error-free essays to 2-4 editing sessions. They are well on their way to editing as professionals who revise for content and then edit all at once before sending their texts out to be read.

This is mainly accomplished by strategic organization. For instance, let's look at chapters 16-18 which concern creating stylistically mature sentences with coherence techniques, sentence variety, parallel structure, and correct punctuation. Chapter 16 gives students the necessary definitions to discuss these editing strategies. Chapter 17 discusses stylistic issues such as coherence, variety, and modification problems. Chapter 18 is aptly titled "Anyone Can Punctuate Correctly." Most handbooks put style concerns in one section and punctuation concerns in another. *Writing Successfully* creates a seamless learning experience because the relationship between a mature sentence style and the proper punctuation for this style is so interrelated. The chapters build organically from one to another. Each of the handbook chapters (13-22) build on each other, and the suggestions in the chapters even alert students to how they can begin joining strategies as they become more experienced.

Traditional handbooks separate sections on editing for connotation, word specificity, and wordiness from sections on spelling problems (though they are similar tasks); sections on improving coherence and sentence variety from sections on punctuation (again, similar tasks); and editing for action verbs and active voice from sections on verb problems. Experienced writers combine skills that naturally work together, and *Writing Successfully* has a unique organization that puts skills together in an order that allows students to learn all these skills and begin combining them. Most professors feel lucky if students edit for the most grievous punctuation and spelling errors. I believe they would like students to actually edit for those skills that produce sentences with attention paid to coherence, conciseness, and clarity also.

Writing Successfully proves to be an excellent rhetoric to teach students the all important skills of critical reading, synthesizing source materials, and writing various kinds of researched writing including persuasive researched essays, reports, synthesis essays, and essays incorporating primary research. There are excellent sections on both in-text documentation and works cited/ reference pages in MLA , APA, and CSE styles, with example student essays using MLA and APA formats.

Acknowledgments: First Edition

First of all, I would like to thank Ken Davis, who at the birth of this text was the Director of Composition at the University of Kentucky: he allowed me to try out the very rough early versions when I was not but a Ph.D. student. He was followed by William Campbell, who also allowed me latitude. I would like to thank Chris Cetrulo, who helped me immensely as I moved through drafts at the University of Kentucky.

I want to especially thank Joe Opiela, Editor-in-Chief for Humanities at Allyn & Bacon, who "held my nose to the grindstone" and shaped this book's first edititon with countless helpful ideas. I would also like to thank his editorial assistants, Brenda Conaway and Carol Alper, who answered many questions and provided in-depth editorial comment.

At Jefferson Community College I would like to thank, in addition to my colleagues (Pam Butsch, Diane Calhoun-French, Alice Cleveland, Ron Horvath, Mark Johnson, Rafe Johnson, Dan Kline, Michael Misbach, Mary Mulder, Rita Recktenwald, Larry Rees, Betty Shiffman, Betty Weldon, Michelle Whited, Mike Zalampas, and Sherree Zalampas) with their valuable suggestions and encouragement, Cathy Fields, who supervises the bookstore and put up with innumerable problems as I produced various printings of drafts-in-progress. I could not have done this without you. I also want to thank Thomas Rogers and Jeff Taylor, computer wizards *extraordinaire*.

Finally, I would like to thank my children – Chris, Jason, and Troy – who put up with a father who writes. And thanks to my parents, who supported me spiritually, emotionally, and financially when I could not.

Further Acknowledgments

Colleagues at Jefferson Community & Technical College have helped me immensely with their encouragement and advice. Many talks about teaching strategies make this book what it is, though of course all faults of *Writing*

Successfully are my own. I would also like to thank: Adria Bryant, Barbara Blackburn, Laura Dearing, Susan Erdmann, Chris Graney, John Gass, and especially Jo Zausch and Linda Klein who read drafts for more than one edition, and gave me much encouragement and many useful suggestions.

I would also like to thank Judy Dial, who helps get prototypes of editions out to students at the bookstore, and another new colleague, Elizabeth Chambers-Gaw, who creates a seamless office environment. And finally, I would like to thank James Swindler, who as always, is of immense help with all printing matters. A regular Ben Franklin.

I want to thank newer colleagues. Brian Wixom, B.J. Wilson, Meg Matheny, Stacy Taylor, Jill Adams, Michael Estes, Marlissa Austin, Annie Lotz, Tiffany Young, Sandra Eubanks, David Cooper, Quanisha Charles, and Claud Rogers.

For this new sixth edition, I would like to thank my new family at Kendall-Hunt, and especially Sean Skinner and Megan Drake

I would love to thank the support of my life, who takes care of the mundane when I am driven by deadlines. Lory Decker is also my spiritual support. My children are now grown. I want to thank them again. Finally, I would like to thank my students (who are my best teachers) for helping develop a pedagogy that works.

1

College Genres: Writing and Learning Styles

Welcome to the world of academia. Students today are of course preparing for careers, but more importantly, for future success college teaches 1) learning how to understand *and* analyze *any* difficult ideas and texts found in this sometimes complicated modern world and 2) learning how to communicate well orally and with visual and written texts. These are the basic requirements for college educated adults, and future employers (as well as college professors) expect competence with these two broad skills. It could be argued that thinking about and analyzing difficult subjects and communication skills are the two activities that make us human!!!

Some students have come from an academically rigorous high school atmosphere and some have come from a less rigorous setting, but college demands that students complete most work on their own time outside of class. High school courses usually last 50-60 minutes all five days of the school week. Depending on the class, homework may or may not have been assigned, but there was much more time to do the learning and the work during the class period; however, in college, professors create assignments so that students well prepared for the course will spend an average of two hours doing homework for every hour in the classroom. Most college classes are 2 ½ hours a week, so for success students should expect to work at least 5 hours a week on homework for each class, more if they are not as prepared for the course.

Here are some basic suggestions for academic success – to learn how to negotiate courses and analyze *any* difficult ideas or texts:

- **Study the syllabus carefully** – it tells you specifically what is expected of you, and there are often specific due dates with descriptions of any reading and writing assignments. The syllabus will explain for you the exact outcomes required of you for a grade in that class. If you do the required outcomes, you get the A.
- **Study and follow the directions, or learn the material, of any handouts** – Professors explain essential content or essential processes to learn (or do, for homework) in handouts, and professors do not give these to you to make your backpack fuller. They are essential for success.
- **Attend and participate in class, and *take careful notes*** – College professors might go over reading assignments, but often the learning during class time is in addition to the assigned readings, not covering the same material.
- **Carefully read any assigned reading** – Study chapter 6, "Critical Reading: Summary, Evaluation, and Response," and learn those essential skills. Read the readings for the day they are assigned because a professor's classroom activity or lecture assumes that you have read the assignment, and if you haven't you will not understand that class with the complexity it deserves.

- **Use a daily calendar** – at the beginning of each week, mark down the times you will be in class, at work, or leisure activities, and then find the exact hours where you will be doing the assigned reading, writing and study/ test preparation for all your classes that week. (Remember that if you are a student with a full-time schedule, you should expect to spend approximately 25 hours on homework to be a success. *Full-time college is a full-time 40 hour work week!!!*
- **Ask questions!!! (when they come up, not when it is too late)** Most professors – especially in first year writing courses - see themselves as coaches, helping you achieve the learning outcomes of successful critical reading, writing, and research skills. Professors want you to ask questions, or they wouldn't be teachers; however, most do not "suffer fools." If you are asking a question that was plainly answered on a handout or in a reading, the professor might not answer. They are not at school to do your work for you.

Academic Reading and Writing –
Encountering New Genres and Learning Their Styles

Colleges expose you to the kind of writing that you can expect to do in your chosen discipline; moreover, in the general studies courses you take in the first few years of college, classes expose you to a variety of styles in the varied courses you take in different disciplines. The kinds of texts read and the kinds of papers written by a psychology major (experiments or case studies) would be different than a Fine Arts major (analysis of a work of art or a period), or a business major (statistical studies or reports on a business or industry). However, you need to be comfortable in a variety of styles because of the overlap: a business major studying marketing – to understand how to market - would have to be comfortable studying and reading psychology-style essays to understand human behavior and would have to be comfortable studying and reading art analysis to know how to design the visuals of advertising. Let's add another skill that will help you do well in college:

- **Learn the technical language and the writing styles (genres) of each of your courses' disciplines** – When you begin taking courses in a new discipline for you, keep a log of the definitions of the jargon (specialized words) they use, note the kinds of research and analysis they use in their writing (as you will probably be asked to do this type of research also), and notice the degree of formality they use in the tone of their essays.

For instance, *genre* is a technical term used in composition studies meaning "a particular category of writing with its own style and set of expectations," and most of the rest of this chapter discusses both the various genres you are probably already familiar with and the ones you will probably encounter in college and your chosen career field. In order to become an accomplished writer, you must learn to study the particular context of each of your essays: you write and read texts using one set of genres in a science course and another set of genres in a humanities course. All

2

professors expect you to become proficient in the genres and the particular jargon of their disciplines, and a beginning college writing course is where you learn a necessary skill for your entire college and career life: to be able to differentiate among and quickly learn how to read and write in new genres in new disciplines each with their own technical jargon and style.

Before college, you wrote in several genres. You probably first learned – even in elementary or middle school – to write *reports*. Reports are essays where the writer studies several encyclopedia/ textbook articles, and then writes a summary of those articles to define or describe the subject of the essay. They answer a question: Who was Woodrow Wilson? What were the causes of the Civil War? How do solar panels work? Middle and high school teachers assign reports because when we study a subject and then describe it in writing, we retain the knowledge much longer. Writing a report activates memory centers in the brain. You also have probably written *essay exams*. In high school, you also could have written *lab reports* in science classes, *personal experience narratives* that tell a story from a writer's life or analyze a situation in life or world culture, and *argument* essays where the writer takes a position and perhaps defends it from the ideas of an audience who disagrees. You will also do these in college. Although you might be asked to think about your essay's subject and fulfilling the genre's requirements more thoroughly than before college, you essentially already know these genres.

One difference you could experience: in real life choosing a specific audience (or having the audience chosen for you because of the point you are making or because the genre of the writing demands a certain audience) is one of the most, if not the most, important decision you make when working on a writing project. All writing has a specific audience it is directed toward. Many students still write as if they are writing high school reports, making sure they define and describe everything like they would for an encyclopedia-type essay. In reality, whom your audience is determines all the content you include or exclude in an essay. If the subject of an essay was Facebook, would most audiences really need to be told that it is an extremely popular social networking site that everyone seems to be using? No. All that information would bore readers to tears. They would want to read a specific analysis of the site. As a matter of fact, encyclopedia-type information on Facebook would not be necessary for anyone unless perhaps your audience included people over 80 in nursing homes, or visitors from space. So, with all writing, writers need to carefully examine the needs of their audience, and their audiences' depth of knowledge concerning the writers' subjects. Analyzing audience is very important. Since college courses are teaching you how to communicate effectively in the real world, it is necessary to pay attention to the demands of the genre (including your professor's expectations) in considering your audience. Fortunately, with the explosion of social networking and gaming sites, users of those sites (like most college freshmen) have intuitively become much more aware of communicating to different audiences for different occasions, so you actually already know a lot about audience and audience analysis. When you are asked to do this analysis in college classes, don't mistake it for a foreign concept. Use what you intuitively know about writing and communicating to your audience when you develop and write papers for college classes.

You also need to consider whether your professor is the audience – sometimes she is for college essays, but not always. If you are writing in one of the genres used in an academic discipline, the audience is probably an academic audience which would

3

include your professor, other students, and scholars in that discipline. The style would be objective, fairly formal, and writers would use the specific jargon associated with that discipline; however, student writers must learn that knowing what your audiences already know and believe about a subject as well as what audiences need to know to understand your thesis is the most important feature for deciding what content to include.

Particularly in college composition courses, instructors will ask you to decide for yourselves what audience needs to hear your message. For instance, if your essay argues that video games are not all bad, these three audiences would each have their own set of expectations and knowledge, and your essay would have different content for each of these audiences, even if your message stayed the same: younger teens, conservative old fashioned parents and educators, or more liberal parents and educators. If your audience included both of the last two, you would have to carefully strike a balance to appease both of those groups. As pointed out above, this isn't as foreign as it might sound: with your friends, your parents, and your parents' generation you have to appease different groups with different beliefs and wants.

After you pick and analyze an audience appropriate for your unique message, you choose your content and the tone you use with them based on that audience. This concern of college composition courses makes you ready for writing in the real world: if you were asked to explain a new software system at work, you would write one set of explanations for new hires who don't know the system at all; another set of explanations for workers who know the older version of the system, emphasizing only the similarities and differences; and a third explanation to managers who would not need to know how it worked, but would want to know why features of the new system will improve the workplace. Same subject (the new software), but three completely different essays. In summary, college writing courses make sure you understand that the genre you are writing in and the purpose for which you have been assigned an essay force you to carefully analyze the demands of the particular audience you are writing for. Different disciplines use different genres, styles, and tone/language with their writing.

- **When writing, choose an audience based on the expectations of the genre and your instructor** – Study chapter 2, "Developing a Writing Context: Subject, Audience, Writing Situation, Thesis, Tone" for methods to analyze your audience.

College has different disciplines, or majors, grouped in several categories:

Humanities and Fine Arts: Majors in English, history, classics, languages, cultural studies, women's studies, philosophy, studio art, art history, music, music history, theater, film, dance, pre-law.

Social Sciences and Media/Communication: Majors in psychology, sociology, anthropology, political science, social work, pre-law, media studies, communication, journalism, radio/television/film studies (some would place history and economics here also).

Natural and Applied Sciences, Engineering, Computer Science, Health Sciences: Majors in chemistry, biology, physics, geology, ecology, building and industrial trades, engineering (civil, electrical, chemical, biomedical, aerospace, industrial, mechanical), information management and computer systems, nursing, respiratory therapy, physical therapy, pharmacology, pre-med, veterinary, dentistry.

Business: Majors in finance, management, accounting, marketing, economics, public relations.

Each of these disciplines uses different genres. To be successful in college, you will have to learn to navigate these different genres with their differing expectations, as well as revising content and editing sentences and words successfully. The following contains a definition of the major genres encountered in college classes, with the types of courses that use them.

Genres common to all four: Sciences, Social Sciences, Business, and Humanities

Analysis This common type of college and real world assignment asks you to analyze causes and effects or the how and why of a process. If it is a subject you know well (how to keep from falling when riding a skateboard or what happens when a computer crashes), you would not do any outside research. If you are not an expert (Why global warming? What are the causes or effects of a slow economy?), you would need to become knowledgeable before writing this causal essay. In the natural science, social science, or business disciplines, you would be formal, academic, objective. In the humanities, you might use that tone, but you might write to another audience where you could be less formal.   (For a complete definition and the process for completing, see ch.10; for examples see ch. 7 & 10.)

Rhetorical Analysis With rhetorical analysis, you look at an advertisement, a visual text, a cultural artifact (a Coke can, the flag, tennis shoes), or a written or spoken argument, and analyze who the creator's target audience/consumer is, what the creator's meaning is, what rhetorical tools does the creator use to send the message, perhaps whether the message is true or not, whether the subject is successful getting its meaning across, and what the ad/text says about either the creator's culture or the consumer's culture. For example, any political advertisement has been sent by a specific group and it is meant for a specific audience. (Are they drumming up support within their own party or are they attempting to convince the undecided?) It has a specific message, and it uses either appeals to logic, appeals to emotions, or appeals to authority, but usually NOT logic. They also usually have some half-truths, or at least some slanted information, embedded in the message. Often a political advertisement says more about its intended audience than it does about the candidate when the advertisement is analyzed with all the complexity it deserves. Or a scientist might look at an argument about global warming and analyze who the message was targeting, and how the information has been slanted to produce a specific response. The purpose of a rhetorical analysis would be to analyze all of these conditions of the advertisement/written argument. Most rhetorical analyses are written to a formal, academic audience.   (For a fuller definition and the process for completing, see ch. 10; for examples see ch. 8 & 10.)

5

Evaluation This is another activity you have been doing since you were little, so you will just need to learn how formal written evaluations work. We evaluate all the time: friends, enemies, books, films, cups of coffee, cars or electronics to buy. We often compare and contrast several similar items when we evaluate, but the overwhelming feature of an evaluation is a value judgment where you rate the item good, bad, or indifferent with reasons, or if there is a comparison involved, better than, equal, or not as good as. Of course, everyone has an opinion about most things; what elevates evaluation to a higher level of thinking is your ability to give *thorough* reasons and *convincing* evidence to support an evaluation.

(For a fuller definition and the process for completing, see ch. 10; for examples see ch. 3, 4, & 10.)

Argument/Persuasion You have done this before too, though perhaps not formally in writing. With argument/persuasion, you are almost always writing to an audience who disagrees with whatever your thesis is; however, most people think that with argument/persuasion you are trying to get your audience to change their minds. The truth is, that is only one sub-genre of argument/persuasion. Most people are fairly stuck in their belief systems, though hopefully people do change their ideas with more education on the subject. Other much more common sub-genres include:

1) Convincing people who will never agree with you that at least you have a logical argument even though they disagree with you.

2) Trying to reach a common ground with the audience who disagrees with you.

3) Many persuasion essays have a thesis where there IS no one right or wrong (*Huckleberry Finn* should have had the last hundred pages cut – the climax is when Huck decides to "go to hell" and not turn in the escaped slave, Jim.), and your job is to persuade the reader that you have a defensible argument against the other possible counter-arguments.

4) A problem/solution persuasive essay where you identify a problem and/or propose a solution.

(For a complete definition, the process for completing, and examples, see ch. 11.)

Essay Exams Even more than your past experiences with essay exams, in college you will need to quickly grasp what the professor specifically asks you to do, quickly organize your thoughts and a plan for the response, make sure you have several reasons to support the point(s) you are making, and write edited paragraphs quickly.

(For a fuller definition, the process for completing, and an example, see ch. 10.)

Types of writing used by all disciplines when conducting research

Synthesis (Called a *Literature Survey* in the sciences and social sciences.) When professors ask you to write a synthesis essay, they want you to research and analyze the range of reputable sources on one subject, and then write an essay in which you discuss the relationship between the reputable sources' positions on an issue (Which ones agree or disagree? Which ones have the strongest evidence and why is it stronger? Does evidence in one source support or refute a claim in another source?) The end result of this synthesis should be, in addition to your essay itself, that you are knowledgeable in the range of opinions on the subject of your essay and that you

would be able to enter into an informed, scholarly discussion of the subject, and that you would know the expert opinions on that subject. In simple terms, you would be able to discuss the subject with other people knowledgeable in the field, and thus would be nearer to the basic goals of a college education.
(For a fuller definition, the process for completing, and examples, see ch. 7-8.)

Abstracts You will read abstracts during research more often than write them. An abstract is a paragraph summary of an article. It does not evaluate the article; it has a tone of objective reporting. Abstracts are useful tools to quickly skim the content of, let's say, one hundred articles on your subject. You read the abstracts and from them pick the most relevant articles on your subject to read the entire articles.
(For a fuller definition and the process for using, see ch. 7, 8, 9.)

Literature Reviews (summary/evaluation of a source) You are already familiar with some kinds of literature reviews: movie, book, and song/album reviews perform the same function as college literature reviews. In the college literature review, scholars read an article (or sometimes a book) and write
/ a thorough, objective summary (What is the main idea? The main sub-points and the major evidence used?)
/ an evaluation (What are the source's strengths and weaknesses and what specific evidence do you have to prove that they are, in fact, strengths or weaknesses?)
/ a response (Do you agree or disagree with the source and why? What is your position on the subject of the source, and what evidence do you have for your position?)
(For a fuller definition, the process for completing, and examples, see ch. 6.)

Annotated Bibliographies A *bibliography* is a thorough list of the sources you consult to create any essay that has a subject you must research before developing your essay. The listing uses the citation format of the discipline you are writing for. (For instance, MLA documentation for an English class or APA documentation for a psychology class.) *An annotated bibliography* is a thorough list that includes short summaries and evaluations of each source, and possible uses in the planned essay.
(For a fuller definition, the process for completing, and an example, see ch. 7.)

Genres common to the Sciences, Social Sciences, and Business

Observations Many times you will be asked to specifically observe a group of people (or animals/plants in biology), and then in writing describe exactly who they were and what they were doing, followed by an analysis of what you observed. For instance, a business marketer would want to know how people react to a new storefront or a new product. A child psychologist might want to know how a specific child in his care reacts with given stimuli. Sometimes *interviews* or *surveys* might be used in addition to the observation.
(For a fuller definition, the process for completing, and an example, see ch. 9.)

Informative (reports) Whenever you begin researching a subject you know little about, it would be wise to go to encyclopedia and textbook articles (informative reports) to read and become knowledgeable about your subject before doing in-depth research, so you will still be reading reports, but you have been writing these for a long time,

7

and unless your professor specifically asks for a report, this is not what he is looking for in college. Informative reports are used in the real world to give a group who know nothing about a subject specific information on that subject. It will rarely occur in college that you are writing to an audience who needs basic information on your subject, so informative reports do not occur unless the instructor specifically asks for one; nevertheless, see ch. 12 if asked for a report.

Case Studies You will more likely read case studies, or if you are in the social sciences in an upper level course help a professor conduct one, than actually write one yourself, though in freshman composition courses or introductory social science courses you might be asked to write a brief one, to give you a taste of what the social science disciplines do. A case study is like – and has all the qualities of – an observation, the difference being in a case study a variable usually has been inserted into the "case." (Does a new test – the variable – help students learn?) And in a case study, the writer might or might not be doing the physical observation herself; she can also use collected data. For instance, if a town put in extra traffic lights, a case study could be done by comparing accidents before and after the lights (the variable) to see if the lights had made the roads safer. The writer would have to account for other variables when analyzing the results. Case studies are used by companies, by government, by educators, and by social scientists to analyze and improve society.
(For a fuller definition, the process for completing, and an example, see ch. 9.)

A Genre common to Sciences and Social Sciences

Lab Reports College and professional lab reports of experiments follow a specific organizational format: introduction, materials and method, results, and discussion. The tone is formal and must use the jargon of the discipline you have done the experiment for.
(For a fuller definition, the process for completing, and an example, see ch. 9.)

Genres used in Business

Business Letters Anyone in the business profession needs to learn the specific conventions of this important genre, and learn to develop a suitable formal tone for getting her purpose across and getting the receiver of the letter to do what is wanted. But those in other school disciplines will use this convention also. To be successful with letters of complaint, letters of application, or proposals to get something done in a community you belong to, any educated person should be able to write a good, solid, persuasive business letter.
(For a fuller definition, the process for completing, and an example, see ch. 12.)

Memos While business letters are external communications, memos are internal communications between members of the same firm. The same qualities of formality, conciseness, easily found specific purpose, and call for the receiver to do something appear with memos. The difference is one of audience: with memos writers need to be careful not to give too much unneeded information the receiver already knows, and needs to recognize the psychology of the relationship between the writer and his audience (are they equal, or is the receiver above or below the writer in terms of

8

corporate structure?), adjusting the tone and content of the memo in accordance with these considerations.
(For a fuller definition, the process for completing, and examples, see ch. 12.)

Business Proposals Many times in a business, a worker or owner needs to write a proposal for action-change and this can occur within a company or between companies. The writer needs to study previous case studies that are similar to the proposal and summarize, evaluate, and synthesize them; then describe exactly what the proposed project needs in terms of material, employees, and cash; there needs to be a specific outline of a time table for the proposed project; and finally a discussion of proposed outcome, its benefits, and possible problems.
(For a fuller definition, the process for completing, and an example, see ch. 12.)

Resumes and Letters of Application Being able to write a professional resume and letter of application will be one of the most important tools any college educated person should be able to do. It is not necessary that you have the genre memorized, but you should understand the relationships between writer and audience and know how to analyze audience, and take this knowledge of writing context and writing situation into the composition of resumes and letters of application.
(For a fuller definition, the process for completing, and examples, see ch. 12.)

Genres used mainly in the Humanities, though occasionally the Social Sciences

Literary (or Art/Music) Analysis An essay that looks at a literary or artistic creation and analyzes either what features of the text make it beautiful or expressive (the brush strokes of a painting, the setting of a novel, the symbols used in a poem) or what the work of art means.
Sub-genres of literary essays are, strictly speaking, textual analyses (see below) that focus on
1) the writer/artist (biographical literary analysis)
2) the culture or the artistic milieu the work appeared in or describes (historical literary analysis)
3) feminist criticism (discussing what the work says about gender relations)
4) psychological criticism (using Freud's or Jung's ideas to analyze the work)
(For a fuller definition, the process for completing, and an example, see ch. 10.)

Textual Analysis Similar to a rhetorical analysis (look at its definition above), a textual analysis looks at a literary or scholarly text, poem, art, song lyric, cartoon, television or film, and examines the stance of the creator, her audience, the message, the methods for getting the message across, and what implications can be drawn about the creator's or the audience's culture from the text. Usually, textual analyses are written for a formal, academic audience.
(For a fuller definition and the process for completing, see ch. 10; for examples, see ch. 3 & 10.)

Personal Narratives From your experiences and observations, and your careful analysis of these experiences and observations, you develop a specific thesis that is informative, interesting, humorous, provocative, emotional, argumentative: the key here is to turn your experience into a specific point about human nature. That is how audiences connect to your narrative – a shared sense of humanity. After developing your thesis (the point), careful attention to specific detailed description of the scenes and a narrative of the carefully chosen details will turn your great idea into an excellent personal narrative that proves your thesis.

(For a fuller definition, the process for completing, and an example, see ch. 10.)

Memoirs/Reflective Memoirs are like personal narratives, but they are much more personal. Many of them focus on the specific socio-economic-cultural background you live/lived in. You are the first audience for the memoir/reflection. You use writing to come to a greater understanding about a stage of your life. In a final draft, the instructor might then ask you to decide on an audience and revise your personal memoir into an essay that has a thesis your chosen audience needs to hear. Like a personal narrative, memoirs can be informative, interesting, humorous, provocative, emotional, argumentative, and they have specific, detailed description of scenes and narratives of carefully, chosen incidents to create meaning.

(For a fuller definition and the process for completing, see ch. 10.)

Literacy Narratives Literacy narratives ask you to explore, in depth, your own (or others) experiences with writing and language. Where and how did you/they acquire dialects? Where and how do you/they acquire writing habits and what works? When using new forms of expression like gaming or social networks, what kinds of communication cultures do users create? How has language informed your/their world?

(For a fuller definition, the process for completing, and an example, see ch. 10.)

- **Choose your major!!!** If you haven't chosen a major, or still want to explore other opportunities, as you study these different genres which use different types of research and writing, look at the disciplines associated with each genre. Which kinds of genres and which discipline's content interest you the most? The art of joy in life consists of picking activities that you enjoy to do. Let this introductory composition course, along with your other general studies courses, help you decide what you want to do in life to be happy. Work CAN be "not work."

2

Developing A Writing Context:

Subject, Audience, Writing Situation, Thesis, Tone

Many people think of writing ability as a mysterious, sometimes awe-inspiring "gift" conferred on a precious few at birth. They picture a writer sitting at a desk creating flawless prose day after day; however, professional writers and successful writers point out this is just not the case. Occasionally an experienced writer will produce a page or two of polished prose with very little revision, but this is certainly a rarity. Most of the time writers produce successful prose with multiple drafts and extensive revision. Two essentials promote a writer's success: *experience* with drafting, revision, and editing processes and *hard work*. Anyone who works at the writing craft conscientiously, with an honest eye for needed changes and a willingness to try new methods of composing, will become an extremely proficient writer. Reading quality writing (whether essays or fiction) and practicing writing (whether formally or informally) will give you the needed experience to communicate well. *Practice* makes good writers, or in other words, hard work.

Good Writing Habits

Though all writers at times suffer from "writer's block," successful writers have *confidence* they can work through their block and find the important viewpoint they are struggling for. In addition, writers must have faith in their *writing habits*; they know enough work habits to overcome anxiety and revise for quality. If you lack confidence, discover writing habits that work. Investigate! What makes you comfortable? Could it be idiosyncrasies like covering your head with a blanket as you sit on your bed composing onto your laptop? Hastily writing a first draft onto a PC and printing it; then with a pencil meticulously adding content, scratching out content, and changing words for specificity until the printed words are almost unused?

Find the best places, the best times, to write. Try searching for a quiet, comfortable place with no distractions — preferably one that you can return to every day at the same time. It might be your bedroom, but it also could be at a library, a cubby at one end of your school's writing center, student center, or computer center, or at a comfortable, quiet coffeehouse or restaurant. (Everyone is different: the occasional writer might find a noisy, crowded coffeehouse best. You won't know until you investigate.) Find the time of day that seems most congenial to you — early in the morning, after dinner, late at night. Even find favorite body positions for writing — in bed, at a desk, sprawled on a floor. Experiment and discover which writing tools — pen, pencil, typewriter, computer, or laptop; looseleaf paper, notebook or legal pad — work best for you. *Writing Successfully* will give you many specific suggestions for developing your particular habits, and also will discuss the ***writing processes*** successful writers use. Relax. Writing well is a habit that, once formed, stays with us all our lives.

EXERCISE 2.1
Discovering Good Writing Habits

A) What writing tools do you usually use? Where and at what time do you usually write? Answer those questions, and analyze *why* you use those particular tools, times, and places. Also for this assignment: investigate. Experiment. Find a new place and use it to write. Describe the place you found and why you chose it. Analyze the best time to write, given your schedule and your writing habits. Consider when you do your most productive thinking and analysis. What time, *each day*, would be your best time to write, and why? Prove it with evidence. Try a computer if you usually compose with a pen, or vice versa. More than once, try new places, times, and tools until you can answer this question: which work best, and why?
B) Write a 250-500 word letter to yourself, describing and analyzing your confidence or lack of confidence concerning writing. What are your strengths? What are your weaknesses? What are your feelings concerning writing?

Writing Processes

Writing unfolds in a ***four-stage process*** of discovery and clarification. In the early stage of a writing project, which we will call ***predrafting***, you study your *subject* and learn the demands of the *writing situation* (what is the forum you are writing for? an editorial? a chemistry lab report? an article for a gaming magazine?) Given that writing situation, decide on and analyze the *beliefs, needs, and knowledge level of your audience*. As you study your subject and think about the writing situation and possible audiences, discover your *thesis* (the point you are going to prove with evidence - the content - to that audience about the subject). As you finalize these considerations, you begin to decide on an appropriate *tone* to use for this audience and your thesis, and the content you will use in this writing. We will call the five essential elements (subject, audience, writing situation, thesis, and tone) an essay's ***writing context***.

At some point, you write an initial ***rough draft***, the second stage, which is really just a trying out of possible content and a first stab at writing to an audience with a possible thesis. After writing a draft, in the process of clarifying and revising, you either move back to the predrafting stage or forward to the third stage.

You might move forward into the third stage, ***revision*** or postdrafting, if you are fairly satisfied in the initial draft with your thesis, your tone toward your audience, and your overall content. If you are fairly satisfied with these essentials of good writing, in revision you add and clarify content and develop efficient organizational patterns for your essay. You will often discover new content during the *first few* drafts until you are finally satisfied with the purpose and content for the essay.

But for most writing situations, after an initial draft you first move backward to reclarify and rediscover purpose and tone, and also to rethink some, *or even all*, of the content. You must *make sure* you have settled on a thesis and an audience before revision for content. How do you know what you are going to say (your content) until

12

you are absolutely sure what your point is (the purpose/thesis) and who you are going to say it to? Decide absolutely on these elements of the writing context before doing revisions for content.

In the final stage, after finalizing in revision ALL the content for a specific context, you *edit* by polishing individual sentences and words and by correcting grammar, usage, punctuation, and spelling problems. Of course, some editing of sentences and diction naturally occurs while you are concentrating on content; clear sentences and proper words help clarify your ideas and examples. But repeat the editing cycle for sentence and diction style after you have found your writing context and have revised thoroughly for content and organization. By then your essay will have great ideas, so craft the individual sentences and words into perfect expressions of those ideas. Successful writing has great ideas stated well.

Writers generally move in the following order when discovering their writing context and developing content; however, sometimes the writer realizes purpose first; other times, audience. Using your judgment, complete these essentials in any order your discovery process creates. The conscientious writer returns again and again to these first steps until the writing successfully achieves its purpose:

- Picking a Subject
- Learning about a Subject and Developing Content
- Focusing the Subject and Analyzing Audience and Situation
- Developing Specific Content for the Focused Subject/Audience
- Deciding on a Thesis (a purpose for your writing) and Tone
- Arranging and Adding to the Content, and Developing Organization

Predrafting Techniques: Journals

Many writers keep a journal to record ideas they have, and to focus and develop ideas when and if they decide to use them in their writing for any class. Journals also keep writers writing every day. Some professors may ask students to keep a journal as a class assignment. A journal is not a diary, but a notebook in which the writer writes on any topic that comes to mind for sessions of ten to thirty minutes, analyzing an occurrence, something learned, or a thought of the day. It doesn't take much time, and just the practice of putting thoughts to paper will increase confidence. Describe an unusual event of the day. Summarize a new idea that you read about or that was discussed in a class, and then analyze it. The summary and analysis help you learn and understand it. If nothing happens in a day, nothing was learned (certainly an impossibility), then describe a person, place, or thing. Write about and analyze a personal relationship. Just write. Frequent journal writing builds confidence, and on a more practical level, it gives you a wealth of topics to write about with at least some of the content already on paper in rough form.

You can also use journals to store all your predrafting in one notebook.

Finally, use journal writing to take stock of how you perceive life, not only your personal world, but the world around you. Journals help you analyze how you perceive this world. Most writers who use journals either carry them all the time and write in them at least once a day or they set aside a specific time of the day and write for ten to thirty minutes.

13

Buy a small spiral notebook (5X7 to 7X9), one you can carry comfortably if possible, and begin a journal. Before buying, look over different sizes, colors, width of lines. Pick a notebook that you feel fits you, one that you think you'll be comfortable with (you are picking a writing tool, as was suggested at the beginning of the chapter). You can practice any of this chapter's predrafting suggestions in your journal, and here are some other activities you can use a journal for:

Describe —

an unusual experience of the day	a person you have met
a beautiful scene in nature	an event from the past

Analyze —

a good classroom discussion	a personal relationship
a thought of the day	something you read
a film, T.V. show, news report, video, advertisement	
a C.D., concert, story, poem, novel	

Write —

a story	a poem
a song	a screenplay
an autobiography	an essay

Subjects

Every day, events and communication require a response, often a written one, that might be informative, persuasive, or simply entertaining. Writing is a two-way communication between writer and audience; it can focus on any possible subject. The subject does not have to be "special" or earth shattering. Successful writers don't try to find "perfect subjects" — there aren't any. They spend their time developing the subjects they do have, allowing them the complexity they deserve. To do this writers analyze and study their subjects, breaking them into parts as well as examining *all* related issues.

Early in the predrafting process, two fundamentals concerning the subject must be addressed:

- **Focusing the Subject:** Good writing discusses a subject with the complexity that it deserves, so learn to focus your subject. A writer could not discuss a complex subject like "child care" in a four page essay, but he could make one point about child care and defend this thesis with support. A focused subject developed into a thesis might be: child care workers need more education before working with children. He would defend this thesis with evidence.
- **Knowledge of the Subject:** Make sure you know enough about the subject to write about it. If writing about child care, a writer would use predrafting techniques to remember his own personal experiences, he might study television programs or movies concerning children, he would observe how children and child care providers interact, and he would do some reading to get expert opinions on, and facts about, child care.

14

Focusing the Subject

You cannot try to say everything about a complex subject in a short essay, so narrow the scope of the essay to a sub-topic manageable for the length of the writing project. Writers must always make choices as they write, and good writers control their writing partly by deciding what their writing *won't do*. When you narrow the scope of your essay, you must also consider the demands of the situation. Is there a suggested word length? What type of essay is expected? Are there other essays of the same kind that you can look at? These questions can help focus the subject and limit the length and scope of your treatment of it. Deciding on your audience and thesis can also help narrow your topic. Study your audience to decide which approach to the topic would interest them most. To be completely certain that your subject fits the assignment, make sure your professor approves it — and ask if it is focused enough.

Whatever you do, don't simplify a complex subject; this will offend the intelligence of your audience. The next section of this chapter demonstrates four methods for focusing a subject: brainstorming, lists, clustering, and looping.

Activities for Focusing a Subject

- Become interested in your topic. What portion of the more general, broad topic do you want to discuss in detail? If a professor has assigned the topic and you are bored with it, look for a subtopic that you do identify with.
- Ask the reporter's questions (who, what, when, where, why, how) to investigate the complexity of your subject.
- Divide a broad subject into parts using library sub-headings, lists, or clustering (demonstrated in the next section, predrafting techniques). What subdivisions of the larger topic are there?
- Pay careful attention to the requirements of the assignment. Are there suggestions for narrowing the subject or determining the audience? Is there a suggested word length? Make sure that the professor approves your focused subject.

Knowledge of the Subject

Always make sure you know enough about your subject to write intelligently about it. During predrafting, be sure that you have *thoroughly* analyzed all the ramifications of a subject, and learned all you need to know to write about it. Use whatever combination of writing, reading, and observation necessary to fully explore your subject and know it well. In practice, while you are writing about your subject, you are learning, or relearning, about that subject so that you know enough to write successfully.

Chapters 2-3 will give you multiple predrafting techniques to describe and analyze experiences, the media, and informal observation (of the present or of memories). Chapters 6-8 will demonstrate how to do in-depth analysis of your reading and how to use a college library. Chapter 9 will discuss more formal, scientific methods of observation, survey, and interview.

Activities for Studying a Subject

- Experience (Memory)
  Our experiences contain a well-spring of knowledge. The predrafting techniques that follow and in the next chapter will discuss techniques to recall specific details from experience.
- Television, Movies, the Internet
  We have become a visual culture. We learn a lot about who we are from watching the visual products of our culture. There is also a wealth of informational programs released today. Be careful, however, that you critique and analyze these informational shows for accuracy.
- Observation and Interview (from memory or done specifically for the writing)
  Recalled observations and conversations are another wellspring of knowledge. Later in this and the next chapter, we will discuss methods of recalling details. Also, you might choose to use scientific techniques for vivid observation and solid interviews (discussed in chapter 9).
- Reading (Newspapers, Magazines, Books, Internet, or Library Research)
  Knowledge of a subject is a must! If you need to do research, DO IT! When readers read something and it is obvious the writer does not understand the subject, readers stop reading. When writers express opinions, the reader expects writers to have studied the facts as well as outlooks other than their own. If your knowledge of the subject is not apparent, the reader stops reading.
- *Analysis of these Activities*
  The most important activity involved in studying a subject has to be the analysis. As a successful writer gathers ideas, whether from memory, observation, or research, the writer synthesizes, compares, and analyzes to decide what more to learn, and then to say, about a subject.

Predrafting Techniques: Brainstorming, Lists, Clustering, Looping

Four often used predrafting techniques (brainstorming, lists, clustering, and looping) can help you pick a subject, focus a subject, gain knowledge of a subject, and develop content for an essay.

Brainstorming and Lists

You can brainstorm either in paragraph form or in lists, and you can use these techniques from the very beginning of a writing project. Set a five-minute time limit and write constantly: whatever your mind thinks, write it without worrying about grammar, spelling, or punctuation, never letting the pen leave the paper. If your mind rambles or you seem to be thinking nonsense, still write it down. No one will see it, and it is good practice for getting thoughts from mind to paper. As a variation, make a list — whatever your mind thinks, write it. Again, never let the pen leave the paper. Quantity, not quality, is important at this stage. At the end of three or four five-minute sessions you will have many ideas.

16

The pages following demonstrate the process Matthew Moore, a freshman writing the first essay of his first semester composition class, used to find, focus, and know his subject.

The requirements for the essay included:
4-5 pages word processed. MLA Documentation if essay uses sources.
Broad Subject: American Identity -- Analyze a quality of Americans or a segment of Americans.
A specific thesis, with adequate evidence/content to support this purpose.
Provide a specific, detailed audience; and pick a magazine or journal this audience would read (a writing situation) that the essay would be published in. The tone of the essay should be appropriate for the purpose, audience, and the magazine.

The genesis for what became Matthew's essay came from a series of brainstorming sessions in his journal, written in his dorm late at night:

> Do exercise 2.2: List of 20 possible subjects -
> American identity what can I write about? american identity I'm just a regular middle class white kid what can I . . .
> 1. growing up middle class white kid in suburbia
> Boring what do I have to say?
> 2. Divorce as part of american identity today
> 3. Green Day - American Idiot - I think they even made a broadway show out of it
> 4. what do other music groups say about identity? - broad. list some if I need to. What's his name, Dad's man - Tom Petty
> 5. Bruce Springstein is an american icon: song Born in the USA
> 6. What do I think another group thinks about American identity - what can I say from my viewpoint about what it LOOKS like growing up Latino or African? - probably do african. never knew many Latinos
> 7. What about poverty - what does someone living in - or what does poverty itself - say about America?
> 8. red state blue state 2 americas? discuss

At this point Matthew stared off into space for a few minutes and nothing came, so he went to the next part of assignment 2.2 (p. 24) which said take three of the subjects from the list, brainstorm on each of them for five minutes, and then pick a focused subject. If that didn't work, add to – or pick others from – the list, and try to find a focused subject from one of them.

> Red state blue state. Does seem like everyone is polarized in one of those two, but wait a second the red states seem more polarized within themselves too. There's the kind of old time Republican that grandpa is - keeping spending down for a small

govt, but taxes should be high enugh so that there is no deficit. Then there is the religious republican who is in it for no abortion and as much Xianity into the govt as can go. And then there is the newest republican who is for no taxes period (hardly any) and reduced social security/medicare, but they still want us to have a huge military. What's up with that? the math doesn't work.

I can vote for the first time and don't even know whether I want to - maybe there is another entire topic for identity: voting and how young americans don't even want to it is so messed up. (#9 topic)

But what about blue states - democrats are splintered too though not as much as the repubs - there are a few old time liberal dems left that want govt to do everything. And then there is the faction that is the pro-labor and unions.

(Heh topic #10 - American identity as labor with discussion of Dad and his being an electrician. Made a good middle class wage, but has been out of work for some time now)

And then a third - perhaps majority - new democrat that is much more like the old time fiscal republican. I could do something JUST about how old time middle of the road conservatives have become the new centrist Democrat/liberals. (#11) Maybe. It's worth some thinking and writing about. Time's up. Good. Do I want to focus on this?: I hate politics, but it will force me to really take a look at it. And red state blue state is an important component of who America is right now.

Notice in brainstorming sessions how ideas generate more specific ideas (in this example the classification of different types of red staters, which of course suggested that Matthew must do a contrast and also classify blue staters). Lists can help create more and more specific ideas, and the more ideas a writer has, the easier it is to pick and choose the best - whether the ideas are for focusing a subject or a little further on the discovery path, looking for the best content once a subject and thesis have been created. Matthew is up to eleven great possible topics in less than twenty minutes.

After a five minute rest, Matthew repeated this brainstorming exercise with a description and analysis of Green Day's album and Broadway play, *American Idiot*. As Matthew walked across his room to get a bag of potato chips during his next five minute rest, he walked past his bookshelf. Looking over, he saw a copy of his favorite book: Walt Whitman's *Leaves of Grass*, the ONLY poet he had ever liked. Matthew froze. That's it, he thought. We get our subjects from something that interests us - even if you don't like the broad subject, with some analysis and thought writers can always find a sub-topic that interests them. As Matthew searched, it could have been a film, a television program, a song (like the few he considered), a leisure activity or sport, a conversation at a party or in the dorm, or a topic discussed in class or read about. Subjects come from life. But in order to find one of the many subjects that will interest you - especially if you don't like the broad subject - you have to investigate like Matthew did to find his focus.

Matthew did one more brainstorming session to formalize his idea for a focused subject: Walt Whitman and his philosophy would be a perfect method for Matthew to say something about what it means to be an American. In this final brainstorming session he also developed some of the possible ideas he would analyze to produce the content for the essay. Many students waste days and days trying to decide which of their possible subjects will become their actual subject. Consider this suggestion: When an essay is assigned, brainstorm and then pretend you are in class and the essay must be finished during that class period. In other words, with time restraints what would your choice be at that particular moment? Spend no more than five minutes weighing your decision (as if in a test situation). Then, *and this is the most important part of the suggestion*, continue your brainstorming on the subject you have just chosen for at least another half-hour to an hour — generate ideas for focusing the subject and adding content. At the end of the session, decide whether to keep the subject. If you decide not to keep the subject (or that focus), *immediately* repeat the steps: pick another and rewrite on that subject/focus. Don't spend days or weeks fumbling with your choice of subject. Good writing does not come from picking the perfect subject, but from revising the writing on the subject you picked.

Remember another important tool for studying and focusing a subject: reading and library research. On his way to class the next day, he stopped in the library to get a biography of Whitman, and discovered several shelves of critical studies and biographies. He looked through each one for a minute or so, and since he was writing about American identity and culture, he chose a cultural study of Whitman: David Reynold's *Walt Whitman's America: A Cultural Biography.* Since he already knew Whitman's poems, he could use this one study to compare Whitman's America to what he had observed himself of twenty-first century America. Matthew had the beginnings of a focused subject. The next day he finished his focusing during class, and began deciding on thesis and developing content.

Clustering

In class, the instructor demonstrated clustering, another predrafting technique, which Matthew used to help focus his subject further. Walt Whitman's poetry would be the content Matthew used to discuss American identity, but what ideas in Whitman's poetry would produce a specific thesis and the content to validate the thesis Matthew would create?

With clustering, you draw a "map" of ideas, with lines connecting clusters of circles, to make connections between ideas. Some writers need a visual picture of groupings of ideas, and this method works for them. In the center of a piece of paper, write a topic word or phrase. Divide this topic into parts by surrounding the first idea with related ideas, and draw lines connecting ideas. Repeat this again and again.

As you study your expanding map,
a. you will sometimes notice connections you have not made before,
b. you will discover and analyze many sub-topics to focus your subject or support your main thesis, and
c. you will generate additional content areas for your complex subject.

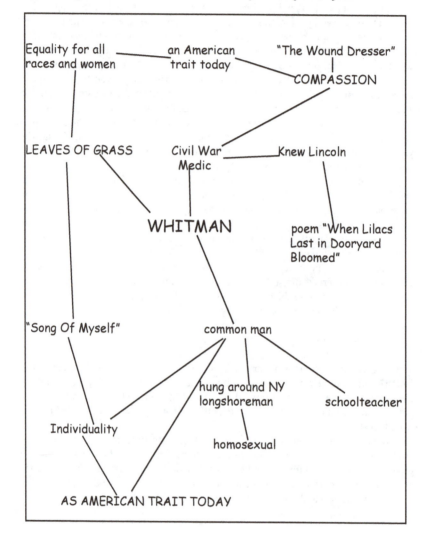

Looping

Another way to find and narrow a subject or to generate content is a form of thinking-while-writing called either focused brainstorming, focused freewriting, or looping. With this method, start with a subject that you want to focus on and give a descriptive title to your first focused freewriting topic. Write on the focused subject for five to ten minutes, again not paying attention to grammar, spelling, etc. As in other forms of brainstorming/freewriting, write anything you are thinking about. If your mind strays off the topic, finish writing out the thought (it might be useful for some other writing), and then go back to the original topic. When you finish a looping exercise, relax, stretch, and then read over what you have written. Mark ideas and examples you could possibly use for your writing, and notice whether there is a general train of thought about the subject running through the writing or whether any of the trains of thought lead to an idea more specific or different than those previously explored.

Then, pick a second focused topic from an idea in your first looping session, one of the trains of thought or an idea more specific or different from those explored, one that you could explore more fully. Write on the paper a descriptive title for your second looping topic. Freewrite on that focused topic for five minutes, repeating the instructions above. When you have finished the second looping session, pick a third focused topic from your second freewriting session; again pick a looping topic that you could explore with more complexity. Continue this pattern for at least five looping exercises in a row.

Looping can be used in one of two ways:

- If the topic is still undecided or unfocused, looping can be used to focus and narrow the topic by finding the most specific thought in the first looping exercise and exploring it at greater length in the second exercise, then finding the most specific thought in the second looping exercise and exploring it at greater length in the third. Repeat the looping exercise several times until the subject is focused. In this process, writers always develop content while they focus the subject, and many times also discover their thesis.
- If the topic has already been sufficiently focused, use the looping exercises to explore the topic and its various sub-topics and side issues, analyzing its complexity and generating quality content for the essay.

When you do a looping exercise, don't worry about being so specific at early discovery stages of the writing process. Let your mind wander — there is no right or wrong with these looping sessions. You are just moving ideas from mind to paper.

The following is a looping example that Matthew wrote after he did the clustering exercise. He picked one of the American traits he had discovered using the clustering exercise, individuality, to begin the looping exercise. Notice how with the looping exercise Matthew discovers content he might use, but more importantly he further focuses his subject with the clustering and the looping. He needs to find what specific American traits he will develop in his essay exploring American identity, and only then will he begin to decide what his thesis will be and what content he will use.

21

Individuality and Whitman

Beginning of his "Song of Myself" opening <u>Leaves of Grass</u>: "I celebrate myself and you - what I assume you shall assume. Every atom belonging to me belongs to you." Whoh - haven't picked up the book in over a year and I still remember how it begins. Powerful words. Atom in me is a part of you - that's what current physics says - all matter is the same stuff. What a visionary. That's not what they believed - where did he get that idea from? hope the book answers it.

wait a second - we are all the same is the opposite of individuality. No. that is not what he says. He says he celebrates me and I celebrate him and assume . . . assume . . . assume like "take on" what I "take on" you "take on" makes more sense in terms of what he's saying than everyone assumes the same thing - but isn't that like we are all now - we all believe and "assume" the same thing, or believe one of two polarized opposites.

So what does he say about individuality - he celebrates the equality of ALL people including the slaves and women. He celebrates his own unique personality and also talks about the unique personalities of each individual person - there's some poem about the unique grain of sand as metaphor for individual humans.

He was certainly an individualist if he was a homosexual in mid-nineteenth century culture. Five minutes past up. Stop.

Matthew rested for five minutes. The instructor told everyone to get up, walk the hall, get a coke or candy bar. Rest a few minutes. Celebrate the hard work of letting thoughts flow. When Matthew returned and looked over what he'd written, he began trying to think of a focus that came out of his first looping exercise. To repeat, there is no one right answer for what the next looping session has to be. It might be one point from the previous exercise that can be explored in more detail. It might be an opposite topic from the one just explored. It might just be a look at a subject from a different angle. Matthew decided that he would focus on twenty-first century notions of individuality and see whether they were similar to Whitman's or different. He immediately began his second looping session:

Individuality Today

Everybody talks about it, but where is it? Get up. Go to work. Come home and eat dinner and watch tv. 2.5 kids- or is it 1.5? Look at everyone in the room. Everyone has on either blue jeans or sweat pants. Everyone wants to do the same things. Beer bong parties. Hooking up. Yeah - some guys have earrings and some don't. the daring ones - guys and girls - all do the same thing: tongue piercing. Where do we all want to go for spring break? Florida. Where is the individuality? But we all SAY we are unique individuals. I'm saying I'm different because I picked one poet I like, and you aren't supposed to like poetry.

But was it any different in Whitman's time? Probably not. I guess we have more ability to choose the area of the country or the world that we live in. Is the huge choice of television stations and utube to watch what makes us different? When most of us my age don't go to church is that a stand for individuality? - maybe it is. And Whitman also celebrated finding God on your own - all the transcendentalists did that too.

There is much more sexual freedom now than in Whitman's time - does sexual freedom equal individuality? I guess with more choices - whether it is television or sex or the kinds of jobs you can get - there is greater individuality. But I just don't see it. We all think and act the same, or in one of two ways - more liberal or very conservative. Just two ways. Is there a way to make my readers more individualists through discussing Whitman's poetry?

Matthew and the class rested. Class was over. The instructor said that for this to be a true looping session, students had to repeat the looping exercise at least three more times, and students should do brainstorming, lists, clustering and looping over and over until each student had a narrowed topic and had enough knowledge (and some of the content) to be able to start the essay by the next class. As Matthew walked out the door, he had already decided what his next focused freewriting session would concern: the common man in Whitman and how that topic relates to today.

The Common Man

Whitman hung around the bars with the longshoremen in the ports of New York City - Brooklyn I think. The hardworking common man whom he celebrates. He hung around the common soldier during the Civil War, tending to their wounds and helping these common men mostly die. A lot like Dad.

Spent his time working hard and then going to the union hall or the bar for an hour or so to celebrate. to celebrate what? freedom from work? Not really. He loved his work, working with his hands. Perhaps this was like Whitman - didn't he hang around with his fellow MALE workers because he just loved the friendships that evolved over the years working on different projects. America acts like they love the common man, but in the 50s-70s they got a decent wage and good retirement, but that's all going away now - or has gone away. Has America gotten away from celebrating the common man. The politicians - especially the democrats - SAY they love and respect the common man. but do they? Thank you sir for your service fighting in Afghanistan AND Iraq, but sorry you can't get a job now with your PTSD. I know you worked for twenty years, but your job is going overseas now. Your unions have too much power - we're not supporting them anymore.

What does this say about us NOW? Do we need to start celebrating the common man, or is the common man a man of the past? That just can't be true. We'll always need plumbers and construction workers.

Matthew did three more looping sessions after class, but you get the picture of how they work. He finally ended his sessions because he realized he was beginning to encounter a problem that must be solved first before any successful writing can occur: attaining a thorough knowledge of the subject. Matthew's next task was to read some of the biography of Whitman he had checked out, and also he began to immerse himself again in his much loved poetry, the sole poetry volume Whitman added to again and again throughout his life, *Leaves of Grass*. This entire work Matthew had done so far had lasted less than three hours, and he had already focused his subject and a few hours of reading with the all important analysis of what he read would give him the needed knowledge of his subject and most of the content for his essay.

EXERCISE 2.2
Picking the Subject and Knowledge of the Subject

A) *Picking a Subject*: In five minutes make a list of twenty subjects. Then pick three of the topics and spend five minutes on each choice, writing whatever comes to mind to generate ideas about (and reasons for writing on) the subject. After you have finished this twenty-minute session (perhaps thirty minutes with breaks), decide whether you would like to write on one of the subjects you've been working on. If you don't want to work with one of those three subjects, repeat this process until you have picked a subject.

B) *Knowledge of Subject:* Make a thorough list of what you would need to know to write an essay on either two of the subjects below or subjects of your own choice:

Friendship	Buying a car	Political changes in Europe
Terrorism	Farm Price Support	The Next Election
A Film Review	A CD Review	College Applications
Democracy	Freedom	Drinking
The newest stereo equipment		The latest computer innovations

EXERCISE 2.3
Focusing the Subject and Knowledge of the Subject

For the essay you are working on, use the activities (brainstorming, lists, clustering, and looping - pp. 16-24) to complete the activities for focusing the subject (p.15) and studying the subject (p.16).

Audience

Know who your audience is. *Try to picture them and know something about them, especially what they already know and believe about your subject. Your audience greatly affects the choices made as you write.* Choosing a specific audience and then evaluating it allows you to decide precisely what content to include. Also, your style — how you address your audience — will be different for each audience. For instance, your style and tone would be different in a love letter, hopefully, than in either an essay on Central American foreign policy or a letter to your parents. If the professor wants to be the intended audience (he would say: "write to a scholarly [or academic] audience"), you have a ready source of knowledge concerning the audience. You have observed the professor in class, which should help you make writing choices. If you have already written an essay for the class, re-read it and carefully note the professor's comments concerning its strengths and weaknesses.

Evaluating Audience

Some writing occasions begin with a specific audience. (A letter to a boss asking for a raise, a complaint letter for a dress that tore the second time you wore it, or some college assignments: "Write a three page critique of one of the assigned essays to share with other students in our class" or "Write a fifteen page research paper on some aspect of abuse in America. Assume an Academic Audience.") The academic audience in the last example suggests that the writer should assume an educated audience familiar with the terms and concepts of the discipline. In this instance, because the subject is abuse, the discipline would be psychology or sociology; the audience would be readers familiar with the terminology and concepts of psychology and sociology. However, with many writing situations in college classes, as well as in pieces for magazines, writers need to decide specifically *whom* they are writing to as they decide *why* they are writing. For instance, if you were going to write an essay defending handgun control, you would focus on different points if you were writing to members of the National Rifle Association, who would disagree with you, than you would to an audience of teenagers, who perhaps haven't looked at the facts and made up their minds yet. You would focus on yet different concerns and have a different style if the essay were for an audience who already agreed with your views.

If you are not sure whom you want to write to, make a list of different groups of people whom you think would be interested in your subject. You could also imagine your essay being published in a particular magazine, newspaper, or website; this can help you choose and imagine an audience. When you have picked an audience, you need to analyze it. You can make a list of traits describing the audience (age, sex, ethnic heritage, religion, socioeconomic and educational background); then make some decisions. What can you reasonably expect that they already know *and* believe about your subject? What do they need to know about your subject? Are they already experts on your subject or do they already have a pre-conceived view on your subject? Use these questions as starting points for predrafting to decide specifically how you will approach the audience in terms of tone (discussed in this chapter) and the content you will need to use to keep your audience interested.

Analyze specifically your relationship to the audience, your role as the writer to a specific set of readers. The easiest audience to write to is usually your peers (people

25

you actually know and who are members of your peer group – with similar ages and interests — perhaps people you work or socialize with); next easiest would be members of your peer group, but not specific people you know.

Next in order of difficulty would be an audience you know but who differ in age, sex, or lifestyle (an owner of a store, a college professor, a minister, a parent). Even harder as an audience would be a specific person or group that you don't know at all. If you know your audience well, or are a member of your audience, it is much easier to decide exactly what to include in your writing and what is unnecessary. If you are not a member of the audience you are writing to, you must carefully analyze the audience-- to know what they need to know about your subject, and more importantly, to leave out what they already know about it.

The most difficult group to write to is the general reading public. *Always try to limit your audience to a more specific one than the "general reading public," even if you sincerely want everyone to read your message.* There are so many differences in the general reading public that a careful median must be reached in order to make the writing understandable and enjoyed by a majority of readers. The best method to approach writing for a general audience is to pick a more specific audience and write to it. By making an audience as specific as possible — even if your writing will actually be read by others outside the audience, the choices for necessary content and tone decrease and the writing correspondingly improves. Selecting a specific audience allows you to choose appropriate content more confidently. Readers outside your target audience will still respond to writing not pointed directly at them. Do you ever read magazines pointed at audiences you are not a member of — *Guitar Player*, even if you don't play guitar; *Seventeen*, even if you are older, or a male? A male can learn from an article written for women on subjects such as how to get a date or how to keep a relationship growing, and so can women from an article written for men. As readers, we often read articles written to audiences we aren't members of, and as writers. In summary, we have to be aware of the complex demands of audience analysis.

Analyzing the Writing Situation

What kind of writing is your essay? Every type of writing follows certain forms and conventions, so study the demands for each writing situation carefully — it usually only takes a few minutes. If you remind yourself from the beginning whether you are asked to write a newspaper editorial, a scholarly research paper, a lab report, an article for a small segment of the population, you save time deciding what to say and how to say it. You can also examine samples of the kind of writing you are being asked to write, to help you understand forms and conventions of that particular kind of writing.

There are too many forms of writing to list, but to illustrate the writing situation here are a few forms that you are familiar with:

- the personal letter
- the resume and job application letter
- a letter to the editor of a newspaper
    informative or analytic
    persuasive/argumentative, centering on
    complaint or praise

- a "how to" essay describing a process (such as at a business)
- a record review
- a movie review
- a book review
- a report

Some specific forms of writing used by scholars in university situations include:

- lab reports
- reports of case studies, experiments, and surveys in the social sciences
- literature reviews in the natural and the social sciences
- literary analysis in the English, Humanities, and Language disciplines

Chapter 1 discusses the genres of writing you will probably encounter in college, and chapters 6-12 give you specific points about navigating the conventions of these genres written for specific kinds of employment and scholarly research. Writers follow specific conventions in each of these forms (and with almost all forms of writing), and if you simply remind yourself of the format, vocabulary, style, and tone already established for that style of writing (elements of the writing situation), this will help you choose and arrange content and diction. A simple illustration: if you are asked to write a research paper, you know you must do some kind of research that will form the centerpiece of your writing. For academic writing, the professor often details the writing situation when giving the assignment. If the professor asks you to analyze, compare, describe, synthesize, summarize, argue, persuade then arrange your content to do so. He or she is suggesting a particular writing form by describing what the writing needs to do.

Finally, one method to help envision both audience and situation is to pick a specific magazine, journal, or newspaper you are writing for. You can look at the publication's articles and decide which audiences would read it, to help choose a thesis and content that suits that audience.

Here are some sample types of magazines, journals, and newspapers, with notes on audiences they draw and the content they would expect:

Popular Magazines
- For instance, *Sports Illustrated*: Although the magazine has a fairly general audience, you can assume that most readers of the magazine read it on a regular basis, that they like sports, and that they have at least a basic knowledge of major sports. When choosing a popular magazine, imagine the audience: *Cosmopolitan* would have an educated female audience, ages twenty to forty. *Rolling Stone* would have an audience that follows contemporary rock music closely and ranges from twenty to thirty-five (with some who have been reading it since it began in 1967, so some as old as sixty or seventy).

Scholarly Journals
- For instance, *The Mark Twain Journal*: a scholarly journal designed for teachers and literary critics who specialize in Mark Twain. There are thousands of scholarly journals, usually published quarterly, for all specialized subjects studied in academia. Any college research library has these, usually in databases. This audience (which would include a professor who teaches Mark Twain's fiction) knows Mark Twain's life and writings well, so writing for this journal you wouldn't need to give biographical details or plot summaries. You *would* analyze Mark Twain's writing or life using examples to justify your thesis. In writing an essay on Mark Twain, you would study and research your topic, thus becoming a scholar of his writing. Though you are a novice scholar, you need to conform to the conventions of professionals, and research and write with the clarity and thoroughness of a professional.
- Don't shy away from writing for professional scholars as an equal. If you have a good analysis or a persuasive argument — whether it be on an issue in history, literature, the social sciences, or the natural sciences — communicate that idea clearly and confidently, following the forms and conventions of the genre used by that academic field. Care in following the conventions set by a discipline will gain the respect of your audience.

Your college newspaper
- You are a member of the audience and can assume what they should know.
- You should have a natural understanding of their thoughts and feelings concerning the topic you are writing about.

Your hometown newspaper
- If you come from a city your audience is diverse, so you must compromise and strike a balance – focusing the piece on a narrower audience, yet making it engaging and accessible for a broad appeal. An exception would be a subject affecting all the city's citizens equally. If you come from a smaller town, your audience will be easier to envision. You can choose purpose and content according to the town's general attitudes toward a subject (if there is a prevailing attitude).

Activities for Analyzing Audience and Situation

Use these questions to help make decisions about how to convince an audience that you have a valid thesis, and what content should be used to convince them.

- *Who is the audience? Describe their age, sex, ethnic heritage, religion, and socioeconomic and educational background. Be specific and detailed.*
- What is your relationship to the audience? Are you a member of their group or not? How are you similar and dissimilar? Should your tone be formal or informal, humorous or serious, sympathetic or non-sympathetic?

- Why will the reader be interested in your writing? How can you interest the reader in your writing?
- What does your reader know about your subject? Make a list. What does your reader need to know about your subject? Make another list. What details from the lists should be in your writing, and what can you assume the reader would find unnecessary?
- What are your audience's views or beliefs on your subject? Are they like or unlike yours? Will you need to persuade your reader to accept your thesis?
- What magazine, newspaper, or journal would publish your essay? What is the writing situation?
- Given the audience's educational background and the purpose for the writing, how formal should the language be and how many technical terms (if applicable) need to be defined?

Here is the list Matthew made of possible audiences:

> 1. People my age - they aren't going to like Whitman subject. Will have to interest them.
> 2. English teachers/the professor - kind of scary - he knows a lot
> 3. People of my grandparent's generation seem more in touch with Whitman's values than people today.
> 4. People who are really "for" equality and individuality
> 5. Non-reading "common men"

During the next class, the professor broke the class into small groups to discuss their subjects, and all the students in Matthew's group rolled their eyes when he talked about Whitman, so this made him firmly decide: THEY would be his audience. He quickly moved to talking about concerns of Whitman's, individuality and equality, and they all leaped on these as good topics.

To help plan content, Matthew did an in-depth audience analysis using the questions above. Notice that the analysis centers on making decisions about the tone he should use (as in "tone of voice"), and deciding what content to include or leave out based on this audience. *Audience analysis is an important time saving step in the writing process. How do you know what content to include if you have not analyzed what your audience knows and believes or what they need to know to validate your thesis?* Here is his analysis:

> Exercise 2. 5 Analyzing Audience and Situation
> Who is the audience? College students, 17-22, male and female. Mostly fairly liberal, and at least middle class. A minority from poverty and a minority from wealth. All ethnicities but approximately the same as the general population. I am going to focus on my own: middle class, white.
> what is relationship to audience? I am a member of the audience: I should stay pretty informal, but not slangy. Should use a tone of concern and desire for making the world a better place without sounding lame

<u>Readers will be interested? How to interest them?</u> Teens will not be interested in Whitman, but as I discovered I will have to interest them in equality and individuality as part of American identity, and I have to make a connection with Whitman so they will maybe get a little interested in Whitman. I mean come on - his lines sound like a rap song

<u>Reader knows about</u>: most really believe that THEY work for equality - and some think we are free while others believe that America has a way to go. They know basically that we are taught from childhood to believe in individuality. They have heard of Whitman probably - they think poetry has regular lines unlike Whitman's. They know about the Civil War, but not much else about Whitman's time period.

<u>Reader needs to know about</u>: This is hard. Maybe I should change the subject. Give up - No! They need to be validated in the beauty of Whitman's proclamations. They need to see that we aren't there in individuality, equality, and certainly not compassion these days. I need to plead to my audience's better natures. I need to just give them the enthusiasm I'm feeling now - light on the facts and heavy on the emotional plea!!!!! I need to give them Whitman's words/poetry. I need to have them connect to the common man which doesn't happen so much these days. He is ignored and thought of as a servant - not the free individual he is!!!!

<u>Audience's views</u>: they really agree with me that there should be more individuality and equality like Whitman calls for. Not so sure about the compassion - help them get there. America is not lost.

<u>Writing Situation</u>: a fanzine, or maybe the literary magazine of the college. Certainly not a literary analysis, more a personal narrative perhaps. (But do need some historical analysis and comparison between the 1850s and today.)

<u>Tone</u>: Informal, subjective – very. A tone of enthusiasm: that is the dominant impression I want to leave the reader with.

EXERCISE 2.4
Learning About Audience and Writing Situation

A) Evaluate Matthew's essay at the end of chapter three in terms of audience. Who is the audience? Does he evoke emotions in the reader? How is the essay most successful? least successful? What changes would you propose?

B) Imagine you have a job at a medium-size corporation in which you are an entry-level office manager, and you report to both immediate supervisors and upper-level management. Invent a problem at the job and write three letters concerning the problem, one to co-workers, one to your immediate supervisor (whom you work with closely), and one to the vice-president of the company. After completing the letters, write an analysis of the differences in choices of content, style, and language you made because of the changing audience for the letters. If you find that there are not substantive differences, revise the letters to reflect the differences in audience and then write an analysis.

C) Go to the library or go on-line, and look at issues of three or four of the magazines listed below. Examine the table of contents, read at least two articles in each magazine, and look at the advertising. Who would read each magazine? Describe the audiences in detail, including age, sex, education, and socioeconomic group. What kinds of writing, or writing situations, are in the magazine?

Psychology Today	*The New Yorker*	*Time*
Cosmopolitan	*Science*	*The National Enquirer*
Gentleman's Quarterly	*Journal of Popular Culture*	
The Smithsonian	*Journal of New England Medicine*	

EXERCISE 2.5
Analyzing Audience and Writing Situation

Make a list of possible audiences for the essay you are working on. On some occasions you decide on the thesis first; others you will decide the audience you want to talk to about the subject first. Either is correct, but do one or the other, and both are going to need to be done. Choose the audience you think you want to write to the most. Use the Activities for Analyzing Audience and Situation on the previous three pages to study that audience. Make a list, or write a response (whichever seems more appropriate), for each of the seven questions. There will probably be some you can't answer yet, but making sure you answer them at some point in the predrafting and drafting process will help insure successful writing. After this ten minutes of thinking, decide if this is your preliminary audience. If you aren't sure, repeat until you have decided.

Purpose: Thesis and Tone

Writing is a form of communication. If you listen to a person speak and there does not seem to be a point being made, or if the person cannot support ideas with logical proofs, you eventually stop listening. Like all good communication, spoken or written, your writing should have a purpose and the purpose should be supported with examples, evidence, illustrations, and supporting ideas in the text.

Some writing projects are born ready-made with a purpose: an email to friends and family to tell them what has occurred in your life while you are away, a complaint letter to get a specific problem corrected, a letter to co-workers to explain a process for solving a problem. In these letters, the purpose itself needs little thought, but the *choice of details* requires effort: what should you say to convince the dress company that the dress was bought torn? In other writing situations, particularly in college, you must discover the purpose (what you want to say about the subject, your point).

Creating a Thesis Statement

Many writers call the purpose a ***thesis statement*** for the writing — a declaration of what the essay is attempting to do. Until you know the answer to the question, "what is my point?," you will just be stringing together ideas about a subject, you won't be truly communicating. The more precise the point (or thesis), the more precise the actual essay will be. Most writers begin with fairly vague thesis statements, but

31

in the course of predrafting and drafting, their purposes become clearer and more specific. Before coming up with a thesis, an essay begins with a *research question or questions*. Many people mistakenly think this will serve as a thesis statement, but that isn't true. A question isn't a statement! The thesis statement is the answer to the research question, whether the question had to be answered through library research, or just through the analysis of predrafting. For instance, Matthew started out with this research question:

> What does Walt Whitman's philosophy say about what it means to be an American?

This is not a thesis statement, it is a question that needs to be answered to discover what an essay's thesis might be. As Matthew did predrafting exercises to discover the many possible answers to this question, other research questions occurred as he wrote.

> Whitman celebrates individuality, but he also celebrates the common man doing communal things together. Isn't this a contradiction?

(He ended up, with this question, deciding that it wasn't a contradiction.)

> Americans talk about individuality, but doesn't American society make us conformists?

He answered these and thought of other research questions as he analyzed American identity through the lens of Whitman's poetry and beliefs.

So, when you begin an essay and the thesis statement isn't apparent from the beginning, you start by deciding on a subject, focusing it, and making sure you have analyzed it enough, and when you have thoroughly learned about and analyzed a subject, you finally reach a stage where you can answer the next questions: what is my point going to be? (the thesis statement) And whom am I going to communicate this thesis to? (the audience) Only then can you finalize decisions about what content to use to validate a specific thesis to a specific audience.

As Matthew neared the end of his discovery process, he began to write thesis statements until he finally created one that he knew was what he wanted to communicate to his audience, college students. Compare these thesis statements, which Matthew wrote at various times during his composition process, and notice how they came out of answers he discovered to the research questions that began his discovery process. Also notice his own astute comments [bracketed] on the thesis statements that he abandoned:

> Three traits shared by almost all Americans are individuality, a desire for equality, and compassion.
> [entirely too broad - this would have to be 3 separate essays, not 1. I could pick one of them.]

Whitman is the most American poet, celebrating individual freedom and the beauty of the common man.
[better, but I want the focus to be more on the American character and less on Whitman, though I don't want to lose Whitman as the way to see us.]

Whitman celebrated the "common man," but in today's America it seems that no one cares for the working man, and he is looked upon as ignorant, poor, and uneducated, even though that is not true. The common man is the last frontier for equality and compassion in America.
[better, a specific focus for the thesis, and one that examines a facet of the American character, but I really want to focus more on Whitman's philosophy of America's character, and how it encapsulates America.]

[How can I do something with how equality and compassion are missing from the political discourse today? How can I SHOW the equality and compassion as Whitman envisioned it to make readers excited about them again?]

Today America is divided into two ideological camps, and we have no one spokesperson for American values. Walt Whitman was that spokesman in the last half of the nineteenth century, and he believed that his two central ideas were, and I believe they still should be, the true philosophy of the United States: Equality and Compassion.
[Yes. That encapsulates what I want to say! Will of course have a section on the common man. Writing Situation: I realize now that I am not going to be writing a personal narrative, but really a textual analysis of what Whitman's poems and thoughts say about Americans then and now.]

Excellent thesis statements like this last one not only state the main point, the driving force behind the essay, but also forecast the main content of an essay and even show the organizational pattern. When you read Matthew's essay at the end of chapter three, you will see that the essay mirrors the structure of the thesis statement, beginning with a discussion of the two ideological camps in today's society, then moving to a section concerning Whitman as a spokesman for America and its belief in individuality; third discussing how Whitman saw equality and compassion, and concluding with a bringing together of the two time periods of the essay: Whitman's vision as applied to today. Notice also that he finalized the genre of the essay he was writing, a textual analysis as opposed to a literary analysis or a personal narrative as he had thought previously. Notice also that the final thesis statement is a reworking of the third preliminary statement.

Excellent thesis statements *make a point*, and the essay supports the statement with evidence. Writers write and rewrite in a process of discovery until they find the purpose, or thesis, for their writing. Sometimes the purpose is found after one draft (or is already known before the writing commences); for other occasions, writers must try multiple possibilities before they find the purpose that best conveys their message. Almost all writers, however, ask for second opinions as they explore their subjects for the right purpose for them and their audience. Ask fellow readers for help as you search for your thesis statement.

Finding an Appropriate Tone

Remember who you are as you write. If you know your audience well, and the writing situation is informal (a letter to a girlfriend or boyfriend, for instance), you can adopt a familiar tone. If the writing occasion is more formal (a researched college essay), adjust the tone to fit the audience. Successful writers have analyzed how familiar they can be with their readers in an essay, as well as the demands of the genre and writing situation, and they adjust the tone accordingly. They wouldn't adopt a familiar, conversational tone in a lab report or a rhetorical analysis, nor would they sound stiff, stifled, and overly analytical in a personal narrative trying to evoke feelings in the reader. There would be no room for jokes or sly irony in a scientific essay, nor would there be a reportorial, persuasive tone in an essay whose purpose was comedy. Students today really understand more about tone than previous generations: take what you know about tone when talking to people in your peer group versus talking to people your parents' and teachers' ages, in other words, what you know about responding with an appropriate tone of voice.

Tone reveals the writer's attitude toward the subject and the relationship between the writer and audience. Ask these questions of your relationship to your subject and audience: Are you sympathetic, antagonistic, or ambivalent toward your subject? Should you use humor, anger, a tone of sadness or longing, a tone of separation from or identification with the audience? Should you be objective (as most college essays are), or subjective (as personal experience essays usually are)? One of the most important aspects to search for as you write preliminary drafts is the tone you will use to best convey meaning to the reader; however, this decision usually isn't finalized until you are revising your text. Other words could describe your tone:

How are you emotionally connected to your subject *and* to your audience?

Are you: angry sad hostile uncommitted enthusiastic joyful friendly?

Some styles invoke a tone:

comic satiric ironic argumentative persuasive analytic informative

All writing falls on a continuum somewhere between subjective and objective.
And on a continuum somewhere between informal and formal.

While revising, adjust your tone to fit your audience and purpose. The graph on the next page shows words that describe types of tone, moving from left to right from the informal to the formal, to an overly formal, stilted tone.

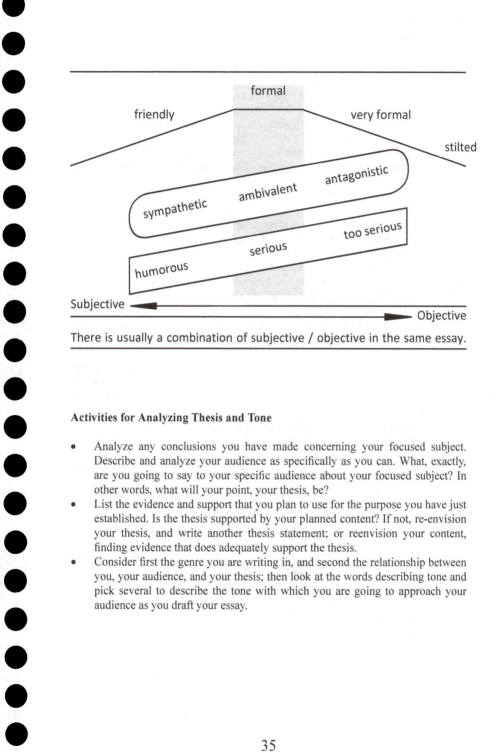

There is usually a combination of subjective / objective in the same essay.

Activities for Analyzing Thesis and Tone

- Analyze any conclusions you have made concerning your focused subject. Describe and analyze your audience as specifically as you can. What, exactly, are you going to say to your specific audience about your focused subject? In other words, what will your point, your thesis, be?
- List the evidence and support that you plan to use for the purpose you have just established. Is the thesis supported by your planned content? If not, re-envision your thesis, and write another thesis statement; or reenvision your content, finding evidence that does adequately support the thesis.
- Consider first the genre you are writing in, and second the relationship between you, your audience, and your thesis; then look at the words describing tone and pick several to describe the tone with which you are going to approach your audience as you draft your essay.

EXERCISE 2.6
Developing Context Cards

Context Cards are 3x5 index cards that you can create to focus your writing context. You write your focused subject, audience, writing situation, thesis, and tone on them, but your card could change many times during predrafting and drafting until you finally discover *precisely* what you want to say to whom. Use Exercise 2-3: Focusing the Subject and Knowledge of the Subject (p. 24), Exercise 2-5: Analyzing Audience and Writing Situation (p.31), and the Activities for Analyzing Thesis and Tone (p. 35) to discover the elements of your writing context. Work on refining the card by discussing your subject, audience, situation, purpose, and tone with others until your choices are precise and clear.

After you have discovered these context elements, then your card becomes finalized and you and your peers can use it in its final form as you revise. When you are revising your draft, keep the finalized card where you can see it to keep your revision focused. When a fellow student or the professor reviews your essay, the card will explain exactly what your context is so they can better evaluate your essay.

You might use both sides of the card to give yourself and your peer reviewers enough information to analyze your writing. Using context cards will really help you focus your writing, and are invaluable for helping peer reviewers critique your essay.

Here is Matthew's context card:

Matthew Moore
English 101
Dr. Janovitch
1st Draft

Subject: Walt Whitman's philosophy of Americans
Audience: People my age college students. More of a focus toward white middle class.
Writing Situation: A textual analysis. An essay in the college literary magazine.
Thesis: Today America is divided into two ideological camps, and we have no one spokesperson for American values. Walt Whitman was that spokesman in the last half of the nineteenth century, and he believed that his two central ideas were, and I believe they still should be, the true philosophy of the United States: Equality and Compassion.
Tone: fairly formal and analytic. Scholarly. But also ENTHUSIASTIC - convincing readers that Whitman's vision is still possible!!!!!

3
Developing Content To Organization And Drafting

As a writer develops a writing context (a focused subject, specific audience, writing situation, thesis, and tone), he/she also thinks about and looks for the supporting evidence for the thesis, the content necessary for communicating this thesis to the audience. As chapter two points out, at first a writer will complete a thorough study of the subject. Remember, writing well usually comes after one has some knowledge of the subject. But while doing this study by both writing about (analyzing) and often researching the subject, while thinking about and finalizing decisions about the context, a by-product of this discovery process is that the writer usually has done enough brainstorming and research on paper to have also developed more than enough content to satisfy the demands of the audience and thesis he finally decides on.

Chapter three contains more predrafting techniques to develop content for an essay (the reporter's questions and the rhetorical patterns), then discusses strategies for organizing this content, and finally gives tips for writing the initial draft of an essay.

Discovering Content

EXERCISE 3.1
DEVELOPING CONTEXT AND CONTENT

As you read about the predrafting techniques in chapters two and three (brainstorming, lists, clustering, looping, the reporter's questions, the rhetorical patterns, re-thinking audience and context cards, and outlining), use each of them to help you develop context and content for the essay you are writing. Even if you don't see how it could help your present essay, experiment and use each strategy anyway. The difference between successful writers and not as successful writers is that the former have more "tools" in their toolbox to pull out when they need them. By using each of these strategies as you develop your essay, you will implant the "tool" in your brain (your "toolbox"), and can then pull it out again whenever you need it.

Predrafting Techniques: Brainstorming, Lists, Clustering, Looping (again)

Writers, besides using brainstorming, lists, clustering, and looping to develop subject, audience, and thesis (the writing context), can also use them to develop content for their essays. In chapter three, we are going to use the predrafting for content that Gerald Gardner did to write an essay for his composition course. We are at a point where he has already developed his writing context.

The requirements for the essay included:

4-5 pages word processed. MLA Documentation if essay uses sources.
Broad Subject: Gender or Race/Multi-Cultural Issues.
A specific thesis, with adequate evidence/content to support this purpose.
Provide a specific, detailed audience; and pick a magazine or journal this audience would read (a writing situation) that the essay would be published in. The tone of the essay should be appropriate for the purpose, audience, and the magazine.

Gerald made lists and did some freewriting exercises to arrive at his focused subject. As you will see from the predrafting here as well as the draft of the essay which appears in chapter four, he initially resisted the topic, but he worked his way through his reluctance by speaking with fellow students, his professor, and looking back at his own small town America lack of experiences with other cultures, comparing his hometown with the more cosmopolitan university culture he attended.

Gerald didn't use them with this essay, but clustering and looping are also good processes for developing content. Try them also.

Gerald's Context Card:

Gerald Gardner
Eng 150
Professor Robinson
First Draft

Subject: Racism
Audience: white people like myself who ignore racial problems
Writing Situation: hometown newspaper editorial
Thesis: Racism, mostly unconscious, still occurs in America today, and we need to work – as a nation – on relieving it.
Tone: serious, persuasive, objective

Again, the key to brainstorming is to write whatever thoughts cross your mind, expressing them openly without worrying about organizing them, whether they are good ideas, or whether they are expressed well. Also, Gerald knew little about his topic when he started this project, so he began doing research and reading the articles in his class's anthology, but one does not always do library research first before using these predrafting techniques. These predrafting techniques also serve as great tools to remember details from, or analyze thoroughly, experience or observations. You will also see Gerald analyzes his own experiences and observations as he thinks about race for the first time.

Brainstorming/Listmaking for Content

I don't even think about how African-Americans are treated because everyone in our small town treats the two or three African-american families fine, or at least that is what I see. Yeah there was talk on the news when I watched it about issues with unfairness in prisons, or in housing. A lot of whispers that 'they' keep taking 'our' jobs - and it is said with whispers and quotation marks in white society because we know that this idea is somehow suspect, that you aren't supposed to say it because it really isn't true. So what did I learn about African americans

38

when I was growing up? Not much. We just didn't spend too much time on it in history. In literature I remember reading Toni Morrison's The Bluest Eye and a poem by that black poet ---- Langston Hughes, That"s it. We spent a day listening to Duke Ellington, Miles Davis, and Aretha Franklin. With hip hop, knew more about music than teacher.

What all did I learn in high school American history? And I need to preface this with African-Americans are about 14% of the population, and their families have been here a lot longer than most white people, and I surely didn't spend 14% of my time in american history talking about African-american issues. That ain't right. Never thought of that before.

1 class on slavery

1 on Reconstruction

1 on racism/KKK of 20s and 30s

1 on Civil rights

1 on Martin Luther King and the race riots of the 60s

Wow!!!!! So the teacher connected the peacekeeper with rioting. I'm not sure what that means yet, but it's significant.

And that is it!!!!! FIVE classes, six with the one on music.

Let's see, in middle school I remember a few minutes on George Washington Carver, Harriet Tubman, Frederich Douglass, Sojourner Truth, Jackie Robinson, Thurgood Marshall.

So what does it mean that I grew up insulated in my own culture? That we didn't study other cultures than our majority culture. I'm feeling kind of lop-sided right now. I feel the rush of empty space that needs filling up with knowledge from other cultures, starting with African-Americans. Come on now. They MADE American music. They ARE American sports. and I don't really even know any of that other than a few basketball stats.

I hated this at first, but I'm liking this road to greater understanding I've started on.

Notice that this exploration contains private thoughts, a self-analysis of Gerald's experiences. When you are brainstorming or writing in a journal, you should feel free to write whatever comes to mind, even if you know the thought you are writing has no business in an essay that will be read by others. When you let your innermost thoughts on a subject come out, it can help you decide whether to write on that subject or not, and it will help you become completely knowledgable on your subject by helping you remember your deepest feelings and thoughts (even if they won't be used in your essay). Writing is an avenue to learning about, analyzing, and organizing your thoughts on a particular subject — whether the subject is personal or public.

But when you read Gerald's essay in chapter four, you will see that he used many of the more public predrafting ideas directly in the draft of his essay – this predrafting helped him form his content. (The portions he ended up using will be underlined.)

**Predrafting Techniques: The Reporter's Questions —
Who? What? When? Where? Why? How?**

With Matthew's predrafting in chapter two, we saw one use for the reporter's questions: the questions to analyze audience and writing situation are a form of the reporter's questions. Secondly, they can be used to find out and list what you still need to know about a subject. Thirdly, you can also use the reporter's questions to find content by exploring all aspects of a topic, remembering details from observations you have just made or from memory, or as in the examples below analyzing research on a topic. The reporter's questions help create more than enough specific, detailed content. *If we don't record details, we tend to forget them, and good writing has vivid, specific details.* Use these reporter's questions like focused brainstorming sessions, focusing on details of the whos (the people in your writing), on details of what happened, on the when, where, why, and how of a subject. Remember to use these techniques to find out both *what you know* and *what you need to find out.*

Sometimes, one or two of the reporter's questions are not relevant, or not as relevant as others, because of your choice of subject. Usually one or two will be very important. If one of the questions is extremely important for your subject, spend the majority of your predrafting time analyzing that question as it pertains to your subject and purpose.

A portion of Gerald's predrafting using the reporter's questions follows. Knowing that he was going to have to understand affirmative action to write his essay, after reading two encyclopedia/textbook articles for basic information and two pro and two against Affirmative Action articles, he used the reporter's questions to reflect and analyze the subject, to see what he thought.

Affirmative Action   Where: U.S.

What and When
Various early stabs at Affirmative Action, but solidified with Civil Rights Act of 1964. It protects discrimination against people in employment for race, sex, religion, national origin. Added over the next 15 years or so were amendments protecting discrimination for age, pregnancy, and disbility.
Fed govt, including contractors, is the largest employer by far in the country, and Pres Johnson immediately signed executive orders making sure that all federal agencies and contracts complied, so Aff Act quickly spread.
Within a few years, via lawsuits, discrimination in college acceptance was put in force.
To make sure that these worked, there was a quota system in that if 2 candidates applied for a job, preference should be given to the under represented race, sex, religion, national origin. Of course, they had to be able to do the job. University of California vs Bakke 1978 (supreme court case) said that quota COULD NOT be the only factor in decisions, but could be one factor.

Why

The problem is what if one candidate is better than the other, though the lesser can do the job. Actually, an employer should employ the lesser of the two qualified. Rationale: You can't really quantify what one person will do on a job til they are there. An early supreme court case, Griggs Vs. Duke Power 1971 (remember that court cases are italicized!!!) found that Duke Energy could not demand a HS diploma and an IQ test for employment because there was proof that employees with these did not do a better job than employees without them, and thus the tests were being used to keep african americans from being employed.

Over the last half century Affirmative Action has moved MANY more women into places of power, and has assured a middle class lifestyle for many African-American employees.

Who

does not agree with affirmative action -

/ whites passed over for a job

/ men passed over for a job by a female

/ people who work at a job where they see someone who barely works and claims discrimination if they are reprimanded

/ some african-americans think that it holds people of color back because they will never know if they got a job because of their merits, or to fulfill a law requirement.

Reverse discrimination is a fact, so is it right and what could be done to lessen its impact?

How

How do we make affirmative action irrelevant?

First, we are never going to end racism, or even the unconscious racism where an employer hires someone who looks and thinks like the other employees. Yes, it makes life 'easier,' but it discriminates. Think of a few types of jobs now worked by women: car salesmen, plumbers, factory workers. Yes, men now have to guard against off-color jokes, but is that a bad thing? Speech is important for shaping culture. Should women still be just 'breasts'? Men might have to lift bigger objects bcause women can't. So what, women - as a group - are more nimble with their fingers. I read that there have been tests with air force pilots, and women's reaction time and reflexes, as a gender, are much more finely tuned and quicker than men's.

Second, we need to make GREAT education something ALL Americans receive. This will improve all Americans, especially those in poverty.   Enough for now. Take a break.

From this session using the reporter's questions, Gerald did some of the analysis necessary to firmly convince himself that he had the thesis he was going to stay with, and from this and the predrafting below, also developed some of the content that eventually appears in the essay.

Predrafting Techniques: The Rhetorical Patterns

The traditional rhetorical modes are *narration* (what happened?), *description* (what does it look like and what senses does it invoke?), *exposition* (what is it? what is it similar to? how and why does it happen or work?; i.e., explanation, analysis), and *persuasion* (arguing a point against opposing arguments). Exposition has usually been subdivided further into these patterns: *example/illustration, comparison/contrast, classification/division, process/process analysis, causal analysis,* and *definition.* Other useful patterns that explain and analyze include: *question-answer, problem-solution, statement-support,* and two useful persuasive techniques, *induction* and *deduction* (explained in chapter eleven). These rhetorical patterns can be used to develop ideas and content about a subject, and also to organize an essay. To use these modes to develop ideas and content, brainstorm using each of them as the basis for your exploration.

For each essay you work on, brainstorm during predrafting to find how these patterns help you think about and develop content for your essay.

Narration/Description

Good writing uses specific details, and in terms of narration/description those specific details include precise narrations of what happened, what a situation or an object looks like, what it sounds like, what smells and tastes are there, and what do objects tactilely feel like? This example has description and specific narratives, with analysis of what Gerald got out of this remembrance from the past. Helped with his life more than the essay, as good critical thinking and writing will do.

> Just went to the football game, and was observing the pockets of African-Americans cheering on our team. The typical African-American ends and defensive backfield. The BIG African-Americans on the line. Always seems like white quarterbacks and running backs, well not always. Always only one token African-American coach. The players making the touchdowns are almost always white, and they were PROTECTED by those men of color. Really, that is just the plantation system of another era.
> In high school we had TWO people of color on the team (out of three male African-Americans in the entire school). Tells you something about expectations. These guys were the typical, stereotyped African-American sportsmen. Quiet in school. Didn't seem to worry about, or do much to get, grades. Everything was smooth. I remember Ernie being confronted by Mrs. Harris about his biology grade, and he just sat and listened. When she finished he just nodded. When she said, "aren't you going to respond?" I can hear him now, softly, "Nome." His look said he knew he was good enough to get a college scholarship somewhere, and he would do just well enough to get a degree, without learning much. AND would end up contributing to society. I always thought his

attitude was a great attitude to have, and now that I think about it, I am just now moving to emulate it.

Example/Illustration

What specific examples could you use to illustrate your subject? Can you think of an analogy (something is like something else: going to the forest is like going to church for me). Good writing is based on evidence. Make sure you are using specific evidence to prove your points.

> My English instructor demanded a final research unit on some aspect of gender or race. I went to him to complain. What he said smacked me into awareness. 'If racism and gender inequality still exist, and you are aware of it, if you aren't doing whatever you can to stop it, then you are a misogynist and a racist.' Wow. For a moment my defenses started going into battle, but then a calmness sunk in. He was right. I knew it.

When you read Gerald's essay in chapter four, you will see that he used this specific example in his final essay.

Comparison/Contrast

What and how is the subject similar to and different from other things? Can you compare and contrast two or more items relating to your subject? One often used form of comparison is the simile, a comparison of two unlike items using *like* or *as* to make a point: The housing projects are like a war zone.

Be sure to compare similar points; otherwise, you are not comparing. In this example, Gerald contrasts the comments he received on an essay with comments received by an African-American peer. To make sure his contrast was valid, he looked at sets of essays for both him and his peer from two professors. The principle of comparison, the similar points in this predrafting, is the types of comments elicited for their essays. We use this common tool — comparison — all the time in our daily lives.

> I was sitting with a few peers from my history class. The history class had an essay assigned, and we had just gotten ours back. On mine, the professor had made some astute comments on using evidence more effectively, and a couple comments on stylistic concerns like eliminating wordiness and using action verbs. I looked at Jeremiah's essay. It not only had a lower grade, but it was filled with red marks over grammatical and punctuation concerns, with not one single comment on the content of his essay except at the end 'Pretty good. Work on learning to edit.' Now this struck me because I am no editor. I am learning in the composition class, but I'm still pretty weak. I looked again at my essay and I noticed many, many editing errors that had not been

> marked. Wow. With my new opening eyes, I realized that this was a mark of unintentional racism. How can they be their best if they are never challenged? If they are just told repeatedly that they are not up to par? We share a class with Professor Robinson, who was the challenger of us to look at gender and race, so I asked to look at some of his papers from Professor Robinson. I couldn't believe it. Professor Robinson focused more on surface editing issues with Jeremiah and less on content than he did with his comments to me. And this is from a professor who obviously is trying hard to right problems faced by women and people of color!!!

Gerald continued this comparison, predrafting for another page because he found for this particular essay he was getting a lot of content he could use in his essay.

Classification/Division

Just as with comparison, we use classification and division all the time in our everyday life as we look at something and decide if it shares traits with a larger group of objects (classification) or if we can subdivide this thing or idea into smaller sub-groups that share some trait or traits. To use classification, a writer needs to decide on a category or a general concept that the subject is a part of, and also name other members of the category. For instance, vertebrae all have backbones (a category or general concept). Fish, birds, and mammals are all members of the category *vertebrae*.

For classification and division: what are the characteristics of each group and subgroup? Are some characteristics or groups more or less important than others and why? Picture the pie diagrams of the federal budget often seen in magazines and IRS publications, and draw a pie diagram of your subject. Do looping exercises for each of the parts.

In Gerald's example here, the principle he uses to classify groups are the belief they have about racism, and after two brainstorming sessions he defined the characteristics of each group and analyzed their reasons by evaluating their strengths and weaknesses.

> Classification - let's see - I do need to make sure I identify all the groups of ideas people have about racism:
>
> People who pretend that they do not see color - wow, that's a judgement, and that for them personally racism is a thing of the past. They, however, see racism in the world as a real thing.
> People of color actually have SEEN racism. They know it is a real thing. White parents do not have to give 'the talk' to their children 'be nice to cops' (or you could get shot). White teens do not get followed around shopping malls by rent-a-cops. Etc.
> People (like many in my hometown, my audience) who think racism is a thing of the past.
> People who think racism is real, but there is nothing they can do about it (like me a couple weeks ago).

People who think racism is real and there are things you can do about, the power of the voting booth, the power of aid to people of poverty, the power of actively speaking out about it, and calling unconscious racism when they see it.

People who are 'a little racist,' as in they don't try to be racist, but they just do not care what happens to minorities, and most actually wish minorities would just go away so America could be this vast great white continent.

KKK type racists and proud of it.

When you use classification/division to discover content, go further than just breaking a subject into groups: define, describe, analyze, compare/contrast, and/or evaluate each of the groups to help you understand and develop content with the complexity it deserves. Gerald later went back and analyzed each of these categories for completeness.

Process/Process Analysis

Many times you need to decide how or why something was done or how/why it works. Process: how is/was something done or how does/did something work? Process analysis: why does something work or why do each step in a process? (Why is it necessary?)

When predrafting, be complete to have a thorough knowledge of the subject. Make sure that you have listed

1) all the materials or preconditions for the process to occur

2) all the steps in the process

3) what the result is. Then,

4) analyze why each step occurs. Explore both how and why, doing research if necessary.

When you use process or process analysis in your essay, depending on your reason for using it you might not be as complete, but in predrafting make sure you understand the process completely by creating a through description and analysis of the process. In this section from Gerald's research notes, he uses a quotation from a source that illustrates what happens when blacks and whites commit a crime. He knew that this could serve as the most telling example of how the justice system is not just.

"Although less than 40 percent of Georgia homicide cases involve white victims, in 87 percent of the cases in which a death sentence is imposed, the victim is white. White-victim cases are almost eleven times more likely to produce a death sentence than are black-victim cases.

When the race of the defendant is considered too, the following figures emerge: 22 percent of black defendants who kill white victims are sentenced to death; 8 percent of white defendants who kill white-victims are sentenced to death; 1 percent of black defendants who kill black-victims are sentenced to death; 3 percent of white defendants who kill black-victims are sentenced to death" (Amsterdam 262).

45

Causal Analysis

The world works via cause and effect, so you already intuitively understand this pattern. Every action or idea has causes, and every action or idea has consequences, or effects. Studying the causal relationship between two actions or ideas helps us understand. When parents get divorced, there were multiple causes for this breakup, and not only are the effects felt by the parents, but by the children, by each of the parents' workmates, and by all their friends and acquaintances. There were multiple causes for Madonna's fame, and her fame had effects on other musicians and music, and on the audiences for all American music genres whether they liked and listened to Madonna or not. Many times, finding causes is identical to analyzing a process, so don't get too caught up in definitions here. If you have predrafted a process analysis that as a byproduct identifies causes, for this exercise focus on effects.

For causal analysis, be careful not to oversimplify or exaggerate the cause-and-effect relationship. Do not identify a single cause for a complex issue when there are in fact many causes; do not exaggerate the significance of simple coincidences. These are not true causal relationships. Touch a hot stove, and the effect is that you get burnt. Go near a hot stove when you are young, and the effects are you like the warmth, you become curious, your parents get worried, and they discipline you. (A complex chain of effects: if we went a step further, you might have liked the effect that your parents became worried over your behavior, and you either returned to the hot stove or looked for other avenues to gain their concern. One effect of this could be that you began to like being punished, and so on.)

When exploring causal relationships, *patterns include moving from a general cause or causes to specific effects, moving from a specific effect or effects to general causes, or demonstrating that two events or ideas have a cause and effect relationship.* For instance, poverty (or poverty coupled with lack of education) can cause hopelessness (or a combination: hopelessness, homelessness, and criminal behavior). Moving in the other direction, one could argue that criminal behavior is caused by poverty, lack of education, and substance abuse/alcoholism. Or, one could show the causal relationship between poverty and criminal behavior.

Make lists of causes, of effects, and ask for help from others in classroom or study group settings to fully analyze the web of causes and effects surrounding a subject.

Notice how Gerald is not only creating a thorough analysis of African-Americans and crime/the 'justice' system, but he is also studying how causal analysis works by labeling all of the effects of the numbered causes that he lists.

What causes African-American men to be commited to prison for longer periods?
Of course, 1) poverty, EFFECT: so they get public defenders.
Public defenders mostly try, EFFECT: but they have way too many cases to be effective.
2) An article said that black men are just angry because of mistreatment and so EFFECT: they are viewed by law enforcement AND the judicial system as dangerous.
3) Gang activity EFFECT: laws give African-Americans longer

sentences. Study says gang activity is caused by the need to feel safe in the un-safe world of the city streets, so why shouldn't young black men band together?

4) Related: causes of gang activity - gives men power, or feeling of power anyway.

5) Power and safety related: guns EFFECT: longer prison terms.

As long as being cool means being tough, a gangsta, men are still going to be involved in gangs. I know guys who act like thugs, like 'gangstas,' but yes they are posing; on the other hand, when they get busted doing petty crime stuff they do not get the sentences that young black men get, even if they did the same stupid crimes.

Definition

Do words or concepts need to be defined in a special way? Just as with comparison, classification, and analysis, definition is one of the prime activities of the human mind. You have already been doing this since you first identified the sounds and look of your parents and labeled them, "Mommie" or "Daddy" (or two "Mommies" or "Daddies").

There are multiple possible uses for definition as you predraft for an essay and as you write an essay. You might give an extended, thorough definition of a word

/ when you use it for a specialized purpose

/ when a specific group defines it in a special way

/ when defining it for an audience that doesn't know the word

/ when stipulating which of several definitions of a word is intended

You might give a lengthy definition of a familiar word (such as *heroes, fatherhood, liberty*)

/ when you want to explain what the word means to you personally

/ when defining to help an audience understand a concept

/ when you want to achieve a humorous or ironic tone using a familiar word or concept comically

You might want to define a new or slang word

/ when technology or society has created a new word

/ when one of the social groupings you are in uses a slang word (especially if two groups or generations use it differently)

/ when you create a new slang word (be careful–it must make sense in the context)

In order to define, use any of the rhetorical patterns we have discussed so far, narration, description, illustration, comparison/contrast, classification/division, and process or causal analysis.

Here is just one page of Gerald's predrafting using definition:

Define unconscious racism, that invisible knapsack of white privilege that whites didn't do anything to get, that for the most part is not in and of itself racist, it just IS. It is all the things in daily life that makes it esier for whites to succeed in America

that people of color just do not have. Things like when I get a job, I know that I got it because of my merit. In the back of every woman's and minority's mind is the question 'am I the most qualified or did the employer just fill a quota?' In other words, they are made to question their self-worth. With women, it can even be 'did I get it because the employer thinks I'm cute?'
Whites can buy a house almost anywhere and they can assume their color will mostly be represented. This is also true of the schools white kids go to, the job possibilities in the world. Nothing we whites can do about these numerical truths, but we can recognize that they exist and acknowledge our privilege.
I'm depressed for now. Come back to this later. It's important.

Organization and Outlines

Readers crave a sense of order as they read. Logical patterns of thought (or experience in the case of narration and description) help them make sense of the content. All good writers, at some point in the writing process, attend to organization and arrange and rearrange their writing until the content flows smoothly from one point to the next. At times, a piece of writing will suggest an organizational scheme (explaining how to enroll at your college would use process analysis; telling your best friend about your new friend at school would use narrative, description, and perhaps comparison). Even if the demands of a particular writing situation call for a particular rhetorical strategy, you will still need to decide specifically what content to use and the exact order of ideas and examples within the parameters of the overall organizational pattern or patterns. Some writers outline elaborately before they begin a draft; others usually discover organization as they draft or revise. Anytime you make a list of possibilities for content and then think to yourself "I will discuss this first, this second," and so on, you are in fact making a rough outline.

In addition to discussing how to organize the rhetorical patterns discussed in the previous section, this section describes four kinds of outlines (scratch, forecasting, traditional, and descriptive).

Organization for Rhetorical Patterns

After choosing a thesis and content to support it, use the patterns to arrange the content. Some writing situations use only one of the patterns; for instance, you might write an essay that is centered around one of the modes, such as a process analysis essay or an essay that narrates an experience. Most writing, however, uses a variety of the rhetorical modes (as you will see in a student essay used in this section of the chapter); one section or a single paragraph of the essay might center around description, while the next section centers on causal analysis. Even an essay that uses one overall pattern, for instance, a comparison essay, would probably also use description and example to illustrate the comparison. Whatever patterns you use, the content should support the thesis, the purpose for the essay.

Most of the rhetorical patterns have basic organizational structures that can be used with success. This section contains exposition on how to organize each of the rhetorical patterns, and also contains an example paragraph or short essay using the

48

pattern. *When you pick one of these strategies to use as the overall plan for your essay or for a section of an essay, review the suggestions that follow to help organize your draft.*

Narration/Description

For narration, two usual patterns are **chronological narration** (a straightforward ordering of events) and **flashback narration** (where you show how an event in the present of your narrative triggers a memory from further in the past).

For chronological narration, you might narrate one event in detail or you might narrate a series of events. In either case, *when choosing details to narrate, keep your purpose/thesis and audience in mind.* Pick only content that is necessary for the purpose or that the audience needs to know to understand your narration. Too many writers try to tell the whole story, when only some of the details are necessary for the reader to understand the writer's purpose; in fact, non-essential details confuse a reader. This is especially true if you are picking several events over a span of days, months, or years to illustrate a point.

Usually, description and narration are combined, so the reader can visualize a scene. If you are describing the visual, again pick only the essential details. As for order within the sentences, pretend you are a camera: move from foreground to background, background to foreground, right to left, or left to right, always "zooming in" on only the details necessary for your purpose. Use smells, sounds, tastes, and what something feels like, but only if they are relevant for your purpose. *What is your purpose for using description? Decide on the **dominant impression** you want your reader to get from your description, and choose only concrete, specific details that add to this impression.*

The example following uses **chronological narration**, Examine the way this selection uses a descriptive "camera's eye," as well as other sense impressions and the emotions of the student writer, Lory Decker, to capture this scene of life and death.

> Working in a nursing home taught me many life lessons, and some of the most important ones were about life and death. The long hallway walls were a bright white accented by a dull, yellowish floor the cleaning crew just could not keep clean: too many scuff marks from all the walkers and wheelchairs. The urine odor never completely left the air. Half the doors were closed and the other half opened to a patient either sitting in a wheelchair in front of the television or a patient lying in bed. (Sometimes moaning incoherently, or more painfully, coherently, "help me. Please, help me.") The staff learned to tune those out as they never wanted anything, except the few who never did call out. When they yelled "help," we knew they needed something. I got to where I could work through a code where the patient expired, someone I might have known for a year, take them down to the cold storage where the funeral home picked them up, and then go on to eat my dinner as if I hadn't just spent the last hour in the presence of death. Sometimes I was the one doing CPR, and sometimes they lived, though there were times when I heard every rib crack with the chest compressions.
>
> One old, old German lady had come to us from the independent living section. Beautiul, ninety-seven year old great-great-grandmother. But she

couldn't get around anymore. She couldn't go out to the beach anymore. Couln't read the bingo cards anymore. Couldn't even eat candy anymore with her diabetes. But she took her situation stoically. Still told clean jokes and had an appetite. Loved her family's visits. One morning we found her unresponsive and coded her, and she came back. Her comment when she opened her eyes, in that lilting German brogue: "Why? I was in such a beautiful place. Then you brought me back with your bag of tricks!!!" Such is life. It wasn't her time.

Notice the wise choice here of mostly description with very little narration. The writer carefully chose details: a detailed description of only the hallway, as if everyone is on a journey. We get enough of the colors, the sounds, the smells. In a few words, we seem to know the German lady intimately. From the choice of details, we know something about the darkly comedic philosophy of the writer. All these work together to give the desired overall *dominant impression* of stoicism combined with despair that everyone will some day die that is the purpose of the essay.

The next example illustrates *flashback narration*:

Camille had just bought her first house with her husband, Gerald, and their infant daughter, Jade, and it was December. As Camille and Gerald removed the boxes of ornaments from the new-smelling garage and carried them into the living room, Camille looked over at Jade standing at attention, eyeing them from the playpen. Suddenly, Camille was awash in the memories of her childhood. She remembered most coming home from church Christmas Eve, warm in the glow from the Christmas carols. Her and her mother would set out cookies they had baked and milk for Santa, and then she and her mother and father would all lie on Camille's bed and her father would read Christmas stories. He was always working, but he was there for Christmas. Camille thought that she had to get the recipes and ingredients for Christmas cookies, and she was glad that her husband was not the workaholic her father had been. She leaned over the playpen and gave Jade a kiss.

Example/Illustration

Use specific examples and illustrations to make a point. Sometimes a *single detailed example* works better for your purpose; other times, a series of *closely related examples* provides better evidence. If you have a series of examples and illustrations, think of your audience and the relative strength of your examples to organize them logically. Reasonable patterns include:

- *Least important to most important* point (if there are several).

- *Most important to least important* (if there is one particularly strong example and several lesser ones or lesser ones that support the main point).

Or if all the points in the example are equally important:

- *Least familiar to most familiar* point or *most familiar to least familiar* (in terms of what your audience knows).

50

For each of these patterns, use trial and error: if one doesn't work, revise and use another.

A *single detailed example* (also moving from most familiar to least familiar):

> When many of America's major cities were laid out in the nineteenth century, landscape architects made sure that even in the densest population areas there was greenery. Of course there are the great parks like New York's Central Park, but what I like are the little neighborhood parks strewn throughout cities like the one I grew up near. The park in Lyndon was home for some of my fondest memories. It had a playground that I spent hours at as a young boy. There were two softball fields, and leagues played there on Saturdays with practice on Wednesdays. The rest of the week we could play pick up games there every evening as the sun went down and the fireflies came out, and of course there were basketball courts. There was several wooded acres, where I pretended to be Daniel Boone when younger, and then when I got older my first youthful dalliances with the fairer sex occurred under the shade of these trees. These are the memories of youth.

A paragraph with a series of *closely related examples* (also moving from most familiar to least familiar):

> When many of America's major cities were laid out in the nineteenth century, landscape architects made sure that even in the densest population areas there was greenery. New York's Central Park is almost two miles long and a half mile wide, and it includes two large lakes, wooded areas, footpaths, athletic fields, and stages for concerts and performances. Several blocks from the densest urban office spaces in America, it is surrounded by brownstone condos that allow these city residents to experience the trees and fields of the country without leaving the city. In New York alone, there are several other parks not as famous but almost as big: the Bronx Park (including the Bronx Zoo), Van Cortlandt Park, and the Brooklyn Museum and Botanical Gardens in Prospect Park. Washington D.C., of course, has the Mall, visited by millions of visitors each year and containing not only the famous monuments, the Capitol, and the Smithsonian museums, but it also serves as home to numerous festivals a year. On days with nothing planned, you still see college students and occasionally government officials playing softball, football, or soccer on its fields. Chicago, Boston, Philadelphia — every major city — has parks both large and small to accommodate the human need for fresh woods and sloping fields.

Classification/Division

As with narration, description, illustration, and comparison, classification/ division is a tool we have used all our lives. It is one of the first things a baby's brain starts to do: does this thing I am looking at fall into a larger category? Yes, mother and sister are female and father and brother are males. Trixie the dog and Felix the cat are both different categories, and they aren't male and female humans. Can I divide a thing into parts? Yes, the entire building I live in is a house, and it is divided into rooms. We usually use classification to either define or explain something, and definition and explanation are two of the primary reasons for writing.

Classification and division must have these organizing features:

- **Consistency**: Use the same principle to define each category. For instance, if you created a list to classify types of drinkers using the principle of amount – heavy drinkers, moderate drinkers, beer drinkers, light drinkers, non-drinkers – you would delete *beer drinkers,* a category that does not state amount.

- **Completeness**: Make sure that no major categories or parts have been left out – an audience recognizes such omissions. This lack of completeness destroys the credibility of your writing. If you were going to divide the category types of schools, you might start with the categories preschools, elementary schools, middle schools, high schools, and colleges. But as you analyzed and described these categories in your predrafting, and you decided that your principle was types of degrees, you would probably add junior colleges (associate degrees), technical schools (technical degrees), and graduate schools (to differentiate between bachelors and graduate degrees in college).

- **Order**: Arrange the categories in the order that most effectively illustrates your purpose: *least important to most important* or *least familiar to most familiar* are often used. The principle: there *must* be organization.

Sara Curl wrote an essay analyzing why women are becoming victims of anxiety, and in the middle third of the essay (included here), she uses classification to analyze the types of negative messages and how they are judged. She is consistent and complete, looking at women in the work/education sector, as persons in groups, and in the family, and for each one she analyzes how situations create anxiety. For further consistency, each of the paragraphs end with a personal experience/ observation following the analysis of the situations. (Readers LOVE organizational consistency.)

> Adults tell young women if they work hard they can be anything they desire. Many have taken this to heart; consequently, they now put all this pressure on themselves to be the best in everything. College proves to be exceptionally difficult for many young women. Not only worrying about grades, homework, and tests, they also deal with personal issues from work, love, and home. Because some women take on too much, they end up not finishing school. Instead of spacing classes out to have more time for them, they take on five or six classes at once. My freshmen year did quite a number on me, and it took me a year out of college to get my anxiety back under control. Since I was taking five classes, I was constantly working on school work and had no time for any leisure activities. I didn't have any friends or even the drive to make any. I became depressed and started having these weird spells come over me. I didn't know what was going on until I had a small break down. I ended up going to

the emergency room, where they told me what was wrong and suggested I needed to talk to a counselor.

Another aspect to consider, adding layer upon layer of stress, is the pressure, conscious or unconscious, to maintain a standard of beauty. This standard is flaunted in front of us all the time with models on T.V, books, and even on our phones. Women even judge other women on their appearances. They'll either downgrade someone to feel prettier, or they'll put themselves down and feel undesirable. Our culture has built up the image of beauty to such a high pedestal that women are having a hard time fitting into social groups, because they don't fit up there with a few who got lucky with genetics. Being socially isolated because of their appearance is not only humiliating, but also hard on a young women's self-esteem. Scars, acne, and cellulite are all considered flaws. I deal with all three. My self-esteem is rather low since all I can see, when I look in the mirror, is all the flaws and not the whole picture. I actually feel emotional pain because I don't fit into the category we have all set. Real beauty is on the inside even if no one but you can see it. We all need to remember that, whether it's for ourselves or for when we look at others.

In addition, the burden of being a good housewife has increased because women are breaking out of old traditions. First, society pressures women into feeling they have to have excellent careers (while being the traditional mother/ housewife). The truth is women are doing it to themselves. Working AND raising kids makes it hard to keep up with cooking and the cleaning. Having other people see their house is a fear some women have because not only are they afraid of other women seeing that they can't keep up with it all, but they are also afraid of being judged for it. Not only is it affecting working moms, but it's a problem for stay-at-home moms too. Working individuals have become condescending toward the stay-at-home moms because they don't respect the decision to not become successful in a workplace setting. They don't understand that keeping a clean house, laundry, and kids is also a full-time job. Stay-at-home moms deal with anxiety just like other women do, if not more. When anxiety is not handled successfully, some women may become overwhelmed which can lead to problems with their husbands, or if they work it can start to show in their performance and escalate from there. Humans are social creatures, but when you stay at home with your kids the majority of the time it's hard to find the time to socialize. My cousin is a stay-at-home mom who has three beautiful children. Her husband works on electric towers all over the state, while she's taking care of their kids at home. Her kids are her world. She doesn't get the chance to get out much or take any time for herself. This isolation causes her to become lonely, but she tries to make the best of it. At night, after she gets her kids put to sleep and all taken care of, she has anxiety attacks. They aren't the little ones that you can brush off, keep going, and be fine. She sometimes has to have a close friend come over to watch her kids, just in case they wake up, while someone takes her to the emergency room.

Process/Process Analysis

To demonstrate how something is done or how something works, use chronological order. *Important content, in this order, includes 1) all the materials, equipment, and preparation, 2) a step-by-step description of the process, and 3) either what the completed project should do or look like, or what the results of the process are.* Explain all steps and be sure to define all terms that might confuse the reader. Analyze your audience carefully: how much they already know about the process and the particular needs of this audience help you decide how much content and explanation is needed. (A mechanic would not need the level of detail that an auto repair student would in a description of rebuilding a specific carburetor.) Also, decide whether the audience just needs to know how (process), or if they need to know why (process analysis). Use your purpose, audience, and writing situation to decide if you need to analyze the process in addition to describing it.

Process analysis asks why something works and/or why to do each step in a process. Unless your audience is an expert in how to do the process, you will also have to explain how to do something/how it works. In other words, you are going to include process in the process analysis.

Patterns include:

- Discuss how the first step works, then if needed discuss why the step works. Then discuss how, then why if needed for the next step. Go through all the steps using this organization. OR

- Discuss all the details describing how in the first section followed by a discussion of all the details describing why in the second section.

The following example comes from a written final examination in a composition class asking for process analysis. In the first draft, Jim Koroski described how to predraft for a successful writing project; in revision *(the italicized portions)*, he described why each step is done.

The first goal in your agenda for completing an essay is 1) picking a subject. After you have picked a subject, you need 2) to learn everything about the subject you'll need to write intelligently about it and 3) to focus the subject. *If you haven't studied your subject, your audience will recognize that you really don't know what you are talking about, so study your subject. The faster you focus your subject, the less work you will have to do. For example, if your subject is television, it would take less time to study and write about the subject if you first focused to television sitcoms of the nineties, and then perhaps to one specific sitcom. Is it easier to research television, or just one show?*

After you have focused a subject and you are learning about it, you need to do three activities; however, each writing assignment is unique and you will find yourself completing these projects in a different order with each essay. In other words, as you analyze your subject and prepare to write your paper, complete these activities concurrently: 4) analyze your audience, 5) develop a thesis statement, a purpose for the writing, and 6) develop content for the essay. *All good writing addresses a specific audience, and has a specific statement that the writer is making to the audience about the subject. As Professor Hanson says, "until you have a specific audience and purpose, until you know what you are going to say to whom about your subject, you are just stringing words together into sentences about a subject, you aren't communicating. All good writing addresses audience and purpose."* Sometimes you are able to decide on audience first; other times you decide on your thesis first. On the other hand, no matter how much content you have developed for an essay, you need to re-evaluate the content after you have decided on audience and purpose. *A writer decides on content based on who the audience is and what the writer wants to say.* So, while you might be deciding on and analyzing audience, purpose and content together, you need to rethink content after you have finalized audience and purpose.

Whether you finish these activities before you even start a draft or not until after you have written six drafts, they must be done to have a well-written essay.

Question-Answer

At the simplest level, ask a question, answer it, and support your answer with evidence. However, in many situations, there will be more than one answer to a question, so don't oversimplify. In the instance of multiple possible answers, you might have to argue with evidence that one answer is better than others.

The **question and answer** organizational pattern is exemplified in this excerpt from a student essay. It is, at the same time, a causal analysis response as well as an exercise in definition.

What happens when a lesbian comes out while still in high school? First, from parents and most adults, the reaction is "you are too young to know what you are," or "this is just a phase you will grow out of." No amount of explaining using documented research will convince them otherwise. This is of course the best possibility: Some teen gays are shunned altogether by parents and relatives. From some kids the reaction is just rude: guys saying "can I watch?" or girls doing their "what EVER." In my rural high school, I was mostly just ostracized from everyone and spent the rest of my high school years pretty much alone, though happier than if I had lived a lie. I read a lot of literature on the movement, and watched what was going on on-line. I also participated in blogs that helped me create my already strong personality. But, the good news I am learning in college is that the experience is usually much more accepting in urban high schools - that it is as accepted as multi-racial dating. Perhaps in another generation, all indications seem to point at acceptance for a large minority segment of the population.

Problem-Solution

Problem/solution essays usually have two parts: convincing the reader with evidence that there is, in fact, a problem; and convincing the reader with evidence that you have a workable solution to the problem. In some instances, you will discuss several solutions, and demonstrate, with evidence, which solution makes the most sense. Of course, if the problem is widely acknowledged, you would only focus on the solution(s). Furthermore, some subjects are so complex and controversial that it would take many pages just to convince readers that there is a problem (for instance, global warming), so some essays in this pattern only focus on proving that a problem exists.

55

The *problem/solution* organizational pattern is employed in the following paragraph discussing recovery from alcoholism.

> I am a recovering alcoholic with several years of recovery, and would like to discuss the disease of alcoholism from the perspective of not only my views, but also the views of most long-recovering alcoholics. Alcoholics present problems not only for themselves, but everyone they come in contact with, and most directly, their loved ones. First off, the use of alcohol is only a symptom of a psychological and emotional disease, and once we stop ingesting alcohol, we have only curbed the physical manifestations of the symptoms (the need to drink alcohol). To recover and live happily, we have to deal with the psychological/emotional symptoms. Most alcoholics define the alcoholic not as "someone who uses alcohol addictively," but as someone who suffers from a disease of perception: over and over again we describe ourselves as people who feel like "we don't fit in" and that "people don't like us." To combat these basic identity fears, we gravitate to one or both of two poles: we are either ego-maniacs or have inferiority complexes. These last two sentences define the disease as we understand it, and describe why we drink — we self-medicate ourselves with alcohol. After "putting the plug in the jug," dealing with these problems on a consistent basis is what alcoholics call recovery.
>
> To find a solution to this seemingly insurmountable emotional, psychological problem, alcoholics in recovery band together to help each other recover, and what they help each other do is the twelve steps of Alcoholics Anonymous. In brief, the solution is to stop drinking, to ask a power greater than ourselves to help us stay stopped, to do an inventory of the wreckage we've made of our lives, to ask that higher power to relieve us of the character flaws we found in the inventory, to make amends to those we've harmed, and to continue this program on a daily basis while helping others. A life-long project, but well worth it. What is the alternative?

Statement-Support

On the simplest level, all paragraphs make a statement and then support the statement with evidence, but not all paragraphs fall into one of the rhetorical patterns demonstrated in this section, so the following is an example of a complete paragraph that uses several of the patterns, including narrative, example, comparison, and problem/solution. Useful patterns for the support include least important to most important support, most important to least important, least familiar to most familiar, and most familiar to least familiar. Examine the paragraph that follows, as well as the penultimate paragraph to Rob's essay on utopias (pp. 59-62).

> I have found that if I want to lead a lifestyle I enjoy, I can only take three classes a semester, and that is pushing it. My first semester I took five classes and worked forty to forty-five hours a week to support my partying, my car, and my shopping. I had to drop two classes, and I got two Cs and a B in the other classes. The next semester I talked the boss into reducing my hours to thirty, and took five classes again. I still partied just as much, though I didn't

go shopping as much. It was Springtime so I went to Florida for Spring Break, and I felt real constrained in my partying because of my budget down there. I still had to drop two classes, and got three Cs for my other classes. I was just so sick of school that I didn't take any classes over the summer, and I picked up a steady boyfriend. When Fall came, I almost didn't go to school, but my parents and boyfriend encouraged me. This semester I only took three classes, I kept up my hours working, shopping, and going out with my boyfriend, but I got a planner and made sure I spent enough time to get my work done. It has been extremely hard to devote the hours to studying that I need to, but I am making it. The counselors in college were right: I need to study about two hours for every hour in class, so three classes is about a twenty-seven hour work week in addition to my forty hours at the job and the hours I spend for my recreation. I am one busy woman.

Most essays written, however, do not use just one rhetorical pattern, like some of the examples above. Instead, writers use a combination of rhetorical strategies in a single essay to create the content and organization needed to support a thesis. The essay following, by Rob Watson, uses all these organizational patterns: comparison, contrast, causal analysis, definition (within that definition it uses description, comparison, and causal analysis), and statement/support. So first there will be descriptions and definitions of these rhetorical modes, as well as comments on their organizational structure, followed by Rob's essay with a discussion of how he melds these patterns together in a wonderful essay on utopian societies.

Comparison/Contrast

The most important concept to remember for valid comparison: discuss the same points for all items that are compared. When comparing two cars, if you discuss engine efficiency, interior space, and options for one of the cars, you should do the same for the other. The only exception to this suggestion occurs when your audience is very familiar with one of the items compared. If you contrast American and British secondary schools for an American audience, you need only describe the significant differences in the British system. Readers can make the contrast themselves.

In terms of organization, *most comparisons move from least important to most important points*, and there are two organizational patterns for comparison that work well: the *divided pattern* and the *alternating pattern*. The *divided pattern* discusses everything about point A, and then discusses everything about point B. The *alternating pattern* discusses the items to be compared point-by-point (AB AB AB etc.) The divided pattern should usually be used for shorter comparisons, whereas the alternating pattern can be used for shorter, as well as longer, comparisons.

Notice that these outlines use the same points for both of the items being compared:

- **The Divided Pattern**

I.   Small Colleges
    A.   Choice of classes
    B.   Extracurricular activities that lead to job placement
    C.   Quality of educational experience
    D.   Student's ability to find a job after graduation
II.   Large Universities
    A.   Choice of classes
    B.   Extracurricular activities that lead to job placement
    C.   Quality of educational experience
    D.   Student's ability to find a job after graduation

- **The Alternating Pattern**

I.   Choice of Classes
    A.   Small colleges
    B.   Large universities
II.   Extracurricular activities that lead to job placement
    A.   Small colleges
    B.   Large universities
III. Quality educational experience
    A.   Small colleges
    B.   Large universities
IV. Student's ability to find a job after graduation
    A.   Small colleges
    B.   Large universities

Causal Analysis

Causal relationships can be very complex, so don't oversimplify. On the other hand, don't worry about their complexity for you have been studying causal relationships since you were born. Many causal essays, while they point out there are multiple causes and effects, focus on one. The writer has decided, through analysis, that one cause or one effect is more important than the others, so he mentions the others but focuses on what he has decided is the primary cause (or effect). Others discuss a pattern of causes or a pattern of effects.

Causal organizational patterns include:

- Picking an event or situation and showing the effects it creates (usually from least to most important, but sometimes most to least).

- Picking a result of an event or situation and analyzing its causes (usually from least to most important, but sometimes most to least).

- Tracing a cause and effect chain: A happens and causes B, C, D; B causes E and F, and so on.

58

Definition

Paragraphs that define use narration, description, example, process, comparison, classification, and analysis to create their content, and they serve several purposes: some definition paragraphs give an extended, in-depth definition of a word, some define how the writer or a specific group of people use a word, some define a new word or a new way of using a word, and some give a special way of using a word. Some definition essays give extended definitions of commonly used words like *love*, *friendship*. Examine how Rob defines utopias in his essay that follows.

Context Card for Rob Watson's essay:
Subject: Utopias
Audience: College Students
Writing Situation: a textual analysis in a blog that discusses the future
Thesis: Utopian society may be the ultimate goal to which civilization aspires to ascend, but in evaluating the media that entertains this grand idea, it is an impossible goal.
Tone: objective, studious, fairly formal for a blog

This rough draft would be six pages double spaced plus the works cited page if printed on 8 1/2 X 11 computer paper.

Rob Watson
English 102
Dr. Rita Recktenwald
Rough Draft

The Utopian Facade

George Jetson lives a life to be desired. Each day, he wakes up to a machine that brushes his teeth, washes, shaves, and dresses him, and to a robot that makes him breakfast. His job at Spacely Sprockets consists of nothing more than pushing one button an hour, three days a week. High in his spacious home resembling Seattle, Washington's Space Needle, George and his family live a very comfortable life, with little or no work, stress, or problems. It seems that life could not get that much better for George, and the year is 2062.

In 2012, flying cars will be available for purchase ("Aircraft"), a resort hotel located in low Earth orbit is scheduled to open (Galactic Suite), and a modest $200,000 will take passengers to it (Virgin Galactic). With the rapid advancement in technology, the acceptance of racial equality, and a deeper understanding in the medical field, the future feels closer than ever imagined. Eric Schmidt. CEO of Google, says "we create as much information in two days now as we did from the dawn of man through 2003" (Galactic Suite). Indeed these are amazing feats, but current society needs to leap forward to reach the status of the Jetson family utopia.

The idea of a utopia, or the ultimate society enriched with equality and supple wealth, has been discussed as early as 380 BC. Illustrated by Plato in his celebrated dialogue, *The Republic*, he describes an imaginary city, Magnesia,

Comparison: divided pattern. Rob expects his readers to make an implicit contrast between the Jetsons and their lives, and a comparison between the cartoon described in the 1st paragraph and the futuristic plans already here described in the 2nd paragraph.

3rd para: Comparison implicit. Rob expects reader to compare Plato's ideal society to our own, and to notice the parallels with communism.

59

where population is controlled to prevent crowding and underworking. In Magnesia, citizens own slaves to perform the trading and manufacturing of the city, along with other humble tasks throughout the city. Lawmakers not only enforce laws, but persuade the lawbreaker what he/she did was illegal and convince citizens of the "correct" beliefs and true principles that they should be following. The location of Magnesia is geographically perfect for fruitful agriculture and productive commerce. Enabling the use of each of these ideas, Magnesia would be a city where no poverty exists and individual labor duties are minimal, allowing all citizens (slaves are not citizens) the opportunity to grow socially and educationally (Bobonich).

Comparison: alter-
nating pattern - of 3
movies. Notice Rob
discusses the same
concept for each
of the 3 movies he
compares (which
is the only true
comparison).

Children's cartoons are not the only medium today that portrays society as a futuristic paradise. Many adult novels and films feature a similar theme, though it may not appear so without paying close attention. M. Night Shyamalan's *The Village*, released in 2004, featured a small village separate from other civilizations, where crime, famine, and poverty were all but eliminated. A teen novel written in 1993, Lois Lowry's *The Giver*, tells a story about a future where there is no war, disease, famine, poverty, or pain. Fritz Lang's classic 1927 *Metropolis* illustrates (quite literally, as it was a silent film) a city divided into two classes, one of which lives luxuriously with no menial tasks to be performed (or disease, poverty, crime, etc), while the other works to support the extravagant lifestyles of the first class. As classic movies and books win awards and fame, more are produced with different plots, characters, and time frames, but the basic utopian fantasy remains the same.

Rob switches to
causal analysis in
this paragraph.

When analyzing a movie or book about utopian society, it is impossible for observers to ignore that each civilization has a specific fault to it, thus transforming a utopian society into a truly dystopian society. In *The Village*, the entire town's ignorance of the outside world (and the current year) is the price tag of a life without chaos, famine, or crime. Perhaps it is very obvious, such as in *Metropolis*, where the enforced labor is the fuel for the upper city's wealth. Recognizable or not, almost every utopian story brings light to a very undesirable price for which the utopia's grandeur exists. The cliché "nothing in life is free" is the lesson learned and is impressed upon present day society's greatest fear for the near future: to enjoy a life full of ecstasy and freedom, a great and terrible payment will be necessary.

Another causal
analysis paragraph
on a different
subject.

Using semiotics, each utopian/dystopian piece can be analyzed to identify different expenses society fears to pay. One of these can be recognized as the fear to regress to a familiar practice of America's recent past: the fear of becoming slaves of the powerful or wealthy in order to fashion a Utopia. In America, Europeans permeated the land and decreased their own personal workload by using both the indigenous people and Africans as slaves doing grueling labor. America was not, of course, the first country to use slavery to promote industry; ancient Egypt, Greece, and Rome all actively used slaves for agriculture, household chores, as soldiers, and even as sacrifices to appease gods.

Slavery defined
with examples,
description, and
comparison.

Although the thirteenth amendment abolished slavery in 1865, the fear of being owned or doing work for someone else's luxurious lifestyle still remains. This was the exact fear represented in *Metropolis*. If this 1920s silent appears dated, this same fear was displayed in the 2005 *The Island*, where humans live

60

in a safely regulated future only to discover they are clones secretly used for organ harvesting by the rich. More recently, *Daybreakers* (2009) features Sam Neill and Ethan Hawke in a utopian world inhabited by vampires. In this story, vampirism is a trait to be desired, as sleep is no longer necessary and disease is eliminated. However, when it seems as if the world is now perfect, viewers discover that the last surviving humans are harvested as a food supply, and the population dwindles.

Throughout utopian novels and movies, scientific advancement plays a major role in the plot. These advances invite another underlying terror in the exultant future: that humanity's scientific constructions to create utopia will ultimately destroy their creators. In Isaac Asimov's adaptation, *I, Robot* (2004), the world is a less overworked place thanks to the employment of the robot workforce. Daily lives depend on the assistance robots provide, and because they cannot violate their programming, humans are free from the fear of robots gaining power from them. However, a "technophobic" cop discovers that the robots have found a way to overcome their creator's software design and they plot to overthrow the human race. The original story for *I, Robot* was written in 1950, and in 2009 the movie grossed $144,795,350 ("*I, Robot*" imdb). For a movie based on a sixty year old theme to do as well as it did in the present suggests that people still connect with technophobia today. In *I Am Legend* (2007), Will Smith (again) plays a scientist who discovers a cure for cancer, only to find that it instead created an unstoppable plague which destroys most of humanity. While this future doesn't employ self-aware machines to improve the quality of life, the cure comes from genetic research that scientists today are attempting to gain more control of in the near future. Both movies feature the same theme representing a fear Ted Peters discusses in *Playing God? Genetic Determinism and Human Freedom*, that all scientific achievements of the future are too good to be true and the human race should not "play God."

Definition of utopian movies using description. causal analysis, and comparison-contrast of 2 movies.

If utopia isn't created by slave labor nor giant leaps in scientific achievements, than it must be maintained by an omniscient body with absolute control over population, lifestyles, industry, and knowledge. However, the term "control" doesn't normally correspond with society's current liberties such as freedom and choice. To successfully apply this strict nature of administration without igniting revolt, ignorance would have to be the primary tool used. This is featured in *Logan's Run*, where unlimited food, drugs, and sex are at any citizen's disposal, but everyone is taught that at the age of thirty they must perform a specific ritual in order to be reborn. This ritual was a ploy by the city's designers to end life at thirty in order to maintain a manageable population density. This occurs also in *The Giver*, where all careers and family units are prearranged by a council, and the ability to see color is also genetically taken away to eliminate racial distinctions. Chaos, famine, and disease are virtually eliminated in these two stories, but at the cost of having practically no choice in a lifetime for anyone. Perhaps the most celebrated and recognizable dystopian story known today is George Orwell's *1984*. Written in 1949, the term "Big Brother" from this novel is frequently used today in discussions of cell phone and internet privacy. Its plot conveys a "future" of 1984 where the government uses surveillance and mass media manipulation in order to maintain a totalitarian system of government.

Statement/support paragraph with multiple examples for support.

Utopian society may be the ultimate goal to which civilization aspires to ascend, but in evaluating the media that entertains this grand idea, it is an impossible goal. Other than in children's cartoons, Utopias are a facade, a dream out of reach, protected by society's fears and morals. Reflecting back to Plato's *Republic*, his ideal city uses all three mentioned practices: slavery, totalitarianism, and scientific advancement, thus becoming not a utopia but a dystopia, one that would be immediately rejected by today's culture. Whether humanity will enjoy a Jetson's-like lifestyle by 2062 remains to be seen. The more interesting question is what it will cost society in their pursuit of perfection.

MLA Style Documentation   Works Cited

"Aircraft." *Terrafugia*, 2008, www. terrafugia.com/faqs, accessed 11 Oct. 2011.

Asimov, Isaac. *I, Robot*. Doubleday, 1950.

Bobonich, Chris. "Plato on Utopia." *The Stanford Encyclopedia of Philosophy*, edited by Edward N. Zalta, Stanford UP, 2008, pp. 1429-36.

Daybreakers. Directed and written by Michael and Peter Spierig, performances by William Dafoe and Ethan Hawke, Lionsgate, 2009, DVD.

Galactic Suite. 2011, galacticsuite.com.

I Am Legend. Directed by Francis Lawrence, performance by Will Smith. Warner, 2007, DVD.

"I, Robot." *Internet Movie Database*, www.imbd.com/IRobot.

I, Robot. Directed by Alex Proyas, performances by Will Smith and Bridget Moynahan, Fox, 2004, DVD.

The Island. Directed by Michael Bay, performances by Scarlet Johansson and Ewan McGregor, Dreamworks and Warners, 2005, DVD.

The Jetsons. Directed by William Hanna and Joseph Barbera. Hanna-Barbera, 1962-87, DVD

Logan's Run. Directed by Michael Anderson, performances by Michael York and Jenny Agutter, MGM, 1976, DVD.

Lowry, Lois. *The Giver*. 1993. Laurel Leaf, 2002.

Metroplis. Directed by Fritz Lang, performances by Brigette Helm, Alfred Abel, and Gustav Frohlich, UFA, 1927, DVD.

Orwell, George. *1984*. 1948. Signet, 1994.

Peters, Ted. *Playing God? Genetic Determinism and Human Freedom*. Routledge, 1997.

The Village. Directed by M. Night Shyamalan, performances by Sigourney Weaver, William Hurt, and Joaquin Phoenix. Touchstone, 2004.

Virgin Galactic. *Virgin Galactic*. 2009. www.virgingalactic.com.

The revision of this rough draft can be found at the end of chapter five.

Outlines

Some writers swear by outlines; others rarely use them, but you won't know what works for you unless you try them. Use the methods in this section and find out. Also, remember from the preceding section that organizational patterns help suggest a thesis and logical content for your writing. There are no rules for deciding when to use certain patterns. *Writers discover the best organizational scheme using trial and error.*

They try out patterns for the overall structure until they find one or two that help the audience understand the thesis, and then they use trial and error again at the paragraph level to arrange each paragraph's individual ideas, examples, and support.

Here are some general points on outlining:

- Specific outlines usually take some time, but less time is needed for revision when they are used.
- By constructing a specific outline, you have already decided on the major content for the essay.
- *Never, Never*, slavishly follow an outline you have constructed.

As you begin writing, if it appears that other ideas need to be added, or moved, or deleted, by all means do so. Just because an outline looks suitable, that doesn't always mean a successful essay will follow from the outline. *Always be ready to change organizational plans as you write and revise.*

Discussion of four types of outlines follows.

Scratch Outlines

If you don't use the more formal types of outlining in your writing process, it is nevertheless wise to at least make an informal scratch outline before starting a draft. When you have a tentative idea for the purpose of your writing, even if you really haven't decided on specific content, simply ask yourself: "With my preliminary thesis, what should I talk about first, second, and third to give purpose to my writing?" Sketch a quick list and then look over the order of ideas; reorder them if necessary; scratch some out, and add some. These few minutes will probably save you time later. It takes less time to write a list of possible main ideas than it does to try out a series of ideas in paragraph form. Here is a student example preceding a rough draft on the subject of older siblings abusing younger siblings. Bill felt he had been abused by his older brother, and wanted to ask parents to help prevent older siblings hurting their brothers and sisters. He constructed the list and then reordered it in the left margin, also deleting one of the sections he had planned:

1	Introduction	set up my situation and introduce myself
		describe my family situation and give thesis
	Thesis: Parents should more actively stop fighting
		between brothers/sisters
4	Reasons why I think my brother hit me and strangled me
3	Reasons he said he did it
2	How it made me feel
CUT	~~How it made me feel toward my parents~~
5	How I felt toward my brother
6	What parents should do

This outline is vague and tentative, but in the end it saved Bill time because he could more quickly write a draft based on the outline; he had already considered the main areas of content he wanted to pursue with the scratch outline. Later, using

63

descriptive outlining while revising his essay, he added content and removed two more subtopics from this original draft, but the preliminary search for structure with the scratch outline helped Bill find the content for his thesis.

Forecasting Outlines

While drafting, when you finish a writing session, it is always wise to write a note to yourself, a forecasting outline, to remind yourself where you are heading and what you need to be doing next. Here is an example from the end of Jason Robertson's writing session, when he was composing the rough draft of an essay on Nathaniel Hawthorne's *The Scarlet Letter* for an American Literature survey:

> . . . It is the combination of the errie, surreal, strange setting — the lights and darks of the forest and the town (some critic said this: Foyle or Fogel?) — and the fairy-like angel/impishness of little Pearl, the unearthliness of her character, that keeps her father, the doomed minister, and her mother, the lonely outcast, so on edge and out of touch with the light of common day.
> To come next:
> Dimmesdale — how Pearl affects him
> / her questions to him
> how this affects Dimmesdale's relationship
> to Puritan community
> Hester — how Pearl affects her mother
> / reread scene in the forest
> (also, isn't forest where Pearl questions minister, so is the forest important? — the scene certainly is for my interpretation)
> how Pearl's relationship to mother affects
> mother's relationship to society — end of novel?
> Hester and Dimmesdale together — don't think I'll use it, but — maybe use their relationship to Pearl as conclusion. There isn't enough, I don't think.

Re-examine the last sentence Jason wrote in the draft (beginning the example). It came at the end of a long paragraph, and it both serves as a conclusion to the preceding paragraph and forecasts what will occur next in the draft. Examine how, from this sentence, Jason expanded the ideas: the outline expands on the root idea in the sentence and lists possible areas to discuss in more detail. Notice that this forecasting outline is very tentative. Jason reminded himself ("re-read scene") that he must first return to the subject of his paper, Hawthorne's novel, to make sure he has evidence to substantiate his point. In other words, he uses the forecasting outline to remind himself that he must research his support before using it. Second, several of Jason's ideas are tentative (the importance of the forest and the relationship between Dimmesdale and Hester); in fact, he states in his outline that he doesn't think they are relevant for his thesis. However, *he wrote them down*. Too many good ideas are forgotten because we don't write them down. Use a forecasting outline like any other predrafting technique — you are just listing and exploring possibilities. Forecasting outlines will help you get restarted in researching or writing when you return to your project.

Traditional Outlines

Traditional outlines are the most detailed outline forms and work best when a writer has already discovered exactly what the elements of the context are (focused subject, audience, thesis, writing situation), as well as most of the content to support the context. Because their structure is so logical, creating specific traditional outlines before starting a draft could help you see if any major ideas or areas of support are lacking. However, even with a precise outline, be prepared for changes in context, content, and organization as you write. Writers come up with new ideas throughout the writing process.

Many professors, especially those asking for longer research papers, may demand an outline with the assignment. If they do, the traditional form is the specific form they are asking for. Follow the structure below closely.

Each heading can use an abbreviated phrase to describe the section of the paper it is referring to, unless the professor asks for a *sentence outline*. A sentence outline uses the same organizational format, but each heading describes its section of the paper in a complete sentence. You probably should not mix sentence and abbreviated phrases in an outline; use one or the other. Michelle Brown uses the traditional outline form to make her descriptive outline, illustrated below and on the next two pages.

    I. Major Idea
       A. idea supporting I.
           1. illustration or idea supporting A.
           2. illustration or idea supporting A. (there can be as many of these as are necessary, but traditionally at least two)
               a. illustration supporting 2
               b. illustration supporting 2 (there can be as many of these as are necessary, but traditionally at least two)
       B. second idea supporting I. (there can be as many of these as necessary, but at least two)
           1.illustration or idea supporting B.
               a. illustration supporting 1
               b. illustration supporting 1
           2. illustration or idea supporting B. (continued)

    II. Second Major Idea
       A. idea supporting II.
           1. illustration or idea supporting A.
           2. illustration or idea supporting A.
       B. second idea supporting II.
           1. illustration or idea supporting B.
           2. illustration or idea supporting B.
       C. third idea supporting II.

    III. Third Major Idea   (and so on)

Descriptive Outlines

If you are fairly certain of your writing context and have written a draft, one method to check the overall content and the organization of the writing is to make an outline of the draft you have just written. With this method, you "clear away all the leaves so you can see the forest." You are reducing the draft to its main points, so that you can see if any of the major ideas and their support need more specifics, or, on the other hand, should be eliminated because they do not clearly relate to the overall purpose for the writing. You should use the traditional outline form to make this descriptive outline, as it is the most detailed, and allows you to look at the relationship between the topic and the sub-topics, and the relationships between sub-topics and support (evidence, examples, illustrations). After you construct the outline, analyze the content and organization in terms of the subject, audience, and purpose. Does any content need to be added? Deleted? Moved? Revise the outline and the structure of ideas and support *before* revising your draft.

The following outline is a descriptive outline Michelle Brown constructed after she wrote her rough draft. She thought that overall the organization worked, but after she constructed the outline, she penciled in three places where she thought she could add more evidence and analysis. She used this revised outline to finalize the essay for content and organization.

I. Comparison/Contrast: Madonna and Woman's Movement
     A. Madonna is controversial, breaking stereotypical molds, which is what the women's movement does; however, Madonna focuses too much on her physical attributes.
     B. Feminists: unity, pushing ahead in fight
     C. Madonna pushed self ahead
          1. Arrington quote Madonna as star, successes

          2. but <u>Truth or Dare</u> intolerant of women
           a. the rape of the girl
           b.??????? Need another example.
II. Madonna sees <u>self</u> as the center of modern feminism (Anderson quote)
     A. ~~Madonna's rise to fame~~ CUT THIS SECTION
     B. Grizzuti-Harrison quote Madonna's degredation not okay
          1. dismisses Madonna justifying of masochism
          2.?????? Need more on Madonna's feminism
     C. Conservative <u>Praise</u>
          1. Papa Don't Preach Video:
          some conservatives like
          2. Various conservative praises
            a. Tipper Gore, others
            b. Planned Parenthood antivideo.
              It says "pregnancy is cool"

III. Feminist praise for opening up the entertainment business for women
        A. <u>Forbes</u> magazine Madonna worth $39 million
        B. Crotch grabbing Michael Jackson - comparison shows Madonna not really feminist
IV. NEED TO EXPAND CONCLUSION

EXERCISE 3.2
Refining your Writing Context and Developing an Outline to Decide on Content

You have done a lot of thinking and predrafting to develop your essay. Now:
A) Look at your writing context. Has your thesis become more specific in this predrafting process? If it has, re-write the thesis. A good thesis usually describes in one or two sentences EXACTLY what your essay will say.

    Vague: Harrison Ford is a good actor.

    Specific: Harrison Ford is an American icon as an actor because of his rugged manliness, his hero roles in many movies, and his softer side that shows the emotional depths and humanness of his characters.

Do you think the audience you decided on before is still the best audience for your essay, or is there another one or a more specific one to read your essay? If there are any changes, do another audience analysis (pp. 28-30) to help you decide whether you have enough content to convince your audience of your thesis. In this audience analysis, decide what tone you should use as you write the essay.
B) With your revised context in mind, from your predrafting pick the best and most relevant content by making an outline. When finished, look over the outline and decide whether you have enough content to support your thesis for that audience. If you don't, predraft some more. If you do, begin your draft.

Drafting

    The first three chapters of *Writing Successfully* discuss predrafting techniques: methods for developing context (subject, audience, writing situation, thesis, tone, and genre) and developing content and organization suited to that context. But at some point in the drafting process, an initial draft with paragraphs and linked sentences and ideas must be written. Some writers, especially if they know a lot about their subject and have a well-defined purpose, skip most predrafting, start with a rough draft, and then spend the majority of their time revising this first draft. Others write first drafts, throw them away when they are unhappy with them, and then write another rough draft, and then another, until they have developed a draft that has a specific context and content. These methods, however, usually work best only when they already have a specific context, and their main thrust is to find suitable content to match this context. In practice, since most writing involves first deciding what you are going to say about a subject, most writers do some predrafting or planning (focusing a subject, developing at least a preliminary purpose, creating content, and a rough outline) before they start an initial draft. The greater the amount of time spent predrafting and planning, the lesser the amount of time spent revising.

Since 1) most of the writing done by students has a timetable, a date when the initial draft is due, and 2) all writing must have a well-defined context with suitable content to match the context, you can use these two points to evaluate how much time you will need to spend to create a successful essay. If during predrafting you are able to develop a specific context and content, you are "ahead of the game," and will spend less time revising. However, each writing situation is different: some essays come easily; some take much more work. If your draft is due the next class, and during predrafting you are still uncertain about the specific context and content, just write the draft. You will discover new ideas as you write, and you might discover the exact focused subject, purpose, and audience as you write. Realize, however, that since your goal remains a well-defined context and suitable content for that specific context, you will probably have to spend more time revising than in situations where you have already developed a context and content.

Many writers are hesitant when starting a draft; these are tips to overcome "writer's block."

- Find the best time of day and place to write, and decide what you write best with (pen and paper or computer). If you find that you write best in longhand rather than on a computer, when you revise your first draft, type it into a computer. As soon as you get a draft on a computer file, it makes it much easier to revise and edit the draft.
- Create a context card with a preliminary focused subject, a possible audience, and a possible thesis, even if you aren't completely sure of your context. This will focus your writing. On the other hand, during the first draft and the initial revision stages, you are still analyzing context and content. Allow yourself as you write to change the context card. You are still discovering what you are going to say, and this is often a process of trial and error!
- A first draft is a discovery draft. To repeat, even if you think you have a specific context and content, new ideas will come as you compose. Get them down on paper; you might decide that your new ideas are better than the ones with which you began the draft, and your context and content will improve.
- Just write, don't worry about whether it is "right" or not, or whether what you are saying is "good" – DISCOVER as you write. In many cases, the key to good writing is discovering what you *are not* going to say, before you find what you *are* going to say.
- How many times have you spent hours staring at a blank page trying to decide how to start an essay? Stop it! The beginning of the essay is an introduction. How can you introduce something when you haven't written it yet? The last thing writers revise, after they have developed suitable context and content, is the introduction. Then they know they are introducing what the essay actually contains. If you do write an introduction at the beginning of your discovery draft, be prepared to revise it after you have finished writing the essay. If you stare at a blank page for more than five minutes trying to decide what the first sentence will be, decide what the first main section of your essay will discuss (look at your preliminary outline which you should have), and start with the first section of the essay after the introduction.

- Until you have written and revised drafts to the stage that the context, content, and organization are successful, don't worry about sentence style, word choice, grammar, punctuation, spelling, and proper form. Too many inexperienced writers write one sentence, and craft it to "perfection" checking for spelling, punctuation, and grammar, then they write a second sentence, crafting it to "perfection," and so on. This is a waste of time. What if the hours you spend crafting each sentence to "perfection" are wasted because you later decide that you don't need those sentences anyway because their content doesn't match the final context? Don't edit at the sentence, word, or grammar level until you are sure the sentences will, in fact, stay in the final draft of the essay.
- *Do not wait until the last second* to write your essay, believing that you always work best under pressure. Perhaps in some cases you do, but what if nothing comes at the last second? To get the feeling of pressure, if this is what you want, set a specific length of time to write the draft, and create pressure that way. ("I need to be finished drafting by 8:00 when my favorite show comes on.") All successful writers leave themselves plenty of time to revise and polish their essays. If you have allowed plenty of time, you can wait several days before revising a draft, and this lapse of time allows you to see your essay anew and come up with better ideas and ways to express the ideas. Professional writers try to allow a length of time between all their drafts, and this allows them to truly create and polish their best work.

EXERCISE 3.3
Writing the First Draft

You have now developed enough ideas to write your rough draft. With your writing context in mind, write your first draft. Do not follow your outline slavishly. Many more new and better ideas, evidence, and content will come to you as you write your initial draft.

Student Example: Drafting

We will no longer be using Mathew's Whitman essay from chapter two — the first he ever wrote in college — as an illustration. From the predrafting you read in that chapter, he developed a draft of the essay which is printed here. To give a preview of the revision processes of chapters four (revision for overall content and organization) and chapter five (revision at the paragraph and precise word use level), here is the initial rough draft, with **precise words added, various spelling and usage corrections,** and the notes to himself for revisions for content penciled in. This essay would be five pages double spaced on 8 1/2X11 printer paper:

Matthew Moore
English 101
Rough Draft

An Old Voice for a New Generation

In the second half of the 19th century, a period when Americans

PARAGRAPH COMPLETENESS & WORD SPECIFICITY -- 1) Go to history book, find examples, and list. 2) Need specific examples of values, like Uncle Joe the right wing wingnut. 3) Need to go to history book to find comparisons of 1850s and today

And in that philosophy that transcends individual beliefs on issues, in those paradigms of equality and compassion, Whitman was a man who spoke for all men, and particularly all Americans.

PARAGRAPH COMPLETENESS: Need examples, perhaps a couple lines from "Song" for support.

More lines from "Salut"?

were divided more than ever before or since, Walt Whitman took upon himself the role as the spokesman for the American people. From the darkest times in our nation's history, **the time of the Civil War and the massacres of western Indian tribes,** arose **one of** the most optimistic voice**S** our nation has ever produced. ~~In current times,~~ **In the twenty-first century, it seems** Americans have spokesmen for each side but there doesn't stand a single person that speaks for ~~every~~ **most** Americans**, ~~rather~~ whether** they are on the left or right side of the political fence. Today, what Americans perceive as our nation's "values" or "traditions" differ from person to person. Our differing definitions of such terms has made it very unlikely that any two Americans, no matter what party or philosophy they claim to adhere to, will agree on all issues. **, nor did they in Whitman's time.** The current political and social situation in America is not very different from that time period Whitman and the other transcendentalist writers lived in. Whitman, though he wrote on nearly every topic of his time, decided to focus much of his writing on two of the ideas he believed were, and should still be, the true philosophy of the United States: Equality and Compassion.

Walt Whitman is often considered to be one of the leading proponents of individualism in American letters, and although this is true he never claims that he is any way superior or more significant than the common man. His "songs," he writes, are not only to "celebrate" himself but to admit "I am not an earth or an adjunct of an earth, I am the mate and companion of people, all just as immortal and fathomless as myself" (397). Throughout his work, Whitman speaks of his belief in the equality of every human being. He repeatedly celebrates the differences between every member of society. Whitman felt a connection with the common people and expressed this in a letter to the senator John P. Hale. He told Hale he did not know "the great men" in politics, but declared "I know the people. I know well the real heart of this mighty city" (Reynolds 135). As a white male in the mid-nineteenth century, Whitman was a member of the privileged class in the United States, but instead of fearing those different from him and fighting to protect his place as a superior in American society, he openly embraced and spoke of the need for equality among not only Americans but all people across the globe. Whitman believed that every person born was a member of one race, man, and that only when united can people reach their true potential and achieve what he calls the "Great idea": perfect and free individuals. In "By Blue Ontario's Shore" he declares that the true goal for America is to "produce great persons, the rest follows." and to "lead the present with friendly hand toward the future" Although he considered himself the spokesman for a generation, he also displayed a ~~humbleness~~ **humility** due to his belief that his audience, the American people, were just as important as himself; declaring in the opening lines of "Song of Myself": "I celebrate myself and sing myself, And what I assume You shall assume, For every atom belonging to me as good belongs to you." He continues, in later passages of the same poem, to celebrate the existence and importance of nearly every member of American society: carpenters, deacons, immigrants, husbands, wives, prostitutes, the young, the old, etc. However, Whitman not only speaks of the greatness of what we would now consider "Americans" but, in "Salut Au Monde" he equally treats members of every country around the world: the English, the Slavic, Africans, Spaniards, French etc. Today it is taken for granted that this is a basic "American" ideal, but once again immigration has become an issue among Americans, and throughout

70

the country we see huge differences in what American citizens believe it means to be a "real American." Even ~~the~~ President **Obama** is constantly attacked for not being what some consider a "real American." We seem to have forgotten that, still to this day, America's welcome sign reads: "Give me your tired, your poor, Your huddled masses, yearning to breath free, The wretched refuse of your teeming shore, Send these, the homeless, tempest tost to me, I lift my lamp beside the golden door."

Along with the belief of equality between nationalities, Whitman spoke openly of his belief in equality for the women and slaves of his time. He writes in section 21 of "Song of Myself": "I am the poet of woman the same as the man, and I say it is as great to be a woman as to be a man." In others he speaks of what can be argued as the only superior being he mentions: "the mothers of men." In the preface to the original edition of *Leaves of Grass* he argues for the equality of women, coining the term "workwomen" to promote ~~there~~ **their** presence in the workplace. He later coins another term, "freewomen," defending women's right to freely choose their sexual partners. In a letter to his friend, Horace Traubel, he wrote: "Indeed, I think the best women are *always* the best of all: the flower - the justification of the race - the summit, crown" (qtd. in Reynolds 198). Also known as being strongly against slavery, we can see evidence of Whitman's views in "I Sing the Body Electric." Here Whitman tells of a man being sold into slavery, a man, he declares, who is equal to his buyer and seller with "the same old blood, the same red running blood" running through his veins. Throughout *Leaves of Grass* Whitman tells of the unjust act of slavery and it is believed that the original opening line of the entire collection was in fact: "I am the poet of the slaves and of the masters of slaves." In a later poem he dreams of a time when everyone in America will be "answering our equal friendship and calling no man master." He believed that slavery could cause the downfall of democracy in America, and in an unpublished piece warned the Southern states that "you are either to abolish slavery or it will abolish you."

Although considered by Thoreau as "probably the greatest democrat that ever lived," Whitman's own political views are not directly stated anywhere in the poems of *Leaves of Grass*. However his belief in equality as a fundamental idea to America and Democracy is apparent throughout all of his work. Along with this belief in equality, there is a constantly underlying tone of ~~humbleness,~~ **humility,** where Whitman reminds us of the importance of acknowledging your own unimportance. He continually speaks of the need for "comrades" to "march into battle" with. Although hoping that one day "every American will carry a copy of my leaves in his back pocket," at one point he tells the reader that if they do not find value in his poems to "release me and depart on your way," for, no matter the importance of the individual; it is the majority, the common people, who are the life and future of society. Unlike previous poets, Whitman decided not to write his epic based on the adventures of one particular man, but instead chose all of the American people as the "hero" for his work. In "I Was Looking a Long While," Whitman states his work is "all for the modern - all for the average man of today."

Arguably, the most important theme Walt Whitman ever wrote about, and the one that encompasses the majority of his work was compassion for his fellow man. In his own life he worked in numerous hospitals as a nurse treating wounded

Whitman seems to be 150 years ahead of his time, Even abolishionists of his time did not think of the black or red races as equals. Nor did most whites of the 1950s and 60s who pushed for what eventually became the Brown case or Voting and Civil Rights Acts of 64. 4% believed in interracial marriage.

DOCUMEN-TATION: After "that ever lived" need (Reyn-olds)

71

soldiers from both the Union and Confederate armies. In his poem retelling his time in the hospitals, "The Wound Dresser," he describes his compassion for the wounded, describing them as "unsurpassed heroes (was one side so brave ? The other was equally brave)." He was known by some soldiers as "Santa Claus," always bringing treats and presents to the patients of the hospitals. In our busy lives today, it seems the common American has forgotten that our country was based on the idea of the common man helping in the progress and preservation of the nation. Whitman claims in "The Base of All Metaphysics" that the underlying message behind all philosophies, Christian or otherwise, is truly that of "the dear love of man for his comrade."

In this current time Americans are constantly bombarded with political advertisements attacking candidate's rivals, and the daily news seems only to focus on the negative events that take place from day to day. There is very little mention of any type of social progress throughout the world, and the works toward peace throughout the world seem to have become of a much lesser importance to the common people than whatever horrible event that happens each day. The workings of the mass media and political figures together do nothing for the common people but scare them into fearing one another. We are told by our politicians that "our enemies hate us because we believe in freedom" or, by the previous president, that we must "confront every threat from any source that could bring sudden terror and suffering to America" without ever being told exactly what that "threat" or what it's "source" actually are. Our country is developing an increasingly paranoid point-of-view, believing that every outside nation wishes us harm and that a vote for the wrong candidate will result in the collapse of our nation, the death of our "values," and (as we are commonly told) the doom of our children. At a time when the vast majority of Americans are experiencing similar difficulties, we continue to remain divided on what are seemingly unimportant issues. Even today debates are held on whether or not certain Americans, depending on their ethnicity, sexual orientation or place of birth, should be allowed the same rights as the rest of the population. Is there not a simpler answer to the questions being raised? Can we not look on some of these issues not as a question of "values" or "traditions" and decide that what is really needed is understanding and compassion towards every member of society. Until we openly accept others right to exist, and to exist how they wish, how will we ever begin to tackle more pressing and more complicated issues? In such a turbulent time, isn't it necessary for Americans to put aside their differences on so many vague and truly unimportant issues and return to the simple philosophy that America was founded on and that Whitman's works preached? The most important matter is to love, respect, and help your fellow man. In Whitman's words: "Be not dishearten'd, affection shall solve the problems of freedom yet."

Works Cited

Reynolds, David S. *Walt Whitman's America: A Cultural Biography*. Knoph, 1995.

Whitman, Walt. *Leaves of Grass*. 1855-1893. Barnes and Noble, 2004.

4

Second Draft and Peer Review

Revision

Revision of the Writing Context Before Revising the Content

Checklist Questions
WRITING CONTEXT
A. Is the subject focused (for suggested length)? Can you discuss this subject with the complexity it deserves in the length and time allotted?
B. Is there a specific audience and writing situation that it is obvious you have analyzed?
C. Is there a well-defined, specific thesis?
D. Can you describe the tone appropriate for the genre, audience, and thesis?

So you've written a draft; what do professional writers do after they've written theirs? First drafts are in many cases still predrafting; writers are still trying to focus the subject further, decide specifically on audience, and find exactly what the thesis for the essay will be. So after finishing a rough draft they rethink their context, and only after any final changes to context do they then revise the content to match this finalized context. Even if writers were very sure of the context before starting, there will usually still be some refining of the context before improving the content. Writers almost always refine and qualify their thesis more, and either change the audience or analyze them more thoroughly. Until writers are *exactly* sure what they are saying (thesis and tone) to whom (audience and writing situation) about a subject, only then can they assuredly revise the content and organization to match this finalized context.

The inner front cover of *Writing Successfully* has a checklist of questions to use for revision of context (also see checklist above for a summary of inner cover checklist). This section on revision will discuss what to do if you need to rethink and/or finalize your writing context before revising the draft, and the next section discusses what to do AFTER you have finalized your context with the questions you need to ask yourself in order to revise the content to match the finalized writing context.

How do you know what content to use if you don't know who your audience is or what the point of your writing is? Also, if you haven't yet focused your subject enough, you will waste time writing paragraphs on ideas that you will later take out because they aren't relevant for your focused subject. The following is a discussion of the first questions you ask yourself after finishing the initial draft, with two examples of students asking other students their thoughts about the context of the initial draft. The answer to most of the four checklist questions above after a first draft will probably be "not yet." Your goal is to revise your context until the answer to the questions is "yes, this is exactly what I want my essay to do." Only after making these decisions can you revise the content of your essay using the content and organization questions.

A.   Is the subject focused (for suggested length)? Can you discuss this subject with the complexity it deserves in the length and time alloted?

Whatever the subject of your essay, you need to discuss it with the complexity it deserves. When you are researching a subject, when you are analyzing a subject, and often in the initial draft on a subject, you are exploring and trying out many possibilities. As soon as possible, focus your subject so that you can discuss it in detail, exploring all its ramifications. Good writing consists of tightly focused, detailed writing, not many great undeveloped ideas on a larger, unfocused subject.

Sometimes, you will have focused the subject before beginning the essay. Other times, especially when your predrafting has not been as extensive as possible, your first draft will have too many good ideas and undeveloped subtopics. *After writing a draft, consider this focused subject question first. If your draft has many ideas not fully developed, decide on the focus for your subject, write a new focused subject on a context card, delete everything in the initial draft that does not directly concern the revised focused subject, and decide whether you need to go back to predrafting to develop more content or a specific thesis for your new focused subject.*

B.   Is there a specific audience and writing situation?

When the professor assigns a specific audience and situation, you do not have to worry about this question. Sometimes, the purpose for the essay will demand a certain audience and writing situation, so you do not have to worry about this question. But most of the time, you will have developed an audience and writing situation during predrafting, and you need to reconsider it before starting any revision.

With this last possibility, after writing your first DISCOVERY draft, you need to rethink your audience and writing situation after focusing your subject. Given your subject, is this the right audience, the one you feel most comfortable talking to or the one you have something you want to communicate to concerning the subject? After deciding on audience, what is the forum, the writing situation, that you see your essay being delivered in? Where would it be published?

Revise your context card to reflect any changes in audience and writing situation, and be sure to redo the audience analysis (pp. 28-31) in detail for the new or more specific audience. Without knowing what your audience knows and believes about the subject and what they don't know and you want them to believe, how are you going to develop the proper content? As a matter of fact, even if your audience has not changed, or has only become slightly more specific, the wise writer still re-does the audience analysis to help develop content for the revision. This saves much time.

C.   Is there a well-defined, specific thesis?

After deciding on your focused subject, audience, and writing situation, consider your purpose. Sometimes, you will know exactly what you want to say before beginning a writing project. More often, the thesis statement evolves as you predraft, write, and revise. In most cases, the point could evolve and change, or at least become more specific, with each of the first few drafts until you know exactly what you want to say and to whom about a subject. *After writing a discovery draft, and re-analyzing subject, audience, and situation, rethink your thesis and rewrite the more specific or different thesis on the context card. Rethink this question again after the second draft, and be prepared to change the purpose again and again until you have developed a specific thesis you can live with for your writing. Record changes on an updated context card.* **When you change the thesis, be sure to cut irrelevant content from your draft.**

D. Can you describe the tone appropriate for the genre, audience, and thesis?

Only after you have finalized audience, situation, and purpose can you be sure of the tone to adopt. For instance, if you were writing a literary analysis in a literature class, your professor would be your probable audience, the kind of analysis found in professional scholarly journals would be the likely situation, and because of this audience and situation, your tone would be serious, formal, and objective. If you were writing an essay about the rise in vulgarity in television advertising and your audience were older, conservative Americans your parents' age, your tone would probably be more formal and objective than if your audience were people your own age. With people your own age, you could be less formal, less serious, more subjective, and if you chose could be more humorous or irreverent. *After you have developed a tone for the essay, which often takes several drafts, describe it on your context card.*

In writing courses, not only the teacher but other students often critique classmate essays. The examples that follow show the comments two students had for other students to help them finalize decisions about their focused subject, audience, and thesis. Whether your professor asks you to get critiques from other students at this stage of the writing process, or you are asked to make these decisions yourself, you need to ask yourself the following questions and use the questions to finalize your writing context before you can complete a successful content revision of your essay.

A. Is the subject focused (for suggested length)? Can you discuss this subject with the complexity it deserves in the length and time allotted?

> Bob, I can see you are trying to find a focus with this first draft. You're trying a lot of good topics; as a matter of fact, there is a good focused subject in every paragraph and in some instances every couple of sentences. We are supposed to write 3 or 4 pages, not a book. Remember what the prof said: focus your subject so that what you do write about, you explore it with the complexity it deserves. Of the many good possibilities in your draft, two I especially liked were the girl overcoming gender bias or an expansion of the section on men's feelings about women bosses. Choose & cut the rest.

B. Is there a specific audience and writing situation?

> Women in the workplace is certainly an appropriate and interesting topic for your audience, the women in this class (mostly 18 year old middle class females). It is especially interesting for those

a few years older who have had problems in the working world. Though I'm a man, I found your many thoughts on the topic interesting and commendable, especially your illustration of the girl overcoming gender bias on the job. Of course, you could change to a male audience – which one would you rather write to?

C. Is there a well-defined, specific thesis?

Develop a specific purpose: perhaps expand the section on overcoming gender bias and argue to women, as a male writer, that many men also want this gender bias to end.

D. Can you describe the tone appropriate for the genre, audience, and thesis?

Even though you aren't entirely clear on a thesis yet, if you stay with girls about our age as an audience I think you have the perfect tone: you let them know that you have concern for their issues, but as a male you certainly don't presume to speak for them, only to relate your subjective experience. The best part of this early draft is its tone.

Notice that while the peer reviewer is essentially saying Bob should pick only one short passage from the original draft and write an entirely new draft around that focused subject, he has continued commenting with a positive tone. His comments focus mainly on focusing the subject, because until the writer chooses a focus he will never be entirely sure whom the audience should be or what the thesis will be. This is a good example of a comment which gives concrete criticism while maintaining a positive tone. Do the same if you are critiquing your own drafts!!! Be truthful and constructive, whether you are looking at your own writing or someone else's — but give yourself or your peers a *valid* criticism of the writing. Remember, "It's pretty good" doesn't help the writer at all. The peer reviewer above does not comment at all on the strengths of the content because the writer has not focused his subject yet.

The next example shows a peer review comment when the writer HAS finalized decisions about subject, audience, and purpose.

A. Is the subject focused (for suggested length)? Can you discuss this subject with the complexity it deserves in the length and time allotted?

Yes – Math Anxiety, but you even focused to Math 070, the class that most of us who aren't very good at math take to prepare for 109. I like your contrast between your older brother and his anxiety, and yourself who used to be anxious but was taught how to overcome anxiety by the H.S. teacher and that book she gave you.

B. Is there a specific audience and writing situation?

> Math anxiety and steps to overcome it is certainly an interesting and appropriate topic for your audience, us in the class. I need it especially, so I'm a good person to peer review. I can SEE the essay's writing situation as being in the school newspaper. Get it published when you're done!

C. Is there a well-defined, specific thesis?

> Yes – giving some specific steps to overcome math anxiety, a process/process analysis essay.

D. Can you describe the tone appropriate for the genre, audience, and thesis?

> The tone is objective and serious; however, you let us into your subjective fears when you had math anxiety, and this helps the reader relate to your essay.

EXERCISE 4.1
Revision for the Writing Context

Take the essay you are working on now and ask yourself the four questions for developing a writing context:
A) If the subject is not focused enough, focus the subject and find out what you need to know to write on that focused subject.
B) After doing this, decide on your audience, make them as specific as possible, do an audience analysis, and decide on a writing situation.
C) Rethink your thesis, and decide EXACTLY what your point is.
D) Finalize the tone you should use to get your message to your audience.

Global Revision for Content and Organization

Checklist Questions
CONTENT AND ORGANIZATION
1. Make a descriptive outline of the draft you are looking at. Does an outline demonstrate there is a logical flow of ideas in the essay? Using the outline, examine for any important ideas/evidence missing. Revise until the content is organized.
2. Does the draft discuss only content necessary for thesis and audience (no straying off on tangents)? Does the draft have enough content for the audience? Does it have content the audience does not need to understand your thesis? Cut and add until it does.
3. Does the draft use a tone proper for the purpose and audience? Revise for tone.
4. Does the draft make the point (with specific evidence) that the thesis says it will? Does it achieve this specific purpose? If not, revise.

It is probably important to decide on a focused subject before you begin a revision for a second draft, and it saves considerable time to have finalized audience, writing situation, and thesis (though this does not always happen). *If, however, you are not successful finalizing decisions concerning audience and thesis before beginning the second draft, write this second draft with the knowledge that your primary concern as you add to and change the first draft is that you need to discover audience and thesis.* Until you finalize decisions about your audience and purpose for writing to them, you can never be entirely successful deciding on tone, content, and organization. How do you know what content to include until you know what an audience already knows and needs to know about a subject? How do you know what content to include until you are completely sure what you want to say or prove (the purpose for your writing)?

Use the questions following to revise the content of your essay, and after completing the second draft, use both them and the context questions again to recheck your writing. When are you finished revising for context and overall content and organization? When the answer to ALL these questions is "Yes. Good work."

1. Make a descriptive outline of the draft you are looking at. Does an outline demonstrate there is a logical flow of ideas in the essay? Using the outline, examine for any important ideas/evidence missing. Revise until the content is organized.

Make a *descriptive outline* (pp.66-7) of the draft you have just written. Looking at the ideas in outline form might help you discover the direction you are going, and help you create a specific thesis. If you have already finalized the context (subject, audience, situation, thesis, and tone), use a descriptive outline to decide whether the ideas and examples flow logically (supporting the thesis) and whether any important ideas or evidence to support this purpose are left out. Using the outline, add or delete content and reorder sections of the essay, until you believe that the ideas and support necessary are all included and there is a logical flow of ideas.

2. Does the draft discuss only content necessary for thesis and audience (no straying off on tangents)? Does the draft have enough content for the audience? Does it have content the audience does not need to understand your thesis? Cut and add until it does.

The first two questions are a check to make sure that you only use content for your focused subject, audience, and thesis. A section of your essay might have a great idea, with adequate support, but if it doesn't help demonstrate your thesis, it needs to be cut. Also, you need to think about your audience; take out information that you can assume they already know (unless, of course, you need it to set up a point you are making). For instance, if you were talking about the American educational system to Americans, you would not need to describe kindergartens in detail. On the other hand, do you have enough content so that your audience completely understands your claim? Add/delete content until these questions have been answered satisfactorily.

3. Does the draft use a tone proper for purpose and audience? Revise for tone.

Give a last evaluation to your final audience, writing situation, and tone. The kind of writing (the writing situation) appropriate for your subject, audience, and purpose will help you decide on the tone to adopt. By the time you have developed this specific context, and adequate content and organization to convince the audience of your thesis (finalized decisions about all the previous questions), you will have decided on a style, a tone, to help convince your readers. Become your audience! Have you used a tone that helps convince them of your thesis? Edit until the tone is appropriate for the audience. When you are utterly sure you have convinced your audience that you have a valid thesis, then you are probably using an appropriate tone.

4. Does the draft make the point (with sufficient evidence) that the thesis says it will? Does it achieve this specific purpose? If not, revise.

Give a final check to all the previous questions to make sure the support for your ideas substantiates the thesis. If it doesn't, add content to make the essay successfully prove the validity of your thesis.

Student Example: First to Second Draft

Gerald Gardner
Eng 150
Professor Robinson
First Draft

Subject: Racism
Audience: white people like myself who ignore racial problems
Writing Situation: hometown newspaper editorial
Thesis: Racism, mostly unconscious, still occurs in America today, and we need to work – as a nation – on relieving it.
Tone: serious, persuasive, objective

WRITING CONTEXT
A. Is the subject focused (for suggested length)? Can you discuss this subject with the complexity it deserves in the length and time allotted?

> While the subject is very broad, the thesis pointed to that specific audience makes essay acceptable. I have become very knowledgeable in the last weeks, and feel ready to revise this.

B. Is there a specific audience and writing situation that it is obvious you have analyzed?

> Perfect audience and writing situation - I know this audience and their beliefs, and I am arguing to them.

C. Is there a well-defined, specific thesis?

> The thesis is specific and I am happy with it and the evidence I have to prove it.

D. Can you describe the tone appropriate for the genre, audience, and thesis?

> The tone is perfect for editorials in the Tribune. I am being persuasive, analytical, and much of this is observation and data.

Since Gerald has written several essays in this first semester class, he is able to combine steps. After writing a quick first draft based on the outline and preliminary context card, he combines the revision steps for overall content and paragraph revision/using specific language, doing them at the same time. So this second draft has revisions using not only questions 1-4 for overll content and organization (front inner cover), but also questions 5-8 (which are discussed in the next chapter). For the first college essay of your lives, use each question A-D and 1-8 individually, but when revision becomes second nature you may begin to combine steps. BUT THEY ARE *ALL* NECESSARY STEPS FOR QUALITY CONTENT.

CONTENT AND ORGANIZATION

1. Make a descriptive outline of the draft you are looking at. Does an outline demonstrate there is a logical flow of ideas in the essay? Using the outline, examine for any important ideas/evidence missing. Revise until the content is organized.

1) Intro: <u>needs race statistics for my town</u>, but otherwise lets reader know subject of essay and <u>sets up logical organization for the essay</u> with the listing of what I learned growing up (though I don't reveal yet that this is the organization I will use).

2) Short paragraph setting up how I got to this subject. <u>Add sentence to demontrate my initial reluctance</u> to confront the subject (audience can relate). Personal Experience grabs audience.

3) The statement that if i'm not fixing racism I'm a racist that hit me in the gut. <u>Add how this propelled me into the research</u>.

4) The story about how I observed racism in action with my peer's essays.

5) discussion of affirmative action and why it needs another generation. <u>ADD what grandmother said about how affirmative action helped white women in the 60s-70s to make point clear.</u>

New para: <u>5a Use para 5 as set up to argue here that African-Americans need another generation getting out of poverty before Aff Action should be dismantled.</u>

6) What African-Americans say about economic, educational, and crime/punishment racial problems. <u>Add evidence and statistics in this paragraph for completeness,</u>

7) Brief paragraph on racism in the justice system. This is in and of itself its own topic, so I think wisely just choosing a quotation proving statistically the racism is all I should have. Must include this brief section so that I discuss the introduction's 4 points I was taught growing up (so organization is consistent).

8) Conclusion blah!!!! <u>Re-write</u> with specifics using McIntosh's "Fifty Privileges Whites have in their knapsack that people of color don't have" (title?) Go for the personal privileges my white audience receives that they haven't even thought of.

80

2. Does the draft discuss only content necessary for thesis and audience (no straying off on tangents)? Does the draft have enough content for the audience? Does it have content the audience does not need to understand your thesis? Cut and add until these questions haave been answered.

<u>See underlined notes in outline and additions and deletions in the revised text below. I think I have it now with the revision.</u>

Rough Draft with revisions penciled in after considering writing context questions A-D and content and organization questions 1 and 2. As stated before, Gerald already has practice with revision. So questions 1 and 2 assure him that his overall content and prganization stand up, so they actually point toward essential revisions outlined in questions 3-8 (specific word use and paragraph revision). Since he spent so much time planning this draft, the overall content and organization was acceptable with the first draft. His decision to organize the essay based on refutations of the four ideas about racism he learned growing up, as you can see, works well to give an overall organizational framework to the essay.

1) I grew up in small town mid-America, Missouri to be exact. There were 1% African-Americans in my town and 5% Latino farmworkers (United States Census Bureau). White bread America. I didn't think too much about color in the town I grew up in. America. Didn't have to. In American History, we spent an hour on slavery, an hour on Reconstruction, an hour on racism and the KKK in the 20s and 30s, an hour on Civil Rights, a half hour on Martin Luther King (the peace keeper) with the other half hour on the race rights of the 60s. Go figure. Oh yeah. I remember in the eighth grade we had a few minutes each on George Washington Carver, Harriet Tubman, Frederick Douglass, Sojourner Truth, Jackie Robinson, and Thurgood Marshall. Here is what I was taught by the culture I came from: 1) Affirmative Action is now taking away jobs from white people and people of color use it to get jobs they aren't qualified for. 2) Racism is a thing of the past. 3) The preponderance of American-Americans and Latino-Americans are in prison is because they committed crimes. 4) Always be nice to minorities and treat them as equals. As long as I did the last 4), I would be free of racism.

2) When I got to college, I was bombarded with new information. My African-American black female sociology instructor and my lily white grad student composition instructor both hit me with units and readings on gender and racial inequality. I ignored it and went on being a college freshman as long as I could. I wasn't the bad guy.

3) Here is what happened: first, my English instructor demanded a final research unit on some aspect of gender or race. Second, I went to him to complain. What he said smacked me into awareness. 'If racism and gender inequality still exist, and you are aware of it, if you aren't doing whatever you can to stop it, then you are a misogynist and a racist.' Wow. For a moment my defenses started going into battle, but then a calmness sunk in. He was right. I knew it. So I decided to use the research and analysis for this paper to become knowledgeable in the ways racism still occurs in the United States. Gaining knowledge would be my first step toward combating gender and racial problems. As I left his office, I felt like a warrior for truth and justice. Yeah, perhaps that is fishy, but nevertheless, that is what I felt.

81

4) It just so happened that a few days after my conversation with Professor Robinson, I was sitting with a few peers from my history class. The history class had an essay assigned, and we had just gotten ours back. On mine, the professor had made some astute comments on using evidence more effectively, and a couple comments on stylistic concerns like eliminating wordiness and using action verbs. I looked at Jeremiah's essay; **he is a thoughtful African-American.** It not only had a lower grade, but it was filled with red marks over grammatical and punctuation concerns, with not one single comment on the content of his essay except at the end: 'Pretty good. Work on learning to edit.' Now this struck me because I am no editor. I am learning in the composition class, but I'm still pretty weak. I looked again at my essay and I noticed many, many editing errors that had not been marked. Wow. With my new opening eyes, **with the rose tinted glasses off,** I realized that this was a mark of unintentional racism, **the racism of low expectations for a student of color.** How can they be their best if they are never challenged? If they are just told repeatedly that they are not up to par? We share a class with Professor Robinson, who was the challenger of us to look at gender and race, so I asked to look at some of his papers from Professor Robinson. I couldn't believe it. Professor Robinson focused more on surface editing issues with Jeremiah and less on content than he did with his comments to me. And this is from a professor who obviously is trying hard to right problems faced by women and people of color!!! I was beginning to think that racism, especially unconscious racism, still does run deep in our culture.

5) So let's look at the first idea I was taught growing up: Affirmative Action should be an idea of the past. Women and people of color have made amazing strides in career possibilities (many more doctors, lawyers, professionals), and with these amazing strides has come SOME positive movement toward equalizing pay disparities. There have been many more opportunities for these groups in college also. **I remember my grandmother talking to me before I left for college, and she says when she went to college in the early 60s, most women went to college for one reason, and one reason only: to find a college educated husband who would provide for them. There was actually a degree many of them took in Home Economics!!!! Of course, even then, a woman could become a doctor, lawyer, entrepreneur, but they were often considered freaks. We have come a long way. But in terms of affirmative action, I want to make a point. Notice I have been mainly talking about the successes of white women (and we still have a long way to go).** Many people forget, or never knew, that Affirmative Action helped women who had been treated unequally in the workplace also. So since 1964 when the Civil Rights Act was passed, white women, who already came from the more affluent and educated homes, were much more quickly able to use Affirmative Action to get into medical schools and get preferential treatment when applying for jobs or new positions. Within a generation these new opportunities for women had become ingrained in our country's values. **New paragraph 5a:** However, African-Americans, even with Affirmative Action, cannot get a job they are not qualified for. It will take a generation or two before African-American family and cultural structures can reach an economic and educational starting point similar to white women's in 1964. **5a cont: So it is my supposition that when that occurs, African-Americans will be on a level par with whites, and by then hopefully, women, men, anyone has equal parity in college and the workforce, and then Affirmative Action can be done away with. In my first act of rebellion to end racism**

I declare: it is the height of injustice and racism for white people, when their economic stature has raised considerably with the rise of the wife's income over the last generation, to call for an end to Affirmative Action right at precisely the time when another generation will bring African-Americans to a level commiserate with their worth.

Need to have specific evidence for all the claims about problems Af americans have in para below:

6)   As I read a few articles by African-Americans (Knowles and Pruitt, Muhammed, McKissak, and a well-known Caucasian educator, Kozol), I furthermore realized that it was the height of folly for me – for all white people - to assume that racism has become a thing of the past because we don't see it, and that the few bad apples among whites were the last vestiges of an old racism that no longer exists. African-Americans still have unequal educational opportunities, more crime in their neighborhoods, stiffer prison sentences, less access to medical care, and their pay gap has hardly moved in the last decades. **NEED EVIDENCE for all of these.** Of course, much of this is not because of overt racism as occurred before the 1960s, it can be attributed to poverty; however, the result is the same. Caucasians in poverty are lower on the scale than their more affluent numbers, but they are still higher than African-Americans. **NEED STATISTICS.** Could this be the result of low expectations on a massive scale like the ones already discussed? Moreover, if white children and families were suffering from the problems of black communities, I can assure you that politicians would find the money and programs to correct the problems.

7)   In terms of crime, I am not going into an in-depth argument over unequal practices from a lack of decent representation of poorer African-Americans as well as an unconscious racism, a fear of black males prevalent in our culture, I am going to let one set of statistics prove my point, and the figures are borne out in all states:

> Although less than 40 percent of Georgia homicide cases involve white victims, in 87 percent of the cases in which a death sentence is imposed, the victim is white. White-victim cases are almost eleven times more likely to produce a death sentence than are black-victim cases.
>
> When the race of the defendant is considered too, the following figures emerge: 22 percent of black defendants who kill white victims are sentenced to death; 8 percent of white defendants who kill white-victims are sentenced to death; 1 percent of black defendants who kill black-victims are sentenced to death; 3 percent of white defendants who kill black-victims are sentenced to death (Amsterdam 262).

8)   ~~We need to help prisoners get out of the revolving door of prison–the streets, make educational opportunity a reality for all, and all should learn about that invisible package of white privilege even the poorest white carries at all times. Only then can we begin to see an America that is beginning to free itself of racial bias. We need to vote for politicians who will promise these essentials.~~

What I need to do – what we whites need to do – is begin to realize the many invisible privileges we have as members of the majority culture of America. There is a famous article by Peggy McIntosh that lists fifty ways that whites have an innate privilege over people of color in this country. As examples, I list the first eight:

1. I can if I wish arrange to be in the company of people of my race most of the time.

2. I can avoid spending time with people whom I was trained to mistrust and who have learned to mistrust my kind or me.

3. If I should need to move, I can be pretty sure of renting or purchasing housing in an area which I can afford and in which I would want to live.

4. I can be pretty sure that my neighbors in such a location will be neutral or pleasant to me.

5. I can go shopping alone most of the time, pretty well assured that I will not be followed or harassed.

6. I can turn on the television or open to the front page of the paper and see people of my race widely represented.

7. When I am told about our national heritage or about "civilization," I am shown that people of my color made it what it is.

8. I can be sure that my children will be given curricular materials that testify to the existence of their race.

See what I mean? There are fifty of these aspects of white privilege we enjoy that help us achieve success and the American dream which people of color do not have, even if they are born wealthy. But let's begin to think about what we can do. Most of the answers to lessening the racism still prevalent in our nation are beyond our individual control EXCEPT through the ballot box. We need to look for, and elect only, politicians who are ready to A) Stop the prison industry and help prisoners become productive members of society (it costs much less to educate a prisoner than to repeatedly incarcerate him); B) Create less poverty in the United States through home ownership campaigns, teaching economics to students in high school and college, and education opportunities for adults; C) Train ALL teachers in all levels of the educational community to recognize when they are unconsciously harming a student of color's success. The thirteenth amendment was a long time ago!!! Let's realize its potential.

NEED A WORKS CITED PAGE

After thoroughly revising using questions 1 and 2 of the checklist questions, Gerald did a final check for overall content and organization by looking at questions 3 and 4:

3. Does the draft use a tone proper for the purpose and audience? Revise for tone.

I think I am using a tone consistent with the Tribune. My essay treats readers like thoughtful adults and uses reputable sources so that they will acknowledge I have done my homework. I have been analytic, using evidence, and have been persuasive. Confirm with peer reviewer and prof.

4. Does the draft make the point (with specific evidence) that the thesis says it will? Does it achieve its specific purpose? If not, revise.

> After this completion of revisions for questions 1-8, I am pretty sure this essay fulfills its purpose with specific evidence. Need to get a peer review from someone in class, and maybe the prof.

EXERCISE 4.2
Revision for Content and Organization

Take the essay you are working on now, and ask yourself the four questions for developing content and organization. Revise your content and organization until the answer to the four questions is "yes":

1) Make a descriptive outline of the draft you are looking at. Does an outline demonstrate there is a logical flow of ideas in the draft? Using the outline, examine for any important ideas/evidence missing. Revise until the content is organized.

2) Does the draft discuss only content necessary for thesis and audience (no straying off on tangents)? Does the draft have enough content for the audience? Does it have content the audience does not need to understand your thesis? Cut and add until these questions have been answered.

3) Does the draft use a tone proper for the purpose and audience? Revise for tone.

4) Does the draft make the point (with sufficient) evidence that the thesis says it will? Does it achieve this specific purpose? If not, revise.

Peer Reviewing

Many people think writing is a lonely occupation: that there is a mysterious connection some writers have with words making them successful writers, and that these writers write and revise by themselves. This is just not true. *Writing Successfully* discusses the steps — the processes — necessary for successful writing. The steps debunk the mystery, so just learn these processes *through practice*. (Use the revision guidelines on the inside front and back covers.) This section discusses how professional writers *peer review* each other's writing to make it better. Students can peer review with success too. Together with your classmates, use the revision and peer review guidelines to help each other notice areas of excellence and also to improve compositions that need work. Writing does not have to be a lonely craft.

Most of the time spent writing should involve the predrafting and postdrafting stages. Writing becomes successful by revision (from the Latin word *revisere* meaning "to look back"). Rethinking the content to discover the most effective ideas for the audience and purpose, reforming the sentences to achieve the most exact phrasing to express the desired meaning, using the most appropriate word for the audience and the purpose: this attention to detail creates successful writing. Gathering second opinions from others helps reveal details that need attention. Remember that writing is a form of communication: what seems clear to you may not be clear to others, so use other writers to help you evaluate your writing. Published writers have editors who suggest changes, and they value their editors' suggestions, so why shouldn't you?

When to Gather Peer Reviews

Peer reviews can help you at all stages of the writing process.

- If you are having trouble picking a subject, talk about the pros and cons of your possible choices and get feedback from peers.
- After you have picked a subject, let peers suggest additional sources of information on your subject or more ways to subdivide the subject and analyze it.
- As you discover content, you will probably need to focus your subject, talk about pros and cons of possible choices, and get feedback from peers.
- Peers can help you think about your audience and make your thesis more precise.
- After you have gathered content or written a draft, peers can evaluate whether the content is appropriate for the subject, audience, and thesis.
- Peers can offer suggestions for content and organization revisions as you draft and revise your essay.
- Peers can point out awkward sentences, word choices, and problems with grammar and stylistic conventions.

Preparing for Peer Reviews

- If you have any questions about your draft, write them at the top of the page as specifically as possible for the peer reviewer to see. ("Does paragraph 4 need more detail?" "Does the introduction signal to the reader what the essay is about?" "Am I being too strong in my argument and chasing readers away?") You can also ask specific questions in the draft. ("Is this the right word?" "Do I need transitions between these paragraphs?" "Do you understand what I am saying here?")
- Encourage your readers to be tough on you — and let them know that you will also be truthful concerning their writing.
- Remember that the essay isn't finished yet, and the peer reviewer knows it isn't finished yet, so the peer reviewer is expecting that there will still be problems with the essay.

How to Peer Review

- Ask for the context card, identifying the focused subject, intended audience, writing situation, thesis and tone. You need to know *exactly* whom the writer is writing to and *specifically* what the writer is trying to say before you can evaluate the essay. If the writing is an early draft and the writer is not yet sure of the context elements, focus your peer review comments on helping him or her find subject, audience, situation, purpose, and tone. If the writer has identified these elements of context, read the essay with audience and thesis in mind; in fact, *become* the audience to better evaluate the content and organization.
- Use the guidelines on the inner front and back covers of *Writing Successfully* to guide your peer review.

- If the writer is still struggling with context, it is too early to comment specifically on content.
- If the writer has identified the context, comment on content and organization, but do not attend to details concerning sentence style, word choice, punctuation, grammar, and spelling.
- Peer review for sentence style, word choice, punctuation, grammar, and spelling only after the essay is successful for context, content, and organization.
- When you comment, praise first. Tell the writer something that is being done well before commenting on areas that need improvement.
- Especially when peer reviewing for style and punctuation, reading the essay aloud can help you analyze the flow of the sentences and the punctuation for the essay.

After Your Essay Has Been Peer Reviewed

- Carefully evaluate the comments. Remember, however, the essay you are writing is *your essay*, so do not slavishly follow all the suggestions. Sometimes when a peer reviewer offers a suggestion, he or she is getting a sense that something is not right, but the suggestion for change is wrong. Learn to evaluate your prose so that you find the essential problems underlying the reviewer's suggestion rather than always following the suggestions for change. Realize you are the boss.

The more you help other writers evaluate their writing, and the more conscientiously you study what others have said about your writing and revise accordingly, the better you will become at evaluating your own writing. As your peer review skills develop from helping other writers, you will develop more confidence. Practice brings success, so take whatever opportunities occur to peer review.

When we discussed revision for context earlier, we had a peer review for a student essay on math anxiety, and the peer reviewer had commented that the context was fine. We repeat her comments below for context questions, and add the comments she made for the writer's revisions for content and organization.

A. Is the subject focused (for suggested length)? Can you discuss this subject with the complexity it deserves in the length and time allotted?

> Yes – Math Anxiety, but you even focused to Math 070, the class that most of us who aren't very good at math take to prepare for 109. I like your contrast between your older brother and his anxiety, and yourself who used to be anxious but was taught how to overcome anxiety by the H.S. teacher and that book she gave you.

B. Is there a specific audience and writing situation?

> Math anxiety and steps to overcome it is certainly an interesting and appropriate topic for your audience, us in the class. I need it especially, so I'm a good person to peer review. I CAN see the essay's writing situation as being in the school newspaper.

C. Is there a well-defined, specific thesis?

> Yes – giving some specific steps to overcome math anxiety, a process/process analysis essay.

D. Can you describe the tone appropriate for the genre, audience, and thesis?

> The tone is objective and serious; however, you let us into your subjective fears when you had math anxiety, and this helps the reader relate to your essay.

1. Make a descriptive outline of the draft you are looking at. Does an outline demonstrate there is a logical flow of ideas in the essay? Using the outline, examine for any important ideas/evidence missing.

> The only thing missing in this excellent draft is that you need many more specifics of <u>exactly how</u> to overcome anxiety. You describe how you used to be (which we relate to), you describe how it is now, but give us more on the ins and outs of overcoming the anxiety.

2. Does the draft discuss only content for purpose and audience (no straying off on tangents)? Does the draft have enough content for the audience? Does it have content the audience does not need to understand your thesis?

> See note above.

3. Does the draft use a tone proper for the purpose and audience?

> Tone appropriate. I especially like the way you personalize the anxiety makes us as readers feel like you are one of us (which you were).

4. Does the draft make the point (with specific evidence) that the thesis says it will? Does it achieve this specific purpose?

> After you provide more details (I'd keep the same informal, talkative "one of us" tone), the essay should achieve its purpose.

Throughout, this peer reviewer discusses specifics about the draft she read, and discusses good points as she points out the first large problem that should be addressed (a single major suggestion for more detail). When you peer review in class, model your peer reviews after the ones demonstrated in this chapter.

Students might say, "I'm only a student, how can I comment on another student's work?" This practice not only makes you a better reviewer of your own work, but it also allows you to see how an audience reacts to YOUR work. This helps you revise.

5

Third Draft: Revising Paragraphs

and Precise Word Use

Here is one of the big "secrets," one of the most important tools for turning great ideas into great essays (essays that *prove* your essay has a valid thesis): what essays usually lack after your context has been finalized and your overall content and organization proves the essay's point is enough SPECIFIC, DETAILED EVIDENCE AND ANALYSIS to support ALL the sub-points of your paragraphs. So, for excellent writing that supports great ideas, do a second round of content revision. You do this by revising at the paragraph level and for precise word use (precise diction creates specific content). Each paragraph contains one sub-idea of an entire essay, right? After you have completed your revision for context and overall content and organization, look at each individual paragraph, decide what the main point of that paragraph is (we will call this the *topic sentence*) and then make sure you have ALL the content necessary — *complete paragraphs* — to prove the point of that paragraph, and then revise the organization, the *order* of evidence and support in each paragraph. This attention to detail helps turn great ideas into excellent writing.

This chapter looks at the individual paragraphs as microcosms within the whole essay. Just as the entire essay is centered around a thesis statement (its purpose), has adequate content for the thesis, and has developed a suitable organizational strategy, each paragraph should also contain these features. To differentiate discussions of components of the overall essay from discussions of individual paragraphs, we will refer to paragraph features by different names. The major areas to revise at the paragraph level (with their complements in the essay) are:

Terms for Essay	**Terms for Paragraph Discussion**
Thesis Statement	**Unity**

A paragraph should be unified by one controlling idea (*a topic, or implied topic, sentence*), just as the entire essay has a purpose, a controlling thesis.

Content	**Completeness**

A paragraph should have enough information to support and explain its topic sentence.

Organization	**Order**

A paragraph's content should be arranged in a suitable, logical pattern.

As you read this chapter, study the unity, completeness, and order of the example paragraphs, and their precise and specific use of words. Then revise the paragraphs of the essay you are working on for unity, completeness, order, and precise diction.

Topic Sentences

Paragraphs are groups of sentences that center around one main idea, and just as the entire essay has a purpose, each paragraph should also have a distinct purpose, one sub-point that helps the overall thesis. To assure that each paragraph has a controlling topic and purpose, construct a *topic sentence* (or sentences) describing this subject and purpose for each paragraph.

To help you understand this concept, the topic sentences are underlined in example paragraphs A-F. (Unless the topic sentence is implied. Implied topic sentences are discussed next.)

EXERCISE 5.1

Analyzing Topic Sentences and Support
With examples A through F in this chapter, examine the relationship between the topic sentence and the paragraph's content — all content should discuss and explain the specific topic. For a class discussion, pick one paragraph that achieves adequate content for its topic particularly well and one paragraph that could use additional content. Write a short rationale for your choices with specific details to support these choices.

Example A

Examine each sentence and each idea in this paragraph. They all add to the main idea, the viewpoint expressed, in the topic sentence.

> Let the good times roll! When the levees broke, my church loaded up a bus full of construction workers and teens and headed for "Nawlins." We worked our tails off all day every day. But we have a pretty cool church and pastor, and at night the workers went out to have a drink of cold beer. That's how I know there's always going to be a New Orleans, and it is always going to be the coolest city in America. It will always recover: We got there the day after the flood, and the French Quarter was already open for business. A local cop said, "how we going to keep the clean-up crews happy if we don't have the Quarter open? *Laissez le bon temp roule.*" While the men had a beer, the teens roamed the quarter. I have never seen happier, or more bizarrely dressed and acting, citizens who knew that their beloved town was coming back. It was the very best weekend of my life. I will be back. I HAVE to experience a Mardi Gras. If what I saw is what New Orleans does when it has suffered an unparalleled disaster, the Mardi Gras must be ... well, I can't wait. Indeed, let the good times roll.

Implied Topic Sentences

The topic sentence, though, does not *have* to be included in the paragraph; in fact, many successful paragraphs have *implied topic sentences*. You should be able to read a paragraph and say that it has *one central, controlling idea, a point-of-view or purpose all its content points toward.* This is the topic sentence, whether the sentence is actually written in the paragraph or implied by the cumulative effect of the paragraph's content.

Example B

What is the implied topic sentence of this paragraph?

> Mary always liked working with her hands. This made her seem weird to both guys and girls, but she wasn't about to quit something she loved. In middle school she always puttered around with old computers, becoming pretty talented at finding malfunctioning parts and putting replacements in. She liked the precision work she performed with a small soldering pen. She mostly outgrew that and moved on to "girly things," but she was still more apt to be helping her uncle work on cars on Saturday afternoons than be at the Mall. She began college at eighteen - just like good students were supposed to do. Two years later, passing but hating every minute of it, she did what all school counselors should do for their students, let them look through qualifications, schooling, pay scales, and job outlook for ALL jobs, not just those requiring a college degree. While Mary is still getting a degree - a 2 not a 4 year degree - she is taking the robotics courses needed for a job starting at 40 to 50K, in much demand, where she gets to spend the days working with her hands.

Doesn't this specific narrative example have all the content necessary to make a specific point? This content has the cumulative effect of suggesting this implied topic sentence: High school guidance counselors should direct students toward their aptitudes, and many jobs that don't require college, or at least not a 4 year degree, would better serve many teenagers.

To summarize, paragraphs don't always have a topic sentence written directly in them, but *all successful paragraphs* have a single idea, whether it be expressed directly in the paragraph (a topic sentence or sentences) or indirectly, a single idea that controls their content (an implied topic sentence or sentences).

Paragraph Unity

The surest method for assuring unity within individual paragraphs is to have a clear topic sentence for each paragraph. If a paragraph doesn't have a topic sentence, decide what the paragraph's controlling idea is, write an implied topic sentence in the margin of the draft, and then check every sentence to make sure it contributes to the purpose and viewpoint of the topic sentence. A sentence or group of sentences in a paragraph may be related to the overall thesis of the paper, but if they are not related to the controlling idea of the paragraph remove them. What do you do with them?

If they more clearly belong to an idea in another paragraph, put them in that paragraph. If they do not clearly relate to another paragraph, make a decision: If the idea of the sentence(s) seems essential for the thesis of the essay, make a new paragraph, deciding on its place in the overall organizational scheme of the essay and *adding more information* if necessary. On the other hand, the idea could be a very good idea, but if it is not *essential* for the thesis of the essay, then it should be deleted. Good writing is always tightly focused around fully developed ideas, not a collection of many "exciting" ideas not fully developed.

Example C

Examine how this writer chooses to remove two ideas concerning the actor and director. This paragraph focuses on the main character's revenge, so they don't belong; however, she created new paragraphs and developed them at length.

> Max Cady, in *Cape Fear* (the 1993 movie), spent fourteen years in prison planning revenge against his attorney. Played in the movie by Robert DeNiro, this psychotic maniac served his prison term for the rape of a teenage girl. While incarcerated, Cady, who during the trial we imagine was an uneducated "country bumpkin," zealously studied law books and the *Bible*, all the while planning revenge on his attorney, played by Nick Nolte. (This psychotic role of DeNiro's fits in a long line of madman roles) he has played in his film career. (Many of the films were, like *Cape Fear*, directed by Martin Scorcese.) Cady's plan of revenge includes terrorizing Bowden (Nolte), his wife, and his teenage daughter, played respectively by Jessica Lange and Juliette Lewis.
> **(Create 2 new paragraphs - DeNiro's madmen and relation to Scorcese - and add more details on Cady's revenge in this para.)**

Many times you will also find that two or three paragraphs can be combined — that they actually have a unified central idea. If the topics are clearly related, combine the paragraphs. The example that follows illustrates two related paragraphs that should probably be combined. Although the first group of sentences below discuss Cady's indestructibility and the second group discusses his religious fanaticism, most writers would combine these two paragraphs because they both discuss the Cady character. If, however, one or both of these were elaborated on at much greater length (two to three times as much detail and analysis), then the paragraphs would remain separate.

Example D

> The main flaw in Robert DeNiro's character is that he appears indestructible, quite unbelievably I might add. He wards off three thugs wielding tire irons and bicycle chains, allows a flare to melt over his hand, and survives being doused with lighter fluid and set on fire. Reviewer Scott McKain states: "DeNiro should play Superman," implying that that is what his character reminds you of. I agree completely. **Combine with next paragraph to show connections between Cady's indestructibility and religious fanaticism, and discuss connection.**

DeNiro's character places great emphasis on the religious aspect of his revenge. He intends to make Nolte suffer so that he can be redeemed and go to heaven. This religious aspect was not included in the 1962 version of *Cape Fear*. It was added by director Martin Scorcese and writer Wesley Strick to "pump up Cady's role as an angel of death" (Travers 101). **But it is just this religious fanaticism that creates the indestructible, though totally evil, insane man. He had spent too much time in the eye of the devil, and he has become one. Cady burns with the fury of a hell and brimstone preacher.**

Notice in the note the student commented that she realized there was a connection between the ideas of the paragraphs she combined into one, and she wouldn't have realized this without studying the unity and completeness of each individual paragraph.

Example E

Not all topic sentences begin a paragraph. Examine the following paragraph, "America's Fascination with the Automobile." If we took off the last sentence (the topic sentence), wouldn't the paragraph still be unified? Wouldn't we, if asked, write an implied topic sentence for the paragraph much like the one ending the paragraph?

Everybody wants a Ferrari, a Corvette, a high speed sports car, but why? We want so much to look good in front of our friends. We want to be able to say, "I am so proud of my car. Isn't it wonderful? Don't you wish you had a car like that?" We want so much for our friends to notice us and think that we are "cool." It can ruin our lives. It can become dangerous because some people are willing to spend their entire life savings on a car that can very well cost more than two years worth of family income. People can live in a ramshackle house and have barely enough money to eat, but you wouldn't know it because they have a car they look good in driving to and from work. Most of us aren't nearly as foolish, so since we can not or will not buy a Porsche or Ferrari we settle for a Ford. Buying an expensive car for its looks, performance, style, and quality is one thing, if you can afford it, but buying it just for "bragging rights" is another.

All ideas in the paragraph are unified around its central idea. The paragraph makes an opening general statement that appeals to the audience to identify with it: "*Everybody* wants a Ferrari . . ." It uses invented dialogue and example to develop the opening statement and then argues for the foolishness of the many who spend too much on expensive cars. The writer ends the paragraph by "dividing" his audience into those who spend too much and those who buy cars suitable for their economic conditions. The final forceful sentence uses jargon ("bragging rights") to reinforce his conclusion analyzing the rationale for buying cars that cost too much.

Notice that the topic sentence appeared in the middle of paragraph A, was implied in paragraph B, began paragraph C, appeared near the end of D and at the end of E. The placement of the topic sentence is determined by the effect you want to achieve. The New Orleans paragraph needs to start with the situation. The writer of the career placement paragraph wants her readers to discover for themselves what they need to do personally with their own situations, so she leaves the main idea implied. As readers discover the implied topic sentence, this will make them look at their own experiences. The author of paragraph C uses a statement ("Max Cady is a psychotic maniac") followed by support. In D, the writer in revision saw the connection between the two paragraphs, which led her to discover a topic sentence that joins the ideas of the old paragraphs. The content on sports car fascination implies and supports the topic sentence throughout the paragraph, but he states it firmly at the end for effect. The choice of placement for topic sentences is yours and it is based on your rationale for the paragraph, but all paragraphs must be unified around a central idea. *Concern for details like this guarantees successful writing.*

Completeness and Precise Word Use

While checking for paragraph unity, make sure that there are enough evidence, examples, and details to thoroughly illustrate the viewpoint of the topic sentence. Have you ever written and revised an essay, until you are sure of your thesis, audience, and content, but you keep reading over the essay thinking, "it just feels like something is missing"? Usually, what is missing is not any more sub-ideas, but specific evidence and illustrations to support each of those sub-ideas.

Do a paragraph revision check for the essay after you have satisfied the checklist questions for context and overall content and organization. Reminding yourself of the overall purpose for the entire essay, look at how the topic sentence and content for each paragraph fit into the overall plan. Will your intended audience want or need any more content - evidence, examples, illustrations - in any of the paragraphs? Ask this one paragraph at a time. Add content as needed. We just looked at three paragraphs that had enough content to support their topic sentences (Paragraphs A, B, and E). In paragraphs C and D, the writer, as she made decisions about paragraph unity, decided at the same time where she needed more content in the paragraphs.

At the same time you are revising the paragraphs, check for use of precise, specific words. Vague words create vague content. Many times you make a paragraph's content thorough enough just by eliminating vague words, so edit for specific words to help with paragraph completeness.

Paragraph Completeness

Fully develop the controlling idea, the topic of the paragraph, with persuasive evidence. Notice how adding just a few specific details and rearranging ideas adds so much to this paragraph: in this case, the writer is using a narrative to make a point, so the first addition - the lines to the song - bring the reader into the bus. The sentence she added is the topic sentence she developed after looking at her rough draft.

Example F

When I was a little girl, my mother ~~was~~ [**drove**] a bus ~~driver~~.
She always took me with her wherever she went. Even though I was

94

only four years old, I still remember joining in with everyone on the bus singing "Rocky Top." **"Rocky Top, you'll always mean, home sweet home to me, Ro ro Rocky Top - Rocky Top Tennessee."** It was the only country music I ever knew, that is, until a couple of years ago**. (TO END -** For years ~~people~~ [**Americans**] have been tapping their feet to country music. I had once thought that country music was for old people who sat around and drank beer while listening to it. Boy, was I wrong! **)** Now as an eighteen-year-old, after several years listening to pop and a stint enjoying metal, country music is the only style of music I listen to. **Don't get me wrong:** <u>**there is nothing wrong with Bruno Mars or Nine Inch Nails, or even Aerosmith or Metallica, but put them up against the excellent singing, musicianship, and lyrics of a Kelly Clarkson, a Trisha Yearwood, or a K.D. Laing, and there isn't any comparison**</u>.

Eliminating Ambiguity by Choosing Specific Words

Your writing will improve immensely if you begin to look at your writing for general, vague words — words that are so general they render your meaning imprecise and non-descriptive. Replace these words for precision and concreteness. In all writing situations, try to be as specific as possible with your choice of words.

Adolph Hitler was born in Europe.

Europe is a very general word that encompasses many countries. Pinpointing the country gives the reader more specific information:

Edited: Adolph Hitler was born in Austria.

Mrs. Goodwin is very old.

Could the writer and reader have different definitions of old? Use more specific words:

Edited: Mrs. Goodwin is seventy-two years old.

Eliminate vagueness.

The class read a Shakespearean play.

Edited: The class read *As You Like It*.

Or if the audience is not familiar with Shakespeare's plays:

Edited: The class read Shakespeare's *As You Like It*.

95

Her mother has an incurable disease.

Edited: Her mother has terminal cancer.

Concrete and Abstract Words

Concrete words refer to things perceived by the senses — sight, sound, smell, taste, touch. Abstract words refer to qualities such as values and feelings (joy, anger). Concrete diction is preferable in most writing situations.

Mr. Johnson was *angry* when the truck hit his car.

Be descriptive. Use concrete images.

Edited: Mr. Johnson slammed the car door shut and began screaming at the driver of the truck that hit his car.

John weighed much more than his brother, Bill.

Much more denotes a relative difference that is vague. How much more?

Edited: John looked like the middle linebacker that he was, while his brother, Bill, was a tall, thin, long-distance runner.

The revision not only lets the reader visualize the size difference, but also gives the reader more specific information about the two brothers.

Words that describe a writer's feelings toward a person, place, or thing are often abstract.

Jimmy was funny.

Edited: Jim tells jokes constantly, ones that leave a person rolling on the floor in laughter.

Watch for vague, abstract words and edit for specific, concrete diction:

Vague adjectives that denote
a positive evaluation - *cute, fantastic, fine, glamorous, gorgeous, lovely, marvelous, neat, nice, pretty, terrific, wonderful*
or emotion - *happy, glad, interested, joyful, excited*

Always decide how you can *show* this positive quality rather than telling us the vague adjective.

I had a *terrific* meeting with my new boss. [You could fill in most of those words here.]

96

Edited: After all my hard work, the new head of the department praised me and gave me an assignment my superiors usually do. Am I being groomed for a raise?

Not only do we know exactly what happened that is so *terrific*, but *boss* has been edited to the more specific *new head of the department*.

That painting is the most *gorgeous* art I have ever seen. [You could fill in most of the other vague words instead of *gorgeous*.]

Edited: Van Gogh's *Starry Night* has some blurring of the lines that fascinates me because it seems that this is what the universe does: it blurs how we perceive it. I have never seen a work of art before that takes me to the edge of the universe and leaves me to think.

This writer has also replaced the vague g*orgeous* (what gorgeous means to one person is different than what it means to another) with specific details so that we think as we read his sentences "this writer thinks *Starry Night* is gorgeous," but at the same time we know exactly why the writer thinks that. He also, of course, replaced the *that painting* with the specific title of Van Gogh's masterpiece.

Vague adjectives that denote
a negative evaluation - awful, peculiar, terrible, weird, ugly
or emotion - sad, angry, mad, confused, bored, unhappy

Show us, don't tell us with a vague word!

That was the most *peculiar* date I ever had.

Edited: I barely knew Lindsey when I asked her out on a date, and when I got to her dorm first she wanted us to play with her guinea pig for an hour, then we went to Cameron's to eat, but after she ordered she decided she didn't want to eat. Finally, we went to a Sigma Chi party, and she wouldn't get off my arm. Needless to say, we won't be repeating that one.

After the funeral, I was *sad*.

Edited: After the funeral, I wanted to run away and cry.

Five of the most overused vague words - stay away from them - good, great, best, bad, worst

That was the *best* game I ever saw.

How is anyone supposed to know what criteria the writer used to call the game the *best*? And this sentence doesn't even state what kind of game it is.

97

Edited: I have never seen a closer basketball game than when State played its rival. The score went back and forth seven times, and it went into double overtime. Both teams had never played with the intensity and skills they played with that night.

The three most overused vague words in the English language -
thing, a lot, society

There are so many *things* that teens who don't ever read books are missing.

Edited: When teens don't read, they don't become knowledgeable in the history of humanity and they miss the beauty that comes from a well written passage or book.

Be specific in your writing. How much is "a lot"? How is the person, place, or thing "good," "great," or "bad"? Give your reader meaningful details with concrete, descriptive words.

EXERCISE 5.2
Editing for Precise Word Use

Edit this passage- Answers will vary:

All the great movie heroes have a beautiful way of expressing themselves. I have been watching movies for a long time and really like them a lot. I get excited watching some of them over and over. Some of the things they do amaze me. When I want to have a good time I just lean over to the box and turn it on. What a way to spend some time! It is better than just about anything else I do. Come on over and you can watch them too.

Paragraph Order

Paragraphs should each have a logical, overall organizational pattern, just as the entire essay does. For each paragraph in your essay, both as you plan and revise it, decide on a logical pattern for the order of ideas in the paragraph. *Writing Successfully* describes logical patterns for narration/description, example/illustration, comparison/ contrast, classification/division, process/process analysis, causal analysis, definition, question/answer, problem/solution, and statement/support in chapter three (pp. 48-62), and patterns for induction and deduction in chapter eleven. There is not one right order for a paragraph you are revising; there are many successful, logical orders and many wrong, illogical orders. Your job is to revise unclear organizational patterns until you do find any successful order for each paragraph.

Read the first and then the edited draft of this paragraph. Examine this writer's revisions for a more logical order, as well as some edits for precise word use:

I used to smoke ~~a lot of~~ pot **several times a day**. After ~~awhile~~ **two years**, I began taking pills. I became so drug addled that I almost failed ~~school~~ **high school** and the state took away my driver's license. **(** ~~Pot~~ **Marijuana** makes ~~you~~ **users** absolutely unable to read anything and remember it. And all ~~you~~ **smokers** want to do is watch TV, play video games, and eat junk. **)** Drugs are even worse. I spent all my time trying to find money to buy drugs, and when I wasn't doing that I was trying to find drugs. Life became a miserable insanity. I'm sure glad I decided I had to quit if I wanted a life. **(** Many of my friends are still stuck in ~~a~~ **the drug** rut. **)** I have gone on to college, and I assure you all users and experimenters that I still have a life, I'm playing sports again, and I am preparing for an adult career. Life has never been better.

Edited: I used to smoke pot several times a day. Marijuana makes users absolutely unable to read anything and remember it, and all smokers want to do is watch TV, play video games, and eat junk. After two years, I began taking pills, becoming so drug addled that I almost failed high school and the state took away my driver's license. Drugs are even worse: I spent all my time trying to find money to buy drugs, and when I wasn't doing that I was trying to find drugs. Life became a miserable insanity. Many of my friends are still stuck in the drug rut, so I'm sure glad I decided I had to quit if I wanted a life. I have gone on to college, and I assure all users and experimenters that I still have a life, I'm playing sports again, and I am preparing for an adult career. Life has never been better.

Two re-arrangements of sentences and a couple of words edited for specificity make all the difference in this paragraph, changing it from a paragraph that makes a valid point with evidence to one that also makes the point with the same evidence, but also with more logical organization. Readers crave order for ideas, so practicing revision for paragraph order (organization) turns good ideas into more fluent writing understood much better.

EXERCISE 5.3
Unity, Completeness, and Order

1) Underline the topic sentence or sentences in each of the paragraphs of the writing you are working on now. If the paragraph's purpose is implied, write an implied topic sentence in the margin of your draft, and underline the implied topic sentence.
2) Decide if the paragraphs are unified and if any paragraphs should be combined or separated.
3) Then analyze each paragraph for completeness. Is there enough information to support the topic sentence? There should be evidence and illustrations for every idea in each paragraph. Are any words so vague that the reader does not know exactly what your content is saying? Edit all words in each paragraph so they are precise and specific, and add content until the paragraph is complete.
4) Examine the order of ideas and evidence in the paragraph. Does it have a logical order? If not, revise. Remember that there are often-used organizational patterns for most rhetorical patterns (pp.48-62).

Introductions

Introductions can be short or long. A shorter piece of writing might use one sentence at the beginning of the first paragraph; a longer piece of writing might use two or more paragraphs. A book can have an entire introductory chapter, though there will be introductory paragraphs at the beginning of each chapter. But short or long, introductions must do two things: *they must interest the reader enough to spur continued reading, and they must give some sense of the writer's subject.* They also usually suggest the order of the main ideas. For college essays you might say, "The professors have to read my essay; I don't have to interest them." You don't. But they will grade your essay, and if you haven't interested them, and interested them from the beginning, your grade will suffer. So sometimes introductions employ a "hook" to entice the reader, though writers of scholarly prose for classes other than freshman composition courses (where teachers often encourage a variety of styles) generally don't try to flamboyantly hook their audiences.

Introductions (and conclusions also) are often the last segments of an essay to be written. Why? If an introduction "introduces" the rest of the essay, it makes sense to write and revise the essay until it is practically finished before you can introduce what it is going to say. Conclusions signal that an essay is finished. You have to know in your mind as you re-read your essay that it is, in fact, practically finished, before you can write a conclusion. This should be a big relief in your concerns over composing style! Many writers, foolishly, spend hours and days trying to get "started right" by writing the perfect introduction. Introductions usually aren't composed before the essay's content is complete, unless the writer knows *specifically* what he or she is going to say before starting. *So, in practice, if you stare at a blank page trying to start the introduction for more than twenty minutes, decide what the first major supporting idea is going to be (or have it ready with a scratch outline) and just start with the first paragraph after the not-yet-written introduction.* You can go back later, after you've written and revised the essay, and write an introduction. Don't let writer's block stall you!

After you have developed your ideas thoroughly throughout an academic essay, and have completed revisions for your essay, in the introduction you should simply:

- *Give your audience a sense of the subject* (what you are going to explore in your essay) *and some sense of the overall purpose and organization* of your essay, so they can know what to expect as they read.

Sometimes, the subject itself is enough to interest a reader; at other times, a "hook" must be used to keep your reader reading. Popular magazines often employ "hooks." A "hook" can be

- *A question* posed to arouse interest or to provoke the reader to answer it.
- *A curiosity provoking statement* that challenges the reader's imagination.
- *An especially dramatic example* to entice the reader to keep reading.

is flying a drone near the village and he gets the order. A minute later twelve civilians - three shopkeepers, four retired men playing chess, two mothers, and three children - and four Al Qaeda terrorists have been killed. Do you think the people of that village, the families of those killed, look kindly on Americans? Are we saving them from terrorism?

According to sketchy reports, drones have killed 3000 civilians in the last twelve years of the war. That's 3000 X however many relatives those civilians had who probably now hate the United States. . . .

A dramatic example is another method of bringing your reader immediately into caring about your subject. This one grabs the reader immediately, and then at the end of the paragraph asks a question based on the example (though not all dramatic example openings end with a question).

So remember that readers should be interested in your writing from the first sentence. Write and rewrite until you discover a strategy for your essay's introduction to assure the audience that they are not going to be bored to tears.

Conclusions

Much damage has been done to inexperienced writers by the insistence that conclusions should summarize what has already been written in an essay. For longer writing, a summary can sometimes be useful as the reader has confronted a lot of material; however, for essays shorter than twenty pages a summary is usually unnecessary. Your audience's memory span is not that short; do not offend their intelligence with a summary. So what does a conclusion do? A conclusion needs to create a sense of finality, of closure. All audiences need to feel a sense of order, of organization, as they read a piece of writing. The introduction signals to the reader that the writing will be about _____ and that certain ideas concerning _____ will be discussed; the body of the essay should thoroughly consider the expectations forecast by the introduction; and the conclusion should signal to the reader that the writer has finished, has said what needs to be said to get a point across.

Several strategies (which are usually combined) for planning conclusions include:

- *Leave the reader thinking* by using a question, a recommendation, or a projection of the writing subject into a larger context or into the future.
- *Give a sense of closure*, by restating the thesis more dramatically after it has been discussed fully in the body of the essay.
- *Present the end of an argument or investigation* by arriving at a conclusion to a line of research or a solution to a problem. In some essays, this is the first time the essay's thesis statment occurs, after the evidence has been laid out clearly building to the end of the argument, its point.

Leaving the Reader Thinking

This concluding paragraph, which makes a recommendation and a projection into the future, is excerpted from Lisa Benningfield's essay analyzing rude customers:

I really hate to sound off, but it's all plain and simple. It basically boils down to this: My job is to serve customers, not to receive verbal outbursts of anger from them. It is not in my job description, nor do I get paid enough, to take that kind of abuse. I can understand their anger and frustration, but there are many things that occur in my job beyond my control. Whoever reads this paper, I'd like to say this to them: the next time you want to blow up in a clerk's face because something is out of stock or not working right, think about how unnecessary anger and rudeness are. If this paper accomplishes what I meant it to, you will remember that employees are only people too, and we have feelings just like everyone else.

A Sense of Closure

Jarad Pennington's essay, while it discusses the two sides in the global warming debate, focuses on how public predispositions rather than evidence create views. He restates the reasons for the debate and calls for action on the part of the public, a change in how we study, to signal he has said what he needs to say.

> After identifying the underlying reasons for the continued debate on Global Warming (a lack of in-depth knowledge; highly politicized and pre-dispositioned views held by scientists, politicians, and the public; an incredible wealth of knowledge with an equal amount of misinformation; and the confidence-shaking data manipulation by climate scientists in 2009), we, as individuals, must recognize our own habits to absorb information which reinforce our pre-dispositions concerning often politicized subjects. As long as media, scientists, and politicians continue to be politically influenced and unable to take an objective stance (the proper role of politicans and scientists), public understanding of Global Warming shall continue to erratically shift and the debate shall continue. Therefore, nature and human society need each of us to set our predispositions aside and to adopt a neutral stance to allow for an effective evaluation of human industry on Global Warming. Those unable to do so shall arrive at a pre-formed conclusion before any scientific data has been given the opportunity to affect change and enlighten the public.

The End of an Argument or Investigation

Amanda Stevens-Hensley investigates reality television with an in-depth analysis of specific episodes of *Keeping Up With the Kardashians* along with analysis of media coveage of the family. This conclusion signals the end of her investigation/argument by broadening the discussion out to reality television in general.

> Margaret Haggerty explains that Americans say they really, really don't like the influence reality television has on our culture (4). Even disliking it, they keep watching, the shows becoming more and more popular. Jennifer L. Pozner asks what it means to be an American in the twenty-first century. According to her, reality television envisions women as catty bitches, stupid bimbos, and greedy gold diggers whose worth can only be measured by their physical measurements. Straight, single gals are pathetic losers and, we're led

to believe, it's hilarious when they get mocked, dumped or punched in the face. Black and Latina women are violent, "low class" and "ghetto," while men of color are buffoons, thugs and criminals (11). We know that reality programs stereotype and we still choose to engage in them. We, as Americans, continue the stereotypes by agreeing that the way they portray us is ok, that's how the rest of us are. Are all Americans just uneducated, trashy, violent people with a lack of self-respect and dignity? We who watch the reality programs are part of the problem. It's not ok that our youth are growing up aspiring to be trashy, foul mouthed, binge drinking, sex-crazed reality stars. Our children need to know that hard work and education is what they need to aspire to. Also, we don't want the rest of the world to see we are choosing to make these people famous for their crude behavior, nor do we want them to think we are anything like our current form of entertainment. Reality television is ruining pop culture. The next time you turn on your TV and begin to watch a reality show, remember most real everyday normal people do not behave as they do, and that when you choose to watch you are sending a message saying that's how Americans act. Without viewers, these shows would not exist.

EXERCISE 5.4
Writing Introductions and Conclusions

Compose two introductions and two conclusions for the essay you are working on now. Use techniques as described above, or create your own. Introductions introduce what a writer will discuss and conclusions signal that a writer has said what needs to be said.

Student Example: Paragraph Revision

The remainder of this chapter will show the peer review comments Rob Watson received from a fellow student on his "Utopian Facade" essay, after he had completed a second draft refining his overall context and content. The draft he completed after this peer review when he revised at the paragraph and word level follows.

Context Card
Subject: Utopias
Audience: College Students
Writing Situation: a textual analysis in a blog that discusses the future
Thesis: Utopian society may be the ultimate goal to which civilization aspires to ascend, but in evaluating the media that entertains this grand idea, it is an impossible goal.
Tone: objective, studious, fairly formal for a blog

Checklist Questions
WRITING CONTEXT
A) Is there a focused subject?
Yes, and interesting too.

B) Is there a well-defined thesis and writing situation?

I could see this essay in any of a number of blogs. I think that anyone interested in gaming would probably like this essay, as well as any college students in a class looking into the future.

C) Is there a well-defined, specific thesis?
The thesis statement on the context card is a precise summary of the main point you are making in the essay. Good job.

D) Is the tone appropriate for your audience and writing situation?
Your tone is fairly formal for most blogs, at least blogs frequented by college students, but the tone matches your thesis and i think you COULD see a studious article like this one in some blogs.

CONTENT AND ORGANIZATION
1. Make a descriptive outline of the draft you are looking at. Does an outline demonstrate there is a logical flow of ideas in the essay? Using the outline, examine for any important ideas/evidence missing.
Looking at the descriptive outline you created when you revised your essay, I think you generally have the main points down, and the ideas flow in a logical order, but there could be much more detail in some of the paragraphs (which I know you haven't revised for yet).

2. Does the draft discuss only content necessary for thesis and audience (no straying off on tangents)? Does the draft have enough content for the audience? Does it have content the audience does not need to understand your thesis?
In a first reading, I thought you discussed too many movies. On a second reading I think they all fit and if anything you could have more detail and analysis - how these movies' plots and themes fit into YOUR argument. (I would say this is paragraph completeness additions; overall, your content fits your thesis.)

3. Does the draft use a tone proper for the purpose and audience?
Yes - your objective, studious tone fits your argument well,

4. Does the draft make the point (with specific evidence) that the thesis says it will? Does it achieve this specific purpose?
In general, the essay achieves its purpose. It could have more detailed illustration and analysis at the paragraph level.

PARAGRAPH REVISION
5. Is there an effective introduction to the essay? (Does the reader have a sense of the essay's subject, and in many cases also a sense of the order of ideas.)
Intro overall good: opening with a cartoon rather than a movie or book shows how persuasive the utopian theme is in western society.

Re-reading the essay, stop at the end of EACH paragraph, decide on its topic sentence (whether written in the paragraph or implied), and answer the next two questions:

6. Is the Paragraph unified? (Decide whether paragraphs that are separate should be combined because they have one subject and whether any need to be split into two paragraphs.) Is the paragraph complete? (Each paragraph's idea should have adequate support. It should discuss the sub-topic of that paragraph COMPLETELY with thorough evidence, illustrations, and analysis.) For completeness, check each word for precise, specific word use.

Unity O.K.
Paragraph 3 good beginning, but analyze Plato's utopia more thoroughly - I mean come on, it is based on slavery!!!!
Paragraph 5 Needs more!!! a more thorough analysis of the "nothing in life is free."
Para 6 - cut - need info on slavery?

7. Does each paragraph have a logical order for its ideas and evidence? Are logical rhetorical patterns used and organized appropriately?

Paragraphs all seem to have a good logical order.

8. Is there an effective conclusion to the essay? (Writer has suggested in some fashion that the purpose of the essay has been achieved.)

OK Conclusion – I'd try another one though.

The first draft of this essay appears on pp. 59-62. Notice Rob took most suggestions, but also combined some paragraphs.

Rob Watson
English 102
Revised Draft

The Utopian Facade

George Jetson lived a life to be desired. Each day, he wakes up to a machine that brushes his teeth, washes, shaves, and dresses him, and to a robot that makes him breakfast. His job at Spacely Sprockets consists of nothing more than pushing one button an hour, three days a week. High in his spacious home resembling Seattle, Washington's Space Needle, George and his family live a very comfortable life, with little or no work, stress, or problems. It seems that life could not get that much better for George, and the year is in the year 2062. **Combine paragraphs**

In 2012, flying cars will be available for purchase ("Aircraft"), a resort hotel located in low Earth orbit is scheduled to open (Galactic Suite), and a modest $200,000 will take passengers to it (Virgin Galactic). With the rapid advancement in technology, the acceptance of racial equality, and a deeper understanding in the medical field, the future feels closer than ever imagined. Eric Schmidt. CEO of Google, says "we create as much information in two days now as we did from the dawn of man through 2003" (Galactic Suite). Indeed these are amazing feats, but current society needs to leap forward **much further** to reach the status of the Jetson family utopia.

The idea of a utopia, or the ultimate society enriched with equality and supple wealth, had been discussed as early as 380 BC. Illustrated by Plato in his celebrated dialogue, *The Republic*, he describes an imaginary city, Magnesia, where population is controlled to prevent crowding and underworking. In Magnesia, citizens own slaves to perform the trading and manufacturing of the city, along with other humble tasks throughout the

107

city. Lawmakers not only enforce laws, but persuade the lawbreaker what he/she did was illegal and convince citizens of the "correct" beliefs and true principles that they should be following. The location of Magnesia is geographically perfect for fruitful agriculture and productive commerce. Of course there are at least three obvious flaws here: the society is based on slave labor; we know today that humanity being what is, not everyone would or should follow all the laws; and a place with "perfect" farmland and "always" productive industry is a fiction. We can perhaps forgive Plato his use of slaves as this was commonplace throughout the world in the fourth century B.C., and perhaps also his utopian notion of perfectly compliant citizens as he is writing at the dawn of civilization's use of logic and reason, and perhaps he did not have enough information to consider his ideas foolish. The perfect commerce and agriculture is, of course, nothing more than fiction. Nevertheless, Enabling the use of each of these ideas, Magnesia would be a city where no poverty exists and individual labor duties are minimal, allowing all citizens (slaves are not citizens) the opportunity to grow socially and educationally (Bobonich). Let's leave his utopian Magnesia as what it is, in common with all later utopias, a fiction, not a real place. He created with his Magnesia a definition of utopia which really has not changed except in details: an ideal place where problems have been solved, not a real world. The only modification to his utopia, in the last two centuries, has been the use of utopian visions to critique and satirize problems in the world as it really is. Mankind has actually thought it was building utopias at times since Plato created his: America was thought of as the shining "city on a hill," some kind of perfect Christian society, that was at the same time an engine for economic power. The Russian revolutionaries thought they were creating a perfect communist society, later followed by the Chinese after the second world war who dreamed of their own communist utopia..

Children's cartoons are not the only medium today that portrays society as a futuristic paradise. Many adult novels and films feature a similar theme, though it may not appear so without paying close attention. M. Night Shyamalan's *The Village*, released in 2004, featured a small village separate from other civilizations, where crime, famine, and poverty were all but eliminated. A teen novel written in 1993, Lois Lowry's *The Giver*, tells a story about a future where there is no war, disease, famine, poverty, or pain. Fritz Lang's classic 1927 *Metropolis* illustrates (quite literally, as it was a silent film) a city divided into two classes, one of which lives luxuriously with no menial tasks to be performed (or disease, poverty, crime, etc), while the other works to support the extravagant lifestyles of the first class, following Plato. As classic movies and books win awards and fame (Metropolis is regularly listed in 100 best movies of all time lists; The Giver was awarded the prestigious Newberry youth book Award in 1994), more are produced with different plots, characters, and time frames, but the basic utopian fantasy remains the same.

When analyzing a movie or book about utopian society, it is impossible for observers to ignore that each civilization has a specific fault to it - a tragic flaw, thus transforming a utopian society into a truly dystopian society. In *The Village*, the entire town's ignorance of the outside world (and the current year) was the price tag of a life without chaos, famine, or crime. Perhaps it the flaw was very obvious, such as in *Metropolis*, where the enforced labor was the fuel for the upper city's wealth. Recognizable or not, almost every utopian story brings light to a very undesirable price for which the utopia's grandeur exists. The cliché "nothing in life is free" is the lesson learned and is impressed upon present day society's greatest fear for the near future: to enjoy a life full of ecstasy and freedom, a great and terrible payment will be necessary. **Does that mean we shouldn't strive for improvements to our very flawed modern society? No. But perhaps utopian films and literature help keep us vigilant to foresee flaws in forward-thinking ideas.**

Using semiotics, each utopian/dystopian piece can be analyzed to identify different expenses society fears to pay. One of these can be recognized as the fear to regress to a familiar practice of America's recent past: the fear of becoming slaves of the powerful or wealthy in order to fashion a Utopia. ~~In America, Europeans permeated the land and decreased their own personal workload by using both the indigenous people and Africans as slaves doing grueling labor. America was not, of course, the first country to use slavery to promote industry; ancient Egypt, Greece, and Rome all actively uses slaves for agriculture, household chores, as soldiers, and even as sacrifices to appease gods.~~

Combine paragraphs

Although the thirteenth amendment abolished slavery in 1865, the fear of being owned or doing work for someone else's luxurious lifestyle still remains. This was the exact fear represented in *Metropolis*. If this 1920s silent appears dated, this same fear was displayed in the 2005 *The Island*, where humans live in a safely regulated future only to discover they are clones secretly used for organ harvesting by the rich. **This interesting plot development combines the fear of science/genetic engineering run amok with the older slavery as the price to be paid themes**. More recently, *Daybreakers* (2009) features Sam Neill and Ethan Hawke in a utopian world inhabited by vampires, In this story, vampirism is a trait to be desired, as sleep is no longer necessary and disease is eliminated. However, when it seems as if the world is now perfect, viewers discover that the last surviving humans are harvested as a food supply, and the population dwindles.

~~Throughout~~ **For other** utopian novels and movies, scientific advancement plays a major role in the plot. These advances invite another underlying terror in the exultant future: that humanity's scientific constructions to create utopia will ultimately destroy their creators. In Isaac Asimov's adaptation, *I, Robot* (~~2004~~), the world is a less overworked place thanks to the employment of the robot workforce. Daily lives depend on the assistance robots provide, and because they cannot violate their programming, humans are free from the fear of robots gaining power from them. However, a "technophobic" cop discovers that the robots have found a way to overcome their creator's software design and they plot to overthrow the human race. The original story for *I, Robot* was written in 1950, and in 2004 the movie grossed $144,795,350 (*I, Robot* imdb). For a movie based on a sixty year old theme to do as well as it did in the present suggests that people still connect with technophobia today. In *I Am Legend* (2007), Will Smith (again) plays a scientist who discovers a cure for cancer, only to find that it instead created an unstoppable plague that destroys most of humanity. While this future doesn't employ self-aware machines to improve the quality of life, the cure comes from genetic research that scientists today are attempting to gain more control of in the near future. Both movies feature the same theme representing a fear Ted Peters discusses in *Playing God? Genetic Determinism and Human Freedom*, that all scientific achievements of the future are too good to be true and the human race should not "play God."

If utopia isn't created by slave labor nor giant leaps in scientific achievements, than it must be maintained by an omniscient body with absolute control over population, lifestyles, industry, and knowledge. However, the term "control" doesn't normally correspond with society's current liberties such as freedom and choice. To successfully apply this strict nature of administration without igniting revolt, ignorance would have to be the primary tool used. This is featured in *Logan's Run*, where unlimited food, drugs, and sex are at any citizen's disposal, but everyone is taught that at the age of thirty they must perform a specific ritual in order to be reborn. This ritual was a ploy by the city's designers to end life at thirty in order to maintain a manageable population density. This occurs also in *The Giver*, where all careers and family units are prearranged by a council, and the ability to see color is also genetically taken away to eliminate racial distinctions. Chaos, famine, and disease are virtually eliminated in these two stories, but at the cost of having practically no choice in a lifetime for anyone. Perhaps the most celebrated and recognizable dystopian story known today is George Orwell's *1984*. Written in 1949, the term "Big Brother" from this novel is frequently used today in discussions of cell phone and internet privacy. Its plot conveys a "future" of 1984 where the government uses surveillance and mass media manipulation in order to maintain a totalitarian system of government.

Utopian society may be the ultimate goal to which civilization aspires to ascend, but in evaluating the media that entertains this grand idea, it is an impossible goal. Other than in children's cartoons, Utopias are a facade, a dream out of reach, protected by society's fears and morals. Reflecting back to Plato's *Republic*, his ideal city uses all three mentioned practices: slavery, totalitarianism, and scientific advancement, thus becoming not a utopia but a dystopia, one that would be immediately rejected by today's culture. Whether humanity will enjoy a Jetson's-like lifestyle by 2062 remains to be seen. The more interesting question is what it will cost society in their pursuit of perfection

Works Cited

"Aircraft." *Terrafugia*, 2008, www. terrafugia.com/faqs, Accessed 11 Oct. 2011.

Asimov, Isaac. *I, Robot*. Doubleday, 1950.

Bobonich, Chris. "Plato on Utopia." *The Stanford Encyclopedia of Philosophy*, edited by Edward N. Zalta, Stanford UP, 2008, pp. 1429-36.

Daybreakers. Directed and written by Michael and Peter Spierig, performances by William Dafoe and Ethan Hawke, Lionsgate, 2009, DVD.

Galactic Suite. 2011, galacticsuite.com.

I Am Legend. Directed by Francis Lawrence, performance by Will Smith. Warner, 2007, DVD.

"I, Robot." *Internet Movie Database*, www.imbd.com/IRobot.

I, Robot. Directed by Alex Proyas, performances by Will Smith and Bridget Moynahan, Fox, 2004, DVD.

The Island. Directed by Michael Bay, performances by Scarlet Johansson and Ewan McGregor, Dreamworks and Warners, 2005, DVD.

The Jetsons. Directed by William Hanna and Joseph Barbera. Hanna-Barbera, 1962-87, DVD

Logan's Run. Directed by Michael Anderson, performances by Michael York and Jenny Agutter, MGM, 1976, DVD.

Lowry, Lois. *The Giver*. 1993. Laurel Leaf, 2002.

Metroplis. Directed by Fritz Lang, performances by Brigette Helm, Alfred Abel, and Gustav Frohlich, UFA, 1927, DVD.

Peters, Ted. *Playing God? Genetic Determinism and Human Freedom*. Routledge, 1997.

The Village. Directed by M. Night Shyamalan, performances by Sigourney Weaver, William Hurt, and Joaquin Phoenix. Touchstone, 2004.

Virgin Galactic. *Virgin Galactic*. 2009. www.virgingalactic.com.

6

Critical Reading: Summary, Evaluation, and Response

Success in college and in careers demanding a college degree requires a mastery of the following skills:

- to read texts carefully and critically
- to think of questions concerning a subject as you read
- to paraphrase and summarize texts accurately
- to compare, contrast, and synthesize the ideas of several texts
- to think creatively concerning issues discussed in texts

The student who can apply these skills has become a critical reader; moreover, these skills are related and can be learned through practice. We all think critically about situations in our lives and in the world around us, and you can transfer this skill you already know to analyzing written texts. As a matter of fact, you increase your critical thinking ability by learning how to analyze written sources. Close reading skills will arm you with facts and expert opinions, and hone your ability to sift facts from opinions, to distinguish true from false evidence, and to comprehend the nuances of human thought and action. Close reading and careful, critical reading are synonymous – you *closely examine* the text you are reading. This chapter suggests strategies used to read for comprehension and retention, to summarize and paraphrase sources, and to respond to and evaluate sources. These are essential activities for learning *and* for writing essays based on outside sources.

Although taking accurate class notes (in other words, summarizing the lecture) will help you succeed in college, your success also depends on your ability to read accurately *and efficiently*. College professors often assign texts and expect you to understand them without discussing them in class. It is your responsibility to read them closely and analyze them (though most professors will meet with you individually if you need to discuss the readings to understand them).

You need to learn *when* to use particular critical reading skills. For instance, if you know the information in a textbook chapter will be on a test, or you have focused a subject for a research paper and you know the information in an article will be useful for your purpose, use all of the close reading skills explained in this chapter to assimilate the knowledge. If, on the other hand, you are just beginning a research project and you are reading to learn basic information about the subject, then you can usually read more rapidly, skimming through material and taking more general notes. If you are reading the newspaper or magazines for general knowledge about the world or for pleasure, you can read even faster. In other words, you should *determine how you will use what you are reading* and adjust your methods of reading accordingly. But even when you read critically and carefully, which takes more time, you are actually saving time. By taking careful notes and marking important ideas in a text you will be able to review and reread important material with greater ease.

111

Critical Reading: Pre-, As, and Post-Reading Strategies

This section discusses specific processes for critical, analytic reading.

Pre-reading — Before beginning to read a text:

Find out as much about a text as you can before you start reading, and then as you read you will have some idea of what to expect and will understand it with more ease. You will also become more of an active reader as you read if you can anticipate what the text is about to say. When you can anticipate, you will better be able to comment on, respond to, and evaluate the text. Looking at these will, in the long run, reduce the amount of time you spend studying:

- The title – does it tell you anything about the subject or purpose?
- The author – see if there is any information included about the author and the author's credibility to discuss the subject. Also, see if you can find out the author's point-of-view (for instance, John McCain would have a middle-of-the-road Republican viewpoint; Hillary Clinton would have a pro-women Democratic viewpoint). If there is no information about the author with the source, you could use these reference tools: the *International Who's Who, Contemporary Authors, America's Who's Who*, or the *Directory of American Scholars*. If you are looking at a book, see if there are any professional reviews of it in the *Book Review Digest.*, or even Amazon. Many unauthoritative books are published every year: make sure you have a book that experts recognize as an addition to the literature on your subject.
- The introduction – good introductions to essays and books let you know what the writing will be about.
- Sub-section headings if any (or chapter titles in the table of contents of a book) – subheadings and chapter titles orient you to the major areas discussed in a work. If you have a general idea of the organization and content of the essay or book, you will understand better as you read.
- If a book, use the index – if you have already focused your subject, use the index to help find the pages of the book relevant to your focused subject.

You are looking for clues to the main ideas in the text. After analyzing the items above, think about the subject and author of the text you are about to read and do the following pre-reading activities too.

- Write your preliminary thoughts on the subject of the text. Describe what you already know or think about the subject — facts and opinions.
- List any questions you want answered by the reading.

By pre-reading, you determine reasons for reading (questions you want answered), and you have listed ideas, facts, and opinions you already know or believe that you can compare with the ideas, facts, and opinions in the text you read. You use your previewing notes after you read to evaluate your prior knowledge and your reading selection for accuracy, strengths, and weaknesses.

112

As you read (to summarize, understand, and remember):

- With a pen or highlighter, underline/mark important ideas and examples.
- Summarize (in the margins or in extensive notes) major ideas and indicate important structural changes from one sub-section to the next sub-section.
- For easier comprehension, examine the structure, the order of ideas, in the text. All writing has a structure, an organization constructed to help a reader understand the text. Common structural strategies writers might use that you will see:
  / using headings or italics to emphasize ideas;
  / beginning or ending paragraphs with the most important ideas;
  / usually presenting the thesis in the introduction; or
  / presenting the thesis at the end, after examples/evidence are presented.
- Find key words that represent major concepts in the essay's discipline and write the meaning in the margin if necessary.
- Analyze the rhetorical situation: who is the author's audience and what is the author's purpose for writing? What are the purposes of the sub-sections of the writing, both as sub-sections and in relation to the overall thesis?

As you read, evaluate the text's strengths and weaknesses in the margin:

Careful readers also evaluate the text (examining its strengths and weaknesses) as they read. Not all texts are equally persuasive, authoritative, and well written. Even excellent writing has weak points.

- Does the writer use facts or opinions? (Both can be valid — but judge their reliability.) Are the explanations sound?
- What biases does the writer have?
- Is the piece well written? How well are the ideas supported? Is it persuasive?
- What are its strong points? its weak points?
- If you have read other articles or books on the same or related subjects, comment on the similarities, differences, and connections among the texts, and weigh the strength of the arguments propounded in the writing in comparison to the strength of the arguments in the other readings on the subject.

As you read, respond to the text in the margin:

During your pre-reading notes, you have already jotted some preliminary thoughts on the subject, and you have written what you already know about the subject. Critical readers are not passive, but active – they engage and question the text. Write in the margins of the text (or however you are taking notes) using all of these considerations:

- Challenge your previous ideas about the subject as you read and let the text challenge you to think of the subject in new and innovative ways.
- Decide if you share the views of the writing, and why? What sections do you agree with and why? Disagree with and why? Support your positions with evidence.
- Make connections to your experience, to knowledge you already have on the subject, and to any related subjects.

113

Post-reading — After you finish a text, do these suggestions:

Summary and Understanding the Reading

Write a one-two sentence summary of its thesis, the main idea. If you can't write the main idea after looking at what you underlined/highlighted, you need to use the close reading techniques to study the text more; you don't understand it yet. Also, by writing a summary of what you've read, you remember it better, thus decreasing study time.

- If you think you don't understand everything in the text yet, or if the text has proven to be essential for your purpose, write a longer summary, outlining the main ideas of the text.
- Return to your pre-reading notes and your notes taken while reading (whether they are in your notebook, a journal, or in the margin of your text), and clarify these initial ideas. Since you have read the entire text, you should have more knowledge to connect together and clarify your thoughts on the text.
- Use questions to help you clarify your thoughts on the text. Decide which previewing questions were answered, and which weren't. List any additional questions that the reading itself asks but doesn't answer or that you think of from the reading. Consider where to search for answers to unanswered questions.

Evaluation of the Reading

- Do the supporting ideas adequately illustrate, examine, and strengthen the main idea(s)? What are the specific strengths and weaknesses of the text? For each strength and weakness, provide evidence from the text and your own experiences to prove that it is, in fact, a strength or weakness.
- Is the writer leading you toward a certain idea, a set of ideas, or a course of action? Sometimes these ideas are not directly stated: if so, can you infer an argument from the essay?
- Compare, contrast, and synthesize articles you have read on the same subject. Especially note connections among the articles (agreements, disagreements, and one essay giving support for another essay's ideas) and evaluate the strengths and weaknesses of their arguments. (Discussed at greater length in chapters 7-8).

Response to the Reading

- What do you think about the reading? What parts do you agree with and what parts do you disagree with and why? Overall, do you agree or disagree with it and why?
- Can you relate any of the ideas or examples in the text to your own experiences or observations? Compare and analyze in terms of your own experiences and observations.

114

The following example by Joan Barnes, a student, contains the pre- and post-reading notes she made before and after an article she read called "The Cruel Logic of Teen Violence."

Pre-reading:

Title: Definitely leaves reader thinking, a question to answer: what is the cruel logic of teen violence he is going to discuss?
Author: newspaper reporter for a very small newspaper. Not a known authority or expert on child psychology or criminal behavior, so I will have to carefully analyze the strengths of his argument.
Introduction: doesn't tell much – just a graphic picture of youth violence. but grabs reader's attention!!!
Preliminary thoughts: Violence in youth is caused by poverty, by entertainment from cartoons to movies to video games, and by lack of contact with adults. For the poor kids by lack of hope. Also, peer pressure. Nobody seems to be doing much about youth violence – locking them up just makes them career criminals. Someone needs to care!
Questions: What is the "cruel logic"? Does O'Brien offer any solutions?

Post-Reading:

Thesis: William O'Brien suggests that two American cultural values, violence and materialism, combine to produce youth violence, and these values are transmitted by entertainment and advertising.
Summary: O'Brien uses anecdotes about video games, teens murdering, and "heroes solving problems by killing" to prove what we already know, that Americans are violent – and he argues that this comes, to a great degree, from the media. He discusses materialism, and argues persuasively that we are materialistic, and that there is a connection between violence and materialism. The introduction and conclusion both cite other often used explanations for youth violence (economic, social, family, community), but O'Brian asks us to also recognize materialism as creating a moral philosophy that promotes violence.
Connecting and Clarifying thoughts: This essay is brief and to the point: most important connection is the one between violence and materialism.
Initial Questions answered: The "cruel logic" is that Americans think of materialism as a good thing, so it is "cruel" that our cherished materialism has a connection to youth violence. O'Brian's solution is a greater awareness by Americans, which he is providing with this essay.
All in all, from a logical standpoint, his argument seems convincing.
Questions left unanswered: If he is correct, how should, how can, the American people change?
What proofs could there be to support his connection?

Evaluation: No hard evidence that we are a violent and materialistic nation (though in a brief article like this, who needs it? audience would already agree), and no hard evidence for his connection between the two ideals, but from a logical standpoint his argument convinces. (For instance he cites youths who shoot others for tennis shoes or drug money, both commodities. Also logical are his connections between movies, video games, and violence.)

Author leading reader toward idea/action?: yes, though not enough info in the essay for how to achieve this move away from violence through becoming less materialistic (perhaps I could provide some of these in an essay?)

Compare and Synthesize: info on violence is repeated (with statistics) in my sociology textbook, in the encyclopedia article on "violence," and in the article by Males, "Public Enemy Number One?" Ideas about materialism and how pervasive it is in American society discussed in much more detail in the Solomon article, and in sociology textbook. Could easily synthesize these ideas together for a longer, researched essay.

Response: Connection between violence and materialism is the most interesting idea of the essay. He does mention, early in the essay, that most people assign causes like poverty, race, and breakdown of morality to youth violence, and then he offers his thesis. I agree with this essay 100%, and notice that even our politicians seem to glorify violence in the Middle East, even though it could be argued that we are only there for oil (cheap oil=materialism). What do small kids think of all the patriotism of this era? Does it contribute to them being more violent?

Finding Meaning in Difficult Passages

But what if you are reading a sentence, a passage, or an entire text that you must study and analyze to understand? All readers, especially if they are reading pieces written for audiences and situations they are unfamiliar with, need to apply themselves to understand difficult passages. This will happen to you repeatedly in college as professors expand your horizons. You should be able to paraphrase these passages (rephrase them using your own words); if you cannot, you need to analyze them again more thoroughly until you understand them better.

Begin by identifying those parts of the writing you do understand, and those you don't. If the reason for not understanding occurs because of unfamiliar words or concepts, follow these steps:

- Before looking up words in a dictionary, try to understand them by studying the context, the ideas of the sentence and the sentences surrounding them.

For example, here is a section from Charles Darwin's *Evolution of the Species*:

Man is descended from some less highly organized form. The grounds on which this conclusion rests will never be shaken, for the close similarity between man and the lower animals in *embryonic development*, as well as in *innumerable points of structure and constitution*, both of high and

116

of the most trifling importance — the rudiments which he retains, and the *abnormal reversions* to which he is occasionally liable are facts which can not be disputed. [*italics added*]

When studying context to analyze a passage, first keep in mind the overall subject. In this case, it is Charles Darwin's theory that man evolved from an earlier animal form. A student, Mary Shoemaker, made educated guesses and, writing in her journal, deduced these meanings from context:

> Embryonic development? — the theory is that man evolved or developed from a lower form. The word development is included — so embryonic development probably means "growth.
> Innumerable points? — points is plural, so innumerable probably means "in numbers of" points, or "many" points?
> Structure and constitution? — passage concerns similarities between man and apes, our similar structures are our skeletal systems and body organs. The constitution is a system of laws for living, so in comparing man and apes "constitution" probably means the way we live
> Abnormal reversions? — abnormal is not normal, so how does reversions (which means reversals) fit into the context of the sentence?

Mary decided to try a preliminary, partial paraphrase to help discover the meaning of "abnormal reversions":

> Man is similar to apes in important and trifling ways, and when he retains these rudiments he is liable to "not normal reversals."

"Reversals back to acting like animals," she thought. "That is probably the meaning." She then attempted a more formal paraphrase. Compare the original phrasing and Mary's phrasing:

The original phrasing: between man and the lower animals
    Paraphrase: Charles Darwin contends that mankind's similarity to lower forms of animals

 in embryonic development, points of structure, and constitution
    in growth,   body form,   and systems of living,

    and the abnormal reversions to which he is occasionally liable
    and also man's occasional reversal to animal acts,

    man is descended from some less highly organized form
    leaves no doubt that man evolved from animals.

To double-check for accuracy, Mary checked *embryonic* in the dictionary: "of or pertaining to the early stages of development, in mammals to early stages passed within the mother's body; later the young is called a fetus." Next, she looked up *constitution*, and found that it could mean "makeup." Studying context with these definitions in mind, Mary revised the paraphrase for accuracy to read:

> Charles Darwin contends that mankind's similarity to lower forms of animals in early fetal growth, bodily form, and makeup, and also man's occasional reversal to animal acts, leaves no doubt that man evolved from animals (133).

Finding meaning through studying context not only saves time, it helps insure accuracy. When you look up a word in a dictionary or thesaurus, it usually has multiple meanings and you still have to decide which meaning is appropriate for the context. Though a thesaurus lists words with similarities in meaning, the original word must be understood in context before a suitable synonym can be employed. Dictionaries and thesauruses are essential tools for successful writers, but when you use them *be sure you study the context*.

- If you do use a dictionary when analyzing a difficult passage, study the context of the word in the passage so that you know you have found the correct definition in the dictionary.
- Sometimes the structure of a sentence makes it hard to understand. In this case, break the sentence into its parts to find its meaning.

For example, here is a passage from Steven Rose's article, "It's Only Human Nature: The Sociobiologist's Fairyland":

> It is against this that we must pose a real science and vision of humanity — one which says that it is the biological and social nature of humanity to transform itself, reach beyond itself constantly: that what seems fixed or constant is so only in the historical moment which itself is always in flux, that the human nature of feudal, preindustrial society was not the human nature of the industrial revolution, is not the human nature of today's advanced capitalism — and will not be the human nature of the transformed societies of tomorrow — those that will at length have truly achieved that old goal, the freedom of necessity.

What a sentence! Heavily embedded with clause after clause after clause. To begin "deciphering," John Frisca, a freshman, cut out the beginning "it is." From a grammatical standpoint, the it is-there are structure usually points the reader toward the main assertion in the sentence (in this case, "that we must pose a real science and vision of humanity"). If you can't find such a structure, look for the main subject and verb of the independent clause of the sentence. The main assertion in the sentence suggests what the sentence will be about. After discovering the main assertion of the sentence, cut out all that isn't entirely essential in the rest of the sentence — get to the kernel, root idea(s) of the sentence. John found the main assertion, cut out all that was not essential to the meaning, and then outlined the progression of ideas:

It is against this that we must pose a real science and vision of humanity one which says that it is the biological and social nature of humanity to transform itself, reach beyond itself constantly: that what seems fixed or constant is so only in the historical moment which itself is always in flux, that the human nature of feudal, preindustrial society was not the human nature of the industrial revolution, is not the human nature of today's advanced capitalism and will not be the human nature of the transformed societies of tomorrow those that will at length have truly achieved that old goal, the freedom of necessity.

As John outlined the main ideas, he thought of synonyms (in parentheses) for some of the words:

I. Posing (suggesting) a real science and vision of humanity,
   A. the biological and social nature of humanity transforms itself
      (physically and socially humankind)   (changes)
      1.what appears fixed (unchanging) is actually changing
      2.human nature of the past is not the same as modern society
      3.and will not be in the future
      4.where society will have achieved the goal of "freedom of
      necessity."

Here is a rough paraphrase of the Rose sentence after John understood the main assertion and had outlined the ideas:

> Steven Rose suggests that a new view of humankind will appear as we physically and socially change. What appears unchanging, actually changes. Human nature in the past is not the same as it is today, nor will it be in the future when people have reached their goal: "the freedom of necessity" (413).

Writing Summaries and Paraphrases

Most academic writing includes other people's ideas, but the ideas are usually expressed with paraphrase and summary rather than with direct quotation. Direct quotation should be saved for particularly significant ideas that are stated so well in the original that by paraphrasing or summarizing them their poignancy and force would be lost. When you use summary, paraphrase or quotation, however, integrate

119

the source into the text using proper format. You must credit the original source, using phrases like Karen Rowe believes or Karen Rowe discusses to introduce direct quotation, paraphrase, and summary. At the end of the direct quotation, paraphrase, or summary, put the page numbers of the original source in parentheses using the form demonstrated at the end of this sentence (347). Notice the placement of the period. If the idea you are crediting is a direct quotation, place the number in parentheses after the closing quotation mark, like this: "this is the proper form" (241).

There are many specialized types of summaries used for different purposes, but the primary purpose for all of these is the same – to condense the content of the original source without changing the meaning. When you take notes or write in the margins of your textbooks, you are *paraphrasing* if you restate in your own words what the original says. When you write only the main idea or ideas, if you shorten the source in any way, you are summarizing. When you read a *synopsis* of a novel, film, or play, you are reading a summary of its plot. Legal *briefs* are summaries of court cases, and *abstracts* are summaries of articles in professional journals. A *précis* is a special kind of summary that follows the organizational pattern of the original source. It requires, by definition, a one-sentence summary of each paragraph in the original, so if the reader of the précis wants more information than is contained in the précis, he or she knows, for example, that sentence eighteen in the précis corresponds to paragraph eighteen in the original source.

After closely reading the text to be summarized, the next step for writing a summary is evaluation of your audience and writing situation. Ascertaining the needs of your audience is very important, whether the audience for your summary is yourself (taking notes, writing a précis of an article so you have the ideas contained in the longer piece of writing), or someone else (a professor, your class, or other students with the same major).

If a professor has assigned a combination reading-writing assignment, analyze the requirements. If the professor wants your reaction to or analysis of the reading, you can assume that the professor has read and understands the essay assigned; you need to summarize only enough so that the professor can read your essay smoothly without referring to the original text. However, if the professor wants you to summarize the essay, and he or she is the audience, you are probably being asked to demonstrate you understand the essay. The summary should then be complete enough so that the professor knows you understand all its complexities. If the professor wants you to summarize the essay for your class (your classmates are the audience), then you have to provide enough information so they will understand your summary, as well as the original essay. You can no longer assume that your audience has read the essay and must adjust the material in your summary accordingly.

Many times, when you are writing a researched essay that uses multiple sources, to support your thesis you just want to use the original source's main idea, and you summarize the entire text (even if it is a book) in one or two sentences.

Beginning Marker: Reference to original source
William O'Brien argues that two American cultural values stressed in the media, violence and materialism, cause youth violence *(9-11)*.

End Marker (Pages summarized; signals the end of the summary)

120

Other times, when writing an essay, to support your purpose you want to use one specific idea in the original source. If this is the case, then you paraphrase only the portion of the essay that serves your purpose.

> *Original Source*: Possessions are the ultimate measure of a person's worth. Upward mobility and consumption absorb our energies and define our goals.

Beginning Marker: Reference to original source
Paraphrase: *William O'Brien discusses* the consumerism rampant in American culture, where the evidence of climbing the social ladder becomes defined by our possessions *(11)*. **End Marker: page number. One specific sentence on one page paraphrased. Always signal the beginning of a summary, paraphrase, or direct quotation by citing the author's name(s). Signal the end of the cited passage with its page number(s). The chapters on documentation will discuss situations where there are no page numbers identified in your source.**

At times, the purpose of your essay calls for a several sentence summary that includes several of the ideas from the original.
Beginning Marker: Reference to original source
Males in our society get their ideas about heroes from the media. *William O'Brien points* to violent video games and Arnold Schwarzenegger as 1990s versions of the John Wayne western, and indicts the news media, displaying American military action (like Kuwait) on the nightly news. He also makes connections between the cheapness of human life as evidenced in the media and the need to be wealthy as a way to measure human worth, arguing that the result is violence *(10-11)*. Expanding from his ideas, I would argue that possessing material "things" has become one way that males gauge themselves as heroes.
End Marker: The page numbers in parenthesis are the pages summarized, and this parenthesis signals the end of the summary.

Some writing situations call for a complete summary of all the major ideas of the original. This example is the opening paragraph of a summary/evaluation essay written by Cindy Brannick.

William O'Brien, writer for the Sonoma County Press, argues in "The Cruel Logic of Teenage Violence," that violence has become an honored cultural tradition. He places the blame for this serious problem on the mass media, the advertisers, and what he considers a second honored cultural value: materialism. O'Brien states that youth violence, an unusual occurrence a few years ago, has grown into a monumental problem seen daily in the news and affecting all communities. The writer clearly makes the point that our youth behave logically, following the violent ways taught to them by our society. Children have easy access to both violent movies and video games that glorify killing and teach such unrealistic ideals as: violence fixes anything and force overcomes any obstacle. "Why then would society be surprised," asks O'Brien, "when he [the child] picks up a gun?" Secondly, he believes that our society teaches that "possessions are the ultimate measure of a person's worth." Advertisers support this illusion by directing commercials toward children that enforce a belief in materialism. The FCC's deregulation of advertising for children gives the perfect opportunity for advertisers to exploit our children. O'Brien concludes that adults must address the issue of violence and materialism, and take immediate action to change their own habits before we can save the youth of the United States. These changes will not be easy; furthermore, they must first take place within the adults before the children have a chance to learn a better way of life (9-11).

The following three summaries of the same essay are written with different audiences, writing situations, and purposes: evaluate how these changes influence content and organization.

Summary 1

Audience: Fellow students of an Introduction to Film Class
Situation: Professor has assigned thirty essays, each read by a different student. Each student will write a précis of the article read. These précis will be copied and given to each student, so students will have summaries of thirty relevant critiques of classic films. A précis is a summary that shortens by having one sentence for each paragraph of the original source. Since the essay, "Who Killed King Kong?," is a twelve paragraph essay, there will be twelve sentences in this précis.
Purpose: Précis, by their very nature — one sentence for each paragraph — give complete summaries of sources. By assigning a précis, the professor suggests that the purpose is to give a thorough, complete summary of the essay.

Study the audience, situation, and purpose: the audience, like the writer, all are studying classic film. As for the situation, the writer knows that the summary will be used as a study aid by all the students in class, and that each student will get twenty-nine précis of different articles. The summaries need to have the essential information so that classmates, the audience, do not have to read the original. Evaluation of your audience and writing situation in this manner is a very important prerequisite for writing successful summaries.

61-1) X.J. Kennedy finds that King Kong continues to delight audiences as they watch Kong struggle against, escape from, and die because of the forces of urban society.
61-2) Though he dies and the movie is old, his legend still wins large segments of the viewing populace in television showings (Kennedy cites a March, 1955 New York Kongtelethon that beat out top raters of the time like Ed Sullivan and Groucho Marx).
62-1) Fans still go to the theaters to see Kong too, more than any other movie monster says Kennedy.

62-2) He credits this to the fact that *King Kong* outdoes every other monster movie, but he thinks its enduring success comes from deeper sources.

62-3) He notices that Kong, as an ape, is manlike, and suggests American audiences identify with him for the same reasons they identify with Tarzan: "If Tarzan recalls the ape in us, then Kong may well appeal to that great-granddaddy primordial brute from whose tribe we have all deteriorated."

62-4) We empathize with Kong's loneliness; he belongs in the tradition of the "pitiable monster" of Hollywood such as Quasimodo (the Hunchback of Notre Dame) and the Frankenstein monster who plays with the little girl.

63-1) In 1933, the Depression years added a dimension to the film as Fay Wray [the lead actress] is picked from a soup kitchen to portray a heroine in a jungle movie and Kong later smashes that same street where Wray was found wandering at the beginning of the film.

63-2) While this could have satisfied Depression audiences, perhaps in 1960 [essay written in 1960] the impulse (in all of us, Kennedy suggests) to leap out and destroy the machines that make life a drudgery is acted out by Kong swinging the rail car over his head and smashing it.

63-3) Though violent, Kong's actions toward Fay Wray and his pursuit of her remind us both of the hopeless lover and the perfect gentleman.

63-4) He dies a tragic hero: "one of those persecuted near-animal souls bewildered in the middle of an industrial order, whose simple desires are thwarted at every turn."

64-1) In the South, African-Americans watch it every year, perhaps because, Kennedy argues, Kong is a black free spirit attacked by white policemen [essay published in 1960].

64-2) By watching Kong die over and over, the animal in us dies, and Kennedy finds this unsettling (61-64).

Summary 2

Audience: Fellow students of a 20th century American History Class
Situation: Professor has assigned thirty essays, each read by a different student. Each student will write a summary of the article read. These summaries will be copied and shared, so students will have summaries of thirty relevant critiques of classic films.
Purpose: The professor wants the student writer to explain the main thesis of the essay, and then summarize what the critic finds important sociologically and historically concerning the classic film.

Study the audience, situation, and purpose: the audience, like the writer, are all studying American history. However, the writing situation and the purpose for summary 2 are different than the situation and purpose for 1. Summary 1 demanded a specific kind of summary, a précis, that is fairly uniform (one sentence for each paragraph), while 2 asks for a summary with more stringent requirements for content (an emphasis on sociology and history), but less stringent requirements for organization and for supporting content. Part of the writing context is identical: the writer knows that the summary will be used as a study aid by all the students in the class, and that each student will get twenty-nine summaries of different articles. The

123

summaries need to have the essential information so that classmates, the audience, do not have to read the original. Notice that with this summary, the writer has organized the summary to suit the purpose given by the professor. It does not follow the structure of Kennedy's essay; indeed, it shouldn't.

> X.J. Kennedy's 1960 essay, "Who Killed King Kong?," argues that it is not Kong's fated love for Fay Wray that kills him (as the entrepreneur character who marketed Kong said to reporters on the street after Kong's death at the foot of the Empire State Building: "' That's your story, boys — it was Beauty killed the Beast'"), but instead the entire urban, industrial complex we all live in that killed him. Kennedy goes a step further, and suggests that the overwhelming popularity of the movie after all these years rests with our sympathies for the innocent, pitiful monster, the unrequited lover, and most of all the "displaced animal spirit forced to live in a jungle built by machines." Kennedy finds that in the Depression year the movie was released in, 1933, audiences probably identified with the starving heroine, who when she was picked off the street to become a Hollywood actress became their fantasy. He argues that they probably also cheered when, at the end of the movie, Kong decimated the same landscape Wray was pulled from at the beginning of the movie, a Depression landscape they lived in. For the 1960's audience, Kennedy argues it is the destruction of urban, mechanized society by the innocent brute that causes audiences to cheer. He says we all wish to destroy the causes of our "daily grind." He concludes suggesting that it is not any historical period that finds Kong attractive, but the basic animal spirit within us that is slowly dying which empathizes the most with Kong (61-64).

Summary 3

> Audience: The Professor of a 20th century American History Class
> Situation: A ten page research paper using the conventions of academic writing (credible sources, support for ideas, logical structure, conventions of Standard Edited English); the broad subject is Industrialized Society in America.
> Purpose: The student has focused her subject to adverse reactions to mechanization in popular films.

Study the audience, situation, and purpose for assignment 3. They change considerably from 1 and 2. Since the audience is now the student's professor, the student can assume that the audience has an in-depth knowledge of the subject, and wants an interesting, thought-provoking, persuasive essay. The writing situation demands that the researcher survey the main ideas on the subject, synthesize the material, and draw conclusions from the research. In the first two summaries, the professor had assigned a purpose. With summary 3, the writer has researched a subject and must create a purpose for the essay. The summary in this essay is just a small portion of a larger research paper. Only the beginning of the essay, which summarizes Kennedy's article, is reprinted here.

Much has been written about the animal-like reactions to modern industrialization evidenced in plays and screen adaptations of great American playwrights like Eugene O'Neill and Tennessee Williams. O'Neill's play, *The Hairy Ape*, will bear scrutiny on this subject, though it has been overworked, as will Williams' great animal, Stanley Kowalski in *A Streetcar Named Desire*. "Here Stella! The Meat. Catch." But an undercurrent of rage at industrialization also runs throughout the B movies and thrillers of the 1930s. One of the most persuasive critiques of a popular movie on this subject is X.J. Kennedy's "Who Killed King Kong?" He argues that Americans still flock to the movie because Kong is that primordial being within all of us who resists mechanization and longs for the jungle (63). Stanley Kowalski seems to reinforce this theory. . . .

Your audience and the purpose for your essay determine what content to include or exclude from a summary.

Accurate Paraphrase and Summary - Avoiding Plagiarism

There are three major problems associated with summary and paraphrase: incorrectly documenting the source in your essay, not changing the original enough by using your own diction (word choice) and syntax (the way words, clauses, and sentences are arranged), and creating misleading content that is contrary to the meaning of the original source.

- Paraphrases, summaries and quotations must include a reference to the original source. Otherwise, you have committed *plagiarism*.
- Paraphrases and summaries must have your wording and phrasing. Key words (specific nouns that do not have either a synonym or a phrase you can use to replace the original word) can be transferred from the original to the paraphrase, but in general *the diction and syntax of your paraphrase must be yours.*
- Writers of summary cannot change the meaning of the original to suit their own purposes. When you summarize, you must accurately reflect the meaning in the original source.

Writers can have problems choosing appropriate synonyms and syntax. The challenge confronting Joan Smither was to transform 17th century British English into 20th century American English.

Original Source: I have seen Parents so heap Rules on their Children, that it was impossible for the poor little ones to remember a tenth Part of them, much less to observe them. However they were either by Words or Blows corrected for the Breach of those multiplied and often very impertinent Precepts. Whence it naturally followed that the Children minded not what was said to them, when it was evident to them that no Attention they were capable of was sufficient to preserve them from Transgression and the Rebukes which followed it.

125

Reference to the original source

The *seventeenth century English philosopher, John Locke*, notes that when parents give children too many rules the children can't remember all of them, and when they are repeatedly punished either verbally or physically for not remembering the rules, they eventually stop trying to obey the rules (96).

All ideas from the original are contained in the paraphrase. Only three key words are repeated: parents, children, rules.

To paraphrase or summarize accurately, you must first *understand* the original source. First, define any unfamiliar words; this involves studying the context, using a dictionary, and for particularly difficult passages, analyzing the sentence structure.

After analyzing and understanding a passage, then change the passage into your words and phrases (rendering all of the original's meaning for paraphrase; the most important ideas for summary). Also, remember that simply changing the diction is not an acceptable practice for accurate paraphrase and summary: you must also change the syntax (the sentence structure) of the original text. Examine the changes in word choice and sentence structure in the examples on the next pages.

- *Inaccurate paraphrase: no reference to source*

    Source: In the same sense, the entertainment industry's constant depiction of violence and destructive behavior, as perpetrated by some of the most attractive and glamorous human beings on the planet, redefines such conduct as sexy, glamorous, even admirable. We may not instantly copy dangerous or despicable actions we view in movies or on TV, but that doesn't indicate the media images are powerless to alter our notions of what is acceptable – or fashionable – in the world around us.

    Inaccurate: Though most people do not copy intolerable social behavior from movies and television, they cannot help but be subtly affected by "sexy, glamorous" movie stars acting out negative behaviors, which in turn subtly changes for the worse the public's view of acceptable conduct.

No reference to original source, though syntax and diction appropriate for paraphrase. "sexy, glamorous" occurs in the original, so these words appear in quotation marks to indicate that they are the words used by the original source. On the other hand, the word "behavior" is so integral to the meaning, that it can be used in an accurate paraphrase without the quotation marks.

    Accurate: Michael Medved concedes that most people do not copy intolerable social behavior from movies and television; however, he argues that people cannot help but be subtly affected by "sexy, glamorous" movie stars acting out negative behaviors, which in turn subtly changes for the worse the public's view of acceptable conduct (323).

126

- *Inaccurate: shared syntax and diction*

  Source: The hybridization of American teens has become talk show fodder, with "wiggers" – white kids who dress and talk "black" – appearing on TV in full gangster regalia. In Indiana a group of white high school girls raised a national stir when they triggered an imitation race war at their virtually all-white high school last fall simply by dressing "black."

  Inaccurate: According to Nell Bernstein, the "hybridization" of teens in America has become common on talk shows because "wiggers" (whites dressing and talking "black") appear on television wearing gangster clothes. In Indiana, "white high school girls" received national attention when they dressed "black" and started a race war (505).

Accurate reference to original, but neither the wording (to any great degree), nor the sentence structure, has been altered.

  Inaccurate: According to Nell Bernstein, the connections between cultures evident in American teens have been a frequent topic on talk shows, with "wiggers" (Caucasians imitating black clothes and customs) appearing on television wearing gang colors. In Indiana, white secondary schoolgirls received national attention for starting a race riot at their mostly Caucasian school when they wore clothes that were from African culture (505).

Though the diction has been altered, the syntax remains exactly as the original. This creates stylistically unnatural sentences, so is unacceptable paraphrase or summary.

  Accurate: According to Neil Bernstein, when Anglo-American teens in Indiana chose to imitate African-American clothes and customs (slang: "wiggers"), an "imitation race war" occurred in their school which received national media attention. "Wiggers," wearing the "gangster regalia" that identifies them, have also frequently appeared on media talk shows (505).

- *Inaccurate: misleading, altering the source's meaning*

  Source: It is commonly estimated that about 100 million species of plants, animals, and microbes have evolved at various points along the earth's 3.5 billion year biological history. Of all these species, about 99 percent are extinct, so that the one million or so animal and 350,000 plant species that inhabit the world today represent only a tiny fraction of all the evolutionary paths that have been taken.

  To say that all 99 million missing species have gone extinct, however, would be misleading. Every creature that is alive today is a successful adaptation by some previous species . . .

Inaccurate: William Tucker reports that 99% of the 100 million species that have inhabited the earth during its 3.5 billion year biological history have become extinct, with the survivors (1 million animals and 350,000 plants) exhibiting but a minute number of the evolutionary paths taken (558).

The beginning of the source's second paragraph qualifies the meaning of the first paragraph. The inaccurate paraphrase does not take into account the writer's intent when it paraphrases only the first paragraph, thus the paraphrase is inaccurate because it alters the source's meaning.

Accurate: William Tucker reports that 99% of the 100 million species that have inhabited the earth during its 3.5 billion year biological history have become extinct. While the survivors (1 million animals and 350,000 plants) exhibit but a minute number of the evolutionary paths taken, all species contain a part of the extinct species in that the survivors are descendants of extinct forms (558).

A non-productive method to use when paraphrasing or summarizing begins with a thesaurus and changes some of the words. The most productive method begins by making sure you understand the original source, and then just writing the ideas with your own syntax, your own phrasing and sentence style (without referring to the original source). Don't be concerned in this first draft whether you have used appropriate synonyms. When you have written the rough draft, compare it to the original and

- Make sure that you have left out no ideas essential for your audience and purpose.
- Make sure that you have accurately conveyed the meaning of the original.
- Check to make sure that you have used appropriate synonyms rather than the diction of the original source.
- Make sure you have not altered the original.

If you cannot think of an appropriate word to use in a paraphrase or summary, find one in a thesaurus, but always select words from the thesaurus to fit the context in tone and level of formality. A thesaurus lists words with similar, not identical, meanings, so refer to a dictionary to make sure your synonym has the same meaning as the words in your original source. Experienced critical readers know when you have used a word inaccurately or non-idiomatically, so take the time to double-check your word choices. For example, when paraphrasing a recipe, you shouldn't replace the word 'sugar' with the similar, but inaccurate, word 'sucrose.'

When to Cite Sources

A general rule for when to cite sources: if you have borrowed someone else's work and used it in your writing, you must cite the source. Three comprehensive examples include:

a. If you have directly quoted a source, that writer did the work of putting the words in that order, and you need to cite the source and put quotation marks around the borrowed words.
b. If you are reporting information from a study (a survey or any statistical report), you didn't compile the statistics yourself so you have to cite the source.
c. If a source has analyzed and interpreted a subject, they did work, i.e., they thought about it and drew conclusions. You must cite a source when you incorporate these ideas even if you put them into your own words.

For example, if you are researching the battle of Gettysburg, you would not have to cite a source that told you the battle occurred on July 1-3, 1863 because the writer of the text you are reading did not do work to find that information — he/she could have found the dates in many sources. However, if you read a source that argued that Generals Lee and Longstreet lost the battle and the entire war for the Confederacy when they decided not to take the high ground at the end of the first day of the battle, you would have to cite that source, even if you put it in your own words. The reason for this is that the source you were using *did work* to come to that conclusion. (He/she studied diaries and contemporary battle reports and read what other military historians had concluded about the battle, and then from the analysis made the decision that the battle and war were lost that day. In other words, this source *did work* to reach that conclusion.)

Literature Reviews: Writing Summary-Evaluation Essays

Most summary-evaluation essays do three things: they take a written source (an essay or a book) as a subject and

1) summarize it so that the reader of the summary-evaluation knows the main ideas of the source,
2) evaluate the effectiveness, the strengths and weaknesses, of its presentation, and
3) agree or disagree with the views of the source.

Book reviews in newspapers and magazines are essentially summary-evaluation articles; scholarly journals call reviews *literature reviews* (though their subjects are scholarly articles and books, not literature).

The preliminary step to writing a summary-evaluation essay is to apply the critical reading skills discussed earlier in this chapter to the source you are going to write about.

Summary-evaluation essays contain these features:

- A fairly complete summary of the original source. (Approximately one-third of the summary-evaluation essay should consist of the summary.)
- A discussion of the author's credentials to write the piece, if appropriate, as well as any biases the author might have concerning the subject.
- A discussion of the rhetorical situation, the audience for the source, if appropriate.
- Any innovative ideas or features of the text.

129

- An evaluation discussing the strengths and weaknesses of the ideas and their support in the text.
- An analysis of the claims and the support for logical effectiveness, reliable facts, and authoritative opinions.
- If the ideas in the source are sound but the support is weak, some evaluation essays develop support for sound ideas by adding support in the evaluation article. (See the first example student essay that follows.)
- Evaluation essays usually respond to the source, either agreeing or disagreeing with the ideas, and give support (a rationale with evidence) for the agreement or disagreement.
- Some evaluation essays compare the source to other sources that discuss the same subject, or to other writing by the same author.
- Most importantly: The writer of the excellent summary-evaluation essay does not disappear, submerged in the ideology of the writing being summarized. A reader of an excellent evaluation essay easily recognizes the writer's own view: the reader knows what the writer thinks about the essay evaluated, and knows what the writer thinks about the subject of the essay evaluated.

Summary-evaluation essays usually follow this organizational pattern:

- Optional: An introductory paragraph that discusses the subject of the source and gives a thesis statement that reveals your overall evaluation of the source. (In general, is the source accurate or inaccurate, persuasive or not persuasive?)
- A SUMMARY of the source.
- A transitional forecasting statement that previews the key areas you will analyze in the essay.
- An EVALUATION, discussing each section of the source in detail, supporting your contentions about the source's strengths and weaknesses by referring to the content of the original.
- A section that RESPONDS, discussing your overall agreement or disagreement with the ideas of the source you are evaluating. This may serve as the conclusion.
- If the previous response section does not seem to conclude your essay appropriately, conclude with an overall assessment of the work.

On the simplest level, many times you can just write a three paragraph essay (with complete, thorough paragraphs each a page or so in length): a summary, an evaluation, a response. See the student example following. You will be asked to write summary, evaluation, response articles many times in your college career. They will usually be called literature reviews.

130

Student Example: Literature Review

John Logan
English 101
Dr. Richard Hanson
Final Draft

Whenever you summarize, you must begin with a reference to the source OR IT IS PLAGIARISM! (See 125-129).

Literature Review of Valerie Palmer-Mehta's
"Men Behaving Badly: Mediocre Masculinity and *The Man Show*"

Summary

Valerie Palmer-Mehta argues that *The Man Show*, by attacking feminism and alternate masculinities, actually does more to harm white males by fostering narcissism and by avoiding modern gender realities. *The Man Show* (1999-2004), a cable television comedy featuring Jimmy Kimmel and Adam Carolla (followed in the final season by Joe Rogan and Doug Stanhope), made fun of women and men who were not stereotypical white males (such as homosexuals and men of color). Palmer-Mehta points out that this show led the way for other programming that does the same thing, such as Spike Television and MTV's *Jackass*, the shows *Viva la Bam* and *Wildboyz*, and recent Brut men's care ads. She quotes Rob Freakins, the ad campaign manager: "the ads reflect the style of how these young guys feel today ... it's good to be Neanderthal again" (qtd. in Palmer-Mehta 1054). The show uses, and speaks of, women in stereotypical, degrading, and subordinate ways (Palmer-Mehta calls this "emphasized femininity") in order to make white males seem superior. A repeated set of characters are "the Juggly Girls," who act in a stereotypical "dumb blonde" manner, and they are displayed positively against any woman who will not conform to "hegemonic masculinity," the old cultural ideal which puts men in economic, political, social, and familial control. Some of the women treated negatively include Oprah Winfrey, a woman who asks for fiscal responsibility from her husband, and lesbians. To prove her point, the author shows that when a feminist on the show decides to just have fun and dress to please men, the show then puts her in a positive light because she is no longer a threat. Palmer-Mehta analyzes the show's position thusly: free-thinking women must be converted to slaves for men or else be put down for their stances. The next section of the article demonstrates that *The Man Show* not only attacks feminism, it also attacks any men who are not part of the white male patriarchal structure. The attacks on African-American masculinity include Jimmy Kimmel playing a stupid character in "blackface" (like the racist minstrel shows of the nineteenth century) and episodes that allude to the perception that African-American men are hyper-sexual and want to seduce white men's wives. The show, likewise, embraces homophobia; it suggests that any man with a non-normative body (the show uses a dwarf) is a freak; and it also promotes a fear of multiculturalism in our country. In the end, however, Ms. Palmer-Mehta makes the salient point that the hosts of the show are not, themselves, hegemonic, ideal men; as a matter of fact, they are specimens of what she terms "mediocre masculinity" (bodies not strong,

Begins with 1-3 sentence overall thesis of the article summarized.

Rest of introduction gives thorough summary of the original:

Near beginning of the intro summary paragraph, details of the source's subject.

The original has these 3 main sub-sections, so these are all summarized in detail (paragraph completeness):
1) emphasized femininity

2) alternative masculinities

3) mediocre masculinities

131

looks not pleasing, economically and intellectually bankrupt, scared but won't show it). The reason for this, she finds, is that all the changes in gender over the last half-century have created a "crisis in masculinity" manifesting in "fears, concerns and frustrations felt by the hegemonic male as a result of the increasing public presence and power of women and minorities." *The Man Show*, though "denying reality," is a response to these circumstances and emotions (1068). In conclusion, she finds that *The Man Show* does nothing to address these fears and concerns, and thus by hiding behind resentment rather than working for solutions, the show hinders men by avoiding and minimizing the big problems men face today (1053-1072).

The end of any summary has the page numbers in parentheses.

Evaluation

The biggest strength of this article is the in-depth analysis of multiple examples that prove Palmer-Mehta's points. For one instance, she spends over a page analyzing exactly what Jimmy Kimmel does when pretending to be a black basketball player, making him sound like an ignorant black man (horrible English, no intellect, not being able to count, even forgetting his brothers' and sisters' names), embodying all the negative stereotypes American culture has towards black men, even successful ones like the Utah Jazz star, Karl Malone. And for a white man to do an African character in minstrel show blackface is the height of racism. A second strength is the use of experts to make her arguments stronger (the Works Cited is two pages long). For example, after her extended description and analysis of homophobia on the show, she quotes a scholarly expert on homophobia, Michael Kimmel, who says, "homophobia is a central organizing principle of our cultural definition of manhood . . . The fear . . . that others might perceive us as homosexual propels men to enact all manner of exaggerated masculine behaviors and attitudes to make sure that no one could possible [sic] get the wrong idea about us" (qtd. in Palmer-Mehta 1064). I only once, near the end of the article, decided that she was perhaps giving too much detail and analyzing too much. She discussed for a page how men were now being marketed to for clothes and body image (with her noticing that *The Man Show* thought this was to be satirized too – I guess men shouldn't have to worry about how they look from a hegemonic perspective). My problem with this section is that men's body image and how that has evolved is a paper in and of itself, and I didn't feel it belonged in this essay. Also, and most importantly, she did not fully answer the opposing argument: that the show is merely comedy and should not be taken seriously. A brief biography of Palmer-Mehta shows her to be an Associate Professor at Oakland University, and that her field of expertise is mass media and culture criticism.

The 2nd paragraph is an in-depth analysis of the strengths and weaknesses of the article with specific evidence to show why a point is a strength or weakness.

Notice that in the evaluation, examples to prove strengths or weaknesses often come from additional specific summary from the article.

Now begins discussing two weaknesses - evaluation should be thorough. Any article has many strengths and weaknesses. Evaluations often mention whether the author is an expert, as this one appears to be.

Response

I agree with Palmer-Mehta with reservations. Her analysis of *The Man Show* is one hundred percent correct: the show is entirely misogynistic, and furthermore, its characters and their attitudes are so loathsome that they give men a bad name. Sadly, many men are this loathsome. She points out the many shows that depict men as utter buffoons, including *The Simpsons, Family Guy*, and *The Drew Carey Show*. I could add to this number: there are absolutely NO male characters on sit-coms who are not utterly despicable as men. They might be funny, they might have a few or many endearing qualities, but they are definitely not "real men." The only other male type is the cops and soldiers *The final* of television and movies, the strong, silent, violent heroes. Where do men *paragraph is a* who are just regular guys get a sense that what they are doing – in their *response: do you* families, their work, their political leanings, their intellectual pursuits, even *agree or disagree* their sports– is good and right? Secondly, by not answering the opposing view *with the source* that *The Man Show* is just comedy, she presupposes that modern men do not *and why? Can you* understand the concept of satire. Most men who aren't those stereotypical, *you read to your* ignorant "hegemonic" - - -holes recognize the characters of *The Man Show* and *own experiences or* the other comedies mentioned as the caveman idiots that they are, and while *observations? This* modern men might not have many positive role models around, they certainly *is where you say* recognize that the show is satirizing the modern "hegemonic" man. Satire: to *what YOU THINK* exaggerate problems with people through characters so that viewers recognize *about the subject* these traits in themselves and say "I do that sometimes. I need to quit it!" Give *you are evaluating.* men a break. We aren't that dumb (or most – or a few - of us aren't anyway).

Works Cited

MLA style docu-mentation

Palmer-Mehta, Valerie. "Men Behaving Badly: Mediocre Masculinity and
    The Man Show." The Journal of Popular Culture , vol. 42, no. 6, Dec. 2009,
    pp. 1053-1072. *Ebsco Host*, www.0e10l78uq.y.http.web.a.
    ebscohost.com.libproxy.kctcs.edu

7
Secondary Research Techniques:
The Library and Internet

All research begins with a question or questions that need to be answered. Some research questions allow for definitive answers; others don't. A student writing in a natural sciences class might be asked to describe a process and choose to explain how gold is refined from base metal and made into jewelry. The student can research this process and write a paper giving a definitive answer. On the other hand, the student essay included in this chapter, Gary Hughes's "A Connection Between the Media and Violent Behavior," cannot give a definitive answer to this question, but he does give his informed opinion based on evidence gathered from both *secondary sources* (reading views by media experts) and *primary sources* (a published essay with a writer's observation of her nephew, paralyzed in a shooting incident).

Secondary research is *library research*, used in your writing when you synthesize, critique, evaluate, or report other writers' ideas or research to either inform or persuade your audience. The term library research, now that we are firmly in the twenty-first century, has wider implications than simply entering a library to find information in a book or journal. First, much secondary research can be completed with computers. Second, many industries and businesses, newspapers and magazines, and the government and judicial systems have their own sources of information, their own libraries. As a matter of fact, the largest compiler and publisher of information *in the world* is the U. S. Government. *Primary research*, or *field research*, is what scientists actually *do* — experiments, surveys, observations, interviews. Writers of secondary research look at events and information obtained through primary research, and then explain, analyze, and draw conclusions. Examples of secondary research include articles in magazines like *Psychology Today* or *Scientific American* that describe and define the latest trends and the latest research on a particular subject. Examples of primary research occur in scholarly journals like *The New England Journal of Medicine* or *Nature*, where researchers report on experiments they have conducted. Some courses might ask you to perform primary research (observation, experiments, interviews) and then report your findings. Other courses will just ask you to read scholars' primary research and use their findings to argue your points.

When you read either secondary or primary sources, you are entering the world of scholars and experts in the field of your research. You should begin to know what experts think about your subject. One word of caution: you want to read carefully and analytically, staying alert to avoid overly biased opinions and distortions of fact. Using critical reading skills and a skeptical mind, carefully evaluate the sources you have chosen for your subject. When still in doubt concerning the authority of a source after applying the techniques for critical reading in chapters six and seven, ask your professor or a professional in the field you are studying if it is reliable. Most of the research you do as an undergraduate will be from secondary sources, so you need to learn the intricacies of analytic reading and library research early.

Writing Situations for Researched Writing

Since you will be expected to write several kinds of research papers in college, before you begin you should find out the kind of research expected for each situation and class. *Ask your professor to clarify the aims and methods of your research.* Notice that the types of secondary research papers listed here also have applications that you will use in the world beyond college.

The report (Informative) asks you to study a subject and report facts concerning the subject: how something works, how an event occurs, what happened, a summary of another source. This, in many ways, is the simplest form of research paper. You are simply reporting, neither critiquing nor evaluating (except as you decide whether a source is reliable or not). Most research papers you wrote in high school were reports, and if you are planning a career in business or engineering you will probably be asked to write reports on topics like the following:

- A mining engineer is asked to research the soil studies (primary sources) in a given area for the last thirty years and write a secondary research report.
- A writer for *Time* magazine reports (secondary research) the findings of a series of experiments (primary sources) conducted on the next generation space rockets.
- A physics student is asked to study the design advances of particle accelerators, and report (secondary research) on their development and uses.

But in college, you will commonly be asked to critique and evaluate your findings as you would in a synthesis or a persuasive research paper.

The synthesis (or in the social and natural sciences called a *literature survey)* asks you to review both facts and opinions in a field of study, and to critique, compare, evaluate, and interpret the strengths and weaknesses of information and critical opinion on this subject. You will be asked to write a synthesis in many academic settings: in the natural sciences, the social sciences, and the humanities. Many managerial jobs, as well as jobs in the medical field and in education, require preparation of such papers.

- A government economist synthesizes the various reports concerning imports and exports to a Third World Country and contrasts the current reports with those from ten years ago.
- An art professor asks students to pick a style of art, research the opinions of important scholars on the style, and comment, critique, compare, and evaluate their positions.
- A student proposes a psychology experiment using music therapy to teach special ed children. The first section of this essay surveys and critiques the studies already done by psychologists in two areas: teaching of these children and music therapy for these children. (Conventionally, most social science and natural science primary

135

research reports of experiments begin with an introduction that surveys and synthesizes studies and experiments already done on the subject.) *Writing Successfully* contains this essay (pp. 209-14).

Argument papers, whether taking a position, proposing a solution, or persuading an audience, usually involve researching a subject to construct a logical position and defending the position against opposing arguments (which you also often find with library research). This type of research takes place in all academic branches of the natural sciences, the social sciences, and the humanities. Besides the obvious applications in fields related to the law and politics, there are applications for engineers, medical personnel, business managers, entrepreneurs, and educators.

- A professor asks a literature class to research critical opinion on a well-known character in literature, present the arguments (notice this also includes synthesis), decide which critical position has the most validity, and argue that position.
- A sociology class researches problems connected with the homeless (primary sources), and together they draft a proposal to relieve the homeless problem in their college's town, arguing with evidence that the solution will work.
- A group of townspeople research the various arguments to ban *Huckleberry Finn* in their high school, and then draft an editorial to persuade townspeople that *Huckleberry Finn* is not only a great American novel, but also that one of its most pervasive themes is the end of racial prejudice.

Analysis essays ask you to examine causal relationships. If you are doing a *rhetorical* or *textual analysis*, you will at minimum do primary research, analyzing the object that is your subject, but you will also probably be asked to do secondary research into the culture or audience the subject comes from or is addressed to. You could also be examining the causal relationship of any activity or situation, which would take either primary research (if you participate or participated in the activity) and secondary research if you did not.

- For a freshman composition course, students are asked to do a *rhetorical analysis* of an advertisement, and they would study the ad itself in detail as well as other ads of the same type (primary research), as well as doing secondary research from business sources to find out about the company the ad came from and sociology sources about types of readers who would use the product.
- A professor of a cross-cultural course in Latino culture asks for a *textual analysis* of a Spanish film, analyzing the film (a primary source), the director (secondary research) and the culture for which he produced the film (secondary research).
- A married couple in therapy must pick a significant experience related to their gender or race and analyze the causes and effects of the experience (primary sources - observation, perhaps interviews with people who were at the student's experience).

- A person getting ready to vote in her first election analyzes the probable causes and effects of each of the candidates' positions to make her decision.

Actually performing *primary research* - experiments, observations, interviews, surveys, case studies, lab reports - will be discussed in chapter 9.

Analyzing the Research Requirements and Picking a Subject

As with all writing, for essays employing research make sure you understand the rhetorical situation (the requirements for the essay, its intended audience, genre, and the writing situation). At the simplest level, make sure you understand all the details of the written assignment, asking questions if you need more information:

- Do you use primary or secondary research, or a combination?
- Is the assignment requirement asking for a specific writing genre (at the most basic level, is the purpose for the essay after you have done your research to report, to inform, to persuade, or a combination of these goals?) [All writing, to some degree, persuades – you are convincing your audience with evidence that you have a valid thesis; however, more formally, some writing situations are argument style essays that specifically challenge an audience to do something or to change their minds. This style of writing is discussed in chapter 11.] Study the format, style, tone, and diction of the genre requested by the assignment.
- Make sure you understand the length of the essay and the research project it involves: the problem usually occurs when students pick a subject/research question too broad, one that it would take an entire book to answer. Native American treaty violations would be the subject of an entire book. A specific topic for a college research essay might be "What was the nature of the Native American complaints at the Wounded Knee standoff in the 1970s?" Of course as a student did this research other research questions would naturally occur that had to be answered for the writer to be knowledgeable enough to write the essay: what were the FBI and the Bureau of Indian Affairs' positions? What was the longer history of the Lakota people germane to the situation? What was the outcome of the siege? Who were the principal participants?
- Based on either the specific genre or the professor's instructions, study or create the intended audience carefully. (If you give an audience too much information they already know, they will become bored. If you don't give them enough, they will not be able to follow your essay's reasoning. Specifically target your audience [ch. 2] and decide what they know and what they need to know for you to successfully inform or persuade them.)
- As with all writing, you must obtain enough knowledge to write about your subject with the complexity it deserves, and you must develop a thesis statement, a purpose for your writing.
- As for tone, most researched writing has a formal, objective, serious tone.

All these research requirement questions must be answered the first week of the research project, or a student could waste quite a bit of time.

Pick a subject that you want to know more about and for which you can develop questions. Given your broad subject, think of some questions you want to know the answers too. From the research question arrives the focused subject, and make sure to focus the research question(s) to create a focused subject. See the third bullet above, and here are two more illustrations:

Too broad/vague: How do students pick a college? (vague and ultimately too many answers)
More specific question: How are SAT/ACT scores measured and how do they affect college entrance? **Focused Subject**: SAT/ACT Scores
Too broad/unfocused: What were the causes of the Civil War? (This begs a 1000 page book!!!)
More specific: What effects did abolition societies have in the 1850s and 1860s in America?

If you are having trouble choosing a subject, if the requirements allow pick a subject from a possible major you are considering: this will help you decide whether you want to major in that field or not. If you do not pick a subject you are interested in, you will become bored and it will show in your effort. Even if your professor has picked a broad subject area that you do not like, begin researching to focus and find a sub-topic you like better. Procrastination will, obviously, get you nowhere.

As you begin reading articles written by scholars on the subject you are researching, examine how they write their articles. Look at organizational format, style, tone, word choice. Also, at any point during the research or writing process, if you are not sure exactly what the professor expects, ask questions and try to get examples from the professor. If it is a large class, go to your school's writing center. The best research essays are modeled after the articles you are reading concerning your subject. Don't sell yourself short — imitate their style and the conventions that they use. For questions about how to research: *this is going to be repeated several times it is so important - ask a school librarian*, whose entire job is knowing how to do research.

Planning the Research Project

Since researched essays take more time, the wise student, in conjunction with the course syllabus, creates a written timetable to schedule approximate due dates for each section of the project. Follow a schedule using all the steps below and you will successfully complete a researched essay, but be sure to do each step thoroughly. The first four research steps in this timetable are explained in this chapter; the last five are predrafting (chapters two-three), writing, revision (chapters four - five), and editing (chapters thirteen - twenty-six).

Completion date by
2/14   1) Specifically analyze the requirements, genre, and audience: pp. 134-8.
2/16   2) Pick a FOCUSED subject/research question(s) of interest suitable for the audience and writing situation: pp.134-8.

2/18   3) Begin research with encyclopedia, reference, and textbook articles on the subject *for basic information on the subject.* Use encyclopedia/textbook bibliographies to find names and titles of *authoritative* scholars, books, and articles on your subject. Prepare a preliminary bibliography: pp.139-43.

2/25   4*)* Use on-line book catalogs and magazine/journal databases for more books and articles to add to the preliminary bibliography and, having obtained a basic knowledge of the subject, begin *in-depth, specific critical reading* of the books and articles (taking notes, summarizing, responding, evaluating, synthesizing). *Focus Subject* more while reading if necessary. Focusing early and quickly saves time by moving quickly to reading only articles and sections of books relevant to the focused subject: pp. 143-148.

2/28   5) *Re-analyze Audience and Situation* after investigating the subject, eventually arriving at a *preliminary thesis*: chapters 1-2.

3/7   6) Continue research to make sure the thesis is valid. Modify thesis if necessary and continue research until deciding on a finalized *thesis statement.* Prove the validity of the thesis statement with an *outline of content* that would adequately support this thesis. Return to the library and fill in gaps in your lines of reasoning by finding more support. *Submit Annotated Bibliography, Writing Context, and Outline to professor*: chapters 3, 7, 8.

3/14   7) Draft Due.

3/18   8) Revised Draft Due – revised for context, content, organization, and paragraphs.

3/23   9) Essay Due – final content revision, and edited for style and proper documentation.

Developing Content using the Library and Computer

Large research libraries are much more complex and contain much more information than public and high school libraries, *so save yourself time and ask college librarians to help you use your library efficiently.* Librarians are your most important source for finding information. There is absolutely no reason to stay lost in a library.

Since libraries have all joined the computer age (the changes are rapid, even yearly now), learn when and how to use the computer for library searches and, in most instances now, for retrieving periodical articles and government information. Especially learn how NOT to do college level research: it is not in anyone's best interests to do much research using Google or any general internet search engine!!! Anyone can post anything on the web - correct or not, well reasoned or infantile, the latest research or someone's guesses based on who knows? College is not the place to use questionable sources. Fortunately, all college libraries have databases they subscribe to that have had librarians pick reasonably reliable sources for their content (not that most articles won't be biased, but at least they aren't fringe arguments from lunatics). Students can, from home, often search these databases on the college library website. Databases chosen by college (and now public) libraries allow access to most mainstream magazines, large newspapers with reputable research staff, and journals written by experts. Different databases have different kinds of material, and it is a requirement of freshmen in college to learn how to navigate these databases on their college library websites. *The best way to learn is go into a library when there are support staff to help you if you have questions, and spend an afternoon exploring.*

So in order to succeed in college, you need to become familiar with a broad base of information-retrieval systems, of which the library will remain central (even if you communicate with the library by computer rather than in person). Using computers for research will be discussed generally in this chapter, but you need to become familiar with the intricacies of the computer systems at the libraries you use. Each library's system has minor differences that can be mastered quickly. *Both librarians and computers will save you much time*: learn to use them well.

Obtaining General Knowledge of Your Subject

A basic knowledge of the subject is essential for any writing or learning activity, and college textbooks, encyclopedias, and other reference works, used together, are a good place to start. What are the questions you need answered to begin to understand your research subject? As you read the first few general information sources, add to your list of basic questions on the subject, and find the answers. Later in your research, you will begin to form search questions that will be directly related to the focused subject of the essay you are planning, but an encyclopedia-type knowledge is necessary before being able to understand more in-depth research.

It is really a good student's job to learn ALL the features of a good library, and a tried and true section of the library is the reference section. You will discover not only the BEST general encyclopedias like the *Encyclopedia Brittanica*, but you will find row after row of specialized encyclopedias and almanacs: how about a 20 volume encyclopedia just for music and musicians, or a multi-volume biographical dictionary, or a listing of all federal or state laws? Each of these reference tools has articles written by experts in their fields, and in addition to good, solid basic information on the topic, they also have bibliographies of the best works on the subject (chosen by the experts).

Most colleges have also begun offering on-line reference databases such as *The CQ Researcher* and the *Credo Reference* database.

As you read basic information on your subject:

- Take notes and summarize major ideas and concepts, and note important people and the major historical changes in your subject's knowledge base. (For instance, information on DNA and how it can be used changes almost yearly now.)
- Use specialized biographical encyclopedias to research important scholars in the subject. (Try to read works only by acknowledged experts and leaders in your focused subject. A leader might not be an expert, but if her voice is important in discourse on the subject, she should be read.)
- Look up unfamiliar words in a dictionary and become knowledgeable in the key words and specialized diction of your subject area. (For instance, a student describing the process of making a film would want to know exactly what the *gaffer* does.)
- Differentiate fact from opinion and use all the techniques of close reading (chapter 6).

- When starting with encyclopedias, use not only general encyclopedias like the *Encyclopedia Britannica* or the *Encyclopedia Americana*, but also specialized encyclopedias like the *International Encyclopedia of the Social Sciences*. (There are specialized encyclopedias and dictionaries for all the disciplines of the humanities, the social sciences, the natural sciences, and business.) See the list below and on the next page.
- *Do not trust Wikipedia or an encyclopedia loaded onto your computer.* A few decades from now, Wikipedia could possibly be the best encyclopedia ever written, but for now there are too many errors, which you would spot if you knew a subject. (But we don't go to encyclopedias for subjects we already know a lot about, only those we don't. So we cannot evaluate the accuracy of a Wikipedia article). Trust the sources listed in this section.

Use encyclopedias and textbooks in three ways:

- Read the articles relevant for your research topic so that you have a basic knowledge of the subject.
- Use their bibliographies as a starting point to find authoritative articles and books on a subject. The writers of textbooks and encyclopedia articles are experts in their field, so with their knowledge they can point you toward authoritative sources.
- Look for sub-topics of the main subject to focus your subject to a topic manageable in a short researched essay.

The pages following contain a *partial* list of specialized encyclopedias, which can be found in the reference section of most college libraries. Do not trust the internet for basic information – go to the experts found in these specialized encyclopedias (whether in the reference room of the library or in a college database). For additional resources, ask a librarian. **Do not read specialized articles and books on your subject until you have a basic understanding of your subject, found in specialized encyclopedias.**

On-line Resources

If your library's databases include these, you can get much basic information from these three sources. Also, ask a librarian what your school's databases have for encyclopedia-type material:

The CQ Researcher. A weekly magazine where each issue focuses exclusively on one subject, good for current issues.

Gale Virtual Reference Library. A good start at the multitude of encyclopedia and reference works only found inside libraries, and now if a school links to Gale databases, a student can research from home what used to be available only in the reference room of the library.

Credo Reference. Like Gale, contains many of the specialized and general encyclopedia articles that used to be found only in the Reference Room of the library and now students can get them at home.

The Best General Encyclopedias

Academic American Encyclopedia. 21 vols.
Collier's Encyclopedia. 24 vols.
Encyclopedia Americana. 30 vols.
Encyclopedia Britannica. 30 vols. – the best by far.

Specialized Encyclopedias

Dictionary of American History. 3rd ed. 10 vols. 2002.
Dictionary of the History of Ideas. 6 vols. 2004.
Encyclopedia of American Foreign Policy. 3 vols. 2nd ed. 2001.
Encyclopedia of Philosophy. Ed. Paul Edwards *et al.* 8 vols.1978.
Encyclopedia of Psychology. Ed. Alan Kazdan. 8 vols. 2000.
Encyclopedia of World Art. 17 vols. 1959-1968.
International Encyclopedia of the Social Sciences. 9 vols. 2007.
McGraw-Hill Encyclopedia of Science and Technology. 20 vols. 11th ed. 2012.
The New Grove Dictionary of Music and Musicians. Ed. Stanley Sadie.
          20 vols. 2004.
Stierlin, Henri. *Encyclopedia of World Architecture.* 2 vols. 1998.

Yearbooks — Current Events/Statistics

Americana Annual. 1923-.
Annual Register. 1758-.
Britannica Book of the Year. 1938-.
Facts on File. 1940-.
Statistical Abstract of the United States. 1878-.
World Almanac and Book of Facts. 1868 –.

Biographical Dictionaries

Contemporary Authors. Can often get this as a database through library databases.
Dictionary of American Biography. 16 vols. and index. 1927-80. Supplements. —
          Entries include only dead Americans.
Dictionary of National Biography. 60 vols. 1882-2004. Supplements.—
          Entries include only dead Englishmen.
Dictionary of Scientific Biography. 8 vols. 2007.
Directory of American Scholars. Rev. ed. 2013.
International Who's Who. 1935- .
Who's Who in America. 1899 -.
McGraw-Hill Encyclopedia of World Biography. 2nd ed. 1997.

Literature

Cambridge History of American Literature. 7 vols.
Cambridge History of English Literature. 15 vols.
Drabble, Margaret. *Oxford Companion to English Literature.* 5th ed. 1985.

Hart, James D. *Oxford Companion to American Literature*. 4th ed. 1965.
Harvey, Sir Paul. *Oxford Companion to Classical Literature*. 2nd ed. 1937-1984.
Spiller, Robert E., *et al. Literary History of the United States*. 4th ed. 2 vols. 1974.

College Level Research

Once you have obtained a general knowledge of your subject, and hopefully have focused your subject as much as possible before beginning your in-depth research, it is time to see what facts there are about your subject and what the experts in your subject say about it. It has already been mentioned that you should attempt to find from your general knowledge readings who the experts are on your subject, and try to find their works to study. Most library reference section encyclopedias have bibliographies that could help you with this.

When you search the library databases (or card catalogs and periodical indexes for libraries not completely connected to the latest research techniques), look for those authors who are experts. As was mentioned in chapter 6, if you find a likely authoritative source by an author, check for his/her reliability in *Contemporary Authors, America's Who's Who,* or *The Directory of American Scholars.*

Find out how your library indexes books, periodical articles, and newspapers. Periodicals, newspapers, and increasingly books can all be retrieved electronically now, but don't ignore printed books, and if you need older periodicals for a historical view you might need to go into the stacks of the library. You should now look for:

- authoritative books
- journal articles (journals are specialized magazines written by scholars for scholars.)
- popular magazine articles (written for the general public and less authoritative than journal articles)
- newspapers (less authoritative than either journals or magazines, not usually written by experts though most try to report objectively. National newspapers like the *New York Times* and the *Washington Post* can be authoritative, though biased.)

Reliability: Books/Popular Magazines/Scholarly Journals/ Newspapers/The Internet

The types of periodical articles most often used in scholarly research are those found in academic *journals* and *government publications*. Journals are written by scholars, for scholars. They are more difficult to read than popular magazines, as a general rule, because they are written for experts, but they also contain more specific information than general magazines. There is also a screening process for articles in journals to assure the article's authority and high quality. As a matter of fact, journalists who write for both newspapers and popular magazines like *Time* or *Psychology Today*, before interviewing experts, read journal articles on their subject, and then they take the information from journal articles and from the experts, and re-write it so that the general population can read it in a popular magazine. However, in freshman composition and other freshman courses, professors will often have you do research not only in academic journals, but also in newspapers and popular magazines (so that you understand the difference in the types of research, analysis, and writing in these differing rhetorical situations), but after freshman courses most research will occur in either scholarly journals or from primary sources in historical or literary research.

When reading in journals for your research paper, it is wise to narrow your subject first — to be able to state precisely what the subject of your research will be. For example, "Mark Twain" as a subject is too broad, but "Twain's Views on Race Relations as Exhibited in *Huckleberry Finn* and *Pudd'nhead Wilson*" has been focused. There are countless articles in scholarly journals on Mark Twain, even on *Huckleberry Finn* and *Pudd'nhead Wilson*. There is even a journal that specializes in the literature of Mark Twain, *The Mark Twain Journal*. If you have narrowed the scope to race relations in those two novels, you can more easily find the relevant articles in scholarly journals.

In summary, be aware that articles in popular magazines and newspapers are written for general audiences, and are often merely summaries of the research done by scholars and reported in scholarly journals. The hard evidence needed to be persuasive in college research will often be found in scholarly journals. Do not limit yourself only to magazines; avail yourself of the research found in scholarly journals and government research. You can be assured of the authoritative nature of articles written in journals; this is not true of magazine articles.

Newspapers also have the same problems that magazines do. The writers are often not experts in the fields they are reporting on. Another problem, with newspapers and magazines, is that they usually have an editorial board with a bias (either toward liberal or conservative tendencies), and while this is to be expected, it makes it harder for a student researching an issue for the first time to sift fact from opinion, and to recognize the biases of an opinion in an article.

Of course, newspapers are your only source if your subject is new and topical. When you do choose to use newspaper or popular magazine articles, try to corroborate the evidence (find the information reported in more than one source); also, choose the most authoritative newspapers. Writers and editors of small town newspapers do not have the resources to check every article. They do the best job that they can to be authoritative. On the other hand, for subjects of local interest only, you have to rely on local coverage. For national and international subjects, whenever possible choose the *New York Times*, the *Washington Post*, or the *London Times* (known for their reliability) rather than local coverage.

What has been said about magazines/newspapers versus academic journals is also true of books. Just because it has been published, it still might not be authoritative. If it is in a college library, you can be somewhat more sure of its authority; however, because libraries rarely throw away books, make sure the book has the timeliest information. A literary analysis can be good whether it was written in the nineteenth century or last year, while a report on conditions on Mars changes every decade as more information becomes available, as with history, psychology, and other disciplines that have a time element attached to them. Studies of dating patterns from the 1950s and psychological evaluations of them have little value unless one is writing a historical view of dating.

The problems voiced about reliability concerning magazines, newspapers, and books triple when using the internet. Magazine and newspaper editors attempt to provide reliable, authoritative information, but anyone can post whatever they want on the web. Use extreme caution when citing internet sources. Having said this, many scholars and universities publish on the internet, and you can find a world of valid information using it: just use all the suggestions for evaluating texts discussed in chapter 6 before relying on any information from the internet. *The best way to avoid problems with internet sources is to use ONLY those databases connected to your school's library website.* However, another warning: even those databases retrieved off a library website do not automatically differentiate between general knowledge articles and articles written by experts. You need to be aware of your source's credibility, so before using any database or card catalog you have to know enough about your subject to be able to differentiate between known authorities and unknown authors, between information with reliable evidence and unsubstantiated information. Good researchers do this by using:

- Reference encyclopedia bibliographies that list specific sources by known scholars in the field, and then using those named sources for information and opinions.
- A biographical dictionary source like *Contemporary Authors* to find out about the credibility of the scholar, and any biases she might have.
- Advanced settings on most databases that let you limit searches to full text articles, to articles only in journals, by title of periodical or by range of dates, as well as other limiters.

For those who ignore the advice of this section and use Google or another search engine to just blindly go out on the web, some words of caution and promise concerning the web:

- Before using information gleaned from the internet, be aware that anyone can post anything they want, whether it is true or not, at a web site. One needs to very carefully evaluate any information found on-line. Having said that, many users of the web do publish factual, important, relevant information on the web. Just be careful, using all the evaluation methods discussed in chapter 6.
- Web sites can be there one day and gone the next, as can information found at a web site. When you find information you might use, print it and carefully record the search path (the web address and the date you found it). Also, be aware that unlike books and magazines, web sites can be constantly changed. When you return to a site, you might find new and interesting material, but information that was once at a site might be gone.
- Many sites and search engines have *chat rooms*, usually discussing a specific subject, where people using the web can discuss issues relevant to the chat room with other users of the chat room, and where people can post information and/or leave questions that they would like answered by other users of the chat room. While intelligent dialogue often occurs in these chat rooms, anyone can post anything on these, factual or not, logical or not, so be very careful and use all of the evaluation methods discussed in chapter 6.
- The world wide web and chat rooms are excellent places to find out the range of opinions concerning a subject, and some search engines are excellent

places to find relevant subtopics of your subject. With the immensity of the web, *IF you carefully evaluate the sites*, it is an excellent place to find many sources quickly. You can ask questions in chat rooms, and knowledgeable participants of the chat room often answer the questions. Ask your professor before using a chat room as a source. In addition, many magazines and newspapers (including the *New York Times*) publish part or all of their contents for free on the web. It is also becoming possible to tie into some of the world's largest libraries without leaving home. Researchers in the twenty-first century need to become familiar with on-line research. For all its flaws, it considerably expands the horizons of anyone's research.

Online Database Periodical Indexes

Periodicals (both popular magazines and scholarly journals) are indexed by various databases purchased by libraries and loaded onto their websites. Different databases focus on different kinds of magazines and journals (as evidenced in the sampling listed on the next page). In addition, most libraries have older printed indexes, which researchers only have to use if they are looking for articles published before the computer age (usually pre-1980s). For instance, if you write an article on 19th century public school systems, or the poetry of the 17th century English poet, John Milton, many of the most important scholarly articles and books could have been written before the age of computers, and to find the most relevant articles you would sometimes have to use the old printed indexes (after saving time by consulting encyclopedia type articles to discover authoritative sources). However, many databases today also include older articles.

Researchers access most of these web-based databases using a subject index, but you can also look for individual writers and articles. The indexes also give you a. original print publication information which you will need to cite your sources, b. an abstract which is a summary of the source, and in most cases c. users can access the article or book itself right from the database.

These abstracts really save time: you can quickly survey many articles - 100 or 200 - on a subject by looking at the titles.

- From the title you can discount half the articles as unpromising.
- If the title seems promising, read the abstract. Unpromising abstracts will eliminate more of the articles.
- The ones with the most promising abstracts and the most authoritative authors and journals are the articles you actually choose to read.

Instead of picking the first ten articles you find whether they were the best or not, this process with practice takes at most an hour or two to find the best fifteen or twenty articles out of 200-400 possibilities.

If the database you are using does not have the article itself stored, it usually tells you whether the library you are in contains the periodical referenced by the database. If you need to read the article, you will have to record the call numbers of the periodical and go to the periodical stacks of the library where you will find the journal. (The issues are bound together by year.) *If your library does not have a copy of the periodical, and you know from the abstract that the article will be very important for your research, college libraries have an inter-library loan system, and*

146

you can ask the librarian to get an article or a book through inter-library loan. This process takes a few days to a week, so make the request quickly.

Each library contracts, and pays for, specific databases loaded into their computer systems. You need to search your library's website to discover which databases your library uses, and more importantly find out the kinds of articles published and the kind of periodicals referenced in each of the databases. Since each database and each library computer system is different, it would be pointless to describe how to use these systems. *You need to study your library website and ask the staff at your library what they have cataloged in their system, and how to use the various sources.* The list below contains ten of the major databases used by many schools (all listing articles by subject), with an explanation of the kinds of articles referenced in them, and words of caution when appropriate.

ERIC or JSTOR: Two databases that contain articles from scholarly journals in all of the disciplines studied on college campuses. These important databases list mostly scholarly articles first published in journals, so the articles tend to be more authoritative. They are the journals used by scholars and professors.

Contemporary Authors: A database that does not list articles; it lists authors. It contains biographical information and book reviews of books by that author. This is a very important source for judging the reliability of the writers you are reading.

Government Documents: Libraries use several types of databases to access government documents, so see if your library has a database with this function. The U.S. Government is one of the most active research systems in the world, and thus they are also the largest publisher of statistical data in the world, a valuable storehouse of information in the natural and social sciences. If you are attending a larger university, major research libraries have an entire department devoted to cataloging government data; use the staff in this department to help you research government documents.

EBSCO Host: A comprehensive database that contain a multiple sub-databases with articles and books on a broad base of subjects from newspapers, magazines, books, and professional journals, including the respected general *Academic Search Complete*.

Newsbank or *Newspaper Source*: Two databases that contains articles on a broad base of subjects from newspapers around the country. Use caution with this database, as local newspapers are not always authoritative sources.

New York Times Index: A database that contains articles by the most respected newspaper in the world, though it has a known liberal bias. The authors tend to be experts in their subjects, but be careful to evaluate whether you are reading an article that is an opinion piece or factual journalism. An opinion piece can also be factual, but it is, of course, biased.

Gale Databases: A collection of databases from one company that includes databases focusing on individual subjects like business or health fields, it has many general information type databases, and it also has the respected *Academic One File* which lists popular magazine, newspaper, and journal articles.

Credo Reference: A database that contains many of the specialized reference encyclopedias and dictionaries formerly found only in the reference section of the library.

Books: Card Catalogs and Online Book Catalogs

Most libraries now have computerized card catalogs, but you should ask whether *all* of the library's books are cataloged in the computer system (especially older books). Often, only books received after a certain date are included in the computer database or "online catalog." In either case, cards or computers, books are cataloged three ways: by title, by author, and by subject categories, using either the Library of Congress system (the call number begins with one or more letters) or the Dewey Decimal system (the call number begins with a number). *Preparing to find a book, be sure to copy the entire number from the card catalog or the database, as well as the author, title, publisher, place, and date of publication.* If you know the title of a book, you can get the complete bibliographical information and the call number by typing in the title (or finding its card with the old system). If you know an author famous in a subject field, you can type in the name (or find the cards) to find the complete information and call number on every book in the library by that author. The subject catalog is more vague. You will find every book on a subject, but 1) you won't know which books are the best ones, and 2) if you are in a large research library, you might find hundreds or even thousands of books listed.

As you look for books on a subject, remember to consider their authority — choose works by known authorities, review the author in *Contemporary Authors* or another biographical dictionary, or review the book in *Book Review Digest*.

Also, before you check a book out of the library, read its preface, introduction, and look at its table of contents and index. This will tell you three things: a. whether the book, in fact, has information relevant to your research; b. if it does, which chapters of the book to read instead of reading the entire book (though you should never skip the opening and closing chapters for an overall view); and c. what particular biases an author has toward his/her subject (no author is completely objective). a. and c. will help you decide if you need the book or not.

When you enter a library for the first time, ask someone to show you how to retrieve books.

Compiling an Annotated Bibliography and Taking Notes

As you research, develop a system you can use and that you are comfortable with, to keep track of the information you find. Teachers for most of the twentieth century usually suggested transcribing information on 3X5 or 5X7 notecards. For the writer of this handbook, notecards are not large enough, but if that is what you are comfortable with, use them. A second option is to record your notes, evaluations, analysis, synthesis, and predrafting in a spiral notebook or in a single computer file. But above all, keep your notes in the same place. When you read articles, this writer strongly suggests making copies of articles that you find relevant to your subject. Then, you can write summary, response, evaluative, and synthesis notes in the margins of the articles.

As you research, your notes should become an annotated bibliography of sources you have read on your subject, whether the sources are books, print articles, or internet sources. These annotated bibliographies should summarize and evaluate your sources. They should also have the complete bibliographic data necessary for you or the reader to find your original source if needed. The next section contains an example of an annotated bibliography. Some professors demand an annotated bibliography with any research essay written. The rest of this chapter and chapter 8 discusses synthesizing these sources into a researched essay.

EXERCISE 7.1
Constructing an Annotated Bibliography

A bibliography contains all the sources you consult to write your essay, whether you used them in your essay or not. Some of the sources in your annotated bibliography might be sources that were very poorly written, poorly argued, even worthless. Conversely, some of the articles in the bibliography might be excellent articles, but you later focus your subject or construct a thesis that doesn't necessitate using the source. The point of the annotated bibliography is to have a record of the sources you looked at, not just the ones you refer to in your essay. In fact, you did use all the sources to become an expert on your subject, even if you don't refer in your essay to every source you looked at. As a matter of fact, *scholars almost never refer to information they find in encyclopedias; they use reference books to learn about their subjects and develop bibliographies.*

Compile an annotated bibliography of sources for the subject of your research essay that contains these features:

1) A complete bibliographical entry using the documentation form assigned by your professor. (Chapters 23-26 demonstrate MLA, APA, CSE, and Chicago styles.)
2) A summary of each entry — longer if it seems necessary for your specific research; shorter if the source will not be used.
3) An evaluation of the strengths and weaknesses of each source, including checking the reliability of the author in *Contemporary Authors*, the *Directory of American Scholars, America's Who's Who*, the *International Who's Who*, the *Book Review Digest*, or any other source that helps you evaluate the author. (Some professors ask you to photocopy or print the information that you find and append it to the annotated bibliography.)
4) Don't disappear into your research. Respond to the source: do you agree or disagree with the ideas? Can you relate what was said to your own experience, observations, or other sources yoou have read?
5) A short discussion of whether you can use the source in your essay or not, and if you can, how you might use it.
5) As you study, summarize, evaluate, and respond to your sources, remember that you are developing a specific thesis for an essay you will write, so have a page where you take notes to remember your developing ideas for what YOUR ESSAY is going to say about your subject, and what research you will use to help you prove your point.
(7.1 continued on next page)

149

7.1 Continued Find at least one source on your subject in each of these categories:

A) a general encyclopedia, preferably *Encyclopedia Brittanica*
B) a specialized encyclopedia from the library reference section/database
C-D) two newspaper articles, at least one of them being *The New York Times* or *The London Times*
E) a popular magazine article
F) a journal article
G) a book
H) an internet website (to evaluate the difference between [originally] print sources and web sources)
I) _____ more articles of your choosing that will help you write the essay
J) When you are finished, write a letter discussing which types of sources were most and least valuable, and why. (Were they credible? Did they rely on fact or opinion? Were the opinions substantiated with reliable evidence and/or logic? Which are best for college level research?)

Synthesizing Multiple Sources

When you are researching a topic using written sources, of course you need to read critically, but you also need to synthesize; in other words, analyze the relationships between the sources that you read. Activities that scholars use to synthesize include summary, comparison, contrast, definition, and analysis.

The first two components of synthesis are:

- Critical reading to understand, respond to, and evaluate each source individually. Use all the pre-reading, reading, and post-reading tools discussed in chapters six and seven.
- As you read, decide on your own views on the subject you are researching. Develop support through your reading and your personal experience and observation to persuade yourself that you are creating a valid, supportable view on the issues germane to the subject.

As you begin to gather multiple sources on a topic, take notes on the relationships among the ideas and the support of the sources you read.

Synthesis research culminating in essays that synthesize contains these features:

- *Create an informal annotated bibliography*: write a short summary/ evaluation/response as demonstrated in chapter six of each source as you read it (either actually writing on the text - or copies of it - or in a notebook or computer file).
- List sub-topics of the main subject, and list which sources (and the appropriate page numbers) discuss which sub-topics.
- Compare: Make a list of authors who agree (with appropriate page numbers). Decide which authors have the most adequate support for the ideas they agree on, and list the best support for each idea. One essay might have the best examples for an idea in another essay.

150

- Contrast: Make a list of the ideas authors disagree on, and summarize, describe, and define their differences. Analyze the strengths and weaknesses of their support, and decide which authors have the most valid reasoning or support. (Include in this analysis support that you know of not contained in the sources. A source might have the most valid thesis, but the writer has not supported the idea as well as he or she should have.)
- Definition: How do various sources define and explain key concepts on a subject? With some subjects, writers define concepts differently. Be aware of the differences as they affect meaning.
- Analysis: Information in one essay can help explain why something occurs or explain a line of reasoning in another essay. (For example, if a source graphically describes a teen killing another teen for tennis shoes, a student notices that O'Brien's essay, another source, makes the connection between violence and materialism, which offers an explanation for the violence. See the synthesis essay on pp.158-60)
- *Most importantly: Do not let your thoughts on a subject disappear. Although your thoughts on a subject may be changing as you research and learn new information and lines of reasoning, be alert to the connections between your evolving thesis concerning the subject and the ideas in the sources you read. Ultimately, you are synthesizing sources so that you can develop your own adequately supported statement about the subject.*

When you choose to copy a direct quotation, be sure to put quotation marks around the quotation and write the exact page number. If you don't, when you write your essay from your notes you will forget the quotation marks in your essay and will have commited plagiarism, which could earn you a failing grade.

Also, clearly label your summaries, evaluations, and responses; otherwise, you might take someone else's ideas and not give them credit for it, which also is plagiariam. Notice how the student in the example below clearly differentiates between his ideas and the summaries of his source material.

Study this annotated bibliography carefully. This is the research path Mr. Hughes took to arrive at the essay that utilizes synthesis at the end of this chapter. He had to read more essays than he actually used to become knowledgeable in, and think about, his subject and to develop a thesis and essay with good supporting evidence.

The section concluding the chapter demonstrates student Gary Hughes preparing an annotated bibliography and writing an essay. His research question was whether or not the media influenced youth violence. While he does not have a definitive answer to this question (as there isn't one easy answer), from this research he develops a thesis and supports it with evidence. The essay itself concludes the chapter.

Student Example: Annotated Bibliography and Synthesis Essay (MLA citations used)

Begins research with encyclopedia / textbook general information articles to gain basic knowledge of subject.

Subject: the media and violence

General Encyclopedia

"Broadcasting." *The New Encyclopedia Brittanica: Macropedia,* 15th ed., vol. 2, Encyclopedia Brittanica, 2007, pp. 272-292.

Begin ALL summaries with the author's name (or title of the article if anonymous) or it is plagiarism.

Summary: "Broadcasting" discusses broadcasting history, science, broadcasting types/systems, relationship to public, to artists, and broadcasting as art.
On violence: westerns, shows involving gangsters and cops, and hospital shows prevalent. Some people have criticized violence on tv as harmful to children, so many broadcast mediums have "introduced codes of practice to minimize these scenes" (2: 279).
From the bibliography, some important books that might be useful: George Comstock et al, *Television and Human Behavior,* R.J. Thompson, *Television Crime-Drama* (1959: early study of adolescent and violence); US Surgeon-General, *Television and Growing Up: The Impact of Television Violence,* Himmelwitt, Openheimer, and Vince, *Television and the Child* (more general on impact of tv).
Evaluation: Good for first read on subject, but can't use, so brief summary.

"Behavior: the Development of Human Behavior." *The New Encyclopedia Brittanica: Macropedia,* 15th ed., vol. 2, Encyclopedia Brittanica, 2007, pp. 302-339. **(publishing company)**
Summary of section on Emotional and Social Development, including "a moral sense":

Put quotation marks around direct quotations, with author and page number referenced (to easily move accurately from notes to proper documentation in the essay).

"Behavior" discusses morality: movement in child goes from threat of punishment to need for adult approval to developing moral standards (which continues into adulthood).
"Others have argued that because even rather young children are capable of showing empathy to the pain of others, the inhibition of aggressive behavior arises from this moral affect rather than from the mere anticipation of punishment" (2: 314).
Evaluation: The *Encyclopedia Brittanica* is certainly the most extensive encyclopedia I have ever seen. Great in-depth articles !!! It has an excellent TWO VOLUME index that shows you all the places a subject is discussed. And broad topics are discussed at length: the topic "Broadcasting" where I found the section I summarized is 37 pages long, with an annotated bibliography listing about 100 relevant books. THIS is THE authoritative encyclopedia needed for general knowledge before starting a research project !!!

Notice that Gary records his own thoughts, so he won't forget them, and he keeps his source's ideas (summary) separate from his thoughts (evaluation and response).

Response: BUT if a child is raised with excessive violence and bad behavior either in his home, his streets, or for some even an over-dose on tv, there will be a poorly developed sense of morality. I don't think we can blame television nearly as much as the community and family he comes from. We certainly can't blame the child. I would like to find out whether children naturally have empathy, that we are born with it, or is it something that is taught. It seems to me that we have innate feelings at an early age. They love dogs. They share toys.

152

Specialized Encyclopedia

Janowitz, Morris, and Joseph Klapper. "Mass
    Communication." *The International Encyclopedia of the Social
    Sciences*, vol 8, Macmillan,1968, pp. 40-90.

Summary: Janowitz reports thousands of experiements (laboratories, interviews, case studies) show that even brief messages produce attitude changes in viewers, sometimes not manifesting until much later than the message (the "sleeper effect") (49). Mass media can be used as a system of social control (8: 51-53).

After summarizing major scholarly opinion, Thomas Hogarth asks pertinent question defending mass media's messages: "Recurrent violence on television seems likely to encourage acts of violence only in the psychotic or mentally disabled ... to what extent can one risk further unbalancing the unbalanced?" [he seems to suggest that the media should not be concerned] (qtd. in Janowitz and Klapper 8: 65)

Joseph Klapper suggests the most common effect of mass communication: reinforcement of audience's pre-existing interests, attitudes, and behavior. Least common effect: changing audience behavior and attitudes. Audiences select for viewing what they want to select, not something they don't (or aren't familiar with) (82-83). Various studies find a "preference for crime and violence material [on television] is not a cause but a correlate of maladjustment" (8: 87).

Evaluation: Excellent in-depth article (pp.40-90). Learned everything I needed to know about mass communication from a psychological and sociological aspect. A couple of pages of bibliography after each sub-section of article !!! Very dated info (1968) when discussing communist mass media and statistics, but theories are important in this article.

Gary has learned the usefulness of specialized encyclopedias.

General Encyclopedia

"School Violence." *Grolier Multimedia Encyclopedia*, 2012. *Grolier Multimedia
    Encyclopedia (EbscoHost)*, www. libproxy.kctcs.edu/MuseSessionID=
    0e10h7fcm/MuseProtocol=https/MuseHost=digital.scholastic.com

Summary: "School Violence" lists school violence incidents. Mentions that public schools and children are no longer safe. Mentions techniques for avoiding school violence including gun control laws, discipline and dress codes, and increased security in schools. Does have a very brief bibliography.

Evaluation: This essay contains very general information already commonly known. No depth to the article at all !!! No specifics or analysis, only brief data. More for middle school students studying social studies for the first time (though great for them). After reading the comprehensive *Encyclopedia Brittanica* article and specialized encyclopedia articles, I see what the professor means: many encyclopedias are nothing more than dictionaries with extended definitions, and only specialized encyclopedias and the *Encyclopedia Brittanica* are relevant for college level research.

Gary also finds that most general encyclopedias do not have much detailed information.

Response: Not useful at all and real eye-opener on non-usefulness of most general encylopedias except for readers 16 and under.

Book - Anthology of readings
Males, Mike. "Public Enemy Number One?" *American Culture and the Media*,
 edited by Anne Cassebaum and Rosemary Haskell, Houghton Mifflin,
 1997, pp. 234-240.
Summary: Males argues the media does not play a major role in youth violence, rather
that child abuse, poverty, and the youth penal system do. Cites "massive multi-national
correlation studies" that show that media violence accounts for 1-5% of child violence.
He cites multiple studies that find 60-90% of prisoners in prison for violent crimes were
victims of abuse. As for prevention: "Ten years of a costly 'get tough' approach to deter
youth violence concluded with the highest rate of crime in the nation's history. Teenage
violence, which had been declining from 1970-1983, doubled from 1983 through 1991
[the years beginning the 'get tough' policy]. It is not surprising that the defenders of these
policies should be casting around for a handy excuse ... [like] television violence."
Evaluation: Though Males is just a student, not an authority, he uses persuasive scientific
studies and statistics to support his points. Very persuasive article.
Response: I was somewhat for toughness for crimes, and this is the first article that
made me start to re-think my views. All the articles I have read after this have continued
to convince me that getting tough is not the answer, but rather prevention of abuse,
education, and reducing poverty ARE the answers.
I can use this article in my essay for support of non-media causes of violence.

Notice how readings are beginning to shape student's
views. Also, he is beginning to make notes concerning
which sources to include in his essay.

Book - Anthology of readings
O'Brien, William. "The Cruel Logic of Teenage Violence." *American Culture and*
 the Media, edited by Anne Cassebaum and Rosemary Haskell,
 Houghton Mifflin, 1997, pp. 9-11.
Summary: O'Brien argues that there is a connection between the American cultural
values of violence and materialism, and this is a major cause of violence, transmitted by
entertainment and advertising. He uses anecdotes about video games, teens murdering,
and "heroes solving problems by killing." He demonstrates a causal link between
materialism and the violence of America. O'Brien states that children behave just like
our society teaches them to behave, and they have much too esy access to violence. He
actually says children act "logically" in their adoption of violence (9-11).
Evaluation and Response: Essay doesn't have much support – but from personal
experience and observation I, and most Americans, would agree with O'Brien (at least
about the value Americans put on violence and materialism, if not on the connection).
I can use this article in my essay for support of non-media causes of violence.

Book
Solomon, Jack. *The Signs of Our Times*, Putnam, 1988.
Summary: Solomon argues that advertising plays on Americans cultural values and desires
to get us to buy. He talks about how they use status symbols and sex to trick us by making
us feel "guilty" if we don't possess their products. the American dream has two sides:
"one communally egalitarian and the other competitively elite." We talk a good game of
equality, but the materialism from advertising and consumrism makes us competitive and

wanting to be thought wealthy. Ads demonstrate this over and over in this book. We all want to "live the fantasy," to have the symbols of wealth that are advertised Advertisers create a fantasy world that plays off the contrast noted.

Evaluation: Well reasoned argument using multiple examples. Very scholarly approach (Solomon is a college professor who has published extensively on pop culture, especially advertising).

Response: I can use this book to support O'Brien's connection between violence and materialism. It's the heavily advertised $100 tennis shoes poor kids are killing for !!!!

At this point in the research process, after reading general information articles in encyclopedias to get general information on the subject, two required readings for the class, and a portion of a book, Gary had made preliminary decisions about a focused subject and the beginnings of a vague thesis, and from this thought process planned the needed research to decide on content and finalize a specific thesis.

Developing Thesis and Research Plan

Preliminary, vague thesis: At this point, I have read enough to know that scholarly opinion agrees that television does not directly cause violence among teens.

Research plan: I need to find some articles on the real causes of teen violence to add to Males article and the connection between Solomon and O'Brien that offers materialism in American culture as a cause, and some recent scholarly articles that describe recent experiments corroborating those early studies I read in the encyclopedias saying that television does not cause violence in children other than those already predisposed to violence.

Article - popular magazine

Canada, Geoffrey. "Peace in the Streets." *Utne Reader*, July/August 1995, pp. 59-61.
    Alt-Press Watch, www. alt-presswatch.com/utne/41369.

Summary: Canada argues that the streets are not safe, especially for children, and offers these solutions: create a corps of peace officers; reduce demand for drugs; reduce domestic violence, child abuse, and neglect; reduce violence in the media; and regulate handguns.

Evaluation and Response: Brief alternative newspaper article. Liberal bias and heart is in the right place, but what world is he living in? Not realistic solutions.

Article - popular magazine

Dickerson, Debra. "Who Shot Johnnie?" *The New Republic*, 1 Jan. 1996, pp. 17-18.
    EbscoHost, www.ebscohost.com/newrepublic/639567.

Summary: Dickerson, a female, black, Harvard educated lawyer shows her anger at the drive-by shooting of her teenage nephew and his ensuing paralysis.

Evaluation: Excellent description of tragedy and emotion.

Response: will be good source for a specific, poignant example. Perhaps start essay with this?

Articles - scholarly journal

Gerbner, George et al. "Cultural Indicators: Violence Profile no. 9." *Journal of Communication*, vol 28, no. 3, 1978, pp. 176-207. *JSTOR*, www.jstor.org/stable/430167.

Gerbner, George et al. "The Demonstration of Power: Violence Profile no. 10." *Journal of Communication*, vol. 29, no. 3, 1979, pp. 177-196. *JSTOR,* www.jstor.org/stable/436214.

Gerbner, George et al. "The Mainstreaming of America." *Journal of Communication*, vol. 30, no. 3, 1980, pp.12-29. *JSTOR,* www.jstor.org/stable/4392582

Gerbner, George, and Larry Gross. "Living With Television: The Violence Profile." *Journal of Communication*, vol. 26, no. 2, 1976, pp. 173-199. *JSTOR,* www.jstor.org/stable/4388142.

Summary: These four journal articles with lead researcher George Gerbner are part of an on-going study using scientific procedure to study the relationship between television and violence. Gerbner et al argue - together - that in only a small sampling does violent television actually cause child violence, but they quite persuasively show that violence on television causes heavy viewing adolescents to be more distrustful and fearful of society than adolescents who do not watch as much.

Evaluation: Man, scholarly articles are hard to read !!!!! I still don't understand the specifics when they describe how they did the studies, but I do understand that they were proving to other psychologists that they were making fair and credible studies.

Response: I didn't see any reason to summarize anything other than the conclusion of these studies. What made me stop and think - the new data I got from them - was the interesting idea (that makes sense logically too) that while violence does not usually add to violence amongst children it does cause them to be more fearful as people. And with the world like it is today, we need children and adults not more, but less, fearful !!! These scholarly studies will be excellent authoritative support for my developing argument.

Newspaper

Wicker, Christine. "Peace of Mind: New York Schools Try to Teach Kids to Resolve Conflict Nonviolently." *Dallas Morning News*, 13 Sept. 2003, p. C1. *Ebsco Host,* www.ebscohost.com/dallasmorningnews/36812.

Summary: Wicker discusses teaching conflict resolution - with description of its effectiveness in individual cases. Students taught breathing techniques and other anxiety/anger reducing techniques, and taught to listen as they talk (C 1).

Evaluation: feel good article. No statistics on success, but sounds like a good idea. Much briefer and less detail than either popular magazine or journal articles.

Response: could use, perhaps in opening or closing. I see what the prof means: newspapers are not a very good source for detailed information.

Newspaper

Jones, Richard and Leslie Kaufman. "New Details in Failure in Child Care." *New York Times*, late ed., 18 Jun 2003, p. B1. *New York Times,* libproxy.kctcs.edu/MuseSessionID=0e11t7fdp/MuseProtocol=https/MuseHost=search.proquest.com/MusePath/nytimes

Summary: According to Jones and Kaufman, NY's Youth and Family Services have 2000 case files on abuse in group homes and residential treatment centers. Files demonstrate that supervision is often inadequate, worker qualifications are sometimes not even looked at, and the files "shed light on [a] sense of defeatism and fatalism prevelant among workers" (B 1).

Evaluation: excellent in-depth article reporting the facts with data to back them up !!!! NYTimes much better than home-town newspaper!!!!!

Response: It's like this all over. The government skimps on those children who need help the most. The more I read, the more I want to pay higher taxes (or have the rich pay more) so that those who need help are not abused as is obvious from this article. This problem has also happened here many times (check local newspaper reports).

Internet source
Parent Universal Resource Experts., 2002, *helpyourteens.com*, Accessed 7 Nov. 2003.
Summary: Parent Universal Resource Experts, an organization with a website, have agenda with their organization to get federal laws regulating residential schools for troubled kids and helping parents find appropriate avenues for their children. Provides some data I have already found to get readers of website to contact their congress members.
Evaluation: would have to do multiple searches to discover whether they are reputable, and since they obviously have an agenda, would have to carefully check their statistics and arguments.
Response: I have always just gone to websites and gotten information, but after studying college research, I see how internet sites especially all have some agenda going so they could skew the facts to reflect their agenda. I hope this is a credible organization as I have seen many reports on residential treatment centers for troubled kids that do not use good tools for helping them. This is a needed website if they do what they say they are doing (helping parents find good treatment centers).

Notice this process has revealed that:
1) Newspapers other than the largest often do not have the in-depth analysis by experts needed in college-level research — though they remain useful for the latest, just breaking, news.
2) Internet websites have to be so carefully checked for bias. Many times there are better, more reliable, sources. Libraries have databases that are better sources.
3) Most general encyclopedias are useful only if a reader has no knowledge of a subject, and for the depth of knowledge needed in college students should refer to the *Encyclopedia Brittanica* and to specialized encyclopedias. These specialized encyclopedias also have in-depth bibliographies of books on a topic, and the bibliographies give an expert's opinion on the most reliable sources. Many specialized bibliographies are now housed within databases that libraries have available.
4) Scholarly journals report data and analysis by experts (preferable); popular magazines report this data, usually without the detail found in scholarly journals.

Gary was now ready to synthesize his sources to decide on a specific thesis and the content to support this thesis. Remember that when you are synthesizing you are comparing and analyzing sources so that you can decide on your own thesis for your essay, and then you use these compared and synthesized sources as content to support your view.

This student began by breaking down his topic into sub-topics that he had read about while becoming knowledgeable in his subject, looking over his annotated bibliography, comparing what his sources thought about the media and violence, and then defining and analyzing this comparison to arrive at thesis and content for his essay.

Sub-topics with comparison/contrast of sources

agreements:

television is violent:	Canada	Gerbner		Males	O'Brien
youth are violent:	Canada	Gerbner		Males	O'Brien	Dickerson

connection between television and violence:

Canada   Gerbner   O'Brien   (Males disagrees)

America is violent:	Canada	Gerbner		Males	O'Brien	Dickerson
America is materialistic:		O'Brien		Solomon	

Connection between violence and materialism   O'Brien

Definition and Analysis (synthesis of sources)

All authors seem to define America and American youth as violent, and want to do something about it. All authors who talk about television say it is violent, and all make a connection between violence and television except Males, who disagrees. He cites studies to show there is not a connection, and Gerbner's studies back this up, but Gerbner says that television does create an unhealthy atmosphere around fear of violence.

O'Brien makes the interesting connection with materialism (which is part of the message of the media), but Males and Canada argue there are other causes of youth violence.

At this point, Gary used the predrafting strategies in chapters 2 and 3 of *Writing Successfully* (clustering, freewriting, lists, the reporter's questions, the rhetorical patterns, and outlines) to analyze his audience, develop a thesis, and content from his sources and his own observations to support the thesis.

Context Card for synthesis essay, drawing on the sources

> Subject: Media and Violence
> Audience: College students
> Writing Situation: A causal analysis, written for a college newspaper or blog, synthesizing sources..
> Thesis: While it has not been proven that television violence directly causes youth violence, it can be shown that the media creates an unhealthy adolescent fear of violence and, more importantly, creates a climate of "desire" for material possessions that directly influences some teens to commit violence.
> Tone: objective, persuasive, serious, fairly formal and studious

Analyze the essay following by comparing the synthesis notes with the completed essay. Most importantly, Gary took the ideas from his sources, and forged his own thesis, his own statement, about the media. Gary's thesis is a joining, a synthesis, of Gerbner's, O'Brien's, and Solomon's ideas. Excellent writers of synthesis essays discover what they believe about a subject when they research and synthesize sources, and the essays become their essays, not reports of what others think about the subjects. This essay would be 3-4 pages plus the works cited if on 8 1/2 X 11 paper.

Gary Hughes
English 101
Final Draft

A Connection Between the Media and Violent Behavior

Debra Dickerson speaks for many in America when she voices the rage she feels against the hoodlum who shot and paralyzed her nephew, a young man who had to live on violent streets but was neither violent nor a druggie. Poignantly, she asks Johnnie at one point as he lay in his hospital bed listening to music and reading *Sports Illustrated*, "'do you still like gangster rap?'" She says she can almost hear him think: "I'm paralyzed Auntie, not stupid," and then he replies, "'I mostly just listen to hip hop…'" (17-18). I had to stop reading as my eyes misted over. Violent movies, violent music, violence everywhere. But there are a lot of reasons for youth violence: poverty, ineffectual schools, child abuse and neglect, the ease of obtaining firearms, some would say a breakdown in families and "family values."

Many lately have hopped on the bandwagon: violence in the media causes violence on the streets, especially youth violence. There is data to suggest violence on television can cause violence: Gerbner et al (1978) found that young children who watch a lot of television are more apt to think it alright to hit someone "if you have a reason" than children who don't watch as much television. The connection also makes logical sense. If an adolescent thrives on violent television and video games, wouldn't they enact those behaviors they see most often? However, the facts don't bear this out. In four studies, Gerbner et al found that violence on television only directly causes violence in a minority of children. Also, Rowell Huesmann studied 1500 youth in America, Finland, Denmark, and Australia, and found only a 5% correlation between media violence and violent actions (Males 236). Both Geoffrey Canada (CEO of Harlem's Rheedlen Center for Children and Families) and Michael Males argue persuasively that there is much more evidence to suggest the causes mentioned in the first paragraph. For instance, adults injure, sexually abuse, or neglect two million children a year (Males 237), and a 1992 California Department of Justice report shows that adults, not other kids, killed 80% of adolescent murder victims (Males 237). The most interesting data from the Gerbner studies, however, is that heavy viewers of television are much more likely than light viewers to have a fear of violence (to believe something is going to happen to them), to believe that people cannot be trusted, and to believe that people only look out for themselves. Perhaps violence in the media does not directly cause violence, but isn't it sad that media violence creates such unhealthy feelings related to violence in our society?

Whether media violence directly causes violence on the street or not, most people would agree that violence could be considered an appreciated cultural value in America: we love football and boxing, John Wayne and Sylvester Stallone, the man who knows how to hunt safely, but after all, violently.

159

Summary of, AND WRITER'S AGREEMENT WITH, O'Brien. Synthesis of similar claims (O'Brien and Solomon). Solomon's specific examples support O'Brien and writer.

William O'Brien makes an interesting connection. He argues, as I am, that violence is an integral part of the American identity and that it is an integral part of the media scene, but he then connects this violence to another appreciated cultural norm: the materialism rampant in our society (9-11). Most would agree with O'Brien that materialism is one of the most valued cultural norms in American society. Jack Solomon argues at length that some advertisements work by making us feel guilty if we don't possess certain things, whether it be the most advanced, slickest car (a Porsche ad), the best detergent (to stop "Ring Around the Collar"), or the latest computer system (to win the biggest market share) (129-132). So, doesn't it make sense that if we feel guilty when we don't have the newest and best product aggressively marketed, that we would do anything to possess that object?

Conclusion signaling that writer is finished, has said what he needs to.

Perhaps media violence does not directly cause violence in America, but the media is the most potent force shaping the lives of Americans. Two facts are certain: the various forms of the media do display violence and they do speak to our desires. Maybe it is time to adjust our lifestyles so that we don't get caught in the latest media trap. Study after study shows how sinfully weak at the knees we become when bombarded by images, whether they be from commercials, entertainment, news shows, or music. We create the madness; maybe, just maybe, we don't have to live with it.

Works Cited

MLA Style Documentation

Canada, Geoffrey. "Peace in the Streets." *Utne Reader,* July/August 1995, pp. 59-61. *Alt-Press Watch,* www. alt-presswatch.com/utne/41369.

Dickerson, Debra. "Who Shot Johnnie?" *The New Republic,* 1 Jan. 1996, pp. 17-18. *EbscoHost,* www.ebscohost.com/newrepublic/639567.

Gerbner, George et al. "Cultural Indicators: Violence Profile no. 9." *Journal of Communication,* vol 28, no. 3, 1978, pp. 176-207. *JSTOR,* www.jstor.org/stable/430167.

Gerbner, George et al. "The Demonstration of Power: Violence Profile no. 10." *Journal of Communication,* vol. 29, no. 3, 1979, pp. 177-196. *JSTOR,* www.jstor.org/stable/436214.

Gerbner, George et al. "The Mainstreaming of America." *Journal of Communication,* vol. 30, no. 3, 1980, pp.12-29. *JSTOR,* www.jstor.org/stable/4392582

Gerbner, George, and Larry Gross. "Living With Television: The Violence Profile." *Journal of Communication,* vol. 26, no. 2, 1976, pp. 173-199. *JSTOR,* www.jstor.org/stable/4388142.

Males, Mike. "Public Enemy Number One?" *American Culture and the Media,* edited by Anne Cassebaum and Rosemary Haskell, Houghton Mifflin, 1997, pp. 234-240.

O'Brien, William. "The Cruel Logic of Teenage Violence." *American Culture and the Media,* edited by Anne Cassebaum and Rosemary Haskell, Houghton Mifflin, 1997, pp. 9-11.

Solomon, Jack. *The Signs of Our Times,* Putnam, 1988.

8

Employing Synthesis to Incorporate Source Materials: Writing the Researched Paper

In chapters 6 and 7, we looked at the research process, including critical reading techniques and finding secondary sources for college essays that incorporate research. In this chapter, we will examine the steps to move from gathering ideas and information to developing the context and content for the researched essay. In practice, writers do these synthesis techniques while they are gathering information. Also, in many ways, the steps to developing a researched essay mirror the steps to developing any essay, researched or not, as outlined in chapters 2 and 3.

As students read articles and books on a subject, while they summarize, evaluate and respond (chapter 6), they also develop a context (focused subject, specific audience, a writing situation, a thesis, and tone: chapter 2) by finding the relationships between ideas in the sources they read. In the end, writers need to develop their own thesis by looking at the strongest evidence and developing their opinions on the subject based on what they have read and what they already think, know, and believe. After and as they develop this context, writers find evidence from their sources to substantiate this thesis.

With this concept in mind, chapter 8 divides into these sections: inferring relationships between source materials, analyzing research to create your thesis and supporting content, and the specifics of integrating and synthesizing these sources into a researched essay.

We will begin the chapter with a student essay that employs synthesis, and then discuss how Robin French created the essay.

Student Example: A Rhetorical Analysis/ Synthesis Essay. MLA Style Documentation

The professor for this class had students read a series of essays on the media, and asked them to develop an opinion on one of the sub-topics they had discussed in class including media influence on culture (in terms of advertising or violence), gender and racial stereotypes as portrayed by various types of media, news coverage by the various forms of media and their effectiveness (especially in terms of politics), and sports as a viewer activity and its relationship to American consciousness. To help you understand synthesis, study the comments in the margin.

This essay would be 6-7 pages long plus the works cited if printed on computer paper. While it was written just before the Iraq and Afghanistan wars and some of the examples are thus dated, all in all the essay still stands up with relevant timely information.

161

Robin French
English 102
Dr. Hanson

Subject: Television influence on Americans
Audience: middle/working class Americans who read and think about culture (mostly college educated)
Writing Situation: a rhetorical analysis in a popular magazine editorial such as in *Entertainment Today*, employing synthesis of views on the subject
Thesis: Television undoubtedly influences our cultural values, but "influencing" is quite different from defining and creating our values, as some critics suggest.
Tone: objective and thoughtful, but not too formal (more for a general than a scholarly audience)

All In the Family Values

Renowned author and poet, Maya Angelou, describes a day in her childhood as she and other African-Americans listened to a Joe Louis fight, which was broadcast on the radio in a local store. It appeared as though Mr. Louis would be beaten:

From Robin's research, she chose a specific example to introduce her subject.

My race groaned. It was our people failing. It was another lynching, yet another Black man hanging from a tree. One more woman ambushed and raped. A Black boy whipped and maimed . . . . If Joe lost we were back in slavery and beyond help.

As she listened, the tide began to turn and Joe Louis became the heavyweight champion of the world:

Champion of the world. A Black boy. Some Black mother's son. He was the strongest man in the world. People drank coca colas like ambrosia and ate candy bars like Christmas . . . . It would take an hour or more before people would leave the store and head home. Those who lived too far made arrangements to stay in town. It wouldn't do for a Black man and his family to be caught on a lonely country road on a night when Joe Louis proved that we are the strongest people in the world. (183-184)

In the violently racist and segregated America of the 1930s, a radio broadcast of a brave, young black man brought hope and promise of success not only to an impressionable girl, but also to an entire race of people. It was Mr. Louis's success that made the impact, but it was the power of the media that informed the world.

The power of the media and the information that it provides has exploded since the 1930s with the advent of cable television, videos, the internet, and live remotes. Neil Gabler, in his essay "Now Playing: Real Life, the Movie," argues that evidence shows "politics, religion, news, warfare, crime, everything are really branches of, well, call it show biz." He says, "Everywhere the fabricated, the inauthentic and theatrical, have driven out the natural, the genuine, and the spontaneous until there is no distinction between real life and stagecraft" (47). Gabler contends that news stories are chosen for entertainment value and presented in a movie-like format, and points out how politicians sell "good vibes" to make us feel safe and use war to distract us or blind our confidence. He points to Ronald Reagan, arguing that the first movie star president was actually creating a performance for the American people, giving us what we wanted. He insinuates that the 1991 Gulf War may not have been about freeing Kuwait, making sure we had oil, OR the elimination of Saddam Hussein, but rather to make Americans "feel good" about themselves (49-51) He also points to American's preoccupation with the lives of celebrities, and how we not only want to look at them, but literally live their theatrical lives (54).

TOPIC SENTENCE of paragraph.

Source supports topic sentence with evidence.

Although it is hard to deny the media's power of influence, does the media, as Gabler suggests, actually define our values? William O'Brien argues that advertisers, by marketing over-priced products to American youth, send the message that "Possessions are the ultimate measure of a person's worth," and so we should not be surprised that our children value materialism (10-11). Although O'Brien acknowledges the media's role in the promotion of materialism and violence, he does not give the media all the credit for influencing values, as Gabler does. O'Brien also blames cultural problems such as poverty, social alienation, and race and class divisions for teaching teenagers to value possessions over, in some instances, another person's life (10).

One-half of central question asked. (TOPIC SENTENCE)

SYNTHESIS: O'Brien's agreement and disagreement with Gabler. Also, different set of specifics (news vs. advertising).

Barbara Ehrenreich would argue that the media plays a substantial role in the cultural problems O'Brien mentions, such as class and race division, by literally ignoring America's majority. In "Working Class Heroes No More," she argues that even though working class Americans represent sixty to seventy percent of the American population (depending on how you define "working class"), the media basically ignores working class issues, and television and movies either delete the working class completely or paint them as "dumb, inarticulate and mindlessly loyal to archaic values." She notes that they are often portrayed as "hard hat bigots," poor dressers, beer guzzlers, and addicted to cigarettes and network television. She gives *Saturday Night Fever* and the more recent *Married With Children* as examples (73-75). *Roseanne, Drew Carey,* and *The Simpsons* are other examples of Ehrenreich's point. Ehrenreich adds that television would have us believe that a doctor/lawyer team heads every household and that the population is made up solely of white collar professionals and "the annoyingly persistent black underclass" (74). This concept is hopelessly lampooned in the extremely successful and endlessly rerunned *Cosby Show.* As I consider Ehrenreich's argument, I must admit that it is much easier for me to think of shows featuring professional, wealthy, and extremely attractive characters, than of shows with average looking, modest living folks with blue collar jobs. Shows that come to mind include *Ally McBeal, The Practice, ER, Frasier, Friends, Chicago Hope, Becker,* and the list goes on.

SYNTHESIS: Ehrenreich's agreement with O'Brien and another set of examples.

Student gives examples as support for Ehrenreich (a quality of good synthesis), and then analyzes her source and agrees.

Jerry Mander, author of several books and articles on the media, helps to make Ehrenreich's point with his compelling argument explaining the limited points-of-view displayed in the media and especially on television. He says seventy-five percent of network television and fifty percent of public television is paid for by the one hundred largest corporations in America, which produces censorship because television producers wanting to sell their shows must consider the views of this elite group of sponsors. He says this small group of corporations has so much control because they are the only ones who can afford it, with a half minute of prime time selling for $200,000 to $300,000. Mander also points out that the average American sees 21,000 commercials a year, giving these corporations "a system of mass brainwashing and political control" (207-209). In other words, they promote the views, opinions, and values of a very rich, small group of people.

Mike Males downplays the media's influence. In "Public Enemy Number One?," he argues that the media is the scapegoat in the argument concerning cultural violence. He agrees with O'Brien that largely unaddressed social problems such as poverty, child abuse, and child neglect are the true causes of violence, arguing that media influence plays only a small part. He cites a 1984 multi-national study by media violence expert Rowell Huesmann of 1500 youth in the U.S, Finland, Poland, and Australia that showed only five percent of violence is associated with media violence, and he says similar studies have shown the same results (236).

So do the media mirror our cultural values, as O'Brien and Males suggest, or do our values mirror the media, as Gabler, Ehrenreich, and Mander suggest? There is some truth in both points-of-view. The point Mander makes about the large amount of money spent on just thirty seconds of airtime proves that television has influence (208). Why would corporations, whose prime object is profit, spend so much money if they were not benefitting their bottom line by convincing the public to buy their products? Gabler's argument that the information news agencies feed us is chosen and presented to entertain is undeniable (49). As I looked at television listings, I counted eight prime time news magazine shows every week, and this doesn't count cable news programs. The choice of news stories presented can affect our thoughts by making us aware of important issues and changing our viewpoint or upsetting us unnecessarily and lulling us into complete apathy. Also, as Gabler points out, there is no denying that politicians use the media to manipulate with "feel good" wars and speeches that say nothing, but are "oh so comforting" (50). Although the media can influence and hit emotional nerves, I do not believe that most people are programmed like robots to believe, act, and value as instructed by the media and those who control it.

Influencing what one values and defining what one values are very different. With the glut of commercialism in all areas of the media, and as Ehrenreich notes, the undermining of the working class, materialism has been promoted as a value by the media and "keeping up with the Jones's" has never been more important; however, this "keeping up" mentality has been around much longer than the media. Since its inception, America has been the "land of opportunity" where people from all over the world have come to build their fortunes. Capitalism, by definition, promotes materialism and the media just exploits that truth. There is no denying the media influences our tastes, introduces new ideas, shows us the best and worst of humanity, and at times even inspires us as it did when Joe Louis became champion of the world. But true values, good or bad, are developed in consort with many other things such as our personality, humor, fears, conscience, and even our physicality. If we were brought up to value life, media violence will not turn us into murderers. If we were brought up to value education, then we stay in school even if our favorite actor dropped out. We continue to live our lives every day, going to school and work, playing sports, doing hobbies, taking care of our families, visiting with friends, attending to our spirituality, grooming ourselves, walking our pets, mowing our lawns, going to the doctor, going to the grocery, reading a book. Oh yeah, and watching television or seeing a movie. Hundreds of people and places have passed, and continue to pass, through our daily lives, shaping and influencing our opinions and values. And then we go home and catch a rerun of *All in the Family*.

Works Cited

Angelou, Maya. "Joe Louis." Cassebaum and Haskell, pp. 182-184.

Cassebaum, Anne and Rosemary Haskell, editors. *American Culture and the Media.* Houghton-Mifflin, 1997.

Ehrenreich, Barbara. "Working Class Heroes No More." Cassebaum and Haskell, pp. 72-75.

Gabler, Neil. "Now Playing: Real Life, the Movie." Cassebaum and Haskell, pp. 46-55.

Males, Mike. "Public Enemy Number One?" Cassebaum and Haskell, pp. 234-239.

Mander, Jerry. "Freedom of Speech for the Wealthy." Cassebaum and Haskell, pp. 207-209.

O'Brien, William. The Cruel Logic of Teenage Violence." Cassebaum and Haskell, pp. 9-11.

When an essay cites more than one source from the same anthology, the Works Cited cites the entire anthology once, and then abbreviated citations for the articles like here.

Mrs. French's essay took sources she read on her subject, the media, and from the evidence presented in those sources and Robin's lifelong viewing of television, she developed her own position on the issue of the media's effect on Americans. This position became her thesis. Notice that she presented the various views on the subject, the evidence each source used, and from this synthesis she showed that her thesis was just as viable as the theses of her sources. Presenting your own view created by studying a subject is the heart of good synthesis.

The remainder of the chapter presents methods to develop ideas to create suitable theses.

Inferring Relationships Between Source Materials

This concept was already introduced in chapter 7 in terms of researching secondary sources, but will be explained fully here with examples from Mrs. French's notes that she took as she did critical reading and actually prepared the content and context for her essay.

Activities that scholars use to synthesize include summary, comparison, contrast, definition, and analysis. The first two components of synthesis are:

- *Critical reading to understand, respond to, and evaluate each source individually. Use all the pre-reading, reading, and post-reading tools discussed in chapters 6 and 7.*
- *As you read, decide on your own views on the subject you are researching. Develop support through your reading and your personal experience and observation to persuade yourself that you are creating a valid, logical, supportable view on the issues germane to the subject.*

As you begin to gather multiple sources on a topic, take notes on the relationships among the ideas and the support of the sources you read.

- *To focus your subject and gain knowledge of your subject, list sub-topics of the main subject and list which sources (and the appropriate page numbers) discuss which sub-topics.*

Here is Robin inferring relationships in her notes and developing a research question:

The Media and
violence: O'Brien (9-11) "The Cruel Logic of..." violence and materialism
      Males (234-239) "Public Enemy Number One?" media not a
         major cause
      Methvin (252-256) "TV Violence" studies show it does
         cause violence
news: McLaugin and Yeoman (35-42) "...What you didn't hear on
        the News"
      Angelou (182-184) "Joe Louis" historical account of
        radio broadcast: importance
      Gabler (46-55) "Real Life, the Movie" news and newsmakers
        Hollywoodize and simplify the news
advertising: Mander (207-209) "Freedom of Speech for Wealthy"
        message controlled by rich
      Steinem (21-28) "Sex, Lies, and Advertising" make up and other
        companies selling women's products control
        women's magazines: censorship

Focused Subject (research question): whether and how much the media influences Americans.

- *Compare and Contrast: Make a list of authors who agree (with appropriate page numbers). Decide which authors have the most adequate support for the ideas they agree on, and list the best support for each idea. One essay might have the best examples for an idea in another essay. Make a list of the ideas authors disagree on, and summarize, describe, and define their differences. Analyze the strengths and weaknesses of their support, and decide which authors have the most valid reasoning or support. (Include in this analysis support that you know of not contained in the sources. A source might have the most valid thesis, but the writer has not supported the idea as well as he or she should have.)*

At the most general level, in terms of comparison/contrast:
Similar - the media describes our values, does not create them: O'Brien and Males
Opposite to above, but similar to each other - the media defines our values, makes us who we are: Gabler, Ehrenreich, Mander.

Gabler and Mander talk about how the news makes us who we are, but Gabler talks about how news is created and

Mander talks about how corporations create what we see on the news, while Ehrenreich talks about how television programs create us by showing untrue stereotypes, there is a connection between Mander and Ehrenreich: both talk about how the media give us limited points-of-view.

O'Brien is the "wild card": he points to the materialism in our culture (from advertising), but attributes violence to the "need" for money to buy things so advertising is, in his view, indirectly related while poverty, social alienation, and race and class divisions are the primary cause.

There is a connection between him and Ehrenreich, who also posits a thesis based on stereotypes (and aren't stereotypes what create images we have of what we need materialistically?).

Males and O'Brien together in discussion of roots of violence, and both downplay the media role, suggesting it is a minor cause.

- *Definition: How do various sources define and explain key concepts on a subject? What are the theses of these authors? With some subjects, writers define concepts differently. Be aware of the differences as they affect meaning. From your analysis of sources' definitions and theses, develop your own thesis. You might totally agree with one source's thesis, and you then borrow it, but more often through your analysis you develop a thesis that has parts of several sources' theses. Your thesis, in synthesis essays, often states what you disagree with also.*

For instance, here is a sampling of the research notes Robin made as she developed her thesis, which as you see is her argument after reading sources with data and sources with differing views of how television influences culture. She ends up disagreeing with most of them in terms of degree:

The more I look at this subject, the more I realize that this is an exercise in definition!!!!

While I am analyzing the media's role in making us who we are, a lot of this exercise comes down to how each source and I define the terms, and our choice of words is the actual creator of thesis: Does the media define? influence? mirror? create? describe? affect? The choice of words affects and determines meaning to a large degree.

/ Gabler would say the news defines (or creates, he calls the news a big fiction) how we see the world and Ehrenreich says that television stereotypes define, meaning create (incorrectly) how we see ourselves.
/ O'Brien and Males would use the words influence or affect, but disagree that the media defines.
/ Mander is big on how corporations influence our views.

What do I think? I am more on the influence side. I don't see friends and family as robots - though I have to admit that every kid who looks like the latest pop star is proof for "defines." But O'Brien and Males are right: the media is a big scapegoat for a complex issue. We are much more defined by race, and class (money, education, culture and part of the country we live in) than by the media.

We are affected greatly in our views by what we see.

/ Tentative thesis: Television undoubtedly influences our cultural values, but "influencing" is quite different from defining and creating our values, as some critics suggest.
/ Plan: Since I do agree that we are heavily influenced, I can present the arguments of Gabler, Ehrenreich, and Mander as true - their arguments are just as valid for "influence" as they are for "define," but just modify their thesis in my own thesis from "define" to "influence."

> • *Analysis: Information in one essay can help explain why something occurs or explain a line of reasoning in another essay. Investigating how ideas in differing sources "feed" off each other is the heart of good synthesis.*

/ Gabler says that almost all news is show biz. O'Brien, though he disagrees with Gabler on extent of media influence, adds to and extends Gabler's view by arguing that marketing plays an important part in creating our views.
/ O'Brien, Males, and Ehrenreich together in mentioning multiple cultural problems (poverty, race and class division, social alienation). Ehrenreich is a specific media example explaining O'Brien.

/ Mander helps to make Ehrenreich's point about limited points-of-view in the media (just showing upper middle class whites) by pointing out that large corporations (run by wealthy whites) control the media.
/ Use Maya Angelou's description of 1930s broadcast of Joe Louis win as opening of essay, to show influence of the media (how important it was for her race to hear about a black man winning). Next would come Gabler, to show how we still are influenced today with news ("Real Life: The Movie").

Analyzing Research to Create a Thesis and Supporting Content

- *Most importantly: Do not let your thoughts on a subject disappear. Although your thoughts on a subject may be changing as you research and learn new information and lines of reasoning, be alert to the connections between your evolving thesis concerning the subject and the ideas in the sources you read. Ultimately, you are synthesizing sources so that you can develop your own adequately supported statement about the subject.*

The goal for synthesis and most researched writing is to become knowledgeable in a subject: to find out what evidence and facts there are about a subject and to compare and contrast what experts think about the subject (including analysis of the logic of their evidence). From this evaluation, comparison, and analysis, you decide what you think is the strongest thesis, based on the evidence and logic, and that becomes the thesis for your essay.

One way of simplifying this, after you have done substantial research, is to decide what the positions on your subject are:

- *Are there two opposed sides? If so, decide which position is stronger and your thesis looks like this:*

  Some people say _____, and this position has some validity because _____, but others say_____, and this is a stronger position because_____.

- *Are there several conflicting sides? If so, pick the evidence from each of them that together make your argument (your thesis) viable.*

As in the example on the previous pages, Robin decided on her thesis while analyzing the definitions used in her sources. If you have finished your synthesis, inferring relationships between source materials, and you still have not created the thesis for your essay, it is wise to do so before developing the content for your essay from these source materials. If you work on this for an inordinate amount of time, and you still cannot create your thesis, it is probable that you have not researched enough yet.

After developing your thesis, decide on the content necessary to explain the various positions on your subject, and the evidence necessary to prove your thesis.

169

Exercise 8.1
Synthesis: Relationships Between Source Materials

As you do your research (critical reading, summary, evaluation, and response to sources) and concurrently predraft (developing your focused subject, thesis, and content), be aware that you should be synthesizing to find the relationships among sources that make your points. As the writer did on the previous pages, take notes that include listing sub-topics, comparison, contrast, definition, and analysis. If your instructor asks you, be prepared to turn in all your written synthesis notes, mimicking the notes of the last section.

Make sure you develop your own thesis out of your newfound knowledge!!!

Integrating and Synthesizing Sources in the Essay Itself

This section of *Writing Successfully* demonstrates the specifics of integrating your sources into your essay, and how to document these sources. There are several proper forms of documentation used in college writing, the most prevalent being MLA (the Modern Language Association), APA (the American Psychological Association), CSE (the Council of Science Editors), and the Chicago system. With these systems, the process of integrating and synthesizing multiple sources in an essay are similar, though there are obvious differences in the specific methods used for documentation. This section will demonstrate synthesis and integration using MLA documentation, but will focus only on similarities in all the systems. If you use APA documentation, refer to chapter 24, if CSE, use chapter 25, and for Chicago use 26 for specifics on using these forms of documentation. You also need chapter 23 for the specifics of MLA.

Whenever you summarize, paraphrase, or use a direct quotation, you must let your reader know the source of the ideas or quoted material. In the text of your writing, identify the author (or the title of the source if anonymous) + verb at the begining of the source material, and the page number (if there is one) at the end of the summarized, quoted information (using parenthetical documentation). The author's last name is required; the first name is optional and can be used to give your prose a less formal tone. (In MLA. In the other forms editors almost always just use the last name.) At the end of your essay, a works cited page gives your reader the author, title, and publication information for the source. The citation in the text would appear like this:

Beginnning Marker: Author

Cornel West argues that African-American slaves created social and religious traditions they needed to survive and to combat the "hopelessness, meaninglessness, and lovelessness" that was destroying their very souls (562).

End Marker: page number

In MLA, the works cited entry at the end of the essay would be as follows:

West, Cornel. "Nihilism in Black America." *Perspectives on Argument*, edited by Nancy Wood, Prentice Hall, 1998, pp. 561-565.

Notice how formal the sentence sounds if you only use the last name. Unless you are writing in a genre with a very formal style, use the first and last name:

West argues that African-American slaves created social and religious . . .

But never use the informal first name only. You don't know the writer:

Incorrect: Cornel argues that African-American slaves created social and . . .

When evaluating in-text parenthetical documentation, check for accuracy using these general guidelines (Explanations follow the guidelines.):

- Most academic writing uses summary and paraphrase rather than direct quotation. The only reasons to use direct quotation are: when the source has said something so well that any attempt to summarize or paraphrase it would lessen its impact, or when you can't rephrase the original passage in your own words because there are so many words (usually technical terms) in the source with no exact synonym.
- References in your text must have an entry on the works cited page. (If you refer to a source by author, "Alisha Jones," in your essay, there must be an entry for "Jones, Alisha" on the works cited page.)
- If you are citing information from a specific page or set of pages in your source, identify the location as specifically as you can by using page numbers, or if you cite from a multi-volume work, volume number and page number(s). If you have summarized an entire source, or the source has only one-page, then page references are unnecessary.
- When reading your essay, from your in-text parenthetical documentation the reader should be able to find the source on your works cited page, and from the information on the works cited page, the reader should be able to locate your source in a library or on the internet (unless your source is unpublished).
- When reading your essay, a reader should know when your ideas stop and a source's ideas begin, and the conclusion of the source is always signaled by either the page number of the source in parentheses (217-219) or the author's last name and page number of the source (Jefferson 219). If there are no page numbers on an internet or database site, you still need to signal to the reader in some way that the summary of the source is finished and your ideas begin again (see below and the relevant in-text documentation formats in chapters 23-25).

Using Verbs and Conjunctions to Infer Relationships Among Ideas

As readers read your essay, they expect the ideas to be your ideas until you indicate that you are now using a source's ideas. Cite the author's name with either a phrase (According to Samuel Johnson,) or a verb that describes what the author is doing (Samuel Johnson believes). This is the preferred method of documenting sources because it indicates clearly where your ideas have stopped and your source starts (Samuel Johnson insists). When using this form of parenthetical reference, at the end of the summary or quotation, give the page number in parentheses. This is a clear marker that shows where a source's ideas stop and your ideas start again. When you use a verb, pick one that accurately describes what the source is doing:

171

Beginning Marker: Author of source's name + verb
Samuel Johnson claims that William Shakespeare is the greatest English dramatist (213).
End Marker: page number

Also, use the present tense: Samuel Johnson claims, not Samuel Johnson claimed. Although Samuel Johnson wrote in the eighteenth century, his books and ideas are still giving us insight and knowledge. By convention, words and ideas within a written work are described in the present tense: "Studies indicate," not "Studies have indicated" (unless you are showing how studies have changed through time and a past or perfect tense would reveal your specific meaning):

> Studies in the past have indicated that the death penalty deterred crime, but modern studies definitely indicate that the death penalty may increase violent crime (Billingsley 313).

Different verbs demonstrate different relationships among sources. Pick a verb that accurately reflects the relationship between sources. All of the verbs listed below have different shades of meaning. Make sure the verb you choose accurately reflects what the source is doing.

- *The author is neutral, reporting what he/she considers facts or opinion.*

Bill Jameson *comments* that the Pacific ocean fisheries are being rapidly depleted (201).

Other verbs that signal neutrality, used when you are not comparing to another writer's ideas or when you are using only one source and one of these verbs accurately reflects what the author is doing in the original text:

admits comments considers declares describes explains illustrates notes observes points out records relates reports says states sees thinks writes

Several subordinate conjunctions, adverbial conjunctions, and transitional expressions can be used to show comparison or contrast with these neutral verbs:

> James Wilson argues that free market economy should rule on the oceans too (417); *however,* Bill Jameson comments that the Pacific ocean fisheries are being rapidly depleted (201).

> James Wilson argues that free market economy should rule on the oceans too (417*); on the other hand,* Bill Jameson comments that the Pacific ocean fisheries are being rapidly depleted (201).

> *Although* James Wilson argues that free market economy should rule on the oceans too (417), Bill Jameson states that the Pacific ocean fisheries are being rapidly depleted (201).
> **Notice that another verb is now more appropriate here.**

172

Subordinate conjunctions, adverbial conjunctions, and transitional expressions that serve to show comparison or contrast include:

although even though ;however, ;likewise, similarly ;on the other hand, unless whereas whether or not

- **The author infers or suggests (a stronger, more assured statement than neutral; often accompanied by stronger evidence)**

    Bill Jameson *analyzes* the Pacific ocean fisheries and finds that they are being rapidly depleted (201).

Verbs that imply or suggest (notice that many of these connote some action on the author's part, usually analysis of data):

analyzes asks concludes finds implies predicts proposes reveals shows speculates suggests supposes

- **The author argues (often these verbs are used in synthesis to show opposing viewpoints)**

    James Wilson *argues* that free market economy should rule on the oceans too (417)

Notice the difference between *argues* (definitely makes a point) and on the previous page *claims* (not definite - just making a statement of belief). **Always ask yourself what specifically your author is doing, and choose the most appropriate verb.**

    James Wilson *defends* the free market economy's rights on the oceans (417), while Bill Jameson *disagrees*, arguing that the Pacific ocean fisheries are being rapidly depleted (201).

Verbs that suggest an author is making a definite statement of belief, an argument:

asserts argues believes claims contends defends denies disagrees emphasizes holds insists maintains

- **The author agrees (these verbs are used in synthesis to show similar viewpoints)**

    Bill Jameson *agrees* with James Wilson that a free market economy is best for the world (201).

    Though defending the free market's rights on the ocean, James Wilson *concedes* that Pacific ocean fisheries are being depleted (417).

173

Verbs that suggest a similarity between viewpoints:

admits agrees concedes concurs grants

- ### The author has a negative view of another stance on an issue

   Bill Jameson *complains* that free market economies are ruining the world's
   fisheries (201).

Verbs that suggest negativity in an author's response to a viewpoint:

belittles complains condemns deplores deprecates derides laments warns

In-text Documentation of Summary and Direct Quotation

   The content in a sentence sometimes signals to the reader that you are using
sources, but make sure that the reader clearly knows where you have begun using a
source. When using this method, both the author's last name and the page number
appear in parentheses at the end of the source. For example:

   Front marker: Research verifies
   Research verifies that both passive music reinforcements (little physical
   response when listening to music) and active music reinforcement (playing
   instruments and dancing) increase desired behavior in special needs children
   (Holloway 58-69).
   End Marker: Author's last name and page number

   The phrase "Research verifies" signals the beginning of the source's ideas; since it
is obvious that a student writer did not him or herself complete the research, the reader
knows where the source's ideas begin.

   When using this method, the reader should clearly recognize when your ideas
stop, and your source's ideas begin. Confusion occurs using this method when you
have employed summary or paraphrase rather than direct quotation. In the following
example, it is not clear where the writer's ideas stop and the source's ideas begin:

   Unclear: The American success story continued into the 70s and 80s. Yuppies
   have wholeheartedly taken the cultural ideal that everyone can be successful,
   though they modified the rationale for it away from the need for competition
   and social status (Manca 50).

A preferred, and more accurate citation would clearly show where Manca's ideas
begin:

Clear: The American success story continued into the 70s and 80s. Luigi Manca believes that yuppies have wholeheartedly taken the cultural ideal that everyone can be successful, though they modified the rationale for it away from the need for competition and social status (50).

Sample References

Author and Title

Though only the author's last name is required, often the writer also supplies the title of the source, especially if the title gives information that summarizes the main idea of the source.

> Brent Staples, in "Just Walk on By: A Black Man Ponders His Power to Alter Public Space," observes that whites often show abject fear when they come in contact with him (17).

Citing Part of an Article or Book

> Lauter *et al* argue that Native American religion and religious tales have to be interpreted using the ideals and circumstances of their cultures, not the culture of Christians (3-4, 7-8, 21-25, 70-73).
> **Page references refer to the pages where Lauter discusses contrasting cultures; this example is a one sentence summary of these pages.**

Citing an Anonymous Work Listed by Title on Works Cited

> The Sixty Minutes episode, "A Case for Global Warming," discusses the problem of global warming in detail.

> Synonyms for lighthouse include two: *beacon* and *pharos* ("Lighthouse").

Television shows, newscasts, and films are usually cited by title, unless the writer is emphasizing one part of the show like a specific editor's comments or the screenplay of a show (when they are cited by author).

Dictionaries and other reference books (like the thesaurus paraphrased in the example above) are cited by title of article when the author is anonymous. The works cited entry for this reference (at the end of the essay) would be:

"Lighthouse." *Webster's Collegiate Thesaurus*, Merriam-Webster, 2003, p. 617.

If the title is long, you can give a shortened version in the text that incorporates the first few words of the title so that the reader can find the source on the works cited page. For example, an anonymous article titled "Indecency on the Internet: Censorship of Student and College Web Pages" (and listed as such on the works cited) could be cited in-text as "Indecency on the Internet."

Citing Two or More Works by the same Author

In the following example, the writer uses quotations from three plays by Shakespeare in her essay, so in the text the writer has to not only identify the author and page number (in this instance, for plays, the act and scene numbers), but also the exact source (the specific play) she is citing. There would be three individual works cited entries, one for each play:

> Shakespeare says, "Life's but a walking shadow, a poor player / That struts and frets his hour upon the stage / and then is heard no more" (*Macbeth* V.v). Perhaps he is heard no more because he decided to commit suicide, like Hamlet: "To be, or not to be, that is the question. (*Hamlet* III. i).

Or if there is no mention of author in the text, the citation would be:

> "Life's but a walking shadow" (Shakespeare, *Macbeth* V.v).

Citing Indirect Sources

Many times, you will find someone's ideas in a source written by a second author; for instance, someone's speech printed in another source. When this occurs, you reference the originator of the idea in your text, and in the parenthetical reference you give the author of the source you got the information from with the page number.

> Sanford Dornbusch surveyed 7000 Asian-American students and found they received better grades than other ethnic groups, even when their parents' level of education or economic success was low (Butterfield 119-120).
> **Sanford Dornsbusch did the study, but the writer found the information in an article by Fox Butterfield. The source listed in the works cited entry would be "Butterfield," since that is the source the writer was specifically looking at.**

Indirect citation of a direct quotation

If you are quoting words that are part of a dialogue or are themselves quoted (and thus in the source they are already in quotation marks), identify the quotation-within-a-quotation with single punctuation marks (the apostrophe key on a keyboard). Like the following:

> Barbara Harris said, "' I don't have a belief in God. I have a direct knowledge of his love'" (qtd. in Genova 105). **The writer found the quotation from Harris in an article by Genova. Genova is listed on the works cited.**

Working With Quotations

Begin quotations with either a colon, a comma, or the word *that*. At the end of the quotation, the usual order is quotation marks, page number in parentheses, and then the period: " (12). If the quotation itself ends with a question mark or exclamation point, the order is: ?" (12)

Bergen Evans says: "Robert Burton is a great psychologist" (12).

Thomas Carlyle's narrator exclaims, "The end of Man is an Action, not a Thought" (158).

Ernest Hemingway concedes that "Huckleberry Finn is the greatest American novel" (28).

President Kennedy asks, "What can you do for your country?" (86)

Another method breaks the quotation into two segments:

"I read Solomon more and more," writes Melville to Hawthorne, "and every time see deeper and deeper and unspeakable meanings in him" (130).

When quoting fewer than three lines of poetry, use spaced slashes to signal the end of a line of verse. Line numbers, rather than page numbers, are cited for poetry.

Keats's great ode begins, "Thou still unravished bride of quietness, / Thou foster child of silence and slow time" (1-2)

A quotation mark can signal the beginning of a direct quotation. When using this method, both the last name of the author and the page number appear in parentheses at the end of the quotation.

Beginning of quotation signaled by quotation mark
The American success story continued into the 70s and 80s. "Yuppies seem to have readily accepted into their way of life a fundamental trait of American culture – namely the belief in success and in the individual's ability to achieve it" (Manca 50). **End of quotation (last name of author and page number)**

Quotations over 5 lines are signaled by indenting quotation 10 spaces; no quotation marks:

The American success story continued into the 70s and 80s.
Yuppies seem to have readily accepted into their way of life a fundamental trait of American culture – namely the belief in success and in the individual's ability to achieve it. For the yuppies, however, success is more a means for pursuing happiness than an end in itself. The thrill of struggling head-to-head to beat the competition and the quest for higher social status and power do not seem to capture the yuppie's imagination (Manca 50).
End of quotation signaled by parenthetical reference

A quotation of longer than five lines from a poem is indented like the previous block form for long prose quotations. The spacing and line breaks should copy the form of the poem.

177

When employing direct quotation, it is extremely important to respect your sources and copy exactly what the original says (even the punctuation). It is possible to change quotations, but only under these circumstances:

- To place your own words or phrases in brackets to make the quotation conform grammatically to your writing or to insert necessary information to make the quote understandable to your readers.
- If the quotation contains a misspelling, or if there could be confusion over whether the word is spelled correctly, spell the word exactly as it is in the original passage and insert brackets surrounding the Latin word sic: [sic].
- To omit irrelevant information from the quotation indicate omitted words or sentences with ellipsis: . . .

The Pequod "shot her red hell [sic] further and further into the blackness of the sea . . . freighted with savages, and laden with fire, and burning a corpse, [it] plung[ed] into that blackness of darkness" (Melville 354).
The Pequod is a whaling ship, so the word expected for hell would be hull; although it is quite possible that Melville meant hell, given the events and characters of *Moby-Dick*, the writer using this source still used [sic] to indicate to the reader that this was the exact spelling of the original, correct or not. The ellipsis [...]indicate the writer chose to take a portion of the original out of the quotation as it was irrelevant to the point he was making about *Moby-Dick*. To make the quotation conform grammatically to the rest of the writer's essay he changed the tense of one verb (plunge) and added the word it. The sentence in *Moby-Dick* says that the ship, "burning a corpse, plunging into that blackness of darkness, seemed the material counterpart of the monomaniac commander's soul."

And with that unusual quotation, we leave you to ponder the universe: research, synthesize, and discover new ideas about subjects on your own. Remember the librarian: your most potent source !!!

9

Primary Research and Essays Employing Primary Research

When an assignment requires that you research a subject (whether in a library, a laboratory, or through observations and interviews), you are joining a company of scholars — both teachers and fellow students — exploring not only what is known, but also what can be discovered concerning the topic.

Colleges and universities are research centers, and students often bring new information to the world, sharing it in their research papers. Sometimes their writing is published. Your professors are also researchers as well as educators, and many of them complete research, write research papers based on this research, and publish their findings. A biology teacher, in addition to teaching, might be studying cancer using rats. An astronomy professor might additionally be mapping a galaxy with a telescope and a computer. In order to engage in these activities, they do library (i.e., secondary) research (keeping abreast of other scientists' experiments and observations published in scholarly journals) and primary research (observations in the laboratory or at the telescope and computer). In the social sciences, a psychology professor might also have a private practice. If she was specializing in abnormal psychology, she might also be comparing and classifying case studies for a paper in which the results call for prison reform. A political science professor would not only be reading current studies and surveys, but could also be designing surveys himself in order to more fully understand conditions in the United States. The results would ultimately be published. In the humanities, an English teacher specializing in composition would be reading studies related to composition theory and writing analyses and syntheses of studies in this field, or conducting studies of students he teaches and publishing the results. A literature professor specializing in Shakespeare would not only have studied Shakespeare's plays and period (historical documents, i.e., primary, research), but would know other critics' views on Shakespeare and his works (secondary research). When writing on Shakespeare, she would be joining the community of scholars — as all the examples in this paragraph do — in enlarging personal knowledge, but more importantly, enlarging the shared ideas and knowledge of the entire human race. You will be asked regularly throughout your college career to join in this enlargement of mind. Learning is not passive; it is active. College asks you to engage in research and analytic thought. As Socrates reputedly said, "The unexamined life is not worth living."

Writing Situations for Primary Research

You could be asked to complete primary research, or at least base some of your evidence on a subject from primary sources. When you perform an experiment, when you interview, when you complete a survey or an observation, you are doing primary research. Even if you don't perform primary research, you will be asked to look at and interpret primary sources. Some examples of primary sources that you might read, or in some cases primary research you would be expected to complete, include:

- Scientific reports, with analysis, of both controlled (laboratory) and field (street) observations
    - A psychologist specializing in preschool children designs an observation in the laboratory to study the increase in violence of 35 year old girls when they watch cartoons with violent content as opposed to two control groups who either watch nonviolent programming or do not watch television at all.
    - A sociology student observes the mannerisms of a group of alcoholics in a homeless shelter. (Field research, in other words, observation conducted "in the field," in a natural habitat as opposed to a controlled laboratory experiment.)

- Observation and analysis of forms in the media: movies, documentaries, television, advertising
    - A women's studies professor observes and analyzes how women are abused in movies and on television shows.
    - A student analyzes how advertising for cars creates desire in the consumer.

- Case Studies
    - A student in a sociology class examines attitudes toward affirmative action with surveys before and after a unit on affirmative action.
    - A secondary school principal studies how much sleep students get on school nights and measures classroom effectiveness. Then the school start time moves an hour later, and the studies are repeated.

- Interviews
    - A student in an economics class interviews an economics professor, a bank president, an accountant, and a counselor at the university's placement service to write a paper on the career paths open to students with degrees in economics.
    - A student calls an advertising executive for Mercedes-Benz to find why they thought a particular advertisement would be effective.

- Surveys
  - A psychology student designs and conducts a survey to find out how much time male and female parents spent with the respondents of the survey when the respondents were in middle school (included in this chapter).
  - A group of students design and conduct a survey to find out the reaction to changes in the Student Code of Conduct.

- Rhetorical and textual analyses - document study: autobiographies, diaries, old letters, old wills and legal documents, old advertising and newspapers
  - A historian studies handbills and county records from farm sales in the two decades after the Civil War to write an essay on the changing demographics of a section of Alabama.
  - A literature professor reads sermons and playbills from Elizabethan England to understand a passage in a play by Shakespeare.

- Experiments in psychology or the natural sciences
  - A physics study group reports on a series of experiments when electricity is sent through resistors.
  - A psychologist measures stress when a subject listens to high-decibel heavy metal music as compared to two control groups, one exposed to the same decibel classical music and the other exposed to no music.

Primary research usually begins with secondary research (to find out what is already known concerning the subject) and then it describes observations, interviews, surveys, and experiments that have been completed by the writer and his/her team. If you are asked to perform primary research, or decide on your own that a detailed observation, an interview, or a survey you create and conduct is essential for the success of your writing, be aware that these activities can best be completed only after a thorough study of the subject using secondary research. For you to construct a valid study, you must already have a good knowledge of the subject. The remainder of this chapter will discuss how to perform six major primary research activities (observations, interviews, case studies, surveys, experiments, and scientific proposals), how to integrate these activities into your writing (including several of the forms often used in the social and natural sciences to report primary research), and the chapter also contains six student examples that utilize primary research.

Generally, there are two basic situations when you would conduct and use primary research in your writing: when in a humanities or social science course you use it in a section of an essay as support for your thesis, and when in a social science, natural science, or business course you write a formal report of primary research you have completed.

When you are developing support for a thesis, any time you need to closely observe an event or a group of people, interview someone, or test a hypothesis with an experiment, do so. Perhaps you are studying television habits of adolescents, and you decide to not let your little sister watch her favorite program until she explodes: you have just created an experiment. (Of course, social scientists have to be very sure that they do not harm their subjects when they perform experiments; siblings do not have the same restraints.) Seriously, many research questions call for detailed observation and interview; less frequently students might actually conduct surveys or experiments themselves (though they frequently read surveys and experiments performed by others and collected through library research, and then use the results as support for their thesis). For examples in this chapter, Nancy Birkla had done secondary research on the differing communication styles of the two genders; to add support for her essay, she made detailed observations of men and women communicating and used this primary research as support for her essay. Kim Reed had been closely observing television advertising, and when she began to wonder why a Mercedes-Benz commercial seemed so effective, she prepared an interview and made phone calls to the national Mercedes-Benz marketing headquarters. They gave her the name and phone number of the New York advertising firm who had designed the advertisement, and the Vice President of the company allowed her to interview him! This is an excellent example of what writers do to research thoroughly and write successfully: they do whatever it takes. In these examples, the essays use a regular statement/support organizational pattern; it just so happens that the best support for their essays included primary research.

However, there is an organizational structure social and natural scientists frequently use to report their primary research (Introduction/Materials and Method/Results/Discussion) and you might be asked to use this format, as an undergraduate usually in science lab classes. The other four student research essays in this chapter use this common scientific pattern: Smith, Hamilton, and Dodd's case study, "Getting Enough Sleep Before Tests," Joan Steiden's survey, "A Study of Young Adults' Memories of the Amount of Time Parents Spent with Them in Middle School;" Mike Whitaker's lab report of a Physics experiment, "The Random Nature of Nuclear Decay and Radioactivity;" and Brian Allen's proposal to do a scientific study, "The Effectiveness of Music as Positive Reinforcement in Teaching Developmentally Handicapped Children to Play the Piano." The final student example in the chapter includes an account of the student's research process as he wrote his scientific proposal.

Writing Topics

Some classes demand that you do some kind of primary research; the following are some suggestions.

Places (observation, perhaps interview or survey)

- A soup kitchen
- The student lounge
- A 12 step recovery meeting
- A pinball or pool room
- A bar
- A church
- A restaurant
- A shopping mall
- A fast food establishment
- A specialty store

People (observation and interview)

For any of these subjects, you must have a focus for your interview, some definite reasons for wanting to interview these people, information that you cannot find from print sources:

- Profile a person who does a job you want to know more about
- A sports figure or community leader
- A favorite teacher or a teacher who teaches your favorite subject

Surveys

These subjects need to be focused with specific questions in mind:

- Attitudes toward gender and gender roles
- The education system — what works and what doesn't?
- Poverty issues
- A current issue on the local, state, national, or international level
- Concerns for social security and the aging of the population
- Child care issues

The Research Process: the Scientific Method and Hypotheses

Social scientists and natural scientists pride themselves on using the scientific method, and you should also use the scientific method when conducting primary research. When observing, experimenting, or interviewing, whether in the laboratory or in the field, study your subjects closely and accurately. Be a careful observer, a student of the details. When conducting an experiment, try to control all the variables in the experiment. For example, if a researcher were studying preschool children, their reaction to stimuli would be different at 10 A.M. then it would be at 1:30 P.M. if they had not had a nap. The good researcher would try to control all variables that could affect the outcome of an experiment. When a researcher conducts a survey, she would construct the survey questions so that they don't lead the respondents to answer in a certain way. For example, "The *immoral* Iraqi occupation makes you feel a. mad, b. sad, c. glad, d. proud, e. scared, f. ashamed?" is a leading question. A response that would elicit a more accurate response of the respondents' true feelings would be: "The Iraqi occupation makes you feel a. mad, b. sad, c. glad, d. proud, e. scared, f. ashamed? Check all that apply."

After doing a general study of primary research already conducted surrounding a focused subject (what is already known?), the main job of the primary researcher is to develop a *hypothesis*: if I did/asked/created a situation for A, would B, C, or D be the result? After deciding on a hypothesis, you would develop the research plan to find out the answer that the hypothesis asks. To be specific, you would decide exactly what interview or survey questions, observations, or experiments would answer your hypothesis. Another more strict definition of hypothesis is when a scientist looks at data and specifically decides what a probable outcome would be in an experiment. Then the researcher develops an experiment that demonstrates without a doubt that the hypothesis is true ("proving the hypothesis"). If the research shows the hypothesis to be false, then the scientist develops another hypothesis based on the new knowledge of what doesn't work/isn't true, and then designs another experiment to prove the new hypothesis. Depending on your classes, you could be asked to develop either type of hypothesis and analyze conclusions based on an experiment you construct.

Social and natural scientists who write a primary research report use a formulaic, unchangeable organizational pattern. You might be asked to write a report that uses this form. The sections are:

- The *Introduction* presents the question(s) that the research is trying to find answers to, it reviews and summarizes the research that has already been done on the subject, and it states a hypothesis (an assumption to prove) that the experiment will study. For lab reports, the assignment itself guides the student: the professor tells the student what the questions are, any relevant background information, and states the hypothesis the lab experiment is studying. The introduction describes the theory tested by the experiment.
- The *Materials and Method* description gives an exact account of the participants in the experiment, observations, interviews, or surveys, and all the tools used to conduct the research. The exact method of the research also has to be described, including a process analysis explaining why the research was done in the manner it was. (The research should be constructed with the least possibility for error.)
- The *Results* section states the findings of the research as precisely as possible.
- The *Discussion* explores and analyzes the implications of the study, including possible ramifications of the study for its subject field, and further studies suggested by the present study.

When your assignment calls for primary research, because of its complexity, consult the syllabus and follow a well thought out specific research time schedule, with these 10 steps:

Completion date by

    3/18 1) Specifically analyze the requirements, audience and writing situation.

    3/21 2) Pick a subject you are interested in that is suitable for primary research.

    3/25 3) Begin research answering general questions about your subject, and use encyclopedias and textbooks to get a basic knowledge of your subject: chapters 6-7.

    4/1 4) As you begin to focus your subject, read more secondary and primary resources on your focused subject. Look for more questions that you want answered: chapters 6-7.

    4/3 5) Develop a hypothesis that your research will answer, and if you are to use the introduction/material and methods/results/discussion format, write an introduction that summarizes and synthesizes the knowledge on your focused subject: chapter 9.

    4/6 6) Study primary research on your subject, and analyze specifically how the scientists developed the details of their research and then develop the material and methods for your research to prove your hypothesis (the interview or survey questions, the controls for the experiment): chapters 6-9.

184

4/13 7) Conduct the research, and decide whether more questions need to be answered after conducting the research: chapter 9.

4/20 8) Analyze the results of your primary research and draw conclusions. Write a draft.

4/27 9) Revised Draft Due – revised for context, content, organization, and paragraphs.

4/30 10) Essay Due – final content revision, and edited for style and documentation form.

Observation

To complete excellent, detailed observation, begin with secondary research: what has already been said about the people or place that you are going to observe? Focus your subject — are you more interested in certain people that inhabit the place observed, kinds of people in the place, the actions of the people, or the place itself? Develop a hypothesis (an idea you want to prove) or questions that you want answered concerning the subject that you will test by close observation. Decide if you also need to do an interview independent of the observation.

Planning and Conducting an Observation

In order to perform a successful observation, memorize the hypothesis and initial questions that you want answered. You must not let the people who are being observed know that you are watching them. Leave a notebook out in the car, at home, or in the dorm if you are observing near where you live, and immediately after leaving the observation site, record these items:

- An overall initial impression — freewrite for 5 minutes
- Description of setting with minute details
- Describe the people — clothes, ages, physical factors, and what they are doing (types of activities and reactions to people and events around them)
- Write answers to questions you want answered that you found either through observation or informal conversation
- A summary impression — after you have recorded all the details above, compare, classify, evaluate, and analyze
- What other questions, observations, interviews, or library research are now necessary to answer your questions or hypothesis?

Continue the process of observing, interviewing, and library research until you have answered your questions and developed a thesis for your essay.

Nancy Birkla, in the essay that follows, had done a considerable amount of secondary research on differences in communication styles between the genders. After she wrote a draft using just the secondary research, she felt that she had not yet proved her point. She took the statements of the experts, and used their ideas about differences in gender styles as the hypotheses that she would prove through observation. She then spent a week observing how the genders interacted, and revised her essay using the observations to further support her points.

185

Nancy Birkla
English 102
Professor Mulder
April 5, 2017
Final Draft

Communication: Creating Shared Meanings

The dictionary definition of "stereotype" is "something conforming to a general pattern," and stereotypes could not exist without patterns or reoccurrences of behaviors significant enough to validate patterns. For years, men have poked fun at women for being "too emotional," and women have chastised men for not "sharing their feelings." Men say women need to simplify their feelings; women claim men need to quit burying how they are feeling altogether. In the meantime, communication between the sexes has progressed slowly throughout history.

Genetically, it appears as if all human beings possess identical emotional components and have the capability of acting alike emotionally. Historically, they have not. Gender roles have played an important part in the great production of life, it appears, ever since the beginning of time. As far back as the Old Testament, women were expected to play a subservient role to man. This was stated in Genesis: "Your desire shall be for your husband and he will rule over you" (*Revised Standard* Version, 1952/1997, 3.16).

History began when men started documenting, by drawing, how their lives were lived. The pictures, or hieroglyphics, that the ancient Egyptians left behind depicted men as warriors and providers (Johnson *et al.*, 1963, Vol. 4, p. 621). They did not portray women exchanging blows or kneeling in triumph, as they did the men (p. 623). Women were practically discounted altogether, only rarely being illustrated at all – and then only to portray elaborate fashions or hairstyles (sound familiar?). Generally, their deaths were recorded also (p.630). This demonstrates the non-significance of the actions and words of women in those times.

One conclusion that has been made over the years is that society has always influenced how we behave and even how we talk (Goldberg, 1988). Goldberg states: "The emotions of both males and females of all societies associate dominance with the male, in male-female relationships and encounters" (p. 26). He further explains that only in recent years has it become at all acceptable for men and women to attempt breaking out of their traditional roles in a stride toward individuality.

Even so, Tannen (1991), Tannen (1994), and Gray (1992) argue that some behaviors have been embedded so deeply for so long they seem to reach our emotional cores. Although there are no set rules governing "how men should act" or "how women should act," there certainly seem to be trends which even today remain prevalent. The paramount factor seems to be that men and women often hear the same words differently. According to these same

186

sources, members of the opposite sexes often seem incapable, or perhaps unwilling, to attempt understanding the way the other perceives things, regardless of the language used.

American men tend to place the majority of their emphasis on their egotistic need for independence rather than on social involvement (Tannen, 1987). In reference to this behavior, Tannen says, "This often entails paying less attention to the meta-message level of talk – the level that comments on relationships – focusing instead on the information level" (p.18). Several of these scholars agree that man's need for gathering and processing information appears to supersede his need for emotional bonding. Men appear to have an inherent need to collect as much information as necessary and then resolve the situation as expediently as possible (Berkowitz, 1991; Tannen, 1987; Tannen, 1991). I have been closely observing a married couple, good friends of mine, as the husband moves into a new job, and their situation illustrates this pattern perfectly. The husband looked at the facts, the main one being that he would probably, and the operative word is probably, make more money at this new job. He was ready, after analyzing the information, to move right into the new job. He could not understand why his wife was so scared and wanted to talk out her fears with him, why she wanted him to analyze whether he would like the new job, or why she wanted them to wait and look at the situation for a longer period of time (so, I believe, she could process the change emotionally through talk) (T. Jones& B. Jones, personal communications, Mar. 20, 22, 25, 2011).

Tannen (1994) expounds on this point when she states, "Men generally take things literally" (p.146). The example she used was of a female executive who frequently initiated the airing of complaints in a roundabout, pleasant way. The woman did a lot of talking as a way of airing her feelings, so perhaps her male associates would understand her better. Instead of understanding, they would quickly offer solutions on how she could improve the situation. They criticized her inability to "cut to the chase" (p.146). All the talking she was doing, in an effort to buffer her compatriot's feelings, was interpreted as chronic complaining. She was left feeling condescended to and frustrated.

Despite the lack of ability on the part of men to talk about feelings, Berkowitz (1991) argues that they do not often show a willingness to change. He states, "Men are often afraid to lower the drawbridge and open up the gate. Other men are rarely allowed to cross the moat and enter his fortress" (p. 36). Even so, Berkowitz goes on to say, men seem to admire and envy women for their ability to have intimate friendships with other women. I observed women in a homeless shelter, and there was much talk about how sad, lonely, and for some, how angry, they were. I observed men in a homeless shelter, and they talked only about information – food, jobs, and for some, liquor. I have observed men who were losing their jobs when a plant closed, and most of the talk was about getting another job and paying bills; a small minority did express anger verbally, perhaps the only emotion a man thinks he is allowed to exhibit. Several talked about how their spouses would react emotionally; most of them wished they didn't have to discuss the emotions with their wives.

Because of most men's inability to relate to women on the emotional terms that women understand, Brooks (1990) concludes that men and women must learn about each other's means of communication and rapport. In reference to this, he states:

> When we match our partners' process words, not only are we speaking their language and being understood, but we're also relating with them as opposed to relating to them. This is because we're in the picture with them; we've become associated – seeing, hearing, and feeling life the way they do (p.92).

He further states that once we become able to communicate in the same way or in a way our partner can understand, we not only become understood, but we can reclaim our integrity.

The argument that one of the keys to communication between the sexes lies in trying to say things in a way that the other understands is one that keeps appearing over and over again as I read books and articles about relationships. Bloomfield & Vattese (1992) assert that the point is not to agree, but to unconditionally accept and support a partner's feelings. They surmise, "It is not about who is right and who is wrong, but appreciating each other's point-of-view; when it comes to feelings, no one is right or wrong (p.66). When people deal with, and communicate about, information, there usually is a right or wrong. When people deal with emotions, they just are.

To me, as a woman, the most intriguing aspect of what I studied was in the writing of Gray (1992). He shifted the focus off men being at fault and constantly being blamed for having the inability to communicate effectively. He wrote, instead, that women seem unwilling to learn and understand the silent communication that is typical of many men. Since nonverbal communication is the most prevalent type of all, he theorizes that women have a lot to learn about men before their relationships can be truly fulfilling. They need to accept that when a man is upset, he automatically goes into "his cave" (p. 68), as Gray calls it, to work things out. Gray challenges women to learn not to be upset when this happens. Not only does a man not want her in his cave with him, but he does not want anyone else in there with him either. Gray uses the following words to make his point understood:

> Women should not become scared that they have done something terribly wrong. They need to gradually learn that if you just let men go into their caves, after awhile they will come out and everything will once again be alright (p.68).

He further explains a variety of reasons why men react this way. Gray's list reads as follows:

1. He needs to think about a problem and find a practical solution.
2. He doesn't have an answer to a question or problem. Men were never taught to say, "Gee, I don't have an answer. I need to go into my cave and find one." Other men assume he is doing just that when he becomes quiet.

3. He has become upset or stressed. At such times, he needs to be alone to cool off and find his control again. He doesn't want to do or say anything he may regret.

4. He needs to find himself. This fourth reason becomes very important when men are in love. At times, they begin to lose and forget themselves. They can feel that too much intimacy robs them of their power. They need to regulate how close they get. Whenever they get too close, an alarm goes off and they are on their way into the cave. As a result, they are rejuvenated and find their loving and powerful self again (p. 70).

Gray asserts that women have an extremely difficult time understanding this kind of language, because one of women's golden rules is to never abandon a girlfriend in a time of need. She then, quite naturally, wants to go into the cave to help her man out. Gray sums up everything nicely when he states, "Both men and women need to stop offering the method of caring they would prefer and start to learn different ways their partners think, feel, and react" (p. 69). The reason this particular piece of information was especially interesting to me was because I saw my and my first husband's behavior reflected in Gray's explanation of men's and women's reactions to each other. When I actually saw the words written in a book, I realized the pattern. I had always felt that I was doing something wrong when he went "into his cave," since when a woman shuts down she usually wants nothing to do with the person she has shut down with. I understand now that his behavior had nothing to do with me. Now, when my present husband displays the same type of withdrawal, I will know that he is just processing information and feelings like men do. As a matter of fact, I asked my husband to read Gray's book, and we now both seem to have a better understanding of gender communication styles. He could process the book because it was "information." He now understands my need to talk everything out and be listened to. We only need to learn how to do this, and how to take turns talking. We cannot very well both do what we feel comfortable doing at the same time, since the type of communication we each understand differs.

Very few issues become resolved by all persons on one side of an issue suddenly jumping to the other. As time goes on, our society is becoming more and more accepting of human beings emoting in whichever way feels comfortable to them as individuals - not as men or women. I believe the answer to this age-old problem is simply a melding together of both styles of communication. If we would all concentrate on the shared meaning of communication, instead of whose way of communicating is best, I bet we would meet in the middle a lot faster.

References

Berkowitz, B. (1992). *What men won't tell you, but women want to know*. William Morrow.

Bloomfield, H. & Vatesse, S. (1992*). Lifemates: The love fitness program for a lasting relationship*. Signet.

Brooks, M. (1990). *Instant rapport*. Warner.

Johnson, E. et al. (Ed.). (1959-1968). *Encyclopedia of world art* (Vol.1-15). Macmillan.

Goldberg, S. (1988). *Opposing viewpoints.* Greenhaven Press.

Gray, J. (1992*). Men are from Mars, women are from Venus: A practical guide for improving communication and getting what you want in relationships.* Random House.

Revised Standard Bible. (1997). Bible Gateway. https://www.biblegateway.com/versions/Revised-Standard-Version (Original wok published 1952)

Tannen, D. (1987). *That's not what i meant: How conversational style makes or breaks a relationship.* Random House.

Tannen, D. (1991*). You just don't understand: Women and men in conversation.* Random House.

Tannen, D. (1994, March). But what do you mean? *Redbook, 76,* 93-95, 145-147.

Interviews

Interviews are one of the most effective means of discovering information, and are often used in conjunction with observations and document study. Imagine the historian's delight when she discovers an elderly person who has lived through a period that she is analyzing, or the delight of a sociologist observing a sub-stratum of American society who finds a member of that culture who will discuss its ways.

Many people have a fear of conducting interviews, but they shouldn't. Just remember a basic human behavior trait: most people like to talk about themselves and about subjects they are interested in. You are asking them for information on a subject they know a lot about, so don't let interviews intimidate you. If you are well prepared, you will do fine — interviews are just informative conversations. The most important thing to remember about an interview is to gain as much knowledge of the person or subject as possible before doing the interview. No one, no one, likes to be asked questions that can be found with a little research. You must find out as much about the subject as you can before the interview.

Planning and Conducting an Interview

1) Arrange the interview at the beginning of your writing project. People are busy and you must work around their schedule!

    a. Make a phone call: Introduce yourself and give a short, simple explanation of your project. Be enthusiastic, but don't monopolize the conversation. The interviewee will not be able to respond if you talk on and on.

    b. Don't hang up without arranging a specific time and place for the interview.

2) Plan your Interview

    a. If the place where the interview occurs is important for the questions you want answered, go there first and observe. The observation will answer some of the questions, and it will suggest other questions to ask. Also observe before the interview to feel comfortable when you actually interview the subject.

    b. Do background reading. Knowledge of the subject is essential.

c. Consider your objectives for the interview. Do you want 1. an "overall picture," 2. to be led to other people to interview, 3. facts/information that you couldn't find out through written means or the public relations branch of the interviewee's organization, 4. more information about a person, or 5. more information about a place?

d. Prepare questions based on a careful analysis of the objectives.

3) For the interview, take a notebook with prepared questions. Listen to answers, and be prepared to ask questions based on responses. Good interviewers listen well and base their next questions more on the responses of their subject than the prepared set of questions (see the example interviews that follow this set of instructions).

After the interview:

- Immediately after the interview, reflect, review notes, add notes, and write a main overall summary impression of the interview.
- Has the interview developed more questions? Is another interview, closer observation, or more library research now necessary to answer your questions or hypothesis?
- Many interviews refer you to books, articles, people, or resources for more information; in other words, most people don't have the answer on the tips of their tongues, but they can tell you where to find the answer. If this has happened, continue your research.

The following demonstrates two sample interviews:

The writer planned to interview a fellow student who lived in another region of the country for her first two years of high school, and then went to the same high school as the writer for the last two years. They both attend the same college and are in the same composition class. His main objective in the interview was to find out the major similarities and differences between the two school systems to discover to what degree school systems are different. He had already done enough library research to know that the experts agreed there were major differences in school systems. He had developed a list of questions:

1) Which school system was better, and why?
2) What were the main similarities?
3) What were the main differences?
4) How did sports and extra-curricular activities compare?
5) Were there any after-school educational clubs or activities?
6) Were the students different?
7) Where were the teachers better and why?

The writer had an advantage in that he knew the person he was interviewing. He was not nervous, and neither was she. When you do an interview for the first time, you might be scared: just remember that most of the people you interview will not be celebrities and probably have never been interviewed either! Break the ice, and make the interviewee comfortable. Introduce yourself politely, and relax so that your subject will also relax. The following is an example of a poor interview:

191

INTERVIEWER: I really want to thank you for taking the time to answer these questions, Cathy. They will really help me put a focus on my study of school systems around the country. Shall we get started? Since we went to the same high school the last two years, what I need to do is learn about your other school for a comparison. So, which school did you think was better?

RESPONDENT: The St. Louis school system that I went to my freshman and sophomore years was much better. We were tested at the end of every year and there were six to eight levels of classes each year.

INTERVIEWER: What were the main similarities between the two school systems?

RESPONDENT: Well — uh — the kids are about the same everywhere. And there were sports, and . . .

Two problems have emerged with the interview so far: the questions are vague, and the interviewer is not listening to the response of his friend and asking questions based on what she is saying. After his interviewee said "there were six to eight levels of classes each year," the interviewer should have questioned her about specifics of these levels. Also, in most cases, the more specific the questions are, the more precise the responses will be, although sometimes the interview situation demands rather general questions, and one can conduct a very successful interview with general questions if one listens carefully to the answer to the question, searching for the next more specific question from the response. An example of a better interview:

INTERVIEWER: I really want to thank you for taking the time to answer these questions, Cathy. They will really help me put a focus on my study of school systems around the country. Shall we get started? Since we went to the same high school the last two years, what I need to do is learn about your other school for a comparison. So, which school did you think was better?

RESPONDENT: The St. Louis school system that I went to my freshman and sophomore years was much better. We were tested at the end of every year and there were six to eight levels of classes each year.

INTERVIEWER: So you mean academically the St. Louis school system was better?

RESPONDENT: Definitely.

INTERVIEWER: Describe the "levels of classes" that you mentioned.

RESPONDENT: Well, for each class there were levels based on the difficulty of the class.

INTERVIEWER: Can you give an example?

RESPONDENT: Yeah, good. For instance in algebra II alone there was a precalculus level, a college prep level, an advanced level, a regular level, and a remedial level for those who had problems in algebra I.

INTERVIEWER: It sounds like your high school was quite a bit bigger than ours.

RESPONDENT: Actually, no — I think it had 1900 students rather than 1400, but the main difference was that there were all these levels — not just a lot of teachers teaching the same Algebra II class.

INTERVIEWER: We had levels at our school too.

RESPONDENT: Yeah. But we could pick our level. They seriously tested you, and you could even switch from one class to another during the semester. They had the learning sequences so coordinated that somehow it was possible to move up a level if the one you were in was too easy. I felt more challenged.

Notice that the interviewer has not gone past the first question, and is asking questions based on the first response. He is actually analyzing one major difference in the school systems, and it is possible that he will finish his interview without asking another question from the list.

When using information from the interview in your essay, as a general rule you should paraphrase rather than use direct quotation (with the exception below). Use only that part of the interview that directly relates to the subject of your essay, not the entire interview.

For instance, although the interview recorded above lasted twenty more minutes, the interviewer decided to use only the beginning:

> Cathy Jones, a student who spent two years at Thomas Jefferson High School in St. Louis, Missouri and the last two years at Westport High School in Augusta, Georgia, found that the St. Louis system was much better academically because they tested students annually and had a highly developed system of levels so that students worked to their fullest capabilities (personal communication, April 4, 2018).

Interviews can be a valuable asset when researching a subject. Authority figures on a subject can help you find appropriate material, and give you opinions on the subjects of your research, and people who have experienced something related to your subject (as in the example just given) can give your writing specific description and a vividness missing from more often used print sources. The student example that follows demonstrates how one can also use interviews and blogs, direct quotations, to strengthen an argument. Veronica is analyzing the popularity of a fashion line, Kate Spade, and so she uses rhetorical/textual analyses of Kate Spade commercials and their website, but to bring another line of reasoning to her argument, she then uses a persoanl interview and two blogs to strenghen her argument. Usually, one summarizes an interview rather than directly quoting (like the example on the previous page), UNLESS one wants the immediacy and force of the direct quotation, which is what is effective in this essay that follows. The excitement of the interviewees grabs the audience.

Often when doing research on a consumer product or television/movie, interviews can be one way of gaining valuable information and insights into the product.

Veronica Heitzman
English 102-Fall 16
Dr. Hanson
Final Draft

Live Colorfully

Live Colorfully came alive as a slogan in 1993 for Kate Spade. According to its website, Kate Spade was also born in 1993 when Kate Brosnahan Spade, an accessories editor at *Mademoiselle*, first designed a handbag. She used six silhouettes combined with "sleek, utilitarian shapes and palettes" to create her masterpiece. The first store opened in 1996 in New York City. People fell for the fresh, modern sensibility, and business was booming. By 2007, Kate turned over control to Kate Spade & Company, newly merged with Liz Claiborne. Deborah Lloyd (the president and chief creative officer) and Craig Leavitt (the CEO) quickly launched "clothing, jewelry collections, bedding, leg wear and fragrance." Today, the company has added "shoes, stationery, eyewear, baby [accessories], … tabletop, … and gifts." Kate Spade has 140 retail shops and outlet stores nationally and more than 175 internationally, but their products are sold in more than 450 stores "in every time zone and every continent" (Kate Spade & Company, 2015).

Kate Spade is known as an upscale brand, advertising to women who dress and act classy. In Kate Spade & Company (2014), the company did holiday commercials starring Anna Kendrick. In these commercials, Anna runs into instances where she is either mistaken for another person, runs into someone accidentally, her date cancels on her, or she forgets her keys to her apartment. Anna, along with her dog, make the best out of every situation because she has the help of all her Kate Spade products. For example, in one of the commercials Anna forgets her keys and is locked out. The locksmith takes forever, but she notices a ladder she can pull her up to the window. So with the help of all her new products from Kate Spade, she is able to reach and pull the ladder down and she makes it into her room. In the commercial where her date cancels on her, she takes a picture of her purse, which looks like an elf, and posts the picture using the hashtag "dating my purse." Now when people post a picture of their Kate Spade purse, they will usually use that hashtag.

In Kate Spade & Company (2016), they launched their new commercial. This one has three classy ladies who go on a trip together. They are getting together for the "perfect weekend," the name of the commercial, and of course they are head-to-toe in their Kate Spade products. They are renting a house and they keep getting packages brought in. The first package that comes is full of bridal accessories from Kate Spade. The next package that comes is a cake, and if you are a Kate Spade fan you know that "Eat Cake for Breakfast" is another one of their biggest sayings (because, of course, cake makes you happy). The third package that comes is a fun, air-driven bouncing castle (for kids). After their first package arrives Anna Kendrick who lives next door comes over and, by the end, they are friends with her. She too is dressed head-to-toe in Kate Spade. Here the commercial tells us that if we buy Kate Spade, we will have the perfect day or weekend because nothing bad can happen with Kate Spade on your side.

Kate Spade makes their products sturdy and long lasting. You can always count on them. I have never had a problem with any of their products and I carry everything in my crowded purse. Whether it be books or my wallet, I have never had a tear in the lining or the fabric. I also have never had a problem with the leather getting weak and the trim coming off. They are consistent with every product they make. There are many brands of purses, such as Coach or Fossil, that advertise the same sturdy products, but do their purses show quality? Does Coach and Fossil inspire woman to be more powerful and successful? From my own personal experience, brands like Coach and Fossils' leather always wears out, the lining rips very easily, and the lining around the straps always rub off. Kate Spade not only shows her quality in her purses, but also shows her quality in what they stand for.

Hailey Owen, a lady I personally interviewed, said, "I love Kate Spade! I will forever be a user of their products. Kate Spade is just so classic and classy. My favorite is their nylon hipster purse. I have one in black. It is just so convenient and it goes with everything. I also like their cosmetic and travel bags. All of their products just have great quality!" (personal communication, April 16, 2016) A blogger posted: "I have ten kate spade bags and numerous small accessories. Kate Spade bags were my favorites about five years ago. What attracted me was there was plenty of pink and she had the cutest initial lining. My initials are also KS so it was a novelty for me. Over the years I have moved on to higher end bags - LV, Chloe and Balenciaga but I still find myself visiting her website monthly to see what is new. All my bags still look fabulous. The only item that hasn't held up well is my large planner but it gets a lot of use. It's probably just wear and tear. Its two years old." (Skyler, 2008) Another blogger posted, "I have recently started buying several Kate Spade Bags. Actually they now over power [sic] my Coach Bags. The designs are simple yet elegant. The feel of the leather is fabulous. I'm in awe of the 14Kt gold accents, and I just love her logo. My experience with Kate Spade has been very positive" (Accessories by Kate Spade, 2012).

Kate Spade not only supports their customers, but the company has a foundation for empowering women to transform their community. The Kate Spade & Company Foundation (2015) tells us, "Four million women and girls call New York City home. One in four of them is economically vulnerable. We're dedicated to empowering low-income New York City women to find trade (their own business, a career path or skill set- not just a job) that will support them and their families, and create positive ripple effects in their communities." The company has created three pillars to accomplish their foundation (para. 1).

The first pillar is women in entrepreneurship. "Men in New York City own 1.5 as many businesses as women, employ 3.5 times as many people and make, on average, 4.5 times as much revenue. Our guarantees are setting out to change that by providing business support, legal and finical assistance and many more invaluable resources to women-owned businesses" (para. 2).

The second is women in technology. "Learning to code is just the beginning. Although the tech industry today is a predominately male industry, we see that as an opportunity: the prospects for women to find employment that can be creative, collaborative, innovative and truly boundary-pushing are immense" (para. 3).

Lastly, the third is women in arts. "Because you need bread, but you need roses too. We believe that the pursuit of art as a career should be available to anyone, no matter their background, and our greatness are giving promising young artists the opportunity to develop their ideas" (para. 4).

I love not only supporting a company that makes good quality products, but I also like supporting a company that gives back and inspires. In today's world, people need a little extra push to follow their dreams and to keep going even when times get rough. We all need a little inspiration and someone to look up to. I love fashion and I plan on pursuing it myself, and this is one of the companies I look up to and follow whether it be through their blogs or just being a loyal customer.

References

Accessories by kate spade. (2012, June 21). [Online forum post]. Purseblog. https://forum.purseblog.com/forums/kate-spade.279.

Kate Spade & Company. (2016, May 28). #Missadventures: the perfect weekend. [Video]. YouTube. https://www.youtube.com/watch?v=CmTfbwJL0Ss.

Kate Spade & Company (2014, November 13). #Missadventures: the waiting game. [Video]. YouTube. https://www.youtube.com/watch?v=CpTfbwTD0Ss.

Kate Spade & Company. (2015). Who we are. Kate Spade. https://www.katespade.com/ katespade-customer-service-ks-about-us/ks-who-we-are.

Kate Spade & Company Foundation. (2015). Kate spade & company foundation. Kate Spade. https://www.katespade.com/katespade-customer-service-ks-about-us/ks-foundation.html.

Skyler. (2008, November 10). Kate spade? Thoughts, experiences good and bad. [Online forum posting.]. Purseblog. https://forum.purseblog.com/forums/kate-spade.279.

Case Studies

In a case study, researchers study the results of research already completed or data already compiled, then they introduce a variable into the situation, repeat the same research or data collection, and compare the two sets of data to draw a conclusion. For instance, a researcher could look at marijuana use in a high school both before and after a special set of activities discouraging drug use (the activities are the variable) to discover what attitudes and activities had changed within various sub-populations after the activities. From this, she would draw conclusions about the effectiveness of the program and perhaps about attitudes of the various sub-populations of the high school.

196

Some case studies find the information compared already done and the researcher analyzes the two sets of data based on a variable found or created between the two sets of data, like the previous example. Other students are asked to, or on their own, create the before and after scenario and actually do the research themselves, as in the example below.

Most case studies use a version of the introduction, material and methods, results, discussion form for scientific reporting:

Sections of a Case Study Essay

Introduction - Explains the essay's purpose by describing the processes used, the variable, and what could be learned. Also in this section would be the *methodology* (the materials and methods) used to find the data used in the case study.

Observations - Specifically describe the results of the interviews, surveys, observations, experiments done to produce the data examined in this "case."

Discussion - Discusses the implications that can be derived from the results of the observations.

Conclusion - does not re-state what has been said!!!! The conclusion takes the case study out into a larger context. For instance, if there was little change after the variable was introduced, another more promising variable or variables could be suggested. (Most scientific inquiry includes much time finding out what does not work!) Or, if the variable suggests a positive outcome, how could this information be used to help the situation studied in the case study?

Planning and Conducting a Case Study

1) If you are doing a case study based on already established studies, do in-depth secondary research on the subject to make sure you understand the implications of the studies, and to help you discover how you can find a variable that explains the contrast or lack of contrast between the two studies.

If you are creating your own case study, look at your subject and decide questions that need to be answered, which usually involves secondary research. Develop a case study and a variable to insert between the two halves of your study. Decide how you will collect the data: interviews, observations, surveys, experiments?

A third method is to discover a study already done that you can introduce a variable to and replicate the study already done.

2) If you are doing your own interviews, observations, or surveys begin quickly as you have to do a set of experiments, introduce a variable, and then repeat the experiments before you can begin writing. You can, however, *write your introduction* as you do this. These are usually narratives.

3) After studying the data from your case study, *write the observation.* (What actually happened before the variable and after the variable was introduced?)

4) *Write the discussion and conclusion sections*. Revise and edit the entire essay.

Bill Smith, John Hamilton, and Tyler Dodd
Intro to Sociology - Spring 2016
Dr. Gardner

Getting Enough Sleep Before Tests

Introduction

This study analyzes the effects of 8 hours sleep versus less sleep on the night before tests. A major variable to this study is that students have many different methodologies for studying, so in order to downplay the role of variables, the research began with informal discussions with students in dormitories at Indiana University, asking about study habits. From these informal discussions a brief survey was conducted in order to achieve the methodology needed to rule out other variables around success. The informal survey allowed us to pick students of both genders that we put into four categories:

1) Students who studied less than three hours for tests and rarely read the material.

2) Students who crammed 6-12 hours the day/night before a test, obviously getting little sleep.

3) Students who read the chapters and did homework when it was assigned, and then studied 2-5 hours the day/night before a test.

4) Students who read the chapters and did homework when it was assigned, and then studied 6-12 hours the day/night before a test.

(If a student was not within these four categories he/she was ruled out as a subject.)

After breaking the students into these groups (that they didn't know about), we asked them to just do the amount of study they said they would do in preparation for the first tests of the semester. After the tests were administered, we asked them two questions: their grades and exactly how many hours they slept the night before their tests. We correlated the results.

For the second set of tests in the semester, we asked all these students to either stay in the same category of study, or since we could not tell students to keep doing poorly, if they wanted to increase their study time, we asked that they move into one of the other categories in terms of study techniques *vis a vis* time devoted to study. The only change we demanded of them was that they HAD to sleep AT LEAST eight hours the night before any tests and refrain from any alcohol or drugs for 24 hours before the tests. After the tests were administered, we asked them two questions: their grades and whether they slept eight hours the night before their tests.

Observations

The students' test grades in all four categories improved, an average of 22%. The students who crammed before tests (groups 2 and 4) had an average of three hours sleep the night before the first test. After the experiment with eight hours sleep, their test grades rose 25%

Discussion

As a corollary, the highest grades were not in the group that did the most homework, but in the group who did the second highest time allotment of homework, suggesting that students who work the hardest possibly do not have the advantages of the students with the highest grades. With little surprise, it is noticed that students who cram and students who do not take their courses seriously suffer the lowest grades. Obviously, this case study suggests that a good night's sleep improves grades irrespective of the amount of time studying.

Conclusion

This case study needs to be repeated with a much larger sampling to make it statistically significant, but even in the meantime, students need to see the results of this case study throughout the school, and in society at large. Students who saw the results stated that they not only were going to stop cramming for tests and spread out the amount of time they studied, but also that they were definitely going to get more sleep the night before tests. The teaching to the test that many students had twelve years of before college, as well as the *laissez faire* attitude toward school promulgated by other students, many parents, and society as a whole has definitely had an adverse effect on student test taking. Sleeping eight hours could be an easy step toward righting incorrect learning strategies.

Surveys

Sociologists, political scientists, and many businessmen and economists regularly use surveys, such as the Gallup Polls, to analyze public opinion and societal norms. The constructing of formal surveys has become a precise mathematical science, but there is no reason students cannot use informal surveys to explore how social scientists approach answering questions concerning the society we live in. By asking questions of a larger cross-section of society, or of one specific segment of society, a researcher finds how people live and what they think today.

Planning and Conducting a Survey

1) Do in-depth secondary research on your subject so that you know the kinds of questions that have already been asked, and what the answers were. For your survey, you might re-ask the same questions to discover what your target audience thinks about the subject, or you could design a set of questions that ask for more specific or different, but related, questions than those already asked.

199

2) Analyze specific target audiences to discover who you want to respond to your survey.

3) As you work on 1 and 2, develop a hypothesis, a question or set of questions that you want to find out about through your survey. For example, in the student survey in this section, Joan Steiden wanted to find out how much time parents spent with their children when they were in middle school, and what activities they engaged in. Her target audience was 18-21 year olds at the university she attended, a group not only easy to get responses from, but also one who is four to six years away from middle school and thus better able to remember the details of parental involvement.

4) Have a specific reason for targeting the group that you will survey. Describe the group exactly so that you know why you have targeted them. Decide how to contact them — phone, personal interview (asking a set of questions), passing out or mailing questionnaires (this third method will bring at best a 50% response). If your target audience is made up of fellow students or co-workers, perhaps a teacher or supervisor will allow you to conduct a brief survey, or hand it out one day and collect it the next.

5) Consider the objectives of your survey. Specifically work out the questions to be asked; ask for help from fellow students to make sure the questions are clear and impartial. Don't force respondents into a certain response with leading questions such as: Real earning power of the average wage earner has declined throughout the last two years. The current political administration is not doing a very good job, is it? (See below on how to plan the survey questions using open and closed questions.) At the beginning of the survey, ask for statistics such as age, sex, and any other background information you need to identify the subjects specifically. For instance, a survey on child care would require that you know, perhaps, the ages of the respondent's children.

6) Conduct the Survey.

7) After the survey is completed:

- Tabulate, correlate and synthesize the results of the survey.
- Did you find answers to the hypothesis you began with?
- Draw conclusions from your findings.
- Write an essay describing the results of your survey, using the Introduction/ Materials and Method/Results/Discussion paradigm that social scientists use. (The essay concluding this section uses this organizational format.)

There are two basic types of questions a survey can ask, **open and closed questions**:

Open questions ask respondents to answer freely, and there is a flexibility and a freedom to the responses.
What would you do if _____?
The major disadvantage of open questions is that a researcher cannot graph and tabulate mathematically the broad range of responses.

Closed questions ask for a specific response, and can later be graphed.
How many times a month do you go out on a date? 1-3   4-6   more
In the last year, have you dated?   no one   1 person   2-3   more

When you construct the questions, revise them conscientiously so that the way you ask the questions will not lead respondents toward a specific answer. If you are doing a survey, it would be very wise to share your preliminary survey questions with a peer review group. The group needs to help you create unbiased questions. Most professional surveys use closed questions, but if your needs call for open-ended questions, by all means use them.

Especially if you are planning a career in sociology, political science, or psychology, try planning, conducting, analyzing, and writing about a survey you have conducted. Excellent students do what they are going to do when they graduate.

Student Example: Survey. APA Style Documentation

Joan Steiden
English 102 - Spring 2004
Dr. Richardson
Final Draft

A Study of Young Adults' Memories of the Amount of Time
Parents Spent with Them in Middle School

Introduction

Many recent studies have lamented the lack of involvement between parents and children in America today (Hewlett, 1991; O'Mara, 1992), including these sub-categories: divorce and single parent households (Heims, Julian, & Sussman, eds,, 1995), distant or divorced fatherhood (Boothe & Crouter, eds.,1998), balancing work and children (Blau, Ferber, & Winkler, 1997), and lack of parental skills (Broderick, 1993; McBride, 1990). Some of these studies offer suggestions for improving parent/child relationships (Bartle, Sabateli, & Anderson, 1989; Blau, Ferber, & Winkler, 1997; Haas, 1993; McBride, 1990; O'Mara, 1992). The reduction in dual parent homes is one obvious major limiting factor in the amount of time children spend with their parents (1980 dual parent homes: 81%; 1990 dual parent homes 76% U.S. Bureau of the Census, 1998). One parent who usually has to work in many cases cannot possibly spend the amount of time with children as two parents. On the other hand, children of 2 parents who happen to be workaholics (or by economic necessity have to work several jobs) cannot spend as much time with their parents. Children lose out on time with their fathers for two major reasons: through divorce when the mother gets custody, and through the ideas of this culture that tell a man to be a strong, silent worker, one who never speaks nor shows emotion.

The present survey finds out how much time a group of community college students remember that each sex of their parents spent with them when they were in their middle school years. Much work has been done (McBride & Mills, 1993; and countless others) on how much time each gender spends with pre-school children, with the debate over whether a parent should stay home with preschool children, and much work has been done on at-risk children concerning parental involvement, but not as many specific studies have been done concerning "average" American children. This study surveys one of the least represented subjects: middle class and lower middle class, mostly first generation, college students at an urban community college, an area without devastating poverty or crime problems.

Materials and Method

102 surveys were administered to male and female community college students, aged 18-25. 3 were not used because the students had lived with relatives during their middle school years (with 2, both parents were dead). 152 were given out, but since the questions required approximately 45 minutes to an hour to complete, some were not returned. One significant problem with the validity of this survey is the amount of time it took to complete coupled with the fact that two of my professors gave extra credit for students completing it. Some students could have filled in any answer. A second major problem is that the survey relies on respondents' memories for very specific questions concerning amounts of time. However, I talked individually with enough students to know that they took the survey seriously because it asked penetrating questions and helped them get in touch with their middle school years.

The survey itself is Appendix A of this report. It asks them how much time they spent with each parent in terms of these categories: eating, watching television and movies, housework, home repair, sports, games, and homework. For each of these categories, it also asked whether the respondent considered the interaction between the respondent and parent to be active or passive (passive being defined as having little verbal contact or interaction).

Students had one week to complete the survey.

Results

Of the 99 respondents:

No contact with father; lived with mother	22%
No contact with mother; lived with father	2%
Some contact with father; lived with mother	24%
Some contact with mother; lived with father	4%
Lived with two parents	71%

(step-parents counted as parental, if respondent indicated closeness)

I asked respondents who considered a step-parent to be a "father" or "mother," even if their biological parent was also in their lives, to consider the step-parent as a parent in terms of this study. Since the purpose of the study is to find out how much parental involvement the students had, it really doesn't matter if some respondents were adding together the time they spent with 2 fathers or 2 mothers.

The numbers in the slots below are the average minutes per week spent with parental figures that students answered on the survey, and they are placed in the active or passive column based on their replies to the active/ passive question. Since there are so many homes without father figures, I averaged the number of minutes only of those respondents who said they had a particular gender in their life. For instance, someone without a mother in their lives would not have had their 0s averaged into the scores. When all respondents are used for these averages, the father averages drop by more than 50%, so it appears America is still being raised by the female.

	Mothers		Fathers	
	Active	Passive	Active	Passive
Eating	100	60	75	65
Television/Film	70	50	40	80
Sports: parental participation	4	0	36	0
Sports: parental observation	24	36	36	8
Games	30	0	42	0
Homework	35	0	10	2
Housework and cooking	18	10	8	2
Home repair	2	0	6	0
TOTALS	283	156	255	157

Discussion

It is interesting, though perhaps to be expected, that the first and second largest amounts of time (for both fathers and mothers) was eating and television/film. These are also the activities where parental/child interaction is more apt to be passive. It is significant to note that mothers spend considerably more time helping their children with homework, while males spend more time with sporting events and games. One would be quick to note that women do more housework than men, but this is an erroneous conclusion in terms of this study. All this study shows is how much time a parent spent with a child while housework was taking place.

Of significance is the amount of time listed as passive activity (defined as having little verbal contact or interaction). Women always lament the stoic quiet of the males, but the respondents in this study judged their mothers to be passive just as much of the time as their fathers.

Further study needs to be done to find out whether the respondents felt this interaction to be adequate, and whether they intend to have more or less interaction with their own children.

References

Bartle, S.E., Sabateli, R.M., & Anderson. (1989). A model of parenting style, adolescent individuation and adolescent self-esteem: Preliminary findings. *Journal of Adolescent Research, 4,* 283-298. https://doi.org/10.1177/0743554887943003

Blau, F.D., Ferber, M.A., & Winkler, A.E. (1997, January). The economics of women, men, and work. *Policies to Balance Paid Work and Family.* https:/doi.org/10.4863921/F48436

Boothe, A. & Crouter, N. (Eds.) (1998). *Men in families: When do they get involved? What difference does it make?* Lawrence Erlbaum.

Broderick, C. (1993). *Understanding family process.* Sage Publications.

Haas, L. (1993). Nurturing fathers and working mothers: Changing gender roles in Sweden. In J. Hood (Ed.) *Men, work, and family.* (pp.238-261). Sage Publications.

Heims, S., Julian, M.L. & Sussman, M.B. (Eds.) (1995). *Single parent families: Diversity, myths, and realities.* Haworth Press.

Hewlett, S. (1991). *When the bough breaks.* Basic Books.

McBride, B.A. (1990) The effects of parent education/play group program on father involvement in child rearing. *Family Relations, 39* (3), 250-256. https://doi.org/10.2307/5840868

McBride, B.A., & Mills, G. (1993). A comparison of mother and father involvement with their playschool age children. *Early Childhood Research Quarterly, 8* (4), 457-477. https://doi.org/10.1016/S0885-2006(05)80080-8

O'Mara, S. (1992, Spring). Considerations for the child. *Mothering, 16,* p.6.

U.S. Bureau of the Census. (1998). *Statistical Analysis of the United States* (118th Ed.). U.S. Bureau of the Census.

Appendix A

Thank-you for taking this survey. It should take approximately 10-15 minutes to complete.

Age: Sex: M   F

When you were in middle school, did you have:

No contact with father; live with mother

No contact with father; live with mother/stepfather

No contact with mother; live with father

No contact with mother; live with father/stepmother

Some contact with father; live with mother

Some contact with father; live with mother/stepfather

Some contact with mother; live with father

Some contact with mother; live with father/stepmother

Live with biological parents

If you spent time with a step-parent and a biological parent of the same gender during middle school, count the time you spent with both of them in these calculations.

During an average week in middle school, how much time, in minutes, did you spend with each parent doing these activities. Consider whether the activity of your parent and yourself was passive (little verbal contact or interaction) or active (verbal contact or interaction) during these times. Assign a numerical amount of time to each of these passive and active divisions:

Mother: Passive Active   Father: Passive Active

Eating
Television/Film
Sports: parent participates
Sports: parent observes
Games
Homework
Housecleaning and cooking
Home Repair

Thanks again for completing this survey.

Experiments/Lab Reports

Usually students only perform and write up experiments in biology, chemistry, physics, and engineering courses, but if you are majoring in engineering or the natural sciences, this genre will become second nature. When students perform an experiment in a laboratory setting, the experimenter makes sure that the conclusion reached from the experiment was not contaminated in any way. (For instance, a chemical experiment performed with unclean test tubes would be contaminated by the residue in the test tube.) In the social sciences, psychologists carry out experiments in a laboratory in order to produce controlled results; they can keep outside forces from interfering with the setting that they have built in the laboratory, but on the other hand they might get false results because the subjects in a laboratory setting may behave differently than they would in a comfortable, familiar environment. Scientists carefully weigh their options when planning experiments, making sure not to harm their subjects physically or psychologically, and also build in strict controls to get accurate results from their experiments.

In science and engineering lab courses, the lab report begins with an 'Abstract' (a summary of the experiment).

The first section is titled either 'Introduction' or 'Theory' (both of which describe the theoretical underpinning of the experiment).

The introduction is followed by the 'Materials and Method,' sometimes labeled 'Equipment Used' and 'Procedure.' This describes with precision what materials are required for the experiment and the method of the experiment.

The 'Results' section gives the results (usually in graphs and tables).

The final 'Discussion' section, sometimes sub-divided into an 'Analysis' (which interprets the results) and a 'Discussion' of the results (often including a discussion of the possibilities for error in the experiment), and usually a paragraph labeled 'Conclusion' at the end.

Of course, a Reference section ends the experiment listing any sources used.

The next page has an example of a lab experiment written for an introductory chemistry course. Many disciplines in college and the work world have their own documentation system, and chemistry is one of them. So the sources are documented using the American Chemical Society (ACM) system for documentation. The in text citations in ACM are similar to the *citation-sequence* format of the CSE documentation found in ch 25. The format for ACM References, however, differs from CSE.

205

Student Example: Experiment (Lab Report)

Jake Lawless
Chemistry 120
Dr. Pruett
Spring 2018

The Hot Chocolate Experiment

Abstract

 Electromagnetic radiation is an important characteristic of the world because it is used in many modern applications, including the microwave. Electromagnetic waves move at the speed of light, and a microwave is an object that utilizes electromagnetic waves in a contained environment. Therefore, the 'Hot Chocolate' experiment was performed to determine if the speed of an electromagnetic wave, and therefore the speed of light, could be accurately calculated using a microwave, four chocolate bars, and a metric ruler. Three mathematical equations were also used to calculate the speed of light and to determine the accuracy of the experiment. Four trials consisting of heating a chocolate bar for 50 seconds and noting the distance between two hotspots were performed. After conducting the trials and performing the calculations, the average wave speed of the microwaves was 2.97×10^8 m/s. When compared to the actual speed of light (3.0×10^8 m/s), the average wave speed had a 1.17% percent error. Therefore, this experiment was a rather accurate measurement of the speed of light.

Introduction

 Electromagnetic radiation is radiation involving waves with an electric and a magnetic field that travel at the speed of light.[1] This radiation is seen in many modern applications, including the microwave. A microwave heats food using microwaves, which are a form of electromagnetic radiation.[1,2] These microwaves are generated by a part called a magnetron, which converts electricity into high-powered radio waves. The magnetron shoots the waves toward the wall of the metal box, and the waves continue to bounce between the walls. Food is heated by the microwaves penetrating the food, thus making its molecules vibrate quickly. A turntable mechanism inside the microwave ensures the food is cooked evenly as it gets rotated inside the device. By taking the turntable mechanism out, food is heated in specific areas that the microwaves touch.[2] This leads to the experiment: heating chocolate bars at a fixed position in the microwave and measuring the distance between the melted areas, or hot spots, to calculate the speed of light. The hot spots of the chocolate bar result from the antinodes (points of maximum amplitude) of a wave.[3] Other key terms that are needed to understand the experiment are wavelength, frequency, and hertz. Wavelength is the length of one complete wave cycle, or the distance from crest to crest (crest is the point of maximum displacement). Frequency is the number of waves that pass a given point in

206

some unit of time, and hertz is a unit of frequency that stands for 1 per second.[2, 3] Each of these characteristics of waves were measured and used in equations to answer the central question of the experiment: can the speed of light be accurately measured using a microwave and chocolate bars? In this case, accurately estimated means the percent error of the average wave speed is less than 5%. The book, *How to Fossilize Your Hamster*, contains a result of this experiment that was used as a comparison. Determining if the speed of light can be accurately measured in this experiment would form a better understanding of the electromagnetic spectrum and how other modern applications use electromagnetic radiation.

Materials and Methods

The following materials were used in this experiment: one microwave with a 2450 MHz frequency (the frequency was found by Googling the model number), one microwave safe plate with a 10-inch diameter, one metric ruler, and four chocolate bars. Each chocolate bar was a different brand and length; these chocolate bars were one Hershey bar (13.81125 centimeters), four Twix mini chocolate bars (3.81 centimeters each), one 'Three Musketeers' bar (19.05 centimeters), and one Milky Way bar (13.97 centimeters).

Three mathematical equations were also used in this experiment. One equation was the wave speed equation, which is ($c = \lambda * f$). The variable 'c' represents the speed of the wave, 'λ' represents a wave's wavelength, and f represents the frequency.[1] An average of the speed of light was found by adding each wave speed together and dividing that sum by four. The third equation was the percent error equation, which is (Actual Value - Expected Value)/Actual Value $\times$ 100%.[1] Percent error was used to determine the accuracy of the experiment, and a percent error of less than 5% is considered accurate. Conversion rates were also needed to convert centimeters to meters for the wave speed, and to convert MHz to Hz for the frequency.

The first step in this experiment was shutting off the microwave turn-table to ensure the chocolate did not rotate. This step was crucial because it kept the chocolate locked in place so hot spots would occur only in certain positions, not throughout the entire bar. After shutting off the turn-table, the Hershey chocolate bar was placed at the center of the safe plate. Next, the plate was put into the microwave and heated for 50 seconds. Once it was finished heating, the Hershey chocolate bar was removed from the microwave and the distance between the edge of each hotspot was measured. This was repeated for the other chocolate bars (the Twix mini bars were placed horizontally next to each other). The measurements were used with the frequency of the microwave in the wave formula to calculate the speed of each wave. Then, the average of the wave speeds was calculated and used with the accepted speed of light value (3.00×10^8 m/s) to determine the percent error.

Measurements (A)
Chocolate Bar Length of Bar (cm)/ Distance between Hot Spots (cm)/ Wavelength λ

Chocolate Bar	Length of Bar (cm)	Distance between Hot Spots (cm)	Wavelength λ (cm)
Hershey	13.81	6.0	12.0
Twix	15.24	6.3	12.6
Milky Way	13.97	5.7	11.4
Three Musketeers	19.05	6.2	12.4

Calculations (B)

Chocolate Bar	Wavelength λ (m)	Frequency (f)	Speed of Light c= λ*f
Hershey	0.12	2.45 * 109 Hz	2.94 × 108 m/s
Twix	0.126	2.45 * 109 Hz	3.09 × 108 m/s
Milky Way	0.114	2.45 * 109 Hz	2.79 × 108 m/s
Three Musketeers	0.124	2.45 * 109 Hz	3.04 × 108 m/s

The average speed of light is 2.97 × 108 m/s, and the percent error is 1.17%.

Discussion

Looking at the results, it appears that most of the speeds of light were close to 3.0 × 108 m/s except for the Milky Way bar. The Milky Way bar might have the furthest value from the actual speed of light due to human error: failing to see the accurate edge of the hotspots. Its value could have contributed to lowering the average speed of light, so human error must be met with repeated trials in future experiments. Despite this error, the average speed of light (2.97 × 108 m/s) and the percent error (1.17%) suggest that this experiment could accurately determine the speed of light. Comparing these results to *How To Fossilize Your Hamster*'s results (speed of light of 2.94 × 108 m/s and a percent error of 2%) supports the conclusion that this experiment could accurately determine the speed of light.[4] For future experiments, conducting more trials with different chocolate bars and repeating trials three or four times will provide more data that can possibly provide an average wave speed closer to the speed of light. Also, longer chocolate bars should be used in future trials so more hotspots can be observed and measured. The findings in this experiment are important because they create a visualization of how fast electromagnetic waves move around the world. This knowledge can be applied to other aspects of society, such as radio waves, visible light, and X-rays, and can be used to calculate the wavelength or frequency of other waves if one of the two variables is known.

Conclusion

In the 'Hot Chocolate' experiment, four chocolate bars were heated at a fixed position in a microwave for 50 seconds to determine the average speed of light, in this case 2.97 × 108 m/s with a percent error of 1.17%. These results demonstrate that the experiment was accurate at determining the speed of light. Future experiments should include more trials and should repeat trials two or three times to produce an average speed closer to the actual speed of light.

References

(1) Kotz J.C.; Triechel P.M.; Weaver G.C. *Chemistry and Chemical Reactivity: 6th Edition.* Thomson Brooks/Cole: Canada, 2006; pp. 34, 296-299.

(2) Woodford C. Microwave Ovens. http://www.explainthatstuff.com/microwaveovens.html (accessed March 4, 2018).

(3) The Anatomy of a Wave. http://www.physicsclassroom.com/class/waves/Lesson-2/The-Anatomy-of-a-Wave (accessed March 4, 2018).

(4) O'Hare M. *How to Fossilize Your Hamster: And Other Amazing Experiments for the Armchair Scientist.* Henry Holt and Company: New York, 2008; pp. 42-45.

Scientific Proposals

Since it would take more than a semester to plan, develop, and execute an experiment more complicated than a lab report (at least for a composition class), instead, if you would like to explore setting up a social or natural science experiment you could write a proposal to do a study, which is what professional scientists do before embarking on the research. Proposals ask for funding for the experiment.

A scientific proposal is organized in the same manner as a primary research article discussing work already done. The introduction summarizes and discusses the studies that have already been done, and states a hypothesis that the experiment will study. The materials and method section will give an exact description of the participants in the experiment (if for the social sciences), all the tools needed to conduct the research, and the method of the experiment. All possibilities for error should be addressed. The expected results will discuss precisely how the experiment will be measured, and the possible implications of the study: what would happen if _____ was the result, or if _____ was the result? The discussion section suggests long-range implications of the study, with particular attention to how it would increase knowledge in the field, and it should also discuss other studies that could be done in the field and which are necessary correlatives to the proposed study.

Planning and Writing a Scientific Proposal

1) Pick a subject you are interested in. Read and summarize basic encyclopedia and textbook articles on the subject.

2) Focus your subject and begin reading articles describing experiments and research already done concerning your focused subject. Decide what needs to be learned concerning your focused subject, and develop questions that need to be answered.

3) Develop a hypothesis — what questions will your experiment try to answer. Write an introduction that discusses research findings and experiments already done leading to your proposal.

4) Design the experiment. (Since it is proposed, and you won't be actually doing it, money is no object.) Write the materials and method section, getting peer review help.

5) Revise the first two sections.

6) Write and revise the expected results and discussion sections.

Student Example: Scientific Proposal. APA Style Documentation

The writer of this proposal, Brian Allen, of course approached this assignment with some trepidation. After all, he was eighteen years old and had never written anything so challenging. But he started by deciding on a topic that he always wanted to learn more about: special needs children with low IQs. He also had an active interest in music (he played the piano) and knew that music therapy was one of the components of therapy for many people, so he narrowed his topic to music therapy in mental health programs. You should pick topics in the same manner. Pick a broad topic that you want to learn more about, and if possible, combine the topic with one you already know something about. For example, if you have witnessed alcoholism or drug addiction in your community or circle of friends and want to learn more about causes or treatment of the disease, start with addiction as a broad topic. Combine personal knowledge through observation with a scholastic study of the disease.

After picking his topic, Brian read articles on both programs for the mentally challenged and music therapy in a recent, library scholarly encyclopedia, and then the chapter on the developmentally challenged in a freshman psychology textbook. He began a bibliography with the bibliographies in the encyclopedia and the textbook. Brian next located scientific journal articles by using a Social Sciences database. If an article did not apply to his more specialized topic he stopped reading and went on to the next article. If one did apply, he marked it to read. By skimming hundreds of articles, he soon had over thirty that, at first glance, seemed promising.

As Brian read the articles, he had one notebook for summarizing the main findings of the study, and a legal pad for sketching notes on possibilities for his own proposed research. If he thought of a possibility for further research, no matter how farfetched, he wrote it down. As he read the articles, besides learning what research had already been done, he observed how the scientific method worked in actual research, and also noted any terms related to the care and education of people with these challenges that he would use in his own paper (each academic discipline uses its own specialized diction). After reading the articles, he examined the ideas for his own proposal, and chose the idea that seemed most plausible. Before working out the details of his proposal, he wrote and revised his introduction, summarizing the research that preceded his own idea. He ended the introduction with a thesis statement summarizing his research plan and hypothesis. Brian took the introduction to class to get feedback from classmates and the professor.

After getting approval for the project, he began designing the study, being very careful to anticipate all questions concerning the materials and method for the study.

He also tried to eliminate all possibility for invalid findings. With a rough draft of the materials and method section of the proposal, he again returned to class to get feedback. His preliminary ideas had some problems, but classmates and the professor pointed out possible problems with the research techniques. He revised the materials and method section, and the revision was better aligned with the scientific methods of research.

The expected results and discussion sections of the proposal were much easier after he had perfected the introduction and materials and method sections. He finished the last two sections and gave the proposal a thorough revision and editing. As one can see, the paper was a success, and was not beyond the capabilities of a freshman.

What you will learn from planning and doing primary research in the social sciences is a way of looking at the world and exploring problems: the scientific method — with its emphasis on objectivity and verifiability — can be used to solve many problems and answer many questions you will encounter in life, whether you become a professional social scientist or not.

The Effectiveness of Music as Positive and
Negative Reinforcement in Teaching Developmentally
Challenged Children to Play the Piano

Introduction

Recent studies have indicated that music can help a child with moderate or severe developmental challenges overcome their difficulties (Greene et al, 1970; Johnson & Zimmer, 1974; Masden & Masden, 1968, 1972). Research verifies that both passive music reinforcements (little physical response when listening to music) and active music reinforcement (playing instruments and dancing) increase desired behavior in children with mental challenges (Holloway, 1980). Other observations also demonstrate that when an individual is involved in a task which involves music, there is a high degree of participant involvement and a reduction of maladaptive behavior (Jorgensen, 1974; Masden & Wolfe, 1979; Reid et al, 1975).

The present study proposes that children with moderate and severe mentally challenges can learn to play simple songs on the piano, and that positive and negative reinforcement, provided by music, can enhance motorskills and also help develop functional speech over a period of time.

Materials and Method

Subjects: Forty individuals, age 10 to 17 with I.Q.'s ranging from 30 to 60, half male and half female, will be tested. Four other criteria will have to be met: 1) Each child possesses adequate hearing acuity to participate. 2) Each child has sufficient motor ability to play the piano. 3) Each child has limited verbal communication skills in comparison to a nonhandicapped peer. 4) Each child must live at home with a family, though not necessarily his or her own.

Setting: The setting will be in the house of the candidate.

211

Treatment Conditions: The music preference of each candidate is critical for the working of the experiment. Their preference will be determined by following a procedure first used by Cotter & Toombs (1966).

Apparatus A: portable electric piano with a rhythm section and a range of D below middle C to B below middle C will be used, because this limited range is the mean singing range of developmentally handicapped children. A chair will be placed in front of the piano for the candidate. Wires from a microphone on the piano will lead to a music decoding unit, where the sound waves from the piano will be translated into either noise or music which will then be transmitted to a receiver. If the subject plays discordantly, white noise will be produced; and if the subject plays melodically, music the candidate likes will result. Three recorders will be used. One tape will contain white noise, one will contain the music of the candidate's choice, and the third will be used by the music therapist to record the session.

The combination of tempo produced by the rhythm section and the music produced by the piano has been shown to lower levels of unnecessary body activity of the mentally handicapped (Soraci et al, 1982).

Procedure: The subjects will be observed individually by a music therapist during each of forty sessions over a three month period. During each session, lasting for thirty minutes, everything that the candidate experiences and produces will be recorded by the therapist. Data, such as the age, sex, I.Q., type of family, musical taste, and the amount of motor control (in comparison to before the sessions started, and before and after each session), will be kept on each subject.

The first twenty sessions will be conducted as follows: The child will be led to the piano, where he or she will be shown how to play a simple song such as "The Saints Go Marching In" or "Mary Had A Little Lamb." After practicing the song for fifteen minutes with the help of the music therapist, the subject will try to repeat the song without help. If the subject produces noise on the piano, the stimuli goes to the decoder, which, in return, produces white noise as a negative reinforcement condition. However, when the subject plays the song that is being taught, or makes melodious sounds, he or she will be rewarded by positive reinforcement the determined musical preference of the subject. The therapist will note if the subject learns songs faster and/or produces musical pieces through these negative and positive consequences.

The second twenty sessions are more complex: During these sessions the music therapist will not play the piano at all. The child will sit at the piano for the entire thirty minutes and will produce his or her own songs. Once again, there will be positive reinforcements if the subject produces music, but negative reinforcement (noise) if the subject hits the keys in a haphazard manner. During this phase, any singing by the subject will also be noted on the therapist's records.

Expected Results

The results of the experiment should show the candidate playing simple songs on the piano keyboard because he or she receives positive feedback. Negative feedback is likely in the first sessions, but during the second half of the experiment, it should be proven that the candidates have the ability to play songs on the piano with positive electronic reinforcement. Motor skills of the developmentally handicapped should improve and stereotypic behavior should be reduced. Because music is a stimulus, verbal behavior of the test group should increase during the sessions.

Discussion

Because of the almost self-teaching method of this idea, developmentally handicapped children can improve in their own homes, outside of an institutional environment. By learning to play songs on the piano through negative and positive rewards, they will eventually increase motor skills, and could develop functional speech through singing. Future experiments should be done to determine whether these improvements are permanent or require regular repetition of the program. In an environment of family members and friends, the handicapped children will be in contact with the "real world" and will probably develop their skills at a more rapid rate than those in a sheltered environment. There is further research necessary, though, to determine what environment and what techniques are most desirable to teach, to develop motor skills, and to reduce maladaptive behaviors for these children.

References

Cotter, V.W. & Toombs, S. (1966). A procedure for determining the music preference of mental retardates. *Journal of Music Therapy, 3*, 55-64.

Greene, R., & Hoats, D. (1970). Music distortion: A new technique for behavior modification. *Psychological Record, 20*, 107-109.

Holloway, M.S. (1980). A comparison of active and passive music reinforcement to increase preacademic and motor skills in severely retarded children and adolescents. *Journal of Music Therapy, 17*, 58-69.

Johnson, J.M., & Binner, C.C. (1974). Stimulus fading and schedule learning in generalizing and maintaining behavior. *Journal of Music Therapy, 11*, 84-96.

Jorgenson, H. (1974). The use of a contingent music activity to modify behaviors which interfere with learning. *Journal of Music Therapy, 11*, 41-46.

Madsen, C.H., & Madsen, C.K. (1968). Music as a behavior modification technique with a juvenile deliquent. *Journal of Music Therapy, 5*, 52-76.

Madsen, C.H., & Madsen, C.K. (1972). Selection of music listening or candy as a function of contingent vs. noncontingent reinforcement and scale singing. *Journal of Music Therapy, 4*, 190-198.

Masden, C.H., & Wolfe, D.E. (1979). The effect of interrupted music and incompatible responses on bodily movement and music attentiveness. *Journal of Music Therapy, 16*, 17-30.

Reid, D.H., Hill, B.K., Rawers, R.J., & Montegar, C.A. (1975). The use of contingent music in teaching social skills to a nonverbal hyperactive boy. *Journal of Music Therapy, 12*, 2-18.

Soraci, S., Deckner, C., McDaniel, C., & Blanton, R. (1982). The relationship between rate of rhythmicity and the stereotypic behavior of abnormal children. *Journal of Music Therapy, 19*, 46-54.

214

10

Genres: Analysis, Evaluation, and Narrative

This chapter contains brief descriptions of multiple genres often used in both college courses and the real world, with student examples attached. However, use the brief instructions and examples defining the genres here in conjunction with the descriptions of the writing process — developing context, content, writing, and revising found in chapters 2-5 — and the descriptions of research processes in chapters 6-9. This chapter does not tell you HOW to do the process of writing essays in each of these genres, it only defines each genre by giving a list of its features and the steps that are individual to that genre for completing thorough predrafting. In most situations, the method of developing context and content for each of these genres is the same: the processes described in those opening nine chapters of *Writing Successfully*. When you read the student essays in this chapter, be sure to carefully study the notes attached to them for information on how each genre is organized and what content occurs in writing of that type.

Analysis

Learning how to break a subject or a chain of events into parts and looking at the parts in detail, analyzing causes and effects, as well as discovering how and/or why a process works, are three essential college and life skills. At the simplest level, analysis answers the questions "how?" and "why?" College students should also learn how to explain — in essays — their analyses of causes, effects, and processes. Most of what you learn in any college class can be described as analysis: in science, how a process in biology, the earth, or the universe works; why one computer system works more efficiently than another. In the social sciences, researchers analyze the causes of childhood obesity, or alternately, the effects. What causes some people to commit crimes and not others? OR is it a "why do people commit...?" and not a "what causes?" In the humanities, what are the causes or effects of an historical event or a literary movement? What processes can writers use to write a poem, an essay, or a screenplay? What causes a character in a movie to react as she does? This chapter itself is a process analysis chapter explaining a series of genres that college students often encounter.

We also use causal and process analysis in real life: if candidate A wins, what will be the effects of her administration? If I buy that computer now, will the negative effect on my cash flow be offset by the positive effect on my ability to finish work more quickly?

As human beings, we just want to know how and why!!!

First, we need to make sure we know how to analyze thoroughly, as that will have a profound impact on writing the explanation.

215

Causal Analysis

Examine multiple causes and effects. An event rarely has one cause or effect; it has multiple causes, and each of those causes themselves had causes. The causal chain goes backwards and forwards into infinity in both directions. When you study causes and effects, do five activities. Do each activity one at a time, and thoroughly complete one before moving to the next:

1) Often, your first job is to *break your subject into parts* and describe, define, and use examples to picture each part of your subject. If it was not complicated, you would not need to analyze it.

2) *Proximate and remote causes and effects.* a. Decide which of the causes are proximate (close) causes and which are more remote. An example of the former would be a bank needs help because it has a negative cash flow and can't pay its monthly bills and an example of the latter would be the worthless bonds it sold the year before causing the present negative cash flow. b. Decide which effects are proximate and which more remote. The employer turned down the man for a job so he kicked his dog so his dog bit the neighbor kid and the neighbor kid punched his little brother.

3) *Form a hierarchy of causes and effects from most to least important.* (Factor into your planning whether the causes and effects are proximate or remote. Sometimes a remote cause or effect has more importance than a proximate one.)

4) *Solid evidentiary or logical evidence.* Make sure you have some (as in more than one) kinds of solid evidentiary or logical evidence to support that they are in fact causes or effects. Hold yourself to a high standard of proof. And the related:

5) *Don't jump to a hasty conclusion.* The man drives by the beautiful woman and wrecks his car, causing the hasty conclusion that he was too busy gawking at the woman. In fact, he had just had his eyes examined and his vision was still blurry. The most important cause is the remote one, that he didn't follow directions to have a driver escort him home.

Process Analysis

Discover in detail how a process works and analyze why it works. You could be either describing a process that occurs, how something works, or how to do something. When you write, because of your purpose and audience, you might only need the "how" described. For other writing situations, you would focus on the "why." Why a student got a low grade on an exam might not concern her nearly as much as how she got it (the process of failing) and how she will create a process to get a higher grade on the next exam. On the other hand, how a boyfriend dropped her best friend might not concern her nearly as much as why he left her. Each situation and each audience demands a different mixture of the how and why of a process. But when analyzing your subject before writing, you must know your subject with the complexity it deserves, so analyze both how and why even if you know you will mainly describe one or the other. If you aren't sure as you start, after you have developed your thesis you will probably focus on one more than the other.

When you study a process, do the following activities. Do each activity one at a time in order, and thoroughly complete one before moving to the next:

216

1) *How: Materials, Steps, and Finished Product*. First, make sure you have a list of ALL the materials needed for the process to work, or all the details of how the process occurred (again, breaking your subject into parts). Then, list the steps in chronological order, a. leaving none out, no matter how small, b. making sure you describe how each mini-step occurs in detail, and c. adding to the materials list as you describe the processes. Make sure you completely describe the finished project or process.

2) *Why a process works or occurs*. This is essentially causal analysis of a process, and again, make sure you have listed all the proximate and remote causes and effects of EACH PART of the process. (See previous section on causal analysis.)

3) With some subjects and audiences, why could also mean *why do the process at all* (when you have an audience who is not thrilled about learning the process).

4) *Solid evidentiary or logical evidence*. Make sure you have some (as in more than one) kinds of solid evidentiary or logical evidence to support that a process does occur, or that your reader should do the process for the reasons you are arguing. Hold yourself to a high standard of proof. And the related:

5) *Don't jump to a hasty conclusion*. Let's say you are writing a process paper describing exactly how to prepare to be an informed voter in an upcoming election. Instead of immediately assuming your audience wants to be informed voters, if you decide your readers might not want to do your steps, you will also have to analyze why they should take the time to do this process.

Student Example: Analysis. MLA Style Documentation

There are student examples on 52-53 (using classification), two on 54-5 (using process analysis and question/answer),107-10 (using extended definition), and an analysis of the media and violence on 158-60:

Clay Witt
English 102
Fall 2012 Final Draft
Subject: Games and gender roles
Audience: Educated young people who are interested in games and their effects on gender.
Writing Situation: An analysis on a gaming blog
Thesis: Games are not to blame for problematic children or creating gender roles. Parents who do not mold their children are.
Tone: objective, analytical, disagreement with a source, serious, scholarly

The Writing Context

Use context to analyze these student essays, and create one for the essays you write so that you know what you are attempting.

Monkey Play, Monkey Don't

For many youth, games provide a venue to escape from the frustrations of reality, school pressures, parental interference, encounters with the opposite sex. The ability to enact their own adventures in a virtual world of their imagination (now often assisted by a virtual world) keeps their heads on straight. It is certainly true that games today have much more realism in their content and objectives than they used to. In the past, games like Sorry and Pac-Man had such placid innocence; however, games today often make

Introduction interests the specific audience noted above and lets them see the writer is sympathetic to their own mind set.

parents cringe. In "Boys-R-Us: Board Games and the Socialization of Young Girls," Jennifer Scanlon appears convinced that board games alter the thought processes of young girls, ultimately creating "limited possibilities" (511). Is it really games that destroy the moral fiber of some kids, or is it a lack of parenting that is to blame? Is it possible that something as simple as a game could cast a gender-stereotypical shadow on young minds? I think she needs to reconsider her argument.

Paragraph
Completeness:

In-depth analy-
sis of opposing
argument with
refutations to
the bottom of
the page. While
refuting oppos-
ing views, writer
makes his own
views clearer.

Scanlon claims that toys and games are gender specific and I agree. There are games for girls and games for boys. I believe, in contrast to Scanlon, that the exclusion of the opposite gender in games promotes a feeling among the players that their gender is special. 'I'm a boy; therefore, I can better appreciate this baseball.' 'I'm a girl; therefore, I can better appreciate this Barbie doll.' Scanlon looks at this negatively: "For boys' toys, camouflage greens and browns . . . war toys . . . sports equipment . . . . [girls on the box] dress in feminine clothing and wear heavy makeup and jewelry" (504). I want to know what the problem is. Of course toys for boys are physical in nature, and those for girls are primpy and petite. Can't we argue that when little girls grow up they want to be like Mommy and boys wish to be like Dad? When was the last time you heard a boy say, 'Mom, I want to be just like you some day,' or a little girl exclaim, 'Daddy, I want to be just like you . . .' Non-gay children naturally relate to adults who share their anatomy. You can't blame games for this. Nonetheless the games are gender specific, and this is just a way to cater to children's natural impulses, not to push a certain stereotype. 'You can't be like Daddy/Mommy yet, but here is something to get you started. You can pretend.'

Scanlon disagrees, stating that "gender is a crucial element in development for girls and boys . . . many of these changes are sex-specific . . . social expectation, even more than physical changes, shape gender roles" (504). She says that games today are a tool society uses to shape the minds and morals of children, like the games are saying, "do this because it's right, and is required of you." I respectfully disagree: games are for fun, and I believe both parents *and* children are aware of that. A testimonial from a twenty-four year old woman claims she remembers playing Girl Talk many times with one of her best friends while in elementary and middle school: "Girl Talk was so much fun! I would recommend any parent getting his or her girl this game to play . . ." Another testimonial claims, "This game is a must for teen and pre-teen girls! I played it with my daughter and I don't know who laughed the hardest" ("Girl Talk - Toy"). This is one of the games that Scanlon has accused of being problematic and sexually demeaning (508). But I'm seeing no problem here: grown adults have given the game rave reviews. They played the game as kids, and as adults they still recommend the game. Now perhaps Scanlon would say that these two women and women like them have been artfully deceived their entire lives, but could they be the normal ones, and the games aren't as corrupting as Scanlon claims?

In interviews with up and coming gaming software gurus in *PC Gamer* magazine, Ken Levine (General Manager and Founder of Irrational Games) argues that most children view 6000 murders on television by age six, so how does a game like Quake where players run a lot and destroy demons desensitize kids to violence? Albert McGee (Director of Electronic Arts) adds that game creators have no more responsibility than film producers, writers, and directors. Brad McQuaid (Producer for Verant Interactive) expanded on the topic of game politics, stating that he agrees with that, but he would "play devil's advocate. [Game creators are] creating these things, and for most normal people it's not a problem. But for a few people who have issues, you can say it's their probem. But let's say there's an alcoholic and you give him a beer. Whose fault is it that he's an alcoholic?" Steve Case (of Ion Storm) adds, "It all has to come back to personal responsibility. We're not responsible for raging kids. People have to be responsible for themselves. [Ratings] allow parents to decide what their kids should play, and that is what [parents] should be doing" ("New Game Gods" 77-78).

Writer uses experts (admittedly biased ones) to bolster his point.

This brings me to a few points:

/ There are literally billions of people playing games. So when someone develops different morals than the norm (or conversely develops social codes that reflect mainstream society but that some have problems with), how can you blame something that EVERYONE is exposed to? It's not like smoking, that people choose to do.

And he concludes by making analytic points to prove his argument.

/ People are supposed to be taught to have morals, to know right from wrong, and to have self-confidence instilled in them by their parents. If a child is learning values only from games, the parent is a lousy parent.

Everyone in her lifetime has played a game. Multiply that by the number of people in the world, and the number becomes billions. If one of those goes on a rampage and starts killing people, how can someone blame a game as THE cause? Just as McQuaid said, it's not your fault if an alcoholic takes a beer from you. Thousands go around and drink beer and only a few can't handle it. But the finger gets pointed at the beer, the game? Real rich. I thought this world is based on the assumption that folks have grown up with basic moral distinguishing skills, the ability to know right from wrong, and the real from the imaginary (the game). Even kids can usually distinguish right from wrong and the real from the imaginary.

Let's talk, parents: you are supposed to be responsible for your children. Game developers can't be held responsible for how a child develops. If we're going to blame games: let's blame movies. Why not blame television? If these are more of a factor in your child's life than you are, something is wrong.

Overall, Scanlon brings some mild and repetitive arguments to the table. She has not gone deep enough to the source of her "problem," this moral warping, gender specifying. People have more of an influence on people (mainly children) than any entertainment. Games and toys have a purpose: to entertain, to escape, and yes, sometimes to educate (but in a positive way if used properly). Games don't – or shouldn't – shape morals. She neglects the importance of the role of the parent.

Works Cited

"Girl Talk - Toy." *realbuy,* www.toy.realbuy.ws. Accessed 15 Nov. 2012.

"New Game Gods." *PC Gamer,* Nov. 2000, pp. 69-100.

Scanlon, Jennifer. "Boys-R-Us: Board Games and the Socialization of Young
    Adolescent Girls." *Signs of Life in the USA,* edited by Sonia Massik and
    Jack Solomon, 4th ed., Bedford/St. Martins, 2003, pp. 503-511.

Rhetorical Analysis / Textual Analysis

Rhetoric is the art of expressing oneself well in speech or writing, of getting a message across, and a rhetorical analysis is an examination of what message is delivered, how a message is delivered, why it is delivered, who it is delivered to, and what it says about both its creator and its audience. If the analysis is of a written text, often of a literary text but it can be of anything written, this is called a textual analysis. Modern theorists do not confine themselves, however, to speech and writing (for instance an analysis of a politician's speech). They often do rhetorical analyses of ads, products, or television programs. Movies and songs often receive textual rhetorical analyses. Even entertainers create a rhetorical stance with their lives: everything they say, do, wear, and own says something about who they are and what they stand for. (And they also say something about their fans. Why does this particular culture like a certain entertainer?)

Possible subjects:

- political speeches or advertisements; the message(s) of political or social movements
- consumer products and advertisements for those products
- anything involving pop culture: songs (including the music with them), entertainers, television shows, movies, art
- any argument in any medium; literary textual analysis: stories, poems, books.

As an example, here is the brief beginning of a rhetorical analysis of Tupac Shakur, for which there is ample evidence if the essay were written.

What message?:
"Real" men of color have a menacing violence about them.
How delivered?:
The biography of his life, followed by the lyrics to his songs, the beat of the music, and finally by his early murder. His clothes, his accessories, his guns.
Why delivered?:
African-American men have been stereotyped as unintelligent, poor laborers by American society since its inception, and on a personal level he wasn't going to let this racism stand. As an artist he took the stand, on a communal level, that this was wrong and racist, so that society would change its racist viewpoint.

Who delivered to?:
First, young African-Americans of both sexes, but whites also accepted his stance and, some would say, unsuccessfully mimicked it.
What it says about him and his audience:
They both seem incredibly angry since they accept the violence as a given. It also shows that American audiences have always accepted "frontier" violence – the way of the gun – as a way of life.

This is the barebones of what a rhetorical analysis does. Choose a subject that you are interested in, that you can examine over and over, and where you have (or can find) some connection to the audience. Youtube and other internet sites will get you most anything you need to view or hear to analyze your subject.

Here are the steps you need to complete in order to develop a thesis with adequate content to complete a rhetorical or textual analysis:
1) Study your subject carefully. Use all the tools of chapters 2 and 3: describe it, compare it to similar subjects, classify it, define it, analyze it. Does the message use appeals to logic, authority, or emotion (see chapter 11), and how effective are these? Especially USE the steps for doing causal and process analysis on the previous pages. Usually, an effective rhetorical analysis asks for causes, effects, or analyses of processes. What are the effects of an ad campaign? What causes people to buy the product, store, candidate, movie, social movement? Why does this subject of yours work on an audience? How does it work on an audience?
2) Decide who the audience for the message of your subject is and analyze them in depth. By their use of the object (the film, the show, the ad) what does it say about them? What audience characteristics does the creator use to get their attention?
3) What is the relationship between the person/people sending the message (its creators) and the culture receiving the message?
4) Read articles that analyze the message and the sub-culture audience it is addressing.
5) Evaluate the message: what are its strengths? What tools are used to create the strengths? What does this say about the creator(s) and audience? What are its weaknesses? What do these weaknesses say about the creator(s) and audience?
6) When you have done these in-depth processes, begin to decide what your message, your thesis, is going to be. Rhetorical and textual analyses occasionally analyze the rhetorical devices (the tricks used to persuade an audience), but more often writers develop rhetorical analyses to make a point about the audience or the creator(s) of the message.

There is a rhetorical analysis on 162-65 arguing that the media influences, but doesn't create, societal values; one on 186-89 analyzing gender communication; and on 194-96 analyzing youtube commercials for a fashion line. The essay following is a rhetorical analysis of a Corvette advertisement:

Student Example: Rhetorical Analysis. MLA Style Documentation

Writing Context:

Subject: The "Still Building Rockets" television commercial for the 2011 Corvette ZR-1

Audience: communications, marketing and humanities students

Writing Situation: a rhetorical analysis that demonstrates the cultural, political nature of advertising; This could be presented as part of a lecture or reading assignment.

Thesis Statement: There are at least three groups of consumers to which the 2011 Corvette ZR-1 commercial speaks and the message becomes progressively more subtle as the intended audience and socio-political relevance grow in scope.

Tone: semi-formal. Analytical and informational, but light. I don't want to put people to sleep!

The Writing Context (above)

Use context to analyze these student essays, and create one for the essays you write so that you know what you are attempting.

Introduction interests an objective scholarly audience noted above by giving them a vivid, visual description of the subject. A vivid opening usually catches any audience's eyes, and in this case also gives the academic audience a specific picture of the commercial being analyzed in the essay. (How can the audience understand the writer's analysis if they can't picture the commercial being analyzed?)

Here the analysis begins:

Michelle Townsend

English 102 Spring 12

Dr. Hanson

From Launch Pad to Living Room:
How the 2011 Corvette Commercial Sells More Than a Car

"Once upon a time, a bunch of guys had a crazy idea…"

That is how the commercial for the 2011 Corvette ZR1 begins. The man in the voice-over sounds like the classic American patriot, and in the background, the sound of rocket engines igniting can be heard. Visuals of a Saturn rocket leaving the launch pad alternate with shots of NASA personnel before the scene changes to show an automotive factory where workers are assembling what is, presumably, a Corvette engine. The narration continues over the sounds of 60's-style folk guitar as more engine building shots are cut together with images of the Saturn rocket.

Go farther, faster than mankind ever had before. They dreamt with their hands, shaped aluminum with their brains, and the world watched and waited with baited breath. While time has marched on, and priorities have changed…

The music builds in intensity as a worker pushes a nearly complete engine toward the camera.

"…it's nice to know America still builds rockets." The narrator finishes his lines in a voice filled with smug satisfaction, convinced (as he hopes to make all of the viewers) that the great *American* sports car, the Corvette, is superior in both speed and technology just like NASA's Apollo program was in gaining the moon. The screeching of tires and the thunder of a revving engine punctuate the announcer's words as money shots of a white Corvette ZR1 peeling around a curve and then burning rubber down a stretch of closed track flash on the screen amid more shots of the Saturn rocket hurtling through the atmosphere in a blaze of engineering glory.

"The 2011 Corvette. Only from Chevrolet," the announcer reminds viewers as a Chevy logo is splashed across the screen along with the Chevy website address before fading to black (Goodby, Silverstein & Partners). The ad seems pretty straight forward: give older viewers warm, fuzzy feelings of nostalgia, a heaping dose of national pride, and the notion that driving the Corvette is like piloting an earthbound rocket to stir their lust for the car.

222

However, there are at least three groups of consumers to which the 2011 Corvette ZR-1 commercial speaks, and believe it or not, not every message is intended to sell a shiny new Corvette! The messages become progressively more subtle as the intended audience and socio-political relevance grow in scope, and with recent events, such as the Obama administration's bailout of GM, there is a great deal to be conveyed.

Writer makes a specific well-thought-out series of organizational choices that create a structure for the essay. Michelle has chosen to analyze the commercial in terms of three audiences for the Corvette commercial, and then further chooses to move from the easiest, most obvious group to one that requires the most thought and analysis.

Before getting to the deeper levels of meaning, examination of the obvious is required to lay some basic ground work. Authors Maasik and Solomon, in a demonstration of analyzing advertising semiotically, point out that context is key in understanding what an ad is really communicating ("Brought to You B(u)y" 172-173). (After all, the exclamation "Get out!" coming from a teen discussing who asked whom on a date means something vastly different than the same phrase coming from a man yelling at his dog for urinating on the rug!) American culture as a whole provides one level of context, but only in a very general way. Since the point of most commercial advertising is to sell a product, it stands to reason that the next step in the evaluation should begin with determining the intended consumer type for the item or service advertised. Then, the obvious message can be decoded ("Brought to You B(u)y" 172-173).

The grainy color footage of NASA engineers and Saturn V launches, the rustic guitar music and focus on American workers all lead to one natural conclusion: GM wants to sell Corvettes to "Baby Boomers." This may seem odd at first, but the aging generation that has grown up alongside the Corvette since 1953 is estimated in the U.S. Census Bureau's "Age and Sex Composition: 2010" online brief to equal more than one quarter of the U.S. population (Howden and Meyer). That is a fairly large chunk of market share! When one considers information presented by Laurence Shames that suggests America has been steadily running out of room for economic expansion -- as measured in terms of real earnings -- since the 1970's (90), the target audience begins to make more sense. "Cutting the Cake," an article by *The Economist Online*, demonstrates that inflation adjusted earnings have not risen significantly for most Americans since the late 1960's. This fact makes the 45 to 65 age group a prime target for luxury goods because that segment of the population is not only the largest, but typically the most financially capable sector due to amassed savings or higher pay from years of climbing up the career ladder.

Paragraph Completeness:

She analyzes each of the three groups with the complexity they deserve, using specific evidence for each point she makes.

The Chevrolet brand's new U.S. ad agency, Goodby, Silverstein & Partners, make heavy use of emotional imagery that evokes a sense of nostalgia in the "Boomer" crowd. The images connect viewers with the sense of national pride that was advertised along with the Mercury, Gemini, and Apollo Programs of the 50s, 60s, and 70s. The tone of the narration lauds American scientists, engineers, and manufacturers, professions that were highly regarded in the golden days of post-war Americana. These attributes help create that comfortable feeling of reliving "the good ol' days," but once that feeling is established the commercial catches its audience off guard with a jolt of action! Rockets careen into the sky and a white Corvette careens around a pristine track. This thrill factor juxtaposed with the warmth of nostalgia produces just the right kind of excitement, and *that* is what they want all those financially stable "Boomers" to feel every time they see a Corvette. The message is this:

The Corvette is exciting, cutting edge, and made in America, so you can be proud to own one (and best of all, you'll feel like a teenager all over again)!

Second group:

Another group the "Still Building Rockets" ad speaks to is the potential Chevrolet brand buyer. It is no great feat of logic to arrive at the conclusion

Again,

that the Corvette, while one of the most affordable cars of its kind, is neither affordable nor practical to the majority of current car buyers. If that is the case,

Paragraph Completeness:

then what would a Corvette commercial have to say to consumers possessing less lofty vehicular aspirations? Plenty! According to the edmunds.com article

Michelle analyzes this group in terms of the commercial with the complexity it deserves, using evidence this time from Chevrolet sources other than the primary commercial she is analyzing.

"Chevrolet Corvette History," the Corvette has long been hailed as Chevy's flagship vehicle, representing the best that Chevrolet has to offer in performance and technology. While looking through some old ads for the Corvette, I noticed that it was common practice for Chevrolet to release what I like to call "catalogue" ads. These long commercials feature a whole line-up of Chevy vehicles, and not surprisingly, the commercials usually lead off with a look at the latest Corvette. Not only did the Corvette lead the Chevy pack, it also led the automotive technology pack on many occasions. Jerry Burton, a columnist for autonews.com, highlights several pieces of automotive technology that were first used in the Corvette before becoming industry wide. The Corvette is an American icon thanks, in part, to Campbell-Ewald's "Baseball, Hotdogs, Apple Pie and Chevy" and "Heartbeat of America" commercials. Even if one cannot afford a Corvette, the message is there that Chevy builds a world-class car like the Corvette here in America; therefore, they can certainly build high-class sedans and compact cars that contain many of the same luxurious goodies in more economically (and environmentally) practical packages. This is a vital concept to sell to conscientious twenty- and thirty-somethings. However, U.S. auto makers are already behind foreign imports which have been years ahead of Chevy (and GM) in marketing to the "green" and "techie" crowds, and those segments makes up a significant portion of the up-and-coming auto buyers who have yet to develop strong brand loyalties. Since a vehicle is a major purchase that consumers only tend to make every few years, brand loyalty is a valuable commodity; consequently, the "Still Building Rockets" ad seeks to inspire loyalty by striving to associate the Chevy brand name with one of the most exciting periods of high-tech exploration and innovation in American history.

Third group:

The third message the "Still Building Rockets" ad conveys is an even broader entreaty to the American public to give the "new" GM a chance. If the Corvette is Chevrolet's flagship, then it is, by proxy, GM's flagship as well. A Jim Campbell

Again,

quote from one article reads, "'as Chevy goes, so goes GM'" (qtd. in Eisenstein). That being said, it is sensible to use the Corvette as a starting place for remolding

Paragraph Completeness.

the GM image. While public relations are not necessarily a function of a company's advertising department, advertising always contributes to public relations, and when it comes to GM's public image, Goodby, Silverstein & Partners have a definite challenge ahead. Brian Laviolette, writing for *thedetroitbureau.com*, alludes to the fact that corporate management at GM has been like a revolving door since the bankruptcy. True to Laviolette's predictions, the company's marketing department has since seen its share of the changes. With the Obama administration practically hand picking more than 50% of the new GM board members, it is no great wonder why many people are now calling GM "Government Motors." Yes, GM does indeed have some image problems to overcome.

Chevrolet's U.S. ad firm of 91 years, Campbell-Ewald, made its mark on the brand by promoting it as "THE" American automobile over a span of many years and several notable ad campaigns, such as "See the USA in Your Chevrolet," "Baseball, Hotdogs, Apple Pie & Chevrolet," and "Heartbeat of America" (Campbell-Ewald). This association with populist culture has been an enduring advertising legacy for decades as GM continued, until recently, to focus on churning out popular full-size cars, trucks, and SUVs. It was in a congressional bailout hearing that GM was heavily criticized for being out of sync with design and marketing trends because they delivered so few compact and hybrid cars (Hargreaves), but even though GM's Chevrolet brand now has plenty of compact and hybrid cars on the market (including an all-electric model, the Chevy Volt). It is up to ad firm Goodby, Silverstein & Partners to convince people to buy them - at least in the United States. Although GM's chief marketing officer, Joel Ewanick, seemed less than completely happy with the agency's first work on the Chevy brand (Colias), agency co-founder Jeff Goodby was not concerned. Goodby is quoted by *AdAge.com* columnist Julie Halpert, saying, "'We will get away from the historic campaigns. It will be more clear that this is a technology brand…'"(qtd. in Halpert). If that is the case, then why did Goodby open up his work for Chevrolet with such a heavy dose of Americana? Perhaps it is because he, like all good ad men, appears to have an innate understanding of today's consumer.

First, there was the Tea Party movement, and now, there is Occupy Wallstreet as well. These are two of the most notable among many "grassroots" socio-political organizations that have sprung up in recent years, and the trend is very telling. Much like the volatile political climate of the 60's, today's political atmosphere is becoming charged and ready for a new revolution. There is a growing discontent with the federal government on both sides of the party lines, and America is in a deep recession where jobs are hard to come by as more companies shift labor overseas just to survive in an increasingly harsh market. These issues, aided by the almost limitless resources for free information provided by the internet, have combined to create an American populace that Maasik & Solomon describe as a "bottom up" society: one that no longer settles for the old paradigm of being fed tailored information by a limited number of corporately owned networks ("Popular Signs" 2). It is this shift in consumer thought, in conjunction with current political and economic tensions, that makes it so vitally important for GM to ditch the "Government Motors" label as quickly as possible.

Here Michelle begins an in-depth conclusion that does one of the things that good conclusions can do (widening the scope of the essay's subject to a broader field of vision): this conclusion widens the scope of the analysis from one Corvette commercial to the zeitgeist of American culture at the present time.

Most everyone has heard the phrase "timing is everything," and Goodby, Silverstein & Partners had the timing for "Still Building Rockets" right on target. Perhaps unintentionally, the ad came on the heels of the Obama Administration announcing cuts to NASA's budget and killing the manned space flight program that was instituted by former president George W. Bush. At least one blogger shares my opinion that the ad appears to be taking a jab at the current administration (Hardigree). Even if the timing was purely circumstantial, the idea has been subtly introduced that perhaps GM is not content with its relationship with the U.S. government, particularly when viewed in light of GM's apparent rush to make a public stock offering. Considering the mood of the nation, this can be nothing but good for GM's public image.

225

One ad with three distinct purposes, Goodby, Silverstein & Partner's "Still Building Rockets" commercial is an excellent start for Chevy's first U.S. marketing campaign under new CMO Joel Ewanick, even if Mr. Ewanick himself didn't see it at first. The ad uses nostalgia and a sense of excitement to sell its product, but it also sells the "American-ness" of the Chevrolet brand at a time when Americans are hungering for both economic growth and a sense of national pride. This old stand-by of Chevy advertising links the "new" GM to the "old" GM in the consumer's mind while a sly (though possibly unintentional) poke at the Obama Administration lends credence to GM's efforts to break away from the government owned image. While some in the advertising industry criticize Goodby for a slow start, I think this subtle sort of multi-level message is just what the doctor ordered for the "new" GM.

Works Cited

Burton, Jerry. "Corvette: A Pop Culture Classic." *autonews*, Crain
    Communications, 31 Oct. 2011, www.autonews.com/corvette/329458.
"Chevrolet Corvette History." *Edmunds*, www.edmunds.com/corvette history.
Colias, Mike. "GM's Ewanick Grades Goodby: 'C and B Work.'" *Ad Age*,
    Crain Communications, 15 Aug. 2011, www.AdAge.com/colias/6945934.
"Cutting the Cake." *The Economist Online*, Economist Group, 14 Sep. 2011,
    www.economist.com/14/9/2011/486395.
Eisenstein, Paul A.. "Can 'Big Dog' Chevrolet Save GM?" *The Detroit Bureau*,
    16 Feb. 2010, www.Thedetroitbureau.com/16/02/2010/3968427819750.
Goodby, Silverstein & Partners. "Still Building Rockets: Commercial."
    Youtube, 15 Jul. 2010, www.Youtube/watch?vAGR.
Hardigree, Matt. "Corvette 'Rocket' Ad Slams Obama's NASA Funding
    Cuts." *Jalopnik*, 14 Jul. 2010, www.Jalopnik.com/3694298157ACGF.
Hargreaves, Steve. "Heated Debate Over Auto Bailout." *CNNMoney*,
    26 Nov. 2008, www.CNNMoney.com/Harg4132AC
Howden, Lindsay A. and Julie A. Meyer. *Age and Sex Composition: 2010.*
    U.S. Census Bureau, May 2011, www.census.gov/2010/Age and Sex.pdf..
Laviolette, Brian. "General Motor's New Marketing Czar Quickly Stamps
    His Own Imprint." *The Detroit Bureau*, 16 Feb. 2010,
    www.The detroit bureau.com/16/02/2010/479368827.
Maasik, Sonia, and Jack Solomon, editors. *Signs of Life in the USA.* 6th ed.,
    Bedford, 2009.
Maasik, Sonia, and Jack Solomon. "Brought to You B(u)y: The Signs
    of Advertising." Maasik and Solomon, pp. 171-181.
---. "Popular Signs: Or, Everything You Always Knew about American
    Culture (But Nobody Asked)." Maasik and Solomon, pp. 1-23.
Shames, Laurence. "The 'More' Factor." Maasik and Solomon, pp. 86-92.

There is a textual analysis of Whitman's poetry as a description of American culture on 69-72, and of films looking at the Utopian ideal in the human mind on 107-110, and of *Forrest Gump* on 285-87. Here is a textual analysis of the film, *X-Men: First Class*.

Stephen Austin Adams

English 102

Dr. Richard Hanson

The Writing Context

Use context to analyze these student essays, and create one for the essays you write so that you know what you are attempting.

Subject: Discrimination and prejudice shown in *X-Men: First Class* is comparable to that minorities received during events such as the holocaust and the Civil Rights Movement.

Audience: Young people who have watched the movie.

Writing Situation: An essay about movies and popular culture for English 102

Thesis: The *X-Men: First Class* movie appeals to mainstream society because the prejudice that is displayed toward the mutants is so closely related to that seen throughout history toward Jews, Blacks, homosexuals, and even those who just look different, and addresses the different ways in which the victims of such prejudice determine to move forward. It can be argued that the mutants' plight is not comparable as it is motivated by fear rather than hatred, but hatred comes from the fear that these racial, mutant or even homosexual groups are better than, or present a danger to, "normal" people.

Tone: Persuasive with presentation of alternate opinions.

Introduction interests the specific audience noted above by mentioning their oft-felt alienation, and lets them see how the subject, X-Men, relates to this feeling.

In the times in which we live, so many of us feel alone or on the fringe because we don't fit into society. Sometimes this is caused by our own feelings of insecurity. After all, is there anyone among us who hasn't experienced being different, mainly because we ARE all different? Although we may not have experienced the deeper prejudice that exists in this world, our experience with feeling inferior makes it easy to identify with those who have. The *X-Men: First Class* movie appeals to mainstream society because the same prejudice that is displayed toward the mutants is so closely related to that seen throughout history toward the Jewish people, African-Americans, illegal immigrants, gays, lesbians, and those who just look different. This movie also addresses the various ways in which the victims of this discrimination determine to move forward. It can be argued that the mutants' plight is not comparable as it is motivated by fear rather than hatred, but it is the same; as hatred comes from the fear that these differences (whether racial, ethnic, sexually diverse, gender-oriented, or even mutant) make those groups a danger to "normal" people.

Statement of thesis with essay's organizational pattern foreshadowed.

The *X-Men* comics of the sixties touched the surface of the racial and feminist issues of their day, but never really delved into the heart of the matter. As Mikhail Lyubansky notes in his, "Prejudice Lessons from the Xavier Institute," the comics brought to light how people fear and hate anyone who is different, even when that difference is something really cool. He quotes X-Men comic writer, Chris Claremont, who says, "The X-Men are hated, feared, and despised collectively by humanity for no other reason than they are mutants.

Paragraph Completeness:

Gives a thorough analysis of the subject from an historical perspective.

227

So what we have here, intended or not, is a book about racism, bigotry, and prejudice" (76). In fact, according to Lyubansky, the very first X-Men comic contains Charles Xavier's immediate revelation that humans are not ready to accept mutants. This opens the door for further exploration in later screenplays. *X-Men: First Class* explores all these issues much more deeply. The mutants were from different countries and races; therefore, representing Blacks, Jews, homosexuals, women, immigrants, etc. Additionally, the way both the Russians and the United States turn on all the mutants in the end of *First Class* due to the actions of a few is reminiscent of the treatment of Japanese-Americans after Pearl Harbor or Muslim-Americans after 9/11.

Comparisons to other discrimination are presented early in *First Class*, beginning with the Jews in the Holocaust. We meet Erik Lehnsherr (later Magneto). He is a young Jewish boy in a Nazi concentration camp. When his mother is taken from him, Erik bends the metal gate with his mind. This draws the attention of Sebastian Shaw, a Nazi scientist, who decides to study him extensively. When he tests Erik's ability by asking him to move a coin or risk harm to his mother, Erik is unsuccessful. Shaw orders the guards to shoot his mother. Erik's anger ensues, and he destroys the lab and kills the guards. Just as he was being persecuted as a Jew, his torture became much worse as a mutant. Raven is seen early in this movie morphed into an acceptable form to try to gain food. This is similar to how a homosexual man might try to appear straight in order to be accepted by his family, or a woman feels she has to look a certain way to be accepted by her peers and men. Xavier, although a mutant, does not have a clearly-seen mutation. He is able to hide it much like mixed races can often blend in, so as to assimilate rather than be accepted as they are.

Just as in life, differences emerge as to how each deals with his or her prejudice. Magneto, having already survived the Holocaust, is intolerant and seeks revenge. Magneto thought the United States would be different than what he had experienced with the Nazis; however, given America's history of making slaves of Africans, later segregation of African-Americans, the encampment of over 100,000 Japanese-Americans after the attack on Pearl Harbor, forcing American Indians to leave their culture behind, and the forced sterilization of any segment of the population deemed unfit, he realized how wrong he was. Magneto comes to the conclusion that humans in general don't accept anyone who is different (Lyubansky, "Racial Politics of X-Men"). All of these issues came to a head during the Civil Rights Movement. Magneto is compared by some to Malcolm X. His experiences have turned him into a reverse-racist when he lumps all non-mutants into one category. It becomes an us-against-them mentality in which Magneto wants to be separate. Malcolm X also believed Africans should have their own society separate from whites. Malcolm X had experienced the burning down of his house by Ku Klux Klan members, the murder of his father, and institutionalization of his mother. He eventually tried to bring African-Americans together just as Magneto tries to gather all the mutants on his side. Sebastian Shaw also seeks dominance and separation of all mutants, but wants to annihilate the humans as well as all mutants who don't share his agenda. This is more comparable to how the Nazis acted toward the Jews.

Charles Xavier seeks peaceful integration by showing the mutants' usefulness. This is much like the teachings of Martin Luther King, Jr. As he notes in his famous "I Have a Dream" speech, King dreamed of an America where children of all colors would play together. He wanted a peaceful assimilation where all had the same rights and possibilities. When receiving the Nobel peace prize in 1964, King spoke of "the need to overcome oppression and violence without resorting to oppression and violence." He stressed becoming the best doctors and teachers, etc. without regard to what race they are (Stephens). Thus he had the same message as Xavier of becoming useful (Hamilton).

Raven and Hank McCoy (Beast) are more like the vast majority of those discriminated against. They don't want to be different. Their desire is just to be like everyone else, even at the expense of losing their mutant powers. How many people would rather not be activists at all? They just want to be accepted.

After a thorough analysis of the essay's main points centered around a comparison with historical events, Stephen moves to a discussion and refutation of a major opposing argument.

Many viewers disagree with the analogy to the plight of the Jews and the Blacks. Their only argument is that the discrimination is not the same. Dr. Mikhail Lyubansky argues that people hated Blacks and Jews and thought of them as incompetent/inferior, whereas the mutants were thought of as competent but hated anyway - but this just doesn't pan out. The hatred for all these groups stems from a fear of those who are different, not competence or incompetence. In other words, as Caleb Rosato argues, people hate that which they fear. Therefore, the correlation exists to all these groups. Mutants are feared because of their obvious power to take over the world and to control everyone. Slogans familiar to the KKK's slurs of the Blacks were present in the movie, such as, "The Only Good Mutant is a Dead Mutant." Humans pass a Mutant Registration Act much like the Alien Registration Act that was used to identify Japanese-Americans ("Jan. 14, 1942: Roosevelt Ushers…"). They are feared so it becomes important to identify them and know where they are. Humans even later offer a "cure" for mutants as if they are flawed or sick. The new SyFy television show *Alphas* is similar to this. Characters in this show have genetic mutations that cause them to have exceptional powers. In this show, all Alphas whether good or bad seem to be eventually targeted by the government. Some groups seek to give pregnant mothers a drug which will prevent such mutations as if there was something bad about being able to do extraordinary things. They let it be known that the general public fears them ("Original Sin," *Alphas*).

Jews were feared by the Germans due to their economic power. Jews owned successful shops and businesses while other Germans struggled. The Jews, generally well-educated and rich, often got the best jobs. Most had held high government offices in the past. But the Nazis began to pass laws to boycott Jewish businesses, forbade Jews to own guns, and kept Jews from holding important public office (Edleheit). Blacks were feared as well. After the Civil War, they began to obtain jobs that had once only been for Whites. Their population grew. By the sixties they were graduating at the same rate as Whites. As they had been segregated for so long, Blacks were erroneously feared to be violent. Some Whites feared being around Blacks, as evidenced by their refusal to drink after them at water fountains, sit close to them on the bus, or attend school with them, as if the group presented a danger (Carson 170-174). Homosexual men were feared even by the Nazis as evidenced by their being targeted during the Holocaust. In the United States, they have often been treated as if they are contagious or plan to convert others. Until 2011, they were unable to serve openly in the military. When the AIDS epidemic grew in the 1980's, people became fearful that all homosexuals had the disease and were a threat. The fear of women gaining equal rights was based on anxiety that they would take men's jobs. Men feared they would no longer be needed. If women made as much money as men, it was feared that they would abandon the home and family dynamic.

The conclusion takes the analysis to a deeper level, suggesting the essay is finished, by discussing how, like in the movie, our culture often lets fear breed hatred.

Thus, it seems more than plausible that all discrimination stems from fear, not different levels of competence verses hatred. Fear breeds hatred. Not only in real life, but also in movies, it is apparent how much we fear mutants or aliens, or Indians, or any group or individual who is different. Just as the Civil Rights Movement helped to stop this discrimination toward Blacks, or the Mutant Rights Movement looked toward the same end in *X-Men: First* Class, another group seems to step into the firing line next because unfortunately this seems to be a timeless way of thinking. For example, even today it has become so easy to start movements that show hatred toward immigrants. This hatred basically stems from the fear of so many that we are somehow being "taken over." It took little persuasion to convince large numbers of people what a danger Mexicans crossing the border present to our society. We are all different from each other, and if we are not cautious toward allowing these groups to be targeted, we might find ourselves the next group on the receiving end of prejudice.

Works Cited

Brothers, David. "The Best and Worst of 'X-Men: First Class' – Moral
     Complexity and Depressing Racial Politics." *Comics Alliance,*
     10 June 2011, www.comicsalliance.com/brothers/ADG43296.
Carson, Clayborn. "Civil Rights Movement." *The Reader's Companion to
     American History,* edited by Eric Fone and John Garraty, Houghton Mifflin,
     1991, pp.161-200.
Edleheit, Abraham. "Anti Jewish Legislation in Prewar Germany." *ushmm.org,*
     United Holocaust Museum Washington, D.C., 6 Jan. 2011,
     www.ushmm.org/germany/legislation/409385.
Gilchrist, Todd. "Who You Calling 'Mutant,' Castro? 'X-Men: First Class.'"
     Box Office Magazine, 25 May 2011, pp. 31-32.
Hamilton, Jason. Review of "'X-Men: First Class." *storyhobby.* www.storyhobby.
     com/AGDSC48372.
"Jan. 14, 1942: Roosevelt Ushers in Japanese-American Internment."
     Today in History, www.history.com/1/14/1942.
Lyubansky, Mikhail. "Prejudice Lessons from the Xavier Institute." *The
     Psychology of Superheroes: An Unauthorized Exploration,* edited by Robin S.
     Rosenberg and Jennifer Canzoneri, Smart Pop, 2011, pp. 75-90.
-----. "The Racial Politics of X-Men." *Psychology Today Blog – Between the Lines,*
     5 June 2011, www.psychologytoday/xmen/43926. Accessed 9 Oct. 2011.
Marable, Manning. *Malcolm X: A Life of Reinvention.* Viking, 2011.

McCalmont, Jonathan. "'X-Men: First Class' – Better Without the Class." *ruthlessmuscle. com,* 13 June 2011, www.ruthlessmuscckle.com/Xmen/493266.

"Original Sin." *Alphas,* written and directed by Zak Penn, performances by David Stratheim, Malik Yoba, and Warren Christie, SyFy, 26 Sept. 2011.

Robinson, Shalom, Rapaport-Bar-Sever, Michael, and Sara Metzer, "The Feeling of Holocaust Survivors Towards Their Persecutors." *holocaaustechoes.com,* www.holocaustechoes.com/495832094. Accesssed 9 Oct. 2011.

Rosado, Caleb. "The Undergirding Factor is POWER Toward an Understanding of Prejudice and Racism." *Critical Multicultural Pavilion Research Room,* www.cmpr.com/297395738cd. Accessed 18 Oct. 2011.

Stephens, Gregory. "Martin Luther King, Jr.'s Message – Move Beyond Racism." *black-collegian.com,* www.black-collegian.com/king/racism/183497fgs.

X-Men: First Class. Directed by Matthew Vaughn, performances by. James McAvoy, Michael Fassbender, and Jennifer Lawrence. Twentieth Century Fox, 2011.

Literary Analysis

There are many types of essays that fall under the rubric, "Literary Analysis." Literary analyses can be rhetorical analyses, textual analyses, or evaluations, the only caveat being that with literary analyses the subject analyzed is some kind of literature. Some literary analyses can be used to analyze the time period of the story, its gender and race issues, or the culture in which the literature originally appeared (historical criticism; gender criticism; or the somewhat dated Marxist criticism). Characters in the stories or poems can be treated as subjects of psychological analysis. (For that matter, some literary scholars use a writer's works to psychoanalyze him/her.) So, sometimes in literature courses you could be asked to perform any of those sub-genres of the literary analysis, but the short discussion here will focus on an older style of close reading, where you look at elements of the story, play, or poem (narrative voice, plot, characters, setting, stylistic considerations like imagery, symbols, use of myth, and tone), and from an analysis of these elements develop a response to the literature, deciding either a) one possibility of what it could mean, with evidence to support your interpretation, or b) a discussion of how you connected emotionally or intellectually with the literature (reader response). Of course, another choice would also be to do historical/literary criticism research and discuss the literature using either the historical or gender method of literary criticism.

Or, as with the example following, a professor might allow students to use a literary text as a jumping off point to analyze a subject in contemporary culture, such as race issues, feminism, gender issues, or basic human emotions and situations. Good fiction discusses the things we do: fall in love, fight, learn, reconcile, win, lose. These essays combine personal experience and observation with an analysis of the literary work.

Here are short definitions of elements of short fiction that you can analyze to create a meaning for a story or poem. (Readers *create* meaning based on the story/poem/play *AS* they read.):

1) Narrative Voice

The first question you should always ask yourself as you begin reading a story, novel, or even a poem, is "who is telling the story?" Broadly speaking, the narrator will either be a disembodied voice (called third person) that the author has created to tell the story, or a character in the story telling the story (called a first person narrator).

Some third person narrators cannot go into any characters' mind; these narrators function like a camera, just showing you what is happening and recording the voices. Other third person narrators are fully omniscient ("all-knowing") and these voices can go into minds, go back and forth in time and space, and even make judgments about characters and their actions. Third person narrators run on a spectrum from fully omniscient through various gradations to the totally objective camera-like narrator. They might choose to hide information from the reader (one of the main reasons we read literature is for the suspense), but by convention what they do tell you is honest and objective.

The reason your first question is "who is telling the story?" is because if the narrator is a character in the story (first person), he or she usually is not telling the truth for one of three reasons: an author chooses first person narrators who are young (and thus don't really know the truth), are crazy or ridiculous (a writer uses these in comedy or satire), or, like in detective stories, we go along with the character as she solves a mystery. (The narrator is trying to find out the truth and we go with the narrator on the truth-seeking.) If it is obvious from what a sixteen year old girl says in a story that she hates being leered at by her friend's fourteen year old brother, and he is telling the story, we know it is youthful innocence, and not truth, when he says, "That girl really loves me."

2) Plot

On the simplest level, you must know what happens in the story/poem. You won't get too far without knowing the "facts." Readers (and characters in a story) could disagree about interpretation of the facts, but it helps to know what actually happened in the story.

3) Characters

Stories, poems, and drama have characters, and you should analyze them just like you analyze people that you meet.

In literature, the only difference is that not all characters are fully fleshed out "people." Minor characters often have one characteristic, and they stand for that human characteristic: that character is a miser, that one a thief. That one is a lady's man. If a main character is one-sided and stereotypical like that, this is an obvious message that helps you interpret the story.

4) Setting

Always look at all the clues you can about setting - this often aids in creating meaning; indeed, the story/poem could entirely center around the time or place it describes. There are two elements of setting to look for.

a. First, look at as many clues as you can to discover the actual time and place of the story, as well as any character's social status. Are there cars, phones, any named famous figures or events? (what decade is it?) Is it a wealthy setting or poverty? What region of the world is it? Analyzing these help you decide what the

232

story is saying. You might develop a thesis that has a historical interpretation of the literature: what does the setting, plot, and characters say about 1) the historical period of the story's setting, 2) the time and place when the story was written (these could be two different historical periods: Hawthorne, writing in the mid-1800s often set his stories in the America of the 1600s), and 3) what does the story say about people, situations, and emotions today, i.e., what does it say about being human?

b. Writers use setting to create mood: we all seem to agree that certain kinds of weather and nature create certain effects: nothing good will come if we ride up to a dreary castle in a storm. A meadow swept with daffodils, sunlight, and two deer grazing: this is fortuitous for the young couple's love in a story. Look for those clues throughout the story. Writers of literature rely on setting to create meaning!!!

5) Style

a. Writers use patterns of repeated images to suggest meaning.

b. Writers use symbols: symbols mostly come from the myths of our cultures and even from the shared beliefs we all carry as humans. If an object seems to represent something else, decide if this is creating meaning. Whenever Huck Finn and his runaway slave friend, Jim, get off the river and meet humans, they are oppressed or witness violence and oppression, but whenever they get back on the raft they are free. From even a casual reading it is obvious the Mississippi River itself symbolizes freedom from the restraints of society.

c. Every story and poem has a tone - meaning the same thing as tone of voice. Is the writer creating tragedy? comedy? irony? satire? suspense? Does the voice evoke sadness? joy? anger? fear? Sometimes it is with a writer's tone that she creates meaning.

Less than two pages do not overly restrain you with theory, but they do provide the beginning basics for what you need to interpret literature. Your purpose in analyzing literature is to decide what the story means and/or what the story says about hunanity. (There are other purposes if you become a student of literature, but for now the focus is just on finding meaning. If you can't decide on a meaning for a work of art, you can't get to other interpretations.)

Here are the steps you need to complete in order to develop a thesis with adequate content to complete a literary analysis:

1) Pick a story that you like (or poem if that is what your class has studied), and re-read it carefully and closely. Take notes in the margins and in a notebook, analyzing in detail each of the elements: narrative voice, characters, plot, setting, and style. You might read it three or four times, adding to your analysis and evaluation with each reading. Focus on what the literature actually says: good literary analysis can point to evidence in the story that shows your ideas about the literature are valid.

2) Focus on what the themes are. What is the story about? Some of the common themes: gender issues, violence, love, madness, youth growing up, alienation, loneliness, leaving home, the silliness of human behavior. Follow your decision about themes with a decision about the meaning for the story. What is the literature saying about the subject, its theme?

3) Read a biographical entry on the author (using a reference source from your library or your library's website), and investigate the historical period and place in which the story was written and was set.

233

4) *If y*our assignment calls for a researched literary essay, begin reading books and journal articles (only) on the literature and author you are analyzing.

5) Develop a specific thesis for your analysis, a specific point that illuminates for your readers something about the story. Do not choose something that is plainly in the open, or that your professor said about the story if it was read by the class. Develop your own theory based on your in-depth critical reading. Also, as you develop thesis and content, make sure you understand the audience criteria for the assignment: if the assignment calls for a "scholarly audience," the professor has asked you to write to other experts on the literature, like her. You know that they know your subject well too, and you don't bore them with basic encyclopedia-type information. If the assignment asks for you to write to an audience of peers at your school, you cannot assume they have as much knowledge about either your subject or its author, so appropriately adjust the level of details you have to report so they can understand your thesis.

6) After developing the preliminary thesis, look through all your notes and make sure you have enough evidence in the story (and your critical readings if the assignment demands research) to prove your thesis. Outlines are great tools to evaluate the strngths of your evidence. If you don't have the evidence, develop another thesis. If you do have enough, let your content notes modify your preliminary thesis until you have developed a final thesis statement. Then you are ready to start a draft.

Student Example: Literary Analysis

J.J. Aylmer's essay on Kate Chopin's "Desiree's Baby" argues that its expose of racism, hatred of miscegenation, and patriarchy contains a still powerful message for modern readers. In this reader-response literary criticism, J.J. assumes the reader agrees on the story's meaning, and focuses on its effect on readers. Nevertheless, he does analyze in detail characters and setting of the story in order to suggest why readers respond as they do to the story. A great essay written in a freshman composition course that uses literature to learn analytic processes.

The Impact of Chopin's "Desiree's Baby" on Modern Readers

In the introduction, the writer sets up the major method of analysis in this essay, reader-response, and states the thesis. J.J. makes the tone of the introduction warmer and more friendly by bringing his personal feelings into the essay.

For some readers, Kate Chopin's "Desiree's Baby" has a far-reaching and deeply affecting impact due to the somber tones of racism, the raging hate of miscegenation, and the brutal undertones of patriarchy emanating from Armand, the protagonist. Sadly, although not as prevalent, these ugly, unpleasantries remain facts of life today. But there is a beauty found by readers who learn from all the ugliness present in this story, and who then go forth and use what they've learned for the betterment of themselves or society. I can't sit here behind this keyboard and pretend to be someone who can share with you how these items impacted all who have read this story, but what I can do is share with you how "Desiree's Baby" affected me both while I read it and the time afterward spent in retrospection. I believe the impact on me is similar to the impacts felt by others who have read our story.

Racially speaking, the story impacts us on a level we easily connect with, and this is taking into consideration the fact that it was published close to 130 years ago, evidence of the fact that a strong message will reverberate throughout time. Armand is a subscriber to multiple racist views quite commonplace during his time. Some of those views include, but aren't limited to: being of the mindset that, even after emancipation, African-Americans were second class citizens; being at peace with a plantation brutalizing African-Americans; refusing to accept his own son when he discovers that his own flesh and blood "isn't white;" and thus by default he refuses to accept his wife because their child "isn't white." All the items just mentioned plus the fact that after learning of his son's mixed race, Armand began taking his anger out on the servants of his plantation (in many ways still slaves) – should be enough to impact all readers of "Desiree's Baby." It should make pristinely clear the ugliness people adopt when they choose to view their own skin color as being superior or above any other skin color.

J.J. defines in detail the racist and patriarchal views of the 1890s setting and characters.

   Armand shows us all that we need to be more open-minded, open-minded like Desiree in our story. Desiree, the anti-Armand in all the best ways, loves Armand without stopping to give pause or consideration to what racial ancestry Armand has. Even after holding Armand's arm up to hers and commenting that Armand's skin is darker, she treats him just as she did before the comparison, electing to let love and spousal commitment guide her feelings rather than the Neanderthal-like viewpoint that any racist allows his beliefs to be guided by. When, as a reader of our story, I was able to put the story down and think about these two characters and the uniqueness of each (especially the fact that we learn it is Armand, and not Desiree, with black ancestry), I was able to reflect on which of the two I would hope every reader of this great story would aspire towards, and that's Desiree.

J.J. begins creating the contrast between the two main characters he will use throughout his essay.

Paragraph Completeness:

   Miscegenation is the issue from "Desiree's Baby" that struck the largest nerve with me. For some it will be the racism, while for others it will be the patriarchal point-of-view that Armand lives by, but for me it was the miscegenation because of how close to home it hit - because of the very personal level with which it connected with me. "Desiree's Baby" takes place in an age where a portion of our population, sadly, view "mixed" blood as an abomination, and even worse it was mostly caused by white racists raping black women. This dark world-view and demeanor that Armand carries all but vanishes once he learns that he is having a child, and even more so after the child is born, and we learn that it is a little boy. Armand is nothing short of ecstatic. However, once a few weeks pass and the child begins to really take on his true pigmentation, it becomes obvious to Armand his son isn't one hundred percent "pure." So the demonic-like plantation dictator returns, literally for no other reason than because Armand's son is partially black!!!

In this and all the next paragraphs, thorough analysis with evidence to prove the main points of the essay.

   So, why does Armand's viewpoint on miscegenation strike such a chord with this reader? That's an easy question for me to answer, because my wife is half-Puerto Rican and thus our son is one-quarter Puerto Rican. My Nephew? He's half-black. My other nephew? He's… Well you see where this is going. And that's just me. Lord only knows how many other readers of this story have inter-racial relatives that they love more than the world itself. I mean it's the twenty-first century, and interracial dating / marriage / having biracial children is commonplace. Sadly, the views held by Armand on all three of these situations are also commonplace in small pockets of narrow-minded people. So there are basically two primary impacts that the topic of miscegenation had on the readers of our story: there are those who are short-sighted like Armand and view miscegenation as an abomination, an unforgiveable sin. And then there are others like myself and the majority of those reading this story where the impact was like our small toe (which we rarely give much thought to) being accidentally rammed into the corner of our bedframe, the searing pain a reminder that "it's" still there, as are the issues with miscegenation, and when it is reintroduced into our minds we remember just how painful that way of thinking can be. It is beyond the realm of all I think possible to cast my wife and son off to some far away land and a certain imminent death. The mere thought of not having either in my life – for no other reason than the color of their skin - is almost more than I can bear, especially if it were of my own doing and desire. I'm confident in my being able to surmise that this is how most, if not all, of those who view Armand's feelings as grotesquely as I, would feel also. We see Armand and his antiquated views through a lens that is a complex mixture of disbelief, pity, sadness, anger, and lastly pride. Disbelief in the sense that we can't understand how someone could EVER view an interracial child as a shortcoming / sin. Pity in the sense that we pity such a narrow-minded way of viewing someone so important in parents' lives. Sadness in the sense we are saddened by the fact that Armand will never have a relationship with his own flesh and blood, nor his wife from this day forward. Anger in the sense of how dare Armand treat someone with no say in the matter so poorly and without regard. And then lastly, we feel pride: pride in the fact that we will never be like the devilish Armand, pride in the fact that we recognize the worth of all children no matter the hue of their skin, and pride in the knowledge we know in our hearts that miscegenation is equally as beautiful as any other relationship. This serves as an illustration that readers can be impacted by the same theme of a story in both positive and negative ways.

Those like Armand who take up this sideways lifestyle that includes a subscription to "Why the Patriarchy is good for you, your neighbor, and your world" should really give more thought to how that way of life impacts those around them, but with narcissism being such a pillar of those beliefs I won't be holding my breath. In 1890 when Armand looks in a mirror, he sees a powerful white man above those who aren't also white men; this includes, I'm afraid, white women. It is here that we find an aspect of our story that will again impact both the men and women reading it, but this time we find an issue that may very well impact the women reading it in a more profound and deeper way than it does their gender counterparts. I can only sit here and do my very best to try and imagine how the patriarchal themes affected the women reading it and make as educated a guess as possible, in regard to how it would make them feel. I say that to say this: I can very easily envision the women reading this story being transported in their minds back to a time when men like Armand genuinely believed these women to be only a rung above people of color. Our lady readers realize just how far things have progressed, while also being reminded the fight that was fought (and is still being fought in some circles) was damn worth it. For this issue the impact would be on a much deeper and emotional level than that felt by us men, and for good reason. For them to see an example of not only what that type of "man" looked like, but also a brief glimpse into the "life" of a woman who was living under the thumb of that sort, would stir within them strong and just emotions. For us men, the impact is that of Armand serving as our illustration of why we should avoid drinking the same patriarchal kool-aid as Armand did. I, for one, was impacted by seeing the importance of not only treating spouses as equals but perhaps even more importantly, women altogether. The demise of Desiree was a direct result of how Armand treated her under the belief that men are vastly superior to their female counterparts. How could we as readers not be impacted in a way that reminds us that women will suffer deep wounds when we allow ourselves to look at and treat women in the same manner that Armand does? How could we not be impacted to want to be the best possible equal to our female halves after seeing the death by suicide of a woman as wholesome as Desiree, a suicide that is due in large part to her husband's beliefs, and treatment as a result of those beliefs? The answer is simple, we couldn't not be impacted by this theme in our story. With the patriarchal theme we the readers (in particular us men), just like we were with the racism and miscegenation themes, were once again impacted in a way that showed us why we must aspire for our world to be ridden of these issues, if for no other reason than a desire to see the betterment that would come as a result of those issues being eradicated from our lands.

The end game of these impacts is more than just choosing to not be a spawn of Satan like Armand was. The impacts lay a double-layered foundation for we, the readers, going forward. The first of these layers is a call for us to all choose to be a "Desiree" and not an "Armand." In choosing to be a "Desiree" we are impacted to love others regardless of their faults, to honor our spouses, and for us to adhere to the belief system that none is above the other. As for the call to not be an "Armand," well the reasoning ought to be as clear as the vision of a recent lasik recipient. Our second foundation is also rather philosophical: to never forget time periods like those in which Desiree and Armand lived. For us to remember these eras, the people that lived during them, and the themes / ways of life present and alive during these time periods. The remembrance of these things will impact us in a manner that will show us that while we aren't living in the 1890's, we also haven't erased these disgusting themes from our earth entirely. Even if they may appear to be on life support, they still have life, and that is a change we should aspire towards making. It is through this impact that illustrates for us to be mindful, to always be aware and watchful for these things in todays day and age, for as soon as we are able to rid our world of these things two things are certain to take place: the first – our world will have more and more "Desirees" walking amongst us, and the second – just as we will have more "Desirees," so too will we now also have more people willing to accept, welcome, and love "Desiree's Baby" – both the story and the beautiful child.

The conclusion takes the essay out into a larger context, asking readers to adopt the enlightened views called for by the story and by the writer of this essay

Evaluation

We evaluate all the time, so the basic process is not new to you; however, there are many tools you can use to improve your evaluative skills. Basically, an evaluation discusses the strengths and weaknesses of something, and usually does so within the framework of similar items. Is something good or bad? Is something comparatively better or worse than a similar object? When we say we like a movie, or a particular item at McDonalds, we are comparing their strengths and weaknesses with other movies/eating establishments. Formal evaluations stay away from focusing on whether you "like" or "dislike" the item evaluated; instead a good formal evaluation sets clear, specific criteria, and uses the criteria to evaluate the item. If you evaluate a car, you might decide that the criteria to focus on is cost, which brings up an entire array of areas to research: a comparison of costs, fuel mileage, the long term repair costs of the model, and its resale value. If economics was your main criteria, your essay would focus on this, but you would also need to compare other facets of the car: its looks and features (both interior and exterior) compared to a. other cars in the same class and b. other cars in all classes. Does it have enough of the features you, and since you would be writing for an audience, most people, would want in a car of that price range? Sometimes an evaluation compares all the major items in a similar category and discusses the strengths and weaknesses of each. When doing this you might argue one is best, or you might be even more objective than the tone of many evaluations demand, and write an evaluative report where you just explain the strengths and weaknesses of each item, letting the reader decide which item is best based on your unbiased reporting.

Possible Real World Subjects to evaluate:

- A car or a class of cars
- A computer accessory or computers themselves
- Phones, musical devices or viewing/reading pads
- A politician or a public figure with a message, perhaps a professor
- A group of people you are considering associating with
- Places to live, including conditions and rules on the college campus
- An eating establishment, a type of food

Real World Subjects that are often formally evaluated in college courses:

- Films and television shows; actors and directors
- Consumer products
- College majors and the careers associated with them
- Books and articles

Businesses and Business Courses:

- Products a business might buy or produce
- A set of guidelines for employees
- A marketing campaign

Science Courses:

- The plans for an experiment or study – one being planned or one already completed

Here are the steps you need to complete in order to develop a thesis with adequate content to complete an evaluation:

1) After carefully observing, researching, and analyzing a subject, as well as similar items, develop *a specific set of criteria* to evaluate the subject.

2) Use the criteria to compare it to similar items, and to evaluate the effectiveness, the strengths and weaknesses, of the subject. More in-depth observation, research, and analysis will probably need to be done to be thorough. If you are evaluating a set of similar objects to arrive at a comparison (best, worst, similar), create lists that help you analyze. Even if you are focusing on one specific subject, you will probably still need to do this for a thorough evaluation.

3) Analyze your audience and its relationship to the item(s) you are evaluating – what do they already think about, and know about, your subject? What do they need from your evaluation?

4) From the results of your evaluation and your audience analysis, develop a specific thesis. Develop content in an outline to make sure that your thesis contains a valid evaluative statement. Then you are ready to start a draft.

Student Example: Evaluation. MLA Style Documentation

Chapter 6 also demonstrates how to write evaluations of books and articles that you read.

Cecilia Durbin's essay favorably evaluates the Comedy Central series, *Broad City*, and discusses how it describes Millennial attitudes, and contrasts them with the ways other generations look at the world. It looks favorably at *Broad City*'s use of comedy. An extraordinary essay for a freshman, it illustrates all the conventions of good revison for content, organization, and paragraph completeness.

Writing Context

Subject: *Broad City* and the Millennial Generation

Audience: 18-30, in college or college educated, politically and socially aware

Writing Situation: an evaluation of *Broad City*, perhaps published in *Rolling Stone*

Thesis: *Broad City* is the truest voice of this generation's feminists, taking real-life situations and social themes and addressing them in a comical, relatable way. It introduces a non-biased inclusive mentality that reflects the ideals of my generation.

Tone: Formal, but somewhat relaxed with room for appropriate comedic references. Optimistic. Informed and aware of contemporary society, especially the struggles facing young people, minorities, and especially women.

Use writing context to analyze these student essays, and create one for the essays you write so that you know what you are attempting.

Introduction interests the audience by relating to their own political and social views.

With the craziness of American politics now being perennial, politicians on both sides of the spectrum are scrambling to attract Millennial voters, or Americans between the ages of 18 and 29. According to Chuck McCutcheon, managing editor of the *CQ Researcher* and long-time political reporter in Washington, this age group is the nation's largest, numbering about 75 million (819). And there is one major notable difference between this youngest voting generation and its predecessors: Millennials generally are more left-leaning on social issues. For instance, 70% of the demographic report they disapprove of Donald Trump because of his racist and sexist antics (823).

Furthermore, the issues that Millennials care about most are social ones: illegal immigration and a path to citizenship, same-sex marriage, climate change, and economic and gender equality (820). For politicians trying to familiarize themselves with the ideologies of this generation, they need to look no further than the "fourth wave, queerish, anti-rape/pro-porn, intersectional [feminists]" of Comedy Central's hit sitcom, *Broad City* (Nussbaum 59).

Second paragraph sets feminism in its broadest historical context, and then states the thesis of the essay.

"If women are silly," states Mary Wollstonecraft in her 1792 groundbreaking feminist piece, *A Vindication of the Rights of Women*, "it is only because society trains them to be irrelevant" (86). At a time when gender equality was considered laughable, outrageous, and impossible in principle, Wollstonecraft's statement was a grave one in a dire new situation; now, however, over two centuries after Wollstonecraft wrote those words, a new kind of feminist is taking over, and *Broad City* creators and stars, Ilana Glazer and Abbi Jacobson, are using their own kind of silly as a means of empowerment and optimism for women, the reality of which their feminist predecessors would have only dreamed. *Broad City* is the truest voice of this generation's feminists, taking real-life situations and social themes and addressing them in a relatable, yet comical, way. It introduces a non-biased inclusive mentality that largely and light-heartedly reflects the ideologies of the Millennial generation.

According to feminist scholar Debra Baker Beck, a major part of the serious on-going struggle for women throughout history has been their portrayal in media (139). From the sensationalism of bra-burning during the 1960s women's rights movement, which was just a small portion of the actual protest going on, the part covered by the male-dominated media, to the slight improvement of the Mom-knows-best genre in the 1980s, women were still confined in the media to their culturally decided domestic roles (146).

Begins analysis of Broad City with quotations from experts and with analysis of specific incidents from the series.

In "Laverne & Curly: The Slapstick Anarchists of *Broad City*," television critic for *The New Yorker*, Emily Nussbaum, notes, "[*Broad City*] is the type of meta-comedy that TV sitcoms often experiment with once they are no longer novelties, when the creators have begun to engage, consciously or unconsciously, in a conversation with the viewers' responses" (59). And that is certainly what Glazer and Jacobson have achieved. *Broad City* is light-hearted and hilarious, but the show also addresses relevant issues. Main character Ilana (played by Glazer) introduces viewers to her roommate, Jaimie (played by actor Arturo Castro), an illegal Venezuelan immigrant who also happens to be gay. *Broad City* dedicates an entire episode to his path to citizenship and ultimately his successful passing of the naturalization test. After his ceremony, the gang revels in Jamie's success. "We are going to sail right past the Statue of Liberty," Ilana says. "Like the true American immigrants did" ("Citizen Ship").

Content Thorough: Multiple reasons with specifics and analysis why Broad City is so effective.

While most Millennials support the legalization of marijuana, one cannot ignore the growing support of the issue throughout the country, and *Broad City* makes pot-smoking a central theme. In one episode, *Broad City* touches on the feminist issue of self-reliance as well as the creators' support for marijuana legislation, when the main character, Abbi (played by Jacobson), takes a stand and is determined to find "her own weed, like a grown woman" ("P…Weed"). Another undeniable theme throughout the show is the "sexual frankness" (Nussbaum 61) of the dialogue and situations. "Sexuality comes from a refreshingly natural place," observes Mike Albo of the LBGT magazine, *Out*.

Furthermore, this sexual openness has encouraged fans of the show to open up and to liberate themselves, according to Albo. Free-loving Ilana summarizes the characters' – and many other Millennials' – opinions on sexuality, stating, "Government-mandated monogamy is for old people, like Facebook invites or network TV" ("Citizen Ship").

Nussbaum might have hit the proverbial nail on the head giving the label "slapstick anarchists" to Glazer and Jacobson (61). The nineteenth century feminist, Emma Goldman, in *Anarchism and Other Essays*, asserts that women will only be liberated "by refusing the right to anyone over her body . . . by refusing to be a servant to God, the state, society, the husband, the family . . . by making her life simpler but deeper and richer" (211). *Broad City* is a moving train of feminism, refusing to stop for anyone and knocking down any social constructs and traditional norms in its way. When Ilana finds out her very casual boyfriend, Lincoln (played by Hannibal Burress), "hooked up" with another woman, Glazer is positively ecstatic ("Two Chains"). In the series's television premier, "What A Wonderful World," Ilana and Abbi are stopped on the street by a man who insists, "You girls should smile more." Their response? Both characters form fake smiles with their middle fingers, scaring the stranger away to the viewer's delight. Another example of feminist initiative occurs in the episode, "Stolen Phone." Abbi and Ilana decide to ask men out on dates themselves rather than traditionally waiting to be asked out. "This is so great!" Abbi exclaims. "Why are we waiting for guys to come to us, Ilana? Did Amelia Earhart wait to be asked to fly around the world? Definitely not. She asked. And then they said 'no.' But she still did it. I'm doing it again. I'm asking someone else out."

"Even when its characters fail epically, as they often do, the show feels optimistic a daydream of two goofy slobs pinballing through life, every obstacle they meet just something new to ricochet off" (Nussbaum 61). LGBT rights advocate and founder of the Arcus Foundation, Kevin Jennings, in "American Dreams," recalls when, as a young man, he decided he wanted to be the voice of the underdog. "Inequalities were part of the game, the rules of which were such that gays, blacks, poor people, women, and many others would always lose" (520). Ilana Glazer and Abbi Jacobson have acknowledged the same and, through their comedy rather than traditional political activism, address numerous social issues by highlighting the very many advantages of diversity in our world. The character, Ilana, craves "different colors, different shapes, different sizes. People who are hotter, uglier. More smart, not so smart. Innies. Outies" ("Coat Check").

Advocating for diversity, equality, and the necessity of optimism are arguably the main themes of *Broad City*. Ideas that certainly resonate with the Millennial generation. The show is not merely a sitcom intended to make us laugh; it gives insight into today's political and social conversations and what they mean to the nation's youngest voters. The emphasis on hope and change are how Barack Obama baited Millennials in 2008 and again in 2012. In the episode, "Two Chains," Ilana accidentally gets her bike chain locked around her waist. She struggles to free herself throughout the episode, and when boyfriend, Lincoln, offers to help her remove it, Ilana refuses. "You know, as a woman," she states, "I feel it's important to cast this chain off myself."

Paragraph Completeness"

Cecilia brings up yet anothr issue germaine to Broad City, feminism, and analyzes it thoroughly using evidence from historical sources, contemporary sources, and episodes of the show..

Cecilia ties the show to another of the Millennials main social arguments: the equality of all groups, especially maringalized ones. Notice again the thorough analysis using multiple threads of evidence.

241

Through their comedy, their advocacy, their optimism, *Broad City*'s Ilana Glazer and Abbi Jacobson are empowering all those who are marginalized and are inspiring us to take the chain off ourselves.

Great conclusion signaling completion.

Works Cited

Albo, Mike. "How Broad City Became the Greatest Show on Television." *Out,*
       25 Feb. 2016, *Out.com*, www.out.com.
Beck, Deborah Baker. "The 'F' Word: How the Media Frames Feminism."
       NWSA Journal, vol. 10, no. 1, 1998, pp. 139-153, *JSTOR*, www.jstor.org/jgr41378.
"Citizen Ship." *Broad City*, directed and performance by Ilana Glazer and Abbi Jacobson,
       Comedy Central, 15 Feb. 2015, *Hulu*, www.hulu.com/watch/432965.
"Coat Check." *Broad City*, directed and performance by Ilana Glazer and Abbi Jacobson,
       Comedy Central, 11 Mar. 2015, *Hulu*, www.hulu.com/watch/432965.
Goldman, Emma. *Anarchism and Other Essays*. 1911. 2nd ed.,
       Mother Earth Publishing, 2015.
Jennings, Kevin. "American Dreams." *Signs of Life in the USA*, edited by Sonia Massik
       and Jack Solomon, 8th ed, Bedford, 2015, pp. 519-523.
McCutcheon, Chuck. "Young Voters: Can White House hopefuls win over Millennials?"
       CQ Researcher, vol. 25, no. 35, 2 Oct. 2015, pp. 817-840. *CQ Researcher*,
       www.library.cqpress.libproxy.getpdf41362.
Nussbaum. "Laverne & Curly: the Slapstick Anarchists of Broad City." *The New Yorker*,
       vol. 92, no. 4, 7 Mar. 2016, pp. 59-61. *Academic Search Complete*,
       http.web.a.ebscohost.com.libproxy.kctcs.edu/ehost/pdfviewer/320597.
"P ... Weed." *Broad City*, directed and performance by Ilana Glazer and Abbi Jacobson,
       Comedy Central, 28 Jan. 2014, *Hulu*, www.hulu.com/watch/432965.
"Stolen Phone." *Broad City*, directed and performance by Ilana Glazer and Abbi Jacobson,
       Comedy Central, 26 Jan. 2014, *Hulu*, www.hulu.com/watch/432965.
"Two Chainz." *Broad City*, directed and performance by Ilana Glazer and Abbi Jacobson,
       Comedy Central, 17 Feb. 2016, *Hulu*, www.hulu.com/watch/432965.
"What A Wonderful World." *Broad City*, directed and performance by Ilana Glazer and
       Abbi Jacobson, Comedy Central, 22 Jan. 2014, *Hulu*, www.hulu.com/watch/432965.
Wollstonecraft, Mary. *A Vindication of the Rights of Women*. 1792. Empire, 2012.

Some features of this MLA Works Cited page include
* *Every television show has an episode title, and the original airing date and its title should be listed. This information can be found at imdb.com.*
* *When using an older book in a newer, modern edition, the original publication date should appear after the title (as with the 1911 and 1792 dates above with the Goldman and Wollstonecraft books.*
* *Always follow the system that has been regularized by the 2016 MLA style, including punctuation:*
    Author. Title of article or book. Title of Contaner if there is one, edition and editors if there are ones in a book, if a periodical volume (vol.), and issue (number: no.), publisher if a book, publication date, page numbers of an article. If the source came from the internet, you would then begin a second listing, that usually only contains the name of the website/database and the url.

Narrative

Personal Narratives / Memoir-Reflective Essay

In a memoir, a writer describes and narrates an experience, making sense of the experience and developing a thesis that reflects the new understanding that comes from the analysis of the experience. For instance, perhaps you had a very volatile relationship with a relative, a sibling, a parent, a friend, or even an enemy in your neighborhood or school. Some time has passed since this relationship occupied your life on a daily basis. You would spend as much time as necessary to analyze this experience (using the predrafting exercises of chapters 2 and 3), to come to terms with this experience which, when it occurred, just made you mad, sad, scared, or ashamed. With a little distance, you could decide what parts of the experience were caused by your thoughts, feelings, actions, and beliefs, and which parts were caused by the thoughts, feelings, actions, and beliefs of the other person/people involved. Through this greater understanding, you become a more mature human being. When you write about this in a memoir-reflective essay, your general purpose is to get your audience to relate to the feelings and experiences you experienced, and to witness your present exploration and greater understanding of the experience. Of course, memoirs do not have to relate a negative experience. You could choose to analyze a positive experience, or one that just confused you at the time (but again, with distance, you could make sense of the experience through thorough analysis).

There are also examples of narrative on pp. 42-3, 49-50, 52-3, and 55-7.

A personal narrative could be a memoir-reflective essay like the one just described, but a personal narrative, as a genre, is somewhat more broad. In a personal narrative you describe and narrate an experience that you experienced, but it could also be one you observed. And the thesis does not always reflect a personal growth experience; it could be a thesis that makes a point about humanity or about a particular culture, leaving the growth of you, the writer, in the background. Indeed, the personal narrative you use could be just one element of your content in a researched essay, as both essays in this section are. The first essay uses Caleb Monyhan's negative personal experiences in advanced plcement programs as just one line of evidence suggesting that the program needs improvements. He also uses scholarly sources to make his points. In the second essay in this section, a specialized narrative genre called a literacy narrative, Sherita Watson draws more on her experiences as a mother of a black male student than Caleb does with his essay, but she also use sources to suggest that her experiences are typical for an African-American student in school.

Here are the steps you need to complete in order to develop a thesis with adequate content to complete either a personal narrative or a memoir-reflective essay:

1) Use all of the predrafting suggestions from chapter 2 and 3 in order to analyze your subject with the complexity it deserves. When looking at an experience, writers describe the people and the places where the action occurs, narrate the events of the particular situation (or situations) to be focused on, as well as a narrative of the entire situation and what came before and after. Within both of those time frames, an analysis of causes and effects and processes that occurred becomes of paramount importance. Writers developing a narrative compare and contrast the event and the people involved

243

to other events and people. Writers often need to do extended definitions. To prove the thesis, the essay following uses extended definition, causal and process analysis, comparison, narrative, illustration/example, and persuasion (to answer opposing arguments). Wriers use whatever is needed to accomplish their desired results.

2) As you do all of these pre-drafting activities using the details of chapters 2 and 3, at the side have a note to yourself that you have to be developing a focused subject (you can't say everything about your subject in a few pages!!!!), a specific audience to deliver your message to, and a specific thesis (a point for the details you will be narrating). You work on this preliminary context, and the content to match the evolving context, until you reach a point where you have a final writing context (focused subject, specific audience whom you have analyzed, a thesis that makes a statement, and a tone commiserate with that audience and thesis) and you have content that illustrates and illuminates the context fully for that audience. Then you are ready to start a draft.

Most subjects for narratives and memoirs in college courses concern gender, race, and school issues, or depictions of specific cultures students have lived in or been exposed to. Another often used subject is a literacy narrative, discussing how a person or a group he/she belongs to acquires language (speaking, listening, reading, or writing skills), uses language, or interprets language from other groups who use it differently. Literacy narratives have their own section following this example student narrative.

Student Essay: Personal Narrative / Memoir-Reflective Essay. MLA Style Docu.

Caleb Monyhan

The Writing Context Writing II

Dr. Estes

Use context to analyze these student essays, and create one for the essays you write so that you know what you are attempting.

Subject: The Advanced Placement Program's Issues

Audience: Two: 1) Anyone against the program as a way to get a head start in college. 2) Those who believe the program is fine the way it is.

Writing Situation: Analytic, persuasive memoir. Using personal experience as evidence.

Thesis: The advanced placement program is a fantastic resource for students interested in higher education; however, due to many flaws with acquiring credits, student favoritism, and only a slight advantage when entering college, many believe that this program should be overhauled or dissolved altogether. Dissolving the program is not necessary when it motivates so many students to excel; nevertheless, it is time for an overhaul.

Introduction interests the audience by giving the historical background of the subject, and then paragraph two mentions the issues being discussed now to bring essay into today.

Tone: Formal and analytic. Very enthusiastic about the program and its good qualities while also critical of its missteps.

Advanced Placement: The Solution

Originally conceived as The Kenyon Plan in 1952, the advanced placement program was primarily intended to give high school seniors a chance to study college level material while also earning credits for their degree track. It initially covered eleven disciplines (composition, literature, math, history, biology, chemistry, physics, French, Spanish, German, and Latin). After three years, a non-profit organization called The College Board formed to develop, manage, and maintain the advanced placement program's curriculum and exams. School systems used advanced placement exams so high school students could be tested for knowledge learned in the courses. These exams were not free, however. A fee wall charged would cover the exams as well as the courses themselves, so the advanced placement program, including the college board, could remain non-profit.

Though this sounds like a very good system that every student should use, there are naysayers. Many scholars take issue with the fee wall, the favoritism that can happen, and the big edge it gives to those who take it. None of these opposing arguments hold up under scrutiny. First, most programs have a way for poorer students to take the course for free. The problem is with school systems not alerting parents to the benefits to this system. To make this even easier for parents, the pell grant system should be extended to high schools. This would not only make sure that all disadvantaged students would have the money to use advanced placement, but it would also save the government pell grant system much money, as each $100 payment for an advanced placement course would save the pell grant system the cost of one or two classes for a student in college ($400 to $2400 depending on how much the school's credit hours cost and whether the advanced placement earns the student 3 or 6 credit hours). Parents of middle class students also reap these financial benefits. And this saving is multiplied for EACH advanced placement course a student successfully completes. *Caleb takes the issues today, the opposing arguments of his audience, and refutes them with evidence and analysis one by one.*

Opposing Argument # 1's refutation.

Second, favoritism does occur for students taking advanced placement courses, the 'teacher's pet syndrome,' and it does cause problems as will be discussed later. But favoritism is going to happen in high schools anyway. Teachers are only people. They are of course going to appreciate students who will work toward learning from the teachers. Third, yes, students who avail themselves of the advanced placement program do have a big edge. That all students should have such a problem!!! Advanced placement, with the overhauls discussed here in place, should be the norm, not the exception, for high school students. For those on a technical degree track, more of those classes should also be available in high school. My father tells me of the many technical courses in auto repair, carpentry, bricklaying, plumbing, electrical, heating and air conditioning that were available in his high school. Off the subject, but as the new mantra that is occurring throughout the country says: not everyone should be on a four year college track. Many well-paying jobs are trade jobs. *Opposing Argument #2's refutation.*

Opposing Argument #3's refutation.

First general statement of thesis, that Advanced Placement, with changes, should be the norm.

One of the main problems with the high school advanced placement program, or rather with the rigidity of local school systems: I will give my experience, but there were others in my school, and so I'm sure in every school system that uses advanced placement. In elementary and middle school, I was always known as the teacher's pet. I always seemed to do well in my classes, and teachers often said I was a grade higher than the rest of the class. They would recommend that I skip, but my parents didn't agree thankfully. I would not have fit in with students a few inches taller and a year or more older *First major problem with advanced placement using personal narrative.*

245

Narrative (cont.)

Analysis of experience.

than me. So once I got to high school, advanced placement courses were inevitable, and I did very well in these classes. The problem was once I was done with those classes, the school required me to complete the lower level general courses as well to graduate. How ridiculous!!!! I had passed the pre-calculus college level advanced placement math, but since I had skipped Algebra 1 completely when I started high school to complete higher level math courses, I still had to waste my time in Algebra 1 as a senior just to fulfil some silly box on my transcript. Talk about a ridiculous waste of time. And as I was a captive, I'm sure I gave that poor Algebra teacher much more grief than she needed, and she could have been spending her time helping freshmen who needed it, not a bored senior who was acting out. As a student, I felt duped. My parents were not happy either. I stopped taking those courses shortly after, and actually graduated with a GED as I was not going to let the system's idiotic rules waste my time. The counselors themselves saw what an idiotic rule they had sending me to freshmen courses I had skipped for college-ready advanced courses, but their hands were tied.

Widens his experience out to solutions for creating positive experiences for all students.

I want to make sure that students who participate in advanced placement programs are a. not put in any situation that makes them feel like they need to work harder, more, or as a waste of time than they need to, and to b. make sure that parents know what they are getting their children into. Finally, I want to clarify that I have no hard feelings when speaking of this program. I have seen instances where fellow students had to work harder than they needed to to get the benefits of advanced placement (for instance, six classes including puff ones, when five would have been fine). My parents really stayed up with my schooling and fought for me unsuccessfully because of a flawed set of rules in the system; however, I saw many students whose parents just did not understand the system and/or just left it to the school to make all the choices, and there is no need for that. Simplify the system and explain it to parents when their children are just starting school, and more students will be prepared!!! The advanced placement program is a fantastic resource for students interested in getting a higher education in life. Dissolving the program is not necessary when it motivates so many students to excel. However, it is time for an overhaul.

There are many scholars who believe that the advanced placement program is fine the way it is. This group includes The College Board. Referring back to my personal experience, being the student in that scenario was very disheartening. I felt I had accomplished nothing and was not motivated to continue college until a year and a half after I got my GED, so instead of being two years ahead of my college graduation date (14 years from 1st grade to college graduation) I will probably graduate when I would have if I had never taken advanced placement and had just gone to college (16 years from 1st grade to college graduation). This is a discouraging problem with the program. A major goal of the advanced placement program promises to motivate students to pursue a higher education through college and universities. However, if high schools can require students to take classes they don't need, students like myself – the ones who will benefit the most from advanced placement - may get a late start on their education if they go at all. I know more than a handful of students who completed a year or two of advanced placement in high school and it so soured them that they have not gone to college at all, or dropped out after a semester.

Another issue is with the colleges students transfer to. In Warne et al's "The Impact of Participation in the Advanced Placement Program on Students' College Admissions Test Scores," the four professors' research uncovers the fact that just because students take advanced placement courses doesn't mean they are guaranteed college credits. Some colleges accept advanced placement and others don't (400-416). The colleges themselves should accept the courses as credits, as students who pass advanced placement with a 3-5 generally have more knowledge, in my experience, than students who took the course at the college. Some colleges do not accept some advanced placement credits even if the course occurred on their college campus (412). I myself only received credit for 3 hours of the college freshman composition sequence, although The College Board stated I should receive all 6 of the hours. When I took the second semester course at the college, it covered research tools I had in the high school Advanced Placement course I took and passed. That is just not right, and must be changed. The organization that runs the program is known as The College Board. This implies credits. Added to the fact that students have to pay for these courses, colleges should be required to accept the courses for credits. It is not as if the schools do not have similar courses since advanced placement courses are almost all general studies courses offered at all colleges.

Second major problem with Advanced Placement, mentioning the personal problem but then providing evidence that the problem is widespread.

As you can see, the advanced placement program is not fine in its current state. However, some scholars believe that the program overall should be dissolved. Other scholars believe that it should offer less reward. In Rodney LeBrecque's "Unfair Advancement," he begins with commending Harvard and Princeton for doing away with their early enrollment program. He believes other colleges and universities should follow in their footsteps. LeBrecque proposes that with this, they should also revert the advanced placement program to its original purpose. This purpose was not to get a head start in college, but only to learn more in high school. He even says, verbatim, "AP score aren't meant for college admissions." He tells of the "metamorphosis" of the AP program. Today, it is meant to give privileged high school students a way to get a head start on college. He sees the point-of-view that those who work hard for these programs deserve it, but doesn't think it's fair for the others. He concludes by saying advanced placement is a great program needing to be simplified. Students can still use their test scores, but for advanced placement only, not for college credits. He wishes for those students to want to learn more, but also have an appreciation for patience and discipline. Others do not agree with these ideas. Though I have negative personal experiences with advanced placement, I still recognize its value. In the eyes of a student, the only reward offered being higher learning in high school is not satisfying. Putting in the extra work with no reward is not at all worth the trouble. High School students have enough stress without worry about more difficult classes that they don't have to take. It's nothing but a waste of time for the students and teachers involved. At that point, it's like my personal experience. If this is the way some want to take it, we may as well dissolve the program.

Content completeness and Audience Awareness: Since some scholars in Caleb's reading called for dissolving Advanced Placement altogether, Caleb devotes a paragraph to their concerns and evidence.

That is not the way to take this. This is about improving the program. Charlie White reports on Southern High School in Louisville, Kentucky. White interviewed the school's principal who says,

"The school's goal is to find a way to keep the students interested in learning so they'll pursue an education beyond high school – at technical schools, trade schools or colleges." Only half of Southern's graduates pursue education after high school. They hope to enroll more students into advanced placement so they will be motivated to pursue a higher education. White concludes by reporting that Southern already has thirteen advanced placement courses (A7). Southern High School's approach is the way of the future for the advanced placement program. It gives students an incentive to seek more learning through advanced placement.

Conclusion leaves the reader thinking.

Some worry that motivation is a factor. They ask if students can ensure motivation to continue from the advanced placement program through college. This is where I concede. There is no guarantee that the students will love the classes. The best that can be done is to try our best and get more feedback from the students. Due to the issues of acquiring the credits earned, student favoritism, and unfair advantages, the program has gained a negative reputation amongst scholars. As said many times, the advanced placement program is a great system that needs an overhaul. If we want our future to be a bright one, we must have scholars at the earliest age possible. The Advanced Placement Program not only ensures this, but assists in the procedure. If we were to dissolve this program, we could be sealing the fate of many would-be scholars everywhere.

Works Cited

LeBrecque, Rodney. "Unfair Advancement." *New York Times*, 30 Sep. 2006. *New York Times,* www.newyorktimes.com/49263208.

Warne, Russell et al. "The Impact of Participation in the Advanced Placement Program on Students' College Admissions Test Scores." *The Journal of Educational Research*, vol. 108, no. 5, 2015, pp. 400-416. *EBSCOhost*, www.ebscohost.com/edures/492683.

White, Charlie. "Working for Student Success." *The Courier Journal* [Louisville], 4 Feb. 2009, p. A7. *courierjournal.com*, www.courierjournal.com4022009/studentsuccess.

Literacy Narratives

Research and predrafting analysis for literacy narratives ask you to think at not only the broadest, but conversely the most specific, terms about how you and the culture(s) you have been associated with communicate meaning to other individuals and groups. The best way to understand this is to state a series of research questions that would lead to excellent literacy narrative essays:

- How did you first learn that writing was a different way of communicating than speaking? What is the difference between writing in blogs, emails, and Facebook, as compared to what you were asked to write in high school, and what is being demanded of you in college?
- When did you first learn that your specific cultural group had its own way of communicating, and it was different from other groups? How do you navigate these differences? For instance, these high school cultural groups all speak, write, read, and communicate (verbally and non-verbally) differently from each other: wealthy male jocks, lower middle class/poor male jocks, female jocks, wealthy male intellectuals, wealthy female intellectuals, middle/lower class intellectuals both males and females; this grouping also breaks down along racial lines – Asian, Latino, and African-American intellectuals interact differently with each other as opposed to communication with the majority race; gang kids have their own method of communicating. Kids who focus on dance, drama, music, art, and creative writing all communicate amongst themselves differently than they do with other groups, as do students preparing for technical careers. The list goes on – a good literacy narrative could discuss how you or others you have observed navigate differences.
- In what ways do you and your friends communicate more effectively in ways other than writing or speaking? (Looks, clothes, body signals, actions, activities?)
- If you come from a culture whose dialect is quite different from the one used at college, or if you have moved from one area of the country to another where the dialects were extremely different: How did you navigate the changes in terms of understanding (especially with slang that you didn't understand) and communicating? What did you do that was successful? unsuccessful? What were you taught at the time about navigating differences? Was one dialect privileged as being "better," and how did you relate to this?
- If your first language is other than English, how have you learned the new ways that people communicate and how language communicates meaning about a culture? For instance, a traditional "see you later" in some Latino cultures is "*Vamos con dios*," or "Go with god." That would be a very unusual good-bye to English speakers, and it says something about the Catholic underpinnings of Latino society, that there is more religious feeling in that culture than in Anglo culture. Even a murdering drug lord would say "*Vamos con dios*," and it is so widespread that he would not be thought ironic for saying this. What ways have you learned about the culture you came from or your new culture based on how the two cultures' languages communicate?

249

Literacy narratives contain – in varying degrees – sociology, psychology, linguistics, composition, education studies (reading and composition), and you are asked to become sociologists, psychologists, linguists, and education specialists as you write these narratives from your experience or observations about how language works. Here are the steps you need to complete in order to develop a thesis with adequate content to complete a literacy narrative:

1) Deciding on a focused subject from your life experiences or observations is one of the hardest tasks, as you have probably never been asked to reflect on how you and others learn or use language. But think about it – language is something you began using before you could talk (reading verbal and non-verbal cues), and you have probably done more studying in your life about how to communicate to others and what communications to you actually mean, than any other activity. Is the way that girl flicked her hair at me a sign she likes me? How many times do we actually analyze language? Now, in college, if you are going to do a literacy narrative you are doing something you are already expert at. And if you are one of those people who does have a hard time reading signs and communicating – this analysis is a way to discover what cues you've missed and how you can rectify problems you have with communication. Start with brainstorming and listmaking (chapter 2) to find one of the many topics available to you from your life.

2) After finding a focused subject, use the rest of the exercises in chapters 2 and 3, and the analysis, evaluation, and narrative suggestions in chapter 10, to remember what happened when this communication you are studying occurred, and also to analyze and evaluate these remembered situations with all the complexity they deserve. As you work, be deciding on a specific thesis and an audience to communicate this thesis to. Sometimes literacy narratives become mainly causal or process analysis essays based on an analysis of remembered language development (and the audience is usually a scholarly audience) and other literacy narratives become problem/solution essays discussed in chapter 11 (and the audience usually becomes a group you are a member of where you identify a problem your group might have with language, and solution[s] to the problem).

3) As chapter 2 and 3 suggest, you work on this preliminary context and the content to match this evolving context until you have reached a point where you have a final writing context (focused subject, specific audience whom you have analyzed, a thesis that makes a statement, and a tone to communicate with that audience and thesis) and you have content that illustrates and illuminates the context fully for that audience. Then you are ready to start a draft.

Student Example: Literacy Narrative. MLA Style Documentation

Sherita Watson
Subject: African-American Low Test scores
Audience Analysis: The audience is educators and parents of students especially in grades K-12. The audience's ages will vary with an intended focus on educators in their first few years of teaching. I am a member of my audience on two fronts: I am an educator and a parent of two Black students. The reader should be interested in my writing because I understand the

250

obstacles that parents and teachers face in education. The reader should know and understand the implications of Black students scoring lower than white students consistently from kindergarten to college. The audience probably believes African-American students do not do as well because either they do not want to or their parents think it is unimportant. The paper should be written in clear and precise language to appeal to the target audience.

Writing Situation: a literacy narrative, an article in a national magazine or newspaper.

Thesis Statement: Some people argue Black students consistently score lower than their white classmates because of socio-economic status while others argue the low scores may be a product of institutional racism. I agree that the low test scores are a product of an educational system that perpetuates racial stereotypes.

Tone: Should be formal, serious, persuasive. In some of this there will be a controlled outrage!!!!

The Writing Context

Use context to analyze these student essays, and create one for the essays you write so that you know what you are attempting.

I am a mother of a Black student. I used to think that if I sent him to school and did everything the teachers asked to supplement what he was taught during the school day, he would get a good education. He went to school in our neighborhood, a good school. So, I figured I would provide a stable home environment, a good night's sleep, a nutritious breakfast, a positive attitude, and teach him to be respectful. Sounded like a formula for educational success. I thought, like most parents, that my son was progressing. His grades were good. Parent-teacher conferences went well. I was always told he was no problem. One of his teachers only comment was he should smile more. When he was in the second grade, we moved. The school was different. The racial make-up was more diverse. At his previous school, he was often the only Black student in his class. To my surprise, at this school he was part of the majority and several teachers, including the Principal, were Black. Unfortunately, that was not the biggest difference. At the first parent-teacher conference, I was told my son was two grade levels behind. That meant in the second grade he was reading on a kindergarten level. I could not believe what I was hearing. I panicked. The primary grades are the foundation to a good education and my son's foundation was unsteady. After several meetings with the Principal, I had more questions than answers. I went back to his previous school and met with the Principal. I wanted to know why I was never told he was behind. The answer I received astonished me: the reading teacher and Principal both looked me in the eye and said, "Sometimes it is to be expected that some students progress at a slower rate." They went on to say he wasn't a behavior problem and he was very polite. I had two questions and they both went unanswered: Who are some people? And why wasn't my son expected to achieve? Some people argue Black students consistently score lower than their white classmates on standardized tests because of socio-economic status; however, I believe low test scores are a product of an educational system that perpetuates institutionalized racism.

Introduction interests the more general audience noted above by making a statement about beliefs in rearing children that almost all would heartily agree with.

The rest of the introduction has an in-depth narrative to explain the situation of the essay to her audience.

The crisis that informs this entire narrative and starts the action rolling.

251

Paragraph Completeness:

Three in-depth thorough paragraphs, each with their own subject, outlining the problems African-Americans still have in terms of literacy in many US schools. Writer uses evidence and analysis from experts to bolster her own conclusions.

I was determined to find out how my son fell behind and why it was accepted and expected by his educators as well as what role I played. The first information I found was truly a surprise. In the United States, black students do score lower on standardized tests than white students. Most of the research I discovered pointed to socio-economic factors. Let's examine economics: economically disadvantaged – a fancy way of saying poor – families may have one parent or two working parents which leaves less time to spend on educational reinforcement with their kids. Education cannot be the number one priority if a family is struggling to eat and maintain a roof over their heads. This led me to examine our situation. We were definitely living on the edge of the poverty level. I had to evaluate our priorities and decide how much emphasis I placed on education. I determined it was a priority in our home. Just like most low income families, I realize education is the key to ending the poverty cycle. No matter the situation, we put education at the top of the list. Teale wrote a report on education that claimed examining a family's current situation may not go far enough in explaining educational disparities. He suggested also examining the economic situation of the grandparents. Teale claims overcoming poverty's effect on education would take more than one generation, but that it was not the lone factor in low tests scores in black students (qtd. in Condrone 697-699). The most convincing argument that poverty alone is not to blame for low test scores in Black students is an examination of the scores of Black children adopted by middle class white families. Christopher Jenicks demonstratess the black children adopted by white middle class families had scores equal to their white peers. Unfortunately, as the students reached the fourth grade their test scores were lower than their white counterparts. While there are strong arguments that socio-economics play an important role in the educational gap, there has to be another factor. Jenicks's research leads us to a different conclusion because the economic situation as well as the social aspect are both removed, yet the disparity continues.

According to the National Education Association, the shortfall in test scores is called the education gap. What is even more surprising is that the gap supposedly exists as students' enter grade school (Kazdin). How is that possible? What form of testing decides children are educationally behind as they enter the educational system. Phoebe Kazdin wrote that standardized testing arose from a social need to categorize or track the ability of students. I believe the disparity in the test scores is a result of an educational system filled with institutionalized racism. Unlike other forms of racism, institutionalized racism is hard to pinpoint because it is racism ingrained into the fiber of an institution by its policies and practices. The encyclopedia article that defines testing also claims the tests are written from the white middle-class perspective. The perspective issue is not just a minor point, but a major problem. Perspective is reality. As our culture emerged, the myth of the melting pot had led us to believe that all people think and analyze information in the same way. Unfortunately, that myth leads people to believe they are inferior. Dr. Na'im Akbar outlines how perception of ourselves changes how we perform as individuals. Trying to achieve on a test that by its design and definition was written from a standard that is not innate to the test-taker can create a convoluted image of self-worth. "The implication of this is that the mind's possibilities are limited by its concept of its potential" (113).

252

Second, let's examine discipline. A student breaking a rule is wrong no matter the race of the student. However; Black students are often identified as problems before they have an opportunity to impress upon the teacher their true natures. Rowley and Wright discuss a case study concerning a Black male student who transitions into high school and faces teachers who have deemed him a problem before meeting him. He is singled out and sent to the office for problems other students are given a warning about. Several teachers even claim they sent him out of class because they were afraid of him. The atmosphere at that high school is not an isolated situation. According to Nichole Dobo, the US Department of Education Civil Liberties department is investigating school districts in Delaware. The investigations stem around two incidents where students brought weapons to school. Neither student intended to hurt anyone. The white student involved in the incident was given a mild consequence whereas the Black student was expelled from school. The investigation uncovered startling statistics about the school district. According to this article in *USA Today*, 33% of the student population is Black and they account for 55% percent of the suspensions and expulsions. The investigation also uncovered evidence that indicated the Black students were not breaking more rules than the other students in the school, they were just suspended and expelled more (Dobo). This relates to test scores because if the student is suspended or expelled, they lose valuable instruction time. I believe it is more insidious than missing class time. The previous expulsion was affirmed by the school board. They are the policy-making body of the entire school. Henceforth, the hostility perceived may become real because of the unfair policies. As these decisions based upon race become the norm, they become institutionalized as part of the general policy. A survey of Black students conducted by the NEA found that 68% of Black students feel some form of discrimination while at school. I think this may have a profound effect on the academic performance of those students. Students may feel no matter what they do it will not be good enough. Imagine a school of 2000 students with 75% of the students being Black. If 68% of those 1500 Black students feel they are treating unfairly on a daily basis, that would translate to 1020 students who feel inferior. Moreover; the teachers of those students have low expectations of their Black students. I am a firm believer that children do and believe what they are expected to do and believe. Kids by nature want to please and they will rise to the level of expectancy.

My son prospered at his new school because he was expected to achieve. In an environment where the educators' number one goal was educating not disciplining he has excelled. I explained to him that the standardized test he would have to take did not define or measure his worth. He has now over-achieved and is in the advanced program. All Blacks students need is a place to flourish and the educational gap will close. Low test scores are not just students and parents who need to put a greater emphasis on education. Low test scores are not caused by poor families. Low test scores are a product of an educational system based upon institutionalized racism.

The conclusion signals the writer has finished by taking the reader back to the narrative concerning her son and his schooling that began the essay.

Works Cited

Akbar, Na'im. *Chains and Images of Psychological Slavery*. New Mind, 1984.
Condron, Dennis. "Social Class, School and Non-School Environments
    and Black/White Inequalities in children's Learning."*American
    Sociological Review,* vol. 74, 2009, pp. 683-708.
Dobo, Nichole. "Discipline Rate of Black Students in Del., Elsewhere
    Is Probed." *USA Today,* 7 Oct. 2010, *Newspaper Source (EbscoHost),*
    http://web.a.ebscohost.com.libproxy.kctcs.edu/ehost/search/
    basic?vid=0&sid=0ebfe8c0-c80f-4081-a03c-ed5a71ee9d6b%40.
Jenicks, Christopher. "America's Next Achievement Test." *The American Prospect,* vol. 29,
    14 Nov. 2001. *prospect.org,* http://prospect.org/11142001ANAT.
Kazdin, Phoebe. "Education." *Encyclopedia Americana. Grolier Multimedia (EbscoHost),*
    libproxy.kctcs.edu/MuseSessionID=0e10h8aex/MuseProtocol/40219745.
National Education Association. *National Educational Statistics.* NEA, 2010.
Rowley, Rochelle and David Wright. "No 'White' Child Left Behind:
    The Academic Achievement Gap Between the Black and White Student."
    Journal of Negro Education, vol. 34, no. 3, 2011, pp. 93-107. *JSTOR.,*
    http://jstor.org.libproxy.kctcs.edu/ehost/search/42910673.

Essay Exams

There are several concepts and definitions you should learn that will help you write excellent essay exam questions throughout your college careers.

1) Make sure you DO what the essay question asks you to do: make sure you understand EXACTLY the action verbs that a professor might ask you to perform. For instance, if he asks you to compare, do so. If he asks you to define, do so. Here are the terms that you will probably encounter (and all of these are defined, with descriptions of the content needed and any organizational strategy you must use on the pages listed below, and if an argument is asked for, review chapter 11):

    compare (which includes contrast) 43-4 57-60
    define 47-8 59-62
    analyze 5 46-7 58-62 215-37
    describe 42 49-50
    argue 257-94
    evaluate 6 237-42
    classify 44-5 52-3
    illustrate 43 50-1

2) Since good exam answers have a thesis, and content to support the thesis (like all good writing), before you start writing the response spend a few minutes developing a specific statement, and make sure you have several points that prove this statement with specific content when the question is based on knowing specific evidence. (Notice in the example below that in revision Charles's additions were all to make the thesis more prominent in his response.)

3) Great essay responses use transition words to make the connections between ideas clearer. Use when appropriate:

;however,	;nevertheless,	;moreover,
;indeed,	;in contrast,	;in comparison,
Since...	because...	after
when/whenever...	what/whatever...	which
For example,	;for instance,	

There are many other words, and students who can use these transitions effectively raise their grades immensely. See chapters 16-17 for details.

4) When you write, skip a line so that you have room to make revisions to the content or to correct editing problems before finishing the response.

Student Example: Essay Exam

For this response, Charles Peck was in a course that watched the Sam Shepard play (made into a movie), *Curse of the Starving Class*, and then discussed it in class for a week.
This is one of the questions on the mid-term:
Use an in-depth character analysis of one of the characters in *Curse of the Starving Class* to illuminate what the play/movie is saying about family.

The revisions that Charles added as he read his draft over are <u>underlined</u>, and as is customary there will be comments in the margins concerning features of this response.

Critique of Wesley Tate from Sam Shepard's Curse of the Starving Class

Wesley Tate is the oldest child of Weston and Ella Tate. He is seen playing the cello, at night, several times throughout the play. I believe he does this as a way to bring balance to his life, in contrast to the chaos that he encounters in his personal life during the day. <u>A major theme of the play is the chaos in American families, and thus in American life today</u>. Wesley is in the mode of the type of American ~~that~~ <u>who</u> refuses to admit defeat in the face of all odds. He wants to continue the farm despite the apparent fact that the farm has not been a growing concern for some time, as evidenced by the rundown appearance of the farm.
(cont.)

As with all good writing, Charles uses specific evidence, even in the opening which serves as an introduction.

He added in his thesis after writing the first draft and deciding his exact point.

Makes a specific overall analysis of Wesley, including evidence to strengthen the analysis.

255

In reading over the rough draft, Charles found sentences that were vague bordering on unclear. In his editing of the obscure sentence, he realized a related point which he added to his essay exam.

"This" in the rough draft was an unclear pronoun, which Charlie expanded, and he added "Nevertheless" to better show the connection between ideas. "Latter reason" is vague, so Charlie replaced it with the specific response.

After finishing his revision, Charlie added a final concluding sentence to make the essay sound more complete and finished.

The determinedness may stem from his desire to make something - <u>anything in his stifling life</u> - work ~~if only they were in charge. They know better than anyone else how to make the endeavor succeed, if only given the chance.~~ <u>A secondary theme in the play is the plight of American farm families who know how to make their farms work , but they are stopped by Big Farma, big business, and real estate hustlers.</u> ~~This~~ <u>This desire to make the family farm work</u> could also manifest itself from the idea that people, as a generalization, abhor change. <u>Nevertheless</u>, If he cannot make the farm successful, which is to say that it at least sustains the family, then he must come to the conclusion that he will have to do something else <u>with his life</u>.

I believe ~~this latter reason~~<u>this desire to know if he has to find something else to do</u> is what drives Wesley to make the farm viable. Wesley also plays the peacemaker of the family. He makes excuses for the failings of both parents to the parents when discussing the other one. He does this several times in the play. Of course, he does not play the peacemaker when it comes to his sister, Emma. Natural rivalries exist between the two, probably to express competition between people, whether healthy or not. <u>All in all, in trying to bring some balance to his own life, Wesley brings the only balance to the play, and its misfit family</u>.

256

11

Developing Persuasive Essays

Learning how to develop and organize effective support for your position on an issue — whether it be applying for a job, deciding whom to vote for, or getting an extension on a term paper — is an important skill you develop in college. In conjunction with this skill, you need to learn the art of gentle persuasion. Rarely do we bring about what we propose, or convince our audiences to change their minds, by making demands. Most persuasion occurs when we acknowledge others' viewpoints and use logic and authority to strengthen our position. To teach these skills, this chapter focuses on anticipation of opposing views, development of content for persuading an audience, and the structure of argument. The final section of the chapter discusses examples of faulty logic, not only those often used when people write, but those regularly used in advertisements and by politicians to trick people into buying a product or voting for a certain candidate.

An argument should demonstrate the sound reasoning of the claim you are making, using not only evidence but also logical, authoritative, and emotional appeals to support the argument. The thesis, or claim, you are making could concern:

- Questions of fact:
    / if something exists:
        Does a terrorist organization have nuclear weapons?
    / if a claim is true or false:
        Does a product or an organization do what it says it does?
    / if ideas or events have a causal link (does X lead to Y?):
        Does voting have an effect on a person's personal life?
    / how to define something (how can we define X and
    does Y fit that definition?):
        What are Republicans and what groups have similar views?

- Questions of value:
    / what something is worth:
        Will an idea for helping students become better students work?
    / whether an idea has validity:
        Do lower taxes create more opportunities for poor people?

- Questions of policy:
    / what action should be taken (proposing a solution):
        Would stricter drunk driving laws lessen highway fatalities?

Obviously, some or most of the arguments above could concern more than one question of fact, value, and policy.

Aristotle's *Analytics* and *Rhetoric*, written in Greece in the fourth century B.C., have been the basis for most discussions of argument and persuasion from the time they were written until into the twentieth century. The *Analytics* argues that one can determine the truth of a claim, using a precisely defined system of logic to mathematically analyze evidence and judge truth. For occasions when writers cannot prove a proposition absolutely, Aristotle's *Rhetoric* explains how to use appeals to logic, authority and emotion to refute opposing arguments and convince an audience.

The most important addition to the Aristotelian system of logic occurred in the twentieth century. A British philosopher, Stephen Toulmin, pointed out in his *The Uses of Argument* that most claims cannot be found either true or false. Evidence will suggest a conclusion, but most arguments cannot be mathematically found to be absolutely correct. He suggests that most arguments convince audiences with general, not absolute, evidence. In other words, as in the legal system, we use evidence to convince beyond a reasonable doubt, not beyond any conceivable doubt. In some arguments, there even could be many contradictory, though valid, claims. One example for Toulmin's idea of conflicting yet valid claims is claims made by literary critics, who persuade their audiences that they have valid interpretations of a novel or play. They recognize that others in their audience have different criteria for creating meaning in the work of fiction and so make different claims by emphasizing other evidence. Rather than trying to prove contradictory views wrong (unless, of course, they are either extremely illogical or morally wrong, as with prejudice or dishonesty), the wise persuasive writer acknowledges that there could be valid, alternative viewpoints or claims, and acknowledges that not only are the readers' views logical, but the writer's claim is logical too (and possibly preferable).

Writing Situations for Persuasive Writing

As with all writing situations, to create compelling argument and persuasion, you need to decide specifically what your focused subject will be, you need to learn about and analyze your subject, you need to analyze your audience and their opposing positions on the subject, and you need to adopt a viable thesis (a purpose, or using Toulmin's terminology, a claim) for your essay. We can divide argument/persuasion writing situations into three broad categories that produce different types of purposes for argumentative writing.

- **Taking A Position**

This situation does not involve actively trying to change your audience's mind, though if your argument is strong enough you may effect a change. To begin this mode of persuasion, you definitely have developed a position (a claim or an argumentative thesis) on an issue, and you must be able to demonstrate with evidence that you have a reasonable, well-supported position. You will need to acknowledge the strengths and weaknesses of the opposing positions, and your purpose is not suggesting to your audience that they change their minds, but that they accept your thesis as a valid conclusion concerning the topic. Examples of writing that take a position include these:

- A student or literary critic analyzes a work of literature and proposes that it means (pp. 234-7). (Great works of literature have many possible meanings.) The critic's essay would show that the thesis of the essay was a reasonable and valid interpretation, although he or she would acknowledge there were other readings and could discuss them as viable alternatives.
- A psychologist (or a psychology class) analyzes a case study and finds several behavioral causes for a neurosis. ("His father beat him and his mother left him.") The position taken in the resulting paper does not suppose that there are not causes working on an unconscious level that could be found in analysis; the argument only involves one set of possibilities — behavioral causes — and takes a position only from that set of possibilities.
- In a political science paper, a student takes a position on outlawing trade embargoes to Third World countries.
- A group of citizens takes a position, in a letter to the Mayor, that a newly built bridge has altered the demographic structure of their community.

The student essay, "Life Is Like A Box of Chocolates," in this chapter (pp. 285-87) takes a position.

- **Proposing A Solution**

This situation usually involves action on the part of the audience. You intend to convince your audience through logical, problem-solving analysis and persuasive techniques that you have a valid solution to a problem. You intend to persuade a more specific section of the audience, those who would be affected by your solution or those who would implement your solution, to adopt your solution. Quite possibly, you could suggest an outline of how they would implement your solution. In the course of your proposal you will usually look at counter-proposals, evaluating their validity and strengths as well as weaknesses, showing why yours is the best. As you can see, this type of argument includes not only taking a position, but also proposing a solution — in other words, problem solving — one of the most important tools of the successful student. Some essays (where many people argue whether there even is a problem or not) might focus just on the problem: whether it exists or not. Other subjects would be one where everyone agrees that there is a problem, so the essay would not have to prove that there is a problem, the focus of the essay would be arguing for a viable solution or solutions. In other words, you might be asking the audience to DO somethng, so you will probably have to convince readers why they should do it. Examples of writing that propose a solution include:

- A student in a physics class proposes a method to perform an experiment that has foiled her lab partners repeatedly.
- The psychologist (or psychology class) proposes a method of treatment for the neurotic case study.
- In a political science paper, a student proposes a solution to the trade imbalance in developing countries.

- A group of citizens studies alternative methods for rehabilitation of drug offenders to counteract the cycle of prison, parole, and back to prison, offering an alternative solution and convincing county judges and prison personnel of the wisdom of the changes.

The student essay, "Universal Preschool" (pp. 288-92), presents problems because some people don't see the problems, as well as solutions.

- **Persuading an Audience to Change Their Minds**

Changing people's minds requires tact, control, and a reasonable attitude. When an audience does not agree with you, always try to reconcile differences rather than quarrel. Acknowledge the strengths of their opposing arguments and respect their concerns and viewpoints. Never criticize, unless, of course, their views are immoral or unjust. For persuasion, use logical, authoritative, and emotional appeals (discussed in this chapter) to develop an argument that convinces an audience that your view has more weight than their view. Examples of argument that ask an audience to change their minds include:

- A letter from a student to the college newspaper's editorial page arguing that freshmen should be allowed to bring cars to campus.
- A newspaper editorial that argues voters should vote for a specific candidate.
- A student essay in a sociology class that argues handgun possession should be banned.
- A group of citizens argues that drug offenders are victims of both a physical disease (addiction) and societal factors (poverty and lack of education), opposing the argument that offenders have committed a crime and must be incarcerated as retribution for that crime.

"Health Care Crisis" (pp. 279-84) and "Alternative Energy" (pp. 274-77), in this chapter, try to persuade an audience to change their minds.

Educated people arrive at their convictions by analyzing all the available views on a subject, and then deciding which has more validity. The key word here is more. This is not an "either/or world" wherein one truth is the only truth and all others are falsehoods; it is a world of ideas with varying degrees of truth or falsity. A case could be made that America has too much debt now to finance universal health care, that its deficit should be addressed before beginning a far-reaching, expensive program of such magnitude. Equally valid opposing cases could be made: that citizens deserve universal health care or that health care savings from the universal care program could actually save money for the country in the long run. But it is only by analyzing all the possibilities for solutions and all opposing arguments that a viable argument can be decided on and argued successfully. Whatever stand taken in an argument paper, opposing views must be answered in the writing.

260

- Analyze political candidates in a campus, local, state, or national race and argue which one would be a better office holder.
- Analyze a campus or dorm issue and propose a solution.
- Read the local newspaper every day for a week to find issues that call for a solution or a change of mind.
- Pick your favorite book, television show, movie, CD, or music group and argue for its greatness and/or permanent worth.
- Explore one of these social issues, and argue for a policy that would alleviate related problems, or against one that is ineffective or harmful:
  - Gun Control
  - A Military Draft
  - Poverty
  - Stopping Drug Abuse
  - Taxation
  - Race or Gender Inequality
  - Environmental Issues: animal rights, pollution, global warming, human impact

Knowledge of the Subject and Audience: Gathering Facts/ Opinions

In order to write successfully, you must study the subject in all its complexity. For successful persuasion, you must find the following information through prewriting, logical thinking, and research:

- Facts and opinions concerning your subject (including analysis of their validity and reliability). Be sure to distinguish carefully between facts (objective, verifiable, reliable) and opinions (interpretations of facts).
- Can you corroborate facts by checking a reference source (an encyclopedia or specialized reference book) or a scientific research essay in a journal?
- Are the facts verifiable by observation? Are these facts confirmed by the experience of different observers? If the facts are from a survey, experiment, or scientific study, was the scientific method used to safeguard their reliability? (Professional surveys, experiments, and studies usually are reliable, but to check them, read reactions or contrary opinions published after your fact sources appeared. Also, professionals will usually acknowledge flaws in their studies.)
- Do several scholars in the same field make the same statement? Disagreements indicate you are looking at opinions, not facts. However, opinions backed with strong evidence have almost the weight of fact. Many ideas just cannot be proven, especially those concerning human or societal thought and action, and well-reasoned, logical opinions strengthen arguments. Still, opinions interpret facts, and are likely to be debatable. Decide how authoritative a source's opinions are.
- To what degree does the source rely on logic and facts for its conclusions? Study the logic of an opinion. Is it based on sound, reasoned, logical

thinking? Does it use verifiable facts (you should corroborate and verify them yourself) to arrive at the opinion?

- How authoritative, reliable, and expert is the source? Check in the library or its databases for reviews of the writer and his or her ideas in *The Book Review Digest, Contemporary Authors, The International Who's Who, The Directory of American Scholars* — ask your librarian what is available.
- As and after you arrive at a thesis from your study of the facts and opinions, find and analyze the opposing arguments that counter it.

You should always weigh the relative strengths and weaknesses of opinions in order to arrive at the thesis for your writing. For that matter, this critical examination of alternatives should precede all important decisions. Consider the presidential elections: many people vote without examining in detail the facts behind the opposing opinions expressed by the candidates. America is poorer for our inadequate study of argument and persuasion and the distinction between fact and opinion.

When writing argument, you aren't trying to convince people who already agree with your thesis. You are trying to modify the opinions of a group who don't agree (asking an audience to accept the validity of an alternate position or solution) OR are convincing people who have not yet formed an opinion that your thesis and/or solution is the most valid AND why they should do what you propose if action is required. So when predrafting and generating content, always have audience in mind. With each opposing view — and some will probably have a lot of validity — you must decide why your view is better. This is a very complex undertaking. By all means don't attempt this without adequate research and predrafting (especially analyzing the logic of the views you have decided on, the claim you are making concerning your subject). There are usually many positions on an arguable issue.

In summary, when you are researching always do these three activities:
1) Always look for opposing arguments to your preliminary view on a subject. Do not slavishly look for fact and opinion to justify only your belief; also investigate the strengths and weaknesses of opposing arguments.
2) Don't be afraid to change your viewpoint during the predrafting process. Analyze all the positions logically, and decide on the thesis with the most logical, authoritative evidence. Sound reasoning and solid evidence create meaningful arguments.
3) Your goal in an argument essay is to defend your position or solution as being more valid, reasonable, and desirable than other claims.

When you turn to writing, make it evident that you understand and sympathize with opposing views. On what aspects of an issue do all sides agree? What evidence supports claims contrary to your view? Be sure to list them: predraft specifically to list opposing arguments and their strengths and weaknesses. Then choose the claim with the most validity as your thesis.

Developing Content: Appeals to Logic, Authority, and Emotion

After analyzing subject and audience, and while deciding on a thesis based on research and logic, also plan how best to present the strengths of your evidence. Three common methods to reach your audience are appeals to logic, appeals to authority, and appeals to your audience's emotions.

Appeals to Logic

The most reliable method for argument is to address a reader's objective reasoning faculties through appeals to logic; the stronger the logic, the more reliable your thesis will be. Appeals to logic can use *either inductive or deductive reasoning. Inductive reasoning* begins with particular statements, facts, and evidence, and draws general conclusions from these. *Deductive reasoning* begins with general statements, or premises, and draws a particular conclusion from these premises. Scientists and police officers use inductive logic. For instance, a psychologist who studies a survey of divorced people giving their reasons for divorce can make a generalization on the reasons for divorce based on the responses. A police officer looks at a crime scene and draws inferences from the evidence at the scene. Critics, politicians, and lawyers, on the other hand, generally use deductive logic. They make a broad claim based on a set of principles, facts, or evidence. For instance, a politician will decide to vote for a new tax by constructing a deductive argument:

Premise 1: Cigarettes are the leading cause of cancer.
Premise 2: Cancer research and treatment cost billions of dollars.
Claim: Cigarette smokers should pay for cancer research and treatment with a new tax.

The key to effective inductive and deductive reasoning is to present valid evidence and premises. The three examples above might, or might not, be valid. The study of the divorce survey, an inductive argument moving from data to generalization, would be valid only if the survey itself asked the right questions and if the generalizations the psychologist made were logical. For the second inductive argument to be valid, all the evidence at the crime scene would have to be recovered. The deductive argument concerning cigarettes simplifies a complex issue and assigns only two premises to it. The argument still could be made, but opposing arguments would have to be addressed as well as a multitude of other factors, such as other causes of cancer and the amount of support for research already given by smokers.

A third often-used effective argument strategy reaches conclusions by analyzing the cause-and-effect relationship between events.

- *Inductive Reasoning*

For inductive reasoning to work effectively, you must, of course, make sure that the evidence you use is factual or at least authoritatively plausible; but secondly, the conclusion you draw from the evidence should be logical. For example:

Most students' home residences are within one hundred miles of campus.

This sentence could be a statement of fact. The writer could ask for information at the dean of students' office. If the statement was verified, then the argument would be strengthened, and the sentence could be revised to reflect it as a reliable statement.

The dean of students' office records show that 83% of students' home residences are within one hundred miles of school.

Whenever possible, base your arguments on reliable, objective facts, and use not only supporting content to verify them, but also specific data to show that your proofs are reliable.

What we have so far, however, is a statement of fact, the kind of evidence necessary for strong persuasive essays. An inductive argument draws conclusions from evidence, so when you use inductive reasoning, analyze its logic. For example:

> Since the dean of students' office records show that 83% of students' home residences are within one hundred miles of school, the school should fund a weekend bus service so students can go home on weekends.

This statement, by itself, would be an inductive argument, but not a very strong one because there is only one reason given. A stronger inductive argument would use several kinds of evidence to strengthen the argument:

> Since the dean of students' office records show that 83% of students' home residences are within one hundred miles of home, a student newspaper survey shows that only 23% of students have a car, another survey shows that 60% of the students go home for the weekend, and one of the stated missions of the college is to create a more ecologically friendly planet, the school should fund a weekend bus service so students can go home on weekends.

Conversely, readers also respect writers when they acknowledge that their information or thesis is open to debate. Notice how this writer points out problems with a usually objective measurement of reliability, the survey:

> My thesis is difficult to prove conclusively because surveys on cocaine abuse are generally thought to be more prone to error than most. However, based on both my personal observations and a survey administered by the University Health Department, the use of cocaine has decreased fairly dramatically in the last two years at this school.

The Health Department survey mentioned that the results could be erroneous, so the student also reports this information in the paper. This strengthens her credibility as a writer. She still uses the results of the survey, but adds other evidence to support her opinion. In the entire six-page essay, she uses personal experience and the opinions of an authority on the subject, a narcotics detective, to strengthen her thesis.

- ***Deductive Reasoning***

Arguments from generalizations are useful if they are logical. If you look at several representative examples of a group (of people, things, or actions), you can infer a generalization about that group. Honest analysis will prove whether or not your generalization is logical. For instance:

Air bags in cars were made standard equipment because preliminary reports and studies showed that they saved lives. Over the years, numerous reports suggested that people, especially small children, were seriously injured by these air bags. After several years, enough reports occurred so that the generalization could be made that air bags can cause serious injury, and furthermore, that the people affected adversely by air bags were small passengers. These conclusions prompted changes in air bag safety features including sensors that change the velocity of air bag deployment based on the size of the passenger and cut off switches to use when small children occupy the car seat.

The deductive reasoning pattern occurs like this:

Premise 1: Many people are killed in car wrecks, which is unacceptable.
Premise 2: Preliminary studies show that air bags save lives.
Claim: We should make air bags mandatory to save lives.

This law occurred. However, there was now more evidence as more and more air bags were deployed in wrecks. As the evidence mounted, another deductive argument occurred:

Premise 1: Air bags save lives, so we should keep them in cars.
Premise 2: Small children and low weight people are often hurt when air bags deploy.
Claim: We need to keep air bags as standard equipment, but we have to regulate them in some way so small people are not hurt when they deploy.

- *Causal Reasoning*

When you argue using causal analysis as one of the bases for your argument, explore the complexity of the causal chain. An effect is the result of a multitude of causes — and to ignore the multiplicity of causes in your argument weakens it.

For instance, to argue that "Johnnie can't read because of a poor school system," even if you have many indications that the school system is indeed weak, would of itself be a simplistic conclusion. A thinking reader would ask "what about his poverty, his poorly educated parents, his hunger, his inability to speak English, and many more causes of this complex problem?" A good argument essay would recognize all of these causes, though it might suggest a hierarchy of problems and analyze only one of the causes in detail and propose its solution. Make sure when you use causal reasoning that you examine the causal chain – causes each create effects and effects create causes. For instance:

Johnnie's poverty could be caused by any, or any combination, of these:
parental lack of education
a one parent family
parental physical, emotional, psychological problems
    (including for many, addiction problems)
economic problems in the area he lives in

265

Parental lack of education or physical, emotional, psychological problems would cause Johnnie's home to be a place not as conducive to good learning behaviors.

One parent families; physical, emotional, psychological parental problems; and economic problems would cause parental figures to be absent more from the home, producing the effect that Johnnie does not get the help he needs to learn.

Conclusion: The rise in parents who cannot give adequate support to their children suggests school systems should have a lower student-teacher ratio, so students can get the one-on-one help they need to succeed. If a school system does not have funding to create lower student-teacher ratios, the effect is more students who cannot read.

This example of a complex causal relationship could be extended. Realize when you make a causal argument that you need to examine the subject with the complexity it deserves, though your actual essay might focus on one area of the causal chain. When you focus, however, let the reader know that you realize the complexity of the chain:

While there are many problems that cause a student to fail in school, including poverty and lack of ability in the parents to help children (because of lack of education, personal problems, or economic reasons), many of the failures of school children could be alleviated by the school system itself.

Appeals to Authority

When Aristotle first suggested three methods to persuade (logic, authority, and emotion), the section of his philosophical tract discussing authority argued that successful persuaders should demonstrate their own authority to argue their point. This is still true today: you need to show that you are an authority on your subject. But, you might say, I'm just a college freshman, not a real authority; however, you can still demonstrate your authority by showing the reader that you have a solid knowledge of your subject, that you are being fair in your analysis, and that you recognize viewpoints other than your own. As long as you don't prove to your audience that you do not understand the complexities of your subject, you are satisfying Aristotle's suggestion.

However, you have another method of using authority to bolster your argument: make sure that your sources of information are reputable, and you can "stand on their shoulders," using their authority to bolster yours. Readers respect the opinions of experts and you can use their testimony to strengthen your argument. The biggest problem for a writer is determining whether the source is indeed an expert: use all the critical reading strategies found in chapter six to verify your sources. Is the authority well known as an expert? Does a textbook or professor acknowledge the expert as such? Also, check for reviews of the writer and his/her ideas in the *Book Review Digest, Contemporary Authors, The International Who's Who, The Directory of American Scholars* or numerous database programs at your library for information on the writer to judge his/her authoritativeness. Prefer books by standard publishers or those books found in academic bibliographies on your subject. Prefer articles in scholarly journals to articles in popular magazines, though don't discount popular sources. Just be more careful to verify their content.

Researching conscientiously, you also will need to investigate the bias(es) of the authority you are using. All writers have biases, sets of beliefs they are promoting in their writing either consciously or unconsciously. A simple example would be a political speechwriter who would choose evidence to make a politician look more favorable. The evidence could be valid, but the wise researcher would see whether there was evidence contrary to that presented by this biased source. Most biases are more subtle. For example, an astronomer might write a fairly objective essay discussing conditions on Mars, but if he wanted more money for research he could (perhaps even unconsciously) emphasize the possible uses for a colony on Mars. Most biases are not stated by the writer. You have to decide how a writer's preconceived notions shape the essay and whether a writer's biases interfere with his/her testimony as an expert. Read, study, and evaluate sources carefully.

Give your reader the necessary information they need to know how authoritative your sources are:

> Deborah Tannen, one of the foremost authorities on gender and communication styles in the world, argues that men and women need to learn and appreciate the differences between male and female argument style, and apply this knowledge as they communicate with the other gender so that members of both genders understand each other better.

Appeals to Emotion

Using appeals to emotion, you decide how to evoke emotions in your audience to persuade them to adopt your view. Many times with emotional appeals, you are appealing to your readers' sense of honesty, decency, and fairness, their sense of humanity. For instance, you might marshal all the evidence in the world to convince your readers that "Johnnie can be taught to read" by developing after school programs. However, if the programs would necessitate a tax increase, and your audience balks at tax increases (as most do), to convince them you might need to give an emotional picture of "Johnnie" in a den of drug users after school. Many contemporary social and political issues are decided with emotional appeal much more than logic or the testimony of authority. The most valid, objective methods for argument/persuasion are logical and authoritative appeals; however, audiences don't always accept logic and the testimony of experts. You might need appeals to your readers' emotions to convince them to accept your thesis.

Examine your writing situation: if you are writing a scholarly research essay in a college course (where the audience is your professor and/or classmates or you see it being published in a scholarly journal read by college professors who specialize in the field), you would be wise to not use appeals to emotion in this persuasive essay. They are just not used in this type of writing. If, on the other hand, your writing situation is a popular magazine or a letter to the editor, some appeals to emotion could be used.

Common effective appeals to emotion (if they have validity in the real world) include:

- The "bandwagon" approach: everyone believes (or doesn't believe)____ or everyone thinks ____ should occur, so you should to.
- Appeals to authority or prestige: a famous person (though not necessarily an expert in the field) believes ____ or thinks ____ should occur, so you should to.
- The *ad populum* approach: appealing to people's emotions, prejudices, beliefs. Wouldn't it be a great, humanitarian action if ____occurred or if people believed ____? ____ is just plain, obviously wrong.

EXERCISE 11.1
Appeals to Logic, Authority, and Emotion

Look at the predrafting content for your argument essay: your view and support; the opposing views and their support. Analyze your audience to decide the methods of persuasion — logic, authority, emotion — to use. For each supporting idea, develop logical, authoritative, and emotional proofs, and then decide which combination of proofs would be most effective. How strong is your argument? Use all the bulleted criteria on pp. 261-62 to evaluate your sources, their evidence, and your evidence. Can you think of any more support for your argument or any more opposing arguments?

Opposing Arguments

So far, we have discussed methods to develop support for your claim. This section will first discuss analyzing your audience and their warrants, and then discuss how to organize your persuasive essay based on the opposing arguments of your audience.

Understanding Opposing Arguments, Warrants, and Qualifiers

We have already discussed researching an issue and discovering the opposing claims, and the support for the opposing claims. Next, the wise persuasive writer develops his or her claim, finding the strongest of the arguments among the differing claims. Stephen Toulmin's description of argument has two more important definitions that need to be addressed for a writer to persuade successfully: the warrant and the qualifier. All arguments have them.

Warrants are the beliefs, values, and assumptions underlying any argument, and are almost always unstated. For example:

Fact: Joan took Jimmy's puzzle away from him without asking.
Claim: Joan should be put in time out.
Unstated warrant: Children should be taught not to take other people's belongings.

For someone to make the claim "Joan should be put in time out," the audience must also agree with the warrant that "children should be taught not to take other people's belongings." The audience still might disagree with the claim and suggest another action, but they must agree with the unstated warrant or the claimant will never be able to convince the audience. In this instance, almost anyone in America would agree with the unstated warrant.

But not everyone agrees on warrants for most issues people argue about, and the reason most argument is not resolved is that claimants try to convince audiences based on the claimant's warrant rather than the audience's warrant. For example:

> Fact: Motorcycle helmets save lives.
> Claim: The government should make motorcycle helmets mandatory.
> Unstated warrant: The government should regulate people's actions to make the world safer.

Many people who oppose motorcycle helmet laws do not argue the point that helmets save lives, but they have a different warrant: they believe the government should be as unobtrusive as possible in the private lives of citizens. So, they are not convinced by claims that call for increased government control. People develop their warrants from philosophical positions, and often arguments remain unresolved because the sides cannot agree on the warrants, the assumptions they make about an issue. For instance, let's take one of the most unresolved issues confronting the United States today: abortion.

Pro-lifers' warrants include: Abortion is murder so the teachings of the Bible outlaw abortion.
Pro-choicers' main warrant is: No one can tell women what they can do with their bodies.

The issue remains unresolved because the two sides argue using completely separate warrants; the most thoughtful people involved in this debate have at least looked at the warrants, then have decided that their warrants are more persuasive than the opposing warrants. Unfortunately, some people make claims without ever even looking at the warrants of the opposing sides; these people create very poor arguments. Perhaps the two sides in the abortion issue would reach agreement if they would argue a solution coming from a warrant both sides would agree with, such as: there should be no unwanted pregnancies, hence, no need for abortions.

When you are ready to argue a claim, decide what your warrants are, and decide what the warrants of the opposing sides are. For some persuasive essays, if the warrants are vastly different, your claim might become that one set of warrants is stronger than another, and you don't ever argue the issue at all. In an argument as complex as abortion, if you are a pro-lifer, your claim might be that life begins at conception and you would muster all the evidence to support that view, but also argue philosophically that this warrant is stronger than opposing warrants. If you were a pro-choicer, you might marshal evidence to make the claim that, with the history of crimes against women, they cannot be told what to do with their bodies, but also argue philosophically that this warrant is stronger than opposing warrants.

In most persuasive essays, you need to acknowledge that you understand warrants opposing your warrants, and first argue that your warrants have more validity than opposing warrants before you argue that your claim has more validity than opposing claims.

Carl Rogers, a psychologist who developed argument strategies calling for reconciliation, suggests that the way to win an argument is to find a "common ground." Some persuasive topics call for you to find those warrants, claims, and support that all sides can agree on, and then convince an audience by getting the opposing sides to agree on what they can. This is what was suggested in the abortion debate with the idea of ending the need for abortions, a solution that pro-lifers and pro-choicers could use as a beginning "common ground" on which to build a reconciliation.

Qualifiers are words that help make a claim valid; remember that argument does not usually demonstrate a certainty, but rather a probability. Examples of qualifiers include:

- ***Using** many, most, **or** some **instead of** all*

All football players at State University are dumb jocks.

This statement needs qualifiers: it just isn't true.

I hate to admit it, but some football players at State University are dumb jocks.

Depending on the writer's claim and the facts, the statement might need further qualifiers.

I hate to admit it, but some football players at State University might be considered by many to be dumb jocks.

- ***Some qualifiers are stipulative definitions that qualify a statement.***

The television news presents a biased opinion.

This statement needs qualifiers: for the most part, it just isn't true.

Most of the news talk shows on the cable news networks present biased opinions.

- *may **or** might **instead of** is **or** are*

The President is wrong about the economy.

Can anyone be definitive about this? - if so than half the United States is wrong. When writing effective persuasion, you admit when you are stating a statement you consider probable.

The President may be wrong about the economy.

- *probably **or** possibly **instead of** absolutely*

That student who doesn't do his homework will absolutely fail.

Never does? Absolutely?

That student who seldom does his homework will probably fail.

Carefully evaluate your claims and support to make sure that you have used words that accurately reflect the truth about a situation. When you use qualifiers appropriately, you are demonstrating your authority to make a claim. If you don't, your audience may not trust you.

Exercise 11.2
Predrafting and Outlines for Persuasive Essays

1) Using the checklist below, create a worksheet that proves you have all of the items on the checklist. For each of the items on the checklist, write a summary of the claims, warrants, support, and opposing arguments you have found. If you find that you do not have everything from the checklist or that there are areas where you need more support or analysis, do more research and predrafting until you have completed your preliminary work. After completing the worksheet, develop a persuasive outline using the information from the next section of the chapter.

The checklist contains everything you should have found in the predrafting and research to write a successful persuasive essay, so if some is missing, find that information and create content for the missing data before continuing.

This IS NOT a suitable outline, it is a listing of all the content you need for effective persuasion. From this list, you will develop an outline (discussed in the rest of this chapter).

A Claim
- The warrants underlying your claim
  1) Support for your warrants (are they logical?)
- Support for your claim (logical, authoritative, and emotional proofs to back your claim)

The Opposing Argument(s) to your claim

- The warrants underlying the opposing arguments
  1) Support for opposing warrants (be fair – what validity do they have?)
  2) Your refutation of the warrants (demonstrate the problems with their warrants and show why your warrants have more validity)
- Support for opposing arguments (be fair – what validity do they have?)
  1) Your refutation of the opposing arguments and your refutation of their support (demonstrate the problems with the opposing arguments and their support, and show why your claim has more validity)

2) From the list you have made, develop an outline using one of the patterns discussed on pp. 272-92. Modify one of these patterns as necessary for your audience, claim, and the support you will be using. See the example outline on the next page.

271

Arranging Content: Placing the Opposing Arguments

After you have completed your research and decided on a claim, it would be wise to construct an outline of your persuasive essay. This saves time because before starting the draft you can see whether you have discussed and answered all opposing arguments and their warrants, and can see whether you think you have enough evidence to prove your point. This section of the chapter shows four possible outline structures that are based on the placement of opposing arguments in your essay, along with four sample student persuasive essays that model the organizational patterns. Read this sentence: these models are meant to be suggestive, and since each writing situation is unique feel free to modify any of the patterns to suit your purpose.

A sample persuasive outline follows with enough detail for the writer to know that he has answered all opposing arguments and presented enough evidence. Notice how specific the context and the content is. This writer knows exactly whom he is persuading, exactly what his claim is, and how he will prove this claim.

Writing Context:

Subject — *Home Improvement* (the TV show) and male bashing

Audience — People who think that the female gender should be treated with respect by Hollywood, but haven't thought about the negative images of men.

Writing Situation — an article in *The Journal of Popular Culture* (a scholarly journal discussing popular culture, so this audience is college professors who have already thought and read in-depth concerning gender issues and television, and are knowledgeable in the subject.)

Tone — serious, objective, persuasive (the proper tone for a scholarly article)

Claim (purpose/thesis) — While it is certainly deplorable when women are portrayed in less than favorable circumstances, there are strong women on television situation comedies. Men on these shows are always treated as bumbling and incompetent, and this leads to negative impressions of the male gender.

Outline

I. Introduction: introduce claim with specific descriptions from *Home Improvement* as evidence.
  A. Tim as an incompetent talk show host and as a tool craftsman.
  B. Tim as unable to parent without Jill's expertise.
II. Opposing Argument #1: It is just a comedy.
  A. Agree with opposing argument, that the show is just a comedy, and
    very good comedy too: a sophisticated satire on marriage and family in the 1990s.
      1. Evidence from show (appeal to logic).
      2. Evidence from critics (appeal to authority [experts] and logic).
  B. Refutation: If this were the only show that bashed men, it would be acceptable,
    but *Home Improvement* is just an example: all television situation comedies
    have bumbling, incompetent men.
      1. compare *Home Improvement* males to *Married With Children* males.
      2. compare *Home Improvement* males to *Seinfeld* males.
      3. compare *Home Improvement* males to *The Cosby Show* males.

272

III. Opposing Argument #2: Men ARE bumbling and incompetent, especially around family issues.
    A. Agree with opposing argument, but qualify: some, not all, men.
    B. Refutation: even if this is true, how are we ever, as a culture, going to change and become better if we don't revolt against painful truths?
        1. why we need to change, using research to make point.
        2. how watching male bashing sitcoms perpetuates a negative cultural ideal, using research.
IV. Other male stereotypes in Hollywood.
    A. Rambo/Clint Eastwood/Vin Diesel types — cops/soldiers/renegades who are on adrenaline rushes are an equally odious image. Discuss and give examples.
    B. Workaholics — equally odious. Discuss and give examples.
V. Conclusion: Children get many of their images of masculinity and femininity from the media. If we, as a society, are ever going to reach a state of true equality between the sexes, we are going to have to stop looking at the opposite gender in negative ways.

Study these four patterns and use them to develop your own persuasive outlines:

Opposing Arguments First

I. Introduction: Framing the issues and giving the background necessary to discuss the subject. Also, any discussion of warrants, and the opposition's warrants (if they are in dispute).

II. The Opposing Argument(s): "Some people say. . ."
Sometimes I and II can be combined. In describing and defining the opposing view, with some essays you can also give the necessary background on the issue.
    A. Support for opposing argument(s) (Facts and ideas that are not questioned).
    B. Refutation: discuss the ideas and support for the opposing side, discussing why there are problems with the reasoning of these points.

III. Your Claim: "However, _____[state thesis]"
    A.-? Support for claim – usually building from weakest to strongest support.

This option is especially useful if there are two primary opposed sides to the argument and you want the other side to change its mind, though it can also be used if there are several arguments that are not strongly contested (when you are taking a position, as with the student example that follows, rather than the type of argument that asks readers to change their minds).

An essay using this option begins by discussing an opposing thesis, so that those readers agreeing with that view begin reading with the impression that your essay agrees with them. These are the readers you want to persuade to accept your view. When they read your claim after you have discussed theirs, they realize that your essay opposes their view. But by this time, if the writing has shown them that you are sympathetic to their views too, they will continue reading, in fairness, to see what you have to say. If your argument is strong enough, you might persuade them that their view should change. This option is also useful if there is a widely held thesis or position on a subject, and you want to introduce a new or controversial idea. By beginning with the familiar idea, the reader is not immediately shocked by controversy, but reassured with the familiar, with what is already known or believed (as with the student example that follows).

Student Example: Opposing Arguments First MLA Style Documentation

Charles Shaffer
Dr. Taylor
Subject: Alternative Energy
Audience: Conservatives who believe that alternative energy costs too much, carbon energy still has 200 years left, or that our science can change the atmosphere to stop global warming.
Writing Situation: persuasive editorial/article in a conservative magazine
Thesis: Alternative energy has been shown to have the potential to do wonders for the current state of the world. Our reliance on fossil fuels has blinded many of us from their finite nature and it may be too late to turn back. Alternative energy has infinite resources and applications so long as we are able to develop it further. Humanity has to remove its rose-tinted glasses when gazing into our impending energy crisis and provide incentives and funding to develop new technology and advancements.
Tone: persuasive, objective

Alternative Energy

Introduction frames the debate and the opposing sides.

Advocates seek to create clean and sustainable energy sources that provide more than just the benefits of electricity to humanity in a world of diminishing coal/oil resources and the growing environmental impacts of human society on the world; others may question the feasibility or even necessity in switching our current energy system. A multitude of factors led us to our current system

Opposing Arg I

Agreement with evidence for opposing argument.

of natural monopolies and a constant need for fossil fuels. Economists have argued that the funding needed in order for alternative energy to become competitive would be too expensive when considering a nation's economy as a whole. The potential spending allotted to the development of alternative technologies would indeed be larger than the current spending on fossil fuels and any attempt to do both could imbalance or harm the economy. In June of 2015 the arguments against funding alternative research were acted upon in Denmark. Journalist Melissa Eddy claimed that Denmark is widely known as a leading power in developing alternative energy and their success is largely due to a government fund solely dedicated to the development of alternative technology. The government decided to cut the fund in an attempt to improve the Danish economy (A 12).

Refutation of I

In terms of development costs alternative energy is more expensive for a nation; however, when subsidies are taken into account alternative energy is actually cheaper to a consumer and worth the money in the long run. One of the Danish government's main justifications for cutting the fund was that Denmark had been "a step ahead in green technology" and allowed itself room to cut back. The way I see it, the government acknowledged the need for green technology and only cut its support after numerous projects improved the

274

nation's sustainability; they just couldn't justify the costs when they compared themselves to the rest of the world. The government of Cyprus also weighed the economic impacts of such a fund, yet determined the fund necessary for the future. Robert Fri and Stephen Ansolabehere declared that in 2013 Cyprus was able to support the installation of renewable heating and cooling systems thanks to a fund generated by a nearly miniscule tax of 0.005 Euros per kilowatt hour. The cost of fossil energy is not comparable to alternative energy due to the fact that subsidies are rarely taken into account. The US subsidizes coal to such a large extent that its price to consumers is half of what they should be in order to reflect their impact on human health (5).

Others suggest that since the current method of production has worked for the past seventy years, there may not even be a reason to switch our energy sources. Fossil fuels and natural gas have been able to satisfy America's growing demand for energy as well as its rapidly growing population and can continue to do so for the foreseeable future. The Senate Committee on Energy and Natural Resources concluded that America's current coal reserves can last about 200 to 250 years if the consumption rate stays the same (Sovacool 115). Our current system can produce enough energy to last well beyond our lifetime which causes us to become unable to create a sense of urgency surrounding energy. That urgency will arise once our current sources run out, and they will. Natural gas and fossil fuels are finite resources that took millions of years to create the quantities we currently have on earth; they won't suddenly appear in 200 years simply because we need more. Our current system is perfectly fine when considering the lifetime of the current generation, but it is too inefficient to support the generations who will follow. The current energy system relies on power plants to generate all of the energy in one location and distribute it across its designated region to every outlet available. This centralized production of energy causes substantial losses in energy during the transportation. A study by the US Energy Information Administration (EIA) found that an average of around 7% of gross energy production was lost due to transmission and distribution and these losses can exceed 40% when in rural areas (Sovacool 112). These losses show that we consume almost a tenth of our energy pool for absolutely no benefit or outcome. The current energy grid remains too reliant on natural monopolies and is unstable when introducing new energy sources. Kevin Begos states that independent rooftop generation of energy has begun to damage the financial infrastructure of utility companies (812). If sporadic switches in energy generation is able to cause widespread concern over the stability of the energy grid, the current method of production should not be considered a useable system. And of course the idea that we can wait 200 years to fix the problem ignores what the current system of energy production will do to our planet.

When discussing ways to mitigate fossil energy's harmful impact on the environment, some suggest that switching the source of energy is not the only way to accomplish it. The burning of fossil fuels causes an increase in the amount of greenhouse gasses in our atmosphere and contribute to global warming. Scientists have begun to suggest that we attempt to artificially tamper with the Earth's atmosphere to modify its initial reflection of solar radiation or removing the CO_2 in the atmosphere. These processes will definitely have

Opposing Arg II

Agreement with evidence for opposing argument

Refutation of II

Opposing Arg III

Refutation of III

an immediate impact on reducing the effects of global warming especially in comparison to the low financial costs associated with them. These projects, however, only focus on these short-term benefits and fail to consider any environmental disadvantages in modifying the atmosphere. In 2007 the Intergovernmental Panel on Climate Change concluded that the proposed projects largely had no scientific support and did not include accurate estimates for their costs (Hermerschmidt et al 213). And I really don't think we should mess with the atmosphere we breathe, especially since all we have to do is change the way we get and use energy.

Support for
Claim

Alternative energy can support new methods of production that focus on local benefits and greater control over the energy supply. It serves as a great solution to the problems currently facing humanity due to our reliance on fossil fuels, but it may require greater incentives or funding in order to become a competitive option to conventional energy. Sovacool explains that nearly every phase of energy production that turns conventional materials into electricity damages the environment: mining, waste management, and emissions all have negative impacts on the environment and are implemented on a massive scale (110). These processes pollute the surrounding environment and slowly contribute to global phenomena that threaten our current way of life. Thousands of tons of nuclear waste could cause entire regions to become uninhabitable due to radioactive risks. Alternative energy sources nearly eliminate every harmful process of conventional production. Solar and wind generation facilities will have nearly no harmful airborne emissions or waste since energy sources like coal and natural gas are not being burned in order to generate energy. The resources used by alternative energy sources are also freely available and do not require extensive mining in order to access the fuel source.

Support for
Claim continues
with evidence
and analysis
until the clearest
statement of
the thesis in the
conclusion.

Alternative technologies do tend to have higher initial installation costs when compared to an energy grid that is already in place, but these costs are offset by the fact that renewable generators have much lower lifetime costs when compared to conventional energy. The Virginia Center for Coal and Energy Research found that renewable wind and landfill gas generators had the cheapest generation of energy when the lifetime cost of a generator was divided by the total number of kilowatt hours produced (Sovacool 119). This suggests that if initial funding for the renewable infrastructure and generators was provided, alternative energy serves as the cheapest source of electricity currently possible. Incentives to develop cost-efficient methods to produce alternative technology can easily allow renewable energy to replace fossil fuels in our everyday life.

Traditional energy systems depend on the centralized method of production discussed earlier in the essay and are unable to attempt any other means. Steven Cohen claims that renewable energy allows for decentralized production where electricity is generated near the point of consumption which reduces the energy lost in transit and can save money in power line maintenance (695-7). The International Energy Agency has noted that producing electricity on-site has the potential to lower energy prices by more than 30% (Sovacool 119). Decentralized production can not only lower costs, but make our energy sources less susceptible to natural disasters. With centralized production when a natural disaster hits a power plant, it causes an entire region to lose electricity for the foreseeable future. Decentralized production has a much greater resistance to these disasters; only the generators and areas directly in the natural disasters would be affected. Sovacool states that decentralized production also allows utilities to cope with rapid growths in consumption by moving portable energy generators or by quickly building new decentralized generators in the areas they are needed (113-4). It is easier to produce and move small scale wind turbines and solar cell than it is to update and create large-scale power plants. These also create a huge new industry that provides good paying jobs. Alternative energy can also relieve us of our reliance on foreign nations for our energy supply. America will become increasingly dependent on foreign nations for our energy supply and may shift troop deployment to protect friendly exporters of natural gas and oil. Our need for energy may start controversial wars and skirmishes such as the Iraq War and cause needless casualties. Alternative energy sources have an abundance of fuel in every nation on the globe. Sunlight, wind, water, and waste are the only tools needed to generate clean and sustainable energy once the technology advances. Sovacool suggests that renewable energy technology can also be used to insulate the American economy from fuel shocks and shortages and can increase the overall security of America's energy grid (116). Alternative technology can allow America to have an isolated energy market that is unaffected by affairs in foreign countries.

Alternative energy has been shown to have the potential to do wonders for the current state of the world. Our reliance on fossil fuels has blinded many of us from their finite nature and it may be too late to turn back. Alternative energy has infinite resources and applications so long as we are able to develop it further. Humanity has to remove its rose-tinted glasses when gazing into our impending energy crisis and provide incentives and funding to develop new technology and advancements. There is a solution to our energy problems, it just takes some work to get there.

Works Cited

Begos, Kevin. "Solar Energy Controversies." *CQ Researcher*, vol. 26, no. 17, 2016, pp. 797-843. *CQ Researcher*, http://0e1061yvf.y.http.library.cqpress.com.libproxy.

Cohen, Steven. "What Is Stopping the Alternative Energy Transformation and What Can the US Government Do?". *Social Research*, vol. 82 no. 3, 2015, pp. 689-710. *EBSCOhost*, http://0e1050k1x.y.http.eds.a.ebscohost.com.libproxy.kctcs.edu/ehost etail/detail?vid=7&sid=9aa25b97-935c-486f-8970-eeeaa50aec5b%40sessionmgr400 6&bdata=JnNpdGU9ZWhvc3QtbGl2ZQ%3d%3d#AN=112817925&db=a9h.

Eddy, Melissa. "Denmark, a Green Energy Leader, Slows the Pace of Its Spending." *The New York Times*, late ed. (East Coast), 6 Dec. 2015, A 12. *New York Times*, https://libproxy.Kctcs.edu/MuseSessionID=0e11t1svl/MuseProtocol.

Fri, Robert, and Stephen Ansolabehere. "The Alternative Energy Future: Challenges for Technological Change." *Daedalus*, vol. 141, no. 2, 2012, p. 5. *Academic One File*, http://0e11k1uat.y.http.go.galegroup.com.libproxy.kctcs.edu/ps/retrieve.do?tabID 02&resultListType=RESULT_LIST&searchResultsType=SingleTab&searchType

Hermerschmidt, Felix et al. "Beyond solar radiation management – The strategic role of low- cost photovoltaics in solar energy production." *International Journal of Sustainable Energy*, Vol. 34 no. 3, 2015, p. 211-220. *EBSCOhost*, http://0e1051m d9.y.http.web.a.ebscohost.com.libproxy.kctcs.edu/ehost/detail/detail?vid=31&sid

Sovacool, Benjamin. "Coal and Nuclear Technologies: Creating a False Dichotomy for American Energy policy." *Springer*, Vol. 40, No. 2, 2007, p. 101-122. *JSTOR*, https://libproxy.kctcs.edu/MuseSessionID=0e1011yo5/MuseProtocol.

**Opposing Arguments Throughout Essay: Many points in dispute
or multiple opposing arguments**

I. Introduction: Framing the issues and giving the background necessary to discuss the subject. Usually, end the introduction with your claim.

II. Discussion of warrants (if appropriate).
    A. Opposing warrant(s).
          1.support for opposing warrants (when valid).
          2.refutation of opposing warrants (problems with the warrants).
    B. Your warrants and especially any warrants you share with your audience.
          1.support for warrants.
Sometimes the discussion of warrants occurs with each opposing argument below if there are different warrants relevant to each opposing argument.

III. Opposing Argument #1.
    A. support for opposing argument (when valid).
    B. refutation of opposing argument (problems with the argument)..
    C. if you have a counter-argument related to argument #1 that better addresses the subject than the opposing argument, introduce it here.
          1. support for your counter-argument.

IV. Opposing Argument #2.
    A. support for opposing argument (when valid).
    B. refutation of opposing argument (problems with the argument).
    C. if you have a counter-argument related to argument #2 that better addresses the subject than the opposing argument, introduce it here.
          1. support for your counter-argument.

V. Opposing Argument #3 – continue pattern

    As you can see, this is a very broad framework that you will need to mold to fit the particulars of your argument and the opposing arguments concerning your subject. Not all writing situations will follow this pattern exactly. In some instances, you might agree with some of the opposing arguments; you might agree with some of the support for some of the opposing arguments; some opposing arguments might not have very valid support. In other words, organize each section using logic and proportion, but don't leave any holes in your argument. In terms of overall organization, create a logical pattern that works: move from points where all agree to points you make that are your strongest, or move from your weakest point to your strongest point, or invent any logical progression that persuades your audience.

    For example, David Butch's essay below follows the pattern of opposing argument/support/refutation for the first half, and then in the second half focuses on building support for his claim, which actually most of his audience would agree with. He continues to point out problems with his claim (many points in dispute), and then in the conclusion brings up a final opposing argument with a refutation for it.

    Also notice how David approaches his audience by agreeing with almost all of the opposing arguments' warrants, and by his careful use of qualifiers. He knew that many in his audience were unhappy with the Affordable Care Act but were also unhappy with traditional insurance, so in his evidence he focused on warrants he had in common with his audience, that people should have to take an active part in their own insurance AND health.

If there are several valid, or partially valid, opposing arguments/positions to your thesis, this opposing arguments throughout the essay option could work well. This option answers an opposing argument with your refutation (your analysis of opposing arguments' strengths and weaknesses, showing why your ideas are better) in each section of the essay.

Student Example: Many Opposing Arguments MLA Style Documentation

David Butch
English 102
Professor Taylor

Subject: The Healthcare Crisis in the United States
Audience: People concerned with health care, so audience includes people who are against the Affordable Care Act, but also single payer enthusiasts and ACA supporters.
Writing Situation: A persuasive piece based on research
Thesis: Compared to other developed nations, America has higher healthcare costs with worse outcomes. We need to reform our healthcare system, but many issues have plagued attempts at healthcare reform, including economics (ability for individuals to afford insurance), political differences and personal agendas (in the last decade around the Affordable Care Act), and varying opinions on solutions. By reviewing successful healthcare systems around the world, we can overcome our issues and create a health system that provides government infrastructure and makes healthcare every individual's responsibility.
Tone: Casual to connect with the audience but using persuasive and factual points.

The Healthcare Crisis in the United States

Introduction frames the issues with statistics.

America is facing a continuing and worsening healthcare crisis, with costs continuing to increase in a system that is litigious and biased, with flawed, inflated processes, and low health outcomes. According to Helen Darling, we currently utilize an employer-based insurance system with three types of healthcare payors: government, insurance carriers / employers, and the individual (92). Unfortunately, "The United States has the highest health care costs in the world, far higher than other countries." Additionally, health care costs have been rising approximately 6% per year. This is becoming a substantial portion of our GDP because the GDP has been falling (87). The rising costs make it hard for both the employer and employee to afford. Employees are having to refuse coverage or only cover themselves, not their families, when premiums increase (91). This increase in the cost of care does not correlate with improved outcomes either. Other countries are healthier for half the cost that the United States spends (90).

The US has similar service utilization and growth (how providers reach the health customer) to other countries, but disease prevalence is growing at a much faster rate in the US. Costs are increasing regarding chronic conditions due to

279

Prob I that all sides of audience can agree on. Use of reliable soures, with statistical and logical analysis.

1) the types of treatments required, 2) the length of care needed, and 3) an increased number of visits due to the conditions. Currently we are a sick-care system where we give care only after a person becomes sick, which is more expensive to treat. We should focus on primary care and the cheaper care to prevent people from getting sick. 31% of all healthcare expenses are due to hospital visits and Darling cites a PricewaterhouseCoopers' Health Research Institute study that shows 1.2 trillion dollars in identified healthcare spending waste related to individual behaviors, clinical waste, and operational waste. Obesity, defensive medicine (doing excessive testing or spending to prevent a malpractice lawsuit) and claims processing account for the largest waste in each category (98-99). One genuine issue with American healthcare is the lack of technology in hospitals due to lack of funds and inflated prices. Much of the government spending has gone toward administrative costs such as paper and pens rather than improving our hospitals and the care they provide. According to David Cutler, an economics professor at Harvard University, 200 billion dollars is spent annually on administrative services and nothing has been done to resolve the cost (2). This won't be solved overnight, but goals need to be set to overcome this issue.

Prob II that some in audience would disagree with, so evidence that there is a problem.

Frustration within the healthcare system occasionally leads to discrimination and biased opinions from healthcare providers. According to the Institute of Medicine's "Discrimination Leads to Healthcare Disparities," stereotypes can sometimes lead to minorities not getting the proper treatment they deserve. African-Americans and Hispanics are less likely to have private health insurance than whites. Some of these patients aren't even being asked and it is just assumed they don't have it. However, it has also been shown that ethnic minorities sometimes receive lower quality healthcare even if they do have the same types of insurance. Furthermore, language barriers tend to lead to frustration and possibly an incorrect diagnosis as well. Many healthcare plans do not provide translators for patients who don't understand English. Information can easily be misconstrued and that can lead to an incorrect diagnosis which could lead to much more serious issues (1-2). It is very troubling and disturbing, but many doctors work with the fear of being sued. This sometimes leads to doctors making the safe choice rather than the correct one. Doctors and nurses have enough on their shoulders, including at times my health. They don't need to question themselves while this is going on.

THESIS

We need to reform our healthcare system, but political differences and personal agendas have plagued attempts at healthcare reform. In 2009, with the Obama administration, a major attempt was made at the government level to reform the healthcare system. This attempt resulted in The Patient Protection and Affordable Care Act, generally known as the Affordable Care Act, or Obamacare. "The Patient Protection and Affordable Care Act" from the *Gale Encyclopedia of Everyday Day Law* highlights key components of this reform effort. These include: a tax penalty given to those who do not obtain health insurance (excluding those with financial hardship, lapses in coverage for less than 3 months, religious objections and American Indians); tax credits available for small business and large employers who must enroll employees into health insurance plans; and expansion of Medicaid to cover those ineligible for Medicare. Health insurance exchanges were created

Solution I ACA defined and described in this initial paragraph.

to allow uninsured individuals or small businesses to buy health insurance. Subsidies were made available on the exchange for low income families (2). Private insurance changes included a medical loss ratio component, temporary high-risk pool, dependent coverage prohibiting limits, summary of benefits and coverage, and uniform glossary. There are many essential benefits that must be included as a part of insurance plans and preventive health services must be covered at 100% (3).

Evidence supporting Solution I

Since the enactment of the law, approximately 20 million uninsured people acquired health coverage, according to Bara Vaida's "Is the Affordable Care Act Working?" In a five year span the percentage of uninsured Americans fell from 16 to 9.1 (413). In addition, tax credits have been provided to low income families which has reduced premiums. Finally, the improved access to care has improved health outcomes. Even with the proven successes of the ACA, continued viability of the program is questioned due to cost. Many health insurers have taken a substantial loss on the exchanges. Due to these losses, they will either pull out of the exchanges or they must raise premium amounts to cover the sicker than average Americans who have been utilizing the exchanges for coverage. Lawsuits have been brought against the Obama administration regarding government paid subsidies, given to low income families, to offset premium and other healthcare related costs (418). An additional case has also been brought to determine if religious organizations should be exempt from covering birth control. Another issue with the ACA is that the healthcare plan may change based at any time based on the whims of politicians. The GOP focuses on replacing the ACA and wants to: allow insurers to sell in multiple states, not require healthcare coverage for individuals, and make healthcare costs, including premiums, tax deductible. Democrats, on the other hand, want to focus on continuing the ACA by reducing costs, expanding Medicaid access, and creating a government run insurance agency. Some would like the federal government to run a single payer system.

Opposing Arg to Solution I

Refutation IS Solution II below

Disgreements between ACA supporters and detractors is Problem III

Refutation IS Solution II below

All these issues have created a perfect storm for an inflated cost system that doesn't increase health outcomes, but by reviewing successful healthcare systems around the world, we can overcome our issues and create a health system that provides an enabling government infrastructure for individuals to take responsibility, like the system that was created in Singapore.

THESIS: Solution II Singapore Plan

William Haseltine's *Affordable Excellence: The Singapore Healthcare Story* outlines Singapore's approach to building a system on "individual responsibility supported by an enabling state" (xiii). Their healthcare expenditures make up the lowest percentage of the Gross Domestic Product (GDP) of all the high-income countries in the word. This is an important economic statistic proving the strength of Singapore's system. There are three factors that Hastings attributes to their success. The first two are political philosophies that America would never move towards, but the third is a real possibility. The first, "long-term political unity": Singapore has been under the People's Action Party (PAP) since the country gained independence and this has allowed it to have an uninterrupted healthcare goal (1). Other countries, like the US, often have a change in leadership and political parties. This leads to changes in goals and how to achieve them. Also, when different Singapore government departments meet, it is expected that there will be cooperation to achieve a

Evidence supporting Solution II

(Notice sentence beginning "The first two" where writer acknowledges opposing argument.)

shared goal because health is affected by many areas such as: "housing, water supply, food supply, air quality, waste disposal, road traffic, parks, tree planting, and more" (2). The second success factor William Haseltine states is "the ability to recognize and establish national priorities" (1). Singapore had to focus on national defense and economic stability in the beginning years of the government before they could focus on health. When they achieved some economic stability, they decided to focus on public health. As their GDP grew, so did the health standard (3). The last main factor is "the consistent desire for collective well-being and social harmony of the country" (1). With Singapore's approach to be inclusive and fair, all groups benefit from government social services and economic growth. One program, the Central Provident Fund (CPF), has been instrumental in controlling healthcare costs. This program requires employees to contribute a mandatory percentage of their paycheck into an account and requires the employer to match. People can then use this money for healthcare, buying a house, and retirement. Having this money has allowed people who may not have been able to previously afford healthcare to pay for services while having a sense of responsible spending (4-5).

In-depth analysis of Singapore plan to convince audience that it is workable.

They established an expectation that citizens take responsibility for care and maintenance in all aspects of their life, including physical and emotional well-being (Haseltine 5-6). Yew, founding father of the new Singapore, created the foundation of how Singapore would operate: "the people's desire to achieve and succeed must never be compromised by an overgenerous state" (6). One of the first healthcare steps the county took was to move services outside of hospitals by building outpatient and maternal and child health clinics yielding a "high return for a low investment." They tried free healthcare at these clinics but found that people were non-compliant because they had no investment in their care, so adding a $.50 charge for each visit made people feel more responsible for their health (7). To increase their small number of specialists, they began worldwide partnerships with renowned medical facilities and would send their best doctors for training, resulting in a large number of physicians being highly-specialized in advanced medicine. They invested in improving their existing facilities by making updates gradually across the country and by providing subsidies for organizations to continually make improvements (8). They have added other investments over the years including: "clean water, sanitation services, clean environment, good nutrition, and health education." Singapore introduced the National Health Plan in 1983 stating broad health strategies including: "keeping care affordable, meeting the demands of a growing population, and managing the rising expectations of an increasingly affluent society." National objectives included: leading healthy, fit, and productive lives through active disease prevention and promotion of healthy lifestyle. The plan included changing healthcare delivery to focus more on chronic disease and chronic disease prevention over infectious disease, much earlier than other countries who did not recognize this until around 2010 (9). In the 1980's, public hospitals became more like private hospitals. This allowed for competition against each other, providing a quality and price benchmark for the private sector, and freedom for increasing effectiveness and efficiency, all which stabilized the system. Medisave, an expansion on the CPF, lets the patient pay for medical services and allows for healthcare costs to remain low

Appeal to Audience: Notice how writer emphasizes points in Singapore plan that would appeal to those who DO NOT LIKE the ACA, convincing them of the conservative principles in the Singapore plan. Great audience analysis to add these features of the Singapore plan.

because most of the cost is absorbed by the employer and patient (10).

In 1993 a Ministerial Committee released a White Paper, "Affordable Health Care," containing 5 points to address rising and unsustainable healthcare costs and the growing elderly population (11). The first objective is to promote good health through health education, disease prevention, and motivating the population to adopt a healthy lifestyle. The Health Promotion Board (HPB) was created and the government took the lead to reach out to agencies to conduct targeted outreach. They created national campaigns to build health and wellness into everyday life for increased promotion (11-12). The White Paper's second objective is to "promote individual responsibility for one's own health and avoid over-reliance on state welfare or third-party medical insurance." Medisave could only be used on insurance plans that had co-pays and deductibles to avoid over-reliance on insurance payments. In the US, private insurance costs are responsible for 20% of the entire health expenditure. This leads to over-consumption of care by patients, over-delivery of services by doctors, and favors healthy individuals over risky individuals creating a health disparity (12). The third objective listed is to "ensure good and affordable basic medical services for all Singaporeans." Basic health packages, available to those of all incomes, are offered by hospitals that receive government subsidies. Those that can afford and want more than basic care can get plans in non-subsidized public hospitals and private hospitals. They anticipated that the demand would grow as the economy grew (12-13). The fourth objective of the White Paper is to "engage competition and market forces to improve services and raise efficiency." They want to use market forces "to promote efficiency, improve quality of services, develop more choices for patients, and make sure patients are receiving good value for their money." With this comes the risk of oversupply or too many choices so the Ministry of Health provides price transparency on its website using hospital bills for common illnesses (13-14). The last objective is to "intervene directly in the healthcare sector, when necessary, where the market fails to keep healthcare costs down." The government owns health care facilities and at the same time "encourages the participation of private hospitals and clinics." This allows for a free market that functions between sets of parameters put into place when the market gets off track (14).

Until major reform efforts can be implemented to more resemble the Singapore Healthcare system, additional steps can be made to what we have in place. David Cutler's "The 2010 Health Care Reform Law Should be Improved, Not Repealed" outlines three initiatives that we could implement to improve the Affordable Care Act and help cut our rising costs. The first initiative Congress should enact is improvements on the delivery system through a focus on efficiency. There is currently a lot of waste in the delivery system so a focus on efficiency would work to reduce the amount of financial waste. Second, our malpractice laws need reform. Doctors practice defensive medicine (doing excessive testing or spending to prevent a malpractice lawsuit) and are not always pursuing better approaches for fear of lawsuits. Finally, the country's administrative costs need to be reduced, allowing for higher health care expenditures. Cutler believes the US needs to commit to reducing administrative costs by 50% in the next 5 years (1-2). In order for these next steps to occur, Democrats and Republicans need to settle their disagreements and focus on the end goal of improvements.

Solution III

What Americans can do now.

Many people believe that instead of improving current health care reforms, or creating a state infrastructure with individual responsibility, that we should move completely to a single-payer system. Buerhaus's "Is U.S. Health Care Evolving Toward a Single-Payer System? An interview with Health Care Economist Paul Feldstein, PhD" tells us only three countries have a true single-payer system: Canada, Cuba, and North Korea. Great Britain used to have a single payer system, but had to adapt their system after they realized they could not handle the cost burden of providing insurance for everyone (198). Some say that the benefit of a single-payer system would be that everyone would have health insurance since millions of people in the U.S. still do not carry it (198-199). Unfortunately, the issue with having a government funded health system is that health care has only one unit of funding. This would be an issue for providers to upgrade their technology and would disrupt their prescribing habits. This would also place a significant burden on the US similar to how it affected Great Britain. Nursing is also negatively affected by this system. In our current system there is room for growth and advancement for nurses. If we switched to the single-payer system, there is little room for advancement. In addition, it would affect nurse's wages along with other people in the system (199-200). While this is a good system in theory, very few countries have been able to achieve this system and make it work.

Our current healthcare system needs improvement. Even though we have made drastic efforts toward improvement, more needs to be done. A successful

system like Singapore that provides state run infrastructure that promotes individual responsibility should be considered for the U.S. Overall, economists and politicians need to do a better job of putting aside their biased opinions to focus on an overarching goal of healthcare improvement.

Works Cited

Buerhaus, Peter. "Is U.S. Health Care Evolving Toward a Single-Payer System? An Interview with Health Care Economist Paul Feldstein, PhD." *Nursing Economics*, vol. 28, 2010, pp.198-201. *EBSCOhost*, http://0e1056vbi.y. web.b.ebscohost.com.libproxy.kctcs.edu/ehost/pdfviewer.

Cutler, David. "The 2010 Health Care Reform Law Should Be Improved, Not Repealed." *Health Care Legislation*, 2012, pp. 1-6. *Opposing Viewpoints in Context*, http://0e1026vbe.y.http.ic.galegroup.com.libproxy.kctcs.edu/ic/ovic/439426.

Darling, Helen. "US health care costs: The crushing burden." *Information Knowledge Systems Management*, vol. 8, 2009, pp. 87-104. *EBSCOhost*, https://ebscohost.com.libproxy.kctcs.edu.

Haseltine, William A. "The Singapore Healthcare System: An Overview." *Affordable Excellence: The Singapore Healthcare Story*, Ridge Books, 2013, pp. xii-15. *ProQuest Ebook Central*. https://0e1046vbk-y-https-ebookcentral-proquest-com.libproxy.kctcs.edu/lib/jeffcomm-ebooks/reader.action?docID= 1172722&query=healthcare%20around%20the%20world#.

Institute of Medicine. "Discrimination Leads to Healthcare Disparities." *Discrimination*, 2008, pp. 1-8. *Opposing Viewpoints in Context*, http://0e1026vbe.y. http.ic.galegroup.com.libproxy.kctcs.edu/ic/ovic/ViewpointsDetailsPage.

"The Patient Protection and Affordable Care Act." *Gale Encyclopedia of Everyday Law*, 2013, pp. 413-28. *Credo Reference*, http://galegroup.com.libproxy.

Vaida, Bara. "Is The Affordable Health Care Act Working?" *CQ Researcher*, vol. 36, no. 19, 27 Jun 2016, pp. 413-28. *CQ Researcher*, http://cqresearcher.com/43985.

Opposing Arguments Not Strong, so Last

I. Introduction: State your claim and any necessary background information the audience needs that won't be covered in the body of the essay. Discuss any warrants that are necessary for your claim.

II. Move from the weakest to the strongest point supporting your claim.
   A. support for each point

III. If there are some opposing arguments, address them at the end with support for why these arguments are not as strong as your arguments.

This option is especially useful if the opposing arguments are not very strong, or not especially relevant to your claim.

Student Example: Opposing Arguments Last MLA Style Documentation   *Introduction states claim followed by supporting evidence.*

Veronica Heitzman
Subject: *Forrest Gump* (movie)
Audience: Those who feel they can't be successful or overcome trials.
Writing Situation: A human interest essay to motivate people to get out and accomplish their dreams no matter what trials they face.
Thesis: In life we face many obstacles and we never think we will make it through. *Forrest Gump* motivates people because it shows a character who goes through the same struggles we do today, overcomes them, and becomes very successful.
Tone: Objective and Subjective. Joyful and open to possibilities. Persuasive.

Life Is Like A Box Of Chocolates

In life, we face many obstacles and we never think we will make it through. *Forrest Gump* motivates us because the title character goes through the same struggles we do, overcomes them, and becomes very successful. Today we all strive to live the American Dream, the dream of prosperity, success, and upward mobility for us and our children, but we forget Forrest's philosophy, "Life is like a box of chocolates, you never know what you're going to get."

Forrest Gump is a man who faces many trials. As a little boy, he had walking problems and had to wear braces. Kids made fun of him, but that did not stop little Forrest. One day when he was being chased by mean boys, he overcomes his first obstacle: he runs for the first time and his braces break off. Forrest later achieves success as a football star because he can run so fast. After Forrest graduates from college (another surprise since he has a learning disability), he joins the army, becomes a war hero, and receives the Medal of Honor from LBJ. He loses his best friend, Bubba, in the war, and though he feels the pain does not let this emotional obstacle deter him. Forrest then becomes a Ping Pong Star and travels the world. He later opens up a shrimping business to honor his friend and then a restaurant (Bubba Gump). His mom dies of cancer. So Lieutenant Dan, his friend from the military, takes over the company but Forrest still receives his half. Then one day Jenny, his friend and the love of his life, walks back

Continuing evidence and analysis supporting claim.

into his life, but leaves again after Forrest asks her to marry him. To recover from his heartbreak he just starts to run. Thinking while running, he creates the bumper sticker saying, 'Shit Happens,' and the smiley face icon used around the world, making the two men rich and successful. After three years of running, Forrest suddenly stops and just goes back home.

Towards the end of the movie, Forrest goes on a journey to find Jenny. Forrest not only finds Jenny, but finds out he is a dad. They move into Forrest's house and he and Jenny get married. Jenny later dies of AIDS, but that obstacle still does not hold Forrest down. He finds his joy and happiness in his son and by making his goal to be the best father a son could have, since Forrest himself grew up without his father.

Evidence from professional critic supporting claim.

Rob Humanick comments: "*Forrest Gump* effectively stopped being a movie, transformed by its own success into an unavoidable cultural moment that came equipped with everything from its own line of catchphrases to a tie-in restau-rant chain." He goes on to state that a man with a low IQ score of 75 ends up being one of the most not only successful, but loved, characters in the world. He is a man of bravery, honor, love, and trust. Through all his accomplishments you see that. Forest Gump is the person we all wish we could be, in a society where the culture is about peace, love, and drugs.

Evidence from personal experi- ence supporting claim.

We want all the good stuff, but we can't seem to get past the obstacles in our way. When we face trials, whether it be a death, a failed experiment, a disease, a disability, or that things just are not quite going well, we think it is the end to our goals and our successes. My family owns a bakery called Heitzman's Bakery. When my great-grandfather started it during the 1930s depression, it was not such a success at first. Even though he was struggling, it did not make him give up. He overcame his struggles and found ways to keep his business going. He made it through the depression and we still have a few stores open today. My great-grandpa had passion and he knew that he could do it and so did his customers. During the depression, if he did not sell all the baked goods, he would give them to people in need for free. I believe because of his drive and his loyalty to his customers, his business stayed strong. All you need is a little faith and passion and you can do just about anything. Forrest Gump is that ideal, that perfect example of someone who did not let anything get in his way of becoming successful.

Opposing Argu- ments

Some critics have a different view. They believe that this movie is judgmental and does not depict that era. Max Lindenman, referring to himself as the "Gump grump," points out how Forrest goes through his life becoming very successful, popular, and rich because of the "values of his southern churchgoing mother." Forrest's friend, Jenny, is the rebellious one, protesting against the Vietnam War, becoming a Playboy bunny, into drugs and sex, and in the end is one of the first victims of AIDS. Max feels that the movie is making the era after the Vietnam War seem awful, calling out the movie for making a judgment on everyone who is not a "fool or the lunatic" (139). And of course (in partial agreement with Lindenman), the rebellious girl has to die, just like any wayward college girl in a horror film. Judith Zinsser writes about how she feels toward *Forrest Gump* and how it has affected her opinion about the movie. She refers to the movie sarcastically as the "American Dream" throughout the article. She states she is confused over people who like the

Notice partial agreement with opposing view.

Refutation in next paragraph.

movie. Like Lindenman, she considers the movie judgmental toward the era, and finally claims that *Forrest Gump* contradicts itself over and over: Forrest Gump does not get the girl and his son is another "Little Man Tate" (91).

I believe these writers view *Forrest Gump* in a way that is not in the movie's design. The screenwriter-director-stars are not trying to be judgmental and point out the negatives of the era, rather they are showing the human condition with its many struggles. This movie shows events happening in the latter half of the twentieth century. When you watch this movie, you are seeing events happening through his eyes. Yes, you are seeing a lot of negative events, but that's what he saw and how he saw it. You are supposed to be in his shoes and live it through his footsteps. This movie should have a positive influence on people, how we should face struggles and trials but overcome them. He never lets his struggles get to him. Every single time he moves on, never clinging to the past. Finally, he does all this with a humble heart, and with love. Forrest puts the needs of others before himself and gives back. He not only donates a lot of money to Bubba's mother, but he also gives money to a church so they can do renovations.

Forrest Gump is a person I believe we should all strive to be. He is kind, encouraging, humble, loving, strong, and he doesn't see the bad in people. He is also blind to how society is. He believes in himself and doesn't need the world to be satisfied with him. He is who he is and he has no shame. His personality is something as a culture we should learn and take from. We live in a culture where it seems you have to be like everyone else and you can never just be you because when you do, you are made fun of or looked down upon. Another lesson we can take from Forrest is never let any chal-lenge or trial keep you from accomplishing your goals or stop you from being successful. No matter what it is, let that drive you to do what you want, and to do it better, and with more motivation than before.

Conclusion looks at claim from widest viewpoint: human behavior. Leaves reader thinking.

Works Cited

Humanick, Rob. "Forrest Gump." *Slant*, 4 Sep. 2014, *Slant Magazine,* www.slantmagazine.com/fil/review/forrest-gump.

Lindenman, Max. "'Forrest Gump' Tries to Turn Back Clock but Distorts our Past," *New York Times*, 14 Aug. 1994, p. E14. *New York Times (1923-Current file),* https://libproxy.kctcs.edu/search.proquest.com/109287540.

Zinsser, Judith P. "Real History, Real Education, Real Merit -- or Why Is 'Forrest Gump' so Popular?" *Journal of Social History,* vol. 29, 1995, pp. 91–97. *JSTOR*, https://libproxy.kctcs.edu/Musesession ID=0e10193vz.

Addressing Opposing Arguments in Problem/Solution Essays

There are several possibilities with problem/solution essays.

- If many people disagree on whether or not there is even a problem, one would focus on proving either that there is or isn't a problem with specific evidence proving this claim. Sometimes solutions are not even discussed or analyzed at all, though they are usually mentioned in the conclusion.
- Some subjects are ones that almost everyone agrees is a problem, so a writer with this topic would not spend much time proving that there is a problem,

but rather would analyze the various solutions and argue for one (or more) as the most viable.

- Of course, some topics must discuss both the extent of the problem and the viable solutions to be complete.

As you research and decide on the rational approach for arguing about problems, solutions, or both, also think about the warrants underlying both the problem and the solution. For instance, if you have proved that students do not receive an adequate education in a school district, and one of your solutions involved a cost, you would have to disprove the warrant many people have that more money for education is not the answer to students' dilemmas.

The outline following, of course, must be modified to suit the approach you will take. This outline assumes that you have to prove everything, when in fact some of the concerns in this outline would be irrelevant for your subject:

I. Frame the issue by describing the problem in detail
      A.   opposing arguments (that there isn't a problem) if any
      B.   refutation: proving those that argue there isn't a problem are wrong, and there is, in fact, a problem
II. Discussion of solutions for the problem
      A.   support for the various solutions
      B.   discuss any inconsistencies/troubles with the solutions
III. Your claim: "_____is/are the best solution(s)."
      A.   opposing arguments to your claim
            1.   support for the opposing arguments
            2.   refutation of opposing arguments
      B.   support for your claim (usually building from weakest to strongest)
IV. Conclusion (if needed. Sometimes the strongest evidence is the best conclusion.)

In Cheryl Lynn Myers's example below, the solution is not discussed in great detail, that the United States should have universal preschool. Instead, Cheryl has analyzed her audience and focuses on refuting the problems her audience has with the need for preschool, the problems they believe are built into the preschool system, and the belief that preschool is often ineffectual. Notice how she qualifies some of her arguments to conform to her audience's views whenever she can.

Student Example: A Problem/Solution Argument MLA Style Documentation

Cheryl Lynn Myers
Dr. Hanson
Spring 2017

Context Card
Subject: The benefits and necessity of universal preschool in the United States
Audience: Voting public with a focus on white middle/upper class, and particularly those who think preschool does not help enough, takes away power from parents, and/or is economically too costly.

288

Writing Situation: popular mainstream reading

Thesis: The United States is behind other countries in the world providing universal early childhood education. Studies show that having preschool will benefit the country not only financially but also society itself. Much of the opposition comes from those who feel threatened by the possibility of poor parenting skills, and having the government step in to ensure our children are reaching their full potential academically and socially. I think it is both the fear of admitting we need help and the governmental tug-of-war over funding that keeps preschool from becoming a reality. The data shows over and over again that preschool is a benefit, that even if only a small one, the children are worth the effort. Children should have access to free preschool in this country, which allows parents who do not think it is valuable to choose to keep their children elsewhere.

Tone: A friendly tone with some sympathy to readers including some humor to show that it is not an easy decision. This tone will encourage reading and contemplation about the issue without making them feel defensive.

Universal Preschool

A three-year-old child dips a corn husk in blue paint, then yellow; then she smears it on a sheet of paper. "Oh! Look! Look what I did!" she whispers excitedly, speaking to a child across from her. "You made GREEN! How did you do it? Do it again!" the other child encourages. Both children make green over and over again, creating new shades, learning that blue and yellow together make green. In another setting, a four-year-old plays in an activity using tree bark, river rocks and small toy dinosaurs. He carefully places the tree bark on the rock and works at balancing the dinosaurs on each side, testing the number of dinosaurs that the piece will hold without falling over. He looks up at the teacher when asked: "tell me about what you are doing." He answers: "look, it holds one, two, three on one side and one, two, three, four, five on the other!" This is what happens in a low-income preschool classroom funded by state and federal money, experiences that the children may not have access to before they enter into the world of public education. Experiences such as these help children succeed and thrive in the traditional education system of grades kindergarten to twelfth grade. Studies, many studies, say that preschool can "provide more knowledge of facts and, perhaps, knowing more about how to solve problems and how to learn, and other cognitive advantages" and "these advantages were building blocks for the accumulation of more knowledge and skills in school." Research has shown that "children from poor families will have heard more than 30 million fewer words than their counterparts from professional households" (Barnett 279+) So, with this information, it is easy to see why these kids start off behind others when entering school. With the studies have come questions: is it worth the cost? Does it really benefit the children and, if so, do the benefits last? And how is it going to be funded?

Introduces subject with specific, direct observation to grab audience's attention,

followed by testimony of studies for preschool's effectiveness,

and ending introduction with the audi- ence's main questions.

Statement
of Opposing
Argument 1

John Miller writes from the perspective that universal preschool is not the fix all for what is needed in the school system and society. While this is a partially politically motivated article, it does bring to light that not everyone is on board for universal preschool. A statement he makes is almost enough to refute his article though: Miller writes that it is a good thing that children of the United States scored better than "26 of 35 countries" among peers on standardized language tests and that if we are doing better than average, why mess with preschool? (48) Ninth is good for what is supposedly the most advanced country in the world? No wonder our jobs are being shipped overseas. Are we heading for third world status?

followed by
refutation.

Still, there are questions about how beneficial universal preschool can be, and if the cost is worth the massive undertaking to our school systems. There was a study completed to support the concept of "too much preschool" where there were indications of increased aggression in children. The study completed by Canada's C. D. Howe Institute published a critique saying that preschool, "could possibly turn [boys] off to education," who do not develop at the same rate as girls (Miller 50). Miller also points out that a below average preschool can be more harmful than helpful for a child's development in a middle class family (52). Probably so. Steven Barnett describes the research started in the 1960's as a response to children entering school from poor families not as prepared as their classmates. This response to the need to prepare poverty children led to the creation of Head Start in 1965. With this program in place, research could study the effects on a large scale program. When data was collected on IQ of children showed that there were no permanent effects, some researchers decided that "preschool failed to help disadvantaged children" (279+).

More detail
for Opposing
Argument 1

Notice the
'Probably so'
where Cheryl
agrees with
part of oppos-
ing argument

Opposing
Argument II

Refutation
of previous
paragraph's
Opposing
Arguments.

However, the problem with testing what children are learning in preschool with the old style "drill and skill" method: it does not take into account the backgrounds of impoverished children. The errors some find could be found in who administered the tests, different tests could have been given at different schools, and schools only tested by grade, not with their original group (Kirp 3). And other studies, cited in the next paragraph, disagree with the findings that preschool does not help, especially with children of poverty.

Opposing
Argument III

A third concern: many parents feel offended, believing that universal preschool suggests they are not good parents. But in the twenty-first century, parents need all the help they can get from whatever the source. You can't argue with success: Bracey and Stellar use studies to show that the exposure to preschool greatly influences later years of schooling, higher graduation rates, home ownership, and successful marriages. The children of the studies were more likely to go to college and complete "more years of schooling" than those who did not participate. Steven Barnett agrees with evidence showing that, overall, there are benefits making preschool an "economically efficient public investment." The benefits are long-term, but not always measurable with an IQ test. There are also the benefits for society, with lower teen pregnancies, higher employment rates, and less welfare assistance. Barnett points out there is an "implication for other human capital" that "finding that IQ test scores do not adequately capture the effects of preschool education on cognitive human capital suggests that economists risk serious errors if they

Refutation,
which is also
evidence for
the claim of
the essay.

290

do not account for the complexities of cognitive abilities in research on human capital." From what the studies show, having children score one to two grade levels ahead after participating in a preschool program for children in poverty compared to children not included is so dramatic that it draws attention to the need for preschool (279+). Children, especially those in poverty, need to have access to universal preschool. Perhaps what America should have is free ACCESS to preschool. If parents decide to teach their children at home, after all, we are the land of individual choice and freedom.

Lynn Karoly provides proof of economic benefits for preschool programs along with the challenges for deciphering the evaluations conducted over the years. There were economic and non-direct economic benefits with the evaluations (39). Economic studies show savings to a school district when a child would not have to repeat a grade, and also when less special education classes would be required. There is also data available to show the income earnings for preschool participants increased for lifetime earnings at different ages in life. The non-direct economic issues already mentioned include situations like high school graduation rates, less welfare assistance, lower teen-pregnancy rates, and lower substance abuse rates. Other benefits would be that working mothers could have a more stable working experience that would equate to earning "$133,000" more over their lifetime (44). Imagine the savings in day care with universal preschool!!!

But Bracey and Stellar do warn that the cost of high-quality childcare education is expensive, with the initial sticker-shock needing to be overlooked to see the benefits of early childhood education (782). David Kirp states that "it costs about $8000 a year for a child to attend a Child-Parent Center." That is a lot of money, but, "when measured against the results, that's an amazing bargain-for every dollar invested, there's a $7.10 return to society" (3). Miller does point out that it is not financially realistic to have every child in a prestigious preschool to become prepared for kindergarten. He also states that the control group for today in comparison for the original study cannot compare because preschool is available more now than when the study was started (50).

Bracey and Stellar contrast the United States' daycare programs to other countries like England, Italy, and Sweden by stating the United States has a "non-system" for education while "the other countries, especially Sweden, have coherent, comprehensive programs based on a set of assumptions about the positive outcomes of early education." These countries look at early education as an investment, while the United States "has historically resisted major government intrusions into the early years of education because such intervention would signal a failure on the part of the family." While this may be the case, the data from the studies show that the U.S. needs to get over such beliefs and digest the positive benefits of early childhood education (781). Kirp writes in his article "All My Children" about the preschool programs that have been put in place in Chicago, and about how well they are performing. Children have been shown to learn best through a hands-on approach where they experience and explore the environment around them (1).

More evidence for claim which also refutes opposing arguments.

Cheryl discusses one problem with universal preschool, cost, but gives statistics (with evidence from previous paragraph)to demonstrate that the cost is a good investment.

Placing subject of universal preschool in a wider world-wide context (with continued support for claim).

This way of learning is in contrast to the way Head Start has shifted its teaching. They used to be focused on "social-emotional development and problem-oriented learning" with them now focusing on "decoding language and numbers." There is a push for testing of this information, in spite of proof that "skill and drill" teaching merely helps "poor kids catch up" while it "didn't help middle class kids in the first place" (Kirp 2).

Readers love honesty: discusses problem with universal preschool that should be addressed.

Kirp shows in a 2004 study that "while preschoolers whose teachers took a didactic approach [the skill and drill method] did better at the end of kindergarten, the reverse was true later on. Children who were in preschool classrooms that emphasized child initiated learning had higher eighth-grade reading scores and higher rates of high school graduation" (3). So preschool programs need to be brought up to date with the latest research.

And concluding with final call for support for universal preschool.

While universal preschool is not a magic potion to complete educational success, it is a step in the right direction. It is expensive, just like anything of worth or value, but it is shown over and over again in studies to reap benefits for children. It is common knowledge that the American taxpayers pay for federal programs to save endangered species, why is it so hard to expect Americans to help pay for universal preschool? The funding issue is a non-issue; the money is there. The amount of children and families' universal preschool benefits outweighs the initial start-up cost.

Works Cited

Barnett, Steven W. "Benefits of compensatory preschool education." *Journal of Human Resources,* vol. 27, no. 2, 1992, p. 279+. *Academic OneFile,* go.galegroup.com/ps/i.do?p=AONE&sw=w&u=kctcsjcc&v=2.1&it

Bracey, Gerald W. and Arthur Stellar. "Long-Term Studies of Preschool: Lasting Benefits Far Outweigh Costs." *Phi Delta Kappan*, vol. 84, no. 10, Jun. 2003, p. 780-788. *EBSCOhost,* search.ebscohost.com/login.aspx?d irect=true&db=a9h&AN=9928697&site=ehost-live.

Karoly, Lynn A. "The Economic Returns to Early Childhood Education." *The Future of Children*, vol. 26, no. 2, 2016, pp. 37–55. *JSTOR,* www.jstor.org/stable/43940580.

Miller, John J. "Preschool for All!" *National Review*, vol. 59, no. 18, 08 Oct. 2007, pp. 48-52. *EBSCOhost*, search.ebscohost.com/login.aspx? direct=true&db=a9h&AN=26898590.

Kirp, David L. "All My Children." *The New York Times,* 31 Jul. 2005, *New York Times*, libproxy.kctcs.edu/Jefferson?groupID=1&action=source&source ID=/docview/4331055.

Fallacies and Problems with Logic

Illogical thinking creates faulty prose. As you read, carefully evaluate each claim to see if it contains faulty reasoning, and as you revise your own writing, evaluate each of your own claims for the same flaws. Many of the mistakes in logic that will be discussed in this section are fallacies that people succumb to each day; in fact, politicians and advertisers regularly use these fallacies to help sell their ideas or products. Use this section as a reference guide for revising your writing, but as you read it also become aware of the influence that these shoddy arguments have on you and the public. After studying this section on logical fallacies, you might change the way you buy products, evaluate political candidates, and decide important issues.

This section lists sixteen types of fallacies. 1 and 2 are false appeals to authority; 3 is an appeal to emotion; and 4-16 are false appeals to logic, i.e., they are illogical.

1-3 examine fallacies usually found in advertising ; 4-11 often appear in written essays; 12-14 often appear in journalistic writing; and 15-16 are everyday problems with logical thinking (though they also appear in essay writing). Politicians frequently use all sixteen: pay attention from now on.

Logical fallacies are sometimes referred to by their Latin names (in parentheses).

Study the first three fallacies carefully. They can be used with emotional appeals, and while strictly speaking they are "cheating" (using emotions to sway an audience rather than facts, truth, and logic), on the other hand, they are very effective (which is why advertisers use them so much). Emotional appeals do have their place in persuasive writing, though they should be a third minor component of an argument in addition to logical and authoritative appeals.

4-16 need to be eliminated from your writing, and when people try to use 4-16 to convince you, don't be fooled.

Product Advertisement

1)   Bandwagon or "join the crowd": This argument states, in effect, that "Everybody else believes this — so you should too."

> Faulty: *Beavis and Butthead* has been at the top of the Neilson ratings since it began; it should be your favorite too.
> Better: Since *Beavis and Butthead* is such a favorite with the public in the Neilson ratings, maybe those who don't like it should re-evaluate it and try to see what makes the show so popular.

2)   Appeal to authority or prestige: A famous person is used to endorse a product, or an authority that has no special knowledge in the field endorses a claim in that area of knowledge.

> Faulty: Bill Cosby says "Coke is it."
> (Bill Cosby might be a fine actor, but are his taste buds superior to other people's?)

Faulty: Dr. Melvin Jones, the respected writer of many famous novels, has stated that the world will be overpopulated and we could die of starvation near the end of the next century.

(Dr. Jones might be a fine novelist, but is there any evidence that he is an expert on population predictions? Notice that his title, Doctor, adds to this "authority," leading careless readers to allow his statement as fact, not opinion.)

3) Appealing to the people (*ad populum*): This device uses popular emotions, prejudices, and beliefs to convince — "buttering up" the audience.

Faulty: The majority of Americans today are intelligent, compassionate, and sensible people; to reflect the will of the people, censorship laws should be implemented.

(This is also an example of *non sequitur* (see #4 below). Not only is the writer appealing to the audience's vanity, but also the conclusion does not follow from the opening statement that "Americans are intelligent, compassionate, and sensible people.")

Faulty: Chevrolet - the Heartbeat of America

(Americans want to be thought of as warm, emotional, full of heart, and this "heart" connection to Chevrolet subconsciously drives consumers to buy Chevys.)

Fallacies of Logic

4) It does not follow (*non sequitur*): The "evidence" in the opening statement (the premise) is irrelevant to the conclusion.

Faulty: *Rocky* was a successful movie, so *Rocky 5* will be a successful movie when it opens.

(Just because *Rocky* was successful, does not ensure that *Rocky 5* will be successful.)

Better: Since *Rocky* was a successful movie, that increases the chance of *Rocky 5* being a successful movie.

5) Begging the Question (*petitio principii*): This fallacy presents the same ideas in both the premise and the conclusion.

Faulty: Poor training in public schools causes poorly trained students.

Better: Poor teaching methods in public schools are one of many reasons for students not learning.

6) After this, therefore because of this (*post hoc, ergo propter hoc,* usually called *post hoc* reasoning): This fallacy holds that merely because one event followed another, the first event caused the second. Actually, it could have been a variety of complex reasons or even chance or coincidence that caused the second event.

> Faulty: The witch doctor did a rain dance and then there was a great clap of thunder, proving his power.
> Better: The villagers thought they saw proof of the witch doctor's power when a clap of thunder followed his rain dance.

7) Self-contradiction: This sort of argument contains mutually exclusive ideas (or premises).
> Faulty: The Army should manage the uncontrollable situation in Africa. ("Uncontrollable situations" cannot be "managed.")
> Better: While the Army cannot control an uncontrollable situation, it should try to do what it can to preserve peace in Africa.

8) Ambiguity: An ambiguous statement or argument can be interpreted in two or more ways.

> Faulty: Lee Marvin is a poor actor.
> Better: Lee Marvin does not act well. or Lee Marvin is on the verge of bankruptcy.

9) False Division (either/or): This type of statement oversimplifies the complexity of a situation by eliminating the possibility of an answer between two extremes.

> Faulty: All politicians are either good or bad.
> Better: Some politicians are called "good" and others are termed "bad," but this is rarely the case. There is a bit of good in the worst of them, and a bit of bad in the best of them.

10) Attacking the person (*ad hominem*): This fallacy attempts to disprove an argument by attacking the person who formed it.

> Faulty: Bob Dole is handicapped from a World War Two injury, so he couldn't make the kind of dynamic, energetic President he suggests he would.   (Just because Dole is handicapped does not mean he would not make a dynamic President.)

11) Ignoring the question or rambling: Details that do not support the conclusion are cited as if they do.

> Faulty: Profanity, even on cable television, should be strictly abolished. Of course, there are a great variety of shows to be seen on television today. Many children see shows that I saw when I was a child.

12) Slanting: Sometimes key facts are omitted or rearranged to mislead the reader. A writer cannot present only a portion of a quotation, or rearrange it so that the meaning of the original has been changed.

> Magazine Headline: Secret of Eternal Youth found years ago and Hidden from the Public by Unscrupulous Doctors!
> What was actually said: Medical schools have just begun to include a course in wellness techniques (proper diet, exercise, and stress relief). These techniques have been proven to increase life spans and improve the quality of life, especially in the elderly.

13) Hasty generalization: This fallacy draws a conclusion from too little evidence or from evidence that is biased in some exceptional or unusual way.

> Faulty: None of my friends in high school liked *Star Wars*, so high school kids do not like *Star Wars*.   (One group of friends is not a large enough sampling of high school students to warrant a generalization like this — there is too little evidence.)

> Faulty: "When a robbery occurs in the city, the police are never there," the concerned citizen complained. (The police cannot be expected to be everywhere in the city at once.)

14)   Oversimplification: An oversimplified statement or argument leaves out relevant considerations in an issue. Headlines in newspapers often are guilty of oversimplification.

> Faulty: Actors who are picked for television shows are usually lucky.
> Faulty Headline: Television Actors Lucky
> Better: Actors who are picked for television shows are usually lucky, although in their defense they have also prepared for many years on the stage.

Everyday Problems With Logical Thinking

15) Over-complicated thesis: The best thesis is usually the simplest thesis that explains all the facts. Be suspicions of a complicated thesis. Remember, however, not to oversimplify.

> Faulty: After one week, the gentleman had not heard from the company to which he had applied for work. He began to worry that the employer had not liked him, that he had been too nervous at the interview, that he had asked for too much money, and that his past work record was not good enough. He finally decided to get a much lower paying job and found one the first day.
> Probable Reason: The employer was busy with other tasks that required his immediate attention.

16) False Analogy: A comparison in which the two objects or experiences are not logically related.

> Faulty: The President of the United States is like the head of a household who has a fiscal responsibility for his/her family, i.e., citizens. He or she wants to be generous, but has to have a tight budget for the good of all.
> (The analogy appears to be logical, but when analyzed it has flaws. The head of a household personally loves the members of the family; the President cannot love everyone in the same way. The head of a household should teach children in the house fiscal responsibility which could include both depriving and lavishing presents; the President does not have that same responsibility. Obviously, the sizes of the "households" in the analogy also are too different to be a useful comparison. If you want to use an analogy, analyze it for its effectiveness. Can it bear close scrutiny?)

EXERCISE 11.3
Identifying Logical Fallacies
As with the example below, decide which logical fallacy or fallacies the statement contains, and in a sentence or two discuss what makes the statement fallacious. As you will see, included here are several statements that many Americans hold true. Many people hold positions that have an element of illogic within them. Critical thinkers need to be able to realize they sometimes hold positions that do have an element of illogic in them, and they need to have analyzed these positions so when they do hold positions with an element of illogic, that the premise is so strong they are willing to hold them even if they are not perfect.

1. The students all received poor grades on their quiz, so they did not study enough.
Oversimplification and post hoc reasoning: The teacher might not have taught the information in a way the students could understand, they might not have had enough time to study, or there could have been a school activity or another class's assignment that kept them from studying for the quiz. The reasoning that the students did not study enough could in fact be true, but there needs to be more evidence to support this statement.

2. Joe Smith is a bad candidate for the city council because he did not do well in school and owned a business that failed.

3. One either has to be for gun control or against it.

297

4. President Bush says that the Iraqis have weapons of mass destruction.

5. Raising a family is like coaching a Little League team.

6. There are too many assignments in that class, so it is a bad class.

7. My girlfriend left me so I shouldn't have ever dated her.

8. The Supreme Court should strictly interpret the Constitution.

9. Americans love freedom, so we should protect freedom wherever forces endanger it.

EXERCISE 11.4
Edit Essay for Faulty Logic

Study the previous six pages carefully, and then read your essay slowly, particularly looking for lapses in logic and reasoning. Careful readers spot these fallacies, and when they see one, it often makes them discount the entire argument, so edit your essay carefully to avoid faulty logic.

12

Writing for Business

All types of employment and fields of study in college have individual standards for writing that are followed, and businesses likewise have their own; however, no matter what field you are in, you will sometimes have to use business formats for certain communications. **Business letters** are letters written to a group outside the organization you are in while **business memos** are letters written to a group or individual within the organization. Other types of often used business formats include writing **proposals** and **reports**. We have also included **resumes/letters of application** in this chapter, as getting a job is certainly a business function. Even if you are a psychology or English major, use this section when writing business-type communications. Writers always use the writing style appropriate for the genre they are writing in.

With all the forms demonstrated in this chapter, pay special attention to, and follow exactly, the format used. In other words, placement of addresses and addressees, salutations, dates, and paragraph spacing should be in the exact format as the examples. Readers expect this consistency, and deviating from these formats make the letters harder to read.

Also, pay careful attention to elements of the *writing context*:

- Each piece of writing has a *SPECIFIC purpose*, and all content is strictly aimed at conveying this purpose with evidence, so business writing always has a *thesis* that strictly controls the content. What is the goal that you want the writing to accomplish?
- Also pay attention to the person or people addressed in the communication (*audience*): analyze them carefully. What do they know and what do they need to know to receive your message? Make sure they have enough information to understand everything you are stating. Conversely, if the audience is someone or a group that is familiar with the subject, do not waste their time with information you can be sure they already know. For example, if the letter is from a company that rebuilds car alternators to another company that rebuilds alternators, the writer can assume the audience understands the process and does not have to describe it. Business writing is very tightly controlled: don't waste your audience's time with information that does not add to their understanding of your communication.
- Business writing also has a *tone*: it should be objective, informative, formal, and should NOT be humorous, informal, rambling. Carefully decide the tone for the specific communication you are sending. For instance, if you are writing a complaint letter, you will not be as successful in getting a favorable resolution to your complaint if you are rude or defamatory. Treat them with respect, but state clearly what you want the letter to accomplish. (The audience should understand what you want them to do!)

Business Letters

Business letters are communication to a person or group outside of the organization you are writing for: they could be proposals to buy or sell, to hire or be hired, to work together, to divide work. They could be letters of praise or complaint. They could be letters requesting or giving information. While all of these examples need to be informative and persuasive, the letter could be one that is strictly informative, giving an audience information you feel they need. Since you are writing to a group that you do not belong to (another company), you need to carefully analyze their level of expertise in the subject of the letter: giving them the information they need without boring them with information they already know.

Pay careful attention to the margin notes that discuss specific formatting issues that must be followed for a successful business letter.

Example: Business Letter of Complaint

John Bruhowski
4310 Apple Way
Indianapolis, IN 63555
(555) 413-5555   *Contact Information*
                        (space)
December 27, 2017   *Date*
                        (space)
Bill Horowitz
Shift Manager
Guitar Center   *Complete Address and*
413 31st Street   *Specific Name with title*
Indianapolis, IN 63557

                        (space)
Dear Mr. Horowitz: *Salutation*
                        (space)
I brought my Fender Stratocaster to your store to have the neck straightened the first week of December, and when I got it back it still would not stay in tune.   *No paragraph indent and*
                        (space between paragraphs)
At first I thought perhaps it was just too old and could not be repaired, but a friend told me to take it to Phil Donoway, who does guitar repair work out of his house. He took it from me December 20, and called the next day. The guitar now stays perfectly in tune.

I have always been satisfied with purchases I have made from the Guitar Center, but for this repair job I would like to have a refund of the $45.00 for the repairs you attempted.

I look forward to hearing from you soon.   *Notice the nice tone throughout even if a complaint.*

Sincerely,   *The usual closing: Sincerely,*

John Bruhowski   *Four spaces for signature*

John Bruhowski

Example: Business Letter - A Proposal

Joan Allen   ***Same formatting as the previous page.***
Director of IT Sales
Computer ONE
7608 South Park Pl. Suite 5A
Evanston, Il. 44335
(555) 723-5555

October 1, 2017

Bill Johnson
President
Johnson Computer Programming
4300 Kresge Way Suite 2C
Evanston, Il. 44335

Dear Mr. Johnson:

Our companies have been growing together for the past five years, with, if I may say so, outstanding success. Although we are in competition with each other, we seem to work well in terms of not impeding each other's growth. From what I have heard, you do excellent work developing a client's databases, and have an excellent support service.

Three months ago, we heard that Texco Food Processing was moving into the old Howington Rd. commercial center, which as you know has been empty for several years now. We approached them about setting up their software and hardware, and after preliminary talks we were invited into the center to look at the infrastructure. What a mess!!!! Outdated or non-existent, to say the least.

We could hire more, but as you know both of our companies have stretched the pool of qualified workers to the max for this region. If we moved further afield and started hiring from outside, our HR department believes that it would drive salaries and employee costs entirely out of the range of affordability (for us and your company). Also, would we be able to keep those employees long term? We could also hire people short-term to come in, but as you know that can also be very costly.

The magnitude of work called for here, and the willingness of Texco to pay good money for our support, makes this a golden opportunity.

What I am proposing is that we get together and discuss a way to use both of our companies' resources to together get the job done, with both of our companies reaping the benefits.

I am sending this with the blessing of Bill Smith, our President, who finds the idea intriguing.

I look forward to hearing from you at your earliest convenience.

Sincerely,

Joan Allen

Joan Allen

cc: Bill Smith
Enc: Preliminary Cost Estimate, Texco Food Processing Plant

cc: Tells receiver who else got the letter.
Enc: Enclosed with letter.

Memos

Business memos are stylistically similar to business letters, but they are memos written to members of the organization you belong to. So, again you need to analyze the audience: when writing on the same subject, you would need more information if you were writing to new hires than you would to seasoned employees. When writing to a sales team you would need to supply more information about production details than you would to the production team, and conversely you would expect the sales team to have more information on sales than the production team would. Analyze your audience's needs carefully and content should always conform to audience needs and expectations. Also, make sure you have decided specifically what your memo is to accomplish (its thesis), and direct all content to accomplishing this task. Study the example memo below, written by the same Joan Allen from the previous business letter. Ms. Allen has two specific purposes for this memo: 1) to let the production team know that their company is considering working with a neighboring company, and 2) to ask for any specific information on the strengths and weaknesses of the other company's production team.

Example: Memo

Memo

October 1, 2017

To: Production Team

From: Joan Allen, Director of IT Sales

Re: Possible Work with Johnson Computer Programming to design IT set up for Texco Food Processing opening next year at Howington Road commercial center.

Texco Food Processing is a distribution company opening a plant at the old, abandoned Howington Rd. commercial center, and our company is near signing a contract to refurbish the facility and get it ready for opening. The work load for this project, conceivably, will almost double our billable hours. Of course, if we get this project, you will be able to work all the overtime you would want; however, we do not want to force overtime for those who do not want it.

As you know, there is 100% employment in IT in our area, so we would find it hard to fill all the positions we would need to keep our current work flowing while we do this project. One solution we are exploring is going into business with Johnson Computer Programming to complete the job.

As we enter negotiations with both Texco and Johnson Programming, I would like as much specific information about the production team at Johnson - what are their strengths, their weaknesses? Be specific and if you feel comfortable even include names from their production team. Think about this for the next two days, and I would like us to start our day on Thursday with two hours where you all are at computers writing up your evaluations and discussing your ideas with each other. Following that, we will probably meet for any questions Bill and I have from your initial reports.

Thank you so much for your time and attention to this important concern. Our company will grow because of this, and you all will be rewarded also.

Sincerely,

Joan Allen

Joan Allen

Elements of a Business Letter and Memo

- Use at least one inch margins on all four sides of the letter.
- Use a standard 12 point font like Courier or Times New Roman.
- The writing is single spaced, but double spaced between sections and paragraphs.
- Unless there is company letterhead, begin with your name and address/ phone number, followed by the date, and then the person you are writing to with address. Memos usually use this more abbreviated format::

   Date:
   To:
   From:
   Re: (a brief preview of the memo's subject/purpose)

- A colon follows the salutation (Dear Dr. Smith:), and a comma follows the closing (Sincerely,)
- Content and Organization:

   Introduction: any necessary background information and a statement of purpose for the communication.
   Body: Necessary information as concisely and clearly as possible. Most business communications use short paragraphs so that readers can easily skim the important details.
   Conclusion: If appropriate, clearly state what needs to happen next from you and/or your reader. Do you want or expect anything from the reader of your letter and is that request clear?
   Express appreciation to the reader for having read your letter and considering what you have written. After the closing (Sincerely,) leave four blank lines for a handwritten signature and then type your name.

- Below the signature there are two possible additions:

   cc: Name any other people you are sending this letter to other than those in the address line.
   Enc: (enclosed) Name any other communications or forms sent with the letter.

Resumes/Letters of Application

So you want employment. If you are serious, you need to follow all of the suggestions in this section. Employers say they throw out half of the applications as soon as they look at a resume because it doesn't follow established formats, or tries to be cute or eye-catching. So let's start with the absolute DO NOT include in a resume:

/ unusual formatting or fonts (Use 12 point standard fonts like Courier or New Times Roman.)
/ unprofessional email addresses (cutegirl@yahoo.com)
/ irrelevant personal information (age, medical information, marital status, sexual orientation, number of children, race, religion, height and weight, political affiliations)
/ salary requirements (You might have one in mind, but you don't want to seem like you are applying for the money. And this is just not done - putting information that is usually not supplied will get your application thrown in the garbage.)
/ references (If an employer wants references, she will ask for them. If you included them, it shows you do not even know how to write a professional resume.)

Follow the formatting of this example. Be sure to highlight the activities that you did and any awards you received in the three sections: Work Experience, Education, Activities and Skills. Some companies now begin searches with a computer looking for key words like "trained," "developed," "wrote," "responsible for," "research," so use potential key words that a computer program would look for. In this example, since it is for computer programming, the actual programs Ms. Brown is trained in (COBOL, C++, and Java) would also be considered key words.

Joanne Brown

134 Mulberry Lane
Des Moines, IA 44326
400-555-7261
jbrown6@gmail.com

Work Experience

Start with most recent date.

2012-2013 Programming Associate,
New World Computer Programming, Des Moines, IA.
/ Developed programming for Fortune 500 companies using
COBOL, C++, and Java.
/ Wrote brochures for employees to use the programming.
/ Did market research for New World.   *Notice the brevity AND specificity.*

2011-2012 Computer Repair Specialist, Best Buy, Des Moines, IA.
/ Hardware Repair   *Specifc duties listed.*
/ Consultation on Web Site Fixes for Bugs
/ Customer Service Specialist

2009-2010 Computer and Electronics Sales, Best Buy, Des Moines, IA.
/ Led Sales Team in the home computer department
/ Worked also in the phone sales department
/ Award as Top Producing Salesperson, Christmas 2010

Education   *High School only listed if that is highest degree attained.*

2013   Bachelor of Science, Computer Programming, University of Iowa
/ Minors in Business and Spanish

Activities and Skills

Skills: COBOL, C++, Java, Macbook, MS Word, Excel, Pagemaker, InDesign
Microsoft Publisher. Good writer and editor. Language: Spanish.

2013	Gates Millenium Scholar
Summer 2012	Volunteer - Lutheran World Council
	/ Taught computer skills to impoverished youth, Yucatan, Mexico.
2010-2011	Volunteer - Habitat for Humanity
2009-2013	Apple Club. University of Iowa *Activity relevant to job.*

References
Available upon request.

Here is the letter of application that accompanied this resume:

Joanne Brown   *Same formatting as the previous pages.*
134 Mulberry Lane
Des Moines, IA 44326
400-555-7261
jbrown6@gmail.com

May 13, 2013

John Bradley
Personnel Director
Software and Data Processing Institute of Chicago
436 S. Cook Street
Chicago, Il. 40136

Dear Mr. Bradley:

I am writing to apply for one of the programming positions you advertised in the *Chicago Tribune*. The skills I have developed at the University of Iowa and my first programming job at New World Computer Programming make me a suitable candidate for your company.

I spent two years doing hardware repair as I studied programming at the University of Iowa. I worked hard enough in my first three years at the university to only need three classes a semester my senior year, so I got valuable programming experience working full time for New World Computer Programming while finishing my course work.

I am ready to begin my career, and the services you provide make me want to work at your company. Please contact me at your earliest convenience to set up an interview.

Sincerrely,

Joanne Brown

Joanne Brown   Enc: Resume

Reports

Many positions in the world of business will require you to write objective, analytic reports. These reports could ask you to compare, classify, describe, do causal or process analysis, evaluate (costs, processes, equipment, people, companies), or offer a proposal. When you begin research for a report, make sure you understand specifically what the purpose for your report is (are you supposed to compare? evaluate? analyze?), and as with all writing, do a thorough analysis of the audience who will be reading your report. Are you writing the report for upper management to understand the subject (so what do they already know which you do not have to include?), to new employees, to seasoned employees (who would probably have some knowledge), to members of the specific field the subject of the report concerns, or to the general public (perhaps stockholders). Each specific audience would need more or less detail depending on what you assume they already know. If you are not sure, you need to ask so that when you write you use appropriate content and diction for your audience.

In planning a report, sometimes you do research on the internet or in the library and for other reports you do the observations yourself to find the information necessary. *The key to good research for a report is to have clear questions that you want answered, and you conduct research until you have thoroughly answered the question(s).* The key to writing an excellent report, however, is after you have done the research and described and analyzed what you found, you need to draw conclusions based on your study. Your report shows that you have thoroughly studied your subject, so your readers expect you to be knowledgeable in this subject. They want to know what conclusions you have drawn in order to draw their own conclusions based on your research.

Conversely, other reports are informational only: you are in essence being asked to write an encyclopedia article on the subject so that readers can get basic, factual information. For a report of this nature, a conclusion/thesis is not necessary. With these encyclopedia reports, in lieu of a thesis, you decide how to arrange the information in the most clear, organized manner (chronological order works for some subjects; otherwise most to least important information or least to most; or sometimes most familiar to least familiar). With this clear organization, your audience understands your report's information much better.

Here are the steps you need to complete in order to develop a report with adequate content to create a thorough analysis/evaluation/description (whatever is called for when asked to write the report).

1) *Study the writing context:* Carefully study the requirements for the report (what are you supposed to accomplish through your research and report to your reader?). After making sure that you understand the scope of your report and its research, study the audience carefully: what level of expertise do they already have in the broad subject, so that you know what level of detail you need to make the report understandable to them?

2) *Research*: Study your subject carefully. Use all the tools of chapters 2 and 3: describe it, compare it to similar subjects, classify it, define it, analyze it. Use all the tools of chapters 6 and 7 if you need to do library or internet research. Use all the tools of chapter 9 if you are supposed to do primary research, i.e., you will look at the subject itself and describe, evaluate, and analyze it. If your primary purpose is that you were asked to analyze your subject, use the steps outlined in chapter 10. When are you finished? When you KNOW you are knowledgeable in your subject!

3) *Thesis/Conclusion*: Unless you have been asked to write an encyclopedia article report, analyze all your research and draw a conclusion about the information you have found. Make sure that this conclusion (your thesis) is clear and logical and use it to control the organization of information and the revision of content in the report.

4) Using your thesis and your audience analysis, organize your content, write the report, and then go through the revision and editing steps necessary with all successful writing. After a draft or two, let someone else read it. Make sure this peer reviewer knows the level of expertise your audience has, and what your conclusion concerning your subject is, to help them analyze whether you are using proper content for your audience, and whether your conclusion is clear.

Example: Report

In a business environment, subjects for reports come from either upper management (they ask you to research and analyze an issue and report your findings) or you see the need for a report yourself so that you and the employees you manage have essential information. Remember, that this is one of the first genres of writing that you were asked to accomplish: you probably wrote your first report in the third or fourth grade, and this continued to be the primary genre for writing throughout middle school and high school. So, bring that knowledge to your efforts and just raise the level of detail in research and writing to an adult level, and you will accomplish successful reports.

In college business classes, of course, the professor usually assigns the subject, but remember, anytime you find the need to get more information on a subject (and share it with peers), you will in essence be creating a report. The following example is an instance where Jim Briley found a need for information and wrote a report for the student council, which he is a member of. At a meeting of the Council, they were discussing the poor study habits of students at their college, and Jim decided to research the issue and write a report to present to the Council. Let's look at the writing situation for this report, and discuss the research process used.

Context Card
Subject: Study Habits of College Students
Audience: Student Council members
Audience Analysis: They know their own study habits and, generally, the study habits of the student body. They probably mostly think (correctly) that most students have poor study habits. They want to develop methods of improving study habits, and grades, for their fellows.
Writing Situation: a report explaining good study habits, and proposing that the school creates an inviting place for student study groups to meet.
Thesis: Without much expense, the school could create an inviting place for students to meet and conduct study groups.

Reports in the business world can be anywhere from one page to book length, but for the purposes of this chapter we are purposely giving a very short report, one that would be approximately three pages double spaced. It gives an example of the style and format of a report.

To research this report, Jim first went to the library's databases, discovered that there was much research into study groups, and that the research not only gave specific information on how study groups can be run but also unanimously agreed, with evidence, that study groups produced great results. He then asked around with fellow students in his classes and found several who did participate in informal study groups, and he went to these groups and both observed and interviewed them. What you are reading is an interim report: he did enough research to make the proposal, and if he got approval for moving forward with his idea that the school should support student study groups, he would do more research and write additional reports outlining specifics for how the study groups would work and what the school and the student council needed to do.

Jim Briley
Fall 2016

The University Needs to Implement Student Study Groups to Improve Grades

Most students at State University do not meet in study groups to collaborate in their individual learning processes, but both the literature (Shaw and Kamp et al) and student self-assessment suggest that great gains in student learning occur when students meet together to go over their assignments. One problem for professors to implement this is large class size, so it seems that the school needs to develop a framework for students to create study groups on their own. There is voluminous literature on how study groups and study methods could be implemented: there are thousands of articles - approximately 1/2 relevant - in ERIC, JSTOR, and EbscoHost, three databases in the college on-line library.

I found several students who meet together, in coffee shops, in dorm rooms, and at the library, and I was allowed to sit in with three different groups. While anyplace seems effective, what struck me immediately is where one group met: the second floor of the library. Climbing the stairs, you find a cavernous room in front of the stacks, with individual student carousels on two of the walls, and within the room various tables with chairs and also couches arranged as if ready for student study groups. The room looked like it was designed for study groups, but was mostly empty. How can we get students to see the wisdom of studying in small groups, and how can we make this floor of the library a place to accommodate them?

If I am asked to continue this, I will need to create a committee from our council and we will be charged with developing a flyer: the front will outline with specific evidence why students should create study groups, and the back will have specific information for methods to run effective study groups. This will involve studying the literature on the databases already mentioned, and summarizing the information in a flyer designed to market the advantages of developing study groups.

Here is a vision for the space: The school needs to set up a coffee and soft drink station in a corner of the room. It needs to decorate the room so it is pleasing to be there. I don't know whether this would be possible, but perhaps to make the space really inviting, I believe there are storage rooms in the basement of the library. Could there be a combination pool room, game room, television viewing center set up there? We need to make the library inviting: a place where students want to come to study.

Fully one-third to one-half of the studies on the databases come from the years 1920-1963. Although there has lately been a fury of activity looking at study groups, it seems that the use of study groups has declined until they are almost unheard of today. I want to point out that the level of information in classes has also lessened (as I learned in Dr. Jawowski's sociology course). Perhaps with a new emphasis on student groups, we can revitalize the learning that, after all, is the real reason for attending college.

Works Cited

Kamp, Rachelle et al. "The Relationship Between Students' Small Group Activities, Time Spent on Self-Study, and Achievement," *Higher Education: The International Journal of Higher Education and Educational Planning*, vol. 64, no. 3, 2012, pp. 385-397.

Shaw, Donita. "Promoting Professional Student Learning Through Study Groups: A Case Study." *College Teaching*, vol. 59, no. 2, 2011, pp. 85-92. *ERIC*, http://libproxy.kctcs.edu/ERIC/412692.

13

Connotation: Effective Word Choice

for Audience and Genre

Editing for diction (word choice) does not receive the attention it deserves. Most people look for incorrect usage (such as problems with *to, two, too*), for misspelled words, or for words that are obviously incorrect in the context of the passage, but few spend time during revision looking specifically at the diction, and only the diction, to choose the *precise* word for purpose and audience. Different audiences and genres require differing levels of formality. Since word choice helps create content and meaning, revision for diction should occur *while* content is being created and revised, as experienced writers do. But so you can learn all the concepts for editing diction and improve as a writer, *Writing Successfully* suggests that you isolate and study just the concepts in chapters 13-15, and then after learning them do diction revision at the same time you do your final paragraph revision, discussed in chapter 5. Looking at each individual word will help assure you that the words are the exact, specific word you mean (**denotation**), as well as the perfect word for your audience and genre (**connotation**).

Words have specific meanings associated with them, found in dictionaries. These meanings are known as the *denotative* definitions of a word. For example, a *bed* is a piece of furniture that one sleeps on. But many words also have *connotative* definitions, meanings that change depending on the person using them or the audience reading or hearing them. The denotative meaning of *chauvinism*, from the *American Heritage Dictionary*, is a "fanatical patriotism, [a] prejudiced belief in the superiority of one's own group." The connotative definition of *chauvinism* depends on both the user and the reader of the word. When confronted with the word "chauvinist," a person who believes in the equality of the sexes usually would give a **negative connotation** to the word ("Bill is a *chauvinist* pig!"); whereas people who believe in the superiority of either males or females could give it a **positive connotation** when it referred to a member of the sex they felt was superior. ("I'm certainly glad there are still some oldtime *chauvinist*s around like Bill.")

Purpose and audience are extremely important in governing word choice. Of course, you want to choose the word that means exactly what your purpose requires (*denotation*), but when you spend some of the postdrafting process analyzing diction, you will often find several possibilities for **denotatively correct word choice**, so your choice of audience becomes a determining factor in word choice. For instance, a description of the process of photosynthesis in a school text written for children age twelve would use different words and define more words than a text for college freshmen would. A scientific paper discussing how the photosynthesis process helps create mutations (audience: Ph.D.'s in biology, other experts) would use a greater amount of specific, scientific diction (and would be incomprehensible even to many college educated readers because they don't know the scientific terminology written by scientists for scientists). Writers must always choose words with their audience and genre in mind. Remember that *analyzing audience is extremely important in governing word choice.*

When editing your writing, you must not only choose the most denotatively correct word for your purpose, audience, and genre, but also the word with the most **appropriate connotative meaning**. For example, here is the rough draft of a paragraph describing a mother's love for her husband and the bond between them. The writer's purpose was to adequately describe the attitude of the husband and wife toward the husband's role:

> Mother loved father more than anything. She was proud of the way he could fix things. She liked the security of food on the table and a roof over her head that he always provided. She agreed with the traditional way he raised his son and daughter. She believed that his chauvinistic ideas were proper and never questioned them; they were so synonymous with her own.

Let's examine the word *chauvinistic* in this passage. If the audience for this paragraph accepts *chauvinistic* as a positive, or at least neutral, word (an older, conservative, traditionalist audience), then the word could be proper *if* the writer also wanted to express the view that chauvinism by definition also included the positive traits of the paragraph. However, if the audience imbues the word *chauvinistic* with negative connotations (as most people would today), the writer should revise the word or risk giving a slightly negative connotation to the entire description of his parents (which he didn't want to do). He revised the word using a phrase that would be more neutral for an audience of younger men and women, the majority believing in the equality of the sexes.

> Mother loved father more than anything. She was proud of the way he could fix things. She liked the security of food on the table and a roof over her head that he always provided. She agreed with the traditional way he raised his son and daughter. The traditional mores of Christian society were what my parents were raised with and what they believed in.

Doesn't the revision more clearly relate to the purpose and audience of the passage?

Also note that when you edit at the diction level, if a word's connotation could be inappropriate (your audience would misconstrue your meaning), it might be better to revise an entire sentence to achieve your exact meaning, replacing a word with an explanatory phrase. In the example above, the writer wanted his audience to understand his parents precisely, so he completely rewrote the final sentence to adjust to an audience who would not understand, or agree with, his use of *chauvinistic* in a positive sense.

*A **thesaurus** is probably the most important tool used for finding synonyms* (words with similar meanings). If you are not comfortable with a word choice in your draft, find that word in a thesaurus that lists synonyms and cross-references to related words. Modern thesauruses also briefly define words so that readers may distinguish

310

the minute differences between synonyms. *Always double-check: Use a thesaurus in conjunction with a dictionary*. Also, you should become aware of the time-saving aspects of using computers to edit diction. Most word processing programs have thesauruses and dictionaries built into them, so editing diction, which used to be a more time-consuming process (moving from writing to thesaurus to dictionary and then back to writing), can now be performed quickly on the computer screen. Becoming proficient in these uses of the computer will make editing for diction much easier. Practice using one, but *make sure that the synonym you choose has the denotative AND connotative definition that you desire.*

Any student doing college level work should also invest in a good, **hardcover dictionary**, but by all means carry a paperback edition with you to class or the library, especially if you have trouble spelling words correctly. A hardcover college dictionary at home is specified here because they are more complete and exhaustive than paperback versions, though even they do not contain all the entries included in an unabridged dictionary. If you do not know how to use a thesaurus or dictionary as well as you should, read the directions in their introductions.

Writing Context and Genre: Level of Formality and Tone

Words become appropriate in a writing context only when chosen with the writer's purpose and audience in mind. You should consider your tone, how formal you would like your essay to be given the purpose and audience, and choose words with the proper connotation based on your decision. To illustrate formality and tone, let's distinguish between four classes of words used for different writing situations — *learned, popular, colloquial*, and **slang**. After defining these classes, we will look at applications of these classes in writing situations to examine how you can decide on levels of formality. It is important to note that these four categories are arbitrary constructions: depending on each person's conception of a word, the word could be either learned or popular, or another word could be either colloquial or slang. Also note that all of these classes of words are proper in certain social contexts: nothing is inherently wrong with slang or dialect. As a matter of fact, if you were to choose a category that could be construed as "wrong," it would often be *learned words*. Whenever you use extremely formal diction — unless you are writing to an audience who you know understands and knows the words — you risk the audience's misunderstanding your ideas because they don't understand the words.

Learned words, used more often in the written than the spoken language, are used by educated people, and, most importantly, *are used only when the writing situation demands their use.* For example, a chemist writing a paper (audience: other chemists) would use the term *sodium chloride* (a learned word), but when speaking to a friend or fixing dinner in his own kitchen, he would refer to the same compound as *salt* (using a popular word for the same compound). Most writing avoids formal, learned words, unless you happen to be writing in a genre that demands precise, technical writing or if you are composing a paper in your own major (and you are using specific terms from that discipline).

Popular words are the common words shared by all writers and speakers of a language. Most writing done by educated, as well as uneducated, people consists of words in this class, and most of your writing will consist of words in this class. Every word in this paragraph, as well as the next, are examples of popular words.

Colloquial words and phrases (sometimes referred to in dictionaries as *informal*) are not incorrect; they are simply used in intimate situations, when people speak together casually. They can be used effectively when a writer wants to give the impression of speaking directly to the reader on an informal basis.

For example (*Colloquial speech is italicized*):

> Audience: fellow students at a university
> Writing Situation: the college newspaper
> Purpose: to plead with students to support the debate team
> Writer and his Tone: a peer of the audience showing enthusiasm

> Our debate team has won every match it has entered this year. We support our football and basketball team enthusiastically; isn't it *about time* we supported our debate team also? Be proud of our school. *Come on and get with it everybody!*

In this instance, the audience, situation, and purpose call for an informal tone from the writer, and the colloquial language certainly is appropriate in this context.

Slang words, are not, in themselves, "bad" either. Slang words are either from dialects (*ain't*), from specific cultural groups (*goth punk*), extremely informal ("She's a *babe*."), or words many would call vulgar. You would be wise to stay away from using slang in writing situations, unless your audience is a very select group of devotees to a slang word. By all means use *cool* to describe a new friend in a letter to another friend, but in more formal writing situations avoid the use of slang.

Do not get hung up by the difference between colloquial and slang words. For most linguists, the word *slang* has a connotation suggesting greater informality than the word *colloquial*; other than that, the two classifications are almost synonymous.

All three of the sentences below have identical meanings; however, their diction's level of formality changes.

Learned — most formal
The student's *erudition* verifies the quality of the university's curriculum.

Popular — formal
The student's knowledge proves the quality of the university's program.
The student's knowledge verifies the quality of the university's program.

Using *proves* or *verifies* would depend on how formal the writer wants to be. Words, by themselves, do not belong to one class or the other. While *proves* is less formal than *verifies*, it is possibly too informal in the above situation. As the writer, the word choice is yours, so always select words with audience and purpose in mind.

Colloquial — informal
The student is really *on the ball*. The university must be *real tough*.

Slang — least formal
The student is *all that*. He *aced* the tesst. the university must *rock* students' worlds.

312

Although it is fairly easy to see that writers should avoid colloquial and slang diction in formal writing situations, it is equally important to keep from writing with overly formal diction. The president of a university would not write a sentence such as

The student's erudition verifies the quality of the university's curriculum.

Unless the writing situation was very formal, perhaps a request for an endowment to the school; in most writing situations she would make herself understood clearly, using a sentence such as "The student's knowledge verifies the quality of the university's program."

Another important suggestion: Don't mix levels of diction. If you write an essay using mostly formal "popular" diction, but in an early draft you have written either a very informal sentence or one with very formal, stilted language that doesn't fit the level of diction in the rest of the essay, rewrite the sentence choosing words that fit the language of the rest of the essay. BE CONSISTENT with your level of formality when choosing words.

To summarize: don't use thirty-dollar words if ten-dollar words will do. (Can you hear how awkward this lapse into colloquial diction is?)

Avoiding Sexist Language and Clichés

For over a century, psychologists have been studying how language subtly influences our thoughts and our culture. The language itself has changed with our growing awareness of how the way we label things causes us to continue stereotyping. Some examples of sexist language include: police*men*, sales*ladies* — referring to occupations by gender (a "doctor" is usually referred to as *he*.) Writers should carefully avoid using stereotyped language.

To avoid using sexist language:

- *Switch from singular to plural.*

  A president of a large corporation must protect *his* investment.
  Edited: Presidents of large corporations must protect their investments.

- *Don't assign roles based on gender.*

  Mothers should carefully watch their children for symptoms of Rocky Mountain Spotted Fever.
  Edited*: Parents* should carefully watch their children for symptoms of Rocky Mountain Spotted Fever.

313

If you try to be nonsexist when using pronouns, you occasionally create an awkward phrase.

> A teacher plans and prepares all summer. *She* doesn't get the summer off.

This can be changed to the preferable, though awkward:

> **Edited**: A teacher plans and prepares all summer. *He or she* doesn't get the summer off.

The "He or she," "he/she," "him or her," "him/her" constructions are certainly preferable to the old sexist language that uses a masculine pronoun for gender-neutral nouns; however, in most cases these awkward constructions can be rectified by changing the noun and pronoun to the plural.

> *Teachers* plan and prepare all summer. *They* don't get the summer off.

- ***Use gender neutral designations:*** *police officer, firefighter, sales clerk mail carrier*

- ***Also, as a general rule, do not use clichés.***

Avoid using clichés like *on the ball, blind as a bat*, and *sober as a judge*. They have been repeated so often that they have lost all effectiveness. Even in informal writing situations to family and friends, you risk ridicule for using old, trite expressions. Enough said.

Don't be an old stick in the mud; avoid the following clichés and others like them:

to make a long story short	in this day and age
think outside the box	by the skin of the teeth
a crying shame	beyond a shadow of a doubt
face the music	over and done with
after all is said and done	smell a rat
busy as a beaver	drop a bombshell
bite the bullet	at the crack of dawn
as luck would have it	to the bitter end
the bottom line	take the bull by the horns
on the same page	in the last analysis
green with envy	get in a rut
as happy as a lark	as sly as a fox
as proud as a peacock	fly in the ointment
stick to your guns	the depths of despair
by hook or by crook	in the blink of an eye
the spitting image of	by the seat of the pants
throw in the towel	bundle of joy
hit the bullseye	burn the midnight oil

Occasionally writers do use clichés, but in an original way. For instance:

314

After the impeachment of President Clinton, the cliché "justice is blind" took on new meanings for the American people: the house managers were blind to the fact that 200 years of judicial precedent suggested strongly that Clinton was not guilty of the charges leveled against him; on the other hand, the case also suggested that "justice is blind" in that the court precedents were flawed. Any thinking person would say that Clinton lied under oath and to the American people, even if judicial precedent does not call it perjury.

EXERCISE 13.1
Choose Words for Connotation, Not Mixing Levels of Diction, and Avoid Sexist Language/Clichés

Check the essay you are working on now for words with the proper connotation for your purpose, audience, writing situation, and tone. Make sure that you have not mixed levels of diction or used sexist language or clichés.

EXERCISE 13.2
Exercise on Connotation, Sexist Language, and Clichés

List words that you would change in this paragraph followed by words (or descriptive phrases) you would change them to, including 1) words that do not fit with the connotation of other words in the paragraph, and 2) words that are sexist or clichés. Imagine this as a paragraph in a semi-formal essay for a college class, avoiding colloquial and slang diction.

When my brother jumped the gun and bought a car before he had enough money to do so, I thought he was as stupid as a bag of nails. It was so loud and so fast that a policeman pulled him over and wrote him a ticket the first week he had the car. By the time he had paid his fine and bought insurance and a bunch of CDs, he didn't have enough money to pay the first loan installment. He thought he was getting a good deal when he low-balled the salesman and she took the deal, but if someone doesn't have the money, what good is getting the good deal? He used to have some greenbacks saved to go to school, but I guess that is out of the question. I bet there are a lot of things he is going to be taking back to the store now that he's sinking in quicksand. My brother has to be my best teacher.

1. cut 'jump the gun and'   2.

3.   4.

5.   6.

315

14

Denotation: Spelling, Using the Correct Word, and Adjectival/Adverbial Confusion

When you are at the editing stage where you check for misspelled words, read slowly and carefully, a word at a time. Use a dictionary or other relevant reference source to make sure that the words you use have the *exact* denotative meaning you intend. Is the leader of Pakistan a President, a Premier, or a Prime Minister? Especially when you use technical terms found in academic discourse, make sure the words have your intended meaning. *You should check a dictionary or reference source for any word you are not 100% sure of.* Not only spelling errors, but words spelled correctly but misused, are probably the most prevalent errors in college writing.

Spelling Errors and Glossary of Usage (frequently confused words)

Use the spell check on your computer program, but do not rely on it as your only check. *If you have misused a word, but have spelled another word, the computer will not catch the mistake.* At the risk of sounding repetitive, read your essay *one word at a time*.

Especially watch for frequently confused words and words of questionable usage in college writing situations from the list in this chapter.

Look over this list several times to become comfortable recognizing the words from the list in your writing. Especially single out those words that you know you have trouble with. When you see one of these troublesome words in your writing, check with the list to make sure you are using the correct word:

a-an
Use *a* before the sound of a consonant. – a car, a clown, a U.F.O.[a *yu f o*]
Use *an* before the sound of a vowel. – an apple, an opera, an M.D.[an *em d*]

accept-except
Accept means "to receive something," "to admit to a group," "to regard as proper or true," or "to answer affirmatively." — accept this gift   an accepted custom
Except means "exclusion from" or "if it were not for." — I bought every brand except one. I would have bought that brand except it cost too much.

access-excess
Access means "approach" or "admission to." — an access road
having access to the court files
Excess means "beyond the normal or desirable." — He eats to excess.
The committee reported excess spending.

316

ad

Used in informal situations as a shortened form of "advertisement." Decide how informal the style of your essay is before using *ad* in college writing.

adapt-adopt

Adapt means "to adjust." — The man adapted to subzero temperatures.
Adopt means "to take as one's own." — Congress adopted the motion after a vote.

adverse-averse

Adverse describes something "opposed" or "hostile" to the subject. — Joseph had an adverse reaction to the medication.
Averse describes the subject's hostility toward something. — Bill is averse to buying a new car with his finances in the shape they are in.

advice-advise

Advice is the noun form of the verb *advise.* — He advised me to use my teacher's advice wisely.

affect-effect

These words can both be used as either nouns and verbs, but in most situations *affect* is used as a verb and *effect* is used as a noun.
The verb *affect* means "to impress or influence." — Modern music affects my way of life.
The noun *affect* or adjective *affective* is mainly used in psychology, and is similar to, but not synonymous with, the word "emotional." — The affective behavior of the adolescent was uncalled for.
The verb *effect*, and its adjective form *effective*, means "to accomplish." — The soldier effected his mission. He was very effective.
The noun *effect* means "result" — Modern music has a profound effect on my life.
(As you can see, the noun form of *affect* and the verb form of *effect* are seldom used.)

all ready-already

All ready is two words meaning "completely prepared." — We were all ready to go.
Already means "previously" or "before." — We had already packed.

all together-altogether

All together is two words meaning "all in one place." — The relatives were all together by the fireplace.
Altogether means "completely." — The wreck was altogether his fault.

allusion-illusion

An *allusion* is a reference to something else. — The Senator's speech on foreign policy made several allusions to the Vietnam War.
An *illusion* is a false mental image. — Parents who hit their children have the illusion of power.

317

among-between
Use *among* for relationships involving more than two. — The four senators agreed among themselves.
Use *between* for relationships/connections between two people, things, or points of time. — The two senators agreed between themselves. The train runs between New York and Milwaukee. She eats between meals.

amount-number
Amount is used with a singular noun that names something not countable. — She put a large amount of sugar in the cake.
Number is used with a plural noun that names more than one of a countable thing. — The number of times I fixed the tire is irrelevant.
Be careful not to use amount or number when they can be replaced with specifics: NOT there were numerous as in the class BUT There were 8 As in a class of 21.

anxious-eager
Anxious means "nervous" or "worried." — Jason is anxious about the test results.
Eager means "looking forward to." — John, who has studied, is eager to see them.

anymore-any more
Anymore means "now" and *any more* means "no more," but they can usually be used interchangeably in negative constructions (and the two words usually appear in negative constructions). —
They don't build cars like that anymore. They don't build cars like that any more.

anyone-any one (anybody-any body)
Anyone and *anybody* mean "any person at all." – Anyone can do this job.
Any one means "any one unidentified person or thing in a group." – Any one of these plans could work.
Any body would be rarely used — Any body left in the morgue has to be tagged.

as to
a too formal substitute for "about" — The lawyer questioned the plaintiff about [not "as to"] her alibi.

awhile - a while
Awhile means "for a little while." – I could stay awhile longer.
A while also means "a little while," but it is used as a noun. It is usually preceded by *for*. – I could stay for a while longer.

being as, being that
colloquial for "because" — Because [not "being that"] I spent the money, we came home early.

besides-beside
Besides means "in addition to" or "except for." – Besides the next chapter, there is no other homework.
Beside is a preposition meaning "next to." – My desk is beside my friend's desk.

318

between-among: see among-between

between you and I is colloquial. It should be "between you and me." – "That fraternity is a mess; between you and me, they drink too much."

capital-capitol
Capitol means a building where a legislature meets. – The capitol building for New York is in the state capital, Albany.
Capital means a town/city that is an official seat of government (compare to *capitol*), and can also mean "wealth," "assets," a capital letter (A), "first rate or excellent" (Colorado is a capital vacation spot.), "extremely serious" (That was a capital mistake.), or a punishment by death (capital punishment).

censor-censure
Censor means to remove from public view for moral or other reasons. — The Army censored the public's knowledge during the Gulf Wars.
Censure means to formally scold. – Clinton was censured by Congress for lying under oath.

cite-sight-site
Sight means "vision" and *site* means a place where something was, is, or is going to be. – His sight was perfect. We met at the site of the new building.
Cite means to make a reference to a source you use (I cited Howard Dean in my research paper.), mention someone officially for bravery or meritorious service (The soldiers were cited for bravery [i.e., received a "citation"]), or to summon to a court of law. (The police cited me for speeding.)

coarse-course
Coarse means "rough." — The moon's surface is coarse.
Course has a variety of meanings — "movement in a direction or the route taken in that movement," "part of a meal," "a school subject." – I followed my course toward a culinary arts degree, and this course included taking three literature courses and eating many five course meals.

complement-compliment
Complement is associated with the word "completion." — Mike's new shoes complement his dress suit [in the sense of making the suit complete stylistically].
Compliment is associated with the word "praise." — I complimented Mike on his choice of shoe styles.

conscious-conscience
Conscious means "aware, awake." – The patient remained conscious throughout the surgery.
Conscience means "the thought of humans concerning a sense of right and wrong." – My conscience bothered me when I lied.

continual-continuous
Continual means "always recurring" and *continuous* means "unceasing." — The drip in the faucet went from a continual drip to a continuous stream.

could care less
Non-grammatical slang for "could not [couldn't] care less." Linguistically, *could care less* actually means the opposite of what is intended.

could of, would of
Non-grammatical slang for "could have" and "would have" — I could have [not "could of"] bought the new Chevrolet.

council-counsel
Council is a noun meaning "a group that discusses." – The student council went to the President's council meeting.
Counsel can be either a noun meaning "advice" or a verb meaning "to advise." — The lawyer's counsel helped me reach a decision. I was in trouble and he counseled me.

credible-creditable-credulous
Credible means "believable." — Mary told a credible story about the missing broach.
Creditable means "worthy" or "deserving of credit." — The Beatles gave creditable performances in their early days.
Credulous means "able to trick or able to be tricked." — We knew Jim was lying when he told that credulous story. The credulous fans believed the story that the singer was ill.

decent-descent
Decent means "pretty good." — The pie was decent.
Descent means "to go down." — The plane's descent was rocky because of high winds.

device-devise
Device is "a manufactured item." — That device works quite well.
Devise is a verb meaning "making something." — Can you devise a plan of escape?

discreet-discrete
Discreet means "not calling attention to." (It is the adjective form of "discretion." The adverbial form is "discreetly") — Can you make a discreet announcement?
Discrete means "separate and distinct." — Writers make hundreds of discrete decisions every time they write an essay.

disinterested-uninterested
Disinterested means "impartial." — A disinterested third party who doesn't know the people involved would make a fair decision.
Uninterested means "not interested." — I am completely uninterested in video games.

eager-anxious: see anxious-eager
effect-affect: see affect-effect

elicit-illicit
Elicit means to "bring forth" or "to ask for." — The governor elicited opinions.
Illicit means "unlawful." — Illicit drugs create much misery.

especially-specially
Especially means "particularly." — I especially like my new television.
Specially means "for a specific reason." — That CD was made specially for my birthday party.

eminent-imminent
Eminent means "distinguished." – The eminent scholar published his tenth book on social reform.
Imminent means "about to happen or threatening to happen." – The imminent tornado caused everyone to run for the storm cellars.

etc.
Etc. is an abbreviation for the Latin *et cetera* meaning "and others." First, ~~And~~ etc. is repetitive. Second, many consider *etc.* to be falsely pretentious and avoid its use.

everyday-every day
If you can put the word *single* between *every* and *day* and the sentence makes sense with your intended meaning, use *every day*. If putting the word *single* detracts from the meaning, use *everyday*. – I went to weight training every day. Lifting weights became an everyday occurrence.

everyone-every one (everybody-every body)
Everyone and *everybody* means "every person." – Everyone can do this job.
Every one means "all persons or things in a group." – Every one of these plans could work. *Every body* would be used rarely: Every body in the morgue is dead.

explicit-implicit
Explicit means "fully revealed, not vague." – The judge was explicit: pay the fine or go to jail.
Implicit means "implied, suggested." – The dog's menacing growl was an implicit suggestion to stay out of the yard.

excess-access: see access-excess
except-accept: see accept-except

farther-further
Farther refers to geographical distance. – I walked farther today than I have ever walked before.
Further refers to a greater amount of time, quantity, or degree. – The loan officer required further documentation before approving the loan.

fewer-less
Fewer denotes number and is used only with plural nouns. – There were fewer students in class than there normally are.
Less refers to amount and is used with singular nouns. – I took one less *class* than I did last semester.
Compare: I took fewer *classes* than I did last semester.
                 I ate less *cake* than you did.

idea-ideal
Idea means "a thought." — Bill had a good idea.
[Several dialects of English say "ideal" in this situation when they mean "idea."]
Ideal means "the best that could happen." — The ideal result would be that all Americans would have health care.

illicit-elicit: see elicit-illicit
illusion-allusion: see allusion-illusion

imply-infer
Imply means "suggest without actually stating." – The professor implies that those questions will be on the test.
Infer means "draw a conclusion from evidence." – I infer from your sullen looks that you are mad at me.

irregardless
Non-standard for "regardless."

its-it's
Its means "belonging to it." — The car has lost its shine.
It's is a contraction of "it is" or "it has." — It's going to be a hot summer.
The confusion between these two words arises because most words show possession with the use of an apostrophe (Bill has lost Mary's ring.). An apostrophe is not used with possessive pronouns, and *its* is a possessive pronoun. (See chapter 21: Pronouns)

lay-lie (See also chapter 19: Verb Agreement and Tense Shifts)
Lay (laid, laid, laying) means "to put or place." – I lay the books on the table; yesterday I laid them on the desk. (INCORRECT: Today I laid the books on the table.) *Past and present participles*: I have laid the books on the table many times. While I am laying the books on the table, don't startle me.
Lie (lay, lain, lying) means "to rest or recline." – As I lie on my couch, I remember how yesterday I lay on your couch. (INCORRECT: Today I lay on the couch. Yesterday, I laid on the couch.) *Past and present participles*: I have lain on your couch many times, but I was lying on my couch when you said you loved me.
Lie (lied, lied, lying) means "to tell a falsehood." – Yesterday, you lied to me.
Compare to: Yesterday, I lay on your couch.

loose-lose
Loose means "not restrained" or "not tight." — My dog's collar was loose, so he got loose.
Lose is a verb meaning "mislay" or "not win." — I lose my car keys every day. We are going to lose the basketball game.

maybe-may be
Maybe is an adverb meaning "possibly." – Maybe we can go to a movie tonight.
May be is a verb phrase. – Kim may be the right man for the job.

morale-moral
Morale refers to the mood of a person or group. – The team's morale was high.
Moral either describes conduct and ethical character or it means "the ethical meaning of a story or event." – Estella made a moral judgment. Fairy tales always have a moral that children should learn.

number-amount: see amount-number

passed-past
Passed is the past and past participle tense form of "pass." – I passed the exam.
      I passed the rest area.   [INCORRECT: I have past exams in the past.]
Past refers to "a time before the present." – I have passed exams in the past.
      In the past, I passed the rest area.

percent-percentage
Percent (or *per cent*) follows a numeral and should be written when the number is spelled rather than using the symbol %. - We cornered forty percent of the market.
BUT when using arabic numerals -   He got 125%.
Use *percentage* without numbers. -   We cornered a high percentage of the market.

personal-personnel
Personal means "pertaining or belonging to an individual person." — That is his personal opinion.
Personnel refers to people in an organization. – The military personnel went on a training mission.

prejudice-prejudiced
Prejudice is a regular verb in the English language, but many dialects leave the *-d* off past/past participle endings. — The judge was prejudiced [not "prejudice"] by his relationship to the prosecutor. My upbringing made me prejudiced [not "prejudice"].

principal-principle
Principal means either "chief," "most important," or "a sum of money." — the principal of a school, the principal problem, He lives on the interest in his bank account, rather than spending the principal.
Principle means "rule," "law," or "controlling idea." — The principles of geometry never change. Their code of conduct is the opposite of my principles.

raise-rise (See also chapter 19: Verb Agreement and Tense Shifts)
Raise means "to lift (something), to cause to move upward, or to increase." – The gas stations raised their prices. Raise your hands in prayer.
Rise means "to get up, to ascend." – I rise at seven every morning.

respectfully-respectively
Respectfully means "with respect." — He respectfully submitted the evidence to the judge.
Respectively means "examining at least two things individually," and it can mean "examining things individually in order." — The gun, the knife and the purse were labeled exhibits A, B, and C respectively. [meaning that the gun was exhibit A, the knife was exhibit B, and the purse was exhibit C.]

sensuous-sensual
Sensuous means "responding with the senses to art, music, nature, etc." – The sunset was sensuous.
Sensual means "gratification of the physical senses." – I received a sensual massage.

sight-site-cite: see cite-sight-site

sit-set (See chapter 19: Verb Agreement and Tense Shifts)
Sit means to "position a person on their buttocks." — I sit in the chair.
Set means "to put or place." Many dialects use the word "set" when they mean "sit." — I set the basket of fruit on the table. John sat [not set] and rested for a while.

somebody-some body (someone-some one)
Somebody and *someone* both mean "one unidentified person." — Somebody help me.
Some is an adjective meaning "an unspecified number or part" or "being unknown," and this adjective can modify either *body* or *one*. —
Someone help me stop this tattoo artist before some body gets a bad infection.
(As you can see, "some body" and "some one" are seldom used as words, except occasionally like the previous sentence and: His hair needs some body in it.)

some
Some dialects use *some* when they mean "somewhat" or "remarkable." — His remarks confused me somewhat [not "some"]. That was a remarkable [not "some"] picnic.

sometimes-sometime-some time
Sometimes means "occasionally." – I would like to go to Europe sometimes.
Sometime means "an unspecified time in the future." — Sometime next year, I will go to Europe.
Some time means "an unspecified span of time." – I would like to spend some time in Europe.

stationary-stationery
Stationary means "unmoving" or "unchanging." — The weather front was stationary.
Stationery is writing paper. — He bought a box of stationery.

sure (see the next section of this chapter, Adjective/Adverb Confusion)
non-standard slang when used for the adverb, "surely" — Bill surely [meaning certainly. INCORRECT: "sure"] was right when he stopped the pranksters from defacing the statue.

suppose to, use to
non-standard, incorrect slang for "supposed to" and "used to" — Mary was supposed to [NOT "suppose to"] bring the cherries for the pies.

than-then
Than is used in comparisons. — Jim works harder than I do.
Then means "at that time." – Jim worked for ten hours; then he went home.

their-there-they're
Their means "belonging to them." — That is their house.
There is used with "is, are, was, were, have, and had" to refer to something else. It can also mean "at that place," again referring to another thing. — There are many problems at that apartment complex over there.
They're is a contraction of "they are." — They're going to correct the problem.

theirself-theirselves-themself
Theirselves is not a word; use "themselves."
If you are trying to use *theirself* or *themself*, they are not only not words, but writers who use them are making a pronoun both singular and plural. (See chapter 21: Pronouns.)

thusly
not a word; non-standard for "thus" — And thus, [not "thusly"] the war was won.

to-too-two
To is a part of a verb. — She was going to smile.
Or it means "toward." — He is going to the store.
Too means "more than sufficient." — The meal was too hot.
Or it means "also." — The meal was too hot, and the service was bad too.
2 should be spelled *two*. — I sold two houses in one week.

uninterested-disinterested: see disinterested-uninterested
use to, suppose to: see suppose to, use to

ways
non-standard colloquial dialect for "way" — The farmer had a way [NOT "ways"] to go before reaching home.

your-you're

Your is the possessive pronoun form of "you." — I brought your book to class.
You're is a contraction of "you are." — You're [You are] the prettiest girl on six continents.

Adjectives/Adverbs

Since you are going to be looking at each individual word during this stage of the editing process, we need to define two parts of speech, adjectives and adverbs. You can check for correct usage for these types of words while you edit for word use.

Adjectives describe nouns (people, places, things, or qualities) or pronouns (words that refer to other nouns and pronouns). Most nouns can also function as an adjective when they describe another noun (an army general: the Army - a noun, functioning as an adjective describing "general.") Adjectives either come before the word they describe, after a form of *to be*, or after a verb describing a sensation. Adverbs describe verbs, adjectives, or adverbs. With a few exceptions (too, quite, well, very, really soon), adverbs end in *–ly*.

When we study sentence styles in chapters 16-17, you will learn about adjectival clauses and adverbial clauses, which are word phrases that function adjectivally (describing or modifying nouns) or adverbially (describing or modifying verbs, adjectives, or adverbs).

- *Adjectives describe nouns.*

  Julie has a *kind* smile.

- *A noun (a person, place, thing, or quality) can serve as an adjective.*

  An *African-American* scholar wrote a book on the *Republican political* agenda.

- *Adjectives follow a form of the verb* to be *(am, is, are, was, were, will be) to describe.*

  Robert is *nice*.

- *Adjectives follow a verb describing a sensation (feel, taste, smell, look, sound, become, seem — the last two words indicating the possibility of sensation).*

  The car's exhaust sounds *loud*.
  The cake became *smaller* and *smaller*.

- *An adjectival clause can modify a noun.*

  [A noun, *an adjectival clause describing a noun*,]
  Mr. Johnson, *a chemistry professor for twenty-seven years*, finally decided to make more money and go into private industry.

326

- *Adverbs describe verbs, adjectives, or other adverbs.*

Charles spoke *kindly* to the sick patient.
[The adverb *kindly* describes the verb, *spoke*.]

Joan was *very* tired after the chemistry test.
[The adverb *very* describes the adjective, *tired*.]

Bill listened *quite* sympathetically to the boy's story.
[The adverb *quite* describes the adverb, *sympathetically*.]

- *An adverbial clause modifying a verb.*

[adverbial clause modifying the verb know]
> *When the race has been won*, we know the winner.

With a few exceptions (*too, very, quite, well, really*), adverbs end *in -ly*:

profound (adjective form):
A profound book changed my life. [adj. modifying noun, book]
profoundly (adverb form):
The book profoundly changed my life. [adv. modifying verb, changed]

Adjective/Adverb Confusion

The most common mistakes occur when writers use adjectives instead of adverbs after a verb.

Incorrect: Seth laughed *loud*.
Correct: Seth laughed *loudly*.

Incorrect: The man rested *comfortable* in the chair.
Correct: The man rested *comfortably* in the chair.
[used as adverb modifying *rested*]
Correct: The man was *comfortable* in the chair.
[used as an adjective: *was + adjective*]

Good is an adjective that describes nouns. *Well* is usually an adverb that describes verbs. (*Well* is also used as an adjective to describe a person's health.)

Juan writes *well*.
[*Well* is an adverb describing writes.]

Juan is a *good* writer.
[*Good* is an adjective modifying the noun *writer*.]

Juan wasn't feeling *well* when he wrote that essay.
[*Well* is used as an adjective in this case, since it refers to *Juan's health*.]

327

In some instances you can choose whether to use the adjective or the adverb form (but bear in mind that your choice may affect the precise meaning of your sentence).

The music, soft and gentle, pervaded the room.
[*Soft* and *gentle* are adjectives describing *the music*.]

The music softly and gently pervaded the room.
[*Softly* and *gently* are adverbs describing *pervaded*.]

Comparative and Superlative Forms of Adjectives and Adverbs

- *Adjectives and adverbs show degrees of quality and amount with the endings -er and -est or with* more *and* most *or* less *and* least.

Positive Form (dictionary form)	Comparative (demonstrates a greater or less degree)	Superlative (demonstrates the greatest or least degree)
ugly	uglier	ugliest
awful	more/less awful	most/least awful
quickly	more/less quickly	most/least quickly

- *Usually nouns and past participles of verbs serving as adjectives, and several regular adjectives and adverbs, use* more/most *and* less/least *and cannot use -er and -est.*

I became *more confused*. [not I became *confusider*.]

Native speakers of English can usually tell when a word cannot use *-er* and *-est*, but when in doubt a dictionary gives the correct comparative and superlative forms of a word.

- *Some of the most common adjectives and adverbs are irregular.*

Positive Form	Comparative	Superlative
Adjectives:		
good	better	best
bad	worse [not worser]	worst
many/some/much	more	most
Adverbs:		
well	better	best
badly	worse	worst

- ***Do not use both -er/-est and more/most, less/least. Use one or the other.***

  Juanita fought *harder* [not *more harder*] for her grades.

In speech, some dialects and cultures use both forms of the comparative and superlative in a sentence for emphasis, but it is discouraged when writing.

- ***The comparative is used to compare two things while the superlative compares three or more things.***

  That is the *shorter* of the two races.
  The Indianapolis 500 is the *most popular* car race of the year.

EXERCISE 14.1
Exercise for Adjectives and Adverbs
Correct problems with adjectives and adverbs in the following sentences. Some sentences are correct.

1. I am told frequent that I ought to get a job. frequently

2. He needs a vacation bad.

3. He has the worstest cold I've ever seen.

4. Sleeping light cures my fears about the robbers.

5. She is the most wisest person I have ever seen.

6. Joan was a kindly woman who never harmed anyone.

7. She is the most prettiest girl I have ever seen.

8. Sunita ran quick to the alarm box to call the fire department.

9. He is the shortest of the two of them.

EXERCISE 14.2
Spelling and Correct Usage

Study the preceding chapters of *Writing Successfully* – When you read the list of frequently confused words and problems with adjectives and adverbs, make a list of every word that you personally get confused about.
Then, check your essay one word at a time for vague words to replace with specific language (ch. 5), language that has a connotation proper for the audience and writing situation (ch. 13), and correctly used and spelled words. Also be careful, looking for frequently confused words and correct forms of adjectives and adverbs (ch. 14). ONE WORD AT A TIME, all three diction issues. A two thousand word essay would only take ten minutes, and sloppy word use is one of the biggest detractors for writing.

15

Editing for Concise Sentences:

Eliminating Wordiness and Avoiding Repetition

Eliminating Wordiness

In my opinion, the ultimate goal of all institutions of higher education is to foster an ability in their clientele to think for themselves and to succeed.

WHAT?   Compare that wordy sentence with this revision:

Universities need to teach logical thinking and patterns for success.

Cluttered writing leads to confusion. Let's face it – readers get bored easily. If you can state your ideas clearly in a ten-word sentence, as opposed to a thirty-word sentence, readers will appreciate and understand the communication much better. REMOVE CLUTTER FROM YOUR SENTENCES! Your readers will understand you much better. If an essay has the same content, would you rather read 350 words or 500 words? If the book you are reading has not been edited for wordiness, for the same content would you rather read 350 or 500 pages? Treat your readers with respect and edit for wordiness and repetition!

Some specific types of words and phrases to look for as you eliminate wordiness are discussed here.

- **Cut unnecessary articles**

Articles (*a, an, the*) and *that* are four of the most used words in the English language, but because they are so necessary, they are often overused. Circle every article, as well as every use of *that,* in your essay and re-read it without them. When a sentence sounds correct without the words, cross them out. If the word is needed, leave it in. Most of the words will stay, but you will be able to eliminate some.

- **Cut phrases such as** *I think, I feel, I believe, in my opinion, It seems to me*

You wrote the essay; the reader knows it reflects your opinion. If it is someone else's opinion, you would acknowledge it as such (John Smith believes_____). Since you will tell the reader the name of who wrote or said any statement or idea not yours, as a general rule *I think,* and similar phrases, are not necessary. The exception to this suggestion occurs when you are discussing your ideas and someone else's ideas in the same passage, and you need to clarify who said what. (John Smith believes the campus diner should close at 9, but I think it should stay open until 11 on weeknights.)

- ***Cut intensifiers such as*** *very, really, quite, totally, completely, so*

> The REALLY terrible storm ripped across the bay and TOTALLY destroyed businesses and homes when it hit THE shore. The result was VERY disastrous: SO MUCH wreckage, SO MANY helpless people, SO MANY lost hopes. To see it was REALLY disturbing.

Note the directness and precision imparted by eliminating intensifiers:

> **Edited**: The terrible storm ripped across the bay and destroyed businesses and homes when it hit shore. The result was disastrous: wreckage, helpless people, lost hopes. To see it was disturbing.

The unedited version sounds like a *National Enquirer* article. Unless you are writing to an audience demanding cheapened pathos, like the *National Enquirer*'s, you would be wise to refrain from prose weighed down by intensifiers.

- ***Save the*** *there is, there are, it is* ***pattern for significant information.***

Use it sparingly, as a pointer when you really want to emphasize the ideas that follow:

> There are occasions when the pattern is efficient and occasions when the pattern is inefficient.

The following example is stronger without *there is:*

> The level of discourse in the halls of Congress has reached a new low. There are politicians who constantly lie to their consituents.
> **Edited**: The level of discourse in the halls of Congress has reached a new low. Politicians constantly lie to their consituents.

- ***Cut "Fancy" and "Roundabout" Words and Phrases***

Simplify "fancy" words and phrases. Sounding like the stereotypical lawyer or government official will not improve your prose style. Both the government and the legal profession are well known for obscuring ideas with wordy, unclear jargon or inventing phrases like "pacification of neutrals" when they mean "invasion." Government publications and legal briefs also often use much more formal diction than necessary.

> There seems to be a paucity of disinterested scholars in America's institutions of higher learning.

Why not use this simple and direct sentence?

> **Edited:** Many researchers have left America's universities.

331

Guard against overly ornamented or convoluted writing, and aim for concise, meaningful, simple phrases in your sentences. The examples below show sentences edited for directness.

> The document enclosed is in connection with the letter received on the third.
> **Edited**: The document enclosed concerns the letter received on the third.

> In view of the fact that you have graduated, your employment will begin next week.
> **Edited**: As you have graduated, your employment will begin next week.

- ### *Cut "in his essay" phrases*

Some of the most used wordy phrases in college writing are the "in his essay" phrases that follow:

> In *his essay*, "The World at War," Johann Martin argues . . .

Essay titles always have quotation marks around them, so *his essay* is unneeded.

> **Edited**: In "The World at War," Johann Martin argues . . .

> In *her article*, "Laughing with Groucho," Elaine Showalter finds . . .
> **Edited**: In "Laughing with Groucho," Elaine Showalter finds . . .

Quotation marks signal short story and poem titles too:

> In his poem, "Sunday Morning," Wallace Stevens pictures ...
> **Edited**: In "Sunday Morning," Wallace Stevens pictures ...

Book, film, and television show titles are in italics (preferred) or are underlined:

> In his book, *Notes from Virginia*, Thomas Jefferson describes ...
> **Edited**: In *Notes from Virginia*, Thomas Jefferson describes ...

- ### *Edit Vague Wording followed by Specificity*

> This story is about a husband and wife who just had a baby. Their names were Desiree and Armand.
> **Edited**: "Desiree's Baby" concerns Armand and Desiree, a couple who just had a mixed race baby.

- ### *Edit Wordy Phrases*

Several wordy phrases have crept into common use, and you should look for them as you edit for wordiness. The underlined words below can be used as replacements for the wordy phrases italicized in the sentences that follow:

Wordy			<u>Concise</u>

in connection with   *in relation to*   *relative to*   <u>about concerning regarding</u>
in regards to,   *with regard to* *with respect to*
in reference to   *pertaining to*   *referring to*

The governor's report *in connection with* the school scandal shed new light on the controversy.
Edited: The governor's report <u>regarding</u> the school scandal shed new light on the controversy.

The document enclosed is *in regard to (pertaining to, referring to)* the letter of the 17th.
Edited: The document enclosed <u>concerns</u> the letter of the 17th.

The television news program *concerning the matter of* AIDS programs airs the 27th.
Edited: The television news program <u>about</u> African AIDS programs airs the 27th.

subsequent to   <u>after</u>

Subsequent to the last murder, new evidence surfaced.
Edited: <u>After</u> the last murder, new evidence surfaced.

regardless   *regardless of the fact that*   <u>although</u>

Regardless of the fact that John could not swim, he jumped in the pond to save his dog.
Edited: <u>Although</u> John could not swim, he jumped in the pond to save his dog.

in view of the fact that   *for the reason that*   <u>as   since</u>

In view of the fact that the economy was going downhill, the voters thought about whether to re-elect the governor.
Edited: <u>Since</u> the economy was going downhill, the voters thought about whether to re-elect the governor.

as a consequence of   *as a result of*   *inasmuch as*   <u>because since</u>
for the fact that   *due to the fact that*   *for the reason that*

John repeated the sixth grade *as a consequence of* his rheumatic fever.
Edited: John repeated the sixth grade <u>because</u> of his rheumatic fever.

As a result of the rainstorm, the game was cancelled.
Edited: <u>Since</u> it rained, the game was cancelled.

The Mayor stopped the strike *for the fact that* the garbage workers' union provides a necessary service.
Edited: The Mayor stopped the strike <u>because</u> the garbage workers' union provides a necessary service.

Wordy	<u>Concise</u>
prior to previous to	<u>before</u>

The convention occurred *prior to* the next regular board meeting.
Edited: The convention occurred <u>before</u> the next regular board meeting.

of the opinion that	<u>believes</u>

The professor is *of the opinion that* all students can succeed.
Edited: The professor <u>believes</u> all students can succeed.

by means of by way of	<u>by through via</u>

I reached New York *by way of* the New York State Thruway.
Edited: I reached New York <u>via</u> the New York State Thruway.

make contact with	<u>call write</u>

Can I *make contact with* you via email?
Edited: Can I <u>email</u> you?

inside of outside of	<u>inside outside</u>

John played *inside of* the house.
Edited: John played <u>inside</u> the house.

comes into conflict with creates a conflict	<u>conflicts</u>

Your test date *comes into conflict with* my karate class.
Edited: Your test date <u>conflicts</u> with my karate class.

as long as at the same time as during the period of *during the time that in the time of throughout the time of*	<u>during throughout while</u>

I missed several classes *during the course of* the semester.
Edited: I missed several classes <u>during</u> the semester.

All during the time that we were snowed in, I read.
Edited: <u>While</u> we were snowed in, I read.

For the period of March, I rarely went to parties.
Edited: <u>Throughout</u> March, I rarely went to parties.

present with	<u>give</u>

I want to *present* you *with* this gift.
Edited: I want to <u>give</u> you this gift.

Wordy			<u>Concise</u>
in order that *so that*		*with the intentions of*	<u>for</u> <u>to</u>
in order to *for the period of*		*for the purpose of*	

The 4H Club gave me a banner *for the purpose of* advertising our workshop.
Edited: The 4H Club gave me a banner <u>to</u> advertise our workshop.

Jason explained himself *in order to* bring clarity to the discussion.
Edited: Jason explained himself <u>for</u> clarity in the discussion.

in the event of *in case* *in case of*	<u>if</u>

In the event of a fire alarm, evacuate the building.
Edited: <u>If</u> a fire alarm rings, evacuate the building.

along the lines of *as though* *correspondent with*	<u>like</u>
of a kind with *of a like mind with*	

Wordsworth's "Intimation's Ode" is *in the nature of* Coleridge's "Dejection: An Ode."
Edited: Wordsworth's "Intimation's Ode" is <u>like</u> Coleridge's "Dejection: An Ode."

has a need for *could use*	<u>need</u>

Bill *has a need for* more study time.
Edited: Bill <u>needs</u> more study time.

at this moment *at this time* *at this point in time*	<u>now</u>
at this very moment *in this day and age*	

We need more teachers in the classroom *at present*.
Edited: We need more teachers in the classroom <u>now</u>.

off of	<u>off</u>

Mary jumped *off of* the balcony.
Edited: Mary jumped <u>off</u> the balcony.

It is often the case that	<u>often</u>

It is often the case that thieves are drug addicts.
Edited: Thieves are <u>often</u> drug addicts.

come to the realization that *come to see that*	<u>realize</u> <u>see</u>

After soul searching, I *came to the realization that* I wasn't meant to be a doctor.
Edited: After soul searching, I <u>realized</u> I wasn't meant to be a doctor.

the fact that	*but that*	*but what*	that

Many students refuse to believe *the fact that* low math scores can be overcome.
Edited: Many students refuse to believe <u>that</u> low math scores can be overcome.

at that point in time	*at that time*	then

I lost my objectivity *at that point in time*.
Edited: <u>Then</u>, I lost my objectivity.

of the opinion that	*entertain the notion that*	think

Miguel is *of the opinion that* America should fight terrorism with much force.
Edited: Miguel <u>thinks</u> America should fight terrorism with much force.

Avoiding Repetition

To produce concise, well written essays, remember this human tendency: when composing early drafts we all often repeat ideas, in the effort to state the meaning with the best phrasing. So, as you revise for wordiness also watch carefully for repeated ideas. Here is an example of an unedited paragraph followed by the paragraph edited to avoid repetition:

> Through my youth, baseball has always been a major part of my life. I spent most of my childhood participating in "America's National Pastime." I first took part in this pastime at only five years of age, when I joined Little League Baseball. Through my personal experience, I found Little League to be important and rewarding. It taught me many values through the years, such values as friendship, good sportsmanship, competition, selfesteem, teamwork, discipline, and learning the feeling of winning or the "agony of defeat." But most of all, I remember the friendships I have made through my experience, the fact that I was a part of the team, and that becoming close friends with my teammates built a major part of my selfesteem.

Analyze this revision carefully. *Every* idea from the first draft appears in the revision. When ideas were repeated in the first draft, the writer chose *the most specific* phrasing for the revision:

> **Edited**: From the age of five, I participated in "America's National Pastime." Little League was important and rewarding, teaching me many values including good sportsmanship, competition, discipline, and learning the feeling of winning or the "agony of defeat." But most of all, I remember the friendships I made, I remember I was a part of the team, and becoming close friends with my teammates played a major role in building my selfesteem.

In addition to entire sentences that are repetitive, there can be phrases and words within sentences that repeat ideas. These examples show such redundancies:

In this modern world ~~of today,~~ we need to save the environment.
(The "modern" world is "today.")
It is ~~a~~ true ~~fact~~ Humphrey Bogart never won an Oscar.
(All "facts" are "true.")
The ~~final~~ outcome of the game was 82 to 69.
(All "outcomes" are "final.")

Other frequent repetitions include these:

~~a pair of~~ twins or ~~two~~ twins	fell ~~down~~
climb ~~up~~	reverted ~~back~~
~~new~~ innovation	refer ~~back~~
~~and~~ etc.	bibliography ~~of books~~
~~free~~ gift	~~mandatory~~ requirements
continue ~~to remain~~	blue ~~in color~~
collaborate ~~together~~	tall ~~in height~~
repeat ~~again~~	visible ~~to the eye~~
advance ~~forward~~	~~past~~ history
retreat ~~back~~	off ~~of~~
~~close~~ proximity	expensive ~~in price~~
~~humorous~~ comedy	~~negative~~ complaints

EXERCISE 15.1
Editing for Wordiness Exercise
Edit this paragraph for wordiness and repetition. Answers will vary.

~~There are~~ many times ~~that~~ I wish I had been more studious while ~~I was~~ in high school. When I took the test to enter the college, I found that I had to take three semesters of math to pass the math course necessary for a degree, and it was entirely possible to have taken enough math in high school to not have to take any math in college. In the basic history, social studies, and science courses, I really have to struggle to keep up with the reading homework. I took a study skills seminar the first week of school and was taught simple tools to be a better reader. In twelve years of school I had never learned these simple tools to increase the speed of reading with better comprehension. I wish I had learned more when I was in high school. I see many students in the freshman writing courses who aren't any better thinkers than I am, but yet they spend half as many hours as I do writing their essays because they have already learned all the necessary editing skills that I should have learned in middle school. It just makes me mad to think of all the time I wasted for all those years and all the time I could be saving now, time that I could be using to party away.

EXERCISE 15.2
Eliminating Wordiness and Repetition
Study this chapter. Then edit the essay you are working on now for wordy sentences and repetition. Work toward brevity and concise, clear prose.

16

Definitions: Subjects, Verbs, Conjunctions, Clauses, and Modifiers

Subjects/Verbs and Present Participles

The **subject** is that part of the sentence that is the doer of the action (except in the *passive voice*, where it is the receiver of the action). **Verbs** either express action, or with the verb *to be* link their subject to a word that describes the subject (known as a complement or a predicate adjective).

> **subject** <u>*verb*</u>
> John <u>wrote</u>.

> **subject** <u>*verb*</u> *direct object*
> John <u>wrote</u> a letter.

> **subject** <u>*verb*</u> *predicate adjective*
> John <u>is</u> an artist.

Passive Voice: **subject**   <u>*verb*</u>
> The trees that the men owned <u>were cut</u> down.

Some forms of verbs contain helping verbs. You use them every day in your speech.

> **helping verbs**   <u>**main verb**</u>
> John *should have been* <u>finished</u> when you called.

Forms of verbs with *–ing* endings (**present participles**) cannot impart action in a sentence without helping verbs, nor are sentences that have *–ing* verbs as the main verbs complete sentences without helping verbs.

> **Incomplete sentence**: The student learning to write.
> **Complete sentence**:   The student is learning to write.

But *present participles*, -*ing* forms of verbs, can function as subjects and modifiers.

> *As subject (called a* gerund*)*: *Reading* enhances writing skills.
> *As modifier*: The student *learning to write* should read everything.
>   or: *Learning to write*, the student should read everything.
> *As modifier*: The *talking* bird flew to its cage.

Independent and Dependent Clauses / Coordinate, Correlative, Adverbial, Subordinate Conjunctions and Relative Pronouns

Independent clauses can stand on their own as complete sentences. They always contain at least a subject and a verb.

subject <u>verb</u>
Independent clause: Students <u>learn</u>.

The subject and verb can also each have modifiers and objects attached to them.

subject   prepositional phrase (modifies subject)   <u>verb</u>
The students   of Mr. Harris' freshman composition class   <u>learned</u>
objects of the verb
to write more complex essays.

Two *independent clauses* can be combined into one sentence with a ***coordinate* or *adverbial conjunction*,** or a ***semi-colon*.**

> The students revised their essays twice for content, *but* then they had to edit for sentence style, diction, punctuation, and grammar.

> The children played games all evening; *however*, they still weren't tired.

> Semi-colons can join two independent clauses; this usually doesn't occur without an adverbial conjunction or a transitional phrase.

The third example is grammatically correct; however, it would more directly convey its specific meaning with *;however*, or *;nevertheless*, placed between the two clauses.

Coordinate conjunctions separate two independent clauses, and they are:

,and   ,or   ,nor   ,but   ,so   ,for   ,yet

and or nor but can also connect any group, **but without the comma:**

> John *and* Mary   after the summer *but* before the winter

Some coordinate conjunctions combine with other words to create ***correlative conjunctions:***

> *Both* sugar *and* simple carbohydrates cause obesity.

Common correlative conjunctions:

both ... and	not only ... but also	not ... but
either ... or	neither ... nor	whether ... or
as ... as		

339

Adverbial conjunctions can separate two independent clauses or an independent and a dependent clause, and they include:

;moreover,	;furthermore,	;likewise,	;indeed,
;similarly,	;however,	;nevertheless,	;nonetheless,
;otherwise,	;still,	;accordingly,	;consequently,
;therefore,	;thereupon,	;thus,	

Standard punctuation for an adverbial conjunction separating two independent clauses is:

Independent clause*; [semi-colon] adverbial conjunction, [comma]* the second independent clause.

John went to work; *however*, he became sick and went home.

Conversely, use commas with adverbial conjunctions when the conjunction separates a dependent and an independent clauses.

Dependent clause   adverbial conjunction   independent clause
When we revise conscientiously, *moreover*, we achieve greater success with our writing.

Dependent clauses, as the name implies, depend on an independent clause in the same sentence to complete their meaning. *Dependent clauses can never stand on their own as a complete sentence, even though they have a subject and a verb.* Dependent clauses can occur before, in the middle of, or after the independent clause to which they are connected in meaning, and dependent clauses begin with a *subordinate conjunction* or a *relative pronoun*. Dependent clauses are also called subordinate clauses or, beginning with relative pronouns, relative clauses.

Subordinate conjunctions begin dependent clauses which modify a word in the independent clause or a word in a another dependent clause. The common subordinate phrases and conjunctions include:

after	although	as far as	as long as
as	as if	as soon as	because
before	even though	if	insofar as
in order that	in that	lest	no matter how
now that	once	provided	since
so that	supposing	that	though
unless	until	when	whenever
where	whereas	wherever	whether or not
while			

Relative pronouns begin dependent clauses which serve either as modifiers of another word in a sentence, or as the subject of the sentence. These are the relative pronouns:

who whoever whom whomever which whichever whose that

340

Subject   <u>verb</u>
Dependent clause: When students <u>learn</u> essential concepts

When students learn — then what? The sentence is incomplete. ***These are called sentence fragments.*** All sentences must have at least one independent clause.

dependent clause   ***independent clause***

When students learn essential concepts, the class improves by becoming better editors of their own writing.

Adjectival and Adverbial Modification

Dependent clauses function just like adjectives (modifying nouns, pronouns, or other adjectives) or like adverbs (modifying verbs or other adverbs).

	subject <u>verb</u>
Independent clause (complete sentence):	The trees <u>were cut</u> down
Relative pronoun	*subject <u>verb</u>*
Dependent clause: that	the men <u>owned</u>.

Complete sentence: The trees that the men owned were cut down.
(An independent clause with a dependent adjectival clause modifying "trees")

(relative clause - a dependent adjectival clause modifying *student*)
subject (subj <u>verb</u>)   <u>*main verb of sentence*</u>

The *student* (who <u>wrote</u> in a journal every day) *<u>became</u>* a better writer because of the practice.

(rel. clause modifies *girl* adjectivally) [sub. clause modifies *smiles* adverbially]
***Subject* (subj. <u>verb</u>) [sub. conj   subj. <u>verb</u>]   <u>*main verb of sentence*</u>**

The *girl* (who <u>smiles</u>) [whenever the teacher <u>hands out</u> a test] *<u>must be</u>* a masochist.

In addition to serving as modifiers, dependent clauses, participial phrases (using a present participle), and present participles by themselves can also serve as subjects of sentences, or anywhere a noun can be used.

(relative clause – subject of sentence)
subj.   <u>verb</u>   <u>*main verb of sentence*</u>

(Whoever <u>writes</u> in a journal every day) *<u>will have</u>* more ideas to choose from when selecting topics for papers.

subj. <u>*main verb*</u>   (relative clause as direct object)

The smartest student *<u>must be</u>* (whomever writes in a journal every day).

present participle **(a gerund, as subject)** <u>*main verb*</u>
Praying for grades   *<u>does not bring</u>* success without hard work.

present participle **serving as a noun, used as the object of the preposition "at"**
Bill was good at *cooking*.

341

17

Sentence Coherence, Variety,

Emphasis, and Modification

Using Coordinate, Subordinate, and Adverbial Conjunctions, and Transition Words and Phrases, to Combine Clauses and Create Coherence

Writers use coordinate conjunctions, subordinate conjunctions, adverbial conjunctions, and transition words to achieve clarity in their writing and show the precise relationships between sentences and ideas. These are not mysterious words – they are words you already use every day. After you have revised for context, content, organization, paragraphs, and word use, edit for coherence so your brilliant ideas and examples will realize a new clarity. When you can edit well for coherence, you can join this skill to editing for punctuation (chapter 18), and perform these related skills simultaneously.

Good writing always employs coherence to signal relationships among ideas. Often, we join ideas in our minds, but the ideas are not clear to our readers. Be careful to show the proper relationship between ideas:

> *Confusing*: My essay isn't finished, *and* my mother is going to Florida tomorrow.
> *Clear*: My essay isn't finished, *so* I won't be able to go with my mother to Florida tomorrow.
> *Unedited (six short, choppy sentences)*: Virginia seceded from the Union. Robert E. Lee joined the Confederate army. He was a general in the U.S. army before the war. After war broke out, President Lincoln asked Lee to command the Union army against the rebels. Men were more loyal to their states than to America in the nineteenth century. Lee replied that he had to defend his home state, Virginia, more than America.
> *Edited (two balanced sentences)*: Robert E. Lee, a general in the American army, was asked by President Lincoln to lead the union forces against the rebels after the Civil War broke out. However, men were more loyal to their states than to America in the nineteenth century, so Lee replied that he had to defend his home, Virginia.

The examples following demonstrate how coordination, subordination, and transition words help convey meaning effectively.

342

- *Coordinate conjunctions*

Coordination signals equal emphasis between parts in a sentence. *When coordinate conjunctions separate two clauses in a sentence, a comma precedes the coordinate conjunction.* For example*:*

> Coordination signals an equal relationship between two parts of a sentence, *and* subordination signals an unequal relationship.

Look at the two clauses joined by coordinate conjunctions in the following examples. You will see that each section has equal importance in the sentence as an idea.

To signal addition: *and*

> The All-State fullback went to the state university, *and* his brother followed him two years later.

To signal choice (usually one positive item, one negative): *or nor*

> Summer vacation allows me to take a breather from mental activity, *or* I can work to make money for the next school year.

To signal contrast: *yet but*

> Summer vacation allows me to take a breather from mental activity, *but* most of us have to make money for the next school year.

To suggest cause: *for*

> John studied especially hard for his biology test, *for* he did not do well on the first exam.

To suggest result: *so*

> John studied especially hard for his biology test, *so* his grade was better on the second test.

- *Subordinate conjunctions*

Subordination signals a dominant/subordinate, independent/dependent relationship between ideas in a sentence. Subordinate conjunctions introduce dependent clauses and signal the relationship between parts of a sentence. *When a subordinate conjunction begins a sentence (as with this sentence), the subordinate clause it signals is followed by a comma. No comma is needed when the subordinate clause follows the main clause (as with this sentence).*

Examine the two clauses in the sentences that follow, and study how the subordinate conjunctions signal the relationships they establish.

343

To show contrast: *although   though   even though   as if*

> *Although* I like my new car, I liked my last one better.

To show cause or reason: *because   since*

> John will pass biology *because* he has studied more.

To show condition: *if   even if   unless   provided that*

> *If* I go to school in the summer, I will graduate in three years.
> John will fail biology *unless* he studies more and brings up his test grades.

To show purpose: *so that   in order that   that*

> John will pass biology *so that* he can still apply to medical school.

To show time: *when   whenever   while   as   before   after   since   once   until*

> *Since* the first month of our relationship was stormy, I have still been very careful *when* it looks like we are going to argue.

To show place: *where   wherever*

> Bill worked at two pizza parlors *where* he became the shift manager.

- ### *Adverbial conjunctions*

Adverbial conjunctions, like coordinate conjunctions, join two independent clauses into one sentence. *In terms of correct punctuation, the proper form is:*

> Independent clause*; [semi-colon] adverbial conjunction, [comma]* the second independent clause.

Study the adverbial conjunctions below, paying attention to both their use as coherence devices (signaling the relationship between two ideas) and the proper punctuation for this pattern.

To signal addition: *;moreover,   ;furthermore,   ; in addition,   ;likewise,   ;indeed,*

> John made a lot of money the year after he took his job; *indeed*, he made over six figures.

To show comparison: *;similarly,   ;likewise,*

> Bill graduated in four years; *likewise*, his wife did too.

To show contrast: *;however,   ;nevertheless,   ;nonetheless,   ;otherwise,   ;still,*

> Abraham Lincoln lost six elections in the course of his career*;*
> *nevertheless*, he persevered.

To show result: *;accordingly, ;consequently,   ;therefore, ;thereupon,   ;thus,*

> Students can make money with a nursing degree; *consequently*, it is a
> popular major.

- ### *Transition words*

Transition words and phrases signal relationships between ideas in sentences and paragraphs. *If transitions separate two independent clauses, in most cases, use 1) a semi-colon (as you do with adverbial conjunctions), 2) a period, or 3) a comma and a coordinating conjunction as punctuation between the clauses. If transitions separate an independent and a dependent clause, use commas between the clauses.*

To show addition: *again   also   and   then   beside*
too   further   finally   next   first, second, third   last
equally important   in the first place, in the second place

> *First*, I went to class. *Then* I went to lunch, *and finally* I went back to the dorm.

To show contrast: *although this may be true   in contrast*
on the contrary   still   on the other hand
rather than   even so

> Bill always dresses stylishly; *in contrast*, his brother John is a slob.

To show result: *then   thus*

> People often make decisions based on what their friends say rather than
> examining the issue for themselves, *thus* making it hard to reason with
> them.

To show time: *later   soon   first   next   then   yesterday*
afterward   today   in the future
after a _____   in the meantime

> You are to study for the test *next* week; *in the meantime*, prepare your oral
> reports.

To indicate summary: (Use very sparingly. These are the most overused transitional expressions in the English language.) *to sum up   on the whole*
in brief   for example   for instance

Avoid (overused): *as I have said   in other words   as has been noted*
in fact   to tell the truth   in any event
in summary   hence

345

The federal government has expanded its role considerably since the country was founded; *on the whole*, governors two hundred years ago had more power than the President or Congress.

When a writer uses sentences that constantly repeat either the same grammatical structure or have the same length (like the unedited version below), readers lose touch with meaning, either lulled by the mechanical sameness of the repeated structure, or shaken by the choppy sentences that make readers feel like they are riding on a bumpy wagon. It is very important that you read your essay carefully to check the flow of the prose, and to revise for *sentence variety*.

Here is an example of an unedited group of sentences, followed by the same sentences with a judicious use of coherence words (*italicized*):

Unedited: My roommate went to town at six. Then he dragged home early. His girlfriend had left for the dance with his best friend. He thought about the situation and couldn't decide what to do. Should he punch his friend? Call his girlfriend at three a.m.? Or leave the betrayers to each other? He was sad.

Edited: *After* going to town at six, my roommate dragged home early *because* his girlfriend had already left for the dance with his best friend. *Although* he'd been thinking over what to do for a couple of hours, he couldn't decide *whether* to punch his friend, call his girl at three a.m., *or* just leave the betrayers to each other. He was sad.

Sentence Variety

The best method to check for sentence variety is to read your essay aloud slowly, pausing carefully at each mark of punctuation. Be sure to *read what is on the page*, not how your mind tells you it should sound. You will notice stretches of "sameness" or "choppiness" if you read carefully and *listen*. To illustrate, re-read the unedited sentences above aloud, pausing for punctuation, followed by a reading of the edited sentences aloud. Don't the edited sentences flow more smoothly? Revision can be accomplished by using coordination, subordination, adverbial conjunctions, and transition words. These are the tools that allow you to vary sentence length.

- *Use conjunctions and transition words to create sentence variety*

The example unedited sentences above contain a series of short, choppy sentences. Effective writing consists of a variety of sentence lengths, and you can use coordinate, subordinate, and adverbial conjunctions and transition words to make sentences longer and clearer by joining sentences that are short and choppy. Short sentences then can be used to emphasize important ideas in your writing. You also make the relationships between ideas in sentences clearer with effective use of coordination and subordination.

There was a definite relationship intended between the ideas in the unedited, short, choppy example. The edited version uses four subordinate conjunctions (*after, because, although, whether*) and a coordinate conjunction (*or*) to join the ideas and actually *show* the relationship between the ideas. The revision not only reduces the choppiness of the prose, but also makes the ideas clearer. When we think and speak, linguists find, we intuitively supply coordination and subordination, and in fact when we are writing or reading, if the coordinate or subordinate words are missing our minds usually will supply them. However, if the coordination and subordination are not clear on your page, this imprecision does not create very thoughtful prose. Communication without clear relationships between ideas seems sloppy to readers. When you edit at the sentence level, listen carefully to the relationship between ideas (the best method to discover problems has already been mentioned: find choppy sentences) and supply the proper conjunctions to show the relationship between ideas.

- *Use occasional short sentences to vary sentence length*

On the other hand, a short sentence in a group of longer sentences emphasizes that sentence's ideas, and writers use the *occasional* short sentence to emphasize important statements. Remember that *although a group of short, choppy sentences is awkward, a single short sentence is a valuable tool for emphasizing important ideas.*

Read these examples aloud slowly, pausing at punctuation marks and studying the flow of ideas. Notice how the short sentences (underlined), by their brevity, emphasize their ideas:

> The Rolling Stones are the greatest rock-and-roll band in the world. They started as copiers of American black music, and succeeded in making rhythm and blues acceptable to white audiences in Europe and America. This by itself would make them one of the premier groups who have shaped modern musical taste, but throughout the seventies and into the eighties, nineties, and the present century, they have continued with innovative changes in their style and exciting contributions of their own songs.

> Alcohol and drug addiction drags abusers down a long, dark road that, if the disease goes unchecked, leads to insanity or death. The cycle must be broken. Research has verified that addicted parents pass the disease on to their descendants, and one way to break the cycle is comprehensive education programs as early as the grade school level.

- *Alternate beginnings of sentences for variety*

Beginning every sentence with the subject can also cause monotonous sentence patterns. Most sentences do begin with the subject, but if a series of sentences sounds bland and monotonous, try placing words or phrases at the beginning of the sentence, before *the subject*, as you revise for sentence length. Here is an example of a group of sentences beginning with the subject, followed by the same group of sentences edited to vary the sentence beginnings:

> *Unedited*: The man decided to show his concern. He was, after all, a man of decision. Mr. Jones jumped in his car and raced toward the town council meeting. The meeting had adjourned. He returned home, dejected again.

347

Edited: Suddenly <u>Mr. Jones</u> decided to show his concern. A man of decision, <u>he</u> jumped in his car and raced toward the town council meeting. <u>The meeting</u> had adjourned, so feeling dejected, <u>he</u> returned home.

Sentence Emphasis

This section does not discuss specific editing techniques, but basic methods of constructing sentences. A study of these basic sentence types can give you ideas for methods to rewrite and edit your sentences for clarity and emphasis. By this examination of how sentences in English are usually constructed, you can learn to change sentence types occasionally into unusual patterns. Unusual patterns emphasize the ideas of those altered sentences, lending force to their ideas.

Sentences generally fall into three categories: cumulative, balanced, and periodic.

The cumulative sentence begins with the main assertion of the sentence, followed by phrases and clauses that modify the main idea. This is the most typical English sentence. It has two advantages: the sentence begins by directly announcing its purpose, and the phrases and clauses following the main idea continually add force and weight to the sentence (it becomes "stronger and stronger"). Two examples follow:

> John Billings spent forty-five years teaching — as a young man in the navy instructing submarine crews, later as a good and loving father with six children, and after navy retirement as a secondary school science teacher.

> He [the writer] must teach himself that the basest of all things is to be afraid; and, teaching himself that, forget it forever, leaving no room in his workshop for anything but the old verities and truths of the heart, the old universal truths lacking which any story is ephemeral and doomed love and honor and pity and pride and compassion and sacrifice (from William Faulkner's 1950 Nobel Prize acceptance speech).

Most current written English uses cumulative sentences, so alter an occasional sentence to balanced or periodic when you want to emphasize its ideas.

The balanced sentence has two parallel parts, and can be used to emphasize a comparison or a contrast between two ideas. In balanced sentences, all of the ideas should be of equal value and importance. Often key words and phrases are repeated, and in many instances one small section of the balanced parts might be slightly unparallel, thus emphasizing that one section. Examples of balanced sentences follow; parallel portions are underscored.

> If children do not learn, <u>one can blame the teachers</u> or <u>one can blame the parents</u>. A child is <u>with teachers six hours a day, 180 days a year</u>, but <u>with parents eighteen hours a day, 365 days a year</u>. Blame should not fall on either teachers or parents; they should work as a team, for together they nurture children twentyfour hours a day, 365 days a year.

348

> He who corrects a scoffer gets himself underline{abuse}, and underline{he who reproves a wicked man incurs injury. Do not reprove a scoffer, or he will hate you; reprove a wise man, and he will love you} (*Proverbs* 9:78).

Study the structure of the Biblical proverb carefully. Both of the Biblical sentences are balanced; however, the addition of "himself" in the first sentence makes the second half of that sentence slightly nonparallel, thus emphasizing the admonition "incurs injury."

The periodic sentence withholds the main assertion until the end of the sentence, thus creating suspense in the reader and giving emphasis to the main assertion. For example:

> When I was very young, even when I was playing with dolls or softball in the neighborhood, I knew that when I grew up I should be a writer.

Longer periodic sentences should use parallel construction (discussed in the next section) as the sentence builds to its climax. The subject of the following sentence appears first, but then a series of parallel constructions builds to the main assertion (the establishment of the Constitution) at the end:

> We, the people of the United States, in order to form a more perfect Union, establish justice, insure domestic tranquility, provide for the common defense, promote the general welfare, and secure the blessings of liberty to ourselves and our posterity, do ordain and establish this Constitution for the United States of America (Preamble to the U.S. Constitution).

Parallel Structure and Order of Climax

Two or more elements in a sentence that have the same form have **parallel structure**. Parallel structure occurs between words, clauses, phrases, and can be used occasionally between sentences. When sentences are not parallel, they seem awkward. Here are some examples of non-parallel sentences revised for parallel structure:

> She likes swimming, dancing, and to jog.
> *Parallel:* She likes swimm*ing*, danc*ing*, and jogg*ing*.

> The cable runs across the roof; the north wall is where it runs down.
> *Parallel:* The cable runs *across the* roof and *down the* north wall.

> He admires people with strong convictions and who think for themselves.
> *Parallel:* He admires people *who have* strong convictions and *who think* for themselves. OR
> He admires people who *have* strong convictions and *think* for themselves.

349

To make a parallel structure clear, repeat:

an article (*a, an, the*)

> The man likes a cocktail and three course meal.
> *Parallel*: The man likes *a* cocktail and *a* three course meal.

a preposition

> I studied throughout the night and the day.
> *Parallel*: I studied *throughout* the night and *into* the day.

an infinitive (the form of the verb with *to)*

> He either went to work or play basketball.
> *Parallel*: He either went *to* work or *to* play basketball.

As you revise to insure parallel structure, also check for the ***order of climax*** of ideas in your sentences. When you write a sentence that ends with the main idea, arrange the order from least important to most important.

> These retirees fear death, illness, and poverty.

What do they fear least and most?

> *Edited*: These retirees fear poverty, illness, and death.

> He left the city because his health was failing, taxes were going up, and his dog was tired of the leash law.

What is the order of importance leading to his most important reason?

> *Edited*: He left the city because his dog was tired of the leash law, taxes were going up, and his health was failing.

If the sentence begins with the main idea of the sentence, the usual order is most important to least important.

> Effective sentences, a clear sense of purpose, and proper diction are all elements of successful writing.
> *Edited*: A clear sense of purpose, effective sentences, and proper diction are all elements of successful writing.

In the next instance, the writer would choose what the most important concerns are, but the writer should reflect carefully and then decide which issue is the most important, and place the order of climax from most important to least important or least important to most important:

Poverty in America, the health issue, and the plight of the education system in America are my three major concerns.

Effective writing also uses, when possible, parallel sentence structure. Parallel structure can often help suggest meaning. In this example, the parallel structure highlights the comparison:

When he was twenty, he lived in one room and earned thirty dollars a week. When he was thirty, he lived in a mansion and earned thousands of dollars a week.

Use parallel structure and order of climax to emphasize the ideas in your sentences and paragraphs.

Problems With Modification

Editing for Awkward Structure and Misplaced Word Order

A misplaced, missing, or illogical word or phrase will completely change your intended meaning. On the simplest level, to edit for awkward sentence structure you need to read your essay aloud, slowly. By this time in the editing process, you have read your essay many times, and when we read something silently over and over we begin to read what we think we are saying, not what we actually have written on the page. *This lack of clarity is tricky to spot, so read aloud, slowly.* If any sentence sounds not smooth or even slightly confusing, edit it so that it sounds concise and clear.

Two common mistakes that are difficult to discover are ***misplaced modifiers*** and ***dangling modifiers***.

***Misplaced modifiers** cause confusion; if a modifier (a word or phrase that describes another word) is not positioned correctly, it can change the entire meaning of the sentence*. Notice that in the examples that follow, the position of *only* changes the meaning of each of the sentences. Its position in the sentence *determines* which word it modifies.

Only Jamie said that the novel was inspiring.
Jamie only said that the novel was inspiring.
Jamie said that only the novel was inspiring.
Jamie said that the novel only was inspiring.
Jamie said that the novel was only inspiring.

Other examples:

Chewing gum slowly calms the nerves.

Is the gum "chewed slowly" or are the nerves "calmed slowly"? The revision depends on the intended meaning:

Slowly chewing gum calms the nerves.

351

Chewing gum calms the nerves slowly.

The man and the boy who had been married twice became friends.

Ambiguous! Who had been married twice to whom?

The boy and the man who had been married twice became friends.

Still Ambiguous!

The man who had been married twice and the boy became friends.

"Only," "slowly," and "who had been married twice" modify specific words in the sentences, and modifiers usually modify the closest word that they can. Be sure the modifier you use can refer only to the word it is supposed to modify. Edit carefully!

Dangling modifiers, another problem with modification, are introductory clauses or phrases that do not clearly modify the subject of the sentence. Sentences that begin with *ing* and *ed* forms of verbs, those beginning with subordinate conjunctions, or those with passive voice constructions can lead to dangling modifiers. They are tricky to spot; read slowly and carefully to find them. To correct dangling modifiers, either rewrite the introductory clause to include a subject and verb (as in the first two revised sentences), or rewrite the main clause so that the subject can be modified by the introductory phrase (as in the last revised sentence).

Having heard of the newest terrorist attacks, our trip was postponed.

Who heard of the terrorist attacks, the trip?

Edited: After we heard of the newest terrorist attacks, our trip was postponed.

Or revise the sentence from passive to active voice:

Edited: We postponed our trip after hearing of the latest terrorist attacks.

When only twelve, my mother began to teach me the value of money.

Very young mother, wasn't she?

Edited: When I was only twelve, my mother began to teach me the value of money.

Expecting the announcement any day, the telephone stayed by my side.

Who expected the announcement, the person's side? the telephone?

Edited: Expecting the announcement any day, I stayed by the phone.

Avoiding Faulty Predication

The *predicate* is the part of the sentence including the verb or verbs that says something about the subject. *Faulty predication* occurs when the subject and the predicate together are illogical.

The meaning of the story deals with mother/daughter issues.

A "meaning" cannot "deal with" anything.

Edited: The story deals with mother/daughter relationships.

Starvation is one of the world's biggest problems.

"Starvation" is not the problem, and for that matter "the world," itself, has no problems; "people starving" is the problem.

Edited: People starving is one of the humanity's biggest problems.

In this revision, the subject ("people starving") is the problem mentioned in the predicate.

Love is when you never have to say you're sorry.

Be careful with "is when" and "is where" constructions. Make sure the subject can display time ("when") or place ("where"). *Love* does not denote a specific time; it is a feeling.

Edited: You're in love if you agree that you never have to say you're sorry.
Edited: Love means never having to say you're sorry.

EXERCISE 17.1
Editing for Coherence, Variety, Emphasis, and Problems with Modifiers

Read your essay OUT LOUD, carefully and slowly, LISTENING, pausing at each punctuation mark (they signal pauses), and stopping at the period/question mark ending each sentence. Ask yourself, is it
1) a short choppy sentence
2) a sentence with so many clauses that the meaning becomes confused
3) a sentence that sounds in the least awkward
4) a sentence you know you can rewrite better than its present form, and finally
5) a sentence that sounds incomplete (these are sentence fragments).
Edit until each sentence flows. If you hear a sentence fragment, the following four pages tell you how to identify sentence fragments and make them complete sentences.
All good writing has been edited for sentence style in this manner.

353

18

Anyone Can Punctuate Properly

Punctuation errors and spelling errors are the two most frequent forms of editing errors in writing. Study these concerns carefully. You've spent countless hours crafting your ideas to perfection. Don't you want to spend the additional time necessary to present these ideas in a professional manner?

This chapter discusses methods to find punctuation errors and then presents ways of correcting these errors. If you have trouble understanding any of the concepts presented in this chapter, review chapter 16 (Definitions: Subjects, Verbs, Conjunctions, Clauses, Modifiers).

Sentence Fragments

Sentence fragments occur because of incorrect punctuation. They are either 1) dependent clauses (beginning with a subordinate conjunction or a relative pronoun) that are not in a sentence also containing an independent clause, 2) sentences without a subject, or 3) sentences without a complete verb. (Sentences without a complete verb are usually either phrases with no verb modifying the sentence before or after them or sentences with an *–ing* form of the verb as the sole verb in the sentence.)

To find a sentence fragment, read from one period to the next period. If there is not an independent clause between the periods, you have found a sentence fragment. Almost anyone can HEAR a sentence fragment: they sound like incomplete sentences. Here are the major causes of sentence fragments, with methods to edit them:

- *Dependent clauses cannot be complete sentences.*

If you find a dependent clause (beginning with a subordinate conjunction) by itself between two periods, connect it to the independent clause it belongs with or eliminate the subordinating word.

Fragment:
No matter how a person learns to write, whether with a computer or with a pen. He must carefully revise the finished product to make it easier to read.

> (See? Compare the fragment to the independent clause beginning "He must carefully..." It sounds incomplete.)

> *Edited*: No matter how a person learns to write, whether with a computer or with a pen, he must carefully revise the finished product to make it easier to read.

Fragment:

The use of computer software makes editing of writing much easier. Because you can change punctuation, correct spelling, eliminate awkward words, and revise sentences without retyping the whole essay.

Edited: The use of computer software makes editing of writing much easier because you can change punctuation, correct spelling, eliminate awkward words, and revise sentences without retyping the whole essay.

Fragment:

Our study group worked hard to get good grades. Because we had a drive to succeed.

Edited: Our study group worked hard to get good grades. We had a drive to succeed.

- *Relative (dependent) clauses cannot be complete sentences.*

If you find a relative clause by itself between two periods, connect it to the independent clause it belongs with or replace the relative pronoun with a noun or pronoun.

Fragment:

Carole is a chemistry professor who never seems to run out of ideas. Who has the ability to keep her classes involved.

Edited: Carole is a chemistry professor who never seems to run out of ideas, and who has the ability to keep her classes involved.   *or*:
Carole is a chemistry professor who never seems to run out of ideas, who has the ability to keep her classes involved.   *or*:
Carole is a chemistry professor who never seems to run out of ideas. She has the ability to keep her classes involved.

There are standards for punctuating subordinate and relative clauses (both dependent clauses) to avoid sentence fragments. They are:

If a subordinate or relative clause starts a sentence, it must be followed by a comma before the independent clause. No comma is needed when a subordinate or relative clause follows the independent clause. (The italicized sentences themselves are examples of these standard punctuation patterns.)

355

- *Sentences without subjects are not independent clauses, so they are sentence fragments.*

If there is no subject in the clause between two periods, find the subject (or decide what the subject of the verb is) and connect the subject to the verb to make the clause independent. (Look at the sentences before and after the fragment; the subject can usually be found there.)

Fragment (no subject):
John worked at several low paying jobs. And finally decided to go to college.

Edited: John worked at several low paying jobs and finally decided to go to college.

Fragment (no subject):
The Pell Grant program helps lower income students go to college. Confusing to navigate the website. But most schools have counselors to help.

Edited: It is confusing to navigate the website, but most schools have counselors to help.   *or:*
Since the website confuses many users, most schools have counselors to help.

- *Some fragments occur because there is no verb in the sentence.*

Most fragments without a verb are phrases modifying the sentence that preceded the fragment. Connect them.

Fragment (no verb):
The effect of cartoons is hypnotic. Not only on children, but on adults.

Edited: The effect of cartoons is hypnotic, not only on children, but on adults.

When I was in middle school, for some reason my favorite author was Nathaniel Hawthorne. A famous nineteenth century American author most famous for *The Scarlet Letter*.   *(The second phrase is a fragment - no verb.)*

Edited: When I was in middle school, for some reason my favorite author was Nathaniel Hawthorne, a famous nineteenth century American author most famous for *The Scarlet Letter*.

- *Some fragments occur when the -ing form of the verb is used because -ing forms of verbs never create subject-verb agreement. Make sure that the verb in the sentence can agree with its subject.*

Fragment: The students learning about sentence fragments.

Edited: The students learn about sentence fragments.   *or:*
The students learning about sentence fragments showed great improvement.

356

- *Some fragments have neither a subject nor a verb. They are usually prepositional phrases. Connect the fragment to the independent clause it belongs with.*

                                                  prepositional phrase (a fragment)
Seeing the end strategy in a terrorist struggle is hard. *In a long, drawn-out struggle.*

   Edited: Seeing the end strategy in a terrorist struggle is hard in a long, drawn-out struggle.

- *Occasionally, a writer will use a sentence fragment on purpose to emphasize the idea in the fragment.*

Fragments for Emphasis:
Too many good American boys have died in wars. A shame. A crying shame. We need to carefully decide when deploying American troops is an absolute necessity.

   In review, to find a sentence fragment read from period to period (or other end punctuation, i.e., question marks and exclamation points). If the clause between two end marks begins with a subordinate conjunction or relative pronoun, has no subject, or no complete verb, then it is a sentence fragment. Connect the fragment to the independent clause it belongs with or make it a complete sentence by giving it a subject and a verb.

EXERCISE 18.1
Exercise for Finding and Adding Sentence Fragments to their Correct Place
Make all the sentences in this paragraph complete sentences by eliminating sentence fragments. You may need to rewrite sentences and add or change some words to make these flow while making them independent clauses. There are many edits that will work. Find ones that make the sentences complete, independent clauses.

   Whenever I went into the country. Boy was it a fun time. I climbed the hills

   and lay by the creeks in the valleys. A green verdant stream with many trout

   and bass. Down a path was a patch of wild strawberries. Had not lost their

   flavor as so many do. This was my solitary place. My alone place. I never

   took anyone here because it would have made me feel violated to have

   someone here. Probably selfish. But that's the way I felt. Even now, i am

   struggling with whether to takre my fiance there or not. The lovde of my

   life. I'll figure it out soon.

Comma Splices and Fused Sentences

Comma splices incorrectly join two independent clauses with a comma, and *fused sentences* join two independent clauses with no punctuation at all.

To find comma splices and fused sentences, read from one period to the next period. When you find two independent clauses together with either no punctuation or a comma separating them, correct the error. Standard punctuation for consecutive independent clauses can be summarized:

When two independent clauses occur side by side, they must be separated by
1) a period
2) a comma and a coordinate conjunction, or
3) a semicolon (usually with an adverbial conjunction or a transitional phrase).

two independent clauses:
Comma splice: She likes to buy new clothes, they are too expensive.
two independent clauses:
Fused sentence: He raised the issue she didn't answer it.

Methods to correct these errors:

- **A period separating independent clauses**

  Edited: She likes to buy new clothes. They are too expensive.
  He raised the issue. She didn't answer it.

- **A comma and a coordinating conjunction** (*and, but, or, nor, yet, for, so*) **separating independent clauses**

  Edited: She like new clothes, but they are too expensive.
  He raised the issue, but she didn't answer it.

- **Semi-colons with adverbial conjunctions separating independent clauses**
  Adverbial conjunctions [notice the punctuation]: ; *accordingly,*
  ; *consequently,* ; *furthermore,* ; *however,* ; *indeed,* ; *likewise,*
  ; *moreover,......* ; *nevertheless, ...; nonetheless,* ; *otherwise,* ;*similarly,*
  ; *still,* ; *therefore ..... ; thus,* ; *thereupon,*

  Edited: She likes to buy new clothes; nevertheless, they are too expensive.
  He raised the issue; however, she didn't answer it.

It would not be incorrect to punctuate using a semi-colon like this:

She likes to buy new clothes; they are too expensive.

However, this use of semi-colons rather than periods is rare; it is used mainly when the two sentences' meanings are very closely linked.

Semi-Colons and Colons

Semi-colons either link two independent clauses or separate items in a series that themselves use commas.

- ***Use a semi-colon to join two closely related independent clauses or two independent clauses joined by an adverbial conjunction or a transitional phrase.***
  Transitional phrases that would be used with semi-colons to divide two independent clauses [notice the punctuation]:
  ; in contrast, ; on the contrary, ; in the meantime, ; for example, ; in fact, ; for instance, ; as I have said, ; in summary, ; in other words, ; to tell the truth, ; hence, ; in any event,

  The most inexpensive new cars today cost at least $13,000; fifty years ago you could buy a new Mustang for $2500.

  The median income in 1965 was $12,000 a year; today, it is $38,000 a year.

  ;adverbial conj,

  Most cats are independent; *however*, my cat has to be the most dependent creature on four legs.

  Students can learn to punctuate with just a little effort; *indeed*, punctuation just signals when we naturally pause when thinking in English.

  ;transitional phrase,

  Most cats are independent; *on the other hand*, my cat has to be the most dependent creature on four legs.

  Men in this industry make an average of $32 an hour; *in contrast*, women make only $27 an hour.

- ***Use semi-colons to separate items in a series if the individual items contain commas.***

  Must-read nineteenth-century British novels include: Dickens's *Oliver Twist, David Copperfield,* and *Great Expectations*; the Bronte sisters' *Wuthering Heights, Jane Eyre,* and *Villette*; and George Eliot's *Middlemarch, Adam Bede,* and *The Mill on the Floss*.

359

Colons serve as "pointers" and are used to introduce series, to introduce important statements or questions derived from a statement, to introduce quotations, and they also have some specialized uses.

- **Series or lists**

  John wanted three things out of life: a steady job, a happy family, and a good education.

- **Important statements or questions**

  The work of Martin Luther King has only begun because, in many ways, opportunities for minorities have decreased: racism is still alive and well in America.

  Children are still starving in the barrios of America, and others are still beaten on a regular basis: how can this happen in the world's richest country?

- **Quotations**

  The fanaticism of the colonists during the Revolutionary War is exemplified in Patrick Henry's declaration: "Give me Liberty or Give me Death."

Exceptions to Colon Use: If a phrase or an *–ing* form of a verb introduce a series, or if the colon interrupts the flow of the sentence, omit the colon. Colons signal a complete pause.

If a complete pause is not needed, as in the following examples, a colon is inappropriate.

John wants many things, including a steady job, a happy family, and a good education.

John's goals include having a steady job, a happy family, and a good education.

Patrick Henry's declaration, "Give me Liberty or Give me Death," shows the fanaticism of the American colonists.

Be careful with this widespread incorrect use of the colon:

Incorrect: Three things I disliked about Disney World were: the crowds, the food, and the prices.

Edited: Three things I disliked about Disney World were the crowds, the food, and the prices.

- **Special uses: biblical citations, hours, subtitles of articles and books, salutations**

John 3:16   8:20 A.M.   Dear Mr. Chang:

Title   Colon separating   Subtitle
Declarations of Independence: Women and Political Power in Nineteenth Century American Fiction

EXERCISE 18.2
Exercise for Correcting Fragments, Comma Splices, Fused Sentences
Insert or alter any punctuation, subject, verb, or conjunction to make these sentences complete.

1. A few minutes later. The tired woman mopped her brow.
2. John stood there speechless. His face turning redder and redder.
3. Bill did not recognize Marcia. Her hair shorter and styled differently.
4. His first project was not a success, it was not a failure either.
5. When she left town he went with her.
6. Although you may be rich. You are certainly not famous.
7. Maria didn't see why it was important to write every day, nevertheless, she decided to try it.
8. Kimiko has a friend who is smart. Who is also very handsome.
9. The Wildcats won the football game but lost the tournament.
10. Becky enrolled in the honors sociology class, however, she plans to major in Spanish.
11. The senator went to the Capital. After the news bulletin.
12. I often go to the music store. Usually buying CDs that I never have time to listen to.
13. John is a talented athlete, his brother is not.
14. He was a master of disguise who never seemed to look the same. Who never wore the same disguise twice.
15. Because Tommo likes to laugh so much. He watches Charlie Chaplin movies.
16. I want to go to the movies she wants to go out to eat.
17. Although old habits die hard she tried to quit interrupting people.
18. He watched them. The people working on the road crew.
19. You never try hard enough at school. Because you are too busy with your extracurricular activities.
20. The women worked hard to learn the construction business, however, the men were very resistant to having women work with them.

361

Comma Use

Commas are not meaningless rule-bound punctuation; they either signal pauses in a sentence or clarify its meaning.

Although sometimes whether to use a comma is a matter of choice, there are also times when the conventions of written English *demand* comma use. Readers and writers of Standard Edited English have agreed on certain sentence patterns wherein pauses are always needed, so commas have thus become standard, and furthermore, if you study these patterns you will see that the commas come at natural breaks in the flow of ideas within a sentence. They are logical points for pauses. **Above and below are the nine basic situations when a comma is definitely needed.**

The first three situations below, on this page spread, account for a statistically *large amount of the total usage errors in student essays.* After studying these three situations, check your essay carefully for these types of errors, and continue studying and editing for these three comma errors until you understand these instances where commas are necessary:

- *Use commas after introductory words and phrases.*

one word:
> Bravely, the boy went off to kindergarten.

a phrase:
> Laughing out loud, the woman cheered the performance.

a dependent clause beginning a sentence:
> After the man saw the show, he laughed too.

- *Use commas to mark non-essential phrases.*

Commas are used to set off words and phrases that interrupt the flow of the sentence, but add to its meaning. Decide whether the word or phrase is *essential* for the meaning of the sentence. If it is not essential, commas are needed both before and after the word or phrase. If it is essential, no comma is needed.

> William Faulkner won the Nobel Prize.
> William Faulkner, *a writer of some distinction,* won the Nobel Prize.
> *Useful information, but non-essential for primary meaning* (Faulkner won the Nobel Prize) , *so the commas are necessary.*

> All students suffer for it.
> All students *who don't read the assignments* suffer for it.
> *The meaning changes drastically when the phrase* who don't read the assignments *is added to the subject, so the phrase is essential, and therefore, the sentence* does not *need commas.*

> Bill Smith, *certainly one of the strongest candidates for the position,* has the best chance of becoming manager.

362

- *Use commas to set off transition words, absolute phrases, and contrasting elements.*

Transitions:

Therefore, I will be a better man because of my experience.

On the other hand, I may not get to the game on time.

The first test, *for example*, always comes with extra credit points.

Absolute phrases:

The ball having been dropped, the game was lost.

His self-esteem shattered, he limped home dejectedly.

Having reentered the race, he quickly became estatic again.

Contrasting elements:

The President, unlike the Federal Reserve Board chairman, wanted to lower taxes.

The Office of Oversight, not known for doing good work, missed the main problem with the reactors.

- *A comma preceding a coordinate conjunction (and but or nor for so yet) can be used to combine two independent clauses.*

My father saw my grades. He bought me an old car.
My father saw my grades, *so* he bought me a new car.

The man is handsome. He is also snobbish.
The man is handsome, *but* he is also snobbish.

- *Commas separate items in a series.*

He was a small, dark, homely man.
The girl left the park, went to her home, and gave her dog a bath.
Magazines, books, and stationary supplies are sold here.

Commas are used to separate two items in a series only when you could insert *and* instead of the comma.

Comma needed:	My father was in a long, bloody war.
	(My father was in a long [and] bloody war.)
No comma needed:	Tim saw four big dogs.
	Tim saw four [and] big dogs.
	[Doesn't sound natural.])

363

- *Use commas with direct quotations.*

"I'm mad," the little boy said. "My brother always gets to stay up later than I do."

Notice the position of the comma: ," ." NOT ",   ".

- *Use commas with direct address (when "speaking" to someone), and with dates, addresses, and numbers.*

Remember, Lars, the solution lies in hard work.

March 14, 2014

Louisville, KY 40691

786,329,485

- *Use commas to signal pauses.*

Many times you can decide whether to use a comma just by reading your writing aloud, slowly, as if you were giving a speech. Pause at every comma. If there are too many pauses, there are probably too many commas. On the other hand, when your writing seems to go on endlessly without a break, you might need commas.

If you need a comma why don't you put one there?

There should be a break in thought in this sentence.

Edited: If you need a comma, why don't you put one there?

- *Use commas for clarification.*

Sometimes when you leave a comma out of a sentence or place one carelessly, this changes the meaning of the sentence. Examine punctuation in sentences carefully to prevent distortions of meaning and to decide if adding punctuation would clarify the meaning of a sentence.

When the car hit, Bill Allison fainted.
When the car hit Bill, Allison fainted.

Notice that the meaning is completely changed by the position of the comma.

Overuse of Commas

Commas are usually overused, rather than not used when they should be. Remember that commas should be used only according to the preceding guidelines, to clarify meaning, or to help a sentence read smoothly.

Commas are often overused in these situations:

- **There are either two commas, or no commas, between a subject and its verb, never only one.**

  subject   *verb*

  Incorrect: The tall tree, having grown for a century <u>cast</u> its shadow in the yard.

  Correct: The tall tree, having grown for a century, <u>cast</u> its shadow in the yard.

  subject

  Incorrect: The Congressional Commission that looked into spending

  verb

  problems, <u>met</u> in the Senate Office Building.

  Incorrect: The Congressional Commission, that looked into spending problems <u>met</u> in the Senate Office Building.

  Correct: The Congressional Commission that looked into spending problems <u>met</u> in the Senate Office Building.

- **Use commas OR question marks, exclamation points, parentheses, dashes: never both.**

  Incorrect: The family-owned company bought a new computer system, (giving it a new lease on life).

  Correct: The family-owned company bought a new computer system (giving it a new lease on life).

- **Commas before and after essential elements are unneeded.**

  Incorrect: Jose forgot the screwdriver, he needed, to fix the computer.

  Correct: Jose forgot the screwdriver he needed to fix the computer.
  "he needed" is essential to describe "the screwdriver" in this sentence.

- **Commas between two nouns or verbs joined together are unneeded.**

  noun   *noun*

  Incorrect: Either the *fence*, or the *driveway* needs to be moved.

  no comma

  Correct: Either the fence or the driveway needs to be moved.

<u>*verb*</u>   <u>*verb*</u>
Incorrect: I <u>bought</u> the car, and then <u>sold</u> it the next day.
                    no comma
Correct: I <u>bought</u> the car and then <u>sold</u> it the next day.

- ***No comma occurs after a coordinating conjunction*** (*and but or nor for so yet*).

    Incorrect: Old legends never die, but, they certainly fade away.
    Incorrect: Old legends never die but, they certainly fade away.

    Correct: Old legends never die, but they certainly fade away.

- ***No comma occurs before or after*** *such as, like,* ***or*** *than.*

    Incorrect: I like books, such as *Ahab's Wife, The Corrections,* and *The Biographer's Tale.*
    Incorrect: I like books such as, *Ahab's Wife, The Corrections,* and *The Biographer's Tale.*

    Correct: I like books such as *Ahab's Wife, The Corrections,* and *The Biographer's Tale.*

    Incorrect: These books made me work harder, than I was used to.

    Correct: These books made me work harder than I was used to.

- ***No comma is needed before the first or after the last item in a series.***

    Incorrect: A happy professor will have, attentive students, a modern classroom, and a supportive department, all the time.

    Correct: A happy professor will have attentive students, a modern classroom, and a supportive department all the time.

At the risk of sounding repetitive, the best way to decide whether you have left a comma out, or have too many commas, is to read your essay aloud slowly, pausing at every comma, semi-colon, and period. *Commas occur when there would be a natural pause in the flow of ideas. You will be able to hear if you have too many commas or are missing punctuation that has to occur.*

EXERCISE 18.3
Exercise in Comma Use
Place commas where needed in the following sentences and cross out commas that don't belong in them. Some sentences need no changes.

1. Everyone, who smokes cigarettes, risks lung cancer.

2. The company hires, talented, smart, college, men and women.

3. Whenever we go on vacation my father loses his temper often.

4. All the places all the times that I have been happy, I wish they would return.

5. Please could you hand me that pencil?

6. Before I leave for work, I always drink two cups of coffee.

7. "I will go out and play" Keisha said.

8. After the last waltz the people went to the restaurant.

9. The house cleaned and repainted, is ready to be sold.

10. He might be lost but as a matter of fact, so am I.

11. *For Whom The Bell Tolls*, a novel by Hemingway, is the greatest war story ever written.

12. Ernest Hemingway's novel *For Whom The Bell Tolls* is about love and war.

13. He could be the best, for the company and the business.

14. Although I am small I have a black belt in karate.

15. John wore tight faded blue cutoffs.

16. Paula bit the ripe and juicy apple.

17. Old friends never die and new ones don't go away.

18. Help me Mrs. Garcia, I can't do this exercise right.

19. The dorm needs, a new coat of paint, new ceilings, and an up-to-date wi-fi.

20. The plan being mine won the contest.

EXERCISE 18.4
Editing for Punctuation: Fragments, Comma Splices, Commas, and Other Punctuation

Most problems with punctuation can be *heard* if you read aloud like you are giving a speech. The trick is to pause at every punctuation mark (semi-colons, colons, periods, question marks, and commas) and to not pause if there is no punctuation. You will usually hear when there are too many commas, when there are missing necessary commas, and when you have a sentence fragment or fused sentence. You will also hear awkward sentences.

You were just asked to read aloud after studying sentence style and coherence in chapter 17, and editing for these concerns. Do it again with this chapter, and as you edit for proper punctuation - when there is often a right and wrong choice - also edit again for sentence style. After the first two essays in your class, if you conscientiously do the editing asked for in exercise 17.1 (for coherence, variety, emphasis, modification), and then repeat it with this exercise, 18.4 (comma use), you will be able to combine these two skills and your writing will have improved for the rest of your life.

19

Verbs:
Agreement and Tenses

Verb Forms (infinitive, past tense, past participle, present participle)

Definitions of Terms Used to Describe Verbs

Tense — The time of a verb's action. The main tenses are
present (laugh)   *past* (laughed)   *future* (will laugh)   *present perfect* (have laughed)
past perfect (had laughed)   *future perfect* (will have laughed).

Person — The verb form that indicates whether the subject is
speaking (I run)   *spoken* to (You run)   or   *spoken about* (She runs).

Number — The verb form that indicates whether the verb is
singular (The girl eats)   or   *plural* (The girls eat).

Voice — The distinction between the **active voice**, when the subject performs the action of the verb (*The student read the book.*), and the **passive voice**, when the subject receives the action of the verb (*The toddler was read to by his father.*).

Mood — The attitude of the verb's speaker or writer:
The **indicative mood** - states a fact or opinion, or asks a question.
        (*John wants the apple. Can he have it?*)

The **imperative mood** - expresses a command or gives a direction.
        (*Give me the apple. Go to the store and buy one.*)

The **subjunctive mood** - expresses a desire or suggestion
        (*The principal asked that she write the paper.*)
or an imaginary or hypothetical condition contrary to fact
        (*If I were king, I would institute universal health care.*).

Helping Verbs (sometimes called **auxiliary verbs**) —
is are was were being been have has had create specific tenses (the time sequence of the action of the verb in a sentence) and the passive voice.
may could would should create a meaning of causality or probability in a sentence's verbs.

There are four basic forms of verbs: *the base (or infinitive), the simple past tense, the past participle,* and the *present participle*.

The *infinitive* ([to] smile, [to] finish) is the **base form** of a verb preceded by *to*. Its main uses, without the *to,* occur in the present tense with an *–es* added only for third person singular (or only an *-s* for base forms already ending in *e -*), in the future tense (with **will** added to denote future time), in conditional tenses (with helping verbs that denote causality and probability), and with **do** to signal that someone is/ was performing an action. With the *to,* an infinitive serves as a noun. Irregular verbs with irregular endings are listed and described in the last section of this chapter, and also their endings are conjugated in a dictionary.

- *Present tense*

Person	Singular	Plural
1st	I smile.	We smile.
2nd	You smile.	You (plural) smile.
3rd	He smiles.	They smile.
	(He finishes.)	

- *Future tense*

1st	I *will* smile.	We *will* smile.
2nd	You *will* smile.	You *will* smile.
3rd	He *will* smile.	They *will* smile.

- *Causality and probability*

Helping verbs that signal causality and probability: *can, could, may, might, must, should, would, ought to*

Caitlin *may* smile.
Tom *should* smile.
Jennifer *could* smile.
Tyler *would* smile if he wanted to.

- *Signaling performance of an action with* do

John *does* a good job when he bakes a pie.
They *do* their hair every morning.
The tank regiment *did* a spectacular flanking maneuver.

- *The infinitive serving as a noun*

The boy learned *to swim.*
To laugh is to be human.

369

Regular verbs signal the **simple past tense** by adding an **ed** to the base (or a **d** if the verb ends with an *e*). Irregular verbs, believe it or not, have irregular endings.

Person	Singular	Plural	An Irregular Verb (*be*)	
1st	I *smiled.*	We *smiled.*	I *was.*	We *were.*
2nd	You *smiled.*	You (pl.) *smiled.*	You *were.*	You (pl.) *were.*
3rd	He *smiled.*	They *smiled.*	He *was.*	They *were.*
	(He *finished.*)			

    The past participle is used with a form of *have*, in the passive voice with a form of *be*, or as an adjective. With regular verbs, it is identical to the simple past tense (*-ed* or *–d* added to the base). Irregular verbs have irregular endings for the simple past *and* the past participle. If you are unsure of the form for the past tense or the past participle of a verb, consult the list of irregular verbs that concludes this chapter or use a dictionary.

- **with** *to have*

  Rick *has smiled* at the circus clowns many times.
  Rick *had smiled* at the circus clowns before.

- **in the passive voice with a form of** *to be*

  The circus clown *was smiled* at by Rick.
  The circus clowns *were smiled* at by Rick.

- **as an adjective modifying another word**

  Lisa delivers *completed* work to the boss.

    The **present participle** is always formed by the addition of *-ing* to the base. (There are occasional spelling changes, for instance: *refer, referring; drag, dragging.*) The present participle can be used as a noun, as an adjective, or with a form of *be* to show action in progress.

- **as a noun (a person, place, thing, quality, or act)**

  Smiling is good for you.

- **as an adjective modifying another word**

  The *smiling* man is a happy man.

- **with a form of be to show action in progress**

  The man *is finishing* his work now.
  The man *was finishing* his work when the boss called.

370

Subject-Verb Agreement

Every clause has a subject and verb, and the verb changes to agree with the subject in number (singular or plural) and in person (whether the subject is speaking, first person *I*; spoken to, second person, *you*; or spoken about, third person, any noun or third person or indefinite pronoun.

For example, in the present tense, the verb form changes in the third person singular. The third person singular includes one person (*John, the President, the banker*), one thing (*the dog, the tree, the swimming pool*), or a third person pronoun (*he, she, it, who, that, each, every, all, some*). The verb form for the third person adds *s* or *es*.

Person	Number	
	Singular	Plural
1st	I lift weights.	We run fast.
2nd	You eat slow.	You (pl.) fix cars.
3rd	He sleep**s** good.	They dance every night.
	John guess**es** the answers.	

Verb Agreement Problems

Instances that often present verb agreement problems include the following seven standards that are not followed, and non-use of the subjunctive mode:

Carefully study this and the next three pages for frequent agreement problems.

- ***Use the -s -es endings in the third person singular present tense only***

    rises
    The bay ~~rise~~ every day with the tide.
    sell
    You ~~sells~~ your car cheap.
    play
    The children ~~plays~~ good music.

- ***When words come between the subject and the verb, the verb must agree in number and person with the subject***

    Incorrect: Two doughnuts in the morning is not a good breakfast.
              plural subject   ***plural verb***
    Correct: Two *doughnuts* in the morning *are* not a good breakfast.

    Incorrect: The sports car, along with its T-tops, sell for $2995.
             singular subject   ***singular verb***
    Correct: The *sports car*, along with its T-tops, *sells* for $2995.

371

- **When a verb comes before the subject, make sure it agrees with its subject**

    Incorrect: Inside the locker is the books.
          plural verb plural subject
    Correct: Inside the locker *are* the *books*.
        Compare the placement of the subject:
        The books are inside the locker.

- **In sentences starting with** *there* **or** *here* **and with questions that ask** *who,* *what, which,* **and** *where,* **the subject is not those words, but the subject that comes later in the sentence.**

    Incorrect: There is the lawyers going to the meeting.
         plural verb plural subject
    Correct: There *are* the *lawyers* going to the meeting.

    Incorrect: What is the problems you are finding?
         plural verb plural subject
    Correct: What *are* the *problems* you are finding?

- *Who, which,* **and** *that* **take singular verbs if they refer to singular words and plural verbs if they refer to plural words.**

    Incorrect: A Cadillac is one of those big cars that gives a smooth ride.
    [That *refers to cars (plural), so the verb should be* give *(plural).]*
    Correct: A Cadillac is one of those big cars that give a smooth ride.

    Incorrect: Gregory is in the group of students who is very diligent.
    [Who *refers to a group, so the verb should be* are *(plural).]*
    Correct: Gregory is in the group of students who are very diligent.
    Correct: Gregory is a person who is very diligent.
    [Who *refers to one person, so the verb should be* is *(singular).]*

- **Sentences with compound subjects: Subjects joined by** *and* **usually take a plural verb.**

Except with compound subjects joined by *either. . .or, neither. . .nor, not only. . .but also*, the verb agrees with the subject closest to the verb.

    Incorrect: Sam and Teri is going to town.
    Correct: Sam and Teri are going to town.

    Incorrect: Either Sam or Teri are going to town.
    Correct: Either Sam or Teri is going to town.

    Incorrect: Either Sam or his two sisters is going to town.
    Correct: Either Sam or his two sisters are going to town.

- *Collective nouns – such as crowd, family, group, audience – take a plural verb if the collective noun refers to individuals within the group, but a singular verb if the collective noun refers to the group as a single unit.*

> *plural verb and pronouns*
> The committee *have their* own ideas on the amendment, mostly based on the area of town *they* live in. *[The thoughts of individual members are emphasized in this sentence.]*

> *singular verb and pronoun*
> The committee *has reconciled its* differences and reached a decision.
> *[Although the sentence mentions differences within the committee, the sense of the committee as a single unit dominates the sentence; hence, it takes a singular verb.]*

The Subjunctive Mood

The **subjunctive mood** is used in several specific instances, and it uses different forms of *is, are, was, were, be* than the usual forms of the indicative mood. For other verbs, it uses the base form of the verb whether the time sequence is past, present, or future (*laugh, smile, believe*: If he only *believe* in himself. [not *believes*]). Make sure that you use the correct forms when employing the subjunctive mood.

The subjunctive is used when expressing conditions of doubt; conditions wished for (including suggestions and requirements), conditions that are hypothetical or improbable; or conditions contrary to fact. Many times the subjunctive is employed in an *if* or *that* clause.

> *subjunctive (suggestion/requirement):*
> The professor asks that he *send* the essay via email.
> *compare to the indicative mood:* He *sends* the essay via email.

> *subjunctive (a wish)*: The alumni asks that everyone *contribute* to the fund.
> *compare to the indicative mood:* Everyone *contributes* to the fund.

> *subjunctive (contrary to fact/hypothetical):*
> If Germany *had* won World War II, the world would *be* less free than it is.
> *compare to the indicative mood:* Germany *has* won World War II. The world *is* less free.

Do you see how the subjunctive can be confusing? Check for errors when you have employed the indicative but the subjunctive is necessary.

373

With *to be*, in the subjunctive present tense always use *be* in all persons and numbers (when *am*, *are*, *is* would be used in the indicative mood). In the subjunctive past tense, employ *were* for all persons and numbers, whether *was* or *were* would be used in the indicative mood.

>*subjunctive (condition contrary to fact):*
>If I *were* going to the store, I would buy you the apples you want.
>*compare to the indicative mood:* I *was* going to the store.

>*subjunctive (hypothetical situation, and a wish):*
>I would marry him if he *were* richer than Sam.
>*compare to the indicative mood:* He *was* richer than Sam.

>*subjunctive (a request):* The Senator asked that the rules *be* suspended.
>*compare to the indicative mood:* The rules *are* suspended.

EXERCISE 19.1
Verb Agreement and the Subjunctive Mood
Correct agreement problems in these sentences. Some sentences have no problems.

1. The two men, along with Tim, ~~is~~ *are* going to town.
2. Here is the books that you wanted.
3. Which one of those men dance every night?
4. Either Rita or those men is going to get the contract.
5. When I go to the store, I always buy a popsicle.
6. Either Susan or that man is going to pay the bill.
7. Four good friends at school is all I have.
8. There seem to be a problem with the staffing at the center.
9. I move that Juan be elected to the position.
10. What are the nature of the problems you are having?
11. Two dates in one evening is not a good idea.
12. An old friend and acquaintance who leave when the going gets rough should be avoided.
13. If I was making the rules, I would make them accountable.
14. If he comes to his senses, then I would help him with his homework.
15. If that was my car, I would take good care of it.

Verb Tenses and Sequences

Verb tenses signal when an action occurred or when a subject existed. There are three simple tenses (present, past, and future) and three additional forms of each of these (perfect, progressive, and perfect progressive) that will help you – by using them correctly – describe exactly *when* an action occurred or *when* a subject existed. Defining the tenses and demonstrating how they are formed can best be illustrated by examples:

The present tense: I drive to school.
[action in the present: present tense]

The present perfect: I have driven to school.
[action completed at an indefinite past time: *has/have*+past participle]

The present progressive: I am driving to school.
[a present, continuing action that may continue: *am/is/are*+ present participle]

The present perfect progressive: I have been driving to school.
[an action beginning in the past and continuing in the present that may continue: *has/have+been*+present participle]

The past tense: I drove to school.
[an action completed at a definite time in the past: simple past tense]

The past perfect: I had driven to school when the car stopped.
[a past action that has occurred prior to another action: *had*+past participle]

The past progressive: I was driving to school every day when the engine stopped.
[a continuing action begun, and completed, in the past: *was/were*+present participle]

The past perfect progressive: I had been driving to school when the car broke down.
[a past, continuing action completed before another past action: *had been*+present participle]

The future tense: I will drive to school.
[an action or state of being that will begin in the future: *will*+infinitive]

The future perfect: I will have driven to school by the time you arrive.
[an action occurring in the future before another action: *will have*+past participle]

The future progressive: I will be driving to school every morning next semester.
[a continuing action in the future: *will be*+present participle]

The future perfect progressive: I will have been driving to school for years before you fix my car.
[a continuing action in the future that will occur before some specified future time: *will have been*+present participle]

Sentences with both a dependent and an independent clause must be crafted with care. Since the two clauses in a sentence might denote actions occurring at different times, be sure to clarify the time relationship between the actions. The time sequence is signaled by your choice of tense. Two common tense sequences are listed here:

- *If the action in an independent clause occurs in the present*

I start school today and will also buy my books today.
[present, future]

I have started school today and will also buy my books today.
[present perfect, future]

I start school today and also buy my books today.
[present, present]

- *If the action in the independent clause occurs in the past*

I started school yesterday after I bought my books.
[past, past]

I started school when I had finished my internship.
[past, past perfect]

I started school later than my sister who was traveling around the country.
[past, past progressive]

I started school although I had been making good money for several years.
[past, past perfect progressive]

I started school even though I will soon be traveling to Asia with the Peace Corps.
[past, future progressive]

I started school even though I soon travel to Asia with the Peace Corps.
[past, future – the verb will is understood from the context, so it is omitted]

Also be aware of a convention known as the ***historical present tense***. When referring to an action in an already-existing work (a television show, movie, news broadcast, book, essay, report), and also to report scientific data or information, use the present tense. Examples follow:

Sylvester Stallone *plays* a disenfranchised Vietnam vet in the movie *Rambo*.
　　　　[not played]
Hamlet *wants* to kill his uncle to avenge his father's murder.
　　　[not wanted]
Evidence *indicates* that cancer rates in Australia *increase* as the ozone layer *depletes*.
　　　[not indicated]　　　　　　　　　　　　*[not increased]*

Common Verb Tense Errors

In the English language, verb tenses indicate the precise time sequence of the actions. Make sure that the verbs in your sentence indicate the proper time sequence and that you have used the Ccorrect form of the verb in present, past, perfect, and progressive tense sequences. Common errors include:

- ***Leaving the -d -ed ending off regular past tense and past participle verbs***

    asked
    John ~~ask~~ his teacher for an extension on the term paper.
    sliced
    The ~~slice~~ peach was delicious.

- ***Inappropriate shifts in tense***

              would remind   *is*
    If Cary Grant *were* a movie star today, he ~~reminds~~ us that chivalry ~~was~~ not dead.

       past tense
    John F. Kennedy *was shot* in Dallas, and then when Lyndon B. Johnson
    past tense   *present tense wrong; past correct: swore*
    flew back to Washington on Air Force One, a federal judge ~~swears~~ him in as the new President.

When you write sentences with more than one clause, make sure you have used the proper sequence of tenses. Often, if you are checking for shifts in tense and you read the sentence carefully, you will HEAR that something is not appropriate. If you cannot decide the proper sequence of tenses, review the preceding section.

More often, verb tense shifts occur between sentences separated in a paragraph:

> When John Glenn *became* the first American astronaut to orbit the earth, he ~~spent~~ *[had spent]* more than a decade as a test pilot. He *was* one of the initial seven Mercury astronauts. As he and the first seven *flew* the first manned space flights for America, eight more astronauts *trained* and they ~~have become~~ *[became]*, with the Mercury astronauts, the astronauts in the Gemini and Apollo space flights. Three of them *landed* on the moon a short seven years after Glenn's flight, and we always ~~are~~ *[will be]* grateful for their sacrifice.

- ***Confusion Between the Past Tense and the Past Participle Forms of Irregular Verbs***

Carefully distinguish between the simple past and the past participle forms of irregular verbs. Past participle forms of a verb will either be used as adjectives or with the helping verbs *has, have,* or *had.* Review the list of irregular verbs at the end of this chapter.

377

	present	*past*	*past participle*
sworn *(past participle required)*			
I *could have* ~~swore~~ the money was in the cabinet.	swear	swore	sworn

saw *(simple past required)*			
We ~~seen~~ the money yesterday.	see	saw	seen

gone *(past participle required)*			
Melissa *had* ~~went~~ and then later she *returned*.	go	went	gone

rang *(simple past required)*			
I ~~rung~~ the bell after the robbery.	ring	rang	rung

drunk *(past participle required)*			
Too many people *had* ~~drank~~ the sour mash.	drink	drank	drunk

sprung *(past participles serve as adjectives)*			
The ~~sprang~~ lock revealed the treasure.	spring	sprang	sprung

- ***Troublesome Verbs:*** *lie/lay, sit/set, rise/raise*

Three pairs of verbs – *lie/lay, sit/set, rise/raise* – cause confusion because of their similarities in spelling and meaning. The most troublesome of these are *lie/lay*, mainly because the past tense of *lie* is *lay*.

lie: I *lie* down to sleep. [*present*]   I *lay* down to sleep. [*past*]
lay: I *lay* down the book. [*present*]   I *laid* down the book. [*past*]

Remember the definitions to help you differentiate between the verbs.

lie: to recline (as in a bed)
lay: to put or place

Here are the principal parts of these confusing verbs:

Base	*Past Tense*	*Past Participle*	*Present Participle*
lie	lay	lain	lying
lay	laid	laid	laying

I *have lain* in bed for hours. [*past participle* of *lie*]
I *am lying* in bed now. [*present participle* of *lie*]
I *have* always *laid* the book on the table. [*past participle* of *lay*]
I *was laying* the book on the table when you called. [*present participle* of *lay*]

378

sit: to be seated (as in a chair)
set: to put or place

Base	Past Tense	Past Participle	Present Participle
sit	sat	sat	sitting
set	set	set	setting

She *sat* in her chair. [*past tense of sit*] - NOT She *set* in her chair.
She *has sat* in the chair for hours. [*past participle of sit*] — NOT She has *set* in ...
She *was sitting* in the chair when I called. [*present participle* of *sit*]
She *set* the book on the table. [*BOTH the present AND simple past tense of set.*]
She *had set* the book on the table when I called. [*past participle of set*]
She *was setting* the book on the table when I called. [*present participle* of *set*]

rise: to move up from a reclined or lowered position. (The sun *rises*.)
raise: to move something up from a reclined or lowered position. (Bill *raises* the window.)

Base	Past Tense	Past Participle	Present Participle
rise	rose	risen	rising
raise	raised	raised	raising

The sun *rose* in the morning. [*simple past of rise*]
The sun *has risen* every day. [*past participle of rise*]
The sun *was rising* when I caught the trout. [*present participle of rise*]
Bill *raised* the window and then it fell. [*simple past of raise*]
Bill *had raised* the window when it fell on my hands. [*past participle of raise*]
Bill *was raising* the window when it fell on my hands. [*present participle of raise*]

EXERCISE 19.2
Correcting Verb Tense Errors
Correct tense errors in these underlined verbs. Tense errors usually occur in a sequence of sentences. All the verbs together must have a tense consistency to them. *Some verbs have no problems, and some have several possible answers.*
A.
I (1) have wrote about going into the country to visit my relatives before. All they do (2) is set around and talk about the lack of jobs. But the sun (3) rose in the morning and it (4) sets in the evening, and there (5) are never going to be any changes until the county government does something to bring an industry to the town. Why (6) don't they do this when they (7) had the chance? When they do, that industry (8) would find a hard-working population, which (9) are fast becoming extinct. The County Attorney (10) ask for help from the state, but they didn't answer.

1.

2.

3.

4.

5.

6.

7.

8.

9.

10.

379

B.

World War II (1) <u>began</u> on September 1, 1939 when Germany (2) <u>invades</u> Poland. By the end of 1940, Poland, Czechoslovakia, France, Norway, Denmark, and Belgium (3) <u>have surrendered</u> to the Germans, and there (4) <u>is</u> a battle for air superiority over England, with Hitler preparing to invade England. Hitler (5) <u>has</u> also <u>invaded</u> North Africa and Greece, and in the next year (6) <u>will invade</u> Russia. America (7) <u>stayed</u> neutral until Japan (8) <u>attacked</u> Pearl Harbor in December of 1941. By 1945, allied forces (9) <u>beat</u> the German army, navy, and air force, and Germany (10) <u>surrenders</u>.

1.   2.   3.

4.   5.   6.   7.

8.   9.   10.

Irregular Verbs

Irregular verbs do not employ *ed* or *d* endings in the simple past and past participle forms.

Remember that if a verb phrase has either a form of have *(have/has/had) or a form of* be *(am/are/is/was/were/been) as helping verbs, the past participle or the present participle will be used, never the simple past tense.*

Let's review what causes confusion with verb endings. In regular verbs, the simple past and the past participle are the same spelling:

A regular verb with regular endings:	***Base***	***Past Tense***	***Past Participle***	***Present Participle***
	brag	bragged	bragged	bragging

simple <u>past tense</u>   *<u>past participle (present perfect tense)</u>*
John <u>bragged</u> at the party because he always <u>has bragged</u> when he gets nervous.

The confusion occurs because irregular verbs have different endings for the past and past participle, with several irregularities and several similarities. Some of the most common verbs (like *be*) also have different endings in the present tense. Present participles always end with *-ing*.

To compound the problem, spoken language always is in the process of simplifying how people speak, so in may dialects speakers use the simple past tense when the past participle is called for. In written language, most writing situations encounter situations where the reader expects an educated writer, and one of the methods readers use to decide if the writer is educated is his use of standard written English, with a minimum of usage errors.

So it is important for writers to learn the irregular verb endings of standard English to communicate in most written situations. When you speak, standard format is not as necessary, but when speaking judge the level of discourse you are participating in: if standard written English is required in a speaking situation, by all means use standard English.

An example illustrating the problem:

	Base	*Past Tense*	*Past Participle*	*Present Participle*
irregular verbs with	become	became	become	becoming
irregular endings:	begin	began	begun	beginning

simple past tense   *present participle*
Nellie became a singer in a nightclub by first becoming a keyboard player.

Informal spoken English:
She has became so sought after,
that agents from Los Angeles have began to court her.

Standard English:
past participle (present perfect tense)
She has become so sought after,
        past participle (present perfect tense)
that agents from Los Angeles have begun to court her.

- *Seven of the Most Commonly Used Irregular Verbs:*
  be become begin do give go have

Present and Future Tense Base	*Past Tense*	*Past Participle*	*Present Participle*
be (am/are/is//will be)	was, were	been	being

I am an acrobat, but you are a circus clown, while he is a lion tamer.
I was an acrobat, but you were a circus clown, while he was a lion tamer.
I had been an acrobat the longest, but you have been a clown for the longest uninterrupted time, while being a lion tamer is something he is new at.

As was just discussed, specific verb tenses demonstrate when an action occurred: changing the verb ending from "He has become" to "He had become" signals a difference in when the action ("becoming") occurred. With irregular verbs, a careful editor has to make sure he is using the correct forms of both the helping and the main verbs to signal the time sequence described in a sentence.

become	became	become	becoming
begin	began	begun	beginning

Present and Future Tense Base	Past Tense	Past Participle	Present Participle
do	did	done	doing

Informal spoken English:
Should be simple past tense:

I <u>done</u> that yesterday.
I <u>did</u> that yesterday.

Informal spoken English:
Present participles as verbs need a helping verb:

He <u>doing</u> a good job selling cars.
He <u>is doing</u> a good job selling cars.

Informal spoken English:
Perfect tenses using *have/had* **need past participle:**
OR depending on the time sequence of the event:

He <u>had did</u> the best he could.
He <u>had done</u> the best he could.
He <u>has done</u> the best he could.
He <u>did</u> the best he could.

give	gave	given	giving

Informal spoken English: I <u>give</u> money three times and <u>had give</u> the same last year.
Simple past /past participle required: I <u>gave</u> money three times and <u>had given</u> the same last year.

go	went	gone	going

Informal spoken English: I <u>gone</u> to the store. I <u>going</u> to the store.
Simple past/ Present participle needs *be:* I <u>went</u> to the store. I <u>am going</u> to the store.

Informal spoken English: Bill <u>has went</u> to the store.
Should be past participle with perfect tense: Bill <u>has gone</u> to the store.

have (have/has)	had	had	having

Have is one of the most used verbs because it is used in the ***perfect tenses*** to signal a specific time sequence.

I <u>have</u> a good breakfast every day, but I always <u>had</u> terrible fast food lunches.

Used to form perfect tenses:
present perfect tense using present(have) and past participle of *lost:*
   I <u>have lost</u> my car keys.

past perfect tense using past (had) and past participle of *lost*
   I <u>had lost</u> my car keys when I was in a hurry.

Informal spoken English: He <u>have</u> a good grasp of history.
3rd person present changes from base form: He <u>has</u> a good grasp of history.
(I <u>have</u>; You <u>have</u>; He <u>has</u>; We <u>have</u>; They <u>have</u>)

382

Past perfect ending when have *is the main verb*: Bill <u>had had</u> a good year before the accident.
1st had: *simple past form used as a helping verb to signal perfect tense*
2nd had: *past participle*

- ### *Twenty-seven Irregular Verbs that follow an -n past participle pattern*

These twenty-eight irregular verbs follow a similar pattern making them easy to remember: they change one consonant sound between present and past tense, and they also all end their past participle with an *-n* or *-en* ending. The base of their past participle with some verbs sounds like the base present tense, and with others sounds like the simple past. *Once you assimilate how this pattern SOUNDS, it becomes much easier to correctly use these irregular verbs.*

Present and Future Tense Base	*Past Tense*	*Past Participle*	*Present Participle*
bite	bit	bitten	biting

Informal spoken English: The dog <u>had bit</u> the postal worker three times before.
Perfect tenses using have/had *need the past participle*: The dog <u>had bitten</u> the postal worker three times before.

blow	blew	blown	blowing
break	broke	broken	breaking

Informal spoken English: John <u>has broke</u> his left ankle. He has a <u>broke</u> left ankle.
Should be past participle with perfect tense and when used as an adjective:
John <u>has broken</u> his left ankle. John has a <u>broken</u> left ankle.

choose	chose	chosen	choosing

*Informal spoken English:*Bill <u>has chose</u> the blue tie. Jean <u>was chose</u> class President.
Should be past participle with perfect tense: Bill <u>has chosen</u> a blue tie.
Should be past participle with passive voice: Jean <u>was chosen</u> class President.

draw	drew	drawn	drawing
drive	drove	driven	driving
eat	ate	eaten	eating

Informal spoken English: Joan <u>has ate</u> the whole pie. Jose <u>eaten</u> a whole pie too.
Should be past participle with perfect tense: Joan <u>has eaten</u> the whole pie.
Should be simple past tense: Jose <u>ate</u> the whole pie too.
or the present perfect: Jose <u>has eaten</u> the whole pie.

Present and Future Tense Base	Past Tense	Past Participle	Present Participle
fall	fell	fallen	falling

Informal spoken English: Help. I <u>fallen</u> down.

Correct tense possibilities depend on exactly   Help. I <u>have fallen</u> down.
what time sequence the sentence is describing: Help. I <u>am falling</u> down.
                                                   Help. I <u>fell</u> down.

fly	flew	flown	flying
forget	forgot	forgotten	forgetting

Informal spoken English: I <u>have forgot</u> the homework. I <u>done forgot</u> the book.
Should be past participle with perfect tense: I <u>have forgotten</u> the homework.
do should be simple past, after do *should be base form of main verb:* I <u>did forget</u> the book.

forgive	forgave	forgiven	forgiving
freeze	froze	frozen	freezing
grow	grew	grown	growing

Informal spoken English: Billy all <u>grown</u> up.
                           Billy <u>is</u> all <u>grown</u> up. *or*: Billy <u>grew</u> up. *or*: Billy <u>has grown</u> up.
                           These tense possibilities depend on exactly what time sequence
                           the sentence is describing.

hide	hid	hidden	hiding

Informal spoken English: Jimmy <u>has hid</u> in the closet.
Should be past participle with perfect tense: Jimmy <u>has hidden</u> in the closet.

know	knew	known	knowing
lie	lay	lain	lying
ride	rode	ridden	riding
rise (and arise)	rose	risen	rising
see	saw	seen	seeing

Informal spoken English: I <u>seen</u> the whale from the pier.
Depending on the time sequence: I <u>saw</u> the whale from the pier.
                                       I <u>have seen</u> a whale from the pier.

speak	spoke	spoken	speaking
steal	stole	stolen	stealing
swear	swore	sworn	swearing
take	took	taken	taking

Present and Future Tense Base	Past Tense	Past Participle	Present Participle
throw	threw	thrown	throwing
wake	woke	woken	waking
wear	wore	worn	wearing
write	wrote	written	writing

- **_Forty-three Irregular Verbs that have the same form for both the simple past and the past participle_**

bring	brought	brought	bringing

I <u>bring</u> and he <u>brings</u> the footballs.	*present tense*
Julie <u>brought</u> the football yesterday,	*simple past tense*
but Amy <u>has brought</u> the football in the past.	*present perfect tense so the past participle*
Everyone <u>will have brought</u> a football by the end of the season.	*future perfect so the past participle*
The coach <u>is bringing</u> the whistle.	*present progressive tense so present participle*
<u>Bringing</u> the whistle seems necessary,	*present participle used as a noun*

buy	bought	bought	buying
catch	caught	caught	catching
dig	dug	dug	digging
dive	dived (or dove)	dived	diving
feed	fed	fed	feeding
feel	felt	felt	feeling
fight	fought	fought	fighting
find	found	found	finding
get	got	got (or gotten)	getting
hang (meaning suspend)	hung	hung	hanging
hang (meaning execute)	hanged	hanged (regular)	hanging
hear	heard	heard	hearing
hold	held	held	holding
keep	kept	kept	keeping
lay	laid	laid	laying
lead	led	led	leading
leave	left	left	leaving
lend	lent	lent	lending
light	lighted (or lit)	lighted (or lit)	lighting
lose	lost	lost	losing
make	made	made	making
pay	paid	paid	paying
prove	proved	proved (or proven)	proving
say	said	said	saying
sell	sold	sold	selling

Present and Future Tense Base	Past Tense	Past Participle	Present Participle
set	set	set	setting
shine	shined (or shone)	shined (or shone)	shining
shoot	shot	shot	shooting
sit	sat	sat	sitting
sleep	slept	slept	sleeping
spend	spent	spent	spending
stand	stood	stood	standing
stick	stuck	stuck	sticking
sting	stung	stung	stinging
strike	struck	struck (or stricken)	striking
sweep	swept	swept	sweeping
swing	swung (not swang)	swung	swinging
teach	taught	taught	teaching
tell	told	told	telling
think	thought	thought	thinking
win	won	won	winning
wind	wound	wound	winding

- **Seven Often Confused Irregular Verbs**

come	came	come	coming

This unique irregularity occurs because a past participle is the same as the base form.

The teacher <u>comes</u>. *present tense*

The teacher <u>came</u>. *simple past tense*

The teacher <u>has come</u>. *present perfect tense using the past participle*

drink	drank	drunk (not drunken)	drinking

Informal spoken English: Bob <u>has drank</u> all the iced tea.

Should be past participle with perfect tense: Bob <u>has drunk</u> all the iced tea.

fall	fell	fallen	falling

Informal spoken English: The tree <u>had fell</u> on the car.

Should be past participle with perfect tense: The tree <u>had fallen</u> on the car.

sing	sang	sung (not sang)	singing

Informal spoken English: The baby <u>was sang</u> to by his father.

Should be past participle with passive voice: The baby <u>was sung</u> to by his father.

Present and Future Tense Base	Past Tense	Past Participle	Present Participle
sink	sank	sunk (not sank)	sinking

Informal spoken English: The boat <u>has sank</u> by the pier.
Should be past participle with perfect tense: The boat <u>has sunk</u> by the pier.

Informal spoken English: The raft I was on <u>sunk</u>.
Should be simple past, not past participle: The raft I was on <u>sank</u>.

spring	sprang	sprung (not sprang)	springing

Informal spoken English: The gymnast <u>had sprang</u> over the pylon.
Should be past participle with perfect tense: The gymnast <u>had sprung</u> over the pylon.

swim	swam	swum (not swam)	swimming

Informal spoken English: Bob <u>has swam</u> every morning this semester.
Should be past participle with perfect tense: Bob <u>has swum</u> every morning this semester.

EXERCISE 19.3
Exercise in Using Correct Verb Forms
Using the irregular verb form list, cross out the incorrect verb in these sentences.

1. Did you see the damage the rain (did/~~done~~) to the building?
2. I should have (wore/worn) a jacket to the picnic.
3. I was exhausted because I (swam/swum) all afternoon.
4. I (drank/drunk) at least ten cups of coffee while working on the paper.
5. How long has your television been (broke/broken)?
6. Joan has (rode/ridden) all over town looking for an apartment.
7. Bill has (wrote/written) six papers for his composition class.
8. The little girl (swang/swung) all day.
9. The President is a duly (swore/sworn) official.
10. The robber was (hid/hidden) by his friend.

Use the appropriate form of the verb.

11. ring/come Jack was <u>ringing</u> the doorbell when I <u>came</u> home.

12. steal/see The television was_____and I had no way of

_____

387

13. spoil   Too many cooks were_____the preparations.

14. leave   Someone_____a book in the classroom.

15. throw/leave The pitcher had_____the ball before the
runner_____the base.

16. go/come   Bob had_____when Jim_____.

17. forget/complain The lady had_____the doctor's appointment
and he_____.

18. hang/hang The prisoner was_____after the rope was_____.

19. swear/win John was always _____ that he would_____the lottery.

20. spring   The mousetrap had _____open.

Revise any inappropriate form. If these verbs give you problems, check each verb with
the definitions and forms in this section. Do not revise according to what "sounds"
right — many people use these verbs incorrectly.

lying   correct

21.Just because you are laying down, doesn't mean you can't help raise the screen.

22.She lay the book down next to the folder which had been set on the table.

23.The invalid raised out of the bed and sat in the chair.

24.John was lying in bed when his wife came in and set down next to him.

25.Having risen early, the old woman lay the hoe in the garden and then set the plants

next to it.

EXERCISE 19.4
Editing for Verb Tense and Verb Agreement

Read this chapter carefully as a review – read all the examples aloud, first the incorrect
examples followed by the corrections. Listen for verbs where you use the incorrect
version of the verb (remember that most of the confusion occurs between the use
of the past and the past participle of verbs). Then after taking the hour to study this
chapter carefully, carefully read your essay sentence by sentence checking for verb
errors.
Some of you will discover that you use the correct forms of the verbs, but you never
would have known without this one hour of study/review. More of you will discover
a few verbs that you misuse, and this hour study will alert you to the ones you need
to carefully edit. And some of you will discover that this is an area of editing that you
will need to work on for a time until you know how to edit for proper verb agreement
and tense use.

388

20

Forceful Writing: Using Action Verbs

and Active vs. Passive Voice

In the English language, verbs indicate action, movement, something being done. So, make sure you use action verbs to make your writing much more forceful. One of the most common verbs in the English language is one of the few that doesn't show action: *to be (am are is was were being been)*. In most cases, it is a necessary verb, but because it is one of the most used verbs, it is one of the most *overused* verbs.

Probably the simplest editing technique you can use to improve the quality of your sentences is to circle every form of the verb *to be* (*am are is was were being been*) that you use. First, decide if the sentence with *to be* is in the passive voice, and unless the passive voice is necessary, edit the sentence into the active voice. If the sentence is already in the active voice, decide whether or not the sense of the sentence *requires* the use of *to be*, and if it doesn't edit the sentence to use an action verb.

Using the Active Voice

Most written English uses the active voice. In the active voice, the subject of the sentence *performs* the action of the verb.

> *Active:* **subject verb**
> The Brazilian <u>climbed</u> on the fishing scow.

In the other voice in English, the passive voice, the subject of the sentence *receives* the action (hence the term *passive*). The passive voice, rarely used, should be saved for special circumstances discussed in this chapter.

> *Passive:* **subject verb**
> The sign <u>was painted</u> by the boy in the barrio.

Passive constructions always contain a form of the verb *to be (is are was were being been)*. To change a sentence from the passive voice to the active voice, ask yourself who or what does the action in the sentence (often you can take the noun that occurs after the word *by*, and use it as the subject of the sentence):

> *Active:* The boy in the barrio <u>painted</u> the sign.

In some instances, you have to decide who is doing the action in your sentence. For example:

Passive: The classes for "Maintaining Excellent Health" <u>were begun</u> at dawn.

Active: The "Wellness" Instructor <u>began</u> the "Maintaining Excellent Health" classes at dawn.

Unless you have a reason for using the passive voice, always edit sentences by recasting them to the active voice. When should you use the passive voice? Of course, if you do not know who or what is performing the action, you will have to use the passive voice.

Passive: The gang leader <u>was murdered</u> in the night.

Probably the most useful employment of the passive voice, however, occurs when a writer wants to deflect blame away from an agent or wants to actually hide part of the truth (as you see from the example):

Active: During the Vietnam War, the United States Army <u>killed</u> many civilians.

Passive: During the Vietnam War, many civilians <u>were killed</u>.

Using Action Verbs

- *To Be **as a Linking Verb***

When *to be* as a *linking verb* connects the sentence's subject to an adjective, replace the form of *to be* with an action verb.

Joan <u>was</u> happy when the dean announced the funding of a multicultural arts center on campus.

Instead, have the subject of the sentence, Joan, actually "do something." Verbs, by their very nature, indicate actions.

Edited: Joan <u>clapped</u> loudly and <u>grinned</u> at her classmates as the dean announced the funding of a multicultural arts center on campus.

Note the difference in vividness when descriptive verbs replace forms of *to be*.

Bill <u>was</u> mad at his fraternity brother when the brother stumbled into the dormitory, drunk again.

Edited: Bill <u>fumed</u> and <u>screamed</u> at his fraternity brother when the brother stumbled into the dormitory, drunk again.

390

- *To Be **with Subject and Object***

In addition to being used as a linking verb, the verb *to be* also links a subject to a direct object. In these instances, it usually improves the sentence to replace forms of *to be* with action verbs.

> James Madison <u>was</u> one of the writers of the Constitution.
> ***Edited***: James Madison <u>helped write</u> the Constitution.

> Teenage mothers <u>are</u> often the first students to realize the value of an education.
> ***Edited***: Teenage mothers often <u>realize</u> the value of an education before other students.

> The United States military <u>was</u> in Vietnam from 1961-1975.
> ***Edited***: The United States military <u>entered</u> Vietnam in 1961 and <u>left</u> in 1975.

Be careful with this often overused "who" construction:

> Martin Luther King <u>was</u> a good father and husband *who* always had time for his family.

Tighten the sentence in the following manner:

> ***Edited***: Martin Luther King, a good father and husband, always <u>had</u> time for his family.

These sentences show how one strong verb can replace two forms of *to be* to good effect:

> Joan <u>is</u> a good student and she <u>is</u> always on time.
> ***Edited***: Joan, a good student, always <u>arrives</u> on time.

To revise for action verbs, ask yourself what the subject of the sentence is actually doing, and make sure that the verb *shows* the reader what the subject does.

- *To Be **as a Helping Verb***

Sometimes when *to be* is used as a *helping verb*, it is unnecessary, as is the case in the examples below.

> The Clint Eastwood character *was* smiling at the loitering soldiers until one of them said, "That's the Outlaw Josie Wales."
> ***Edited***: The Clint Eastwood character *smiled* at the loitering soldiers until one of them said, "That's the Outlaw Josie Wales."

> If I *were* going to buy a new car, it would be a Mazda.
> ***Edited***: If I *bought* a new car, it would be a Mazda.

391

The future tense would also be effective here:

Edited: If I *buy* a new car, it *will be* a Mazda.

Be sure to use the proper verb tense or tense sequence, which may require using *to be* as a *helping verb* (see Chapter 19 for specifics on Verb Use). But if helping verbs are not necessary to express your meaning, delete them. Remember that an essay cluttered with unnecessary words, including helping verbs, causes problems with readability.

Use common sense though; some verb sequences require *to be*. Try revisions without the helping verb, and if they make the sentence less clear, return the sentence to its original form. For instance:

I *was watching* late night television, and June moved slowly across the darkened room toward me. She *was going* to surprise me.

Inaccurate revision: I *watched* late night television, and June moved slowly across the darkened room toward me. She *went* to surprise me.

Obviously, in this instance the deletion of the helping verbs causes the sentence to be much less precise. The original, with the helping verb *was* (signaling past progressive tense, expressing a continuing action in the past), suggests that June *moved* (simple past tense) *while* the writer was watching television. The revision merely suggests that both events occur in the past (signaled by the simple past tense) and that it *is possible* they occurred simultaneously. In the second sentence *was going* to *went* creates a much less precise use of tense sequence. The writer did, however, realize that he could use a more precise action verb in the place of *was going*. The final revision of the sentences changed only the second sentence:

Accurate revision: I was watching late night television, and June moved slowly across the darkened room. She *wanted* to surprise me.

EXERCISE 20.1
Using Forceful Verbs

Circle every form of the verb *to be* (*am are is was were being been*) that you use. After finding every use of this verb, whenever possible shift from passive to active voice. When the sentence is already in the active voice, decide whether or not the sense of the sentence *requires* its use. If possible, replace the form of *to be* with an action verb.

392

21
Pronouns: Agreement, Reference, and Shifts

Types of Pronouns and Pronoun Agreement

Definitions of Terms Used to Describe Pronouns

Pronoun – A *word* that refers to <u>another word</u> which has appeared earlier (The <u>man</u> kept *his* pencil.), that refers to an indefinite number of something (*Anyone* can go to the picnic.), that helps ask a question (*Who* is that teacher?), or serves as a subject or object in a [dependent clause]. (The steam roller [*that* hit my car] was huge.).

Antecedent – the word that the pronoun replaces. (The <u>girl</u> lost *her* dog. – <u>Girl</u> is the antecedent of the pronoun *her*.)

Pronouns have three cases:

Possessive – shows possession (*my, mine, our, our, your, yours, his, her, hers, its, their, theirs, whose*).

Subjective – serves as the subject of a dependent or independent clause *(I, we, you, he, she, it, they, who, whoever)*.

Objective – serves as an object of a preposition, as a direct object, or an indirect object (*me, you, him, her, it, us, them, whom, whomever*).

Pronoun types:

Personal – refer to people or things.

Indefinite – refer to an indefinite number of people or things (*anyone, everyone,* and others).

Relative – begin dependent clauses (*who, whoever, whom, whomever, which, whose, that*).

Interrogative – are used in questions *(who, when, why, where, which, whose)*.

Demonstrative – are used to "point" at another word *(this, that, these, those)*.

Intensive – refer to the subject of a sentence in the objective position *(myself, yourself, himself, herself, itself, ourselves, yourselves, themselves)*. <u>John</u> caught the ball <u>himself</u>.

Reflexive – add emphasis, and use the same forms as the intensive (*myself, yourself, himself, herself, itself, ourselves, yourselves, themselves)*. The coach <u>himself</u> clapped.

Pronoun Agreement — A grammatical error: pronouns must agree in person, number, and gender with their antecedents, and must be in the correct case and type.

Pronoun Reference — A stylistic error: there must be no confusion concerning the antecedent to which the pronoun refers.

Pronoun Shifts — A grammatical error: an unnecessary pronoun shift (1st to 2nd person, 3rd to 2nd person: Students [3rd person] should study or you [2nd person] won't succeed. ***Should be:*** Students should study or they won't succeed. *or*: You should study or you won't succeed.)

As you will see from the definitions that follow, you already use pronouns every day. With the definitions, this section will discuss pronoun agreement.

Pronouns, like verbs, must agree in person and number with the words they are replacing, but they must also agree in gender with the antecedent they replace (*his, her, its*), and be in the correct case for their function in a sentence (subjective case pronouns when serving as a subject, objective case pronouns when serving as an object, and possessive case pronouns when showing possession).

masculine plural   plural possessive
The *men* worked at *their* jobs.
[Their *replaces masculine and feminine antecedents.]*

masculine singular	*masculine singular possessive*	*feminine singular*	*feminine singular subjective*	*masculine singular objective*
Bill wrote a letter to	*his*	mother,	and *she* answered	*him*.

feminine singular   feminine singular possessive
Jane wrote a letter to *her* father.

Personal Pronouns

Personal pronouns can serve in all three cases.

• The *possessive case*: possessive *personal pronouns* show possession.

Number: Singular		Plural
Person:		
1st	I want *my* book. I want *mine*.	We want *our* car. We want *ours*.
2nd	You buy *your* car. You buy *yours*.	You buy *your* car. You buy *yours*.
3rd	He uses *his* pen. He uses *his*.	The students use *their* pens.
	She uses *her* pen. She uses *hers*.	The students use *theirs*.
	The bus left *its* parking place.	

A common agreement problem: with possessive pronouns, make sure that the noun that is being possessed is correct in terms of being singular or plural.

Incorrect: The teachers took good care of their class.
Correct: The teachers took good care of their classes.
(Unless the teachers [plural] all taught the same class, then their class.)

Incorrect: On Saturdays, families work in their yard.
Correct: On Saturdays, families work in their yards.

- **The *subjective case*: subjective *personal pronouns* serve as subjects in sentences.**

Person	Number: Singular	Plural
1st	*I* want the car.	*We* can't go.
2nd	*You* must be fast.	*You* must be fast.
3rd	*He* buys a boat.	*They* want one too.
	She couldn't have one.	
	It is too expensive.	

A common agreement problem: using a plural pronoun to replace a singular noun in clauses like this:

Sing.   *plural*

Incorrect: When a football player plays a good game, *they* should be proud.

Correct: When a football player plays a good game, *he* should be proud.
When football players play a good game, *they* should be proud.

- **The *objective case*: objective *personal pronouns* function as objects of prepositions, direct objects, or indirect objects.**

Singular
1st	Jennifer wants James to give the book to *me*.	*(object of preposition)*
	Jennifer wants *me* to give the book to Laura.	*(direct object)*
	Jennifer wants James to give *me* the book.	*(indirect object)*
2nd	Jennifer wants James to give the book to *you*.	*(object of preposition)*
	Jennifer wants *you* to give the book to Laura.	*(direct object)*
	Jennifer wants James to give *you* the book.	*(indirect object)*
3rd	Jennifer wants James to give the book to *her*.	*(object of preposition)*
	Jennifer wants *him* to give the book to Laura.	*(direct object)*
	Jennifer wants James to give *him* the book.	*(indirect object)*
	Jennifer wants James to give *it* to her.	*(direct object)*

Plural
1st	Jennifer wants James to give the book to *us*.	*(object of preposition)*
	Jennifer wants *us* to give the book to Laura.	*(direct object)*
	Jennifer wants James to give *us* the book.	*(indirect object)*
2nd	Jennifer wants James to give the book to *you*.	*[plural] (object of preposition)*
	Jennifer wants *you* to give the book to Laura.	*[plural] (direct object)*
	Jennifer wants James to give *you* the book.	*[plural] (indirect object)*
3rd	Jennifer wants James to give the book to *them*.	*(object of preposition)*
	Jennifer wants *them* to give the book to Laura.	*(direct object)*
	Jennifer wants James to give *them* the book.	*(indirect object)*

A **common pronoun agreement problem** in the spoken language is using objective pronouns when subjective pronouns should be employed. *Don't correct your speech except in very formal situations; people understand you. But be aware of your incorrect usage and be ready to correct it in your writing.*

> *Incorrect*: Joan and me went to the races.
> *Correct*: Joan and I went to the races.
> [**Me** *is not subjective case. It is objective. The subject of* **went** *is* **Joan and I.**]

> *Incorrect*: Bill went with Joan and I.
> *Correct*: Bill went with Joan and me.
> [**Joan and I** *is not the subject, it is the object of the preposition* **with**. **Me** *is the objective case pronoun.*]

> **A special case: an appositive renaming a direct or indirect object**
> The team had two forwards, Jake and me. NOT Jake and I.
> [**me** *refers to* **forwards**, *which is the direct object of* **The team had.**]

Indefinite Pronouns

Indefinite Pronouns: *one anyone everyone someone nobody anybody everybody somebody each neither either*

Indefinite pronouns can function in all three cases, and are always singular, *even if it seems that they refer to plural words.*

> *Possessive*: *Everyone's* house should have a smoke detector.
> *Subjective*: *Anyone* can win the race.
> *Objective*: I would like to go to the dance with *someone.*

>   **singular   plural singular**
> *Correct*: *Each* of the *plans* has *its* own supporters.

>   **singular   singular**
> *Correct*: *Everyone* who goes to school must supply *his* own books.

An important point needs to be considered in the preceding example: What if both males and females go to school? One alternative uses the phrase "his or her," though this is rather awkward.

> Everyone who goes to school must supply his or her own books.

To avoid this awkward construction, it is usually possible to recast the sentence in the plural:

> All students must supply their own books.

A common agreement problem: some indefinite pronouns SEEM as if they should be plural, but they are always singular unless their sense demands that individuals in a group are singled out (as in the examples above and on the next page).

singular   *singular*   *should be singular*
Incorrect: *Every* student <u>needs</u> to get better grades, or *they* will not move on to the next level.
Correct: *Every* student <u>needs</u> to get better grades, or *he/she* will not move on to the next level.   *or switch to plural*:
All students <u>need</u> to get better grades, or *they* will not move on to the next level.

Sounds plural but indefinite pronouns are singular, so his:

Every one of the council members voted to raise *his* salary. [*NOT their*]

Relative and Interrogative Pronouns

Relative pronouns begin dependent clauses: *who, whoever, whom, whomever, which, whose, that.*
Interrogative pronouns are used in questions: *who, when, why, where, which, whose.*

Relative and interrogative pronouns serve either as subjects of a sentence, as objects, or as modifiers. These two types of pronouns cause problems because of subtle differences in each one's function in a sentence and because the same words are used for several purposes in the language. Instead of describing in detail how each one is used, this section will show how they are used by describing the major problems writers have with these words and how to test for correct usage.

The following pronouns, whether relative or interrogative, can serve only in these cases:

Subjective	*Objective*	*Possessive*
who	whom	whose
whoever	whomever	

Relative and Interrogative Pronoun Problems occur in the following situations:

Who and whoever serve as subjects of interrogative sentences.

subject
Example: *Who* is going to the ball? or *Whom* is going to the ball?

Test: Make sentence declarative and choose the subjective form:
              He (subjective) [or] *Him* (object) is going to the ball.
Correct: *He* is going to the ball. *so:*
Correct: *Who* is going to the ball?

397

Whom and ***whomever*** **serve as objects in interrogative sentences.**

> *object*
>
> ***Example***: *Who* are you taking to the ball? or *Whom* are you taking to the ball?
>
> *Test*:   Make sentence declarative, and choose the objective form:
> You are taking *she* (subjective) [or] *her* (objective) to the ball.
> ***Correct***: You are taking *her* to the ball. ***so:***
> ***Correct***:   *Whom* are you taking to the ball?

Who and ***whoever*** **serve as subjects in independent or dependent clauses.**

> *subject of independent clause*
>
> ***Example***: *Whoever* buys the car will get a lemon. or
> *Whomever* buys the car will get a lemon.
>
> *Test*:   Subject of independent clause, so choose the subjective form:
> *She* (subjective) [or] *her* (objective) buys the car.
> ***Correct***: *She* buys the car ***so:***
> ***Correct***: *Whoever* buys the car will get a lemon.

> *subject of dependent clause*
>
> ***Example***: George Washington, *who* was the first President, lived in Virginia.
> or
> George Washington, *whom* was the first President, lived in Virginia.
>
> *Test*:   Subject of a dependent clause, so choose the subjective form:
> *He* (subjective) [or] *him* (objective) was the first President
> ***Correct***: *He* was the first President. ***so:***
> ***Correct***: George Washington, *who* was the first President, lived in
> Virginia.

Whom and ***whomever*** **serve as objects in dependent clauses.**

> *object of preposition*
>
> ***Example***: Send the memo to *whoever* we want to read it. or
> Send the memo to *whomever* we want to read it.
>
> *Test*:   Not a subject, so choose the objective form:
> Send the memo to *they* (subjective) [or] *them* (objective).
> ***Correct***: Send the memo to *them*. ***so***:
> ***Correct***: Send the memo to *whomever* we want to read it.

> *object of* **we want**
>
> ***Example***: Liz Mitchell, *who* we want as the CEO of our corporation, will
> be in the area tomorrow for a speech. or:
> Liz Mitchell, *whom* we want as the CEO of our corporation, will be in the
> area tomorrow for a speech.

Test: Not a subject, so choose the objective form:
We want *she* (subjective) [or] *her* (objective)
Correct: We want *her.*   so:
Correct: Liz Mitchell, *whom* we want as the CEO of our corporation, will be in the area tomorrow.

If the relative pronoun shows possession, use *whose.*

Liz Mitchell, *whose* speech at the university will be attended by many, is top on our list to become the new CEO.

Be careful to distinguish between *whose* and *who's* (*who is*).

The man *whose* car I borrowed is mad.

Who's going to attend the premiere with me?
[Who is *going to attend the premiere with me?]*

Who, *that*, and *which* can all serve as subjects of dependent clauses that rename and refer to a noun they follow.

Who refers to people or specific animals.
That refers to animals or things. It may also refer to people, but in most cases, *who* is preferable for people.

(refers to **Secretariat)**   *(refers to* **record)**
Secretariat, *who* won the 99th Kentucky Derby, set a record *that* was never broken.

(refers to **physicists)**
Physicists *who* study black holes may work for an entire lifetime without finding any definitive answers.

Which refers to animals and thing**s**.

(refers to **John Birch Society)**
The John Birch Society, *which* has mostly disappeared from the scene, was a secret society.

Intensive and Reflexive Pronouns

Intensive and reflexive pronouns: *myself, yourself, himself, herself, itself, ourselves, yourselves, themselves.* The word *theirselves* does not exist.

Intensive pronouns are used for emphasis, and *reflexive pronouns* are used as objects of a verb or preposition. Intensive and reflexive pronouns always refer to another noun or pronoun in the same sentence. They agree in person, number, and gender with the noun they add emphasis to:

399

My mother *herself* fixed the car.
The senators *themselves* gave to the charity.

Reflexive pronouns serve as objects (receiving the action of the verb) and agree in person, number, and gender with the subject:

I criticize *myself*.   We criticize *ourselves*.
He criticizes *himself*.   Estella always looks out for *herself*.

Demonstrative Pronouns

singular — *this   that*   plural — *these   those*

Demonstrative pronouns are four words functioning as pointers, used as subjects, as objects, or as modifiers.

subject   **object**
These are as good as *those*.

modifier
That television is broken.

EXERCISE 21.1
Exercise in Pronoun Agreement
Supply correct pronoun forms for the following sentences and edit any errors with plurality caused by pronoun agreement; with some, you might simply rewrite the sentence. Also, make the verbs agree with the pronouns if there is a verb agreement problem because of faulty pronoun agreement.

1. Me and Mr. Jones went to a movie.

2. Everyone must bring their own sleeping bags.

3. All of the policemen must supply his own uniforms and gun.

4. Neither of the Senators voted for the bills they sponsored.

5. The student must like their dorm room.

6. All job applicants must supply her own car.

7. School, employment, transportation — all of us are tired of it.

8. All of the students like to go to his or her class parties.

9. Everyone must find their place in life.

10. Problems can be solved by studying it.

11. Whomever gets the highest score doesn't have to take the final.

Pronoun Reference

Pronouns must refer clearly to their antecedents (the nouns they replace). Here are some examples of faulty pronoun reference:

> *Faulty*: Bob told Jim that *he* had lost his way.
> *[Who lost his way, Bob or Jim?]*
> *Clear:* After Bob had lost his way, *he* told Jim about getting lost.

> *Faulty*: My sister is a plumber, but I'm not interested in *it*.
> *[It can only refer to plumber, and how can one be "interested in plumber"?]*
> *Clear*: My sister is a plumber, but I'm not interested in becoming one.

> *Faulty*: My mother did not explain the problem *that* made me angry.
> *[Does that refer to the problem or the explanation?]*
> *Clear*: I was angry *that* my mother did not explain the problem.
>   The problem *that* made me mad was not explained by my mother.

Most problems with pronoun reference, however, occur when the pronoun and the antecedent are separated by one or two sentences. You need to be sure that your pronoun refers clearly to its antecedent, and that no confusion could arise over which word the pronoun refers to. For example, here is an unedited, unclear paragraph:

> Ernest Hemingway and William Faulkner were both helped in the early stages of their writing careers by Sherwood Anderson. They later made disparaging remarks about him. After helping Hemingway get his first book published, Hemingway parodied his novel, *Dark Laughter,* with the novella, *The Torrents of Spring.* Faulkner ridiculed New Orleans literary society in his novel, *Mosquitoes.* It was a shame that such great writers would hurl insults at one another. They never knew each other, though Faulkner worked on the Hollywood screenplay of *To Have and Have Not.*

Unless readers happen to be experts in the careers of Hemingway, Faulkner, and Anderson, this vague use of pronoun reference creates various ambiguities. Always check your writing to make sure that the pronouns clearly refer to their antecedents. Methods to correct vague pronoun reference include 1) replacing the pronoun with either the antecedent or a synonym that makes the sentence clear, and 2) adding descriptive, modifying phrases to make the sentences clearer. Closely compare the original and revised versions of the paragraphs.

> Ernest Hemingway and William Faulkner were both helped in the early stages of their writing careers by Sherwood Anderson. They later made disparaging remarks about Anderson. After Anderson helped Hemingway get his first book published, Hemingway parodied Anderson's novel, *Dark Laughter,* with the novella, *The Torrents of Spring.* Faulkner, in the novel, *Mosquitoes,* ridiculed Anderson's New Orleans literary society. It was a shame that such great writers would hurl insults at one of their mentors.

401

Hemingway and Faulkner attacked Anderson independently: they never knew each other, though Faulkner worked on the Hollywood screenplay of Hemingway's *To Have and Have Not.*

Pronoun Shifts

Many writers unconsciously shift from first person (*I, we*) to second person (*you*) or from third person (*he, she, it, they, a proper name*) to second person (*you*) in their writing. By shifting to second they are trying to address the reader, but it is incorrect grammatically, *and good writing is already addressing the reader.* Be careful.

> *Faulty*: *He* works at a job where *you* don't always get all the days off that *you* should.
> *Consistent*: *He* works at a job where *he* doesn't always get all the days off that *he* should.

> *Faulty*: *I* don't like bullfighting because *you* always feel sorry for the bull.
> *Consistent*: *I* don't like bullfighting because *I* always feel sorry for the bull.

> *Faulty*: *We* should love our country because *you* have the opportunity to do whatever *you* want.
> *Consistent*: *We* should love our country because *we* have the opportunity to do whatever *we* want.

EXERCISE 21.2
Exercise in Pronoun Reference and Shifts
Correct faulty pronoun reference and pronoun shifts. Some sentences may not have any problems. **where students study hard.**

1. The school he goes to is one ~~that you do study hard at.~~

2. Residents of our state should help keep it clean because it is your state too.

3. The professor told Jim that he should have revised the essay.

4. I don't like movies anymore because you never cry for the plights of the heroines.

5. My father wants me to go to medical school, but I'm not interested in it.

6. Brad Pitt and George Clooney are great actors. He won numerous awards but the other won an Academy Award.

7. It made me mad when I got lost and Kim made fun of me.

8. The internet company I use saves you money every month.

EXERCISE 21.3
Editing for Pronoun Agreement, Reference Errors, and Pronoun Shifts
Read your essay circling all the pronouns in your essay. Then find the antecedents for each pronoun and make sure that the essay is using the correct pronoun type and case, and that the pronoun agrees in number (singular/plural) and gender. If the pronoun is the subject in a clause, make sure that it agrees with its verb.

402

22

Standard Usage:
Apostrophes and Plurality, Capitalization,
Numbers, Abbreviations, Other Punctuation,
Italics/Underlining and Quotation Marks

Apostrophes and Plurality

Apostrophes are often left out, and it looks sloppy. Don't do it.

- *An s at the end of a noun (a person, place, or thing) signals one of two things: either the word is plural, or the s with an apostrophe signals possession.*

  John Smith is a student.

  There are many John Smiths at the school. *[plurality]*

  John Smith is one of many students at the school. *[plurality]*

  The student's car is here. *[possession]*

  Bill Harris and John Smith's boat is here. *[-s possession for last one only]*

- *If a word is both plural and possessive, the apostrophe follows the s.*

  The students' cars are there. *[multiple students (plurality) and possession]*

Look at the following examples to note how the apostrophe is used. These constructions are often used incorrectly.

  I disagreed with that description of Cara. *[Cara is described.]*

  I disagreed with that description of Cara's. *[Cara does the describing.]*

  Is that book Bill's or Joe's?   *[One of them possesses the book.]*

- *If the noun ends in s, and it also shows possession, add 's,*

  Lois's sweater is pretty.

- *With compound nouns, use 's with the last noun if they possess it jointly, or with individual possession, use 's or s' with both nouns.*

Do you want to go to Bill and Mary's wedding?

Frank's and John's ideas about the election couldn't have been more different.

- *Apostrophes are also used in contractions. The apostrophe is inserted where the missing letter or number should be. Formal writing avoids the use of contractions except with numbers.*

Let us – let's (don't confuse with verb *lets*)	the class of '13
It is/It has – it's	the '70s generation
Are not – aren't (not *are'nt*)	
I am – I'm He is/he has – he's	was not – wasn't
Do not – don't (not *do'nt*)	Does not – doesn't
You will – you'll will not – won't	He would/He had – he'd
I would/I had – I'd	would not – wouldn't
who is/who has – who's (don't confuse with pronoun *whose*)	
cannot – can't	

Apostrophes and missing apostrophes are one of the most prevalent errors in writing today. It looks sloppy to an educated reader, so be sure to edit for proper apostrophe use. DO NOT use the apostrophe when a word is plural, but not possessive:

> *students*
> Some ~~student's~~ confuse plurality and possession.

Capitalization

Use the following guidelines when deciding whether to capitalize a word in your writing.

- *Capitalize the first word in a sentence.*

- *Always reproduce exactly the use of capitalization in a quoted passage or in words in a title of a book, journal, magazine, article, or work of art.*

- *Words derived from proper names are sometimes capitalized and sometimes not capitalized. Check a dictionary for accuracy.*

Americanize   Parisian   plaster of paris   Shakespearean

404

- *Capitalize the names of proper nouns – the names of specific persons, places, and things; but do not capitalize general classes of persons, places, or things. If you aren't sure whether to capitalize a word, look it up in a dictionary; regularly capitalized words are capitalized in the dictionary.*

Lisa McKeen	a freshman
June July Tuesday	spring summer fall
on Main Street	a main street
the Congress	any nation's congress
God, the Buddha	any people's god
the Red Cross	an international relief agency
the Second World War	twentieth century wars
the Haymarket Riots	the riot last year

[though "the riot last year" is a specific riot, it is not being referred to by a special name]

Senator Collins   the senator from Kentucky
[same exception]

Governor Rayburn   John Rayburn, our governor
[When a title follows the person's name it is not capitalized.]

Aunt Paula   Paula, my aunt
[same rule]

Germany Germans Arabs   the two countries, two nations
[Names of nationalities, cultures, and nations are always capitalized.]

Numbers

Sometimes numbers should be spelled out; at other times, they should be given in arabic figures.

- *Usage varies, but a good rule to follow is that if a number can be written in one or two words it should be written out; otherwise, it should be written with figures except with the exceptions noted in this section.*

thirty-two   386   four thousand   4862   ten million   10,800,000

However, the social sciences (APA documentation) use arabic numbers for all but numbers one through nine: Out of 153 cases, there were only nine that displayed this habit.

- *Certain conventions are observed in using numbers for units and ranges of time.*

Centuries are spelled out: the twentieth century, not the 20th century

Years and days of the month use arabic numerals: February 17, 1998
56 BCE (Never Fifty-six BCE.)

1982-1987 is acceptable as is "from 1982 to 1987"
("from 1982-1987" is not acceptable as the "from" and the dash in the same phrase are redundant.)

- *Pages and divisions of books and plays should be written with arabic numerals. (Divisions of plays can also use Roman numerals.)*

  chapter 31   page 12   Act 3, Scene 2 (or Act III, Scene ii)

- *Identification numbers should be written with arabic numerals (except kings and queens, who are referred to with roman numerals).*

  Channel 68   Henry VIII   Interstate 40   scores 7-3
  percentages 55 percent (or 55%)   7600 South Park Place
  exact amounts of money: $106.32 or $200,000

Abbreviations

Use the following guidelines when deciding whether or not to abbreviate a word in your writing.

- *States, countries, continents, days of the week, months, units of measurement, and courses of study are written out, not abbreviated, in most writing situations. Exceptions to this guideline include extremely informal writing situations and articles for particular fields of study (the sciences, mathematics) that allow certain abbreviations in their style manuals.*

- *Frequently abbreviated words such as street, road, avenue, company, volume, chapter, President, Senator and page are written out, not abbreviated, in all but the most informal writing situations.*

- *Some abbreviations are permissible in most work.*

  Mr. Mrs. Ms. Dr. St.(Saint) when used before a proper name, but not when used as common nouns. (He was a saint. Joan, did you see that?)

- *Titles and degrees following a proper name may be abbreviated.*

  Joe Sampson, Jr. William James, Ph.D. Bill Jones, C.P.A.

- *Certain dates and figures may be abbreviated, but only when referring to a specific time.*

  286 BC (before Christ)   286 BCE (before the common era)
  1285 CE (common era)   AD 1285 (abbo domini, i.e., Latin: year of
  our Lord. Note that this abbreviation preceded the date while the rest follow
  the date.)
  $486 [for dollars]   13 mpg
  8:00 A.M. (or a.m.)   8:30 EST (or E.S.T. or est)
  But NOT: I went in the pm. (Doesn't refer to a specific time, so: I went in
  the afternoon.)

- *U.S. when used to describe another word may be abbreviated.*

  U.S. Army   otherwise, write: the United States

- *Organizations or things usually referred to by their initials (acronyms) may be abbreviated – see also next guideline.*

  NASA IBM CIA DNA CD   ABC

- *Agencies and nouns that are usually referred to by their acronym (as with the examples above) do not ever need to be spelled out; however, if you need to use an unfamiliar acronym, write out the full words on the first occasion of its use and put the acronym in parentheses. Afterwards, the acronym alone can be used.*

  During World War II, the Office of Strategic Services (OSS) directed
  the communications between the Allied troops and the various underground
  movements in Europe. Many OSS officers parachuted behind enemy lines
  to coordinate resistance efforts.

- *Certain common Latin expressions are still found in writing, but their use is declining. They should probably be avoided except in fields of scholarship that stipulate their use.*

cf.	compare
e.g.	for example
et al	and others
etc.	and so forth
i.e.	that is
vs. or v.	versus

- *All the forms of documentation used in research essays (MLA, APA, CSE, Chicago) use specific abbreviations, and writers must ALWAYS follow the rules of the documentation style they are using, which supersede the general usage rules on these pages.*

Other Punctuation

Use **periods** at the end of declarative sentences, abbreviations, and indirect questions. Don't repeat the period when an abbreviation ends the sentence.

> She is an M.D. [not: She is an M.D..]

> "Who is that?" she said.

In commonly used acronyms, periods are usually omitted (USAF, IRS, mph, UNESCO).

Question marks follow direct questions. They are also used, usually in parentheses, to indicate doubt or uncertainty about a date, name, or word.

> Where is the book?

> Confucius (551?-448? B.C.) created a system of ethics followed by many Chinese today.

Forgetting to use question marks is a common editing mistake.

Exclamation points are used after sentences of surprise or strong emotion, but are very rarely used by modern writers. Avoid them! (See? They usually produce too strong an emphasis.)

> Modern science has conquered cancer!

Dashes signal a sudden change in tone or a shift in thought, emphasize an added explanation either within the sentence or at its end, and set off items in an introductory series that are followed by a sentence referring to them.

> Still having trouble writing – who isn't?

> Writing is a mysterious craft – some like it and some don't – but I suspect that those who don't like it haven't explored its mysteries.

> Writing is a mystery – a mystery with a solution.

> Confidence, hard work, and patience – these are needed to unravel the mystery.

Dashes are a convenient alternative to the comma for punctuation; however, repeated use of dashes in sentence after sentence is rare in modern usage. Do not overuse them.

Parentheses enclose nonessential but helpful material including examples, explanatory notes, editorial comments, dates, acronyms, and translations of foreign words.

Examples: There are several predatory birds in the region (for instance, red-tailed hawks and even an occasional eagle).

Explanatory comment: We use not only nonverbal signals (comparable to a dog's snarl or a bee's mating ritual) but also word symbols, which we combine in countless ways.

Editorial comment: Some of my friends get drunk every Friday and Saturday night (which I think is just plain crazy, not to mention dangerous), and they don't see what it is doing to their lives.

Dates: Langston Hughes (1902-1967) was one of the great writers of the Harlem Renaissance.

Acronyms: Workers at the Transit Authority of Louisville (better known as TARC) went on strike because of the city council's vote.

Translations: The Greek *polis* (town) had citizens to vote on its *politics* and *policies*.

The end punctuation for sentences should be placed outside the parentheses unless the parenthetical statement itself is a complete sentence, separate from the sentence preceding it.

Faulty: I like my rock-and-roll hard and fast. (as did my father)
Correct: I like my rock-and-roll hard and fast (as did my father).

Faulty: The decision to publish a national newspaper was made in 1981 by the Gannett Company, one of the nation's most successful conglomerates (Circulation for all Gannett papers exceeds 3.5 million nationwide).
Correct: The decision to publish a national newspaper was made in 1981 by the Gannett Company, one of the nation's most successful conglomerates. (Circulation for all Gannett papers exceeds 3.5 million nationwide.)

Faulty: Charles Dickens's *A Tale of Two Cities* begins: "It was the best of times, it was the worst of times." (21)
Correct: Charles Dickens's *A Tale of Two Cities* begins: "It was the best of times, it was the worst of times" (21).

Though a rarely used mark of punctuation, *slashes* are appropriate in the following situations:

- *Slashes show alternatives (either/or, and/or).* Before using a slash in this way, read your sentence carefully to make sure its sense indicates an equal choice between two alternatives.

It was an either/or situation: either fight the intruder or run from him.

It is possible in the context of this situation there were only these two alternatives; however, couldn't the writer also have given the intruder what he wanted? Check to make sure the choice is only between the two items you give.

- *Slashes separate lines of poetry when a brief portion is quoted within the main text of a piece of writing.*

The following extract from John Milton's poem "Lycidas" is first printed as verse and then as a brief quotation within a scholarly paper.

> Weep no more, woeful shepherds, weep no more,
> For Lycidas, your sorrow, is not dead,
> Sunk though he be beneath the watery floor.

> In the stanza that begins, "Weep no more, woeful shepherds, weep no more, / For Lycidas, your sorrow, is not dead," Milton summarizes his concise examination of immortality and death.

All original punctuation in a poem remains when you use slashes. Note the spaces between the slash and the words when separating lines of poetry.

Italics/Underlining and Quotation Marks

When do you underline, italicize, or put quotation marks around titles? First, italics and underlining are interchangeable. In the examples below, *Writing Successfully* will italicize, but underlining is acceptable anyplace that italics are used. Italics are preferred now since most word processing programs have an italics function, but make sure that you are using a font that makes a clear distinction between italics and regular font. Times New Roman is a font often used that has this clear distinction.

The best way to describe how to choose between italics/underlining and quotation marks is with a metaphor: if it is the container, use italics; if it goes in the container, use quotation marks.

Titles of Sources using Italics

All of these sources are the "containers" themselves (they contain the writing):

the name of a newspaper, magazine, or journal (the *New York Times, Newsweek*)
any book, whether it be a novel, a reference book, or a collection of essays, stories, or poems
the title of a CD (or a cassette tape or record album)
the name of a television show (*Seinfeld, NBC Nightly News*) or a movie (*Clueless*)
the title of a play (*King Lear*) or a book length poem (*Beowulf*)
court decisions (*Roe vs. Wade*)
the name of a website (*orpheuspress.com*)

Titles of Sources using Quotation Marks

All of these sources are contained in a larger "container":

the title of an article in a book, newspaper, magazine, journal, internet, or computer source
the title of a short story or a less than book length poem
the title of a song
the title of a particular episode of a television show

For uses of quotation marks to signal direct quotation of a source, see pp. 417-8, 435-6.

Exceptions with neither italics nor quotation marks: Scripture - Bible, Old Testament, Genesis, Talmud, Upanishads; Laws, Acts, Political Documents - Declaration of Independence, The Voting Rights Act; Musical compositions identified by Form, Number, and Key - Mozart's Horn Concerto No. 2. The divisions of a work (introduction, preface, stanza, scene, index, chapter, appendix, index).
Exceptions to exceptions - 1) Court decisions are italicized: *Brown vs Board of Education* and 2) specific editions of scripture (*The King James Version*).

EXERCISE 22.1
Editing for Standard Usage

Edit the essay you are working on for standard usage: correct use of apostrophes, punctuation, capitalization, abbreviations, numbers, italics, and quotation marks.

EXERCISE 22.2
Apostrophes, Capitalization, Numbers, Abbreviations, Other Punctuation

Correct all problems with apostrophes, punctuation, capitalization, abbreviations, and numbers in the following paragraph.

when I went to talk to the pope about the Central Intelligence Agencys report on the situation in Cen. America and the presidents view of the increasing violence in nineteen ninetyfour, he declared that the area needed three things, more education, a stronger industrial base, and more free market economic measures what made him think that He had spoken with the presidents of several countries and the bishops and cardinals in the area, especially Cardinal Marquesea He supported the efforts of american social and religious organizations, both catholic and protestant, as well as the red cross and the United Way the relief effort could cost billions of dollars

23

MLA Documentation

There are several styles of documentation used in scholarly study and *Writing Successfully* includes brief instructions for four of the most common: MLA style (used by English and modern language scholars, and all publications of the Modern Language Association), APA style (used by psychologists, sociologists, and all publications of the American Psychological Association), CSE style (used by many of the sciences, and all publications sanctioned by the Council of Science Editors), and Chicago style (used by historians and several other of the social sciences). *For each class you take in college, always ask your instructor which documentation style to use.* There are other documentation styles, but these are the most prevalent.

This chapter divides into two sections:

- Parenthetical in-text documentation using the MLA style: how to cite sources in your paper.
- Preparing the Works Cited page using MLA documentation.

Remember that this chapter gives only brief instructions showing how to document the most commonly used sources. For complete instructions use ONLY this edition:

Modern Language Association. *MLA Handbook.* 8th ed., Modern Language
    Association of America, 2016.

Parenthetical Documentation Using the MLA Style

Whenever you summarize, paraphrase, or use a direct quotation, you must let your reader know the source of the ideas or quoted material. The reader must be shown clearly where a source's ideas begin and end. The **front marker** usually identifies the author (**author + verb -** Joseph Smith claims). The **end marker** records the page number or numbers of the source when there are ones (using parenthetical documentation). *The author's last name is required; the first name is optional but is usually supplied in MLA Humanities genres to give the prose a less formal tone.* At the end of your essay, a works cited page gives your reader the author, title, and publication information for the source. The citation in the text would appear like this:

Front Marker: Author
    Bruce Ackerman suggests that in 1801 just after Thomas Jefferson defeated
    John Adams, America almost did away with its constitution - our constitution
    that still stands - in arguments over the future of our country (3-5).
    (End marker: page number. NOTICE placement of period after parentheses!)

The works cited entry at the end of the essay would be as follows:

    Ackerman, Bruce. *The Failure of the Founding Fathers.* Harvard UP, 2005.

Notice how formal the sentence below sounds when you only use the last name. Essays in the social sciences and natural sciences often use just the last name, but humanities essays using MLA documentation generally use first and last names:

> Ackerman suggests that in 1801 just after Thomas Jefferson defeated John Adams to become the third President, America almost did away with its constitution - our constitution that still stands - in arguments over the future of our country (3-5).

If an article (the source) is anonymous, the citation is by title of the article, NOT the title of the source's container:

> INCORRECT: *The Washington Post* discusses the statesmanship. . .
> CORRECT: "The President Wins a Round in Congress" discusses the statesmanship President Obama used to win support for the trade bill (A 1).
> INCORRECT: *The Encyclopedia Americana* discusses John Adams's Presidency.
> CORRECT: "John Adams" discusses John Adams's Presidency .
> **"Titles of articles in quotation marks"**
> **"John Adams" is the title of the encyclopedia article. For the name of the container (the newspaper, magazine, or encyclopedia), the reader would look to the Works Cited page.**

When evaluating in-text parenthetical documentation, check for accuracy using these *three specific, IMPORTANT guidelines* for scholarly researched writing:

- Any of your in-text parenthetical documentation sources should have a corresponding MLA citation on your works cited page, and from the information on the works cited page, the reader should be able to locate your source in a library or on the internet (unless your source is unpublished). If you refer to a source in your essay by author, "Alisha Jones argues ...," there must be an entry **beginning** "Jones, Alisha" on the works cited page.) What *appears as your in-text citation IS ALWAYS the first element in your works cited entry. That works cited opening will always be the author EXCEPT when the source is anonymous, then the first item in the works cited entry will be the title of the source. So NEVER cite IN YOUR TEXT with the name of the website, magazine, or newspaper*; always cite by author unless anonymous, and then by source title (see examples above).
  You may choose to also add the publication's name (the source's container) so the reader knows whether your source is reputable, but the publication is not required and must be in addition to the author (or title if anonymous).

  > According to Frank Rich, noted *Washington Post* writer, ...

- When reading your essay, a reader should know when your ideas stop and a source's ideas begin, and the conclusion of the source is always signaled by either the page number of the source in parentheses (217-219) the author's last name and page number of the source (Jefferson 219), or by another syntactic marker when it is a database or internet source with no page numbers or you are citing the entire text. See **3)** in two pages for proper methods to signal the end of the source when page numbers are not available. The **front marker** for a source's ideas or a quotation from the source is usually **author+verb**. The **end marker** is the page numbers in parentheses (19-20) or other identifiers if there are not page numbers. If you cite from a multi-volume work, cite volume number, colon, page number(s) (5: 72-6).

- *Most academic writing uses summary and paraphrase rather than direct quotation. The only reasons to use direct quotation are: when the source has said something so well that any attempt to summarize or paraphrase it would lessen its impact, or when there are many technical words or words that have no exact synonym in the source so that you can't rephrase the original passage in your own words.* Whenever you quote a passage word for word, even if you are only taking notes, ALWAYS put quotation marks around the sentence(s). If you don't do this even in your notes, when you write your essay you will assume you summarized, and then when you insert the quoted passage in your essay without quotation marks, you have commited plagiarism.

Indicate that your ideas have stopped and a source's have begun in one of three ways, the first being the preferred method:
1) Cite the author's name with either a phrase or a verb that describes what the author is doing. When using this form of parenthetical reference, at the end of the summary or quotation, give the page number in parentheses.

As William Franks has found,
As William Franks points out,
According to William Franks,
William Franks adds

agrees	compares	explains	observes	sees
argues	concludes	finds	points out	shows
asks	considers	relates	illustrates	speculates
asserts	declares	implies	reports	states
believes	denies	insists	responds	suggests
claims	disagrees	reveals	thinks	maintains
comments	emphasizes	notes	says	writes

When you use a verb, pick one that accurately describes what the source is doing:

Front Marker: Author of source's name + verb
Jimmy Carter *declared* that America should be energy FREE by the year 2000 (213).
                                                              (end marker: page number)
Two authors: Edward Smith and Joe Baines declare...
Three or more: Andrea Lunsford et al argue convincingly..(et al: Latin 'and others')

Many of the verbs in the "Jimmy Carter declared" paraphrase would fit; however, some wouldn't (*asks, compares, denies, disagrees, notes, points out, responds, sees*).

415

While the rest would be technically acceptable, some would be more accurate than others: Carter is stating an opinion or desire, not a fact, so verbs that connote suggestion would be the most accurate (*asserts, believes, claims, comments, considers, declares, finds, implies, maintains, says, states, suggests, thinks, writes*). Verbs that could connote a fact would be less acceptable (*explains, observes, reports, sees, shows*).

Also, *use the present tense:* Jonathan Swift *claims*, not Jonathan Swift *claimed*. Although Swift wrote in the eighteenth century, his books and ideas are still giving us insight and knowledge. By convention, words and ideas within a written work are described in the present tense: "Studies *indicate*," not "Studies *have indicated*" (EXCEPTION: unless you are showing how studies have changed through time and a past or perfect tense would reveal your specific meaning):

> Studies in the past have indicated that the death penalty deterred crime, but modern studies definitely indicate that the death penalty may increase violent crime (Wilson 314). **(Example of exception)**

The sense of the Jimmy Carter sentence on the previous page is to prove that there were forward thinking Americans in the 1970s who wanted to solve the environmental problem, but they weren't listened to. So in that sentence, since the sentence emphasizes the past, it has a good reason to use past tense.

When citing a source, however, the reader should clearly recognize when your ideas stop, and your source's ideas begin. Confusion occurs using this method when you have employed the preferred summary or paraphrase. In the following example, it is not clear where the writer's ideas stop and the source's ideas begin:

> *Huck Finn* has to be one of the greatest American novels. Another contender is *Uncle Tom's Cabin.*

A more accurate citation would clearly show where Jane Smiley's ideas begin (using the author intoducing his/her source method):

> **(Front marker: author+verb)**
> *Huck Finn* has to be one of the greatest American novels, but Jane Smiley disagrees, nominating *Uncle Tom's Cabin* for having more realistic black characters (318). **(end marker: page number)**

2) Either a quotation mark or the beginning of a long, indented quotation signals the beginning of a direct quotation. When using this method, both the last name of the author and the page number appear in parentheses at the end of the source (*without a comma or a "p."*).

> **Beginning of quotation. Front Marker: quotation marks**
> But some critics do not consider *Huck Finn* the best race novel in America: "It undoubtedly would have been better for American literature, and American culture, if our literature had grown out of one of the best-selling novels of all-time . . . *Uncle Tom's Cabin*" (Smiley 358).
> **End of quotation (end marker: last name of author and page number)**

416

**Long quotation signaled by indenting the quotation one half inch;
with no quotation marks needed.**

> Though many would argue that *Huck Finn* is the greatest American novel
> confronting the racism of America, not all agree.
>> Ernest Hemingway . . . once said that all American literature grew out
>> of *Huck Finn.* It undoubtedly would have been better for American
>> literature, and American culture, if our literature had grown out of one
>> of the best-selling novels of all time. . . *Uncle Tom's Cabin,* which for its
>> portrayal of an array of thoughtful, autonomous, and passionate black
>> characters leaves *Huck Finn* far behind (Smiley 358).

(End of quotation signaled by parenthetical reference)
Ellipsis [. . .] signal portions removed from source as unneeded.

3) For a source with no page numbers or if you are summarizing the entire source,
let the content in a sentence signal to the reader that you are using sources, and make
sure that the reader clearly knows where your use of the source begins and ends.

Sometimes no page numbers are provided by the container, so writers use a
transitional statement (<u>underlined here for identification</u>) to suggest where their ideas
begin again.

> Johnson feels that it is time for an amendment to the Constitution ending the
> Electoral College. <u>On the other hand, I feel</u> that this would create too much
> power in the most populous states, and all the population between New York
> and California would be ignored in Presidential elections.

> Wilson claims that all power is derived from the separation of powers.
> However, <u>the way I see it</u>, the muddled history of Supreme Court decisions
> renders this argument moot.

Without "On the other hand, I believe" and "the way I see it" in the sentences
above signaling that it is again the writer's ideas, a reader could assume that the
analysis of the effects of ending the Electoral College and the "muddled history of the
Supreme Court," in the final sentences also belong to Johnson and Wilson.

Another method to signal a front and end marker creates an alternative front marker,
and then uses the author's name in parentheses as the end marker. In the example
following, the phrase "Research verifies" signals the beginning of the source's ideas;
since the student writer obviously did not herself complete the research, the reader
knows where the source's ideas begin. The student's idea is the first sentence.

> All people love music. Research verifies that both passive music reinforcements
> (little physical response when listening to music) and active music reinforcement
> (playing instruments and dancing) increase desired behavior in special needs
> children (Holloway).

**(Author's last name and if the source has pagination, a page number
without p. No page number here because the entire Holloway article
has been summarized by this sentence.)**

Quotation marks with direct quotations can also signal the beginning of a source.

> Many novels describe ambiguously ideal worlds.. "It was the best of times. It was the worst of times" (Dickens 1).

MAKE SURE every one of your sentences clearly show which ideas come from a source and which ideas are yours.

Sample References

Corporate Authors

Corporations or government agencies can be considered authors, and are named in the text and are listed as the author in the works cited.

> The U.S. Bureau of Statistics demonstrates that a single adult manages thirty-three percent of households in America (431).

Author and Title

Though only the author's last name is required, often the writer also supplies the title of the source, especially if the title gives information that summarizes the main idea of the source.

> Shelley Fishkin, in *Was Huck Black?*, uses detailed linguistic analysis of Huck and other characters in Twain's works to render the controversial decision that Huck was not white.
> **(No page number. This is a one sentence summary of an entire book.)**
> **Two authors: Edward Hallowell and John Ratey find that...**

Citing Part of an Article or Book

> Bertrand Russell shows the rise of Greek philosophy and culture developed out of successive waves of earlier civilizations, including Babylonia, Egypt, Crete, Mycenae, Ionia, the Acheans, and finally the Dorian civilizations (2-11).
> **(Page references refer to the pages where Russell discusses contrasting cultures; this example is a one sentence summary of these pages.)**

Citing Indirect Sources

Many times, you use **someone's ideas in a source written by a second author**; for instance, a writer interviewing or quoting the source you want to cite.
When this occurs, you reference the originator of the idea in your text, and in the parenthetical reference you give the author of the source you got the information from with the page number, like the example:

Tom Browning did a study of traffic patterns and found that many American cities are not equipped for the amount of cars on their roads today (qtd. in Billings 119-120).

(Tom Browning did the study, but the writer found the information in an article by John Billings. The source listed in the works cited entry would begin "Billings, John" since that is the source the writer was specifically looking at. Tom Browning would not be on the works cited.)

Citing a Work Listed by Title of Article/Episode, NOT the source container

The *CNN* episode, "Policing the Border," discusses the problem of stopping drug runners coming in from Mexico.

("Policing the Border" [title] necessary, CNN [the container] optional.)

Television shows, newscasts, and films are usually cited by title, unless the writer is emphasizing one part of the show like a specific editor's comments, the director's vision, or the screenplay of a show (when they are cited by author):

Steven Spielberg creates strong emotion when he films the soldiers coming ashore on D-Day in *Saving Private Ryan*.

Dictionaries and other reference books (like the thesaurus paraphrased here) are cited by title of article or entry since there is not an author.

Synonyms for *racism* include two: *bigotry* and *intolerance* ("Racism" 651).

The works cited entry for this reference would be:

                                 publisher   pub. year page num.
"Racism." *Webster's Collegiate Thesaurus*, Merriam-Webster, 2003, p. 651.

Occasionally, citing by author+verb at the beginning of source material creates an awkward paragraph. *Never write an awkward sentence because of a 'rule'*; instead, create a series of sentences where it is still clear where the source begins and where it ends. The example above beginning "Synonyms for ..." clearly suggests that the source material begins with "Synonyms for . . ."

If the title is long, you can give a shortened version in your text that incorporates the first few words of the title so that the reader can find the source on the works cited page. For example, an anonymous article titled "Ten Long Years: The Middle East Wars and Multiple Troop Deployments" could be cited in-text as "Ten Long Years: Wars."

Citation Using author / page numbers in parentheses at the end

Bill Johnson claims that racism is a thing of the past (413). Jon Smith finds racism still alive and well (217). Jane Courtney cites statistics that show many minorites sufferr what can only be called racism (86).

To avoid the awkward sing song repetition, why not?:

419

Bill Johnson claims that racism is a thing of the past (413) while Jon Smith finds racism still alive and well (217). Statistics, however, show many minorites suffer what can only be called racism (Courtney 86).
Still clear front and end markers for each of these sources.

Citing Two or More Works by the same Author

In the next example, the writer uses quotations from two plays by Shakespeare in her essay, so in the text the writer has to not only identify the author and page number (in this instance, for plays, the act and scene numbers), but also the exact source (the specific play) she is citing:

> Shakespeare's Richard III famously says, "A horse, A horse, my kingdom for a horse!" (*Richard III* V.iii).

or if there is no mention of author in the text, the citation would be:

> "Beware the Ides of March" (Shakespeare, *Julius Caesar* I.ii.).

Working With Quotations

Begin quotations with either a colon, a comma, or the word *that*. At the end of the quotation, the usual order is quotation marks, page number in parentheses, and *then the* period: " (12).

> **(an indirect source: for quotations use "qtd. in")**
> Barack Obama firmly reiterates: "We aren't taking anyone's guns away" (qtd. in Miller 3).
>
> Charles Dickens's narrator begins *The Tale of Two Cities,* "It was the best of times; it was the worst of times." (1).
>
> Rolf Toman argues that "the contrast between the Middle Ages and the Renaissance is usually over-emphasized" (7).
> **(Notice the present tense in all these verbs introducing the quotations.)**

If the quotation itself ends with a question mark or exclamation point, the order is: ?" (12).

> Will and Ariel Durant ask, "What is the role of genius in history, of man versus the mass and the state?" (3).

Another method breaks the quotation into two segments:

> "A trickster," according to M.H. Abrams, "is a character in a story who persistently uses his wiliness, and gift of gab, to achieve his ends by outmaneuvering or outwitting other characters" (7).

When quoting fewer than three lines of poetry, use double spaced slashes to signal the end of a line of verse. Line numbers, rather than page numbers, are cited for poetry.

> Shelley's great ode begins, "O wild West Wind, thou breath of Autumn's being, // Thou, from whose unseen presence the leaves dead // Are driven, like ghosts from an enchanter fleeing" (lines 1-3).

If you refer to other lines of a poem later in the paragraph, leave "lines" out of the parentheses, and just cite the number(s) of the lines (13-15).

A prose quotation of five lines or more or more than three lines of poetry use a *block quotation format* with a further indentation of one half inch and no quotation marks.

> Percy Shelley describes the west wind, and the season of autumn, as:

> > Yellow, and black, and pale, and hectic red
> > Pestilence-stricken multitudes: O thou.
> > who chariotest their dark wintry bed

> > The winged seeds, where they lie cold and low,
> > Each like a corpse within its grave, until
> > Thine azure sister of the Spring shall blow (4-9)

If you are quoting words that are part of a dialogue or are themselves quoted, **an indirect source** (and thus in the source they are already in quotation marks), identify the **quotation-within-a-quotation** with single punctuation marks (the apostrophe key on a keyboard).

> Alexis de Tocqueville said, " 'When all privileges of birth and fortune are abolished, when all professions are accessible to all, and a man's own energies may place him at the top of any one of them, an easy and unbounded career seems open to his ambition' " (qtd. in Solomon 160). **(The writer found the quotation from de Toqueville in an article by Solomon.)**

When employing direct quotation, it is extremely important to respect your sources and copy *exactly* what the original says (even the punctuation). It is possible to change quotations, but only under these circumstances:

- To place your own words or phrases in brackets to make the quotation conform grammatically to your writing or to insert necessary information to make the quote understandable to your readers.
- If the quotation contains a misspelling, or if there could be confusion over whether the word is spelled correctly, spell the word exactly as it is in the original passage and insert parentheses surrounding the word sic: (sic).
- To omit irrelevant information from the quotation indicate omitted words or sentences with ellipsis: . . .

> Leonardo da Vinci studied optics to beome a better painter. In his notebooks,

he wrote, "The true outlines of opague bodies are never seen with sharp precision. This happens because the visual faculty does not occur in a point; it is diffused throughout the pupil [actually the retina] of the eye" (qtd. in Isaacson 270). **Da Vinci was wrong about the pupil so the writer corrects his mistake in the brackets. Da Vinci quote was in book by Isaacson.**

Trump blogged that "Immigrants effect (sic) the nation negatively." **Trump uses the wrong word in his blog. It should be *affect* so writer uses (sic).**

Original: When we allow freedom to ring - when we let it ring from every city and every hamlet, from every state and every city, we will begin to speed up that day when all of God's children, black men and white men, Jews and Gentiles, Protestants and Catholics, will be able to join hands and sing in the words of the old Negro spiritual, "Free at last, Free at last, Great God a-mighty, We are free at last." **The passage with two ellipsis, taking out some of the details to emphasize the main point:**
Martin Luther King exclaimed, "When we allow freedom to ring . . . [all men will want to] sing . . . the old Negro spiritual, 'Free at last, Free at last, Great God a-mighty, We are free at last'" (498) **See quote within quote p.421.**

Italics/Underlining versus Quotation Marks with Titles

When do you underline, italicize, or put quotation marks around titles? First, italics and underlining are interchangeable. In the examples below, *Writing Successfully* will italicize, but *underlining, though rare, is acceptable anyplace that italics are used.*

The best way to describe how to choose between italics/underlining and quotation marks is with a metaphor: **if it is the container, use italics; if it goes in the container, use quotation marks.**

Titles of Sources using Quotation Marks

All of these sources come out of a larger "container":
/ the title of an article in a book, newspaper, magazine, journal, or a computer source
/ the title of a short story or a less than book length poem
/ the title of a song
/ the title of a particular episode of a television show

Titles of Sources using Italics

All of these sources are the "containers" themselves:
/ the *name* of a newspaper, magazine, or journal (the *New York Times, Newsweek*)
/ any *book*, whether it be a novel, a reference book, or a collection of essays, stories, or poems
/ the *title* of a CD (or a cassette tape or record album)
/ the *name* of a television show (*Seinfeld, NBC Nightly News*) or a movie (*Clueless*)
/ the *title* of a play (*King Lear*) or a book length poem (*Beowulf*)
/ court decisions (*Roe vs. Wade*)
/ the name of a website (*orpheuspress.com*) or database (*Academic One File*)

Exceptions with neither italics nor quotation marks:
Scripture - Bible, Old Testament, Genesis, Talmud, Upanishads
Laws, Acts, Political Documents - The Constitution, The Voting Rights Act
Musical compositions identified by form, numbers, key- Mozart's Concerto No. 2
The divisions of a work (introduction, preface, stanza, scene, index, chapter, appendix, index).
Exceptions to exceptions - 1) Court decisions are italicized: *Brown vs Board of Education* and 2) specific editions of scripture (*The King James Version*).

Preparing the Works Cited using MLA Documentation

At the end of a research paper, on a new page continuing pagination from the essay, there should be a Works Cited page (or pages) that lists, *in alphabetical order*, every source referred to in the research paper. **Center the title (Works Cited) one inch from the top of the page**, and double space between the title and the first entry. There are examples of essays with a Works Cited in chapters 10, 11, and ending 3, 5, 6, 7.

Professors may ask, also, for **a bibliography (titled Works Consulted)**, which lists every book and article studied in order to write the essay, but the Works Cited should list only those books, articles, and other sources which are actually referred to in the essay either by direct quotation, picture, graph, paraphrase, or summary.

When you construct a Works Cited list, follow the examples below *exactly* concerning placement of periods, colons, commas, names, and abbreviations. It is unnecessary to memorize this or any documentation style; just refer to this section of *Writing Successfully* or the *MLA Handbook* 8th ed. when you make your list, and follow the examples exactly. **DO NOT TRUST ANY CITATION CREATION SOURCE ON THE INTERNET unless your professor approves it!**

If an entry is longer than one line, every line after the first is indented one-half inch (five spaces). **The list is double-spaced both between and within entries**.

The 8th edition of the *MLA Handbook* has simplified creating works cited pages by regularizing the order of elements across all types of sources. The basic order for creating a works cited citation for all sources (pay attention to the punctuation) – **some sources will not have all of these elements:**

Author.	The author, authors or corporate author.
Title of Source.	The article, story, book, movie, episode, title, song.
Title of Container,	The source's container: title of newpaper, magazine, website.
Other Contributors,	Editors, directors, translators, performers, etc.
Version,	If there is a specific description: 2nd ed. Expanded ed.
Number,	Volume (vol.) and Issue (no.) numbers. TV episodes and seasons.
Publisher,	Name of organization that published the work.
Publication Date,	Self-evident. If more than one date, the one most meaningful.
Location.	Page numbers, URLs, DOIs, location for art or lecture.

There are examples with many more specfic details on the following pages AND follow the punctuation EXACTLY.
For the example citations in the rest of the chapter: when information on an element from the above list is missing, it is ~~marked through.~~

Use these abbreviations and special characteristics:
University Presses use U and P for university and press:

        U of Illinois P   Harvard UP

Book titles, movies, television shows, and websites are in italics.
Essays, stories, articles on websites and in print are in quotation marks.
Any word after a period is capitalized (like the beginning of a sentence).

*Author(s) - also included here: basic information/examples of **Books***

Author. *Title of Source*. ~~Title of Container, Other Contributors, Version, Number,~~
    Publisher, Publication Date, ~~Location~~.

(notice order: last name, comma first name, comma and first name last name)
Brooks, Cleanth, and Robert Penn Warren. *Understanding Poetry.* Holt, Rinehart, 1938.

Campbell, Joseph. *The Hero With A Thousand Faces.* Princeton UP, 1949.

If more than one book or article by the same author is used in the research paper, place them in alphabetical order by title after being placed within the alphabetical order of the entire list by the author's last name; the citations after the first use three hyphens where the author's name occurs.

(another book by Joseph Campbell)
- - -. *The Masks of God: Primitive Mythology.* Viking, 1959.
                          (: *sub-title*)

(two authors - Last name, First name, and First name Last name)
Hallowell, Edward, and John Ratey. *Driven to Distraction: Recognizing and Coping*
    with Attention Defecit Disorder. Touchstone, 1994.

(three or more authors or editors use first name listed and et al)
Kaliski, Burton et al. *Keeping Financial Records for Business.* Thomson, 1982.

(If a corporate or government author, it is listed as the author.)
United States Bureau of Census. *United States Census Figures Back to 1630.* Hardpress,
    2016.

Title of Source versus Title of Container
Anthologies, Websites, Ebooks

If you refer to an article, story, poem, or picture within a larger whole (an anthology, magazine, journal, or website), begin the citation by referring to the writer of the article rather than the editor, using the form below. The title of the article **("Title of Source")** follows the author's name, followed by the larger container it came from, the magazine, journal, website, or anthology *(Title of Container)*.

Anthologies

Author. "Title of Source." *Title of Container*, Other Contributors (editors in these
    examples),Version, ~~Number~~, Publisher, Publication Date, Location.

    ("title of source-the article") *(title of container - the book the essay is in)*

Alda, Alan. "What Every Woman Should Know About Men." *The Gender Reader*,
    edited by Evelyn Ashton-Jones and Gary A. Olsen, 2nd ed., Allyn and Bacon,
    1995, pp. 56-60.   **(Version-Edition)**
    (Location: page numbers of article in anthology)

If you refer to multiple sources in a single anthology, you may cite with author,
title, editor(s) and page number(s). If you do this, there must be an entry for the
anthology with the editor's names listed first: **See p. 165 for example:** a Works Cited
that has several articles by different authors that the writer found in a single anthology.

Kermode, Frank et al., editors. *The Oxford Anthology of English Literature.* Vol. 2.
    Oxford UP, 1973.

Then for all sources from that anthology, use this form:

Shelley, Percy Blythe. "Alastor." Kermode et al, pp. 401-08.

Website

U.S. Department of State. "U.S. Relations with Afghanistan." *U.S. Department*
    of State, 29 Oct. 2015, www.state.gov/r/pa/ei/bgn/5300htm.
(*Title of Container-name of website*, Publication Date, Location: web address)

Ebooks: A book from a college database
(Classic sources can have their original publication date after title as below.)
(Source: *Book* Title of Container: *web database [ebrary]* Publisher: elecbooks)
Defoe, Daniel. *Moll Flanders.* 1720. *ebrary*, elecbooks, 2000, internal.jefferson.
    kctcs.edu:2050/lib/jeffcomm/detail.action?docID=2001791&p00=moll+flanders.

Other Contributors: <u>Editors, Translators, Directors,</u>
<u>*Performers, Narrators*</u>

An edition prepared by a named editor

If you refer to the book itself, as is usual, begin with the author. A named editor,
translator, or other contributor occurs after the Title of Source, or Container if there
is one.
Edited by first name last name, (if following the source title which ends in a period)
edited by first name last name, (if followed by container title which ends in a comma)

Author. *Title of Source*. ~~Title of Container~~, Other Contributors, ~~Version, Number~~, Publisher, Publication Date, ~~Location~~.

Melville, Herman. *Moby-Dick*. 1851. Edited by Harrison Hayford and

Hershel Parker, W.W. Norton, 1967.

(Classic sources can also have their original publication date after title as above.)

With a source that also has a container Page numbers - location within the container.

("title of source") **(*title of container*)**

Jewett, Sarah Orne. "A White Heron." *The Norton Anthology of American Literature*,

edited by Nina Baym et al, vol. 2, Norton, 1979, pp. 462-470.

(number)

If you refer to the editor's comments, such as in an introduction, preface, foreward, or afterward, begin with the editor(s). **Words like introduction, etc. designating the division of a source do not use quotation marks or italics, as with example below.)**

Author. Title of Source. *Title of Container,* Other Contributors, ~~Version, Number~~, Publisher, Publication Date, Location. (page numbers of foreward)

Hayford, Harrison, and Herchel Parker, editors. Foreword. *Moby-Dick*, 1851,

written by Herman Melville, Norton, 1967, pp. ix-xi.

A Translation

If you refer to the text itself, begin with the author. If the translator also served as an editor, reveal this information too.

Author. "Title of Source." *Title of Container*, Other Contributors, ~~Version, Number~~, Publisher, Publication Date, Location. (the page numbers of the poem in the book)

Rilke, Ranier Maria. "I Love the Dark Hours." *Selected Poems*, translated and

edited by Robert Bly, Harper and Row, 1981, pp. 18-19.

If you refer to the translator's or editor's comments, as in an introduction.

Author. Title of Source. *Title of Container*, Other Contributors, ~~Version, Number~~, Publisher, Publication Date, Location.

Bly, Robert, translator and editor. Introduction. *Selected Poems*, written by Ranier

Maria Rilke, Harper and Row, 1981, pp. 3-11.

Other possibilities used in other contributors (capitalized if following title of source which ends with a period; not capitalized if following the title of the container which ends with a comma).

adapted by	introduction by	performance by
directed by	narrated by	translation by
edited by	illustrated by	written by

426

Author. *Title of Source*, ~~Title of Container~~, Other Contributors, Version, ~~Number~~, Publisher, Publication Date, Location.

(original release date)

Star Wars: Episode IV - A New Hope. 1977. Directed by George Lucas, performance by Harrison Ford, special edition, Lucasfilm, 1997, DVD.

(Version)   (Publisher and Publication [release] date)

The Version: Books, Movies, <u>Newspapers</u> in Later or Special Editions

Books with no edition number on the title page are probably a first edition. When you have used an edition other than the first, identify it after the name of the editor or translator (if there is one) or after the title of the book if there is not a named editor.

- The edition of a book is identified in this manner: 2nd ed. 3rd ed. 4th ed., Revised ed., Expanded ed., Abridged ed., Updated ed. or whatever called on the title page.
- Movies might be listed as director's cut, expanded version, or other versions.
- Newspapers are sometimes listed by edition.
- Anything that signals a unique version of a work is listed here, between the title and the number. **See the examples on this and following pages**:

Authors. *Title of Source*. ~~Title of Container, Other Contributors,~~ Version, ~~Number,~~ Publisher, Publication Date, ~~Location.~~

Strunk, William, and E. B. White. *The Elements of Style*. 4th ed., Macmillan, 1983.

If a newspaper with nationwide circulation (such as *USA Today*, the *New York Times*, the *London Times*, the *Washington Post*), describe the edition cited using these abbreviations: National Edition = natl. ed.   Late Edition = late ed.
                             1st Edition = 1st ed.   City Edition = city ed.
                             Online Edition = online ed.

("title of source")   **(*title of container*)**

Smith, James. "Proposal Aims to Encourage Small Business Pension Plans." *New York Times,* late ed., 1 May 1991, p. A2+.

(If the article does not have consecutive pagination (it begins on one page and then skips to a page or pages later in the source), cite the source using the first page followed by a plus (+) sign: 17+)

Number

- If citing a multi-volume book or anthology, list volume number (vol.) in the number position of the works cited format.
- Magazines and journals also usually have a volume number, and sometimes an issue number, and issues are always cited as no. (See examples on next pages.)

Keats, John. "Ode on a Grecian Urn." *The Oxford Anthology of English Literature*, edited by Frank Kermode et al., vol. 2, Oxford UP, 1973, pp. 541-42.

(number)   (location:page numbers of entry)

Articles in *Encyclopedias, Dictionaries, and other Reference Books*

Reference works are now treated just as any other book or on-line material would be treated. Leave blank any information not given.
Begin with title of article or entry unless the author is named.

Author. "Title of Source." *Title of Container*, ~~Other Contributors~~, ~~Version~~, Number, Publisher, Publication Date, Location.

 Title of Container Publisher
Tate, Francis. "Rum." *Encyclopedia Britannica*, vol. 19, Encyclopedia Brittanica, 1951, p. 635.

 Title of Container Publisher
"The White House." *Encyclopedia Americana*, vol. 29, Grolier, 2005, p. 710.

"Nightshade." *The American Heritage College Dictionary*, 3rd ed., Houghton Mifflin, 1997, p. 922.

On-line reference works

~~Author~~ [unless named]. "Title of Source." *Title of Container*, ~~Other Contributors~~, ~~Version, Number~~, Publisher, Publication Date, Location.

If from on-line website (no publisher listed)
"The US Constitution." *Wikipedia*, 28 Aug. 2020, www.en/wikipedia.org/wiki/US Constitution.

"Native American." *Encyclopedia Britannica*, 2018, www. britannica.com/native american.

If from college database - no print edition
 Container, Publisher, publiction date
"Native American." *Britannica Academic*, Encyclopedia Britannica, 19 Jan. 2018, 0e10fy48x-y-https-academic-eb-com.libproxy.kctcs.edu

1st line is citation as if you had the print reference ency. in hand, ending in period.
"Internet Addiction Disorder." *Human Diseases and Conditions*, 3rd ed., 2017.
  Credo Reference, https://libproxy.kctcs.edu/Jefferson?url=https://search. credoreference.com/content/galehuman=2929.
2nd/3rd line starts new citation with just the database (italicized), url. Here also:

***CQ Researcher* is actually a magazine, but it is also a good reference tool for social issues. First *CQ Res* is title of magazine. 2nd *CQ Res* is the database.**
Price, Tom. "Gun Violence." *CQ Researcher*, vol. 28, no. 27, 27 Jul. 2018. *CQ Researcher*, 0e106y4ky-y-https-library -cqpress -com.libproxy.kctcs.edu/cqresearcher201807.

Print AND On-line Articles: magazines, journals, newpapers

Periodical articles are now treated with the same pattern as books: the articles cited are the source and the name of the publication is the container.

Some specifics pertaining to periodicals:
- **Number: Volume number = vol. Issue number = no.**
- **Location are the page number(s) = p. 213 or pp. 213-215.**
- **General editors of magazines (other contributors) ARE NOT given.**
- **Usually both Other Contributors and the Publisher ARE NOT relevant for citations of periodical articles.**

Author. "Title of Source." *Title of Container*, ~~Other Contributors~~, ~~Version~~, Number,
~~Publisher~~, Publication Date, Location.

Print

Updike, John. "Sinclair Lewis: Exile on Main Street." *The New Yorker,* 17 May 1993,
pp. 91-97.

When you have a source that originally was in print, but you are getting it from either a library database (like Ebsco Host, JSTOR, the Gale databases) or from a website for that original source (rollingstone.com, newsweek.com), you cite it as below.

You begin with the pattern just like it was a print medium, and then you repeat the pattern again using the elements necessary to designate the website/database (usually only the title of the container [the database or website] and location [url or doi]). For instance, here is the same John Updike citation except from a college database:

Database

Updike, John. "Sinclair Lewis: Exile on Main Street." *The New Yorker,* 17 May 1993,
p. 91+. *Academic One File,* http//link.galegroup.com/apps/doc/A13870595/
ACNE?u=kctcsjcc@sid=ACNE@xid=s5a3ff66.

Just the database and url added after the period ending the initial citation.

Print

Gore, Rick, and Bill Hamblin. "Neanderthals." *National Geographic,* vol. 190, no. 1,
Jan. 1996, pp. 2-35.

Database

Gore, Rick, and Bill Hamblin. "Neanderthals." *National Geographic,* vol. 189, no. 1,
Jan. 1996, pp. 2-35. *Academic Search Complete,*
http://web.a ebscohost.libproxy.osu.edu/ehost/48234.

Print - Newspaper

Brown, Mike. "Oil Rich Refuge May Fund Energy Studies." *The Courier-Journal* [Louisville],
18 Mar. 1991, p. A1+.

Local newpapers list city in brackets after name unless name includes the place of publication, such as the *Toronto Star*. (+ indicates that the article began on section A page 1 and continues on a page later in the newspaper.)

Database-Newspaper   ***Proquest* is the database.**

Krugman, Paul. "American Democracy May Be Dying." *New York Times,* late ed.,
10 Apr. 2020, p. A 27. *ProQuest,* 0e11ty4-search-proquest-libproxy.kctcs.edu=11686.

Author, A. (unless anonymous). "Title of Source." *Title of Container*, ~~Other~~
~~Contributors~~, ~~Version~~, Number, ~~Publisher~~, Publication Date, Location. If
database/website, then Database/Website, url or doi. **Notice period after location.**

Print - anonymous author. Just skip author and begin with title of article.
"The Who Return to the Road." *Guitar Player*, vol. 41, no. 6, Jun. 2018, pp. 31-33.

**Database - Scholarly Journal article (Citation of print article would be identical
without database and doi.)**
                        Three or more authors, list first author and et al.
Koneswaran, Gowri, et al. "Global farm animal production and global warming:
    impacting and mitigating climate change." *Environmental Health Perspectives*,
    vol. 116, no. 5, 2008, p. 578+. *Gale Academic One File*, doi: 10.1289/eho.11034.

A scholarly journal article originally published on-line (no print analogue)

Abel, Angela, and Michael Barthel. "Appropriation of Mainstream News: How
    Saturday Night Live Changed the Political Discussion." *Critical Studies
    in Media Communication*, vol. 30, no.1, 2013, www.mediastudies.com/4821jour92386.

An article from an on-line magazine or newspaper (no print analogue)

Triece, Mary. "The Practical True Warrior: Reconciling Women and Work in Popular
    Mail-Order Magazines, 1900-1920." *Critical Studies in Mass Communication*, vol. 16,
    Mar. 1999, p. 42+. *Journalseek*. www.journalseek.com/492369244id43cap915.

Ebooks

**An edition of a book that has a print format, but you get it from a database or
website. Format same as for printed book followed by database/website and url.**

Gross, Kenneth. *Shylock is Shakespeare*, U Chicago P., 2006. *ebrary*,
    www.ebrary.com/4125600.

from a database in a later edition   (University Presses are abbreviated UP)
Elton, William. *King Lear and the Gods*. 2nd Ed. UP of Kentucky, 1988. *Proquest
    Ebook Central*, https://0e1049yzm-y-https-ebookcentral-proquest-com.libproxy
    kctcs.edu

from a database with a named editor
Bronte, Charlotte. Shirley. 1849. Edited by Margaret Smith and Herbert Rosengarten,
    Oxford UP, 2007. *Proquest Ebook Central*, https://0e1049yzm-y-https-
    ebookcentral-proquest-com.libproxy.kctcs.edu
**(The Ed. and Editor are capitalized because they follow a period. When following
a comma, they would be lower case: ed. edited by)**
Ed. or ed. for edition. Edited by or edited by for editor.

Editorials, Letters, Reviews, Interviews

An editorial or letter uses the label Editorial, Letter *following the title. An Anonymous article starts with the next item, the title of the source:*

~~Author.~~ "Title of Source." *Title of Container*, ~~Other Contributors,Version~~, Number,
~~Publisher~~, Publication Date, Location. If from database - database, url would be
here.
"Share This Issue!" Letter. *Esquire*, vol. 81, no. 1, Jan. 2013, p. 10.

Heise, Robert. "The It 'Girl.'" Editorial. *Rolling Stone*, vol. 96, 28 Mar. 2013, p.12.

A music, film, or book review

Author. Title of Source. *Title of Container*, ~~Other Contributors,Version~~, Number,
~~Publisher~~, Publication Date, Location.

Rosen, Judy. "Justin's Stoned Soul Comeback." Review of *The 20/20 Experience*
by Justin Timberlake. *Rolling Stone*, vol. 52, 28 Mar. 2013,
www.rollingstone.com/review/3-28-13/Timberlake.
**(If this was the print version, the page numbers would appear as the location
where the url is here.)**

Unpublished Letter

Smith, John. Letter to Richard Hanson, 10 Jan. 2017.

Published Letter

Adams, John. "Letter to Abigal Adams." 3 Jul. 1776. *Norton Anthology of American
Literature*, edited by Nina Baym et al, vol. A. Norton, 2003, pp. 692-694.

Interviews

Jones, Bill. Personal Interview. 12 Feb. 2017.
(the interviewee)

Obama, Barack. Interview with Chris Matthews. *Hardball with Chris Matthews*, MSNBC,
12 Mar. 2016. **(If from YouTube or online - source, url. would be here.)**
(the interviewer)
Welty, Eudora. "Art of Fiction." *The Paris Review Interviews*, by Linda Kuehl, edited by
Philip Gourevitch, vol. 2, Canongate, 2007, pp. 117-142.

An email
(subject line of email)
Matheny, Meg. "Possible Textbook Choices." Received by Richard Hanson. 19 Mar.
2013.

Blog, Listserve, or Discussion Group Posting

Author. Title of Source. *Title of Container*, ~~Other Contributors,Version, Number,~~
~~Publisher,~~ Publication Date, Location.

screenname [author if available]
movie lover 9 [Joan Blandon]. "The Best Movie of 2016." *International Movie Database*, 23
Oct. 2016, www.imdb.com/thread/34862/best movies. Accessed 29 Nov. 2020.
**(Whenever you are citing a source that might not be permanent, like a blog, a
listserve, or a website that might not be permanent, the final entry is the date of
access.)**

Location

You have already seen the location used in many of the citations on the previous
pages. Location is used for
• Page numbers in anthologies of articles, in magazines, journals, newspapers.
• Physical descriptions: DVD, Videocassette, a disk number for a multiple DVD or
CD set, CD, Audiocassette, LP, Television, Radio.
• A location for art at a museum, a lecture attended, a performance seen, by venue
and city (if not in the name of the venue)
• A DOI is THE preferred method (scholarly journals are starting to identify
articles with a specific DOI number.) If there is a DOI, use it for location.)
• A URL if source is located on-line and none of the other locations are relevant.
• An unexpected location: a Transcript, an Address, a physical location of a
museum.
• A bill, report or resolution in Congress could include the number and session
of Congress and specify the document type and number: 107th Congress, 2nd
session, Senate Report 413.
• **If you are citing from a website that does not look like it would be permanent,
that information could change or be removed, the date accessed would be
important:** Accessed 24 Sept 2020.

Sound Recordings

The first person cited depends on the desired emphasis: composer, artist(s), ensemble.
Then list the title, the artist if not listed first, the manufacturer, the year of issue (or n.d.
if unknown), and the medium: audiocassette, audiotape (reel to reel recording),CD,
or LP (record).

Author. Title of Source. ~~*Title of Container*, Other Contributors,Version, Number,~~
Publisher, Publication Date, Location.
Entire album/CD vs. a song
The Rolling Stones. *Exile on Main Street*. Atlantic, 1972. Audiocassette.
Performer.   "Song."   *Album,*   version,   publisher
Pink Floyd. "The Great Gig in the Sky." *Dark Side of the Moon*, deluxe ed., Harvest
Records, 1973, track 5. *Amazon Music*, play.amazon.com/pinkfloyd/3sa26549063.

Author. "Title of Source." *Title of Container*, Other Contributors, ~~Version, Number,~~
    Publisher, Publication Date, Location.

If you refer primarily to the lyrics:

        (Song titles are in quotation marks and album/CD titles are in italics.)
Jaggers, Mick and Keith Richards, composers. "Jumpin' Jack Flash." *Through*
    the Past Darkly, performance by The Rolling Stones, London, 1968, track 1.
    Spotify, play.spotify.com/track/46Cuxy382042?play=true&utm_medium=open.

Davis, Miles. *Kind of Blue*. Capitol, 1959. LP.   **A record**

Kristofferson, Kris, composer. "Sunday Morning Coming Down." *The Best of*
    Johnny Cash, performance by Johnny Cash, Capitol, 1983, CD.
(Kristofferson wrote the song and Cash performed it.)

Audio/Visual: Films, YouTube, Streaming, Art, T.V/Radio Broadcasts

After the title of a film, the director is required, but one may also list performers, screenwriter, producers if relevant. Followed by distributor, year of release, and medium if other than televised or movies: DVD, Videocassette.

(year of original release if different than date of publication)
Casablanca. 1942. Directed by Michael Curtiz, performances by Humphrey Bogart and
    Ingrid Bergman, Warner Brothers, 1981, videocassette.

If you are citing the contribution of a particular individual, begin with that person:

Epstein, Julius, Philip Koch, and Howard Koch, screenwriters. *Casablanca*. 1942.
    Directed by Michael Curtiz, Warner Brothers, 2002, DVD.

"The Cockatoo." *Mad About You*, directed by Paul Reiser, performances by Helen Hunt
    and Paul Reiser, Fox, WDRB, Louisville [KY], 2 Apr. 2013.
(Begin with "title of episode"; include directors and relevant performers, narrators, writers.)

If you are citing from a special edition, give relevant information and name the source what the DVD or website names it.

"The Cockatoo." *The Complete Fifth Editon of Mad About You*, directed by Paul
    Reiser, performances by Helen Hunt and Paul Reiser, Warner Brothers, 2011. DVD.

Radio Programs

"Little Steven's Underground Garage." Narrated by Steve Van Zandt, PBS, KSWD, Los Angeles, 16 Apr. 2013.

A Streaming Service: When citing from netflix, google play, amazon play, hulu

"Rogue." *Legend*, directed and performance by Sean Bean, season 1, episode 5, TNT, 2014. *Netflix*, www.netflix.com/watch/863298493485track-id?4394.

The Avengers: Endgame. Directed by Joe and Anthony Russo, performances by Robert Downey, Jr., Scarlett Johansson, Chris Evans, and Mark Ruffalo, Marvel Studios and Walt Disney Studios, 2019. *Amazon Prime*, www.amazonprime.com/watch/73925815.

YouTube or site that does have control of uploads

"I Have Severe OCD." *YouTube*, uploaded by Lele Pons, 19 May 2020, www.youtube.com/watch?v=USfoQp_ydl4qshtp9862qG1.

Harry Potter and the Sorcerer's Stone. Directed by Chris Columbus, Warner Brothers., 2001. *YouTube*, uploaded by Potter Fan, 24 May 2020, www.youtube.com/watch/49285420.

Art   **date of composition ca=circa location**
Da Vinci, Leonardo. *Mona Lisa*. ca. 1503-09, The Louvre, Paris.

Advertisements

Chevrolet. "Corvette Advertisement." NBC, 15 May 2020.

Proctor and Gamble. "Wisk Detergent Advertisement." *Newsweek*, vol. 86, 3 May 2013, p. 47.

Websites

A personal website

Decker, Daniel. Home Page, 2013. www.louisville.edu. Accessed 13 Apr. 2020.

An entire website

If the website has an editor, director, translator, narrator, begin with name. Otherwise begin with the title of the website. If the sponsor of publisher is different than the site, list that also under publisher (like Yale sponsoring the *Beowulf Manuscripts* below).

Payne, Jake, editor. *HipHopDX*, 2012, www.hiphopDX.com.

Smith, Bill, director. *Beowulf Manuscripts*, Yale U, 2003, www.yale.edu/beowulf.

24

APA Documentation

There are several styles of documentation used in scholarly study and *Writing Successfully* includes brief instructions for four of the most common: MLA style (used by English and modern language scholars, and all publications of the Modern Language Association), APA style (used by psychologists, sociologists, and all publications of the American Psychological Association), CSE style (used by many of the sciences, and all publications sanctioned by the Council of Science Editors), and Chicago style (used by historians and several other social science groups). *For each class you take in college, always ask your instructor which documentation style to use.* There are other documentation styles, but these are the most prevalent.

This chapter divides into two sections:

- Parenthetical in-text documentation using the APA style: how to cite sources in your paper: Author (year of publication) or (author, year).
- Preparing the References page using APA documentation.

Remember that this chapter gives only brief instructions showing how to document the most commonly used sources. For complete instructions use ONLY this edition:

American Psychological Association. (2019). *Publication manual of the american psychological association* (7th ed.). https://doi.org/10.1037/0000165-000

The APA now endorses bias free language in papers and books using APA style around gender, age, disability, racial and ethnic identity. For instance,

Use the singular "they" or "their."
Incorrect: A musician makes little money no matter how many albums he or she sells.
Correct: A musician makes little money no matter how many albums they sell.

Use descriptive phrases rather than adjectives as nouns labeling people:
Not: "the mentally handicapped" or even "differently abled." Definitely not "disabled."
Instead: people with an intellectual disability

Use specific relevant age ranges.
Not: People over 50   *Instead*: People in the age range of 50 to 60 years old

Parenthetical Documentation Using Author (Date) APA Style

Whenever you summarize, paraphrase, or use a direct quotation, you must let your reader know the source of the ideas or quoted material. In the text of your writing, identify the author or the title of the source if anonymous, (the year of publication), and additionally the page number(s) at the end of the source material if a direct quotation or if needed to help reader find the original material in a lengthy source. *The author's last name is used, but not the first name as is used in MLA Humanities genres.* At the end of your essay, a References page gives your reader the author, title, and publication information for the source. The citation in the text would appear like this: **Author (year of publication)**

> Ackerman (2005) suggests that in 1801 just after Thomas Jefferson defeated John Adams, America almost did away with its constitution - our constitution that still stands - in arguments over the future of our country.

The References entry at the end of the essay would be as follows (notice lower case capitalization in title):

> Ackerman, B. (2005). *The failure of the founding fathers.* Harvard University Press.

When evaluating in-text parenthetical documentation, check for accuracy using these four bulleted specific guidelines for scholarly researched writing:

- *Most academic writing uses summary and paraphrase rather than direct quotation. The only reasons to use direct quotation are: when the source has said something so well that any attempt to summarize or paraphrase it would lessen its impact, or when there are many technical words or words that have no exact synonym in the source so that you can't rephrase the original passage in your own words.*
- When reading your essay, from your in-text parenthetical documentation the reader should be able to find the source on your References page, and from the information on the References page, the reader should be able to locate your source in a library or on the internet (unless your source is unpublished).
- References in your text must have an entry on the References page. (If you refer to a source in-text by author, Jones (2007) argues ..., in your essay, there must be an entry **beginning** Jones, A. (2007) on the References page.) What *appears as your in-text citation IS ALWAYS the first element in your References entry. That References opening will always be the author EXCEPT when the article is anonymous, then the first item in the References entry will be the title of the article. So NEVER cite a source IN YOUR TEXT with the name of the website, magazine, or newspaper*, always cite by author unless anonymous, and then by title.
  INCORRECT in-text for citations from anonymous sources:
  IMDB.com (2009) states ...   According to *Sports Illustrated* (2011),
  CORRECT: "Star Wars"(2009) states Lucas made millions.... According to "The Forty-Niners Lose Their Way" (2011), . . . If your reader wants to know where the source came from, she reads the References.
- In text APA citations do not usually have the page numbers EXCEPT for direct quotations OR to help reader find the summarized material in a particularly long source. If a source on the internet does not have pages, but has paragraph numbers, use them (Jullant, 2019, para. 7). If a source has neither page nor paragraph numbers, cite a sub-heading followed by counting the paragraphs to the place cited. If the heading is long, it may be shortened, but in that case use quotation marks around the shortened title.

Use Subheading if no page number
    (Johns, 2012, America First section).
    (Abraham, 2017, William the Conquerer section, para.6).
Quotation Marks for abbreviated long titles:
"Mandatory Testing for Drivers With Poor Eyesight"
(American Teachers Association, 2012, "Mandatory Testing," para. 2)

Count paragraphs yourself if necessary (unless it is pages and pages)
    (Jones, 2020, para. 20).

As a reader reads your essay, they expect the ideas to be your ideas until you indicate that you are now using a source's ideas. The **preferred parenthetical author, date method** has author, year (Jones, 2013) after the summarized source, and (Jones, 2013, p. 14) after a quoted source. However, if this makes it unclear where your ideas stop and the source's ideas start, use the **narrative method**: Jones (2013) argues . . .

1) Parenthetical (author, date) Method. Notice period AFTER parenthesis.

... the end of the summarized section (Franks, 2013).

... the end of the summarized section (Jones&Fink, 2015).   **2 authors**

                                            3 or more authors,
... the end of the summarized section (Branagh et al., 2016). **list first name and et al.**

... the end of the summarized section (Simpson, n.d.).   **no publication date given**

... the end of the summarized section (Department of Labor, 2018). **corporate author**

... the end of the summarized section (National Security Agency [NSA], 2020).
If acronym used, after first citation spells the entity, afterwards citation would be
... the end of the summarized section (NSA, 2020).

Writers in the social sciences show that many scientists agree to support the view of the essay. Use alphabetic order and notice ampersand (&) with 2 authors.
Many sources agree that the ice sheets of Antartica are disappearing (Adams, 2012; Jones & Fry, 2018; Zane et al, 2015).   **See essay example on p. 201.**

For translations, reprinted, republished or reissued works, give original publication date followed by slash and publication date of source that was looked at. .. the end of the summarized section (Faulkner 1932/1986).

Quotations
"...quotations are in quotation marks and add the page number or if no page number another identifier" (Johnson, 2018, p.12).

... the end of the quoted section" (Anderson, 2019, para. 12).

2) Narrative Method

Cite the author's last name or names (and year of publication) with either a phrase or a verb that describes what the author is doing.

> As Franks (2013) has found,
> As Franks (2013) pointed out,
> According to Franks (2013),

If two authors, unlike parenthetical method using &: Jones and Fink (2016) added

> Franks (2013) claimed

agreed	compared	explained	observed
argued	concluded	found	pointed out
showed	asked	considered	illustrated
related	speculated	asserted	declared
implied	reported	stated	believed
denied	insisted	responded	suggested
wrote	disagreed	maintained	revealed
thought	commented	emphasized	noted

When you use a verb, pick one that accurately describes what the source is doing:
Author of source's name (date of publication) + verb
Carter (1978) *declared* that America should be energy FREE by the year 2000.

Many of the verbs above would fit this paraphrase; however, some wouldn't (*asks, compares, denies, disagrees, notes, points out, responds, sees*). While the rest would be technically acceptable, some would be more accurate than others: Carter is stating an opinion or desire, not a fact, so verbs that connote suggestion would be the most accurate (*asserts, believes, claims, comments, considers, declares, finds, implies, maintains, says, states, suggests, thinks, writes*). Verbs that could connote a fact would be less acceptable (*explains, observes, reports, sees, shows*).

Also, MLA *uses the present tense, but APA uses the correct past tense:* Jonathan Swift (1738/1973) *claimed.* Use whichever tense is appropriate to signal the time sequence of what your essay reports.

> Studies in the past have indicated that the death penalty deterred crime, but modern studies definitely indicate that the death penalty may increase violent crime (Wilson, 2011, p. 314).

3) **Quotations** Either a quotation mark or the beginning of a long, indented quotation signals the beginning of a direct quotation. When using this method, the last name of the author, the publication date, and the page number appear in parentheses at the end of the source.

*(***Beginning of quotation***)*
> Some critics do not consider *Huck Finn* the best race novel in America: "It undoubtedly would have been better for American literature, and American culture, if our literature had grown out of one of the best-selling novels of all time . . . *Uncle Tom's Cabin*" (Smiley, 1996, p.358).

End of quotation (last name of author, year, and page number)

A long quotation (more than 40 words) is signaled by indenting quotation ten spaces; no quotation marks needed:

> Though many would argue that *Huck Finn* is the greatest American novel confronting the racism of America, not all agree.
>
> > Ernest Hemingway . . . once said that all American literature grew out of *Huck Finn*. It undoubtedly would have been better for American literature, and American culture, if our literature had grown out of one of the best-selling novels of all time. . . *Uncle Tom's Cabin*, which for its portrayal of an array of thoughtful, autonomous, and passionate black characters leaves *Huck Finn* far behind (Smiley, 1996, p. 358).
> > **(End of quotation signaled by parenthetical reference)**

Sample References

Author and Title

APA style does not give the title in the body of the essay unless there is no author.

Citing Part of an Article or Book

> Bertrand Russell (1945) showed that the rise of Greek philosophy and culture developed out of successive waves of earlier civilizations, including Babylonia, Egypt, Crete, Mycenae, Ionia, the Acheans, and finally the Dorian civilizations (pp. 2-11).
> **(Page references refer to the pages where Russell discusses contrasting cultures; this example is a one sentence summary of these pages.)**

Corporate Author

> The Department of Labor (2018) declared unemployment to be 4.1% (para. 1)
OR   ... unemployment reached 4.1% (Department of Labor, 2018, para. 1).

Citing a Work Listed by Title

> The *CNN* episode, "Policing the Border" (2011), discussed the problem of stopping drug runners coming in from Mexico.

Television shows, newscasts, and films are usually cited by director.

> Steven Spielberg (1998) created strong emotion when he films the soldiers coming ashore on D-Day in *Saving Private Ryan*.

Dictionaries and other reference books (like the thesaurus paraphrased here) are cited by author, which is often a corporate author.

no publication date

Synonyms for *racism* include two: *bigotry* and *intolerance* (Merriam-Webster, n.d.).

The References entry for this citation would be:

Merriam-Webster. (n.d.). Racism. In *Webster's Collegiate Thesaurus*. Retrieved July 12, 2020, from https://www.merriam-webster.com/thesaurus/racism.

Anonymous Articles Cited by Title

If the title is long, you can give a shortened version in the text that incorporates the first few words of the title so that the reader can find the source on the References page.

For example, an anonymous article titled "Ten Long Years: The Middle East Wars and Multiple Troop Deployments" could be cited in-text as "Ten Long Years: Wars."

Citing Indirect Sources

Many times, you will find someone's ideas in a source written by a second author; for instance, someone's speech printed in another source. When this occurs, you reference the originator of the idea in your text, and in the parenthetical reference you give the author of the source you got the information from with the page number.

> Tom Browning (2006) did a study of traffic patterns and "found that many American cities are not equipped for the amount of cars on their roads today" (Billings, 2007, pp. 119-120).
> **(Tom Browning did the study, but the writer found the information in an article by John Billings. The source listed in the References entry would be "Billings, J." since that is the source the writer was specifically looking at.)**

If you were to summarize what Billings summarized in your essay, you would just have (Billings, 2007, pp. 119-120). If your reader needed more specific information, they could find it in Billings, which you would list on your References page.

Working With Quotations

Begin quotations with either a colon, a comma, or the word *that*. At the end of the quotation, the usual order is quotation marks " (author, year, page number) and *then the* period:

Author Date Method   **original publication/source used**

"Four score and seven years ago" (Lincoln, 1863/1991, p. 213).

An indirect source

Barack Obama firmly reiterates: "We aren't taking anyone's guns away" (Miller, 2013, p. 3).

Narrative Method

Charles Dickens's (1859/1983) narrator began *The Tale of Two Cities*, "It was the best of times; it was the worst of times" (p. 1).

Rolf Toman (2007) argues that "the contrast between the Middle Ages and the Renaissance is usually over-emphasized" (p. 7).

If the quotation itself ends with a question mark or exclamation point, the order is: ?" (p. 12)

Will and Ariel Durant (1944/1972) asked, "What is the role of genius in history, of man versus the mass and the state?" (p. 3).

Another method breaks the quotation into two segments:

"A trickster," according to M.H. Abrams (1999), "is a character in a story who persistently uses his wiliness, and gift of gab, to achieve his ends by outmaneuvering or outwitting other characters" (p. 7).

If you are quoting words that are part of a dialogue or are themselves quoted (and thus in the source they are already in quotation marks), identify the quotation-within-a-quotation with single punctuation marks (the apostrophe key on a keyboard).

Alexis de Tocqueville (1824) said, "' When all privileges of birth and fortune are abolished, when all professions are accessible to all, and a man's own energies may place him at the top of any one of them, an easy and unbounded career seems open to his ambition'" (Solomon, 1999, p. 160). **(The writer found the quotation from de Toqueville in an article by Solomon.)**

Quotations from plays use act, scene, and line numbers
Act 1 Scene 2 Line 23
"Beware the Ides of March" (Shakespeare, 1598, 1.2.23).

Specfic Quotations from audio visual works (audio book, TED talk, You Tube video, TV show) use a time stamp
time stamp
"The time for action is now." (Cutter, 2019, 2:12.

Quotations from a classical or religious work include original date, date of your source, and any book, chapter, and line information.
book chapter 6 line 28
She sent me all the "lilies of the field" (*King James Bible*, 1769/2017, Matthew 6.28).

ca.=circa BCE=before common era, Book 1. Line 1
"I sing the wrath of Achilles" (Homer, ca. 800 B.C.E/2017, 1.1).

441

When employing direct quotation, it is extremely important to respect your sources and copy *exactly* what the original says (even the punctuation). It is possible to change quotations, but only under these circumstances:

- To place your own words or phrases in brackets to make the quotation conform grammatically to your writing or to insert necessary information to make the quote understandable to your readers.
- If the quotation contains a misspelling, or if there could be confusion over whether the word is spelled correctly, spell the word exactly as it is in the original passage and insert brackets surrounding the word sic: [sic].
- To omit irrelevant information from the quotation indicate omitted words or sentences with ellipsis: . . .

> The Pequod "shot her red hell [sic] further and further into the blackness of the sea . . . freighted with savages, and laden with fire, and burning a corpse, [it] plung[ed] into that blackness of darkness" (Melville, 1851/1972, p. 354).

The *Pequod* is a whaling ship, so the word expected for *hell* would be *hull;* although it is quite possible that Melville meant *hell*, given the events and characters of *Moby-Dick*, the writer using this source still used [*sic*] to indicate to the reader that this was the exact spelling of the original, correct or not. The ellipsis indicate the writer chose to take a portion of the original out of the quotation as it was irrelevant to the point he was making about *Moby-Dick*. To make the quotation conform grammatically to the rest of the writer's essay he changed the tense of one verb (*plunge*) and added the word *it*. The sentence in *Moby-Dick* says that the ship, "burning a corpse, plunging into that blackness of darkness, seemed the material counterpart of the monomaniac commander's soul."

Italics/Underlining versus Quotation Marks

When do you underline, italicize, or put quotation marks around titles? First, italics and underlining are interchangeable, but underlining is no longer used in APA.

The best way to describe how to choose between italics and quotation marks is with a metaphor: if it is the container, use italics; if it goes in the container, use quotation marks.

Titles of Sources using Quotation Marks

All of these sources come out of a larger "container":

/ the title of an article in a book, newspaper, magazine, journal, or a computer source
/ the title of a short story or a less than book length poem
/ the title of a song
/ the title of a particular episode of a television show

Titles of Sources using Italics

All of these sources are the "containers" themselves:

/ the *name* of a newspaper, magazine, or journal (the *New York Times, Newsweek*)
/ any *book*, whether it be a novel, a reference book, or a collection of essays, stories, or poems
/ the *title* of a CD (or a cassette tape or record album)
/ the *name* of a television show (*Seinfeld, NBC Nightly News*) or a movie (*Clueless*)
/ the *title* of a play (*King Lear*) or a book length poem (*Beowulf*)
/ court decisions (*Roe vs. Wade*)
Quotation marks are used to indicate the above sources in the text of an essay, but quotation marks are not used in the citation on the References page.

Preparing the References using APA Documentation

At the end of the essay, on a new page continuing the pagination from the essay, the research paper should have a References page (or pages) that lists, *in alphabetical order*, every source referred to in the research paper. **Center the title (References) one inch from the top of the page**, and double space between the title and the first entry. There are examples of APA style citations in chapter 9.

Professors may ask, also, for a bibliography, which lists every book and article studied in order to write the essay, but the References page should list only those books, articles, and other sources which are actually referred to in the essay either by direct quotation, paraphrase, or summary.

When you construct a References list, follow the examples below *exactly* concerning placement of periods, colons, commas, names, and abbreviations. It is unnecessary to memorize this or any documentation style; just refer to this section of *Writing Successfully* or the *Publication Manual of the American Psychological Association* when you make your list, and follow the examples exactly. **DO NOT TRUST ANY CITATION CREATION SOURCE ON THE INTERNET unless your professor approves it!**

If an entry is longer than one line, every line after the first is indented one-half inch (five spaces). **The list is double-spaced both between and within entries.**

Books

First name just has the first letter, but corporate authors are spelled out.
Book titles are in italics, and only the first word, the first word of a sub-title, and proper names are capitalized in the title of the book.

Publisher

, Hanson, R. (2020). *Writing successfully* (Rev. 6th ed.). KendallHunt.
Modern Language Association.(2016). *MLA handbook* (8th ed.).
Modern Language Association of America.
Publisher

443

The basic order for book citations: 1) Author, (2 Year of publication), 3) Title of book (including any idenifying information like edition, volume, or report number) 4) source publisher and doi if the book has one. Carefully use the same punctuation as the examples:

1)   **(2)**   **3)**

Author(s). (Year of Publication). *Title of book in italics and only first word is*   **4)**

    capitalized (Edition if other than 1st, volume number if there is one). Publisher.

    Any book with a Digital Object Identifier (doi) should include its number/url here.

Books by a single author or a corporate author

Campbell, J. (1949). *The hero with a thousand faces.* Princeton University Press.

U.K. Community College System. (1997). *1997-98 bulletin.* University of Kentucky Press.

If more than one book or article by the same author is used in the research paper, place them in alphabetical order by title after being placed within the alphabetical order of the entire list by the author's last name; the citations after the first repeat the author's name (not as in MLA which uses use three hyphens where the author's name occurs).
(first word of sub-title capitalized)
Campbell, J. (1959). *The masks of god: Primitive mythology.* Viking.

A Book Published in a Second or Subsequent Edition

Books with no edition number on the title page are a first edition and do not need to be recognized as such.
When you have used an edition other than the first, identify the edition number after the name of the editor or translator (if there is one: see next page) or after the title of the book if there is not a named editor. The edition is identified in this manner: (2nd *ed.*) 3rd *ed.* 4th *ed.*, or *Rev. ed.* for "revised edition," or *Abr. ed.* for "abridged edition."

Books by two or more authors
(No period after title if an edition is given. Notice periods after ed.)
Strunk, W., & White, E. (1983). *The elements of style* (4th ed.). Macmillan.

For three or more authors or editors, list all names up to twenty in the order they appear on the title page (see next page, the Keats citation) with an ampersand (&) between the last two names.

An Anthology

If you refer to an article, story, poem, or picture within an anthology, begin the citation by referring to the writer of the article rather than the editor, using the form below. (The final numbers in the entries are the page numbers of the ENTIRE individual article, story, etc. not the specific page numbers the cited information came from.) The title of the article follows the author's name and date, followed by the editor(s) and the title of the anthology (the book itself.)

Author(s). (Year of Publication). Title of article in the anthology, only first word capitalized. In name the editor(s) as below. *Title of book in italics, only first word capitalized* (edition number, volume number other than 1st and page numbers). Publisher. DOI if book has one.

(title of article)

Alda, A. (1991). What every woman should know about men. In E. Ashton-Jones & G. Olsen (Eds.), *The gender reader* (pp. 56-60). Allyn and Bacon.
title of anthology - book looked at (page numbers of article in anthology. A first edition so not listed and only one volume so not listed.)

(Original publication date followed by date of book actually looked at)

Keats, J. (1819/1973). Ode on a grecian urn. In F. Kermode, J. Hollander, & H. Bloom (Eds.),*The oxford anthology of english literature* (Vol. 2, pp.541-542). Oxford University Press.
(If multi-volume book or anthology, list volume number after title as shown.)

A Translation

If you refer to the text itself, begin with the author. If the translator also served as an editor, reveal this information too.

Rilke, R. M. (1916/1981). I love the dark hours (R. Bly, Trans.). In R. Bly (Ed.), *Selected poems.* (pp.18-19). Harper and Row.

A Book with a DOI
Author, A. (year). *book title.* Publisher. doi

Linton, P. (2017). *The perception and cognition of visual space.* Palgrave Macmillan. http://dx.doi.org/10.1007/978-3-31923-0

A chapter in an edited book with or without doi, newly published or reprinted from a journal

Feldman, D.B., Balaraman, M., & Anderson, C. (2018). Hope and meaning of life: Points of contact between hope theory and existentialism. In M.W. Gallagher, and S. J. Lopez (Eds.), *The oxford handbook of hope* (pp. 353-362). Oxford University Press. **If book has doi it would go here. If this book chapter was reprinted from a scholarly journal this would follow the main citation:** (Reprinted from "Hope and meaning of life: Points of contact between hope theory and existentialism," 2013, *Journal of Existentialism, 31*[3], 123-129)

A volume of a multi-volume work
(See Keats above for multi-volumes without individual titles like below.)
Jung, C.J. (1953/1966).*The collected works of carl jung: Vol. 7. Two essays in analytic psychology* (2nd ed.). Princeton University Press.

Encyclopedias, Dictionaries, and other Reference Books

APA now cites by editor (which could be corporate author), not by name of the article.

Smith, A. (Ed.). (1985). The white house. In *Encyclopedia americana* (Vol. 29, p. 283), Grolier.

Random House. (1992). Seasonal affective disorder. In *Random House Webster's College Dictionary* (p. 1210). Random House.

(If there is a named author of the article or entry in the reference work)
Tate, F. (1950). Rum. In A. Colin (Ed.), *Encyclopedia britannica.* (14th ed., Vol. 21, p. 413).
Encyclopedia Britannica.   **(edition, volume, and page number)**
(last two citations: Ency Britt is name of publisher same as book, so repeated)

If on-line source, if you think information might not be permanent, provide retrieval date. Cite in text by corporate author: (Merriam-Webster n.d.)
Merriam-Webster. (n.d.). *Merriam-Webster.com dictionary.* Retrieved April 5, 2020, from
https://www.merriam-webster.com/

(If no editor:title) Cite date of last change to site so readers can find same version
American trade imbalances. (2020, May 14) In *Wikipedia.* https://en.wikipedia.org/w/
index.php?title=American_trade_imbalances=638467

(Book never in print. Originally published on-line)
Gross, K. (2006). *Shylock is shakespeare.* http://www.uchicago.edu/Gross

Periodical, Database, and On-line Articles

In brief, **for articles you provide four items:** 1) author, (2 date of publication), 3) title, 4) location of source (magazine or journal title with volume, number, page information; if no magazine or journal then website and url.
Also if there is a doi, *always* include it at end of the citation.
1)   (2)   3)
Author(s).(Date of publication). Title of article. Only first word, first word after
                                        4)
    a colon, and proper names capitalized. *Title of periodical in italics*, *Volume*
    also issue number if thee is one, page numbers of article. DOI if there is one.
    Only cite url here if the article was first published on-line and there is no DOI.

Articles retrieved from databases with print analogues (from print journals/ newspapers) are cited just like the print articles (examples on facing page). *The database and url are not listed.*

One author: Johnson, E. (1983).

Two authors: Hallicutt. G. & Browning, F. (1998).

Three to twenty authors: list up to 20 with ampersand (&) between the last two names.

Volume and issue number: the volume is italicized like the title of the magazine and the issue number is in parentheses *112* (3).

No author: If the article is anonymous, begin the entry with the title of the article followed by date of publication (for purposes of alphabetizing the list, do not consider a, an, the).

No publication date: (n.d.)

If the article does not have consecutive pagination (beginning on one page and then skipping to a page or pages later in the source), cite the source using all the page numbers: B3, B5-B6.

Title of Source (magazine, newspaper, journal name):

NOT LOWER CASE LIKE MOST APA CITATIONS. Volume italicized, not (issue).

volume (issue), pages

Weaver, R. (1919). The centennial of Herman Melville. *The Nation, 109* (3), 146-148.

Holloway, M. (1980). A comparison of active and passive music reinforcement to
increase preacademic and motor skills in severely retarded children and adolescents.
Journal of Music Therapy, 17(2), 58-69. https://doi.org/10.1093//jmt/17.2.58

Triece, M. (1999, March). The practical true warrior: Reconciling women and work
in popular mail-order magazines, 1900-1920. *Critical Studies in Mass
Communication, 16*, 42, 48-49. https:// doi.org/10:1027/1618-3169.55.1.1
volume, **non-consecutive page numbers: 42, 48-49**

There is a References page on 203-04 with several citations containing doi's.

APA does not abbreviate any month, and lists month and day for daily/weekly/ monthly newspapers and magazines.

Updike, J. (1993, May 17). Sinclair Lewis: Exile on main street. *The New Yorker,
68,* 91-97.

Gore, R. (1996, January). Neanderthals. *National Geographic, 189* (1), 2-35.

Johnson, P. (2008). An empirical analysis of television habits of teenagers.
Journal of Marketing Research, 37 (8), 110-118.

Citations for newspapers use p./pp. before page numbers - p. 16 and pp. 19-23.

Brown, M. (1991, March 18). Oil rich refuge may fund energy studies.
The CourierJournal, pp. A1, A6.

(Anonymous article begins with title)

Proposal aims to encourage small business pension plans. (1991, May 1). *New York
Times,* pp. A2, A7.

447

Author, A. (Date). Title of work [Descriptor if needed]. Location of source (title of magazine, volume, issue, and page numbers OR website and url OR doi)

Editorials or Letters to the Editor

volume page number

Share this issue! [Editorial]. (2013, January). *Esquire 159*, 10.   **If unsigned,**
begin with title.

If the example were from a daily/weekly source, it would have year, month and day.

Heise, R. (2013, March 13). The it "girl." [Letter to the editor]. *Rolling Stone*, 23.

A music, film, television or book review

(title of review)   [title of CD/film/book reviewed]

Rosen, J. (2013, March 28). Justin's stoned soul comeback. [Review of the CD
The 20/20 Experience by Justin Timberlake]. *Rolling Stone*, 67-68.

Review published on a website

Pitchford, A. (2012). The avengers. [Review of the film *The Avengers*, by J. Whedon,
Dir.]. filmguide. https://filmguide.co.nz/archives/8077

Websites, and Government or Other Organization Reports

American Diabetes Association. (n.d.). *Understanding A1C.* https://diabetes.org/a1c

The Internal Revenue Service. (2020) *Taxpayer bill of rights.* U.S. Department of the
Treasury. https://irs.gov/taxpaper-bill-of-rights

Interviews

Interviews appear in a variety of formats - televison, radio, print, on-line, in person - and you cite the interview using the same format as listed in this section. If a magazine, you use the magazine format; if a YouTube or podcast, you use its format, etc. So the person being interviewed will not usually be the person in the author position. The interviewee or the owner of the site where you got the interview (see below) would be the author. When this occurs, the person being interviewed must be identified in the title (see below).

Unpublished letters and interviews are not listed in the APA References list. Instead, they are cited in-text only: (B. Gaines, personal communication, May 1, 2011)

Koppel, T. (2012, May 12). *Nightline* Interview with Brad Pitt. YouTube.
https://www.youtube.com/watch?v=qt1kc7468Jc9

Coles, J. (2010, October 10). 'Rabbit' at fifty years: An interview with John Updike.
New York Times, p. C13.

TED Talks on YouTube use TED as the author. Title gives evident interviewee

TED. (2017, October 12). Barack Obama: Recovering from the brink [Video].
YouTube. https:// youtube.com/watch?v=sq28639bl42

Advertisements

volume (issue #), page

Ford Motor Company. (2018, May 12). Mustang [Advertisement]. *Newsweek*, 11(3), 22.

Ford Motor Company.(2017, May 14). Mustang [Television commercial]. Stanford, CT: NBC.

Ford Motor Company. (2017, December 14). Mustang [Television commercial]. YouTube. https://youtube.com/watch?v=ks94682ne97

Other Sources

Emails, personal conversations or interviews, telephone, text messages, live speeches, letters, nonarchived message boards or online chats

Any source not recoverable by your readers is cited only in text (D. Johnson, personal communication, March 4, 2020) and is therefore not included in the Reference list.

An on-line forum posting or blog entry   **[Blog post]**
        if no date   **for forum posting:**

Smith, J. (n.d.). Julius Caesar: The bloody fountain? [Online forum post].
        Online Literature. http://www.online-literature.com/shakespeare/4837624.

Twitter Profiles and Facebook Pages
        pages change daily so need your retrieval date

The Democrats [@TheDemocrats]. (n.d.). Tweets [Twitter profile]. Retrieved May 3, 2020, from https://twitter.com/the democrats?lang=en

GOP. (n.d.). Home [Facebook page]. Retrieved May 19, 2020, from https://facebook.com/GOP

Twitter, Facebook, LinkedIn, Tumblr, any social site Posts
        provide day of post to help reader find source

Gaiman, N. (2020, March 16). *Neil Gaiman offers tons of cool stuff for free for you to kill your time with*. Facebook, https://facebook.com/search/links/43986gaimon749

Podcast
        Name host as author and identify as (Host)

Gardner, J. (Host). (2020, February 5). Why color blind doesn't cut it in corporate America [audio podcast episode]. In *Strange Fruit* WFPL Louisville. https:// wfpl.org/category/strange-fruit *identify audio or video podcast series in italics*

YouTube or other streaming Videos (including webinars)
        Corporate Author   **[or Webinar]**

Manufacturing Consent. (2017, November 6). Noam Chomsky and the Media [Video].
        YouTube. https://youtube.com/watch?v=EuwmWnphqll

Audio-Visual Sources

The basic format will be familiar to you:
Author. (date composed or first released). Title of Work [Descriptor: Film, Painting,
    etc. -see below]. Publisher (film or record company, web or museum location).

Author is	if	Author is	if
Director	[Film]	Artist	[Painting, Sculpture, etc]
Executive Producer(s)	[T.V. Series]	Photographer	[Photo]
Writer and Director	[T.V. Episode]		
Composer	[Classical music album/song]		
Recording Artist	[Modern music album/song]		

If the source being cited is part of a larger element (a song on an album, an episode in
a televison series, then in the publisher portion of the citation, name the larger source
(album, series) before the production company (film studio, record company).

The Rolling Stones. (1968). Jumpin' jack flash [song]. On *Through the Past Darkly*
    [Album]. London Records.

The Rolling Stones. (1969). *Through the past darkly* [Album]. London Records.

      date of version used   **[artists in brackets with source used]**
Beethoven, L. (2015). *Symphony no. 9 in d minor, op. 125.* [YouTube recording by Chicago
    Symphony, https://youtube.com/watch?v=r0jHhSSMv] (Original work published
    1824)   **date original work premiered**

Curtiz, M. (Director). (1942). *Casablanca* [Film]. Warner.

Lane, G. (Writer) & Shore, M. (Director). (2003, February 17). The cockatoo (Season
    4, Episode 16) [T.V. series episode] . In P. Reiser (Executive producer), *Mad
    About You.* Twentieth Century Fox.
        If you use special extra information/version
Tarentino, Q. (Director). (2015). *The hateful eight* [Film; special extended version
    on *Netflix*]. The Weinstein Company.
        Museum and Location
Michaelangelo. *David* [Sculpture]. (1501-1504). Galleria dell'Accademia, Firenze, Italy.

If map or photo is untitled, describe in square brackets as below.

The Map Archive. (n.d.). *Central europe 1914* [Map]. https://the maparchive.com/central
    europse/49231

Brady, M. (1862). [Photograph of Dead Soldiers at Antietam]. Matthew Brady and Civil
    War Photography. https://pinterest.com/matthewbrady

CSE Documentation

There are several styles of documentation used in scholarly study and *Writing Successfully* includes brief instructions for four of the most common: MLA style (used by English and modern language scholars, and all publications of the Modern Language Association), APA style (used by psychologists, sociologists, and all publications of the American Psychological Association), CSE style (used by many of the sciences, and all publications sanctioned by the Council of Science Editors), and Chicago style (used by historians and several other social science disciplines). *For each class you take in college, always ask your instructor which documentation style to use.* There are other documentation styles, but these are the most prevalent.

This chapter divides into two sections:

- In-text documentation using CSE style (how to cite sources in your paper). There are three variations used in CSE: citation-sequence, citation-name, and parenthetical name-year.
- Preparing the References page using CSE documentation. There are two variations used in CSE: one for citation-sequence/citation-name, and one for name-year.

Remember that this chapter gives only brief instructions showing how to document the most commonly used sources. For complete instructions use ONLY this edition:

> Council of Science Editors. Scientific style and format: the CSE manual for authors, editors, and publishers. 8th ed. Chicago (IL): The University of Chicago Press; 2014.

In-text Documentation Using Citation-sequence, Citation-name, and Name-year formats

For both citation-sequence and citation-name, the in-text systems are identical except for the order of references on the References page. In both systems, a superscript number [1] or a number in parentheses (1) occurs with each source referred to in the text. The numbers refer to the numbered list of sources on the References page.

On the References page, in *citation-sequence* the sources are numbered in the order (the sequence) that they occur in the body of the essay. The first source is numbered 1 in-text and in References, the second source is numbered 2, the third source 3, EXCEPT that if a source referred to earlier is mentioned again, it receives the same number in-text as it had earlier. For example if the source numbered 2 is used any time again in the essay, it is numbered 2 again in-text.

On the References page, in *citation-name* the sources are numbered alphabetically by the first word appearing in the References citation. The citation number in-text is a superscript number [1] or a number in parentheses (1) that correlates to the number of the source on the References page.

The *name-year* format of CSE uses the author's last name and the year of publication in-text, and on the References page has a different citation format than the citation-sequence/citation-name format.

Ask your professor which version of CSE should be used for an essay.

- *Most academic writing, especially CSE formatted essays in the sciences, uses summary and paraphrase rather than direct quotation.*
- **In CSE, no page numbers are used in-text to signify pages summarized or quoted.**
- **In CSE, a brief version of the essay's title is put in the upper right hand corner of each page with the page number.**
- **If the professor asks for an Abstract, on a separate page before the essay supply a 250 word summary of the essay, with the heading Abstract.**

Examples of In-text Documentation in CSE

citation-sequence or citation-name

Johnson [1] finds that many students have problems following the confusing instructions for developing course plans and registering for classes at community colleges. Other studies [2-3] concur, further finding that at schools with significant advising departments focusing only on advising for classes and majors that the problems of students are much lessened. This present study at a small liberal arts 4 year college will attempt to see how this school's students rate the advising department. The major problems with proper advising occur with undeclared majors; i.e., nursing professors can adequately advise nursing students or English professors can advise English students [2].

While last names in the essay's body are not required in these systems, for elegance and clarity one can choose to use the author's last name to begin the reference, and when that occurs the name is followed by the appropriate superscript number.
The next sentence cites two studies, so there are two superscipt numbers. If they are in sequence (like the above) a hyphen separates the two numbers. If they are not in sequence, they are separated by a comma [3,6].
The final citation in this example demonstrates what MUST occur, a superscript number at the end of the summarized material (as opposed to the alternate format which uses the author's name or signifier like "This study" for the source with superscipt number beginning a source, as in the other examples).
The final citation uses the same number as earlier (2) because it is a second reference to the same source (which has only one entry numbered 2 on the References page whether it is used once or ten times).

name-year format

Johnson (2014) finds that many students have problems following the

452

confusing instructions for developing course plans and registering for classes at community colleges. Other studies concur, further finding that at schools with significant advising departments focusing only on advising for classes and majors that the problems of students are much lessened. (Billings and Hoffmann 2013; Sallings et al. 2014) This present study at a small liberal arts 4 year college will attempt to see how this school's students rate the advising department. The major problems with proper advising occur with undeclared majors; i.e., nursing professors can adequately advise nursing students or English professors can advise English students (Billings and Hoffmann 2013).

In-text with name-year, the surname and date of publication are listed with each source. The names of sources with two authors are separated by "and."
Sources with 3 to 10 authors are listed by the first name and et al. (Latin for "and all.") If no author, list by brief title.
With name-year, a different style of citation is used on the References page (illustrated in the next section of the chapter).

Preparing the References Using CSE Documentation

At the end of the essay, on a new page continuing the pagination from the essay, the research paper should have a References page (or pages) that lists every source referred to in the research paper. Center the title (References) one inch from the top of the page, and double space between the title and the first entry.

When you construct a References list, follow the examples below *exactly* concerning placement of periods, colons, commas, names, and abbreviations. It is unnecessary to memorize this or any documentation style; just refer to this section of *Writing Successfully* or the 8th edition of *Scientific Style and Format: the CSE Manual* when you make your list, and follow the examples exactly.

The list is double-spaced both between and within entries.

In citation-sequence and citation-name, the numbers beginning each citation are numbered as in the examples below.

NO quotation marks or italics are used with titles, and as with APA style only the first word of the title is capitalized.

Second and subsequent lines of a citation in CSE style are not indented as with MLA or APA (see below).

Citation-sequence and Citation-name References

Remember that the only difference between these two formats is the numbering system:

In *citation-sequence*, the sources listed are numbered in the order they appear in the essay (unless a source is repeated and then it uses the same number as used earlier).
In *citation-name*, the sources are listed alphabetically by the first word in the citation, and the numbers on the References page are sequential.

Books - citation-sequence and citation-name

The basic order for book citations. Carefully use the same punctuation as the examples:

Author(s). Title of book: only first word is capitalized. Place of publication, including state initials or country [colon]: Publisher[semi-colon]; date.

Surnames and corporate authors are spelled out, but first and middle names just have initials without periods, and there is no comma between surname and initials..

Books by a single author or an organization

1. Campbell J. The hero with a thousand faces. New York (NY): Princeton University Press; 1949.

In citation-name where the References citations are alphabetical, if more than one book or article by the same author is used in the research paper, place them in alphabetical order by title after being placed within the alphabetical order of the entire list by the author's last name; the citations after the first repeat the author's name (not as in MLA which uses use three hyphens where the author's name occurs).

2. Campbell J. The masks of god: primitive mythology. New York (NY): Viking; 1959.

3. U.K. Community College System.1997-98 bulletin. Lexington (KY): University of Kentucky Press; 1997.

A Book Published in a Second or Subsequent Edition

Books with no edition number on the title page are probably a first edition. When you have used an edition other than the first, identify the edition number after the title of the book. The edition is identified in this manner: 2nd ed. 3rd ed. 4th ed., or *Rev. ed.* for "revised edition," or *Abr. ed.* for "abridged edition."

Books by two authors

4. Strunk W., White E. The elements of style. 4th ed.. New York (NY): Macmillan; 1983.

Books by three to ten, and more than ten, authors or editors

For three to ten authors or editors, list all names in full (see below, the Keats citation). For more than ten authors, list first ten in the end reference followed by et al. For both occasions, in-text list only the first name followed by et al.

An Anthology (Section of a Book with an Editor)

If you refer to a chapter, article, story, poem, or picture within an anthology, begin the citation by referring to the writer of the article rather than the editor, using the form below. (The final numbers in the entries are the page numbers of the ENTIRE individual article, story, etc. not the specific page numbers the cited information came from.) The title of the article follows the author's name and date, followed by the editor(s) of the anthology and the title of the anthology (the book itself.)

Author(s). Title of article: only first word is capitalized. In list editors as below. Title of book: only first word is capitalized. Edition and volume numbers if relevant. Place of publication, including state initials or country [colon]: Publisher[semi-colon]; date. Page numbers of entire article.

Surnames and corporate authors are spelled out, but first and middle names just have initials without periods, and there is no comma between surname and initials..

(title of article)
5. Alda A. What every woman should know about men. In: Ashton-Jones E, Olsen G, editors. The gender reader. 2nd ed. Boston (MA): Allyn and Bacon; 1991. p. 56-60.
  title of anthology - book looked at   page numbers of article in anthology

6. Keats J. Ode on a grecian urn. In:. Kermode F, Hollander J, Bloom H, editors. The oxford anthology of english literature. 2nd. ed. vol. 2, London (England): Oxford University Press; 1973. p. 541-542.
(If multi-volume book or anthology, list edition and/or volume number after title of anthology as shown.)

A Translation

If you refer to the text itself, begin with the author. If the translator also served as an editor, reveal this information too. If there is a separate editor, list after the translator.

7. Rilke RM. I love the dark hours. Bly R, translator and editor. Selected poems. New York (NY): Harper and Row.; 1981. p. 18-19.

8. The Tibetan Book of the Dead. Thurman AF, translator. New York (NY): Bantam; 1994. **(No author so begins with title.)**

Chapter, or Other Part of a Book - same author for book and chapter/part.

9. Jung CG. Man and his symbols. Garden City (NY): Doubleday. Part 1, Approaching the Unconscious; 1964. p. 18-103.
Chapter/Part, and title of chapter, follows publisher.
If chapter/part author and author/editor of book are different, use the format for the anthology at the top of the page.

Periodical and Database Articles - citation-sequence and citation-name

Author(s). Title of article: only first word capitalized. Title of periodical (see note *).
Date of publication; Volume (issue in parentheses) [colon]: page numbers of article.

* Journal titles are generally abbreviated using the List of Title Word Abbreviations of the ISSN International Centre. If a newspaper or popular magazine is not listed, then use its full name in the citation. Journal abbreviations can be found on-line.

Volume and issue number: the issue number is in parentheses 112(3), and there are no spaces between the volume, issue, and page numbers.
For one author, surname followed by first initial of first and second name without periods or punctuation. For two authors, names separated by comma in References, but by "and" if mentioned in-text.
For three to ten authors or editors, list all names. If mentioned in-text list only the first surname followed by et al.
For more than ten authors, list first ten in the end reference followed by et al.

If the article is anonymous, begin the entry with the title of the article (for purposes of alphabetizing the list in citation-name, do not consider a, an, the).
If the article does not have consecutive pagination (beginning on one page and then skipping to a page or pages later in the source), cite the source using all the page numbers: B3, B5-B6, except for newspapers (only list section,first page and column).

A Scholarly Journal

10. Holloway M. . A comparison of active and passive music reinforcement to increase preacademic and motor skills in severely retarded children and adolescents. J Music Ther. 1980;17(2):58-69.
(Abbreviation for Journal of Music Therapy)

No volume or issue numbers for monthly/weekly magazines, just the year.
Dailies give year and month dat. CSE abbreviates any month over three letters.

A Magazine

11.Gore R. Neanderthals. National Geographic: 1996; 2-35.

An Article from a Daily Newspaper

12. Brown M. Oil rich refuge may fund energy studies.
The Courier-Journal (Home Ed.). 1991 Mar 18; Sect.A:1(col.3).

An Anonymous Article in a Newspaper

13. Proposal aims to encourage small business pension plans. New York Times (Late Ed.). 1991 May 1; Sect.A:2(Col.1).

On-line Articles and Websites

Citations are similar to print periodicals with the addition of a date of update/revision (if available), the date of access, the url, and the DOI (if available). Since urls change, many scholarly works assign a Digital Object Identifier (DOI). The DOI, in most databases, usually appears on the first page with the journal's name, and volume, issue, and page number information.

An article or book from a database

14. Triece M. The practical true warrior: Reconciling women and work in popular mail-order magazines, 1900-1920. Crit Stud Mass Comm. 1999 [accessed 2014 Dec 9]; 16:42,48-49. http:// exlibrisgroup.com/primo_library/libweb/action/display.do?frbr V ersion=3&tas=practical+true+warrior&vl(freeText0)=practical true warrior &vid. doi: 0:1027/1618-3169.55.1.1.   **Url followed by doi identifier (if applicable) Name of journal is Critical Studies in Mass Communications.**

An E-book

15. Gross K. Shylock is shakespeare. 2nd ed. Chicago (IL): University of Chicago Press. 2006 [accessed 2015 Jan 19] http://www.uchicago.edu/Gross.
Date accessed/ if there was a revision, its date would go in these brackets also.

An article from an on-line journal, magazine, or newspaper

For scholarly journals, include doi if available.

16. Updike J. Sinclair lewis: exile on main street. The New Yorker. 1993 [accessed 2015 Jun 14]; 62: 76-77. http://www.newyorker.com/Updike/1993.

17. Brown M. Oil rich refuge may fund energy studies. The Courier Journal.1991, Mar 18 [accessed 2015 Mar 17]; http://www.courier-journal.com/486234/energy/63274.

A Website

18. Native Languages of the Americans. Minneapolis (MN): Native Languages of the Americas; c. 1994-2014 [accessed 2013 Apr 13]. http://native-languages.org

An email or letter

An email/letter is cited in text (2015 email from D. Johnson, to me) but not included in References.

A DVD

Give the copyright date, and use the c symbol.

19. Jacobs F, editor. Biodiversity on the pacific rim [DVD]. Los Angeles (CA): American Academy of Bilogy Teachers; c 2009. 1 DVD.

An on-line forum posting or blog entry

author title of post (descriptive word) Blog title   publication date (n.d. no date)

20. PeareShakes. Julius caesar: the bloody fountain? [blog]. Online literature. n.d.. [accessed 2015 Jun 12]. http://www.online-literature.com/shakespeare/4837624.

Name-year References

In name-year, references ARE NOT numbered.

Books - name-year

The basic order for book citations. Carefully use the same punctuation as the examples:

Author(s). Date of publication. Title of book: only first word is capitalized. Place of publication, including state initials or country [colon]: Publisher.

Surnames and corporate authors are spelled out, but first and middle names just have initials without periods, and there is no comma between surname and initials..

Books by a single author or an organization

Campbell J. 1949. The hero with a thousand faces. New York (NY): Princeton University Press.

If more than one book or article by the same author is used in the research paper, place them in chronological order by date after being placed within the alphabetical order of the entire list by the author's last name; the citations after the first repeat the author's name (not as in MLA which uses use three hyphens where the author's name occurs). So for example, the following citation would come after the Campbell citation above as it is chronologically later:

Campbell J. 1959. The masks of god: primitive mythology. New York (NY): Viking.

[UKCCS] U.K. Community College System. 1997. 1997-98 bulletin. Lexington (KY): University of Kentucky Press. **(Organizations are always given an acronym). In-text, the citation would look like this:** (UKCCS 1997).

A Book Published in a Second or Subsequent Edition

Books with no edition number on the title page are probably a first edition. When you have used an edition other than the first, identify the edition number after the title of the book. The edition is identified in this manner: *2nd ed. 3rd ed. 4th ed.*, or *Rev. ed.* for "revised edition," or *Abr. ed.* for "abridged edition."

Books by two authors

Strunk W., White E. 1983. The elements of style. 4th ed.. New York (NY): Macmillan.
 Names separated by comma in References, but by "and" in-text: (Strunk and White 1983)

Books by three to ten, and more than ten, authors or editors

For three to ten authors or editors, list all names in full (see below, the Keats citation). For more than ten authors, list first ten in the end reference followed by et al. For both occasions, in-text list only the first name followed by et al.

An Anthology (Section of a Book with an Editor)

If you refer to a chapter, article, story, poem, or picture within an anthology, begin the citation by referring to the writer of the article rather than the editor, using the form below. (The final numbers in the entries are the page numbers of the ENTIRE individual article, story, etc. not the specific page numbers the cited information came from.) The title of the article follows the author's name and date, followed by the editor(s) of the anthology and the title of the anthology (the book itself.)

(title of article)
Alda A. 1991. What every woman should know about men. In: Ashton-Jones E, Olsen G, editors. The gender reader. 2nd ed. Boston (MA): Allyn and Bacon. p. 56-60.
 title of anthology - book looked at   page numbers of article in anthology

Keats J 1973. Ode on a grecian urn. In:. Kermode F, Hollander J, Bloom H, editors. The oxford anthology of english literature. 2nd ed. vol. 2, London (England): Oxford University Press. p. 541-542.
(If multi-volume book or anthology, list edition and/or volume number after title of anthology as shown.)

A Translation

If you refer to the text itself, begin with the author. If the translator also served as an editor, reveal this information too. If there is a separate editor, list after the translator

Rilke RM 1981. I love the dark hours. Bly R, translator and editor. Selected poems. New York (NY): Harper and Row. p. 18-19.

The Tibetan Book of the Dead. 1994. Thurman AF, translator.
New York (NY): Bantam.   **(No author so begins with title.)**

Chapter, or Other Part of a Book - same author for book and chapter/part.

Jung CG. 1964. Man and his symbols. Garden City (NY): Doubleday. Part 1, Approaching the Unconscious; p. 18-103.
Chapter/Part, and title of chapter, follows publisher.

If chapter/part author and author/editor of book different, use the format for the anthology on the previous page.

Periodical and Database Articles - name-year

Author(s). Date of publication. Title of article: only first word capitalized. Title of periodical (see note *), Volume (issue in parentheses) [colon]: page numbers of article.

* Journal titles are generally abbreviated using the List of Title Word Abbreviations of the ISSN International Centre. If a newspaper or popular magazine is not listed, then use its full name in the citation. Journal abbreviations can be found on-line.

Volume and issue number: the issue number is in parentheses 112(3), and there are no spaces between the volume, issue, and page numbers.
For one author, surname followed by first initial of first and second name without periods or punctuation. For two authors, names separated by comma in References, but by "and" in-text.
For three to ten authors or editors, list all names. In-text list only the first followed by et al.
For more than ten authors, list first ten in the end reference followed by et al.

If the article is anonymous, begin the entry with the title of the article followed by date of publication (for purposes of alphabetizing the list, do not consider a, an, the).
If the article does not have consecutive pagination (beginning on one page and then skipping to a page or pages later in the source), cite the source using all the page numbers: B3, B5-B6, except for newspapers (only list section, first page and column).

Author(s). Date of publication. Title of article: only first word capitalized. Title of periodical (see note *), Volume (issue in parentheses) [colon]: page numbers of article.

* Journal titles are generally abbreviated using the List of Title Word Abbreviations of the ISSN International Centre. If a newspaper or popular magazine is not listed, then use its full name in the citation. An on-line list of the journal abbreviations can be found at http://images.webofknowledge.com/WOK46/help/WOS/A_abrvjt.html.

A Scholarly Journal

Holloway M. 1980. A comparison of active and passive music reinforcement to increase preacademic and motor skills in severely retarded children and adolescents. J Music Ther. 17(2):58-69.
(Abbreviation for Journal of Music Therapy)

No volume or issue numbers for monthly/weekly magazines, just the year. Dailies give year and month day. CSE abbreviates any month over three letters.

A Magazine

Gore R. 1996. Neanderthals. National Geographic: 2-35.

An Article from a Daily Newspaper

Brown M. 1991 Mar 18. Oil rich refuge may fund energy studies. The CourierJournal (Home Ed.). Sect.A:1(col.3).

An Anonymous Article in a Newspaper

Proposal aims to encourage small business pension plans. 1991 May 1. *New York Times* (Late Ed.). Sect.A:2(Col.1).

On-line Articles and Websites

Citations are similar to print periodicals with the addition of a date of update/revision (if available), the date of access, the url, and the DOI (if available). Since urls change, many scholarly works assign a Digital Object Identifier (DOI). The DOI, in most databases, usually appears on the first page with the journal's name, and volume, issue, and page number information.

461

An article or book from a database

Triece M. 1999. The practical true warrior: Reconciling women and work in popular mail-order magazines, 1900-1920. Crit Stud Mass Comm [accessed 2014 Dec 9]; 16:42,48-49. http:// exlibrisgroup.com/primo_library/libweb/action/display.do?frbr Version=3&tas =practical+true+warrior&vl(freeText0)=practical true warrior &vid. doi: 0:1027/1618-3169.55.1.1. **Url followed by doi identifier (if applicable) Name of journal is Critical Studies in Mass Communications.**

An E-book

Gross K. 2006. Shylock is shakespeare. 2nd ed. Chicago (IL): University of Chicago Press; [accessed 2015 Jan 19] http://www.uchicago.edu/Gross.
Date accessed/ if there was a revision, its date would go in these brackets also.

An article from an on-line journal, magazine, or newspaper
For scholarly journals, include doi if available.

Updike J. 1993.. Sinclair lewis: exile on main street. The New Yorker. [accessed 2015 Jun 14]; 62: 76-77. http://www.newyorker.com/Updike/1993.

Brown M. 1991, Mar 18. Oil rich refuge may fund energy studies. The Courier Journal; [accessed 2015 Mar 17] http://www.courier-journal.com/486234/energy/63274.

A Website

Native Languages of the Americans. c. 1994-2014. Minneapolis (MN): Native Languages of the Americas [accessed 2013 Apr 13]. http://native-languages.org.

An email or letter

An email/letter is cited in text (2015 email from D. Johnson, to me) but not included in References.

A DVD
Give the copyright date, and use the c symbol.

Jacobs F, editor. c 2009. Biodiversity on the pacific rim [DVD]. Los Angeles (CA): American Academy of Biology Teachers. 1 DVD.

An on-line forum posting or blog entry
author publication date (n.d. no date) title of post (descriptive word) Blog title
PeareShakes. n.d.. Julius caesar: the bloody fountain? [blog]. Online literature. [accessed 2015 Jun 12]. http://www.online-literature.com/shakespeare/4837624.

26

Chicago (Turabian) Documentation

There are several styles of documentation used in scholarly study and *Writing Successfully* includes brief instructions for four of the most common: MLA style (used by English and modern language scholars, and all publications of the Modern Language Association), APA style (used by psychologists, sociologists, and all publications of the American Psychological Association), CSE style (used by many of the sciences, and all publications sanctioned by the Council of Science Editors), and Chicago style (used by historians and several other social science disciplines). *For each class you take in college, always ask your instructor which documentation style to use.* There are other documentation styles, but these are the most prevalent.

There are two methods of citing sources in the Chicago system, Notes-Bibliography and Author-Date, and this chapter divides into two sections, one for each. Each section will show how to cite in-text and on the bibliography page (as well as the additional Notes page for the Notes-Bibliography format).

Remember that this chapter gives only brief instructions showing how to document the most commonly used sources. For complete instructions use ONLY this edition:

> The University of Chicago. *The Chicago Manual of Style*. 17th ed. Chicago: University of Chicago Press, 2017.

An interesting anecdote for American scholarship: Kate Turabian was the University of Chicago's Graduate School secretary between 1930 and 1958. No one could submit a thesis or dissertation in order to graduate without first getting it past her sharp eyes. She wrote a style 'cheat sheet' book for *The Chicago Manual of Style*, and this style book, *A Manual for Writers of Research Papers, Theses, and Dissertations* is now in its 9th edition. It has sold 9 million copies, and is so famous that the Chicago syle of documentation is also called Turabian style. (Quite impressive for an administrative assistant, don't you think? In the 21st century, she would be a professor or the head of a department, not a secretary.) *So if professors request Turabian style, they are asking for Chicago style documentation. Remember to also ask whether they prefer Notes-Bibliography or Author-Date.*

> Turabian, Kate, Wayne C. Booth, Gregory G. Colomb, Joseph M. Williams, Joseph Bizup, and William FitzGerald. *A Manual for Writers of Research Papers, Theses, and Dissertations*. 9th ed. Chicago: University of Chicago Press, 2018.

When employing direct quotation, it is extremely important to respect your sources and copy *exactly* what the original says (even the punctuation). It is possible to change quotations, but only under these circumstances:

- To place your own words or phrases in brackets to make the quotation conform grammatically to your writing or to insert necessary information to make the quote understandable to your readers.
- If the quotation contains a misspelling, or if there could be confusion over whether the word is spelled correctly, spell the word exactly as it is in the original passage and insert parentheses surrounding the word sic: (sic).
- To omit irrelevant information from the quotation indicate omitted words or sentences with ellipsis: . . .

> The Pequod "shot her red hell (sic) further and further into the blackness of the sea . . . freighted with savages, and laden with fire, and burning a corpse, [it] plung[ed] into that blackness of darkness" (Melville 1967, 354).

The *Pequod* is a whaling ship, so the word expected for *hell* would be *hull*. Although it is quite possible that Melville meant *hell*, given the events and characters of *Moby-Dick*, the writer using this source still used (sic) to indicate to the reader that this was the exact spelling of the original, correct or not. The ellipsis indicate the writer chose to take a portion of the original out of the quotation as it was irrelevant to the point he was making about *Moby-Dick*. To make the quotation conform grammatically to the rest of the writer's essay he changed the tense of one verb (*plunge*) and added the word *it*. The sentence in *Moby-Dick* says that the ship, "burning a corpse, plunging into that blackness of darkness, seemed the material counterpart of the monomaniac commander's soul."

Italics/Underlining versus Quotation Marks with Titles

When do you underline, italicize, or put quotation marks around titles? First, italics and underlining are interchangeable. In the examples below, *Writing Successfully* will italicize, but *underlining, though rare, is acceptable anyplace that italics are used.*

The best way to describe how to choose between italics/underlining and quotation marks is with a metaphor: **if it is the container, use italics; if it goes in the container, use quotation marks.**

Titles of Sources using Quotation Marks

All of these sources come out of a larger "container":
/ the title of an article in a book, newspaper, magazine, journal, or a computer source
/ the title of a short story or a less than book length poem
/ the title of a song
/ the title of a particular episode of a television show

464

All of these sources are the "containers" themselves:
/ the *name* of a newspaper, magazine, or journal (the *New York Times, Newsweek*)
/ any *book*, whether it be a novel, a reference book, or a collection of essays, stories, or poems
/ the *title* of a CD (or a cassette tape or record album)
/ the *name* of a television show (*Seinfeld, NBC Nightly News*) or a movie (*Clueless*)
/ the *title* of a play (*King Lear*) or a book length poem (*Beowulf*)
/ court cases (*Roe v. Wade*)
Exceptions with neither italics nor quotation marks:
Scripture - Bible, Old Testament, Genesis, Talmud, Upanishads
Laws, Acts, Political Documents - The Constitution, The Voting Rights Act, but books of government records italicized, such as *The Congressional Record.*
Musical compositions identified by form, numbers, key- Mozart's Concerto No. 2
The divisions of a work (introduction, preface, stanza, scene, index, chapter, appendix, index).
Book Series (History of the American Nation) or Manuscript Collections (Beowulf Manuscripts)
Websites

Notes-Bibliography Style

In Notes-Bibliography style, the author (or title of source if anonymous) is named in the sentence, and a superscript number [1] is placed at the end of the sentence that you quoted or referred to. Then in either a footnote at the bottom of the page, or an endnote on a page following the last page of the essay, labeled Notes (centered), researchers have a corresponding number followed by the source's author, title, publication information, and the page numbers that the information came from. Most writing software allows one to create footnotes if that is what the professor asks for.

1. The University of Chicago, *The Chicago Manual of Style*, 17th ed. (Chicago: University of Chicago Press, 2017), 111-112.   **page numbers cited**
If you cite the same source again, you may use a shortened form:
2. Chicago, 77.   **But later on the Notes page add the title:**
6. Chicago, *The Chicago Manual of Style*, 145.

In addition to the footnotes/endnotes, there is a bibliography that lists every source you cited in alphabetic order, and in most cases it also includes every source you read whether you used it in the essay or not (with a few exceptions noted on the following pages). The pattern used for the bibliography is different than the format used for the endnote, so for the rest of this section, there will be examples for both endnotes and bibliography on facing pages. The endnotes/footnotes example begins with a number. The following page labeled Bibliography, centered, follows the Notes, or if footnotes were used, follows the last page of the essay, continuing the pagination.

Make sure to follow the format for citations EXACTLY, including commas, periods, and colons. As you look at the examples on the next six pages, notice that the citations for Notes rely on commas while the bibliography relies on periods. Follow the forms exactly, and take your citations to a trained eye WHENEVER you are not sure.

Books - Print and Electronic   If no author, begin with Title.

Notes   **Also May Have Corporate Authors**

first name last name

1. Stephen Greenblatt, *The Swerve: How the World Became Modern*   **One Author**
(New York: W. W. Norton, 2011), 119.

For notes, page numbers actually cited in essay cited after publication info.

2. Sandra M. Gilbert and Susan Gubar, *The Madwoman in the Attic:* **2 or 3 Authors**
The Woman Writer and the Nineteenth-Century Literary Imagination (New
Haven: Yale University Press, 1979), 42-5.

3. Dana Canedy et al, *Unseen: Unpublished Black History from the*   **4 or more Authors**
New York Times Photo Archives (New York: Black Dog and   **(Notice et al in Notes)**
Leventhal, 2017), 33.

4.William Faulkner, *Uncollected Stories of William Faulkner*, ed.   **Book with a named**
Joseph Blotner (New York, Random House, 1979), 215.   **editor on title page**

5. Joseph Blotner, introduction to *Uncollected Stories***Citing an Introduction, Preface**
of William Faulkner, by William Faulkner (New York: **Foreword, or Afterword**
Random House, 1979), xvi.   **(Roman numeral is page number cited:**

6. Pablo Neruda, *Selected Poems*, trans. Anthony Kerrigan, W. S. Merwin, Alastair
Reed, and Nathaniel Tarn (Boston: Houghton Mifflin, 1990), 217.   **A Translation**

7. John 4:3-16 (King James Version)

8. Qur'an 4: 1-12

Article, story, poem in
9. Anne Beattie, "The Lawn Party," in *Anthology of American*   **an Anthology.**
Literature, 8th ed, vol 2, edited by George McMichael, James   **(Notice edition and**
Leonard, Bill Lyne, Anne-Marie Mallon, and Verner Mitchell.   **volume number**
(Upper Saddle River, NJ: Prentice Hall, 2004), 2039.   **when applicable.)**

10, 11, and 12 are electronic or database books
10. Robert P. Marzac, *An Ecological and Postcolonial Study of Literature:*
From Daniel Defoe to Salman Rushdie (New York: Palgrave MacMillan, 2007),
413, Proquest Ebook Central.

11. Elizabeth Downing Taylor, *The Original Black Elite: Daniel Muray and the*
Story of a Forgotten Era (New York: Amistad, 2017), 145-52, Kindle.

12. Margaret Duncan Elmslie and William Burns Thomson. *Seedtime in Kashmir:*
A Memoir of William Jackson Elmslie (London: Nisbit, 1875), chap. 3,   **If no page #s**
Project Gutenberg EBook, 2019. http://gutenberg.org/files/59457/59457-h.htm

13 contains a source quoted in another source
13. Edouard Glissant, *Poetics of Relation*, trans. Betsy Wing (Ann Arbor: University
of Michigan Press, 2000): 75. Quoted in Valerie Loichot, *Orphan Narratives*
(Charlottesville: University of Virginia Press, 2007), 13.

Bibliographies in alphabetical order in essays, not corresponding to Notes like here. Bibliography

last name, first name

Greenblatt, Stephen. *The Swerve: How the World Became Modern.* New York:
W. W. Norton, 2011.

Notice bibliographies rely on periods between elements while notes use commas, and words after periods are upper case.

Gilbert, Sandra M., and Susan Gubar. *The Madwoman in the Attic: The Woman Writer and the Nineteenth-Century Literary Imagination.* New Haven: Yale University Press, 1979.

Canedy, Dana, Darcey Eveleigh, Damien Cave, and Rachel Swarns. *Unseen: Unpublished Black History from the New York Times Photo Archives.* New York: Black Dog and Leventhal, 2017.

Faulkner, William. *Uncollected Stories of William Faulkner.* Edited by Joseph Blotner. New York, Random House, 1979.

Blotner, Joseph. Introduction to *Uncollected Stories of William Faulkner,* by William Faulkner, xv-xvii. New York, Random House, 1979.
Entire range of pages listed in Bibliography, and notice commas.)

Neruda, Pablo. *Selected Poems.* Translated by Anthony Kerrigan, W. S. Merwin, Alastair Reed, and Nathaniel Tarn. Boston: Houghton Mifflin, 1990.

Do not include sacred texts in the Bibliography.

Beattie, Anne. "The Lawn Party." In *Anthology of American Literature.* 8th ed. Vol 2. Edited by George McMichael, James Leonard, Bill Lyne, Anne-Marie Mallon, and Verner Mitchell. 2032-2042. Upper Saddle River, NJ: Prentice Hall, 2004.
(Entire range of pages listed in Bibliography BEFORE publication info.)

Marzac, Robert P. *An Ecological and Postcolonial Study of Literature: From Daniel Defoe to Salman Rushdie.* New York: Palgrave MacMillan, 2007. Proquest Ebook Central.

Taylor, Elizabeth Downing. *The Original Black Elite: Daniel Muray and the Story of a Forgotten Era.* New York: Amistad, 2017. Kindle.

Elmslie, Margaret Duncan and William Burns Thomson. *Seedtime in Kashmir: A Memoir of William Jackson Elmslie.* London: Nisbit, 1875. Project Gutenberg EBook, 2019. http://gutenberg.org/files/59457/59457-h.htm

Glissant, Edouard. *Poetics of Relation.* Translated by Betsy Wing. Ann Arbor: University of Michigan Press, 2000: 75. Quoted in Valerie Loichot, *Orphan Narratives* (Charlottesville: University of Virginia Press, 2007.

Articles in Print Periodicals   **If no author, begin with Title.**

Notes

Print Journal

1. Meredith Holloway, "A Comparison of Active and Passive Music Reinforcement to Increase Preacademic and Motor Skills in Severely Retarded Children and Adolescents," *Journal of Music Therapy* 17, no. 2 (1980): 62.
volume number, issue number (year), page cited

Print Magazine

2. John Updike, "Sinclair Lewis: Exile on Main Street," *New Yorker,* May 17, 1993, 93.

Print Newspaper

3. Mike Brown, "Oil Rich Refuge May Fund Energy Studies," *Louisville Courier-Journal*, March 18, 1991, sec. A.

On-line and Database Periodicals
Begin with author, "title of article, " *Title of Periodical* volume # if any, date, and page numbers. For notes use commas. For bibliography use periods. The locator that ends the citation should be one of these three, in this preferred order:
1) DOI If the source has a doi, cite this. Since urls change, many scholarly works assign a Digital Object Identifier [DOI]. The DOI, in most databases, usually appears on the first page with the journal's name, volume, issue, and page number information. Most articles in science and social science journals now assign DOIs.

4. Steve Ferzacca, "Diabetes and Culture," *Annual Review of Anthropology* 41 (2012): 420. doi 10.1146/annurev-anthro-081309-145806.
page number(s) actually cited

2) Database If the source does not have a doi, but was retrieved from a database, give the name of the database as the locator.

5. Jerry Adler, "Sweet land of liberties; if everyone has his own niche, what do we have in common anymore?" *Newsweek*, July 10, 1995 18+. Academic One File.
page number   database

3) url If the source came from the web and does not have a doi, give the url.

6. Henry Grabar, "What Do We Call It When the Rich Displace the Middle Class?" *Slate*, May 10, 2019, http://slate.com/business/2019/05/gentrification-rich-middle-class-define.html.

Article from a Website
7. Anne Elizabeth Dunn-Vaturi, "Board Games from Ancient Egypt and the Near East," Heilbrun Timeline of Art History. Metropolitan Museum of Art, accessed June 5, 2019, https://www.metmuseum.com/toah/hd/anbd/hd_anbd.htm

Entire Website
8. Shakespeare Birthplace Trust, Shakespeare's Birthplace (website), accessed May 31, 2019, https://www.shakespeare.org.uk/visit/shakespeares-birthplace.

Bibliographies in alphabetical order in essays, not corresponding to Notes like here. To understand differences between magazines and journals, read 143-146. Bibliography

Holloway, Meredith. "A Comparison of Active and Passive Music Reinforcement to Increase Preacademic and Motor Skills in Severely Retarded Children and Adolescents." *Journal of Music Therapy* 17, no. 2 (1980): 58-69.

Updike, John. "Sinclair Lewis: Exile on Main Street." *New Yorker,* May 17, 1993, 91-97.

Chicago prefers that newspaper articles only appear in Notes, not the Bibliography, but if your professor prefers, use the method below.

Brown, Mike. "Oil Rich Refuge May Fund Energy Studies." *Louisville Courier-Journal,* March 18, 1991, sec. A.
Chicago **uses section identifiers, not page for newpapers.**

If city is not in the newspaper's name, add city or region if regional newspaper to its name. The citaton above is for *The Courier-Journal,* **and it is published in Louisville.**

Ferzacca, Steve. "Diabetes and Culture." *Annual Review of Anthropology* 41 (2012): 411-426. doi 10.1146/annurev-anthro-081309-145806.
Entire range of page numbers of article, followed by doi number.

Adler, Jerry. "Sweet land of liberties; if everyone has his own niche, what do we have in common anymore?" *Newsweek,* July 10, 1995. 18+. Academic One File.

Grabar, Henry. "What Do We Call It When the Rich Displace the Middle Class?" *Slate,* May 10, 2019. http://slate.com/business/2019/05/gentrification-rich-middle-class-define.html.

Dunn-Vaturi, Anne Elizabeth. "Board Games from Ancient Egypt and the Near East." Heilbrun Timeline of Art History. Metropolitan Museum of Art. Accessed June 5, 2019, https://www.metmuseum.org/toah/hd/anbd/hd_anbd.htm

Shakespeare Birthplace Trust. Shakespeare's Birthplace (website). Accessed May 31, 2019. https://www.shakespeare.org.uk/visit/shakespeares-birthplace.

Miscellaneous Documents

THE FOLLOWING SOURCES APPEAR IN TEXT OR IN NOTES, BUT DO NOT APPEAR IN THE BIBLIOGRAPHY. When the source is central to your argument it appears in the Bibliography.

Notes   **Personal Communication**

Bill Smithers, in a February 3, 2019 telephone conversation with me, argued that ...

1. Roland Barthes, email message to author, March 15, 2019.

2. John Bollinger, "Really Congress?," Facebook, January 31, 2018. **Copy up to 160** https://facebook.com/johnbollinger/posts/4734291 **characters of post for clarity.**

3. *Merriam-Webster*, s.v. "loquacious," accessed June 30, 2019, https://www.merriam-webster.com/dictionary/loquacious.   **Reference Books**

4. *Encyclopedia Brittanica*, s.v. "Presidents of the United States," accessed April 10, 2019, https://www.briannica.com/event/Presidents-of-the-United-States.

Interviews

5. Barack Obama, interview by Chris Matthews, *Hardball with Chris Matthews*, MSNBC, March 12, 2016.

6. John Brown, interview by author, August 12, 2018.

Blog

7. Andrew Revkin, "Why a Blog, and Why This Blog?," *Dot Earth* (blog), October 24, 2007, https://dotearth.blogs.nytimes.com/2007/10/24/why-a-blog.

Reviews

8. Louis Menand, review of *Paradise*, by Toni Morrison, *The New Yorker*, January 12. 1998. https://galegroup.com.libproxy.ktcs.edu/ps/advancedSearch/59866

9. Alan Sepinwall, review of *Game of Thrones*, created by David Benioff, HBO, *Rolling Stone*, May 13, 2019.   **Movies:DVD/Blueray/Streaming**

10. *Star Wars: Episode IV - A New Hope*, directed by George Lucas (1977: Lucasfilm, 1997), DVD. **If streaming service, like Netflix, name here, or url if from website.**

Sound Recordings

11.The Rolling Stones, *Exile on Main Street*, Atlantic, 1972. CD.

12. The Rolling Stones, "Tumbling Dice," by Mick Jagger and Keith Richards, track 9 on *Exile on Main Street*, 2007: Atlantic, 1972, CD.

13. Lady Gaga, "Shallow," track 12 on *A Star is Born*, Warner Brothers, 2018, Spotify streaming audio.

14. Led Zepplin, "Dazed and Confused," by Jimmy Page, recorded April 23, 1970, Fillmore East, New York, Concert Vault streaming video, http://concertvault.com/led-zepplin/fillmore-east-april-23-1970.html. **Pamphlets, Reports, Brochures**

15. Taoist Tai Chi Society, *Taoist Tai Chi* (Tallahassee, Fl: Taoist Tai Chi Society, n.d.)

16. International Monetary Fund, *Venezualan Economic Policy*, World Economic and Financial Surveys (Washington, DC: International Monetary Fund, 2018), 36.

<u>But ask your professor for her preference concerning inclusion in Bibliography</u>.
If asked for inclusion, follow the *Chicago* formatting pattern that alters the note
for the bibliography (no number or parentheses and periods instead of commas).

Cite personal communications (letters or telephone calls, personal interviews),
emails, AND social media messages PREFERABLY just in the text of the essay,
or can cite in the Notes, but NOT in the Bibliography. Key elements in text or in
Notes: the other person, the date, the kind of communication.

Do not cite reference encyclopedias or dictionaries in the Bibliography, only the
Notes. Include the date the entry was posted, last modified, or if neither of these is
listed the date of access. Since these are alphabetical, no volume or page number
is needed. End citation with the url if you viewed this entry on-line.
> (s.v. : abbreviation for Latin *sub verbo*, 'under the word,' telling reader
> where to find the citation in the reference book.)

Interviews also should only be in Notes; however, the interviewee is listed as the
author, followed by Interview by ...... If it is a published interview, it should be
like the example here, but after the Interview by ... should have the information
listed like the previous pages for whatever source you got the interview from.

Blog posts, videos, and podcasts should be treated as short works from a website.
You may name the medium as the example does.

Reviews (books, television, movies, live or recorded performances): name the
reviewer followed by 'review of' and name the work reviewed and the creator,
and information on where the review appeared including the url if it was found
on-line.

**Bibliographies in alphabetical order in essays, not corresponding to Notes like
here.**   Bibliography

Lucas, George, director. *Star Wars: Episode IV - A New Hope*. 1977: Lucasfilm, 1997.
DVD.   **recording company, release date, medium**

The Rolling Stones. *Exile on Main Street*. Atlantic, 1972. CD. **or if citing a song from:**

The Rolling Stones. "Tumbling Dice." By Mick Jaggers and Keith Richards. Track 9 on
Exile on Main Street. Atlantic, 1972. CD.

Lady Gaga. "Shallow." Track 12 on *A Star is Born*. Warner Brothers, 2018.
Spotify streaming audio.   **Live Recording:**

Led Zepplin. "Dazed and Confused." By Jimmy Page. Recorded April 23, 1970. Fillmore
East, New York. Concert Vault streaming video. http://concertvault.com/
led-zepplin/fillmore-east-april-23-1970.html.

**Information about the author or publisher may not be available, but give enough
information to identify the source. In notes, give page number cited if available,**

Taoist Tai Chi Society. *Taoist Tai Chi*. Tallahassee, Fl: Taoist Tai Chi Society, n.d.

International Monetary Fund. *Venezualan Economic Policy*. World Economic and
Financial Surveys. Washington, DC: International Monetary Fund, 2018.

Author-Date Style

Chicago author-date style is a common tool for many disciplines. In text, writers give the author, year of publication, and page numbers in parentheses (Turabian, 2018, 224). Notice the placement of the period for the sentence after the parenthesis.

On a References page following the essay, an alphabetical list of the sources used in the essay is found. This includes the complete information concerning the source.

The rest of the section will include references for the various types of sources encountered, with a References citation followed by the in text parenthetical citation.

Print Books   **If no author, begin with Title.**
                                   <u>**Also May Have Corporate Authors**</u>
One author   year of publication
Greenblatt, Stephen. 2011. *The Swerve: How the World Became Modern*. New York:
     W. W. Norton.   **page number cited**
                                   (Greenblatt, 2011, 217.

2 or 3 Authors
Gilbert, Sandra M., and Susan Gubar. 1979. *The Madwoman in the Attic: The Woman Writer*
     and the Nineteenth-Century Literary Imagination. New Haven: Yale University Press,
                                   (Gilbert and Gubar, 1979, 119)

4 or more authors
Same pattern as above for References. In text, first author: (Canedy et al. 2017, 113)

Author Plus Editor
Faulkner, William. 1979. *Uncollected Stories of William Faulkner*. Edited by Joseph Blotner.
     New York: Random House.
                                   (Faulkner, 1979, 213)
Introductions, Prefaces, Afterward, Foreward
Blotner, Joseph. 1979. Introduction to *Uncollected Stories of William Faulkner*, by William
     Faulkner, xv-xvii. New York: Random House.
                                   (Blotner, 1979, xvi)
Author with Translator
Neruda, Pablo. 1990. *Selected Poems*. Translated by Anthony Kerrigan, W. S. Merwin,
     Alastair Reed, and Nathaniel Tarn. Boston: Houghton Mifflin.
                                   (Neruda, 1990, 85)

Do not include sacred texts in References. In text: use standard abbreviations and roman numerals. Most sacred texts have numbering like the Judeo-Christian Bible. (2 Cor. 6:2-9) First citation lists translation: (Matt. 6: 3-8 [New Revised Standard])

Work in an Anthology or a titled part of a Book
Beattie, Anne. 2004. "The Lawn Party." In *Anthology of American Literature*. 8th ed. Vol 2,
     edited by George McMichael, James Leonard, Bill Lyne, Anne-Marie Mallon, and
     Verner Mitchell, 2032-2042. Upper Saddle River, NJ: Prentice Hall.
(Entire range of pages listed BEFORE publication info.)
                                   (Beattie, 2004, 2036)

472

Source Quoted in Another Source

Glissant, Edouard. 2000. *Poetics of Relation.* Translated by Betsy Wing. Ann Arbor:
University of Michigan Press: 75. Quoted in Valerie Loichot, *Orphan Narratives*
(Charlottesville: University of Virginia Press, 2007.

(Glissant, 2000, 75)

Electronic Books
From a Database

Marzac, Robert P. 2007. *An Ecological and Postcolonial Study of Literature: From Daniel Defoe
to Salman Rushdie.* New York: Palgrave MacMillan. Proquest Ebook Central.

(Marzac, 2007, 36-9)

E-book

Taylor, Elizabeth Downing. 2017. *The Original Black Elite: Daniel Muray and the Story of a
Forgotten Era.* New York: Amistad. Kindle.

(Taylor, 2017, 73)

On-line

Elmslie, Margaret Duncan and William Burns Thomson. 1875. *Seedtime in Kashmir: A
Memoir of William Jackson Elmslie.* London: Nisbit. Project Gutenberg EBook,
2019. http://gutenberg.org/files/59457/59457-h.htm

When there are no page numbers: (Elmslie and Thomson, 1875, chap 5)

Articles
Journals

Holloway, Meredith. 1980. "A Comparison of Active and Passive Music Reinforcement
to Increase Preacademic and Motor Skills in Severely Retarded Children and
Adolescents." *Journal of Music Therapy* 17, no. 2 (June): 58-69.

(Holloway, 1980, 63-65)

If an article has a doi (given to many science and social science journal essays):

Ferzacca, Steve. 2012. "Diabetes and Culture." *Annual Review of Anthropology* 41:
411-426. https://doi 10.1146/annurev-anthro-081309-145806.

Entire range of page numbers of article, followed by doi number.

(Ferzacca, 2012, 421)

To understand differences between magazines and journals, read 143-146.

Magazines   **no page numbers/complete date**

Updike, John. 1993. "Sinclair Lewis: Exile on Main Street." *New Yorker,* May 17, 1993.

(Updike, 1993, 93)

**If journal or magazine does not have a doi, but comes from a database or
website:**

Adler, Jerry. 1995. "Sweet land of liberties; if everyone has his own niche, what do we
have in common anymore?" *Newsweek,* July 10, 1995. Academic One File.

(Adler, 1995, 20)

Grabar, Henry. 2019. "What Do We Call It When the Rich Displace the Middle Class?"
Slate, May 10, 2019. http://slate.com/business/2019/05/gentrification-rich-middle-
class-define.html.

(Grabar, 2019) **(If webpage had page numbers, then
they would appear here as usual.))**

Newspapers

If the article does not list an author but names a news organization, cite it as the author. If a newpaper article has neither, name the newspaper itself as the author. (See examples below.) As there are usually several editions on one news day, page numbers are left off.

Brown, Mike. 1991. "Oil Rich Refuge May Fund Energy Studies." *Louisville Courier-Journal*, March 18, 1991.

> (Brown 1991) **No commas when no page numbers. If city is not in the newspaper's name, add city or region if regional newspaper to its name. The citaton above is for** *The Courier-Journal*, **and it is published in Louisville.**

Associated Press. 2017. "Students Protest Tuition Hikes." *USA Today College*, March 3, 2017.https://college.usatoday.com/2017/3/3/students-protest-tuition/
> (Associated Press 2017)

Use database rather than url when applicable:

Los Angeles Times. 2018. "California Has Strongest Emission Standards." *Los Angeles Times*, April 12, 2018. Newspaper Source.

Anonymous author   (*Los Angeles Times* 2018)

Interviews and Editorials in Newpapers

Pence, Mike. 2017. Interview by Mike Wallace. *Washington Post*, March 8, 2017.
> (Pence 2017)

Colllins, Peter. 2016. Letter to the Editor, *New York Times*, June 3, 2016.
> (Collins 2016)

Chicago Tribune. 2018. "State Supreme Court Should Uphold Voting Rights Act." Editorial, June 12, 2018.
> (*Chicago Tribune* 2018)

Reviews

Menand, Louis. 1998. Review of *Paradise*, by Toni Morrison. *The New Yorker*, January 12. 1998, https://galegroup.com.libproxy.ktcs.edu/psadvancedSearch/59866
> (Menand, 1998, 92)

Sepinwall, Alan. 2019. Review of *Game of Thrones*, created by David Benioff. HBO. *Rolling Stone*, May 13, 2019.
> (Sepinwall, 2019, 19)

Movies   **Get information on movies and television shows from imdb.com**

Lucas, George, director. 1977. *Star Wars: Episode IV - A New Hope*. Lucasfilm, 1997.
DVD. **If streaming service, like Netflix, name here, or url if from website.**
> (Lucas 1977)

Television

Streaming Services. If watched live, just leave off url.

Legend. 2014. Season 1, episode 5, "Rogue." Directed and performance by Sean Bean. Aired November 4, 2014 on TNT. https://www.netflix.com/watch/863298493485track-id?4394.

Must list director, but can list other performers, writers, etc. that are pertinent to your essay.

Rachel Maddows Show. 2019. Hosted by Rachel Maddows. MSNBC, March 12, 2019.

(Rachel Maddows Show 2019)

Bernie Sanders. 2019. Interview by Anderson Cooper. *Anderson Cooper 360.* May 12, 2019, CNN.

(Sanders 2019)

Radio Programs
Little Steven's Underground Garage. 2013. Hosted by Steve Van Zandt. PBS, April 6, 2013.

(Little Steven's Underground Garage 2013)

If these above are retrieved from an electronic source, end citation with its url.

Sound Recordings

Recording company. Medium

The Rolling Stones. 1972. *Exile on Main Street.* Atlantic.33 1/3 rpm.**if citing a song from:**

The Rolling Stones. 1972."Tumbling Dice," by Mick Jagger and Keith Richards. Track 9 on *Exile on Main Street.* Atlantic, 1995 CD.   **Newer date release of CD.**

Lady Gaga. 2018. "Shallow." Track 12 on *A Star is Born.* Warner Brothers. Spotify streaming audio.   **Live Recording:**

Led Zepplin. 1970. "Dazed and Confused," by Jimmy Page. Recorded April 23, 1970. Fillmore East, New York. Concert Vault streaming video. http://concertvault.com/led-zepplin/fillmore-east-april-23-1970.html.

(Led Zepplin 1970)

Article from a Website
Dunn-Vaturi, Anne Elizabeth. 2019. "Board Games from Ancient Egypt and the Near East." Heilbrun Timeline of Art History. Metropolitan Museum of Art. Accessed June 5, 2019, https://www.metmuseum.com/toah/hd/anbd/hd_anbd.htm

(Dunn-Vaturi 2019)

An Entire Website
Shakespeare Birthplace Trust. n.d. "Shakespeare's Birthplace." Accessed May 31, 2019. https://www.shakespeare.org.uk/visit/shakespeares-birthplace.

(Shakespeare's Birthplace Trust n.d.)

Blog
Revkin, Andrew. 2007. "Why a Blog, and Why This Blog?," *Dot Earth*, October 24, 2007, https://dotearth.blogs.nytimes.com/2007/10/24/why-a-blog.)

(Revkin 2007)

Pamphlets, Reports, Brochures
Taoist Tai Chi Society. n.d. *Taoist Tai Chi.* Tallahassee, Fl: Taoist Tai Chi Society.

(Taoist tai Chi Society n.d.)

International Monetary Fund. 2018. *Venezualan Economic Policy.* World Economic and Financial Surveys. Washington, DC: International Monetary Fund.

If found on-line, end citation with url.

The following sources are usually not included in References, but are cited in a note in the text. If, however, the piece is central to the argument of your essay, include it in References. Central information in the parenthetical information in text includes author, year of the post, some of the text (up to 160 characters to explain the content), the type of post (email, telephone call, Facebook, etc.), the exact date of the post using a time stamp to differentiate more than one post on a single day, and a url.

Personal Communication

Bill Smithers, in a February 3, 2019 telephone conversation with me, argued that ...

(Roland Barthes, email message to author, March 15, 2019)

Social Media, Online Forums

(John Bollinger, "Really Congress?," Facebook, January 31, 2018. https://facebook.com/johnbollinger/posts/4734291)

Well Known Reference Books

(*Merriam-Webster*, s.v. "loquacious," accessed June 30, 2019, https://www.merriam-webster.com/dictionary/loquacious)s

(*Encyclopedia Brittanica*, s.v. "Presidents of the United States," accessed April 10, 2019, https://www.briannica.com/event/Presidents-of-the-United-States.)

Index

479

481

Index for Citation / Documentation Issues